Women's Status in North-Eastern India

Women's Status in North-Eastern India

Sindhu Phadke

Decent Books
New Delhi

Cataloging in Publication Data — DK
[Courtesy: D.K. Agencies (P) Ltd. <docinfo@dkagencies.com>]
Phadke, Sindhu, 1927-
Women's status in North-eastern India / Sindhu Phadke.
p. cm.
Includes bibliographical references (p.).
Includes index.
ISBN 13: 9788186921494
ISBN 10: 8186921494

1. Women — India, Northeastern — Economic conditions. 2. Women — India, Northeastern — Social conditions. 3. Marital status — India, Northeastern. 4. Women — Health and hygiene — India, Northeastern. 5. Women — Education — India, Northeastern. 6. Women in politics — India, North-eastern. 7. Women in development — India, Northeastern. 8. India, Northeastern — History. I. Title.

DDC 305.409 541 22

ISBN 13: 978-81-86921-49-4 **ISBN 10: 81-86921-49-4**
First published in India in 2008

Published and printed by:
Decent Books
D-36/A-1, Mohan Garden
Najafgarh Road, New Delhi - 110 059
Ph. (011) 2535 3435

Distributed by:
D.K. Printworld (P) Ltd.
Regd. office : *'Sri Kunj,'* F-52, Bali Nagar
Ramesh Nagar Metro Station, New Delhi - 110 015
Phones : (011) 2545 3975, 2546 6019; *Fax* : (011) 2546 5926
E-mail : dkprintworld@vsnl.net
Web : www.dkprintworld.com

Foreword

AUTHENTIC information on almost anything in the North-East India is exasperatingly thin — it has yet to be patiently assembled from the data painfully exhumed — even more on a subject, until recently, as unfashionable as women's status.

Dr Sindhu Phadke in *Women's Status in North-Eastern India* has carefully put together stipples collected from personal observations, particularly as a UNICEF Zonal Representative for East India, records of ten ICSSR seminars, inputs from knowledgeable persons, and government documents, and given us the first outline of what must eventually become a fascinating picture.

There are already some surprising conclusions. One of them is that the status of women in the region was generally very low but that it improved with becoming Hindu or Christian. (I always thought the youngest daughter among the Khasis and Jaintias of Meghalaya inherited all the property. But in fact there was no concept of private property among these tribes and so she was merely holding the property in trust for the clan. Therefore even Meghalaya is not an exception.)

We have since realized, of course, that women are the more interesting aspects of humankind. Take one step forward and we all ought to be reading this absorbing pioneering work.

Rangareddy District
Andhra Pradesh
May 1, 2007

J.M. Lyngdoh
Former Chief Election Commissioner of India

Acknowledgement

To my long-time and esteemed friend Mandakini Khandekar I owe a deep debt of gratitude. I have benefited greatly by her many useful suggestions on my drafts. I have known within me that the astute researcher in her would not let any doubtful statement to pass her scrutiny, which was reassuring. Equally important, she took the trouble to provide me many useful references.

In my early exploration of materials on status of North-Eastern (N-E) women, Dr B.K. Roy Burman, the gracious scholar and indefatigable spokesman of the N-E, as well as Dr Tiplut Nongbri of Jawaharlal Nehru University gave me several useful suggestions. My good friend Dr Uma Chakravarty of Lady Keane College, Shillong, arranged with Dr P.S. Datta, Joint Director, North-Eastern Regional Centre of Indian Council of Social Science Research (ICSSR) to permit me access to reports of the various Status of Women Seminars on N-E States conducted during 1988-1989. It was indeed very kind of Dr Datta to arrange for me photo-copies of cyclostyled proceedings of the ten N-E Seminar reports which were in English (a few papers in local languages had to be omitted), besides providing me access to several other materials on the N-E. The dynamic leadership of Dr Vina Mazumdar was undoubtedly a key factor in initiating these seminars on behalf of ICSSR, and Dr P.S. Datta, Joint Director of the N-E Regional Centre gave valuable support in their organization, despite many limitations. These seminars have initiated entirely new thinking on N-E women, a dimension which is conspicuously absent in most previous literature on N-E, and which needs to be carried further.

I had the privilege of receiving many useful suggestions and information from several knowledgeable persons in North Eastern Hill University, including Ms. Sujata Miri and Dr Mrinal Miri, presently its Vice Chancellor, Dr B.B. Dutta Ray of the N-E India Council of Social Science

Research, Dr Satya Chakravarty of the Anthropological Survey of India, specialists in the North Eastern Council Secretariat and many others. In Guwahati, I had the benefit of support from my professional associate and friend Indira Chakravarty, and her brother Tara Prasad Chakravarty who took the trouble to collect some useful information which was not available in published reports. Through their help, I could meet persons with rich experience, such as late Dr B.N. Bordoloi, Director of Tribal Research Centre, Ms. Jeuti Barooah of the Law Research Institute, to mention a few. I cannot resist the temptation of sharing with readers my memorable meeting in Guwahati with the great pioneer in women's education, Indira Miri in 1992. She talked nostalgically about her forays into NEFA (present Arunachal Pradesh) to open schools for girls in villages at a time when there were not even foot-paths. The small band of five or six persons, including an interpreter, had to chop down branches of trees to make their way through leech-infested forests and stop suddenly at times until the crashing sounds of a foraging elephant subsided.

Dr Smriti Mukherjee has been very helpful in providing me many useful sources of information from the library of Gokhale Institute of Economics and Politics, Pune. Mr Rahul Ranade, a young fine arts graduate, helped to prepare the maps included in this book. Chandrashekhar and Manisha Pandit have taken great pains to prepare the manuscript. Deepali Patil prepared the statistical charts and Vilas Mankar prepared the list of sources consulted. My niece Kiran Moghe gave extremely valuable help in putting together the manuscript. I deeply appreciate the several acts of thoughtfulness from friends who are not mentioned here individually.

My heart-felt thanks and gratitude to all of these persons.

Pune, June 2008

Sindhu Phadke

Contents

List of Tables and Maps

Tables

Maps

Abbreviations and Terms Used

AASU	All Assam Students Union
AGP	Asom Gana Parishad
ABSU	All Bodo Students Union
AIDWA	All India Democratic Women's Association
APHLC	All Party Hill Leaders' Conference
CBR	Crude Birth Rate
CHT	Chittagong Hill Tracts
EITU	Eastern Indian Tribal Union
GDI	Gender-related Development Index
GHI	Gender-related Health Index
hA	Hectare
HDI	Human Development Index
IMDT	Illegal Migrants Determination by Tribunal (Assam)
JHUM	Slash-and-burn : a primitive cultivation mode
Kg	Kilo Gram
KWH	Kilo Wat Hour (a measure of electricity)
MHIP	Mizo Hmeichhe Insuihkhawn Pawl (Mizo Women's Federation)
Mithun	A tamed bison
MNF	Mizo National Front
N-E	North-East
NEC	North-Eastern Council
NEHU	North-Eastern Hill University
Nupilan	Women's Movement (Manipur)
NSCN	National Socialist Council of Nagaland
NSDP	Net State Domestic Product
ORS	Oral Rehydration Salts

PLA	Peoples Liberation Army
SC	Sceduled Caste
ST	Scheduled Tribe
TFR	Total Fertility Rate
ULFA	United Liberation Front of Assam
WPR	Work Participation Rate
YMA	Young Mizo Association

Introduction

A succession of striking images race through my mind when I think of the situation of the hardworking and resourceful women of North-East India:

- An attractive newly built Mahila Mandal (women's club) centre in a remote Manipur village, comprising a fairly large central hall for meetings and recreation, with half a dozen handlooms arranged on one side, adjoining a separate enclosure for the *balwadi* (children's centre) and another enclosure for the local youth band's musical instruments etc.; on the opposite side another alcove for storing large cooking utensils generally hired out for village and family celebrations! Asked how the members managed to build such a multi-purpose institution around a rather modest UNICEF grant for the Mahila Mandal, the women clad in their traditional striped Manipuri "puan" explained with obvious pride and excitement how they managed to mobilize enthusiastic community participation, with the *Panchayat* (village council) donating the land, the village mason and carpenter substantially donating their services in building the modest structure with locally available materials such as bamboos, thatching and wooden logs donated by the village community, and their own labour power!

- Small bands of four or five Khasi women with a couple of young children in tow, trekking up the narrow hill paths, with conical baskets strapped to their backs, bringing vegetables and fruits for sale at Shillong markets. Not too far away, some neatly dressed Khasi women catering tea and snacks, skilfully arranged on cane trays, for office workers in Meghalaya Secretariat.

- Members of MHIP (Mizo Women's Federation) show off the low-cost sanitary latrine being constructed for their centre in Aizawl (capital of Mizoram) under a UNICEF-assisted project which required a matching contribution. These women proudly claimed that they had themselves generated the matching contribution by taking a labour contract on the State's road construction project.

- A couple of women in a village in Arunachal Pradesh pounding their daily requirement of rice with utterly quaint and primitive tools such as a thick log roughly spooned out in the middle to serve as a mortar and another little wooden rod for a pestle. Nearby, an older woman weaving a narrow strip on a loin loom, maintaining the tension with a strap going around her back and another in front tied to a tree trunk.

Just a few fleeting glimpses, such as these, from my numerous visits to the seven North-Eastern (N-E) states as UNICEF Representative (United Nations Children's Fund) in East India from 1977 to 1987. In the course of programming UNICEF assistance to development programmes for children and women in these states, I was privileged to have a look at the way women from diverse backgrounds and cultures lived and laboured. The more I observed their industriousness, resourcefulness, tenacity and zest for life even under the most adverse circumstances, the more fascinated I was to learn about them. I could not, however, undertake a systematic study about their situation because of my other official responsibilities.

This deep urge was subsequently re-kindled when the Tata Institute of Social Sciences offered me a Golden Jubilee Professorship in 1992. While initially working on a monograph on North-Eastern women's status in marriage, family and economy, I found myself irresistibly drawn into a wider and deeper exploration of the subject, and realized that my search had just barely begun and that there was a lot more to be learnt. Despite a number of interruptions — both personal and professional — my inquiry kept extending into other related aspects such as religion, health, education, social and political spheres. Discretion, however, demanded that I pause somewhere and present my findings in this book, fully realizing that this inquiry has an ever-widening horizon. If I succeed in motivating some others to take this search further along, I would feel amply rewarded in this effort.

Concept of Status

The term "status" has been used in this discourse in its wider sense, and includes both its hierarchical, meaning relative rank, as well as non-hierarchical, meaning situation or position of an individual. Status is reflected in roles and relationships of a person with respect to others and vice versa, and values attached to these are sometimes specific to a particular cultural context. Certain roles may be vital for the well-being of the family, and yet these may not give much status. N-E women carry the full burden of cooking and feeding the family and yet this does not enhance their prestige very much, since every housewife is expected to perform these tasks. On the other hand, if a wife shows alacrity in keeping "ju" (fermented rice beer) for her husband when he wishes to relax with his friends, she would be rated as a dutiful wife and hospitable hostess. Customs and cultural traditions in each community decide division of functions between men and women. In most N-E groups, major financial decisions are taken by men. On the other hand, ensuring adequate food for the family is women's job and how they supplement inadequate yields from cultivation determines their status as house-keepers. The term status also includes legal position, e.g. right to own and inherit property. In a majority of N-E communities, for instance, women cannot own land. Most of such laws are not codified and are in the form of conventions. Women's status is reflected in the manner in which laws or conventions are interpreted.

Status is an abstract concept and has to be inferred from relationships, attitudes and behaviour. For instance, status of women in the family is reflected in, e.g. how birth of a girl child is received, whether girls are allowed to play with their friends in a relaxed atmosphere, and whether girls have the freedom to select their marriage partners. Roles and relationships are reflected in social practices and traditions. The practice of bride-price in a majority of N-E societies is indicative of a girl being viewed as an asset for her parental family. The groom and his family therefore try to compensate for the loss to the bride's family by giving bride-price, whether in the form of money, a feast for the girl's family or a *mithun* (tamed bison). Once a girl gets married and becomes a housewife there is a sharp change in her status. In a few N-E communities, e.g. the Lothas of Nagaland, if a husband for any reason gets displeased with his wife, he may ask her to leave his house after paying a token compensation. The woman's status after marriage therefore needs to be viewed in the context of a particular community's culture. Furthermore, external influences such as modern education system and contacts with outside communities bring about changes in concepts of status. Thus a Nishing woman of Arunachal Pradesh may well feel satisfied with her position as the senior-most among several co-wives and with the improved economic status of her husband due to greater availability of labour for family cultivation. However, if she receives an opportunity to get education and a salaried job as a teacher, would she still prefer to be one among several co-wives? The impact of new alternatives for enhancing one's status is therefore an essential component for an adequate analysis. Quite often, status in one area influences status in another, and there is no doubt, for instance, that as women achieve economic self-reliance, their status in the family also goes up.

Since status is expressed in a person's roles and relationships within a social context, introduction of new systems or institutions disrupts the status quo. The adoption of Christianity among the Khasis of Meghalaya, for instance, has eroded to some extent the exalted position of the mother as "Ka Blei Ing" — goddess of the household — and as a continuator of the clan. At the same time, adoption of Christianity not only opened the doors for women to participate in religious services but also in church-sponsored social services as well. It is therefore important to note how creation of new institutions influences women's status. In some cases, women's access to some spheres has increased, while in some, the old traditions have eclipsed newer structures. For instance, the customary ban on women's participation in traditional village councils or the councils of elders in tribal communities seems to have inhibited many N-E women from participating in the new autonomous district councils established through Sixth Schedule of the Indian Constitution.

Status is thus a complex concept, which has to be analysed in the context of various spheres, e.g. economy, marriage, family, religion, health, education, social and political institutions. There are many differences among N-E states, and indeed among various communities within each state, in social structures, customs, traditions and women's access to opportunities of enhancing their status. At the same time, there are similarities and common elements, which seem to enhance their capacities to minimize their handicaps and raise their status. This book represents a search in this direction.

Organization of Contents

Chapters 1 and 2 together provide profiles of the N-E region and its seven component states. The general ecology of the region, its isolation from the rest of India, broad demographic aspects and its political integration with India are presented in Chapter 1 - North-Eastern Region: A Profile. This is followed by Chapter 2 - North-Eastern States: Seven Unique Sisters, which provides the backgrounds of each N-E state in two parts. Brief accounts of history in pre-British, British and post-Independence periods are given in the first part, while the second part presents geographical and demographic features of each state, followed by present economic and social contexts.

Perhaps an explanation for giving this background might be useful. A few illustrations follow: In the predominantly hilly areas of N-E states, the most common mode of cultivation so far has been "jhuming," characterised by community ownership and control. This context is essential for appreciating the negative implications for women's status when there is a shift from community to individual ownership of land, and take-over of tribal lands by non-tribal entrepreneurs. Another illustration refers to Mizo women's position in their indigenous faiths prior to Christianity. When missionaries from English Baptist and Welsh Presbyterian Missions tried to introduce Christianity and girls' education in Mizoram in early 20th century, initially there was strong resistance from Mizo men. Why Mizo women avidly welcomed Christianity becomes clear in the background of their marginal status in their native religions. The practice of bride-price, instead of dowry, has generally been viewed as an indication of girls' higher status in marriage in most N-E communities. But among the Wanchos of Tirap district in Arunachal Pradesh, bride-price is viewed by some men as a means of purchasing the woman's body, and her procreative power. A wife who produces more children, especially some sons, gets higher status. On the other hand, a barren woman suffers humiliation and her husband feels justified in discarding her and taking another wife. The context of frequent warfare and the need to replenish population, the prolonged geographical and social isolation of the Wanchos — these circumstances help to explain the degraded status of Wancho women.

The first two chapters thus present the backdrop for succeeding contents, and may well be skipped by readers who are conversant with the N-E region. In an effort to make the outlines of N-E region and its States as concise as possible, some details were eliminated from the text and some are included as the footnotes in each chapter. This procedure is followed in succeeding chapters as well.

Chapter 3 deals with economic status of N-E women, and examines three major aspects: economic status in terms of work participation in the formal sense as used in the Indian Census, the various tasks women perform for family subsistence whether or not these are included in the Cswensus definition of work, and legal rights to ownership and inheritance of property and maintenance, access to means of attaining economic self-reliance, etc. Chapter 4 deals with women's status with respect to marriage, family and religion in each N-E State. This chapter examines customs related to choice of marriage partner, bride-price and dowry, polygamy, divorce, re-marriage, etc., roles and relationships in the family, areas of decision-making, participation in family and community religious worship and special events, etc. in relation to women's status. Chapter 5 brings together information on N-E women's status in terms of certain indicators of health and education. Chapter 6 reviews women's social and political status in each N-E State as reflected in developments such as organization of groups and associations around common social issues, expression of joint protests, participation in political movements, representation in national and state legislatures and in rural and urban local bodies, etc. Chapter 7 recapitulates major findings of preceding chapters and presents some ideas and approaches for enhancing N-E women's status.

A Word of Caution

As will be noted, status is an abstract and somewhat elusive concept and it is inferred from some more tangible forms of behaviour such as roles and relationships. A book such as this, based mainly on reported accounts, cannot do full justice to the topic since it is likely to miss out a number of nuances which are evident only in direct observation of human interactions, not to mention women's and men's subjective feelings of their own and others' status. As I have drawn to a large extent on reports of State level seminars on N-E women's status for some areas, e.g. family, marriage and religion, limitations resulting from unevenness in the quality of presentations and coverage of communities in these documents were inevitable. Despite attempts to supplement with other books and reports, some gaps do remain. In general, coverage on women's status tends to be mostly absent or very thin in writing on N-E States. Furthermore, in an effort to ensure manageability, women's status has been examined selectively in the context of certain broad population groups and clusters of tribes in each N-E state, and several individual tribes were not included. My fervent hope is that this modest effort may help to generate more comprehensive thinking and writing on this subject.

NORTH EASTERN REGION

1

North-Eastern Region
A Profile

Introduction

THE North-Eastern (referred as N-E hereafter) region of India evokes a hazy and enigmatic vision for most Indians. More often than that not, it attracts attention when reports of large massacres and devastation of hundreds of homes by rival ethnic groups hit national headlines. Or again, when a daring raid on a police post by an insurgent group or kidnapping of some prominent personality sends shock waves among the public. Such events are usually followed by a flurry of activities, such as dispatch of relief materials for those rendered shelterless, reinforcement of security personnel, expressions of deep concern over the neglect of this region and announcements of ambitious development schemes by politicians. Very soon when the dust settles down, the N-E region tends to be relegated to its usual marginal position in the national mainstream.

This chapter presents a broad profile of the N-E region,starting with geographical aspects, their implications for transport and communications, and demographic features. This is followed by political and administrative developments in the British and post-Independence periods, salient aspects of the region's economy and a brief note on the North-Eastern Council. Chapter 2 includes the more individual and specific aspects of each of the seven component States. The treatment of contents is analytical, focusing on salient points, and deliberately leaving out details. It is hoped that together Chapter 1 and Chapter 2 would provide the context for an understanding of the situation of women in this region. However, readers who are knowledgeable about this background may wish to skip this content and go directly to Chapter 3.

Ecological Features

The N-E region includes the following States: Arunachal Pradesh, Assam, Manipur, Meghalaya, Mizoram, Nagaland and Tripura.[1] It shares 40,000 km of international border with Bhutan, Tibet and China on the north, Myanmar on the east and Bangladesh on the south and west. It covers an area of about 255,000 sq km comprising 7.8 per cent of India's total land area. Arunachal Pradesh is the largest State of this region with an area of 83,743 sq km while Assam ranks next with 78,438 sq km. The remaining five States are fairly small, ranging between 22,429 sq km (Meghalaya) and 10,486 sq km (Tripura). Table 1.1 gives the details.

More than 70 per cent of N-E region's total area is covered with mountains, hills and plateaus. The plain lands are limited largely to the Brahmaputra and Barak valleys in Assam and a small central valley in Manipur. The Eastern Himalayas which spread across Arunachal Pradesh have high altitudes in Tawang, West Kameng and Lower Subansiri areas, with the highest peak Kango rising up to 7,090 m. The altitudes decrease towards the north and the east, the rest being mostly valleys, plateaus and mountain slopes ranging in altitude between 900 and 3,300 m. A sickle-shaped north-south chain formed by the Patkoi Hills, Naga Hills, Manipur Hills and Mizo Hills marks the eastern boundary with Myanmar and joins Chin Hills and Arakan Yoma towards the south. The Barail Range, which merges with the main mountain chain, goes westward through North Cachar and finally sinks into the Kopili River gorge. The Meghalaya plateau, which consists of Garo, Khasi and Jaintia Hills extends to the Karbi Hills.

Brahmaputra, the most important river of the N-E region, known as Tsangpo, where it emerges from the Kailas Range, goes eastwards for about 1,700 km through Tibet before turning southwards near Namcha Barwa and enters Arunachal Pradesh as Siang. It is joined by many tributaries, e.g. Subansiri, Manas, Sankosh, etc. from the north and several rivers, like the Burhi Dihing, Dhansiri, Kopili, etc. from the southern catchments, before meeting Meghna in Bangladesh. The Barak, which rises in Manipur Hills, is joined by many rivers, which flow through Cachar

1. Although Sikkim ecologically belongs to the N-E region, due to historical and political reasons, it has so far not been included in the N-E region formally, even though Sikkim has been invited to participate in some meetings of the North-Eastern Council (NEC). In the proposed reorganization of the NEC, a suggestion has been made for its inclusion.

plains before joining the Bay of Bengal. A few rivers of eastern Nagaland and Manipur go through the Patkoi Hills and join Chindwin River in Myanmar. In view of the mountainous terrain, and heavy rainfall, many rivers, particularly those in the northern catchment of Brahmaputra, are prone to sudden and devastating floods causing high siltation.

Between 40 and 45 per cent of the total area is covered by forests, although the proportions vary widely among the States as rising pressure of population is leading to denudation of forests. This region falls in the high rainfall intensity zone, with an annual precipitation ranging between 200 to 400 cm. Cherrapunjee and Mawsynram, the places known to have the highest rainfall in the world, reaching up to 1,080 cm, are located in this region. Since the Eastern Himalayas are geologically unstable, this region is highly susceptible to earthquakes and landslides.

Transport and Communications

After the 1947 Partition of India and the creation of East Pakistan (present Bangladesh), the surface links of Assam, Tripura, Meghalaya and Mizoram with Bengal and the rest of India were snapped. A narrow corridor in north Bengal is the only surface link of N-E region with the country at present. In fact, N-E region had suffered the first partition when Burma (present Myanmar) was separated from British India in 1937, thus blocking its eastern outlets and trade routes, and simultaneously dividing several tribal communities among Mizoram, Nagaland, Manipur and Arunachal Pradesh on the one hand, and Burma on the other. The geographical isolation of N-E region from the rest of India has resulted in major hurdles in its economic and social integration. For most N-E States, reaching Calcutta and rest of the country entails long and extremely circuitous journey, not to mention frequent and sudden disruptions due to floods and landslides. Transportation of goods, especially essential commodities is, therefore, extremely time-consuming and expensive.

Travel within the region is also very difficult since the mountainous terrain poses a serious challenge to building motorable roads or rail tracks. The North-Eastern Frontier Railway, after Partition, was left with a very small length of rail track. The total length of railtrack, as of 1992-93 was 2,524.83 km out of which only 266.41 km was broadgauge, according to North-Eastern Council(NEC) (1995) sources. Out of the total rail network, Assam has the largest share, while other States like Nagaland

and Tripura have a very limited share and the remaining have none.[2] The total road length in N-E region in 1992 was 116,551 km, thus giving an average of 45.69 km per 100 sq. km of area as against the all-India average of 62.80 km (NEC,1995:121). The communication prospects are expected to improve since the new bridge across Brahmaputra near Jogighopa, which has been under construction since 1978 has recently been completed. At present, several villages in this region can be reached only by trekking on foot across hills and at times after crossing rivers and streams, which are subject to flash floods.

Demographic Aspects

POPULATION, DENSITY AND RATE OF GROWTH

Pending final and complete analysis of 2001 Census, we look at major demographic features of the N-E region as per 1991 Census. The total population of N-E region, according to 1991 Census was 31.37 million, out of which Assam accounted for 22.41 million (Table 1.1). Excepting Tripura with a population of 2.76 million, all the remaining States had less than two million, and Arunachal Pradesh and Mizoram, less than one million. The total population of N-E region rose to 38.5 million by 2001, with five out of seven N-E States exceeding India's average decadal growth rate of 21.34. As per Table 1.1, the density of population, i.e. average number of persons per sq km, according to 1991 Census, varied between 286 for Assam and 10 for Arunachal Pradesh, which was the lowest in the whole country followed by 33 for Mizoram. Since 2001, the density for Assam has risen to 340, and for Tripura to 304, placing them at 14th and 17th rank, respectively among all States/UTs. Arunachal Pradesh, with a density of 13 continues to be at its lowest rank while the remaining four States range between 42 and 120.

The rate of population growth for N-E region is much higher than that for the country as a whole. India's population, which was 238.39 million in 1901, increased to 846.3 million by 1991, i.e. about three-and-a-half times in nine decades. In 1901, Assam had a population of 3.28 million, which rose to 22.41 million by 1991, i.e. about seven times within the same period. The population of Manipur, Meghalaya and

2. Dharmanagar in Tripura was connected by a rail-head with Assam in 1964, Jiribam near Manipur's border with Assam in 1990 and Tuli in Nagaland in 1991.

Table 1.1 : Area, Populatison & Density of India and N-E States, 1981–1991–2001

India/N-E States	Area in sq. km	Total Population			Density (Population per sq km)		
		1981 *	*1991* **	*2001* ***	*1981*	*1991*	*2001*
India	3,287,263	683,329,097 (Including Assam & Jammu & Kashmir)	846,302,688 (Including Assam & Jammu & Kashmir)	1,027,015,247	230 (Excluding Assam & Jammu & Kashmir)	273 (Excluding Assam & Jammu & Kashmir)	324
Arunachal Pradesh	83,743	631,839	864,558	1,091,117	8	10	13
Assam	78,438	18,041,248	22,414,322	26,638,407	230	286	340
Manipur	22,327	1,420,953	1,837,149	2,388,634	64	82	107
Meghalya	22,429	1,335,819	1,774,778	2,306,069	60	79	103
Mizoram	21,081	493,757	689,756	891,058	23	33	42
Nagaland	16,579	744,930	1,209,546	1,988,636	47	73	120
Tripura	10,486	2,053,058	2,757,205	3,191,168	196	263	304

Sources : *Census of India 1991*, Series-1, Paper-2 of 1992, *Final Population Totals : Brief Analysis of Primary Census Abstract*. *Census of India 2001*, Series-1, Paper-1 of 2001, *Provisional Population Totals*.

* The 1981 Census could not be held in Assam due to disturbed conditions. The population figures for Assam have been worked out by interpolation.

** The 1991 Census was not held in Jammu & Kashmir. The population figures for Jammu & Kashmir are based on projections by the Standing Committee of Experts on Population Projections (October 1989).

*** The 2001 Population of India includes the estimated population of Kachch district, parts of Rajkot and Jamnagar districts of Gujarat and entire Kinnaur district of Himachal Pradesh where census could not be conducted due to natural calamities.

Mizoram increased to nearly three times, that of Tripura to nearly four times and that of Nagaland to six times within just four decades between 1951 and 1991.[3] Arunachal Pradesh, which had a population of 3.36 lakh in 1961, the first time census was conducted in the (erstwhile) Union Territory, rose to 8.64 lakh by 1991, nearly two-and-a-half times in just three decades. During the 1991–2001 decade, the contribution of N-E States to total population growth of India ranged between 2.3 per cent for Assam to 0.1 for Arunachal Pradesh.

RURAL-URBAN DISTRIBUTION

Despite the rapid population growth, N-E region continues to be predominantly rural. The percentages of urban population in the total population of Arunachal Pradesh, Assam, Meghalaya, Nagaland and Tripura in 1991 were considerably lower than the national average of 26.13 per cent. Table 1.2 gives the details. The higher percentage of urban population for Manipur (27.52) and Mizoram (46.10) are explained by the rapid population growth of the capital towns, viz. Imphal and Aizawl after 1972 when Manipur attained full Statehood and Mizoram acquired Union Territory status. The incorporation of villages adjoining the capital towns in the urban category and proliferation of administrative services were responsible for the growth of urban population. The extent of urbanization in N-E region as a whole however, continues to be modest, as noted from the fact that in 1991, six out of seven N-E State capitals had a population of less than one lakh.[4] The only exception was Guwahati with 5.84 lakh.

POPULATION OF SCHEDULED TRIBES AND SCHEDULED CASTES

The predominance of Scheduled Tribes in the populations of some N-E States is a significant feature of this region.[5] Meghalaya, Mizoram and

---

3. Their populations in 1951 and 1991 respectively were as follows: Manipur 577,635 and 1,837,149; Meghalaya 605,674 and 1,774,778; Mizoram 196,202 and 689,756; Tripura 639,029 and 2,757,205; Nagaland 212,975 and 1,209,546.
4. According to 1991 Census, the populations of the following State capitals were: Shillong (Meghalaya) 223,366; Imphal (Manipur) 202,839; Agartala (Tripura) 157,358; Aizawl (Mizoram) 155,240; Kohima (Nagaland) 53,122; Itanagar (Arunachal) 17,320.
5. "Scheduled Castes" and "Scheduled Tribes" are administrative categories recognized in the Indian Constitution as eligible for affirmative action since →

Table 1.2
Percentage of Urban, Scheduled Tribe and Scheduled Caste Population of India & N-E States, 1981-91

India/N-E States	***% of Urban to*** Total Population		***% of ST to*** Total population		***% of SC to*** Total Population	
	1981	*1991*	*1981*	*1991*	*1981*	*1991*
India (Excluding Assam and Jammu & Kashmir)	23.73	26.13	7.83	7.95	15.81	16.73
Arunachal Pradesh	6.56	12.80	69.82	63.66	0.46	0.47
Assam	9.88	11.10	NA	12.83	NA	7.40
Manipur	26.42	27.52	27.30	34.41	1.25	2.02
Meghalaya	18.07	18.60	80.58	85.53	0.41	0.51
Mizoram	24.67	46.10	93.55	94.75	0.03	0.10
Nagaland	15.52	17.21	83.99	87.70	0.00	0.00
Tripura	10.99	15.30	28.44	30.95	15.12	16.36

Source : *Census of India 1991*, Series 1, Paper 2 of 1992. *Final Population Totals : Brief Analysis of Primary Census Abstract.*
N.A. : Not Available.

Nagaland have over 85 per cent of Scheduled Tribes population, and in Arunachal Pradesh their percentage is 63.66 according to 1991 Census, as given in Table 1.2. In Manipur and Tripura, nearly one-third of the total State population belongs to Scheduled Tribes. Assam has the lowest percentage of Scheduled Tribes population, viz. 12.83 per cent These lower proportions are due to large numbers of non-tribal groups from other States of India having migrated to these States, and to the de-tribalization of some communities, e.g. the Meiteis, after they adopted Hinduism. The percentages of Scheduled Castes populations are generally very small in the N-E region as noted in Table 1.2, except in Tripura and Assam, where these are 16.36 and 7.40 per cent respectively, as per 1991 Census. In Arunachal Pradesh, Meghalaya and Mizoram, it is less than 1 per cent, in Manipur 2.02 per cent while Nagaland does not have any Scheduled Castes population.

SEX RATIOS

The 1991 sex ratios, i.e. number of females per 1000 males, were lower than the national average for India, viz. 927, in Arunachal Pradesh, Assam, Mizoram and Nagaland, while these were higher for Manipur, Meghalaya and Tripura, as noted from Table 1.3. As per 2001 figures, all N-E States seem to have registered an improvement over their 1991 sex ratios, and besides the three previous N-E States, Mizoram has out-stripped the Indian average of 933. When one examines decadal sex ratios from 1901 to 2001, at least four States, viz. Manipur, Mizoram, Meghalaya and Nagaland, are found to have had favourable sex ratios for women in the earlier decades.[6] These have, however, declined in later decades as noted from Table 1.3. Assam and Tripura show a slight improvement after several decades of seriously adverse sex ratios for women. Arunachal Pradesh continues to have a significantly low sex ratio for women. The sex ratios for the Scheduled Tribes population are consistently higher than those for the total State populations for all N-E

→ these are regarded as disadvantaged. The present list of about 1700 Scheduled Castes and 450 Scheduled Tribes has originated from the lists of "depressed communities" and "backward tribes" prepared by provincial assemblies following the British sanction of provincial autonomy in 1935 and some changes were made later as needed. The N-E States include about 116 major tribes and 450 sub-tribes. For details see Sengupta (1988).

6. The sex ratios for Manipur and Mizoram in 1961 were 1,015 and 1,009 respectively, and for Meghalaya in 1921 and Nagaland in 1941 these were 1,000 and 1,021 respectively. See Table 1.3.

Table 1.3 Sex Ratios For India and North-Eastern States, 1901–2001

India/ States	*1901*	*1911*	*1921*	*1931*	*1941*	*1951*	*1961*	*1971*	*1981*	*1991*	*2001*
India	972	964	955	950	945	946	941	930	934	927	933
Arunachal Pradesh	NA	NA	NA	NA	NA	NA	894	861	862	859	901
Assam	919	915	896	874	875	868	869	896	910	923	932
Manipur	1,037	1,029	1,041	1,065	1055	1,036	1,015	980	971	958	978
Meghalaya	1,036	1,013	1,000	971	966	949	937	942	954	955	975
Mizoram	1,113	1,120	1,109	1,102	1,069	1,041	1,009	946	919	921	938
Nagaland	973	993	992	997	1,021	999	933	871	863	886	909
Tripura	874	885	885	885	886	904	932	943	946	945	950

Sources : *Census of India 1991*, Series 1, Paper 2 of 1992, *Final Population Totals: Brief Analysis of Primary Census Abstract*. *Census of India 2001*, Series 1, Paper 1 of 2001, *Provisional Population Totals.*

N.A. : Not Available since no Census was conducted in Arunachal Pradesh before 1961.

States for 1981 and 1991, as seen from Table 1.4. However, out of the four States having predominant Scheduled Tribes populations, viz. Arunachal Pradesh, Meghalaya, Mizoram and Nagaland, only Meghalaya shows a favourable State-wise sex ratio for females in 1991, while those of the remaining three are lower than the national average. The reasons for this perplexing finding, and also for declining sex ratios for Scheduled Tribes populations in Manipur, Mizoram and Nagaland are not clear.

Table 1.4 : Sex Ratios for Total and Scheduled Tribe Population of India and the North-Eastern States, 1981-91

India/States	*1981*		*1991*	
	Total Population	*S.T. Population*	*Total Population*	*S.T. Population*
India	935	983	927	972
Arunachal Pradesh	862	1005	859	998
Assam	NA	NA	923	967
Manipur	971	975	958	959
Meghalaya	954	1,002	955	997
Mizoram	919	997	921	982
Nagaland	863	955	886	946
Tripura	946	962	945	965

Source : Census of India 1991, Series 1, Paper 2 of 1992, *Final Population Totals: Brief Analysis of Primary Census Abstract.*

N.A. : Not Available, since 1981 Census was not conducted in Assam due to disturbed conditions.

FOREIGNERS AND OUTSIDERS

The presence of a large number of foreigners and "outsiders" in the N-E region is mentioned briefly here since this has lately become a highly contentious and politically acrimonious issue. To begin with, there is no agreement on who should be defined as a foreigner. Technically, after the enactment of the Foreigners Act in 1947, all Bangladeshi Muslims who continued to enter Assam without valid permits after Partition should be regarded as foreigners. However, before Partition, many of these immigrants were welcomed by local landlords who needed cheap human labour to increase their landholdings and production. The Chakmas who left their habitat in the Chittagong Hills of Bangladesh and sought shelter in Tripura and Arunachal Pradesh, as well as Tibetan refugees who came into the N-E States after Chinese occupation of Tibet are legally foreigners. A large number of Nepalis who have continued to migrate to this region for earning a livelihood are also legally foreigners since most of them do not have valid permits. This whole issue has been complicated due to the large influx of Hindus who sought refuge in Assam and Tripura following communal disturbances in the erstwhile East Pakistan, and later during the Bangladesh war. An equally acrimonious issue has been the migration of people from other States to the N-E region due to new opportunities in trade, business, professions, administrative services, etc. Both the "foreigners" and "outsiders" are perceived by sections of indigenous people of this region as competitors in the race for economic resources and opportunities. The fear of cultural and numerical dominance by outsiders in indigenous social and political spheres has often queered the pitch of hostility. The resultant antagonism has often led to agitations demanding the expulsion of foreigners and outsiders, and at times to violence.

Political and Administrative Developments

The current situation in N-E region has its roots in the policies adopted by the British administration since the first quarter of the nineteenth century. The present policies of the Government of India are a complex mixture of elements of the British legacy and some new departures in the post-Independence period. A broad outline of important political and administrative developments in the British and post-Independence periods is presented here.

BRITISH PERIOD

British occupation of the N-E region began when the Ahom rulers of Assam and the Meitei king of Manipur sought British help to drive back the invading Burmese forces from their territories. The 1826 treaty of Yandabo initiated by the British, following the Burmese defeat, marked the beginning of formal British control in this region. During the next 50 years, the British expanded their base in the Brahmaputra Valley by conquering and annexing other kingdoms, e.g. the Koch, Jaintia, Heramb (Cachar), etc. They, however, allowed some kingdoms and chiefdoms such as Manipur, Tripura and 25 principalities in the Khasi Hills ruled by ßSyiemsû (chiefs) to continue as princely States with some degree of internal autonomy under the supervision of British officers called Political Agents.

The hill areas of Assam and the Frontier Tracts (present Arunachal Pradesh) were inhabited by a large number of tribal groups who were engaged in inter-tribal wars and invasions of each other's territories. The British policy towards the hill tribes was to leave them alone as far as possible and to adopt some containment measures in case they raided the plains people to obtain food grains and other essential commodities to meet their own requirements. As the tribal raids on the plains became more frequent and devastating, the British felt compelled to intervene, especially since some of the tribes, e.g. the Lushais, Nagas, Akas, Daflas and Abors not only took away food and cattle but also abducted several persons besides killing many. The British sent a number of punitive expeditions to subdue the invaders, but the latter often managed to have an edge over the British forces, with their superior knowledge of the mountainous terrain. The British therefore adopted the strategy of establishing permanent posts at strategic points in the tribal territories in order to exercise effective administrative and military control over tribal groups. In course of time, when a particular tribal area was brought under complete British control, it was constituted as a district and annexed to the State of Assam. By the end of the nineteenth century, after conquering major tribal groups, British officers were appointed to supervise the administration of the districts of Naga Hills, Lushai Hills, Garo Hills, Khasi and Jaintia Hills, Mikir Hills and North Cachar Hills. In a similar manner, the Frontier Tracts (present Arunachal Pradesh) were reorganized in 1914 into three divisions, viz. Sadiya, Balipara and Lakhimpur and put in charge of British officers who were to report to the Chief Commissioner of Assam.

EVOLUTION OF "EXCLUDED AREAS" POLICY

While the British administration enforced some restrictions on the tribal groups, e.g. demarcation of each tribe's territory and banning encroachments and head-hunting, the British policy was to avoid interference in the traditional tribal customs and practices. Furthermore, the tribal chiefs and tribal councils were left free to manage internal affairs of their respective tribes and settle disputes according to their own customary codes. A reference to the District Officers or to the Chief Commissioner was to be made only in exceptional cases.

Simultaneously, the British Government introduced a number of legislative and administrative measures[7] to insulate the hill and tribal communities from external political influences. The Inner Line Regulation of 1873[8] restricted entry of outsiders to the tribal regions without a special permit, and prohibited acquisition of tribal land by non-natives. The hills and tribal areas of N-E region were designated as "Excluded" and "Partially Excluded" areas[9] and these were precluded from the application of laws enacted by the central or provincial legislatures. On the other hand, the Governor of Assam had the discretionary powers to decide which laws, and with what modifications, would be applicable to these areas, and when necessary, prescribe special regulations for their governance. Additionally, for the Frontier Tracts (which were also referred as Political Tracts), which covered the present Arunachal Pradesh, the Governor acted as Agent of the Governor-General, and the policies for their administration were to be determined by the Central government, through the External Affairs Department.[10] The Excluded Areas did not have representation in the provincial legislature of Assam, which was intended as a safeguard to avoid external interference but later became a contentious issue (Agnihotri, 1992).

EXPOSURE OF N-E REGION TO EXTERNAL INFLUENCES

Notwithstanding the official British policy to protect N-E region from outside influences, a number of developments in the world and the rest of India were to make significant impact on this region. Christian missionaries of

7. These included: Scheduled District Act of 1874, Assam Frontier Tract Regulation of 1880, Assam General Clauses Act of 1915, Government of India Acts of 1919 and 1935.
8. The Bengal Eastern Frontier Regulation empowered the Provincial Government to specify areas covered by the Inner Line, with the sanction of the Governor General. Assam was previously treated as an adjunct of Bengal. In 1921 it became a Governor's province under provisions of the 1919 Government of India Act.
9. Excluded Areas: North-East Frontier Tracts (present Arunachal Pradesh), Naga Hills (present Nagaland), North Cachar Hills sub-division, Lushai Hills (present Mizoram). Partially Excluded Areas: Garo Hills, Mikir Hills (present Karbi Anglong), the British portion of Khasi and Jaintia Hills other than Shillong Municipality and Cantonment.
10. For details of British policy in the N-E region refer to Assam Government, *The Excluded and Partially Excluded areas of Assam, 1947.*

various denominations had begun to turn their attention to various tribal communities of this region since the middle of the nineteenth century. On the whole, the British administration supported the missionaries' attempts to spread the message of Christianity and thus bring a "civilizing" influence among communities dominated by warfare and superstitions. The missionaries opened schools and prepared scripts for various tribal languages to enable the people to read the Bible. The spread of education, however, achieved a far more fundamental objective of opening their horizons to the wider world of scientific knowledge and learning. A number of persons who were initially enrolled in missionary schools later went to seminaries and institutions of higher learning in other parts of India and abroad and provided intellectual leadership on their return. For the British, many of these educated local people provided a loyal group of employees in government service.

Another important factor in breaking the isolation of N-E communities, was the participation of several men from this region in the two world wars. The direct exposure to World War II operations for people of Manipur, Meghalaya, Nagaland and Arunachal Pradesh made a profound impact on people of this region and marked the beginning of a new awareness among them.

POST-INDEPENDENCE PERIOD

On the eve of Indian Independence in 1947, the N-E region presented a complex and qualitatively diverse picture in its component parts. The plains areas of Assam were strongly influenced by the national movement led by Gandhiji and the Indian National Congress. Despite hectic efforts by the nationalist leaders of Assam to counter the divisive forces unleashed by the Muslim League, Sylhet with the exception of Karimganj, went to East Pakistan (later Bangladesh) at the time of Partition of India, while Cachar remained with Assam. In Manipur and Tripura, popular movements exerted effective pressure on the ruling *maharajas* of these princely States for agreeing on their merger with the Indian Union in 1949. Among the hill communities of Assam, e.g. the Khasis, Jaintias, Garos, Nagas, Lushais, etc. there was considerable insecurity regarding their future in the composite State of Assam. Some British administrators had exacerbated the tribal suspicions by holding out before them the possibility of their forming a joint "Crown Colony" outside the control of India and having direct links with Britain. When India attained Independence in 1947, the hill and tribal communities of this region were apprehensive about their possible exploitation by more advanced societies in the rest of India. They were also anxious to preserve their distinctive cultural traditions and ethnic identities in the new dispensation of free India.

When the national leaders of free India were deliberating on the Constitution, special committees were appointed to ensure the protection of interests of various disadvantaged sections of the country's population. Furthermore, a special sub-committee led by Gopi Nath Bordoloi, a prominent leader of Assam, was responsible for incorporating a number of Constitutional provisions especially to safeguard the interests of Scheduled Castes and Scheduled Tribes.[11] In addition, the Fifth Schedule of the Constitution included special provisions for the administration of Scheduled Areas in order to prevent exploitation of Scheduled Tribes by moneylenders and to preserve their interests in land. A more specific provision in the Sixth Schedule of the Constitution provided for the formation of autonomous district/regional councils for administration of tribal areas of Assam, Meghalaya and Mizoram.[12] The Government of India continued the Inner Line regulation for Arunachal Pradesh, Mizoram and Nagaland in order to restrict the infiltration of outsiders in these States, and to protect local communities from possible exploitation.

The decade following the adoption of the Indian Constitution in 1950 was marked by a series of negotiations between the Government of India and leaders representing various communities of the N-E region. The proposal made by the States Reorganization Commission in 1953-54 was unacceptable to the latter. Around 1960, the idea of a separate State combining the various hilly areas, e.g. Khasi, Jaintia, Garo, Naga, Mikir, Mizo, North Cachar hills, etc. within or outside Assam was perceived as a possibility by the hill leaders. The enactment of a Bill declaring Assamese as the official language of Assam State in 1960, however,

11. Articles 46, 15, 16, 19, 225 and 335 enjoin on the State special responsibility to promote the educational and economic interests and welfare of Scheduled Castes and Scheduled Tribes and to protect them from social injustice. They also provide for reservation of seats in educational and training institutions, representative bodies and in government jobs.

12. The autonomous district/regional councils have been endowed by various State Acts with legislative, financial, executive and judicial powers over several matters, e.g. reserved forests, agriculture, animal husbandry, shifting cultivation, customs regarding marriage, inheritance of property, matters related to education, health, etc. These Acts indicate areas where autonomous councils do not have authority and matters in which State Governments have over-riding powers, which explains variations among States.

came as a jolt and created resentment and insecurity about their future among the hill leaders. Their federation, the All Party Hill Leaders' Conference (APHLC) split at this point and each constituent chose its independent direction.

The Khasi, Jaintia and Garo leaders carried on a Constitutional struggle during the following decade and succeeded in 1970 in ensuring partial fulfilment of their demand of a separate State of Meghalaya within Assam. The leadership among the Nagas and Mizos however went to radical sections that demanded the formation of sovereign republics of Nagaland and Mizoram outside the Union of India. After prolonged periods of armed struggle and insurgency and several rounds of negotiations, Nagaland became a separate State in 1963. After enactment of North-Eastern Areas (Reorganization) Act of 1971 Mizoram achieved the status of Union Territory in 1972, and full Statehood in 1987. Arunachal Pradesh became a Union Territory in 1972, and became a full-fledged State in 1987. Meghalaya too attained the status of an independent State in 1972. Manipur and Tripura, both princely States, merged with India in 1949, and after short stints of being part C States and Union Territories, attained full Statehood in 1972. Even after formal attainment of Statehood, the separatist elements have continued to create disturbances in some areas of the N-E region. While attempts to sort out the grievances of some of the disgruntled sections continue, the process of restoring peace becomes infinitely complicated particularly due to the clandestine support given to them by hostile forces outside India's border.

Economic Aspects

While important strides have been made in incorporating N-E region in the Indian political framework, the challenging tasks of social and economic integration of this region with the rest of the country remain to be adequately tackled. The following section presents some major aspects of the economic under-development of this region and potential resources, which need to be fully developed and utilized.

JHUM CULTIVATION

The economy of N-E region is primarily agricultural. In this context, it is essential to understand the nature of "jhum" or "shifting" cultivation, which is practised extensively in the hilly areas of this region. These include Arunachal Pradesh, Meghalaya, Mizoram, Nagaland, the two hill districts of Assam, viz. North Cachar Hills and Karbi Anglong, and hill areas of Tripura and Manipur. Settled cultivation is practised mostly in the valleys.[13]

In jhuming, which is also called "Slash-and-Burn" cultivation, a patch of hill slope is cleared by cutting down the trees and shrubs, which are left to dry in the sun, and are then set on fire. The ashes are spread over the cleared ground and just before the rains, seeds are either scattered over the field or put in small holes dug with a dibbling stick, a sickle or a "Dao" (large chopper). This system depends entirely on human labour and adequate rains, and does not use ploughs or other agricultural implements, nor does it take the help of manures, pesticides or irrigation methods. Usually paddy and maize are the main crops, and other products such as millets, pulses, vegetables, ginger, chillies, cotton, etc. may be obtained by putting several types of seeds together. The same patch of land may be used for a second year, after which it is kept fallow for some years for natural regeneration, while another patch of a mountain slope may be taken up for jhuming. It may take 10-12 years before the original plot, which is by that period covered by forest, is again taken up for jhuming by rotation. With the growth of population, the jhuming cycle has been shortened to 3-4 years in many areas, thus disturbing the process of natural recuperation of the soil. This has resulted in declining productivity of the land, denudation of forests, heavy soil erosion leading to silting of rivers and streams and consequent flooding.

It has always been customary for most households engaged in jhuming to supplement the food supplies by edible roots, tubers, leaves and fruits, etc. from forests. There are generally no surpluses, but some products from jhum cultivation may be sold to obtain the cash needed for procuring other household requirements. With decreasing yields from jhum cultivation, women have to strive harder to provide food for the family.

It is important to appreciate that jhuming is not only man's adjustment to a particular ecological situation, but also a way of life in terms of systems of ownership and management of land and social relationships. Among most tribal communities, land is usually owned by the tribe, village,

13. A Task Force appointed by the Ministry of Agriculture in 1983 had estimated that the total area in the N-E region under jhuming was 3,865 sq km or 1.5 per cent of the total area of the region, and 4.43 lakh families were involved. (NEC, *Basic Statistics*, 1990).

clan or lineage and allocated to individual households for one or two years on usufructuary basis by the village council or the council of elders representing various clans. The individual has no right to sell or transfer the allocated plot to anyone else. A similar system operates with respect to forest areas, excepting those, which are designated as reserved or protected forests that are owned by the government, and their proportion varies among the States. Excepting some forest areas, which may be owned by individuals or by village chiefs, most others are earmarked for the use of a village, tribe or a clan, whose members can collect fuel, fodder for animals, wood and bamboos for house construction as well as edible roots and tubers for food. These forests are managed by village councils or in some cases by elected members of autonomous district councils, whenever such councils have been established.

There are, however, some variations among N-E States, and even among tribes within the same State. A few tribes have retained the system of chieftains who own all lands within their territory. The Chief allocates plots to individual members for cultivation in return for a share of the produce and free services to be provided to the Chief's household. The Chief is usually assisted by a council of elders who decide on the area to be selected for jhuming. There is another variation prevailing among some tribes, e.g. the Angamis and Chakhesangs of Nagaland and Apatanis of Arunachal Pradesh, who have practised terraced and settled cultivation for several generations, and such lands are owned by individual households.

Irrespective of the pattern of ownership of land, tribal communities of N-E region who are engaged in jhum cultivation have lived at subsistence level, where disparities in income among families were insignificant. But strong traditions of mutual help among members of the same clan, tribe or village have acted as a buffer to meet the needs of labour or food shortages of individual households. In general jhum cultivation is usually associated with joint ownership of land, and introduction of settled cultivation has brought about a shift towards individual ownership of land. Various government programmes aimed at control of jhuming and promoting settled cultivation through introduction of improved technology, e.g. terracing, bunding, irrigation, improved seeds, manures, plantation crops, etc. have usually led to increasing individual ownership of land. The resulting erosion of community management of land and social solidarity has rendered individual households more vulnerable to exploitation by more powerful social sections in the absence of an alternative system of social security.

DEFICITS IN FOOD PRODUCTION

By 1990-91 the annual food grain production of N-E region, as per Indian Economic Survey, was 4.89 million tonnes, which rose to 5.19 million tonnes by 1996-97, which is insufficient for its burgeoning population. The region faces serious shortfalls in food production, and has to depend on supplies brought from other States. The decreasing yields from jhum cultivation are well known. But even in areas such as the Brahmaputra Valley of Assam where settled agriculture is practised, the yields are low because the use of modern agricultural technology has remained limited to a small proportion of land under cultivation.[14] By 1988, around one lakh tonnes of food grains had to be imported into N-E region every month to meet local deficits. It was estimated as per NEC sources that by 1990, this region would need an additional annual production of two million tonnes of food grains (*NEC Journal,* January-June 1988, p. 2). As against 1.40 lakh metric tonnes of annual requirement of fish, the regional production in 1989-90 was only 93,250 metric tonnes, and it could go up to 3.03 lakh metric tonnes. (Sinha, M., *NEC Journal*, 1991). The current requirements of imported food grains are significantly higher.

Low Level of Industrialization

Besides tea and petroleum, there are no major industries here. Less than 2 per cent of the country's large and medium-scale industries and 1.5 per cent of small-scale industries were located in this region until 1988 (Mali, *NEC Journal*, 1988). It contributes less than 2 per cent of the value added by manufacture. It exports raw materials which are processed outside the region and imports finished products. For instance, this region exports Agarwood, which is processed in other States to extract Agarwood oil, which is in high demand in India and abroad. It has the right climate and terrain to produce an abundance of pineapple, citrus fruits and bananas. Most of these are, however, sold locally at a cheap price since

---

14. According to NEC data, irrigation coverage in 1988 was about 15 per cent of the total net area sown. The use of high yielding varieties in Assam during 1986-87 did not go beyond 1,030 thousand hectares for paddy. In other States it was negligible. For details see *NEC journal*, January–June 1988.

fruit-processing facilities are inadequate and transportation of fruits to outside markets cumbersome and expensive. The few small-scale industries which exist in this region, e.g. sericulture, handloom weaving, cane and bamboo crafts, poultry and piggery units, etc. suffer from lack of modern and efficient marketing facilities.

UNDEVELOPED INDUSTRIAL POTENTIAL

One of the factors contributing to slow development of N-E region, apart from difficult transportation facilities referred to earlier, is inadequate power generation despite the existence of very large potential in this region. It is estimated that 37.8 per cent of the total national hydel power potential, or 32,000 MW, is located in N-E region which is endowed with the Brahmaputra and its tributaries. When this is augmented by the power potential from natural gas and from coal reserves, the total adds up to an impressive figure of 50,000 MW, out of which less than 2 per cent was tapped until recently.[15] Another indicator of the lack of development is the low per capita consumption of electricity. In 1988, it was 69 KWH as against the all-India average of 253 KWH.[16] This region possesses rich mineral resources, e.g. deposits of beryl, shale, corundum, copper, iron, coal, dolomite, sillimanite, limestone and fireclay. Except for the oil in Assam, most of these resources remain unutilized so far. A number of factors, such as lack of technical and entrepreneurial skills, unavailability of adequate government and private investment needed for various projects, shortage of banking and co-operative financial institutions, etc. have posed formidable obstacles in speedy industrial development of the N-E region.

North-Eastern Council (NEC)

The establishment of the NEC in 1972 represents a major government

---

15. The natural gas reserves in Assam are estimated to be 135 billion cubic m, which are additional to those in Tripura. Arunachal Pradesh, Assam and Meghalaya have 845 million tonnes of coal reserves (Ahmed, *Times of India*, 20 June 1994). By the end of 1988, the installed capacity of hydel power in the N-E region was 420.30 MW, thermal power 499.50 MW and diesel power 76.86 MW. (NEC, *Basic Statistics* 1990:78).
16. There were wide variations in per capita consumption of electricity in 1988 among the N-E States, ranging between 46 KWH in Nagaland to 113 KWH in Meghalaya. See NEC, *Basic Statistics*, 1990: 79. By 1992-93, the situation changed only slightly, with the lowest in Tripura at 83.9 KWH and the highest in Meghalaya at 159.4, while the national average was 330.6 KWH (NEC, 1995:112).

initiative to promote an integrated and co-ordinated strategy for the development of the N-E region. It was visualized as an advisory body to provide a joint forum for the seven N-E States. It has actively formulated and implemented schemes in transport, communications, water management and power generation sectors. In addition, it has sponsored pilot projects in improved agriculture, control of jhuming, development of horticulture plantations, animal husbandry, sericulture, exploration of minerals and their processing, etc. While NEC has so far placed its major focus on infrastructural development, it has also supported some demonstration projects in the area of manpower development, e.g. training, entrepreneurial skills, management, etc. There is no doubt that human resources development is emerging as a crucial element in accelerating N-E region's development. NEC's efforts were complemented by another specialized organization, North-Eastern Industrial & Technical Consultancy Organization (NEITCO) set up in 1973.

In the course of recent reviews of NEC's performance, the seven N-E States expressed a need to change its organization, staffing and functions, in order to enhance its effectiveness as a competent planning body. It will be expected to prepare technically efficient plans for the development of this region's vast unused potential. But more importantly, the NEC must also play a key role in mobilizing the huge financial resources needed through government as well as private investments. Without massive investments, projects such as the hydro-electric power project on Brahmaputra River, estimated to cost Rs. 54,000 crore, or other ambitious projects for building roads and rail networks and oil refineries, etc. cannot be implemented.

Recapitulation

The foregoing outline has highlighted the difficult geographical terrain, problems of transport and communications and N-E region's physical isolation from the rest of India. Its major demographic features include a high rate of growth of its 1991 population of 31.37 million, which rose to 38.50 million by 2001 (Provisional Population Totals), a relatively small proportion of urban population, a sizeable population of Scheduled Tribes (STs) and its highly heterogeneous composition. Its alienation from the national mainstream can be traced to the British policy of designating large areas of this region as "Excluded" and "Partially Excluded" and keeping them insulated from outside social, cultural, administrative and political influences.

During the post-Independence period, there has been a continuation of the British policy with the avowed aim of safeguarding the ethnic and cultural interests of tribal and hill communities from external encroachment. Simultaneously, the five decades after Indian Independence in 1947 have witnessed a long and at times agonizingly stormy process of political integration of N-E States in the Indian Republic, which is by no means fully achieved. The challenging tasks of bringing about the economic development of this region are yet to be addressed adequately. Only when this process makes a convincing headway, can the social and emotional integration of the N-E region with the rest of India gain momentum.

2

North-Eastern States
Seven Unique Sisters

Introduction

CHAPTER 1 highlighted selected major features of N-E region as a whole. Although the seven component States of this region are euphemistically called Seven Sisters, each sister has a distinct personality shaped by her unique history, culture, assets and liabilities. This Chapter presents brief outlines of the seven N-E States. Each time we do this in two parts: Historical Perspective, spanning over Earlier History, British and Post-Independence period; and the second part, Present Situation, which includes Salient Geographical and Demographic Features, followed by Current Economic and Social Context. These outlines provide the backdrop for understanding various aspects of women's status in each State presented in succeeding chapters. In the interest of making these accounts as concise as possible, many details had to be omitted from the main text and some were included in the notes for the benefit of readers with an eye for details. On the other hand, readers conversant with these backgrounds may skip this chapter and proceed directly to chapter 3. The socio-political and cultural developments in the composite Assam, which previously included Arunachal Pradesh, Meghalaya, Nagaland and Mizoram, have influenced the whole N-E region. This ssexplains why Assam's background precedes that of Arunachal Pradesh in this chapter, while the following chapters take-up the States in their alphabetical order.

ASSAM

Historical Perspective

EARLIER HISTORY

Old Hindu and Buddhist texts, the epics, royal chronicles and stone inscriptions found in the Brahmaputra Valley indicate a close interaction between the inhabitants of Assam and the Aryans and the Indian culture from ancient times.[1] The better known history, however, deals with the period from thirteenth century CE onwards. A number of Indo-Mongoloid tribes from China, Mongolia, Tibet and South-East Asia came to Assam during the medieval period.[2] Between the thirteenth and sixteenth centuries, some tribes had established chiefdoms and monarchical State systems, e.g. Kamrup, Chutia, Koch (Cachar), Jaintia, etc. As their political fortunes fluctuated, they often had to change their habitats, and while some were forced to surrender their territories to the victors, some added new territories and expanded the boundaries of their kingdoms.

One of these groups, the Ahoms, a Mao-Shan sub-tribe originating in upper Myanmar and Yunnan (China) came to Assam in several batches since 1228. During the following six centuries the Ahoms fought with and defeated other kingdoms and chiefdoms and established their supremacy. The Muslims invaded Assam several times between thirteenth and seventeenth centuries. Despite some reverses when the Mughals imposed humiliating conditions on the Ahoms,[3] the latter finally defeated and expelled the Mughals from lower Assam in 1681. By this time, Ahom kingdom covered a major part of the Brahmaputra Valley. During the

1. *Ramayana* and *Mahabharata* refer to the ancient kingdom of Pragjyotish and the "Kiratas." King Bhaskaravarman who ruled over Kamrup kingdom between CE 594–654 was known to be a close ally of Harshavardhana, who ruled over a large part of north India and Bengal during CE 606–647.
2. Acharya (1988) has classified settlers in N-E region into four racial stocks:Veddoid, Dravidoid, South Europoid and Mongoloid and traced the ethnic processes in the formation of various communities. B.P. Singh (1988) divides them into Austrics, Negroids, Kiratas (Mongoloid), Dravidians and Aryans.
3. During the rule of an Ahom king Jayadhwaja Singh (1648–1663), his minor daughter Ramani Gabharu was sent to the Mughal harem after the Mughal general Mir Jumla defeated the Ahoms. She was later married to Aurangzeb's son Sultan Azam. When her maternal uncle Laluksola Bar Phukan was colluding to surrender Guwahati to Azam in return for the latter's help in ascending Ahom throne, Ramani Gabharu stoutly opposed this treacherous move (Borah, 1988).

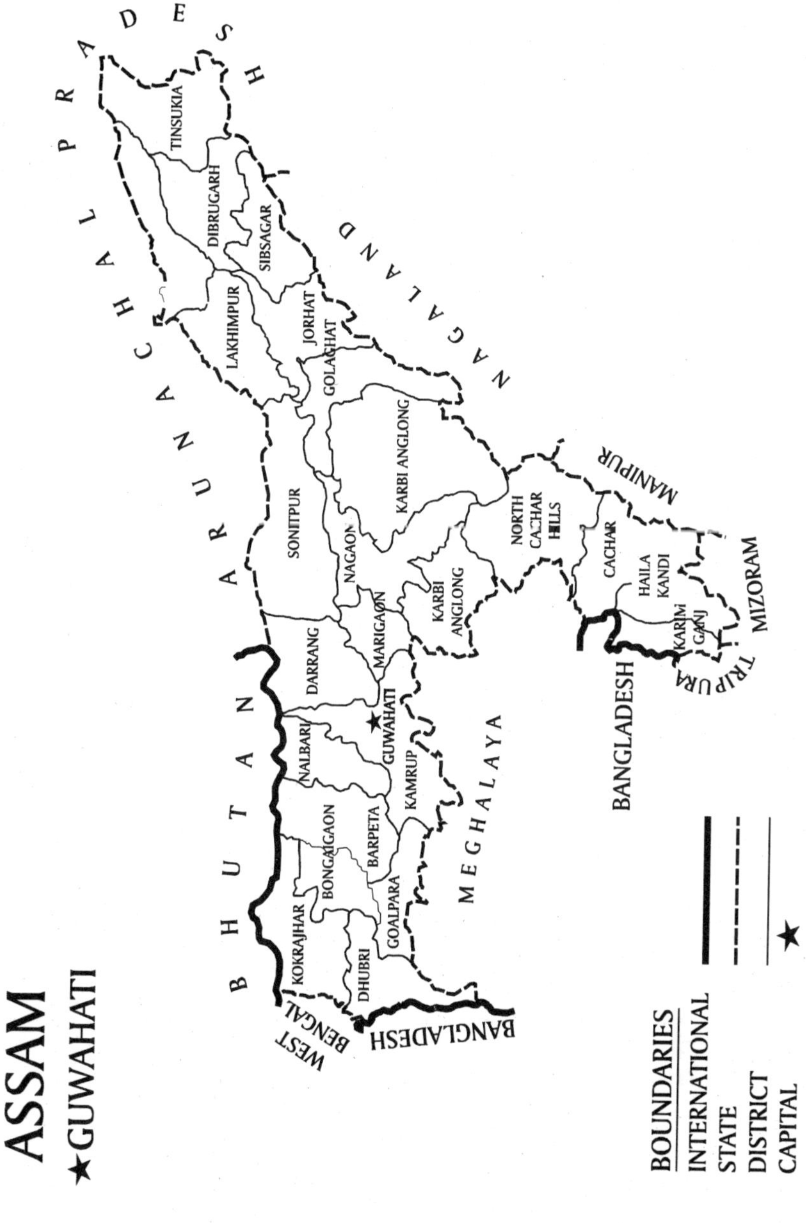
ASSAM
★GUWAHATI
ARUNACHAL PRADESH
NAGALAND
MANIPUR
MIZORAM
TRIPURA
MEGHALAYA
BANGLADESH
BHUTAN
WEST BENGAL
TINSUKIA
DIBRUGARH
SIBSAGAR
JORHAT
GOLAGHAT
LAKHIMPUR
SONITPUR
KARBI ANGLONG
NAGAON
NORTH CACHAR HILLS
CACHAR
HAILA KANDI
KARIM GANJ
MARIGAON
DARRANG
GUWAHATI
NALBARI
KAMRUP
BARPETA
BONGAIGAON
GOALPARA
KOKRAJHAR
DHUBRI
BOUNDARIES
INTERNATIONAL
STATE
DISTRICT
CAPITAL

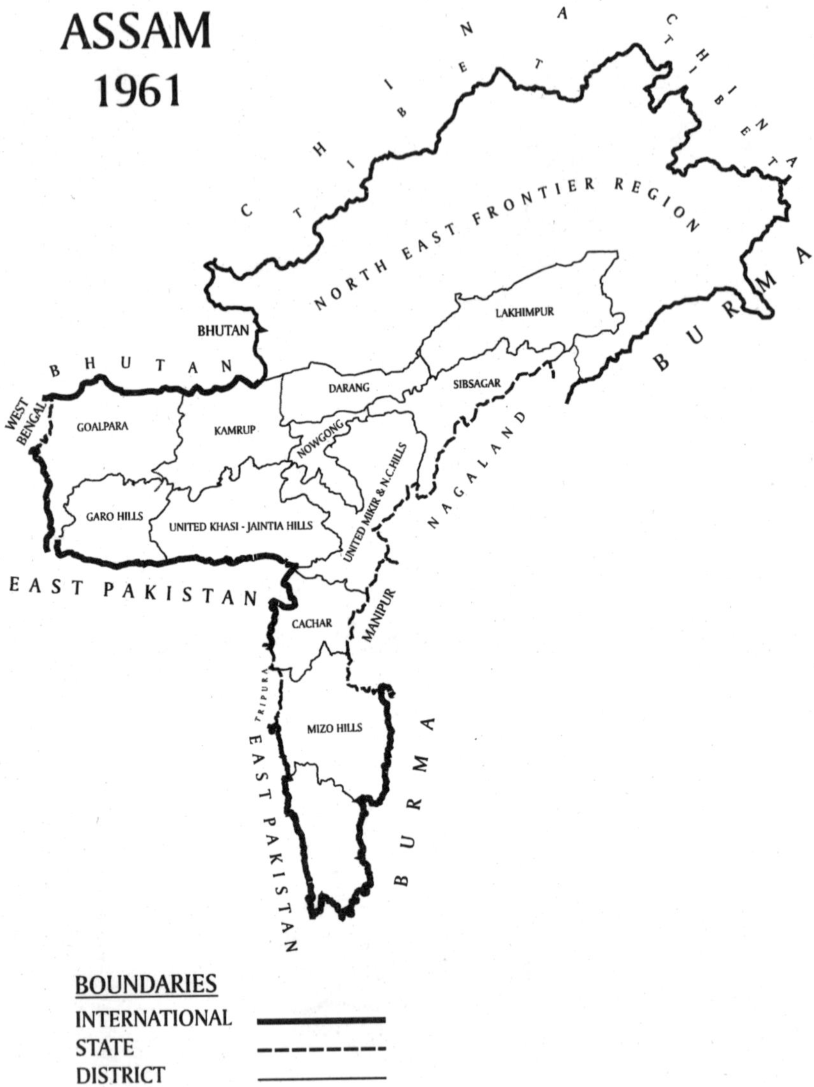
ASSAM
1961
CHINA TIBET
TIBET CHINA
NORTH EAST FRONTIER REGION
BHUTAN
BHUTAN
WEST BENGAL
GOALPARA
KAMRUP
DARANG
LAKHIMPUR
SIBSAGAR
NOWGONG
UNITED MIKIR & N.C.HILLS
GARO HILLS
UNITED KHASI - JAINTIA HILLS
NAGALAND
BURMA
EAST PAKISTAN
CACHAR
MANIPUR
TRIPURA
MIZO HILLS
EAST PAKISTAN
BURMA
BOUNDARIES
INTERNATIONAL
STATE
DISTRICT

period of relative peace which followed, they tried to consolidate their kingdom by setting up elaborate systems for civil and defence services where vassal States and chiefdoms were obliged to provide certain services and tributes to Ahom kings. The Assamese society of this time was highly diverse, representing a wide range of groups characterized by the most primitive subsistence cultivation on the one hand, while adopting elaborate systems of water distribution and wet-land cultivation on the other, besides different socio-cultural traditions.

Assam's adoption of Hinduism played a major role in bringing about some integration in its society. The process of Hinduization had indeed begun even prior to Ahoms' arrival in thirteenth century, as brahmins from the Gangetic Valley and Bengal began to receive the patronage of several ruling families, e.g. Kamrup, Koch, Heramb (Cachar). By fifteenth century, Ahoms had incorporated some Hindu rituals side by side with their native Tai rituals and Hindu temples received royal grants. The formal conversion of the Ahom king to Hinduism in 1648 accelerated the dissemination of Hindu culture in Assam. The eclectic and pluralistic system of Hinduism facilitated different communities to select those deities and rituals from a large pantheon, which could be suitably adapted to their native religion.[4] Another important influence was the advent of neo-Vaishnavism propounded by Shankar Deva, a saint-reformer of the fifteenth century. He and his disciples preached a simple and appealing faith, worship of one god — Vishnu — through devotion and eliminated elaborate rituals to be performed by brahmin priests. They popularized communal worship at "Namghars" (community prayer houses) where anybody, without distinctions of caste or creed could participate. In the liberal ambience of Vaishnavism, it is not surprising that a seventeenth-century Muslim saint Shah Milan, popularly known as Azan Fakir in Assam, found a wide following (Misra, 1999).

Without going into the details of social implications of the adoption of Hinduism, it needs to be noted that the ruling classes, who appropriated for themselves kshatriya caste, tried to super impose the Hindu caste system over the existing hierarchy based on clan and lineage. Nevertheless, Assamese society remained relatively free from some of the extreme forms of caste oppression, such as untouchability and exploitation of women

4. For example, the fearsome Dimasa goddess "Kachai Kati" was suitably re-incarnated as "Shakti." According to one view Shakta and Tantric Hinduism, in turn, incorporated some influences from North-Eastern tribes (Nag, 1995).

of lower castes by powerful land-owning castes as in Bihar and some other States. Furthermore, the greater social heterogeneity and traditions of tribal independence tended to create some space for divergence, despite large scale detribalization within the Assamese society.

By the end of the eighteenth century, the Ahom kingdom was declining due to internal strife and successive Burmese invasions weakened it further. Finally the Ahoms sought British help to subdue the Burmese, and the British found it an opportune development in view of their interest in securing a trade-route into China. With British help, the Ahoms as well as the Manipuris, who were also invaded by the Burmese, finally repulsed the Burmese, but had to accept British dominance in the bargain.

BRITISH PERIOD

The British occupation of Assam started in 1826 after they concluded the treaty of Yandabo with the Burmese. By the end of the nineteenth century they annexed to Assam the following districts: Goalpara, Darrang, Nowgong (presently named as Nagaon), Sibsagar, Lakhimpur, Cachar, Garo Hills, Khasi and Jaintia Hills, Naga Hills, North and South Lushai Hills and Sylhet (presently in Bangladesh). The Frontier Tracts (present Arunachal Pradesh) administration and the "Excluded Areas" policy to insulate hill tribal communities from external political and social influences have been outlined in Chapter 1. Until 1874, Assam was treated as an adjunct of the composite Bengal Presidency, and was later given the status of a Chief Commissioner's province. In 1921, Assam became a separate Governor's province following the passing of the Government of India Act of 1919. Even after this, British rulers continued the use of Bengali language and employment of Bengalis in administrative services, which resulted in persistent Bengali dominance in Assam government bureaucracy.

The colonial orientation of British administration with respect to governance of Assam and utilization of its natural resources disrupted indigenous systems of family-based production and consumption and introduced money economy based on profit motive among people who were ill-equipped to protect themselves from exploitation. A few examples should suffice. The Assam Land and Revenue Regulation Act of 1886, which was ostensibly intended to protect tribal interests, in effect, legitimized the Zamindari and Rayatwari systems by permitting landlords to bring extensive areas under their ownership by leasing land on rental basis and by hiring cheap migrant labour. This attracted land-hungry Muslim peasants from East Bengal to migrate to Assam since 1890s due to adverse local conditions. They were allowed to occupy wastelands and "Char-lands" (river islands). Their superior skills in wet-land cultivation and familiarity with commercial crops and markets helped to establish their dominance over indigenous peasants. The 1931 Census report compared the *modus operandi* of the nearly half a million immigrants to "a mass movement of a large body of ants." Over a period, the indigenous peasants, many of them tribesmen, who were too impoverished to pay the land-rents, or had incurred debts, would mortgage or surrender their lands for a pittance, or become wage labourers. Furthermore, they were also exploited by Marwari moneylenders and unscrupulous traders. Due to the shifting cultivation practised by most tribal peasants, the colonial rulers did not grant them permanent land rights, which facilitated usurpation of their lands by immigrant settlers. Within a short period, the immigrant Bengali settlers occupied substantial wastelands, "char-lands," encroached on village grazing grounds and forest reserves and captured lands belonging to indigenous Assamese peasants wherever possible. As all available lands in Goalpara, Nagaon and Kamrup were exhausted; the Bengali settlers moved to upper districts, e.g. Darrang, Sibsagar, Lakhimpur, etc.

Yet another illustration of colonial exploitation was the system of British forest administration introduced in 1880. It demarcated forest areas into various categories, e.g. Reserved, Protected, Commercial, etc. From now on, tribal communities were restricted from collecting various forest products, vital to their subsistence, from government-controlled forests. On the other hand, the British allowed outside forest contractors to plunder Assam's rich forest resources and to send these raw materials outside the State for processing and selling at highly lucrative prices. The government's role in encouraging British entrepreneurs to set up tea plantations in Brahmaputra Valley by defining vast areas as wastelands and leasing them for nominal rates, as against higher rates on land under traditional cultivation, was another glaring instance of colonial exploitation. The terms of lease were framed deliberately to pre-empt indigenous entrepreneurs and commercial sector was thus empowered to encroach on lands cultivated under subsistence sector (Deb, 1979). The plantations employed migrant labour from Bihar, Orissa, Madhya Pradesh, Uttar Pradesh, etc. The processing of tea leaves and auctions benefited British business, not Assam. The limited network of roads, rail and steamer services developed by the British was controlled mostly by British capital and was designed primarily to serve their trading interests in tea, petroleum and coal.

The British attitude of viewing Assam as a colonial hinterland was echoed by H.S. Suhrawardy when he proposed to the Cripps Mission that Assam should be tagged to East Pakistan to supply raw materials for the latter's industrialization (Bhattacharya, 1984). At the time of Partition of India, Muslim League had repeated this demand. Jawaharlal Nehru, however, stoutly opposed this proposal and Assam remained with India. It is interesting to note that Mohammad Tayebulla, who was President of Assam Congress in 1945, mobilized popular opinion in the State to thwart British attempts to include Assam in Pakistan (Misra, 1999).

POST-INDEPENDENCE PERIOD

This period is marked by an acceleration of important demographic changes, some of which began in the nineteenth century, and by their economic and cultural repercussions on Assamese Society. Secondly, the political changes which led to the carving out of four independent States of Nagaland, Meghalaya, Mizoram and Arunachal Pradesh out of the composite Assam exacerbated ethnic assertion movements deteriorating at times into conflicts among several tribal and non-tribal communities of Assam. The third important aspect is the anti-foreigners movement which rocked Assam during 1979-85 and its aftermath.

The Partition of India in 1947 and creation of East Pakistan led to a large number of Bengali Hindus seeking refuge in Assam as a result of communal riots in Noakhali and other places. The Indo-Pak conflict in 1965 and Bangladesh war of independence in 1971 caused massive flow of Bengali Hindus who sought shelter in Assam. Meanwhile, the influx of Muslim immigrants from East Pakistan, which began from early twentieth century, continued unabated, for reasons which need not be discussed here. Nepalis who started coming to Assam in search of employment as soldiers,[5] herdsmen and porters, etc. since the nineteenth century continued their migration in larger numbers, facilitated by the 1950 Indo-Nepal Treaty of Peace and Friendship (Nag, 1995). The tea

5. Nepali Gurkhas formed the backbone of Assam Rifles and Sylhet Light Infantry (which was later named Gurkha Rifles) and the British used them extensively in punitive expeditions against invading hill tribes in border areas (Nag, 1995).

garden labourers and their dependents who started coming to Assam since 1853 numbered well over 15 lakh by early 1980s. Besides, people from other States of India, particularly Bihar, Uttar Pradesh, West Bengal and Punjab, etc. came in large numbers to seize the new economic opportunities which opened up after Independence.

Between 1911 and 1971, the number of migrants into Assam was estimated to be 5.2 million, out of which 2.4 million came during 1951–71, and their inflow has continued in the following decades (Goswami and Gogoi, 1984; Goswami, 1984). In 1991, among migrants from other States into Assam, the largest number (44.27 per cent) was from Bihar and the next in rank were those from West Bengal (21.48 per cent). Foreign migrants into Assam in 1991 were 3.39 lakh, the preponderant majority (84.85 per cent) being from Bangladesh (Bandyopadhyay and Chakraborty, 1999).[6]

The pockets of concentration of Bengali migrants — both Hindu and Muslim — in certain areas, e.g. Cachar and Goalpara, their air of superiority about Bengali language and culture and their dominance in bureaucracy and educational institutions deeply hurt the pride of the Assamese. The preservation of Assamese culture and language became a major preoccupation among Assamese leaders and made them rather insensitive and indifferent towards ethnic identity needs of hill and plains tribal communities of Assam. The 1960 enactment restoring Assamese as the official State language and how this precipitated developments leading to creation of separate States of Nagaland, Meghalaya, Mizoram and Arunachal Pradesh by 1972 has been presented in Chapter 1. In any case, the separation of these areas from Assam was inevitable since their initial inclusion in Assam by the British was primarily a matter of administrative and political expediency. The tribal communities of Mikir Hills (present Karbi Anglong) and North Cachar Hills, however, opted to remain within Assam and presently form a distinct segment of Assam's population. Under provisions of the Sixth Schedule of the Constitution as mentioned in Chapter 1, Karbi Anglong and North Cachar Hills have

6. Nandi (1997: 21-34), on the basis of analysis of population growth in N-E region between 1971-91, believes that a large number of Myanmari tribal groups entered this region and due to similarity in cultures, got assimilated with local populations making detection difficult, and that the impact of separation of Burma (present Myanmar) in 1937 has so far been largely ignored by scholars.

Autonomous District Councils, which are intended to give a certain degree of autonomy to their inhabitants with respect to tribal customs and traditions (Dutta Ray, 1999). These developments have encouraged a number of other tribal and non-tribal communities to organize movements to preserve their ethnic identity. Some groups started literary and religious revival activities (e.g. Bodo Sahitya Sabha), but later acquired political overtones (e.g. Cachar Sangram Parishad), and some have taken a violent and secessionist stance (e.g. Bodo Security Force).

The Assam Movement during 1979-85 was far from a sudden outburst of anger and rebellion. Indeed, the frustration and despair were building over a long period and Central Government's inaction was perceived as primarily responsible for the situation. The Assamese youth for some time had been feeling dejected that they were not getting a fair share of the already limited job opportunities in government and private organizations, professions, trade, commerce, etc. as a disproportionate number of these were captured by non-Assamese persons.[7] The All Assam Students Union (AASU) which spearheaded the movement had demanded in 1978 that 80 per cent of all posts in government and private undertakings must be reserved for Assamese persons. A related issue was the neglect by Central Government of Assam's economic development, and the continuing colonial pattern of exploitation of Assam's rich resources, e.g. oil, natural gas and tea, which benefited outside capital, but failed to generate local employment. Added to this dismal picture was the longstanding problem of immigrant settlers usurping lands belonging to indigenous Assamese, and the State Government's failure, despite several land reform measures, to restore lands to the latter.[8]

Against this background of simmering Assamese discontent, accumulating evidence of Bengali immigrants' increasing political influence, particularly in the 1978 State Assembly elections, proved to be a flash-point. AASU tried to seek redressal of a number of contentious

7. For data on distribution of employees in private and public sector organizations, refer to findings of Employment Review Committee of the Government of Assam, quoted by Baruah in Abbi (ed.) (1984 : 322-28).

8. Some examples of laws trying to protect sharecroppers and tenants and to restore lands to evicted indigenous owners are: Assam State Acquisition of Zamindaris Act, 1951; Assam Fixation of Ceilings on Land Holding Act, 1956, Assam (Temporarily Setted Areas) Act, 1971; Assam Tenancy Act, 1974, Karbi Anglong District (Land Reforms) Act, 1979, creation of protected belts for weaker sections, like hill tribals, plain tribals, tea garden workers, SCs, etc.

issues in several rounds of negotiations with Central Government representatives including the prime minister, between 1973 and 1979. The breakdown in discussions came towards the end of 1979 due to differences on the cut-off date for defining foreigners and deleting their names from electoral rolls. AASU, which was now joined by All Assam Gana Sangram Parishad (AAGSP), felt there was no alternative except to launch a non-cooperation movement. The next five months turned out to be an extremely turbulent period with a quick succession of events: death of peaceful picketers in police firing which triggered wider protest rallies; deployment of army and security forces by the government leading to a spontaneous mass non-cooperation movement, which forced the State Government to withdraw the curfew in April 1980. Several rounds of negotiations between AASU-AAGSP leaders and Central and State Governments followed, interrupted by deadlocks. The Assam Accord in 1985, which marked the formal withdrawal of the anti-foreigners movement included an important item, Illegal Migrants' Determination Tribunal (IMDT), with 1971 as the cut-off date to decide the status of migrants into Assam.

Meanwhile, the basic issues involved in the movement have remained unresolved. The IMDT has mostly failed to stop illegal infiltration of immigrants into Assam due to several reasons, which include practical difficulties in safeguarding the porous international border as well as procedural wrangles in implementation of IMDT. The period between 1979 and 1985 was marked by a virtual collapse of State Government and extreme political uncertainty. The old animosities and grouses which were kept in abeyance during the Assam movement are coming into open and some sections, who have lost their faith in the government administration, have been resorting to violence to settle old scores. The poor law and order situation and political uncertainty have discouraged outside capital investment in new ventures, thus hampering industrial growth.

Present Situation

MAJOR GEOGRAPHICAL AND DEMOGRAPHIC FEATURES

Assam presently covers an area of 78,438 sq km which is divided into two ecological zones: the plains comprising Brahmaputra and Barak Valley, and the hill areas which include the two districts of North Cachar Hills and Karbi Anglong. These hills constitute a natural dividing line separating

Brahmaputra Valley from Barak Valley. The latter, in view of its proximity to Bangladesh (former East Pakistan) has received the major impact of Bengali-speaking immigrant populations, which explains why it differs in certain social and cultural aspects from the Brahmaputra Valley. Assam is divided into following districts: Barpeta, Bongaigaon, Cachar, Darrang, Dhemaji, Dhubri, Dibrugarh, Golaghat, Goalpara, Hailakandi, Jorhat, Kamrup, Karbi Anglong, Karimganj, Kokrajhar, Lakhimpur, Marigaon, Nagaon, Nalbari, North Cachar Hills, Sibsagar, Sonitpur, and Tinsukia.

Assam population, as per 1991 Census was 22.41 million, the percentages of urban population being 11.10, that of STs 12.83, and SCs 7.4. The religious distribution was: Hindus 67.13 per cent, Muslims 28.43 per cent, Christians 3.32 per cent, and Other Religions and Persuasions totalling 1.12 per cent. As per Provisional Population Totals of 2001 Census, Assam's population was 26.63 million.

The tribal population, mostly Hindu, is divided into hill tribals and plains tribals. The hill tribal groups are concentrated in the two hill districts, North Cachar Hills and Karbi Anglong and include the Karbis (formerly called as "Mikir" which had an association with head-hunting and was therefore discarded), Dimasas and small groups of Nagas, Kukis, Mizos, Jaintias, Khasis, etc. The plains tribals, many of whom belong ethnologically to the Bodo family, include Bodo Kachari (the most numerous group), Miri (Mishing), Rabha, Sonowal Kachari, Lalung, Deori, Barman Kachari, Mech, Hojai, Tai-Phake, Aiton, and some other sub-groups.

Assam's non-tribal population, which forms a predominant majority at present, includes heterogeneous groups of Hindus, Muslims, Christians, etc. Among the Hindus, brahmins, kshatriyas, kayasthas and kalitas occupy a high status. The SCs include Kaibartas, Banias, Jal-Keots, Namshudras, etc. Surprisingly, the Moran, certain sections of Ahoms, Koch and Chutia, who at one time belonged to ruling tribal groups and adopted kshatriya status for themselves, lost their position when they isolated themselves into interior regions after British occupation of Assam, and began to be included among "Other Backward Classes" (OBCs) (Deka, 1982). A presidential ordinance in 1997 declared the Koch and Rajbonshi of Assam as STs, which caused considerable concern among other tribal groups, since this intensifies competition for special benefits provided to STs, including seats reserved for tribal persons in representative bodies such as Bodo Autonomous Council.

A sizeable chunk of Assam's non-tribal population consists of Hindus who include two sub-groups: (a) indigenous or Assamese Hindus, who originally belonged to various tribes which continued coming to Assam over many centuries and became Hinduized and de-tribalized mainly between fourteenth and eighteenth centuries; (b) immigrant Hindus of two types: (i) those who came to Assam from other Indian States mainly during the twentieth century in search of economic opportunities; and (ii) Bengali Hindus who came as refugees following communal disturbances shortly prior to and after Partition of India in 1947. Another important part of Assam's population, consists of tea garden labourers who belong to Santhal, Munda, Oraon and other tribes in Bihar, Madhya Pradesh, Uttar Pradesh, Orissa, and are listed among "OBCs" in Assam.

The Muslims constitute more than a quarter of the non-tribal population of Assam and belong to three streams. Some Muslim soldiers who accompanied Muslim invasions between thirteenth and fifteenth centuries, stayed behind and adopted Assamese language and culture and are called Assamese or indigenous Muslims.[9] By far the largest segment consists of immigrants from East Bengal (later East Pakistan and Bangladesh), who came mainly in the twentieth century and should be referred as immigrant Bengali Muslims. The third stream consists of Pangans or Manipuri Muslims[10] who are concentrated mostly in Cachar and Karimganj districts.

ECONOMIC AND SOCIAL CONTEXT

Most of Assam's vexing social and political problems, even those which are precipitated by ethnic dominance and rivalries, are related to its disappointing level of economic development. According to Planning Commission estimates, in 1987-88, 22.8 per cent of Assam's population was below the poverty line. For various reasons the methodology and assumptions used for this exercise have been questioned (Chandrashekhar

9. Misra (1999) attributes their assimilation in Assamese society to the accommodating nature of Assamese society and a liberal brand of Hinduism influenced by Shankardeva's Vaishnavism, which is reflected in the devotional songs composed by Azan Fakir, a seventeenth-century Muslim saint, who attracted many followers in Assam.

10. Pangans are believed to be descendents of Muslim soldiers who came to Manipur as a part of invading Muslim armies, stayed behind and inter-married with Manipuri women. Why and when they left Manipur and settled in Assam is not known with certainty, however, that Manipuri kingdom at one time included some parts of Cachar is known.

and Sen, 1976). The Agro-Economic Research Centre of the Assam Agricultural University conducted a study on the basis of which the percentage of Assam's population below the poverty line in 1986-87 was 52.29 per cent. The Expert Group appointed by the Government of India in 1989 placed the percentage of population below poverty line for 1993-94 at 40.86 per cent. The number of people below the poverty line in rural areas was 94.33 lakh (45.01 per cent) and in urban areas 2.03 lakh (7.73 per cent).[11]

Agriculture, which continues to be Assam's major production sector, continues to provide low yields since it is mostly devoid of new technologies, such as irrigation, use of fertilizers and high-yielding varieties.[12] The average yield of rice in 1994-95 was 1330 kg in Assam, as against all-India average of 1910 kg (NEC, 1995). There has been no significant increase in total food grain production, which was 3441.80 thousand tonnes in 1990-91 and stood at 3532.10 thousand tonnes by 1996-97 (Banerjee 1999: 29). Assam currently faces large deficits in food grains which need to be met through imports from other States at high costs. Tea plantations and forestry-based units such as match and plywood factories constitute an important sector which currently does not benefit Assam fully since it is managed by outside capital.[13]

Assam is endowed with rich resources of oil, natural gas, coal, limestone, etc. only a small fraction of which are tapped currently. So far

11. For details, refer to *Report of the Expert Group on Estimation of Proportion and Number of Poor,* Perspective Planning Division, Govt. of India, July 1993. For determining the poverty line, a fixed consumption basket including 2400 and 2100 calories for rural agricultural labourers and urban industrial workers respectively was used. Based on per capita monthly expenditure of Rs.49.00 for rural and Rs.56.60 for urban areas respectively for 1973-74, State-specific poverty lines based on consumer price and general indices were used to determine the poverty lines for 1993-94. In the absence of adequate basic data, the Expert Group used Assam's poverty ratios for rural and urban populations as basis for estimating the number of persons below the poverty line in Arunachal Pradesh, Manipur, Meghalaya, Mizoram, Nagaland and Tripura.
12. In 1990-91, the percentage of net irrigated area to net sown areas was 21.14 in Assam, as against all India's 33.35 (NEC, *Basic Statistics,* 1995). According to Assam's Directorate of Agriculture reports, per hectare consumption of fertilizers for Assam in 1990-91 was 14.35 kg as against all-India's 76 kg and Punjab's 162.2 kg for 1992-93.
13. Assam has nearly 800 tea estates and until recently, their production accounted for nearly 60 per cent of India's foreign exchange earning, although the main beneficiary is not Assam, but capitalists outside Assam (Banerjee, 1999, 27).

while the mining units have been located in Assam, the processing was done in other States. With the recent establishment of a petroleum refinery and a few other factories, this is expected to change. Still the number of large and medium-scale industrial units in the State in 1994 was 118 and that of small-scale units in 1988 was 4430 (NEC, 1995), which is very small in comparison with other Indian States. Handloom weaving, sericulture, cane and bamboo crafts and other handicrafts, which are covered in the small and cottage industries category hold a much greater potential in terms of employment and volume of production than available at present. These units need to be strengthened with modern technology to improve the quality of products and institutional support for training, marketing, supply of raw materials and credit requirements. The inadequacy of infrastructure, e.g. transportation systems and electricity, banking and financial institutions, continue to be major constraints in economic development.[14] The Net State Domestic Product of Assam in 1994-95 was Rs. 14,528 crore (Indian Economic Survey, 1996-97), and for 1996-97, the provisional figure was Rs. 17,480 crore, as per State Directorate of Economics and Statistics and Central Statistical Organization.

Meanwhile, the long-awaited multi-purpose Brahmaputra (and its tributaries) project seems like an ever-receding dream with rapidly escalating costs. Consequently, the acute shortage of electrical power cripples industrial development and what is worse, devastating annual floods cause enormous damage to crops and loss of property, while water for irrigation remains scarce. The economic changes in Assam through post-Independence period indicate a lop-sided development of service sectors without adequate expansion of commodity sectors of agriculture and industry, according to Bezbaruah (1999). It is not enough to seek the causes of Assam's underdevelopment on the basis of amounts sanctioned and disbursed by financial institutions,[15] or the extent of Central assistance

14. The cumulative amounts sanctioned and disbursed by all-India financial institutions in Assam up to 1995 were Rs.1,098 crore and Rs. 827.8 crore respectively, as against Rs.54,990.4 crore and Rs.35,323.4 crore for Maharashtra and Rs.35,264.9 crore and Rs. 19,729.9 crore for Gujarat, according to IDBI, 1995 report. (Hazarika,1997).

15. In the Net State Domestic Product of Assam for 1996-97 the service sectors which include transport, trade, banking, business, service, public administration, etc. account for 46.52 per cent, whereas agriculture and allied sectors, mining and manufacturing account for only 38.14 per cent and 15.34 per cent respectively: (Bezbaruah, 1999, 92-100; Assam State Directorate of Economics and Statistics and Central Statistical Organization).

in implementation of five-year plans (Bhattacharjee, 1995). At the same time, there is no doubt that the poor condition of infrastructure and long accumulating backlog in development calls for special consideration, as well as imaginative and flexible procedures on the part of Central Government with respect to Assam.

The current social scene in Assam reflects a serious disillusionment on several counts. Despite the Assam Accord in 1985 which included Illegal Migrants Determination by Tribunal (IMDT), illegal migrants continue to enter Assam largely due to porous international borders and connivance of local people. The economic situation has shown no significant improvement, unemployment continues to be high and no progress has been made in restoring the lands captured by immigrant settlers to their indigenous owners. The emergence of a regional party, Asom Gana Parishad (AGP) and new youthful leadership in 1985 elections for State assembly had generated many hopes about rapid progress of the State and removal of longstanding grievances. Pretty soon, however, the AGP-led government got mired into manipulative politics and personal ambitions. As a result, a number of population sections felt seriously let down and have assumed aggressive postures. A few examples should suffice to illustrate this point.

United Liberation Front of Assam (ULFA) was established by the more militant but disgruntled sections of All Assam Students Union (AASU) leadership. For nearly 15 years, ULFA activists, who include some women, have launched a campaign of sabotage, abductions, ransom, murders, etc. particularly directed against non-Assamese persons, police and security personnel. They have also resorted to sabotage of the key installations like oil pipe-lines, bridges, rail-roads, etc.

Bodos, one of the earliest Indo-Mongoloid groups to settle in Assam, an educationally and socially backward plains tribal group, has recently been jolting the State with outbursts of organized violence against the perceived usurpers of their rights. They have a longstanding grouse against immigrant Bengalis, Muslims and Santhals (who originally came to Assam as tea plantation labour), who have acquired lands in traditional Bodo areas probably aided by their enterprising ability and shrewdness (Hazarikas, 1996). Since the Bodos failed to get the State Government to restore their lands, they have set up militant groups which have been attacking villages inhabited by Muslims and Santhals, burning houses, killing people and forcing their eviction (Banerjee, 1994). Quite expectedly, there have been counter-attacks by Santhals and Muslims, forcing Bodos to leave their villages. Since it has been virtually impossible to provide adequate protection to evicted persons, thousands of people who include Muslims, Santhals and Bodos, have to be sheltered in relief camps in Kokrajhar, Nalbari, Bongaigaon and other affected districts.

When an accord for the creation of Bodoland Autonomous Council was reached between Assam government and All Bodo Students' Union (ABSU) chief, S.K. Bwiswmutiary in 1993, brokered by Central Government, there was jubilation and relief that an agonizingly violent phase had ended. Unfortunately, this has proved to be the thin end of the wedge and the more militant sections among the Bodos are now demanding a fully autonomous separate State of Bodoland. While the violence has continued to erupt in sporadic attacks, sharp differences have emerged among proliferating Bodo outfits, vying for leadership and claiming to be the legitimate representatives of the community.[16] There is accumulating evidence of alignments between different militant groups in the N-E region, and worse still, of clandestine support in arms and funds from hostile forces outside India's borders.

It should not come as a surprise that many other communities, e.g. Mishing, Rabha, Lalung, etc., demanded creation of Autonomous Councils for their respective areas. The Karbis, who are already covered by an Autonomous District Council, are now demanding greater devolution of powers by State Government to the Council, through their front organization, Autonomous State Demand Committee (ASDC). The need for ethnic assertion and a greater share in political and economic power is not limited to tribal groups. For instance, Assamese Muslims, who had initially distanced themselves from immigrant Bengali Muslims, are having second thoughts about their Assamese identification after the 1983 Nellie violence and later disturbances around 1994, e.g. in Barpeta and Kokrajhar where Muslims were targeted.[17] The Assamese Muslims and

---

16. The several Bodo organizations include: All-Bodo Student's Union, Bodo Peoples' Party, National Democratic Front of Bodoland, Bodo Women Justice Forum, Bodoland Liberation Tiger Force, Bodo National Peace and Co-ordination Committee, Bodo Security Force, People's Democratic Front, etc. For information on internecine struggle for leadership, see Guha, *Times of India*, 7 January 1997; also *Times of India,* 2 July 1996.

17. During the controversial 1983 polls in Assam, about 3000 people, many of whom were immigrant Muslims, were killed at Nellie. There was another wave of violence in 1994 when Muslims were targeted, their houses burnt →

Bengali immigrant Muslims together now constitute a sizeable community, which has grown in size from 19 per cent of State population in 1931 to 28.43 per cent in 1991. There are districts where Muslims constitute a decisive majority, e.g. Barpeta (56.07 per cent), Dhubri (70.42 per cent), Goalpara (50.18 per cent) and Hailakandi (55.18 per cent). No political party can afford to ignore them, and they are already demanding their share in jobs and services (Misra, 1999). The tea garden labourers also constitute a sufficiently numerous group at present and can tilt political fortunes in some constituencies.

In summing up, Assamese society at present, even after separation of Nagaland, Meghalaya, Mizoram and Arunachal Pradesh, represents a conglomeration of many diverse groups representing a wide range of cultural, linguistic, religious, social and economic backgrounds. Its current phase of ethnic conflicts and communal violence must not be allowed to make us forget that for several centuries Assamese society has displayed unusual ability for assimilating new and varied influences. Assamese intelligentsia must play a crucial role in reviving the tolerant ethos of the past which helped to hold together communities having sophisticated social and religious systems along with those with primitive lifestyles and animistic faiths. Undoubtedly, the State Government must provide leadership in avoiding past mistakes, deal with social conflicts with forbearance and tact, and above all, assume its full responsibility instead of blaming the Central Government for all lapses. The rich natural resources of Assam and its social diversity can become its greatest assets, if used with care and foresight, by avoiding the temptation of short-term gains. The Central Government will also have to support Assam through a sympathetic and imaginative approach, keeping in view Assam's considerable developmental backlog and social and economic handicaps caused by colonial exploitation and its lingering effects.

ARUNACHAL PRADESH

Historical Perspective

EARLIER HISTORY

A number of archaeological excavations in Arunachal Pradesh testify to the presence of a civilization which goes back at least to the ninth or tenth

→ and they were forced to leave their settlements and seek shelter in relief camps. These events predictably led to revenge where Bodos became victims.

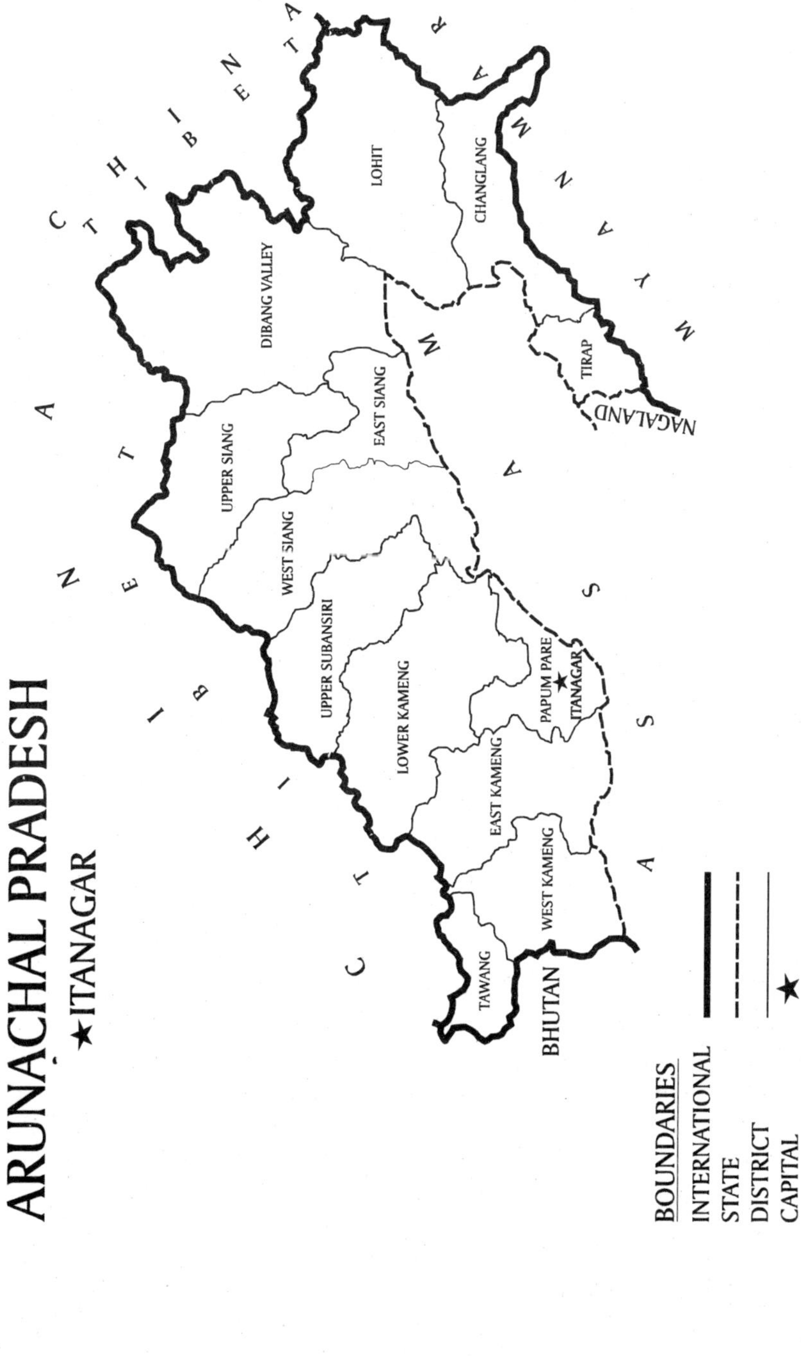
ARUNACHAL PRADESH
★ITANAGAR
CHINA TIBET
MYANMAR
ASSAM
NAGALAND
BHUTAN
LOHIT
CHANGLANG
DIBANG VALLEY
TIRAP
EAST SIANG
UPPER SIANG
WEST SIANG
UPPER SUBANSIRI
LOWER KAMENG
PAPUM PARE
ITANAGAR
EAST KAMENG
WEST KAMENG
TAWANG
BOUNDARIES
INTERNATIONAL
STATE
DISTRICT
CAPITAL

century CE. However, available recorded history relates only to the later Ahom period. A number of Mongoloid tribes of Indo-Tibetan and Indo-Burmese stocks continued coming here from different directions over several centuries and often changed their habitats whenever they were pushed out by more powerful groups or because they were in search of more hospitable lands for cultivation. The Adi legends and folklore refer to their journey from the north across the Himalayas. The Khamti and Singpho came from Myanmar. The Monpa, Sherdukpen, Memba and Khamba tribes came from Tibet side. Some tribes came initially to Brahmaputra Valley and later migrated to Arunachal Pradesh. On the other hand, some tribes such as the Chutia lived originally along the banks of Dibang River in Lohit region and later migrated to Majuli and Sibsagar areas of Assam.

Inter-tribal conflicts were common and tribes having superior skills, e.g. wet-land cultivation or better fighting ability, subjugated the weaker or more peace-loving groups. The Akas who had learnt wet-rice cultivation through their contacts with the plains people and were aggressive fighters, were held in awe by the Miji and other surrounding tribes, who were required to pay tributes to the Akas. The Miji in their turn tried to enslave the gentle Sherdukpens, which provoked British intervention during 1937-39 (Misra, 1982). The practice of keeping persons captured in raids in slavery seems to have prevailed among many other tribes in the N-E region, but became more institutionalized in Arunachal Pradesh.

The system of slavery has prevailed among a number of Arunachal Pradesh tribes at least since the seventeenth century. The Akas and Daflas (currently known as Nishing) generally acquired slaves either from the neighbouring Sulung or Khoa tribes by purchase or by raids. They also raided the plains of Assam to capture persons who were turned into slaves. The Daflas were notorious for their practice of advancing loans to poor Sulungs who remained in perpetual debt and bondage and worked in the fields of their Dafla masters. Slavery was hereditary and permanent and the children of slaves automatically became the property of their masters. As an extension of this practice, the Daflas also procured several wives by purchase, their status being no different from labourers in the fields and domestic servants. Some other tribes, e.g. the Mishmi, Khamti, Singpho, Nocte, Tangsa, etc. were known to impose outright slavery or some form of bondage on weaker sections. In fact, even after the abolition of slavery by legislation in 1955, some vestiges of this oppressive system continue to this day.[18]

The relationship of the tribes of Arunachal Pradesh with the Ahoms fluctuated a great deal according to exigencies on either side. The hill tribes raided the plains villages in Assam whenever they faced shortages of food, cattle or human labour. Sometimes the Ahoms launched punitive expeditions against the raiders. There were, however, times when the Ahoms found it expedient to conclude pacts which permitted the invaders to collect "Posa" — a kind of blackmail levy to keep the peace — from specified plains villages annually.[19] On the other hand, some tribes would enter into alliances with the Ahoms, e.g. the Daflas, sending 600 archers who with their superior familiarity with the hilly and forested terrain made a lightening attack and forced the Muslim invaders to retreat.

BRITISH PERIOD

After the British occupation of Assam in 1826, the Frontier Tracts (present Arunachal Pradesh) came under their hegemony. They now became more directly responsible for protecting people of Assam plains from raids by various hill tribes from the north, e.g. the Aka, Dafla, Abor, etc. Sometimes they too, like the Ahoms, took recourse to pacts agreeing to the collection of "Posa" by the raiding tribes.[20] Whenever the raiders became too outrageous, the British organized punitive expeditions from time to time, sometimes jointly with the Ahoms, Tripuris, etc. At times the raiders inflicted humiliating defeats on the British, as evident from records left by some British officers.[21] The general policy of the British to avoid interference with the internal affairs of the tribes, as well as to prevent external

18. For details regarding the forms of slavery and exploitation among the tribes of Arunachal Pradesh and other N-E areas, see Misra (1982).

19. The "Posa" consisted of annual collection of salt, grains, cloth, cotton thread, cattle, agricultural tools such as the chopper, etc. The British changed it into money. The Ahom King Pratap Singh, (CE1603-47) when beleaguered with successive Muslim invasions, was known to have agreed to collection of "Posa" by the Akas, Daflas and other raiding tribes in return for their co-operation. (Mishra 1991).

20. The agreements concluded by the British with the Akas in 1844 and 1876 included, besides money, allotment of lands for cultivation in the foot-hills and plains for the warring tribes who lived at higher altitudes. See Sinha (1962).

21. The famous Abor expedition of 1911-12 bears witness to this. For an interesting description of the humiliating British retreat against the devastating Abor archers hiding in thick forest in 1859, see Imdad Hussain's (1992) account based on a British soldier's diary.

influences through the "Excluded Areas" policy and the "Inner Line" regulation continued (*Refer to Chapter 1 for details*). At the same time, the intermittent violation of peace by tribes from the Frontier Tracts necessitated extension of administrative control over this area. In 1914, some tribal areas of Lakhimpur and Darrang districts of Assam were separated and integrated in the North-East Frontier Tract and this area was divided into three units: (1) Sadiya, comprising central and eastern section; (2) Balipara, the western section; and (3) Lakhimpur. The first two were placed under the charge of Political Officers and the third under Deputy Commissioner of Lakhimpur (presently a district of Assam). In this same year, 1914, the first administrative centre was established at Pasighat. All the three units were brought under the overall control of the Chief Commissioner of Assam. In 1942 and 1946, these units were further sub-divided and Tirap Frontier Tract was carved out. The "Frontier Tracts" still remained "un-administered" area in British official terminology.

In 1943, there was a shift in British policy, which henceforth had two major objectives: extending administrative control in stages, and promoting development of tribal communities inhabiting this area, which was referred as "Backward Tracts." In 1945, the Assam Governor promulgated the Assam Frontier (Administration of Justice) regulation. This recognized the powers of "Village Authorities" to deal with disputes where both parties belonged to tribal communities. This policy change might well have been due to growing British anxiety over the growth of the nationalist movement in India and the consequent need to appease tribal sentiments. Furthermore, Tirap area had a direct brush with Second World War operations, and the British undoubtedly felt the need to be more alert to developments in this area.

POST-INDEPENDENCE PERIOD

The Frontier Tracts, together with the Naga Tribal Area (present Tuensang) were designated as North-East Frontier Agency (NEFA) in 1951. In 1954 it was reconstituted into six Frontier Divisions: Kameng, Subansiri, Siang, Tirap, Lohit and Tuensang. In 1957, Tuensang Frontier Division was separated from NEFA and joined to Naga Hills, which later became the State of Nagaland. Under the Sixth Schedule of Indian Constitution, NEFA remained under the special jurisdiction of the Assam Governor, who was to act as the agent of the President of India. The "Excluded Area" and

"Inner Line" policy developed by the British continued with minor variations, along with the practice of non-interference with tribal customs and institutions. After the Indo-China border conflict in 1962, there has been a deliberate shift in Indian Government policy towards gradual integration of NEFA into the wider national framework. In 1967, NEFA Panchayati Raj Regulations were adopted to give civil and criminal jurisdiction to village, anchal and zilla parishads.

With the enactment of North-Eastern Areas (Reorganization) Act of 1971, NEFA became Union Territory of Arunachal Pradesh in 1972, thus ending its previous status as a tribal area within Assam. The 36th Constitutional Amendment in 1975 provided for a Legislative Assembly and a Council of Ministers for Arunachal Pradesh. Simultaneously, the Chief Commissioner, who had so far acted as Administrator was re-designated as Lt. Governor on 16 August 1975, and a Council of Ministers was sworn in on the same day.

In 1978, general elections based on adult franchise were held for the first time to elect a 30-member legislative assembly. In the same year the assembly passed the Freedom of Indigenous Faith Act, which was aimed at protecting the indigenous people from external pressure for proselytization. In 1986 the Indian Parliament passed a Bill which changed the Union Territory status of Arunachal Pradesh, and on 20 February 1987 it became the 24th State of the Indian Union.

Apart from the intellectual and emotional isolation caused by "Inner Line" policy, the mountainous and heavily forested terrain and poor development of roads have kept Arunachal Pradesh geographically isolated from the rest of India. The author recalls being accosted by native persons in interior areas with a question whether the visitor came from "India," which in their imagination must seem like a very distant land with which they have no connection. Up to 1981, out of a total number of 3,257 inhabited villages in the State, 2,768, i.e. more than three-fourths, were not linked by roads. It is not uncommon for a government health centre doctor on a home visit to a patient to trek for four days along a mountainous footpath, far away from even a jeepable road. The situation has improved somewhat in the last twenty years. Most district headquarters are now connected by direct road links, thus avoiding to some extent the circuitous routes going through Assam.

Present Situation

MAJOR GEOGRAPHICAL AND DEMOGRAPHIC FEATURES

Arunachal Pradesh covers an area of 83,743 sq km almost all of which is covered by Himalayan ranges, steep valleys and high altitude plateaus with only about 10 per cent being foothills and plains. Besides several major rivers such as Dihang, Lohit, Subansiri, Kameng, etc. a very large number of smaller rivers originating in the Himalayan ranges flow through Arunachal Pradesh before joining the Brahmaputra. When there are heavy rains or when the snows melt, many of these rivers are in spate which throws the already weak road network in complete disarray. The State is bounded by Bhutan on the west, Tibet and China on the north, Myanmar on the east and Assam and Nagaland on the south. The State includes the following districts: Changlang, Dibang Valley, East Kameng, East Siang, Lohit, Lower Subansiri, Papum Pare, Tawang, Tirap, Upper Siang, Upper Subansiri, West Kameng, West Siang.

Its population of 8.64 lakh according to 1991 Census, includes 20-25 major tribes, sub-divided into about 110 sub-tribes, STs constituting 63.66 per cent and urban population 12.80 per cent. In 1997, 16 SCs, which were overlooked in the 1986 Arunachal Pradesh Statehood Act notification, were officially recognized. The various STs speak about 50 dialects and the "Nefamese" — a mixture of Assamese, Hindi and other words — but have no written scripts of their own, the only exception being the Khamtis who use Pali script. As per 1991 Census, the religious distribution of Arunachal Pradesh population was: Hindus 37.04 per cent, Christians 10.29 per cent, Buddhists 12.88 per cent, Muslims 1.38 per cent. A significantly large section of the State's population is covered under Other Religions and Persuasions — 36.22 per cent — which includes 2,75,385 persons belonging to Donyi-Polo faith, a symbol of cultural revival and assertion of ethnic identity among the Adi tribes.[22] Furthermore, 21,020 and 11,720 persons Stated their religion as Wancho and Nocte, respectively. As of 2001, the total population of Arunachal Pradesh was 1.02 million, as per Provisional Population Totals, Census of 2001.

22. Donyi-Polo represents a synthesis of the Sun (female) and Moon (male) principles. Some scholars have found similarities between Adi religion and the Vedic religion of pre-Aryan society, e.g. the concept of immortality of the soul, struggle between the "good" and "evil" elements, the practice of propitiating gods through sacrifices, etc. See Chowdhury (1971).

"Adi," the new generic title of a major population group, includes many tribes, e.g. Gallong, Minyong, Padam, Pasi and several sub-tribes.[23] An ethnic integration movement initiated in the 1960s has brought several groups together under their new Adi identity and revived their ancient religion — "Donyi-Polo." Adis are concentrated in East and West Siang and Dibang Valley districts, and have been promoting spread of education and modernization. Nishings, who include the Dafla, Nishi, Sulung, Miji, etc. inhabit Lower and Upper Subansiri and East Kameng areas. The Monpa and Shredukpen, who are concentrated around Bomdila in Kameng, and the Memba and Khamba tribes in Upper Siang belong to Tibetan Mahayana Buddhist tradition. The Khamti and Singpho groups in Lohit and Tirap districts, on the other hand, follow the Hinayana Buddhist tradition due to their Myanmar origin. Other inhabitants of Tirap are the Nocte (mostly Vaishanavite Hindu), Wancho and Tangsa. Other major tribes are the Mishmis of Lohit, the Apatanis of Subansiri and the Akas of Southern Kameng. A sizeable number of Chakma, Hajong and Tibetan immigrant refugees have settled down in Arunachal Pradesh over the past three decades, which has recently become a disturbing social and political issue.

ECONOMIC AND SOCIAL CONTEXT

The difficult communications and Inner Line regulation restricting the entry of outsiders in the State have kept Arunachal Pradesh isolated from technological and social changes in the rest of India. Indeed, a chance encounter with a habitation in an interior area gives one a glimpse of a lifestyle which could well belong to the hunting and food-gathering phase of human society. About 80 per cent of the State's total workforce is dependent on agriculture. Until 1980s jhuming was the predominant mode, the Apatani Valley and some other areas being the only exception where terraced cultivation is prevalent.[24] Forests, which cover 61.5 per cent of the total State area, constitute a major asset and nearly two-thirds (62.17 per cent as per 1990-91 classification) belong to the community-owned category (Mitra, 1999). Families have always depended on forests

---

23. "Adis" also cover Tagin, Ramo, Bakar, Pailbo, Ahinga, Tangam, Karko, Milang, Panggi, etc. The old name "Abor" suggesting "unruly" or "savage" given to them by others has now been discarded.

24. A 1981 survey by National Council of Agricultural Research revealed 70.77 per cent of the total sown area, the highest in the N-E region, under *jhum* cultivation.

to meet daily requirements of fuel, fodder for cattle, wood and supplementary food such as edible roots, tubers, fruits, etc. In 1987-88, the percentage of population below the poverty line, according to the Expert Group appointed by Government of India, was 37.47 per cent, which rose to 39.35 per cent in 1993-94 and included 3.62 lakh rural and 0.11 lakh urban people.[25]

In the last two decades, Arunachal Pradesh government has launched several schemes to promote settled cultivation through providing incentives such as individual ownership of land, which traditionally has been community-owned, through passing Arunachal Pradesh Land Settlement and Land Reforms Act in 1980. Other measures include agricultural extension services, modern technology inputs such as improved seeds, manures and implements, besides promoting horticulture, tea and coffee plantations, production of medicinal plants, etc. By 1994 settled cultivation was adopted in 56 per cent of total sown area in the State (Roy and Kuri, 1999). Recent harvests of pineapple, bananas, citrus fruits and apples have shown good promise and a beginning has been made in cultivation of walnuts, guavas and plums, according to State Government sources (Directorate of Economics and Statistics, 1998). There is good potential for animal husbandry, e.g. dairy farming and milk production, and rearing of sheep, pigs, poultry. The possibilities of promoting sericulture, viz. eri, mulberry and tussar silk are being explored.

Arunachal's forests constitute a rich resource capable of boosting the State's income besides generating employment. These have so far taken the brunt of shifting cultivation, excessive exploitation of forest products and illegal felling of trees, without a comparable effort in planting new trees and regenerating degraded areas. Nearly 50 per cent of timber supply from the whole N-E region comes from Arunachal Pradesh, and one-fifth of the State's total revenue is contributed by its forests (Mitra, 1999). With the establishment of Arunachal Pradesh Forest Corporation in 1978-79, some forest-based units, e.g. saw mills, plywood and veneering mills have been set up. It is all the more urgent that a long-term and scientific plan for regeneration of degraded areas and prevention of excessive and illegal exploitation of forests is undertaken urgently. Unless this is done on a priority basis, rapid denudation of forests, excessive soil erosion and consequent devastating floods, and above all, permanent destruction of the State's unusually rich biodiversity cannot be avoided.

25. See Note 11, for details on methodology.

So far, industrial development has been rather slow, largely due to a number of infrastructural constraints, such as difficult terrain, poor road network, no rail link and inadequate power supply. The number of large and medium-scale industrial units in Arunachal Pradesh in 1994 was 17, (NEC, 1995) and that of small-scale units in 1998, according to State Government sources was 2004, which included fruit preservation units, oil expellers, rice mills, forestry products units and a few electronic units for assembling radios, television sets, clocks and microphones. The Department of Industries has set up Niglok Industrial Growth Centre in East Siang district to promote production of handloom and handicrafts products. The State has considerable mineral resources, e.g. coal, oil, limestone, graphite, dolomite, natural gas, etc. which so far remain largely unutilized. The Net State Domestic Product in 1994-95 was Rs. 825 crore (*Indian Economic Survey, 1996-97*), while for 1996-97, the provisional figure was Rs. 1,194 crore, as per State Government sources.

Some notable improvements in infrastructural development might well change this rather gloomy picture. In 1992-93, per capita consumption of electricity in Arunachal Pradesh was 128.3 KWH against all-India average of 330.6 KWH (NEC, 1995). In 1978-79, the percentage of villages electrified was 9.9, which rose to 58.43 per cent, covering 2,138 out of 3,659 inhabited villages by 1998 (*Govt. of Arunachal Pradesh, Statistical Abstract,* 1998). Rangnadi hydroelectric project, which is nearing completion, is expected to generate 405 MW of power, which will change the situation completely. Besides, negotiations between Central and State Governments are on for constructing two massive dams on Subansiri and Dihang rivers, which can generate 25,000 MW of hydel power if some snags can be sorted out.[26] Some progress has also been made in construction of roads during the last 20 years. In 1979-80, the total road length was 2,500 km with road density of 2.98 km per 100 sq km, which rose to 12,695 km and road density of 15.10 km for 100 sq km by 1997. Most importantly, all district headquarters are now connected by road, although the roads frequently go across rivers and mountain streams often negotiable only through make-shift bridges.[27] Access to

26. The proposed dams on Subansiri and Dehang were expected to submerge a sizeable section of the plains in Arunachal Pradesh. This is one of the reasons why Arunachal Pradesh government has so far withheld its consent for the project.

27. The author recalls an experience while travelling to Teju, the district headquarters of Lohit, when a shallow river-bed had to be crossed in a jeep. Less than two days later, when she was returning, thanks to a flash flood, the →

safe drinking water supply, which covered 1,281 villages in 1979-80, increased to 3,434 villages, i.e. 85.21 per cent of total villages, by 1996-97 (*Govt. of Arunachal Pradesh, Statistical Abstract*, 1998).

While there is no doubt that many developments hold a promise of substantially improving the quality of life for people of Arunachal Pradesh, it is essential to be alert regarding social consequences of some reform measures introduced by the State Government. For instance, government legislation to prevent *jhum* cultivation and encourage adoption of scientific methods seems to be leading to accumulation of land by a few persons at the expense of others in a society which so far had been relatively free from marked economic inequalities.

The 1980 Land Settlement and Land Reform Act, which was aimed at encouraging settled cultivation, allowed a five-year period during which individual cultivators could undertake permanent cultivation and become owners of the land. The State Government provided subsidies in order to facilitate adoption of improved agricultural methods to develop the land selected for permanent cultivation. Unfortunately some powerful persons have managed to appropriate substantial government grants, and by employing local indigent tribesmen or migrants from Bihar or Nepal as hired labour, they have acquired sizeable landholdings. Similarly, government programmes to develop physical infrastructure through constructing roads and government buildings have served to create an affluent class of contractors. These neo-rich people flaunt a flashy life-style in a society which so far was relatively free from wide income disparities.

In recent years, Arunachal Pradesh, which had so far remained exceptionally peaceful, has experienced disturbances over the issue of infiltration of foreign nationals as in other N-E States. A large number of Chakmas, Hajongs and Tibetans who fled from their native lands have sought shelter in Arunachal Pradesh.[28] Besides, a sizeable number of

→ river-bed was transformed into a 2 km sheet of water which had to be crossed on elephant back to join the road — a common occurrence in this area.

28. In 1890 British Government set aside Chittagong Hill Tracts (CHT) as an autonomous and exclusive area for Chakmas, a Buddhist tribe of East Bengal who originally came from Arakan region. After Independence and 1947 Partition, CHT, although including 97 per cent non-Muslim population, went to Pakistan under Radcliff award. The then government of East Pakistan, and later Bangladesh, adopted a policy of encouraging Muslims to settle in CHT, which led to ethnic conflicts forcing Chakmas to leave CHT and seek shelter in India, particularly Tripura, Mizoram and Arunachal Pradesh (Ghosh, 1987, Saikia, 1994).

Nepalis and Bangladeshi Muslims have also migrated to this State in search of livelihood as graziers and herdsmen, agricultural labourers, petty vendors, etc. The State Government has been urging the Central Government since 1977 to repatriate all foreign nationals who have been living and working in the State without permits, in violation of the Inner Line and Restricted Areas regulations. The situation has become highly contentious since the Government of India had initially permitted 20,000 Chakmas to settle in Arunachal Pradesh, but their number presently is believed to exceed one lakh. Around 1994, the Central Government conveyed their intentions to grant citizenship to Chakmas and Hajongs (both of whom are Bangladeshi immigrants) in line with the 1972 Indira-Mujeeb pact. This provoked angry protests from All Arunachal Pradesh Students Union (AAPSU) which issued quit notices to all foreigners residing in the State. The disturbances were controlled due to prompt State Government action. It is important that Central Government evolves a satisfactory solution of this issue in consultation with the State Government, and not wait for a more violent agitation.

A heartening aspect of Arunachal Pradesh is the emergence of cultural revival movements among some major tribes, e.g. the Adis, and efforts to put new vigour in their original faith "Donyi-Polo" through exploration and reinterpretation of old texts, composing new prayers and creating new places of worship, etc. Despite the Freedom of Indigenous Faith Act, followers of organized religions have been promoting conversions of Arunachalis to their religions. As a counter-measure, followers of Donyi-Polo seek to bring back to their original fold especially those who were reluctant converts or who were converted through coercion or material allurements.

In recapitulation, Arunachal Pradesh has remained a highly under-developed, isolated and at times forgotten State. For a proper development of infrastructure, e.g. communications and transportation, provision of hydro-electric power, excavation and processing of its huge mineral wealth, massive technical and financial resources will be necessary. The Central Government must play a key role here in attracting corporate sector and financial institutions to invest in such projects and in providing technical support. In view of the difficulty in internal mobilization of resources, Arunachal Pradesh has to depend heavily on the Central Government for its non-plan and plan expenditure. Since India accepted the strategy of planned development, the financial allocations for States have been regarded as an indication of Central Government's efforts to boost development and overcome initial handicaps. The outlays for Arunachal Pradesh for Fifth Plan (1974-79) was Rs. 63.10 crore, in Seventh Plan (1985-90) it was Rs. 400 crore and in Ninth Plan (1997-2002), Rs. 3,569.89 crore. This indicates a substantial increase over the past 25 years.

If the Central assistance is matched by the State's initiative, there is no reason why Arunachal Pradesh should not eliminate its developmental backlog and begin to utilize its vast natural resources to make rapid strides. There are immense resources in land, water sources and forests which can be harnessed more fully by the State Government through careful planning and efficient management. The State has some sheep-rearing farms using the most modern technology, highly productive horticultural projects and potato-seed farms which capitalize on high altitude terrain. These are examples which demonstrate what people can do with some technical support from the government, given their capacity for hard work and indigenous talent for self-help. It is essential however, that the State Government, while encouraging individual initiative and entrepreneurship, scrupulously avoids the mistake of sacrificing public interest. Thus, while promoting fuller utilization of the State's immense forest resources, care must be taken to ensure preservation of environmental equilibrium.

MANIPUR

Historical Perspective

EARLIER HISTORY

Meiteis, the major group inhabiting Manipur, belong to Indo-Mongoloid stock of the Tibeto-Burman language group and there are divergent views regarding their origins. References in ancient Meitei scriptures and royal chronicles confirm the existence of an old civilization spanning the history of 74 kings between CE 33 and CE 1949 although the chronology up to eighth century CE is rather unclear.[29] Historically, Manipuris included seven major clans or "salais" having independent principalities, some of which

29. There are several versions tracing the origins of Meiteis to China, and to merging of Manipur's autochthons with the Thais or the Burmese (Sanajaoba, 1988).

MANIPUR

★IMPHAL

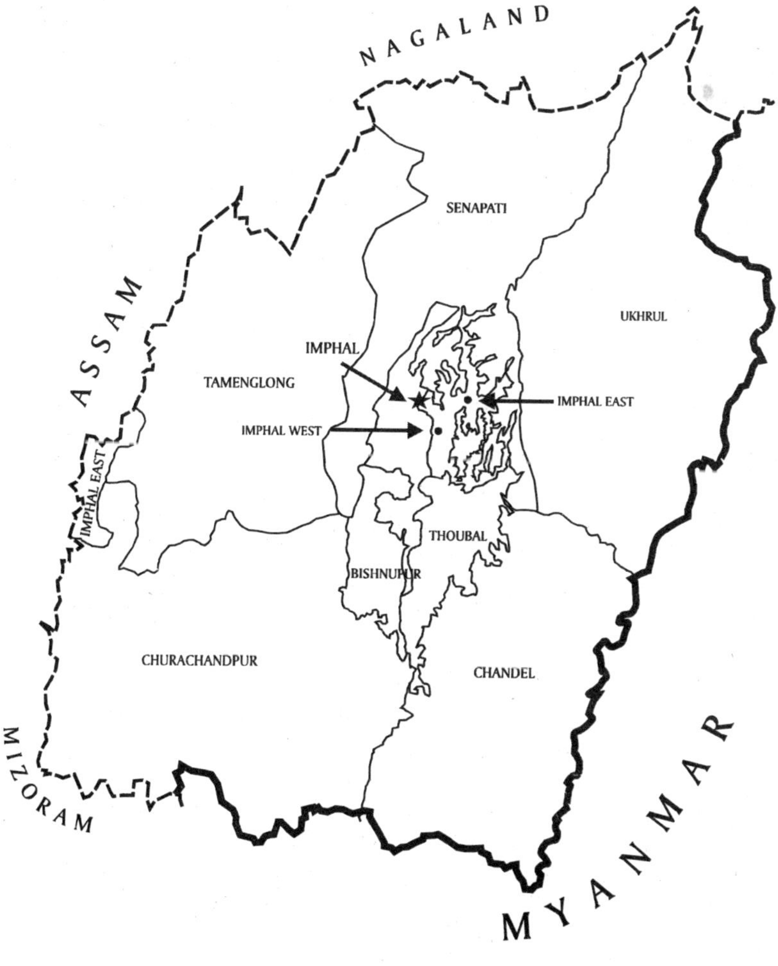

BOUNDARIES

INTERNATIONAL ———
STATE - - - -
DISTRICT ———
CAPITAL ★

go back probably to pre-Christian era.[30] In the continuing struggle for power, Meiteis defeated others and established their supremacy and assimilated other clans. By the time of Charai Rongba's rule (1698–1709), a composite Meitei nationality had evolved and accommodated in its fold some exogenous groups such as immigrants from Bengal, Uttar Pradesh, Orissa, etc. and also from the Shan region of Myanmar.

Besides the Meiteis, a number of Naga tribes started settling down in Manipur since the twelfth century. The Kuki-Chin tribes came to Manipur in the eighteenth and nineteenth centuries, usually due to being pushed out by more powerful tribes. Manipuri kings encouraged Kukis to settle in the hill areas in order to serve as a buffer against attacks by the Nagas and the Burmese. The Kukis who knew the art of making guns and other weapons were definite assets and were recruited in the Manipuri army. The relationship between the Meiteis and tribal groups fluctuated a great deal. At times the Meitei kings attacked and plundered some tribal groups and forced them to retreat into the interior hills and forests. Some Manipuri kings, however, befriended the tribal groups, who joined the former in fighting common enemies. Indeed, Manipuri legends refer to inter-marriages between Meiteis and Nagas.[31] When Meitei kings consolidated the State system, the tribal chiefs paid tributes in kind and services as well as taxes to the former. At the same time the tribal communities were left free to follow their own systems of internal governance and cultural traditions within their respective areas.

Between the thirteenth and eighteenth centuries, Manipuri kings waged a number of wars with neighbouring kingdoms, e.g. Koch, Tripura, Cachar, etc. They also forged political and matrimonial alliances with the Ahom, Tripura and Ava (the former capital of Burma) kings. They successfully repulsed two Chinese invasions around 1250 and 1564 and won Chinese approbation for the Meiteis' bravery.[32] The Burmese invaded

30. The seven "salais" or clans were: Mangang (also known as Ningthouja or Meitei), Luwang, Khuman, Angom, Moirang, Khaba-Ngamba and Chenglei–Leisangthem. Other smaller groups were a part of these larger clans (Manikchand, 1988).

31. According to one theory Meiteis and Tangkhul Nagas in the past shared a common racial origin. The coronation of Manipuri kings and queens included a ceremony where the couple donned Naga dresses and carried a Naga spear (Horam, 1977).

32. The Chinese king visited Manipur with presents for the Meitei royal family. The Chinese soldiers who were captured as prisoners are believed to have imparted the art of sericulture to the Manipuris.

Manipur several times since 1758. The British, who were interested in having access to a trade route to China through Manipur, used this opportunity to sign a treaty with the Manipuri King Jai Singh in 1762 to form a joint defence against the Burmese.

Manipur, like other kingdoms in the Brahmaputra Valley began to receive new cultural influences through the arrival of brahmins from various States, like Uttar Pradesh, Orissa and West Bengal. The impact of Vaishnavite Hinduism on Manipuri royalty had indeed begun much earlier, but it became significant by the fifteenth century. The Meitei King Pamheiba (1709–1748); adopted from Shantidas, his brahmin preceptor Ramanandi sect of Vaishnavism and assumed the title of "Garib Nawaz" (The Protector of the poor). His descendants came under the influence of Gauriya Vaishnavism, due to their close contacts with the Goswamis of Bengal, and urged their subjects to replace Meitei religious practices with Vaishnavite worship. With the patronage of Manipuri kings, the "Brahma Sabha", the council of brahmins, became very powerful and despite protests from "Maiba Sanglen," the highest authority on Meitei religion, exhorted Meitei subjects to replace Sanamahi with Hindu deities, rituals and daily practices. Putting on *chandana* (sandalwood paste) mark on the forehead, shunning meat, adopting Bengali script, disapproving divorce and widow remarriage were some of the brahmin norms which Meiteis were expected to adopt. Persons who failed to abide by Hindu rituals and continued to follow Sanamahi rituals, were punished, ex-communicated and in some cases exiled. Interestingly, while the Meiteis adopted Hindu religious practices, they retained their original pre-Hindu Sanamahi worship at the family level, where women have always played a very active role. The syncretic practice of Hinduism and Sanamahi faiths has resulted in some unique features in Meitei society, and especially for Meitei women's status, as will be noted in Chapter 4. The interaction between Meitei and Hindu cultural streams led to brahmin immigrants partly adopting the worship of local non-Hindu deities and family practices. The intolerance and high-handedness of brahmin preceptors, however, created a strong resentment which found expression in violent protests in later years.

Another effect of Hinduism on Manipur was the attempt to superimpose some elements of Hindu caste system on the existing social hierarchy, in which the ruling family and the nobility appropriated kshatriya status for themselves and adopted Hindu titles. The Maharaja was the owner of all lands and the nobility had access to free land. The "Lois," i.e.

the commoners and those who refused to be converted to Vaishnavism and the "Yaithibis," i.e. those who were punished for violations or were ex-criminals, had to pay taxes in kind and in the form of compulsory labour, called "Lallup" to the king.[33] With the dissemination of Hindu culture among the Meiteis, particularly since the eighteenth century, and the introduction of Christianity among the tribal communities in the hills towards the end of nineteenth century, the cultural divide in the valley and the hills widened further.

Manipur kingdom at one time extended to the east beyond Kabo Valley and Chindwin river and to the west included some part of Cachar plains. During 1819–1826 the Burmese invaded and plundered the State. During the "Seven Years Catastrophe," as this period is referred to, the Burmese killed and captured a large number of Manipuri men and committed atrocities on women. The challenge of liberating Manipur was accepted by Gambhir Singh, who sought British help to raise a crack force of 500 Manipuri and Kachari soldiers and finally routed out the Burmese. The British used this opportunity to establish their dominance over both Manipur and Assam, which was also a victim of Burmese aggression. At the same time, they managed to placate the Burmese by acting as mediators in concluding the Treaty of Yandabo in 1826.

BRITISH PERIOD

The Treaty of Yandabo marked the formal entry of the British into Manipur (as also in Assam, as noted earlier). In 1834, the British, in a shrewd move, allowed Gambhir Singh to occupy Chandrapura area of Cachar on condition that he handover Kabo Valley to the Burmese king, ostensibly as a goodwill gesture. In return, the British agreed to pay a regular compensation of Rs. 500 to Manipur, since they had recognized Chindwin river to the east of Kabo Valley as a boundary between Manipur and Burma (present Myanmar). This manoeuvre ensured for the British a trade route through Manipur and Burma to China (Ibochouba, 1988).[34]

---

33. "Lallup" system required every able-bodied male commoner between 16-60 years to give to the king compulsory labour for 10 out of every 30 days in exchange for about three acres of land for cultivation on usufructuary basis. This system was abolished during Maharaja Churachand's rule and was replaced by house and land tax.

34. The payment of compensation to Manipur was continued by the British until the State's merger with Indian Union in 1949 (Ibochouba, 1988). United

→

In 1835, the British appointed their political agent to supervise Manipuri-Burmese relations. After the death of Maharaja Chandrakirti in 1886, the internal strife among competing princes over succession to the throne provided the British an opportunity to intervene. In 1891, Kulchandra Singh bravely repulsed a British attack on the palace, when five British officers were killed. Soon thereafter, the British attacked with a larger force and defeated the Manipuris and transported Kulchandra for life. To strike terror among the public, the British publicly hanged four main rebel leaders including Prince Tikendrajit and General Thangal. They then selected a seven-year-old boy Churachand, sent him to Ajmer Mayo College for education, and had him crowned in 1907. Manipur was not annexed, but allowed to remain as a subordinate State under the supervision of British Political Agent. Maharaja Churachand's writ was limited to the central valley. The hill areas inhabited by tribal groups were retained under direct control of British officers.

In the tribal areas, the British introduced a system of house tax and compulsory labour which required the inhabitants to provide various services such as carrying luggage and providing food for the comfort of travelling British officers. This rankled the pride of Kukis, who were already disgruntled because of perceived neglect by their British masters, and they rose in a revolt in 1917. The British reprisal was quick and included punitive measures against Kukis as well as Nagas who had distanced themselves from the former. The Nagas, who were frustrated due to their deteriorating living conditions, felt deeply perturbed when Christian missionaries began to convert Nagas to Christianity and to question their native traditional religion as well as the authority of their respected leaders.

Jadonang, a Rongmei Naga youth who had seen action in First World War and was deeply concerned about the plight of his community, launched Zeliangrong movement in 1925 to bring about tribal unity and to initiate religious and social reforms.[35] In the context of the prevailing national non-co-operation movement launched by Gandhiji, the Zeliangrong movement soon acquired the character of a political struggle to resist

→ National Liberation Front (UNLF) and other militant organizations hold the then Indian leaders responsible for failure to restore Kabo Valley to Manipur.

35. "Zeliangrong" symbolizing integration of three kindred Naga tribes: Zemi, Liangmei and Rongmei, advocated an end to inter-tribal wars, reform of traditional religion and elimination of harmful social customs, in a determined bid to withstand the challenge of Christianity (Kabui, 1982, 53-66).

unjust colonial laws and taxes. Jadonang initiated collection of funds and weapons and began to train a group of volunteers for whom he soon became an enigmatic figure endowed with magical powers (Mukherjee et al., 1982). He was soon arrested by the British and executed in 1931. His 16-year old cousin Gaidinlieu quickly took over leadership of the movement. She organized a crack force of armed guerrilla volunteers and openly challenged the British regime by declaring that her community consisted of free people who would neither pay taxes nor obey unjust British laws. She too was arrested by the British in 1932 and sentenced for life imprisonment.[36]

The general climate in Manipur around early twentieth century was characterized by resentment over the feudal and autocratic style of Manipuri royalty, anguish over imposition of Vaishnavite religion and suppression of Meitei traditions by the Brahma-Sabha, and bitterness about oppressive colonial policies of the British. The first "Nupi-lan" (Women's Movement) was triggered when the British Political Agent demanded from Manipuris compulsory labour to rebuild the house of his assistant after it was destroyed by some miscreants. The stiff resistance of Manipuri women forced the British to withdraw their order. The second "Nupi-lan" in 1939 was also launched by Manipuri women to protest against government policy to export rice outside the State when local population faced acute shortage due to poor harvest. Once again the determined struggle of the women, forced Maharaja Churachand to stop the export of rice.[37]

The success of the second "Nupi-lan" undoubtedly helped to mobilize public opinion for demanding a responsible government, articulated by leaders like H. Irabot Singh. Meanwhile, when the Brahma-Sabha expelled some persons for performing Meitei life-cycle rituals, the protest in certain sections gave rise to Sanamahi Movement, which defended a

36. Jawaharlal Nehru visited Gaidinlieu in a Shillong prison in 1937, and bestowed on her the title of "Rani" in his admiration for her unusual courage. When India became independent she was released in 1947. She had advocated a grouping of Naga-dominated areas into Zeliangrong administrative unit within the Indian Union and thus incurred the wrath of Phizo and had to go underground during 1960-66.

37. The second "Nupi-lan" was a combined protest against the greed of Marwari traders engaged in exporting rice at the cost of hardships for local people, British pressure to export Manipuri rice for Second World War soldiers, and also insensitivity of Maharaja Churachand towards the suffering of native population.

revival of Sanamahi worship and an assertion of pre-Hindu Meitei culture. With the backing of H. Irabot Singh and Angom Singh, this movement acquired a political character. The protagonists, called Sanamahis, championed the cause of regeneration of Sanamahi rituals, language and script (in place of Bengali script) and became a symbol of Manipur's sovereign status and distinctive Meitei culture (Saha,1982).

During Second World War the Indian National Army led by Subhash Chandra Bose and assisted by Japanese forces succeeded in advancing up to Manipur. This event, coupled with the freedom struggle launched by the Indian National Congress inevitably helped to build a strong public movement in Manipur against British colonial regime as well as the feudal system of Manipuri royalty. When India attained Independence in 1947, the popular pressure on the Maharaja of Manipur tilted the balance in favour of the State's merger with the Indian Union.

POST-INDEPENDENCE PERIOD

Manipur's merger with the Indian Union was signed on 15 October 1949, and during 1950-56 it became a part "C" State and later a Union Territory, i.e. centrally administered through a Chief Commissioner, initially with an advisory council, which was replaced by an elected Territorial Council. A popular demand for responsible government which gained momentum by 1960 assumed the character of a mass non-co-operation movement in which Manipuri women played an active role. In 1963, the Territorial Council was replaced by an elected Territorial Assembly. The general unrest continued, however, and erupted in the form of a student's agitation in 1965, followed by police firing on agitators, which evoked strong public indignation. Meanwhile, the popular demand for Manipur's attainment of full Statehood continued to gather momentum. Finally, North-Eastern Areas (Reorganization) Act of 1971 conferred full Statehood to Manipur on 21 January 1972 and the status of the Lt. Governor was upgraded to Governor. A Constitutional Amendment in 1971 abolished the privy purse of the crown prince Okendra and he ceased to be a titular head of Manipur.

While Independence led to the end of the British colonial oppression, and feudal exploitation by Manipuri kings, it has not ushered an era of peace and development. Instead, Manipur has been rocked by frequent outbursts of violence, arson and ethnic conflicts necessitating deployment of security forces for long periods and causing disruption of normal social life. At the root of this situation are the ethnic animosities among the State's major population groups — Meiteis, Nagas and Kukis.

The Sanamahi movement which originated among Meiteis in the 1930s acquired a highly political and aggressive stance at the hands of organizations like the UNLF (United National Liberation Front) founded in 1966, and its underground counterpart, Revolutionary Government of Manipur. At times it has deteriorated into destroying Hindu temples and burning Hindu scriptures. Closely allied to this was a demand for secession from India, alleging that Manipur's merger with India was brought about through pressure from Indian leaders. Other militant organizations demanding restoration of Manipur's sovereignty, e.g. PREPAK (Peoples' Revolutionary Party of Kangleipak).[38] and PLA (Peoples' Liberation Army) stepped up armed insurgency since 1976. Their continuing attacks forced the Central Government to declare Manipur Valley as a disturbed area and to launch counter-insurgency operations.

Apart from the unrest among extremist sections of the Meiteis, there is a more general grouse that Meiteis have against tribal communities because of certain safeguards and benefits the Indian Constitution and specific legislations have bestowed on the latter. The Manipur District Council Act of 1971 provided Autonomous Districts for hill areas similar to those created under the Sixth Schedule of the Constitution in tribal areas of Assam, Meghalaya, Mizoram and Tripura.[39] Furthermore, Manipur Land Reforms and Land Revenue Act of 1960, which is applicable to the central Valley, put a ceiling of 10 ha on individual landholding. Since this Act excluded hill areas, there is presently no ceiling on individual holding for Naga and Kuki-dominated areas. There is acute shortage of land in the Valley, whereas in the hill areas there is relatively plenty of land, but the non-tribals cannot purchase land belonging to tribal persons. The Meiteis also resent the special reservations available to tribal persons in government jobs and educational institutions and developmental assistance available under tribal welfare programmes.

---

38. Kangleipak is the old name of Manipur.

39. Autonomous District Councils in the hill areas of Manipur have administrative, legislative and financial powers to protect tribal rights in land, forests, water sources, etc. and safeguard them from exploitative elements. The only exception is: Manipur Autonomous Councils have no authority to legislate regarding appointment and succession of chiefs, inheritance of property, marriage, divorce and social customs (Dutta Ray 1999).

Another complicating aspect which has plagued Manipur in post-Independence period is the longstanding antagonism between the Nagas and Kuki-Chin tribes. Its roots go back to late eighteenth and early nineteenth centuries when Kukis started coming to Manipur from Chin hill areas of Myanmar. Various Naga tribes had settled in Manipur since the twelfth century. In some instances, the Kukis encroached on traditional Naga-dominated areas, aided by their superior weapons, but even more due to the support they received initially from Manipuri kings and later from the British, both of whom wanted a buffer zone against attacks by the Nagas and the Burmese. The Nagas have never reconciled themselves to this perceived affront and have tried to punish the Kukis, which in turn has provoked Kuki reprisals (Patel, 1994).

Present Situation

MAJOR GEOGRAPHICAL AND DEMOGRAPHIC FEATURES

Manipur covers a total area of 22,327 sq km which is divided into two ecological zones. A central valley, about one-tenth of the total area, with an average elevation of 2500 ft above sea level, is surrounded by hills. Manipur shares an international border with Myanmar on the east and the south. It is flanked by Assam on the west, Nagaland on the north and Mizoram on the south-west. The State is divided into nine districts — four in the valley and five in the hills, respectively. They are Imphal East, Imphal West, Bishnupur and Thoubal; Chandel, Churachandpur, Senapati, Tamenglong and Ukhrul.

The total population of Manipur according to 1991 Census was 1,837,149 with nearly two-thirds being in the valley. Urban population constituted 27.52 per cent, STs 34.41 per cent and SCs 2.02 per cent. The percentages by religion were: Hindus 57.67, Muslims 7.27, Christians 34.11, Other Religions 0.77. A high proportion of tribal population has been converted to Christianity, their percentages ranging between 83.23 (Senapati) and 97.50 (Tamenglong) in the five hill districts. Manipur's population, as per Provisional Population Totals for 2001 Census is 2,388,634.

A majority of people in the central valley are Manipuri Hindus, known as Meitei, among whom kshatriyas (who included the royal family) and brahmins enjoy the highest status, other endogenous groups being "Lois" meaning commoners, and "Yaithibis" meaning the degraded classes who include ex-criminals or those pursuing menial jobs. The remaining include Bishnuprias,[40] Pangans[41] (who are also called pangals, Manipuri Muslims or at times Meitei Muslims), Kabui Nagas who occupy foothill areas and who in the past accepted servile jobs from Manipuri kings. The valley population also includes a sizeable number of Nepalis, Bangladeshi immigrants and people from other States of India who are engaged in various trades and businesses, government service, etc. Manipuris refer to "outsiders" and foreigners as "Mayangs."

The hill areas are inhabited by about 29 tribal communities[42] with a concentration of Naga tribes on the northern side, viz. Senapati, Ukhrul and Tamenglong districts and Kuki-Chin tribes in the southern districts, viz. Chandel and Churachandpur. Some Naga tribes, e.g. Tangkhul and Angami trace their origin to Meikhel, a village in Mao-Maram area in Senapati district. The Kabuis and Marings claim that they came from an area in Myanmar. A number of Kuki-Chin-Mizo groups originally belonged to Chin hills area in Myanmar. The point to be noted is the interaction between Naga and Kuki tribes with kindred groups in Nagaland, Mizoram and Myanmar. This also explains the infiltration of tribal immigrants from Myanmar into Manipur and other N-E States during 1971-91 (Nandi, 1997).

CURRENT ECONOMIC AND SOCIAL CONTEXT

Manipur's economy is primarily agricultural with settled cultivation in the central valley and *jhum* cultivation being the predominant mode in the hill areas, with a scattering of terraced cultivation if a water source is available in the vicinity. The State's population increased more than three times

---

40. "Bishnupriyas" emerged as a community in early eighteenth century out of inter-mixing of local Manipuris and Bengalis from Sylhet and Cachar who came to Manipur along with Vaishnavite preachers of Chaitanya school from Sylhet (Acharya, 1988).
41. See note 10. According to one account, Pangans were originally Muslim soldiers captured during Muslim invasions of Assam, who were brought to Manipur from Cachar (some part of which belonged to Manipur Kingdom at one time) by a Manipuri king named Khagemba in 1606. They intermarried with Manipuri women. Presently, they constitute a poor and backward community, numbering about 1.43 lakh.
42. These tribes include: Aimol, Anal, Chiru, Chothe, Gangte, Hmar, Kabui, Kacha Naga, Koirao, Lamgang, Mao, Maram, Maring, Moyon, Monsang, Paite, Purum, Ralte, Rongmei, Simte, Tangkhul, Tarao, Thadou, Vaiphei, Zou.

during 1951-91. At present except for rice, almost all food grains and other essential commodities have to be imported from other States. There is considerable potential for plantation crops, like tea, coffee, cinnamon, cardamom and agar wood, but it remains to be adequately developed. The food grains production in 1990-91 in Manipur was 285.6 thousand tonnes, which rose to 390 thousand tonnes by 1996-97, indicating the need for technical inputs. (Banerjee, 1999). Although Indian Tea Board found hill areas of the State suitable for tea, coffee and rubber plantation, the bigger companies are reluctant to make substantial financial investments as adequately large areas cannot be assured. The particular systems of land ownership in the hill areas present serious difficulties in this respect.[43] There are areas in the State which grow plenty of pineapples and oranges, but with inadequate processing facilities and prohibitive transport costs, profit margins are very meagre.

The growth of industries in Manipur has been poor. In 1994, the number of large and medium size industrial units was a mere six (NEC, 1995). The only other source of non agricultural employment includes small-scale units of handloom weaving, sericulture, cane and bamboo crafts, piggery and poultry units, rice mills, pottery, leather articles, etc. The transportation costs involved in obtaining a steady supply of raw materials and sending finished products are high. Furthermore, the unavailability of adequate technical, financial and marketing support has so far hindered the growth of employment and economic viability of the small-scale sector. The Net State Domestic Product of Manipur for 1993-94 stood at Rs. 1046 crore, and the provisional figure for 1996-97, according to Indian Economic Survey was Rs. 1571 crore. (State Directorate of Economics and Statistics and Central Statistical Organization.)

A good deal of economic potential in forestry, fishing, horticulture and agriculture remains unused at present due to absence of adequate infrastructural development. For instance, even the limited rail link to Jiribam near the Assam border did not exist until 1990. The road journey from Jiribam to Imphal, the capital town, involves nearly 12 hours of bumpy ride across eight to nine hill ranges. It is useful to review the situation of people's access to some basic amenities. The road length per

---

43. In Naga-dominated villages, lands are owned by a particular tribe or clan, whereas in Kuki-dominated villages, they belong to the chief. Even where some lands are owned by individuals, there are no adequate survey records or title-deeds.

100 sq km in 1989 was a mere 26.33 km as compared to the all India average of 47.27 km and by 1992 it still remained at 30.3 km, according to NEC sources, while the all-India average rose to 62.80 km. Per capita consumption of electricity in Manipur in 1988 was 100 KWH against all-India average of 253 KWH, and by 1992-93 it reached 140.4 KWH as against 330.6 KWH for all-India (NEC 1990 & 1995). By 1992, 1580 out of 2035 inhabited villages in the State, i.e. 77.64 per cent were electrified (NEC, 1992), as compared to 887 or 43.59 per cent in 1988 (NEC, 1990). Evidently, the State is making definite progress in providing basic amenities to its population but the pace seems to be slow. In 1980, 1212 villages, i.e. more than half of Manipur's 2035 inhabited villages remained devoid of safe drinking water supply. By 1987, according to State Health Department sources, 125 villages still remained to be covered by this amenity and 275 villages were only partly covered. It needs to be remembered that even the "covered" villages often face problems of disrupted water supply due to thefts or destruction of equipment,[44] not to mention difficulties of transporting materials, like pipes and cement as well as trained personnel to remote villages in the hills.

Despite the unusual initiative displayed by Manipuri women to supplement their family incomes, these tend to be rather low and are even lower among ST families. A tribal benchmark survey conducted by the State Government during Seventh Five-Years-Plan (1985-90) indicated that 47,568 (62.42 per cent) out of 76,209 households in tribal sub-plan areas were living below the poverty line. An expert group appointed by the Government of India estimated the number of persons below poverty line in 1987-88 at 5.53 lakh or 32.93 per cent of the State population (4.68 lakh rural and 0.85 lakh urban). Their estimate for 1993-94 was 6.80 lakh or 33.78 per cent of the State population (6.33 lakh rural and 0.47 lakh urban) was living below the poverty line.[45] Underdevelopment is more pronounced in the five hill districts inhabited by tribal population.

The challenging task of promoting economic development of Manipur and of creating adequate employment opportunities could not be addressed so far due to the chronic unrest which has plagued the State.

---

44. In N-E States it is not uncommon to find pipe-lines of gravity feed schemes passing through hilly areas destroyed by people accidentally during the jhuming operations. At times the disruption is caused by some people just recklessly cutting them midway to avail of water.

45. See note 11 for details of methodology.

More recently, the Nagas and Kukis, who had remained aloof from the disturbances in the valley earlier, have kept the State in so much turmoil that Central Government was compelled to impose President's rule at the end of 1993. The Nagas, who view the Kukis as intruders, and who are accused of marginalizing the Nagas in political and administrative fields, have often raided Kuki villages, massacred and tortured many Kukis. The Kukis, on the other hand, accuse the Nagas of ethnic cleansing and of imposing "Nagaland tax" on Kuki areas. The Kukis' retaliation has been equally brutal. In 1995, a bus carrying 40 Nagas and 6 Meiteis was pushed off a cliff on a national highway by members of KNF (Kuki National Front), a militant outfit.[46]

The repeated process of revenge and counter-revenge among Nagas and Kukis has become more and more menacing due to the alignments of insurgent outfits within and outside Manipur, e.g. NSCN (National Socialist Council of Nagaland) with its rival factions, ULFA, KNA (Kuki National Army) which represents Burmese Kukis and other hostile forces outside India's borders. The latter generally supply training and arms to Manipuri insurgent groups. The Naga-Kuki conflict has recently acquired an ominous dimension due to intense competition to gain control over the extremely lucrative drug trade across the border with Myanmar. As if the Naga-Kuki imbroglio is not complex enough, there have also been violent conflicts between Kukis and Paites, both belonging to the larger Kuki-Chin family, as also among rival NSCN factions.

Meanwhile UNLF and its kindred organizations which champion the cause of Meitei nationalism, have been busy creating public discontent against low levels of Manipur's development, corruption in government departments, high levels of unemployment, etc. Their reports proudly list numbers of weapons seized from the police and security forces and raids on military posts. There is however, one positive element in their aggressive outbursts. They have launched campaigns against alcoholism, drug addiction, gambling and lotteries but they of course use their own fairly drastic methods of punishing the guilty. UNLF has also taken up cudgels

---

46. KNF (Kuki National Front) was founded in 1987 by Nehlun Kipgen, who was trained in Myanmar by Kachin Independence Army, an insurgent outfit. Kipgen launched a movement in 1988 for establishing a Kuki homeland through consolidation of Kuki-dominated areas of Manipur, viz. Sadar Hills, Chandel, Churachandpur and parts of Tamenglong and Ukhrul districts (Chinai, *Times of India,* 28 January 1995).

against rape and atrocities on women which understandably won them Manipuri women's sympathy.

The prolonged presence of military and paramilitary forces in Manipur to deal with frequent breach of peace has brought its own problems, like use of excessive force against suspects and serious disruptions of normal life during combing operations, besides abuse of women. UNLF has been quick to launch retaliatory attacks when such instances occur. Naga and Kuki insurgents too have often ambushed police and army personnel and raided their posts to attract public attention to their demands of southern Nagaland and a Kuki homeland.[47] The lack of co-ordination among various protective agencies, e.g. the police, the Border Security Force, the Central Reserve Police, the army, etc. have seriously hampered their effectiveness, thus losing the respect and support of the public. Meanwhile, there is ample evidence that common people are losing their faith in the credibility of secessionist outfits to achieve their goals of independence of Manipur and are exhausted due to the disruptions and violence as well as extortions they have suffered. They are longing for peace and progress.

It is important for the State Government to use this opportunity to play a strategic role in supporting social sections which are trying to bring about reconciliation among various hostile groups. The example of Kuki-Zomi peace accord in 1998 after ten months of intense violence, is indicative of what can be achieved with local leaders' initiative, if the State Government plays a supportive role.[48] A joint committee for restoration of normalcy comprising moderate elements from Naga and Kuki communities has already initiated some steps, and the State Government, especially the political leadership, can play a decisive role in bringing about a reconciliation. Meanwhile, the State Government must take a lead in evolving a carefully co-ordinated strategy among various security agencies and protect people from violence. The State Government must also launch more determined efforts to fully utilize the immense potential in agriculture, horticulture, fisheries, sericulture, plantations and

47. The Nagas have been demanding a merger of Naga-dominated areas of Manipur and Assam with Nagaland.

48. Zomis include Paite, Tiddim Chin, Vaipei and Simte tribes, all belonging to the larger Kuki-Chin-Mizo family. The clashes between KNF and Zomi Revolutionary Organization began when Kuki insurgents demanded taxes from Paites, and these lasted for ten months in which 300 persons were killed, 1570 houses burnt and 15,000 persons rendered homeless. (Yashwant Raj, *Times of India*, 1 November 1998).

small-scale industries. It would be futile to continue blaming the Central Government for neglect of the State and the State Government must make a determined effort to utilize fully the enhanced Central Government allocations for successive five-year plans.

The Central Government on its part, will need to step up its assistance, both financial and organizational, and adopt a far more supportive role to eliminate the feeling of neglect which at present rankles the Manipuri psyche and which undoubtedly encourages the growth of insurgency. It is indeed fortunate that major Meitei insurgent organizations like the UNLF have so far distanced themselves from Naga and Kuki insurgent groups because of the latter's demands of southern Nagaland and Kuki land, respectively. The Central Government leaders would have to display a much greater sensitivity towards the Meiteis' ethnic identity and pride about their ancient culture. Simultaneously a credible effort to help the State's economic rejuvenation will have to be launched. Ultimately, one of the major causes of continuing ethnic conflict and unrest in the State is the high unemployment, especially among the youth. The opening of border trade with Myanmar in 1994 is expected to enhance the economic prospects of Manipur, besides helping to control the clandestine movement of drugs and arms into Manipur and the N-E region generally. The State's political leaders have been urging the Central Government to end Manipur's geographical isolation — and consequently emotional isolation — by adopting measures to open a transit route through Bangladesh, thus cutting down the distance between Manipur and the rest of the country. Simultaneously, if the National Highway 39 is connected with the proposed Asian Highway, Manipur and in fact the whole N-E region will have access to Myanmar, Thailand, Singapore. When this will materialize, depends to some extent upon Indo-Bangladesh relationship. Meanwhile, a great deal can be achieved by improving internal communications within Manipur and connecting the State to the rest of India by better and more efficient highways and rail-roads.

MEGHALAYA

Historical Perspective

EARLIER HISTORY

Khasi and Jaintia Hills and Garo Hills formed two districts of Assam during the British rule and continued to be so until 1970, when they acquired a

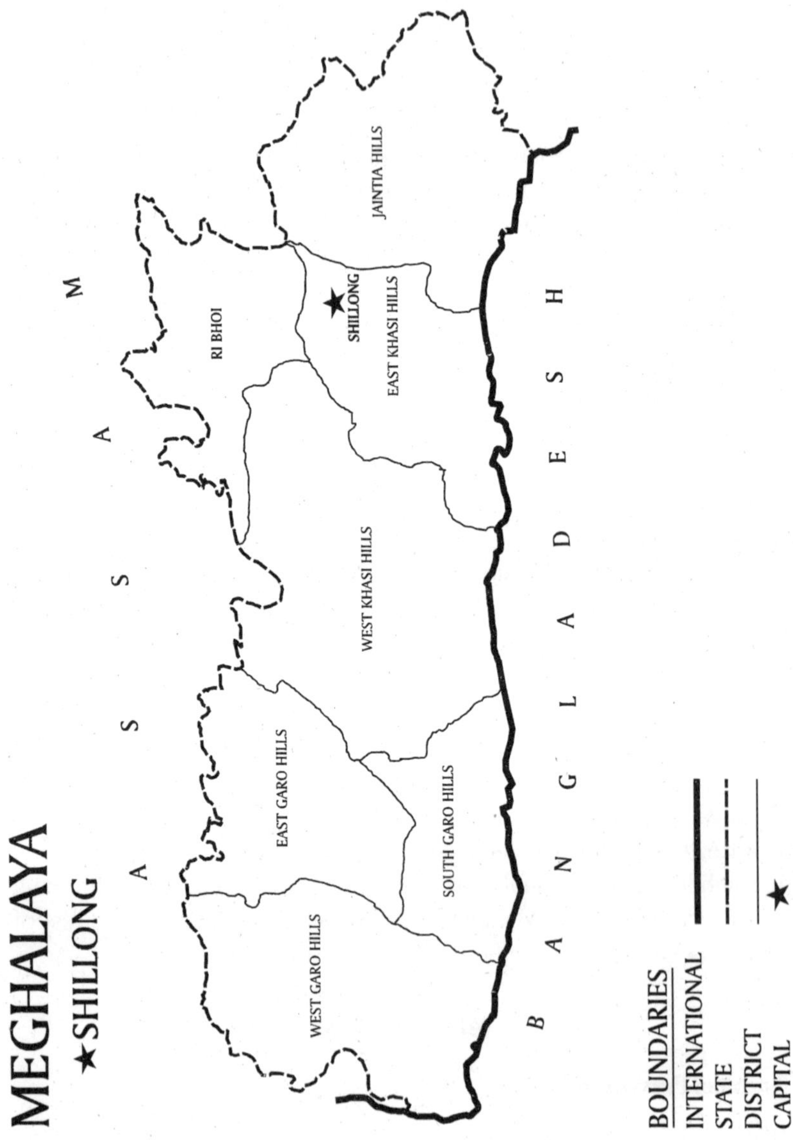
MEGHALAYA
★SHILLONG
ASSAM
BANGLADESH
WEST GARO HILLS
EAST GARO HILLS
SOUTH GARO HILLS
WEST KHASI HILLS
EAST KHASI HILLS
RI BHOI
JAINTIA HILLS
SHILLONG
BOUNDARIES
INTERNATIONAL
STATE
DISTRICT
CAPITAL

new composite entity as Meghalaya. Until British occupation in the first half of the nineteenth century, this area consisted of several independent territories inhabited by tribes and sub-tribes broadly grouped as Khasi, Jaintia and Garo. In the absence of reliable recorded accounts prior to British rule, oral and folk traditions and shared memories of past migrations have been used by scholars to trace their history. Consequently, there are different versions regarding the origins of these three groups as well as sources of Austro-Asiatic influence on their languages.

The Khasi Jaintia people are believed to be South-Mongoloid in racial origins and their language belongs to Austro-Asiatic family. Since there are similarities not only in language, but also in some customs between them and Mon-Khmer people of Indo-China, some scholars believe that the Khasi-Jaintias came from South-East Asian region, and they are therefore classified as Austro-Asiatic. Quite expectedly, divergent views exist both regarding their geographical origins as well as their languages.[49] Das (1978) concludes that while Khasi-Jaintias belong to Indo-Mongoloid group, they probably assimilated the Australoid inhabitants who had previously occupied Khasi and Jaintia Hills but adopted the latter's language. One other explanation of their Austro-Asiatic language is that South Mongoloid race was associated with Sino-Tibetan and Austro-Asiatic speech families since its early formative stage (Acharya, 1988).

The Garos, also known as "Achik" meaning hill people, too belong to the Mongoloid race and are believed to have migrated from Tibet (Roy Burman, 1970) and are linguistically akin to Bodo group. Regardless of the exact origins and the routes followed about which there are differences among scholars, there seems to be a general agreement on one point : Khasis, Jaintias and Garos initially came to the plains of Assam and were pushed into the interior and hill areas in encounters with more powerful groups. Furthermore, inter-tribal and inter-clan conflicts, head-hunting and shifting territorial boundaries were a common feature of their lives. Wars between Khasis and Jaintias erupted off and on, as noted from megaliths erected to mark the occasions (Pakem, 1992). The struggle for

49. One version traces the Khasis to Tonkin, from where they travelled through Yunnan and across northern Myanmar (erstwhile Burma) to Assam plains. Jaintias came in several batches and acquired the names of the places where they settled, e.g. Amwis, Jowais, Nartiangs, Raliangs, Sutungas, etc. (Gassah, 1992). They are believed to have come from Central Asia, according to one view and came through north India to south of river Kopili, from where they were pushed by more powerful groups into Jaintia Hills (Deb Roy, 1981).

survival in the context of inter-group rivalries, particular external pressures and interaction with neighbouring communities led to somewhat different social, cultural and political organization in the three major ethos's — Khasi, Jaintia and Garo.

The Khasis, who were divided into several clans each having a separate territory, had a system of "Syiems" (chieftains), who were designated by clan members. A council of elders and "Lyngdohs" (priests) assisted the *Syiems* in discharging their administrative, political and religious responsibilities on behalf of their clans. The Chiefs of Jaintia clans were known as "Dolois," and were elected by all adult male members of the original founding clans who cleared the forests and established their territories in Jaintia Hills. While Dolois were responsible for secular and administrative matters, Lyngdohs were nominated to provide leadership in spiritual and religious affairs. As the number of Doloiships increased and the need for a higher authority for settling inter-Doloi feuds and also for organizing a joint defence against a common external enemy became evident, the Jaintias created the institution of a Syiem or a Divine king through a suitable myth.[50]

The Jaintia kingdom comprised two sub-divisions: the plains which included portions of Sylhet (presently in Bangladesh) and Nagaon (in Assam), over which the king exercised direct control and the Jaintia Hill areas which were administered by Dolois. A somewhat loose arrangement bound Dolois to pay an annual token tribute (e.g. a male goat) to the king. Old legends and chronicles refer to a succession of 22 Jaintia kings with Hindu names, who ruled over Jaintia kingdom since CE1500. When one of the Hindu kings, Jayant Roy, died, his daughter Jayanti who succeeded to the throne, named the capital Jaintipur which is presently in Sylhet, Bangladesh (Deb Roy, 1981). Although the hill Jaintias followed their native tribal religion — "Niam Tre" — they absorbed a number of Hindu elements.[51] The induction of Hindu and Tantric worship and rituals by Jaintias is attributed to their interaction with the Koch, Ahom and

50. Jaintia legends refer to the miraculous creation of a royal couple, Ka Li Dakha and U Lum Ryindi, out of a mermaid and the subsequent birth of a son who was designated as the Syiem or the Divine king. Since this event took place in Sutunga province, Jaintias are also called Syntengs.

51. The worship of Mahadev and Har-Parvati and Tantric rituals at the temples of Nartiang and Sandai in Jaintia Hills and Kanaighat (presently in Bangladesh) are cited as evidence.

Kamrup kingdoms.[52] This also explains the introduction of human sacrifice in Jaintia rituals.

The Garo Hills were inhabited by a number of tribes, subdivided into clans and kinship groups occupying independent territories called *a'khings*. The "Nokma," i.e. the husband of the inheritress of the clan's property, acted as the principal male head and managed matters affecting the clan in consultation with the "Mahari" (close maternal relatives of the inheritress). Since the boundaries of *a'khings* were not always clear, encroachments by other *a'khings* led to internecine conflicts and head-hunting raids.

BRITISH PERIOD

Following the annexation of Assam by the British in 1826, they established control over some villages in Khasi Hills. The remaining portion, which consisted of about 25 chiefdoms or Syiemships, were also annexed in 1833, but the Syiems were allowed to retain their territories like princely States under British hegemony. The Jaintia Hills too were brought under British occupation in 1835, after the last Jaintia king, Rajendra Singh, was dethroned by the British on receiving a report of a human sacrifice of a kidnapped victim in a religious ritual. The kingship was abolished and he was dispatched to Sylhet (presently in Bangladesh) with a pension. After his death in 1861, Jaintia Hills were brought fully under British occupation. During 1860-63, Kiang Nongbah led a rebellion against British interference with traditional Jaintia practices and taxes levied by the British. Nongbah was arrested and hanged by the British in 1863.[53]

The British tightened their administrative control further by creating Jaintia Hills sub-division with headquarters at Jowai in 1868-69 and incorporated it into the United Khasi and Jaintia Hills district. Simultaneously, they adopted a policy of allowing the Syiems and Dolois to manage the internal affairs of their respective communities.

---

52. A Jaintia king Jasa Malik married a Koch princess. Jaintia kingdom was under the influence of Shakti cult and some scholars believe that at one time it was a part of Kamarupa, known as "Khanda-Kamarupa," which explains introduction of Tantric cult and human sacrifice among Jaintias (Deb Roy, 1981).

53. The British put a ban on the customary cremation of dead bodies in the vicinity of Jowai police station and insisted on burials instead. One of the Dolois, Pakyntein, was reportedly bribed by the British to lead to ailing Kiang Nongbah's arrest and execution. Pakyntein, who was outcast by his native community for his treachery, became the first convert to Christianity.

In Garo Hills, British involvement began during the first quarter of the nineteenth century. In 1821 they introduced a regulation to restore lands controlled by Bengali landlords to Garo peasants. They also sent some missionaries with a view to bringing a "civilizing" influence among the Garos, and thereby started the process of converting them to Christianity. In 1866 the British annexed Garo Hills to Assam, and a year later established the district administrative centre at Tura. One of their earliest steps was to demarcate boundaries of all *a'khings,* prohibit border encroachments and head hunting raids which were prevalent among rival groups. A three-tier hierarchical system of functionaries, viz. *Mouzadars, Lashkars* and *Sirdars* or *Nokmas* was established for revenue and house-tax collection, settlement of disputes and maintenance of amenities such as bridal paths, providing assistance to touring British officers, etc. Furthermore, the *Nokmas* or village chiefs were issued documents of possession of land and they were recognized as absolute owners of lands within their respective *a'khings*. So far, some plain areas were controlled by absentee landlords from Goalpara (in Assam), Rangpur and Mymensingh (both currently in Bangladesh), who used to extract tributes from Garo cultivators through local chiefs. In 1878 the British abolished this system and consolidated the plains and hill areas into Garo Hills district.

During the British period, a number of developments and events helped to integrate people divided into several tribes, sub-tribes and clans into communities with a common identity due to increased interaction among them. The formation of Khasi and Jaintia Hills and Garo Hills districts, emergence of administrative centres at Shillong, Jowai and Tura and growth of urban markets and towns brought people with different ethnic and social backgrounds together. The activities of Christian missions, particularly promotion of education, preparation of scripts for local tribal languages, exposure to new educational institutions and participation in two world wars also expanded the mental horizons of people who had so far lived a fairly isolated existence, both physically and intellectually.

In Khasi Hills, a significant process of re-appraisal and revival of traditional Khasi culture was taking shape towards the end of nineteenth century. This was reinforced by the challenge posed by Christian missionaries' proselytizing activities, their contemptuous attitude and excessive zeal on the part of neo-converts in running down Khasi customary practices. This intellectual ferment received further impetus due to exposure to new ideologies and reform movements in other parts of

India. In 1899 this process gave birth to a new socio-cultural organization called Seng Khasi, led by Jeeban Roy and his associates, to provide a new cultural orientation to the basic tenets of Khasi religion — belief in God as the Creator, respect for kinship and ancestors (Jaswal, 1982).

By the end of 1920s, growing social awareness swept across Khasi Hills with a new political awakening. In 1923, the Syiems along with Reverend Nicolas Roy, a learned Khasi pastor, and some other educated individuals took a lead in organizing the first political party called Khasi National Durbar. With the introduction of provincial autonomy under the 1935 Government of India Act, questions of adequate representation for hill and tribal groups of Assam and apprehensions about the dominance of plains people acquired a new edge. Simultaneously, the political and social divide between the commoners and the privileged class, viz. Syiems, Dolois, Sirdars, etc. deepened further when the latter consolidated their position with tacit support from the British. Taking up the cause of the commoners, Rev. Nicolas Roy broke away from the Syiem-dominated Federation of Khasi States, and decided to organize the commoners under a separate banner.

The Garo Hills had so far appeared somewhat dormant except for a 1902 protest by *a'khing* owners, led by a literate Garo, Sonaram Sangma, against encroachments into the formers' territories by an absentee landlord (Majumdar, 1982). The first political organization, Garo National Conference, was founded in 1946 under the leadership of Emonsingh Sangma, an ex-serviceman, and Singdon Sangma, an employee of the Baptist church. The party was renamed as Garo National Council, which was to play a crucial role not only in bringing together the Garos under one banner, but also other N-E hill tribal leaders on a joint forum under the leadership of Capt. Williamson Sangma, also an ex-serviceman.

POST-INDEPENDENCE PERIOD

While independent India's political leadership was grappling with some basic issues like framing of a new Constitution and reorganization of States, the N-E region was seething with hectic political activity in an endeavour to consolidate numerous fissiparous elements on a common platform. This was essential for ensuring that the interests and aspirations of the hill tribal people were duly safeguarded under the new dispensation. In 1948, Nicolas Roy founded the Khasi-Jaintia Federal States National Conference, while Williamson Sangma rallied the Garos under the banner of Garo

National Council. Nicolas Roy participated in the sub-committee which recommended the provision of Autonomous District Councils for hill and tribal communities under the Sixth Schedule of the Constitution. Under this provision three District Councils were set up for Khasi, Jaintia and Garo Hills. Williamson Sangma became the first Chief Executive Member of the Garo District Council.

In 1950, Nicolas Roy had tried to organize a composite forum of various hill tribal leaders of the N-E region with the intention of putting forward a joint demand for a separate hill State. It did not materialize, however, since the Naga leader Phizo insisted on an independent Nagaland. These efforts succeeded at least partially in 1954 with the organization of Eastern Indian Tribal Union (EITU), which brought together representatives from Khasi and Jaintia Hills, Garo Hills, Mikir Hills, Cachar Hills and Mizo Hills. Meanwhile, EITU succeeded in establishing its political clout in the 1957 elections and joined a coalition government in Assam. As explained in Chapter 1, the enactment of a Bill in 1960 declaring Assamese as the State language seemed to confirm EITU leaders' worst fears about their continuing to be perpetually neglected in Assam.

By this time, the Mizos led by Laldenga had launched a militant movement for a separate Mizoram. At a conference convened by Williamson Sangma in Shillong in 1960, a new organization — All Party Hill Leaders Conference (APHLC) was formed to replace EITU and this new group demanded formation of a separate State of Meghalaya. By this time, the existing rift between the commoners and traditional leaders e.g. Syiems, Nokmas, etc. had become more pronounced in the functioning of District Councils and APHLC emerged as a regional political party representing the former (Mathur, 1982). It not only continued its boycott of the State Assembly but also launched a movement for a separate State of Meghalaya. The agitation was suspended temporarily in 1962 due to Chinese aggression. In the turbulent period which followed when the agitation was resumed, the Government of India held several rounds of negotiations with APHLC leaders.

In 1966, APHLC rejected the recommendations of Pataskar Committee as well as Nanda Committee which had suggested creation of an autonomous Meghalaya State within Assam. By this time, the political rift between the Assamese leaders and APHLC had hardened to a point where any arrangement which continued the hegemony of Assam would be unacceptable to the latter. Finally, an agreement was reached between

APHLC and Mrs. Indira Gandhi, the then Prime Minister in 1967, followed by Parliament passing the necessary Bill in 1969 and in 1970 the State of Meghalaya was born. For a short period, Meghalaya was to function as a State within Assam. However, this position was quickly rejected. Following the passing of the 1971 North-Eastern Areas (Reorganization) Act by Parliament, Meghalaya attained the status of a fully autonomous State on 21 January 1972. The same year a separate Jaintia Hills district was established.

One of the early developments after Meghalaya attained Statehood was the establishment of North-Eastern Hill University (NEHU) in 1973 with the intention of bringing higher education and research within easy reach of tribal students of N-E region. In view of the peculiar geographical terrain and communication problems in the N-E region, a legal provision was made in NEHU's Constitution for establishing other campuses besides its main campus in Shillong. Some colleges in Mizoram and Nagaland operate under NEHU's administration. Unfortunately, ever since its inception, NEHU seems to have been jinxed due to ethnic rivalries among student factions, e.g. Khasi, Naga, Mizo, not to mention vexing administrative and staffing problems. The pursuit of academic objectives has been frequently disrupted due to "Bandhs" (shut-downs), "Gheraos" (which literally means surrounding as a pressurizing tactic), threats and even murders of Vice-Chancellors (Guru Dev, *Times of India,* 2 April 1981). This situation is particularly discouraging because NEHU has so far not been able to fulfil its promise of providing competent and trained manpower badly needed to remove the developmental back log of N-E region and make rapid advances in its integration with the rest of India.

Present Situation

MAJOR GEOGRAPHICAL AND DEMOGRAPHIC FEATURES

"The Abode of Clouds" aptly describes the scenic State of Meghalaya, having an area of 22,427 sq km, consisting mostly of hills and plateaus. The Khasi Hills and Jaintia Hills together form a plateau which includes Shillong peak rising to a height of 1690 m and joining Bangladesh plains on the south in a steep and abrupt slope. The Garo Hills, which include Nortek peak with over 1600 m elevation, are fringed with small plains on the northern, western and southern sides. Meghalaya shares an international border with Bangladesh on the west and south. It is flanked by Assam on the north and east. Meghalaya includes the following districts: East Khasi Hills, West Khasi Hills, East Garo Hills, West Garo Hills, Jaintia

Hills, Ri Bhoi and South Garo Hills (the last two districts were created in 1992).

The 1991 population of Meghalaya was 1,774,775, with percentages of STs 83.53, SCs 0.51, urban population 18.60. Although Khasi and Jaintia societies historically had separate identities, presently they are treated as one community in official classification.[54] The Khasis include various sub-tribes which observed territorial endogamy in the past. The Khynriam Khasis are concentrated on the Shillong plateau, whereas the Wars occupy western and southern slopes. The Bhois occupy the lower foothills towards the north. The term "Jaintia" covers the Phars or Syntengs, and sub-groups like the Biates and Hadems. Lyngnams emerged out of the mixing of Khasis and Garos, and the Garo term for the same people is Megam. They inhabit parts of West Khasi Hills and East Garo Hills districts and have recently been recognized as Khasis. The Bhois and Biates are the only groups who follow patrilineal system in a State which is unique because of its patrilineal system. The terms "Kha-si" and "Syn-Teng" both mean children of ancient or ancestral mother, which indicates the important position assigned to the mother in their culture (Das, 1978). The 2001 population of Meghalaya was 2.30 million as per Provisional Population Totals.

The East, West and South Garo Hills districts are inhabited by Garos who have a lot of similarity with the Rabha, Koch, Mech, Kachari, etc. who belong to the Bodo group. The Garos are divided into three lineage-based divisions: Sangma, Marak and Momin, the last being offsprings of Muslim fathers and Garo mothers. A number of sub-tribes, e.g. Abeng, Matchi, Gara Ganching, Chisak, Atong, etc. have been assimilated in the composite tribe Garo. Besides these major indigenous groups, Meghalaya population includes a fair number of Nepalis, who are engaged in raising cattle, dairying and manual work, Biharis who are engaged in low-paid labour such as road construction and Marwaris, Sindhis and Bengalis who have captured major trades and businesses. Shillong was the capital of composite Assam for several years after Independence, and currently is the capital of Meghalaya, besides being army and air force headquarters and an educational centre. A sizeable number of persons belonging to other States of India reside in Shillong and other district administrative

54. The Land Reforms Commission for Khasi Hills in 1975 defined the Khasi as "a person who is a descendant of people in Khasi and Jaintia Hills, governed by Khasi customary laws of consanguinity and kinship, Christian or non-Christian."

centres. In addition, Meghalaya also received a number of immigrant Bangladeshis before and after Partition. Meghalaya population also includes persons from some other tribes, e.g. Chakma, Hajong, Kachari, Kuki, Mizo, Naga, etc.

The Baptist and Presbyterian missionaries began to convert people to Christianity in Khasi and Jaintia Hills and Garo Hills in the first half of the nineteenth century with support from the British administration. The Unitarians and Roman Catholic missions followed later. The advance of Christianity was faster among the Khasis than among the Jaintias and the Garos. By 1991 Census, the religious distribution of Meghalaya population was as follows: Hindus 14.67 per cent, Muslims 3.46 per cent, Christians 64.58 per cent, other religions and persuasions 16.82 per cent. This last category includes persons professing various faiths, viz. Khasi 111,729; Song Sarek 93,375; Niamtre 61,545; Bhoi 8,723; Synteng 1,884; Garo 1,178; Jaintia 231, etc. (*Census of India 1991,* Paper 1 of 1995).

ECONOMIC AND SOCIAL CONTEXT

Much of the recent unrest among students and hostility towards "outsiders" are symptomatic of a deep frustration caused by intense competition and inadequate employment opportunities due to poor development of the State. Nearly four-fifths of Meghalaya's labour force is engaged in low-yield agriculture, predominantly of the jhuming type. In 1990-91, out of the net sown area of 202,000 acres, irrigated area formed 22.77 per cent. And the yield of rice in 1993-94 was 1094 kg per ha, the next lowest after Arunachal Pradesh, among N-E States, as against the all-India average of 1879 kg per ha (NEC, 1995). In 1990-91 the total food grain production was 154.4 thousand tonnes, and in 1996-97, according to the National Economic Survey data for 1997-98, it declined to 151.9 thousand tonnes (Chatterjee, 1999), causing large deficits in the total State requirement. There is considerable potential for horticulture, especially citrus fruits and pineapples, plantation crops, pisciculture and forestry, which remains undeveloped. Even where cash crops, such as black pepper, cardamom, coffee and cashew nuts are taken up under State Government auspices, such efforts fail to achieve large scale adoption of improved practices by local farmers, as adequate follow-up support is not available.

Industrial growth has remained disappointing although sizeable natural resources are available in forestry, sericulture, fisheries, mining, etc. In

1994 the State had seven large and medium-scale industrial units and in 1988, there were 587 small-scale units. These included a small number of mining and quarrying units for coal, limestone, sillimanite, clay and cement, saw mills, wooden furniture shops, motor repairing and servicing, bakeries, rice mills, etc. There is some increase in sericultural activities, especially muga, eri and tussar (Govt. of Meghalaya, 1987). Meghalaya had 8201 handlooms, according to a 1987-88, All India Handloom Census, the smallest number among N-E States (Mazumdar, 1999). Wholesale and retail trades, hotels and small restaurants provide some employment. While wholesale trade has been captured mostly by Marwaris and Bengalis, retail trade and small tea shops provide employment to women. Growth of medium and large industries is hampered by poor development of transportation (Meghalaya has no rail-link), shortage of electricity and lack of technical manpower and entrepreneurship. By 1992, out of a total of 4824 inhabited villages, 2315, i.e. 47.23 per cent were electrified, which is the lowest percentage among N-E States (NEC, 1992).

According to the estimates of the Expert Group appointed by Government of India, in 1987-88, 5.58 lakh persons constituting 34.60 per cent of Meghalaya population (4.89 lakh rural and 0.59 lakh urban) was below the poverty line. By 1993-94, 7.38 lakh persons or 37.92 per cent of the total State population (7.09 lakh rural and 0.29 lakh urban) was estimated to be living below the poverty line.[55] According to *Indian Economic Survey (1996-97)*, the Net State Domestic Product (NSDP) for 1994-95 was Rs. 1206 crore, and per capita NSDP was Rs. 6136. The provisional estimates for 1996-97 of NSDP for the State was Rs. 1763 crore and per capita NSDP Rs. 8474 (State Directorate of Economics and Statistics and Central Statistical Organization).

Perhaps, a redeeming feature of Meghalaya is the absence of wide disparities in ownership of land and absentee landlordism. M.K.S. Nair (1999) attributes this largely to predominantly community ownership of land, the matrilineal system and kinship-based land relations with relatively rare transferable rights to land. Moreover, large number of regulatory measures undertaken by State Government and District Councils prohibiting sale and transfer of land by a tribal to a non-tribal person have also minimized the possibility of land alienation. The traditional leaders, like Syiems, Dolois, Sirdars/village headmen have acquired some coveted

55. See note 11 for details of methodology.

and sizeable lands in urban or urban fringe areas but this problem does not exist in rural areas, according to a 1979-80 field research by M.K.S. Nair (1999).

A reference has been made earlier to the presence of immigrants from Bangladesh, Nepal, Tibet and persons from other States of India in Meghalaya. The anti-foreigners agitation in Assam had its repercussions in Meghalaya too, when anti-Bengali riots broke out in Shillong in 1979. Unlike Assam, however, the agitations in Meghalaya have been short-lived and usually sparked by some sporadic incidents. In the 1987 disturbances, Nepalis became the targets and some of them were evicted from their houses which were burnt along with their animals. Episodes of communal violence erupted in 1992, 1994 and 1996 in which immigrant Bangladeshis, Tibetans, Bengalis, Biharis and even sweepers from Punjab (who were brought to Shillong by the British) have been victims.

Khasi Students Union (KSU) and FKJGP (Federation of Khasi, Jaintia and Garo People) have either favoured or led most of these agitations against non-tribal people.[56] Recently, some insurgent groups, like Hynniewtrep Achik Liberation Front (HALF) seem to be involved in Meghalaya politics, as evident from death threats issued to some candidates at elections (Saikia, *Times of India,* 4 March 1996). Another vexing problem unearthed recently by the Indian army is the use of Meghalaya's hilly and forested areas by militant groups from other States as safe hide-outs. For instance, NSCN (National Socialist Council of Nagaland), ULFA (United Liberation Front of Assam), ATTF (All Tripura Tiger Force) and others have established camps in East and South Garo Hills and West Khasi Hills, and received clandestine support from a local group, Achik National Volunteer Service (ANVS), a Garo insurgent outfit. The poor road communications pose formidable problems in dismantling these camps (*Times of India*, 31 March 1998).

Meghalaya currently presents a strange scenario. Until the attainment of Statehood in 1972, the State's leadership carried on a determined struggle through entirely Constitutional methods, in striking contrast to some other N-E States which experienced a virtual breakdown of civilian

---

56. The rising unemployment among local population and upsurge in crime rates, e.g. drug abuse and mugging, are attributed to outsiders constituting a majority of Shillong population, which is not substantiated by facts. Between 1971 and 1991, the tribal population of Greater Shillong increased from 41.47 per cent to 53.13 per cent.

government. At that time Meghalaya was way ahead of most N-E States in terms of maturity of its political leadership, growth of educational institutions, responsiveness to external influences and thought currents, and social solidarity among its different ethnic sections. Somehow, the period following 1972 seems to have been frittered away in destructive activities such as strikes to bring NEHU's academic activities to a standstill, and agitations and eviction threats to "outsiders" and "foreigners." The suspicions against "outsiders" and fears of losing out in competition have at times resulted in almost paranoid opposition to establishing a rail-link, opening of new offices and starting new development projects because these might bring more "outsiders" into the State. One of the unusual attempts to find solutions to the State's lack of progress is the attack on its age-old matrilineal system. A section of Khasi men blame its matrilineal structure for lack of initiative and entrepreneurship among men. This group would like to revive an old but defunct organization — Syngkhong Rympei Thymmai (SRT) — Association of New Hearts — in order to restructure Khasi Society into patriarchal pattern (Ahmed, *Times of India*, 28 January 1994).

Today some N-E States have stolen a march over Meghalaya in agricultural and industrial development, education, electrification of villages, etc. It is high time that the people and Government of Meghalaya took determined action to utilize the State's natural resources more fully and boost production. These include modernization of agriculture and horticulture; utilization of the hilly terrain to develop plantations for a variety of cash crops; technological support in mining and processing the State's rich mineral resources; development of roads and rail transport; generation of more electrical power; processing units for fruits and forestry products. These measures are expected to boost the State's domestic product and generate additional employment. Simultaneously, there is a need for the State's political and intellectual leaders to involve themselves fully in the task of motivating their communities for social reconstruction and self-reliant growth, instead of letting the people dissipate their energy in blaming the Central Government or the "outsiders" for their situation. The NEC being based in Shillong, can play a supportive role in obtaining the necessary technical and financial help in these tasks. The Central Government must fulfil their recent promises to develop special packages of aid for N-E States. And yet, there is no doubt that ultimately the people of Meghalaya themselves hold the key to decide their future.

MIZORAM

Historical Perspective

EARLIER HISTORY

The early inhabitants of Lushai Hills belonged to Tibeto-Burmese stock of the Mongoloid race. Historians have variously traced their origins to China, Mongolia, Tibet, South-East Asia, particularly Thailand and Myanmar (erstwhile Burma). There is general agreement, however, that in the course of their roving existence, they settled down for several generations in the Chin Hills area near Tiddim-Falam in Myanmar.[57] Towards the close of the eighteenth century they crossed Tiao river, when pushed out by the more powerful Pawis, and then entered Lushai Hills. They, in turn, pushed out the earlier inhabitants, Thadou Kukis, who shifted to Manipur and Cachar. For some time Tripura kingdom extended up to Lushai Hills, but Sibuta, a Paite chief, threw off the hegemony of Tripura kings and asserted his independence.

The inhabitants of Lushai Hills belonged to various tribes, e.g. Hmar, Paite, Pawi, Lakher, Reang, Lushai, Zadeng, Rengthlai, etc. and territorial conflicts among them as well as with other tribes from Myanmar and Chittagong Hills were frequent. Indeed, the picture of hostilities and alignments among tribes inhabiting Lushai Hills, Myanmar and Chittagong Hills was a constantly fluctuating one.[58]

Around the middle of the nineteenth century, the Sailo clans of Lushai tribe conquered several other groups, established their supremacy and assimilated many smaller groups in their fold. The term "Lushai" replaced "Kuki" in Lushai Hills and acquired a broader connotation by end of the nineteenth century. Since the 1950s the term "Lushai" was replaced by

---

57. Thangura who lived at Falam in Chin Hills of Myanmar in early eighteenth century, is believed to be the ancestor from whom various branches of Lushais, e.g. Zadeng, Paite, Sailo, etc. sprang (Chatterjee, 1985).

58. In 1777, when Mizo tribes raided Chittagong Hills, the Chakma chief of Chittagong asked British help to defend his territory. However, in 1830 when the Zadengs (a Mizo tribe, which previously had several conflicts with Sailos) were invaded by a Burmese tribe, they sought the support of Sailos and Chakmas from Chittagong Hills. Similarly, despite fights between Burmese and Mizo tribes, there are stories about Fanai, a Burmese tribe that made friends with Lushais and continued to live in Mizo Hills until British occupation. According to one version, Raltes are descendants of this Burmese tribe (Goswami, 1987).

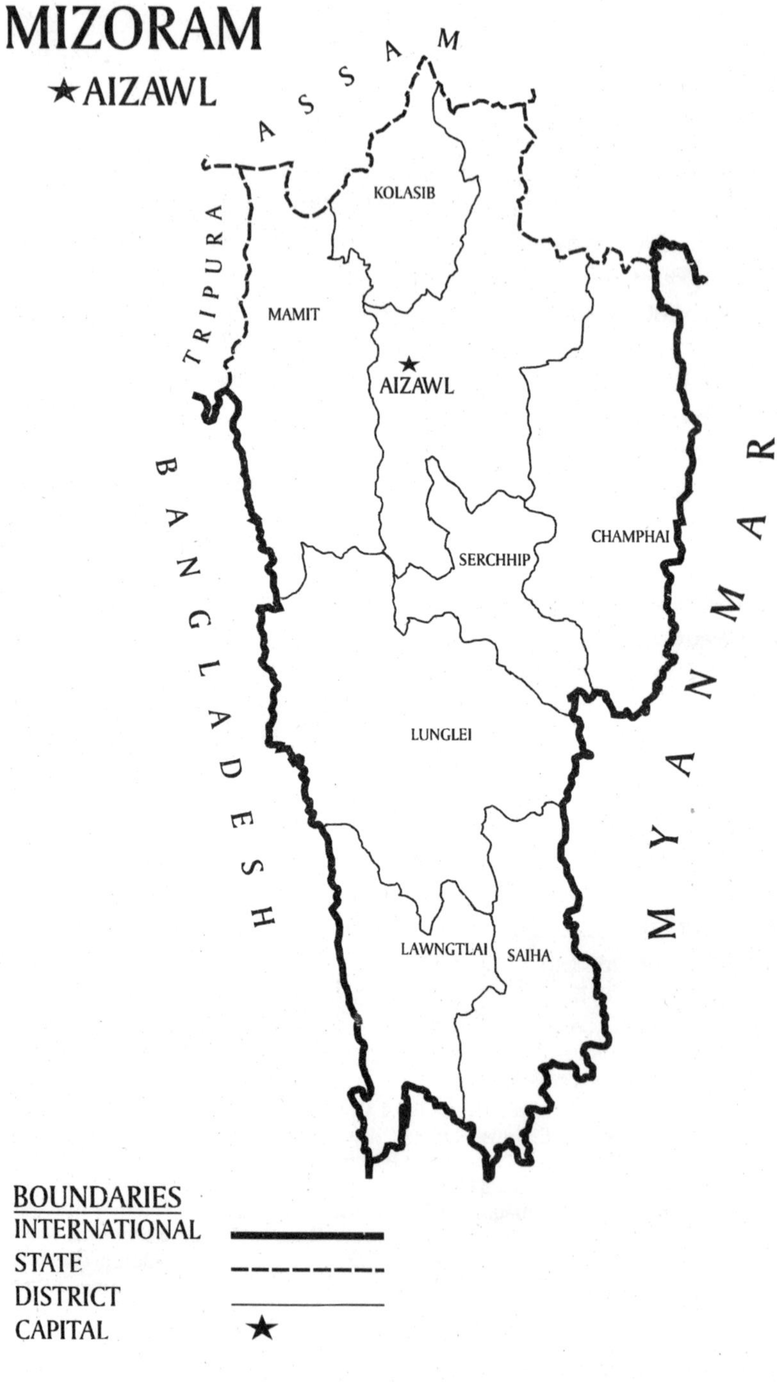
MIZORAM
★AIZAWL
ASSAM
TRIPURA
BANGLADESH
MYANMAR
KOLASIB
MAMIT
AIZAWL
SERCHHIP
CHAMPHAI
LUNGLEI
LAWNGTLAI
SAIHA
BOUNDARIES
INTERNATIONAL
STATE
DISTRICT
CAPITAL

the more comprehensive term "Mizo" (meaning highlander, while "Ram" means territory). In the Chin Hills area of Myanmar, these groups are called "Chin." The ethnic group broadly known as "Kuki" is presently scattered in Mizoram, Nagaland, Tripura, North Cachar Hills and southern fringes of Assam, Manipur, besides Chittagong Hill Tracts of Bangladesh and northern Myanmar.[59]

By the end of the eighteenth century, a fairly formal system of chieftainship emerged and soon became hereditary with the eldest son generally succeeding as the chief. A council of "Upas," meaning elders, assisted the chief, who was responsible for defending the members of the tribe or clan and their territory and settling disputes among them. The chief generally had his house at the highest point on a hill for strategic as well as prestige considerations. All land in the territory technically belonged to his subjects, who in turn gave part of the produce from cultivation, choicest part of meat of hunted animals and services to the chief's household. The chief usually had several wives as well as concubines and slaves who included women captured in raids. The chief typically assumed a parental role towards his subjects, provided shelter to needy widows and children and to social outcasts like criminals or debtors. A part of the collections made by the chief was used to maintain youth dormitories or "Zawlbuks," for construction of public amenities such as water reservoirs and for hospitality of guests, etc. (Nag, 1993). Mizo chiefs usually acquired the best lands for their own use and had traditional powers to attach properties of their subjects and even to inflict capital punishment in case the latter were found guilty of certain serious offences.

BRITISH PERIOD

As mentioned in Chapter 1, the British had their major confrontations with the Lushais when they got involved in protecting people against Lushai raids on the plains of Cachar after British occupation of Assam in 1826. After the devastating Lushai attack on Cachar in 1871 in which a British tea-planter was killed and his six year old daughter, Mary Winchester, was abducted, the British gave up the earlier policy of containment and adopted a more aggressive stance. Whenever the Lushais faced shortages of food, manpower, etc. they continued to raid villages in

---

59. A number of kindred groups belonging to Tibeto-Burman stock of Mongoloid origin are referred as Kuki, Lushai, Mizo or Chin in various regions, and these terms are often used interchangeably (Chatterjee, 1985).

the plains and carried away food, arms, captives as well as heads for the burial of a chief.[60] The British therefore organized a number of punitive expeditions, e.g. in 1849, 1869, 1895, etc. and established two administrative centres at Aizawl and Lunglei by 1890 in order to keep effective control over the Lushais. Two subsequent revolts — the first-led by the intrepid chief Lengpunga and another by Ropoui Leni, the widow of the vanquished chief Vandulla in 1892 — were crushed by the British and the rebels were captured.[61]

In 1897 North Lushai Hills and South Lushai Hills (so far administratively attached to Bengal) were amalgamated into Lushai Hills district and annexed to Assam. In 1930 the area inhabited by Pawi-Lakher tribes in southern Mizoram was brought under British control (Goswami & Mukherjee, 1982).

One of the first steps of the British administration was to demarcate the territories of various chiefs, who previously did not have the concept of fixed boundaries, and to ban inter-tribal raids and head-hunting. Furthermore, the whole area of Lushai Hills was divided into circles and selected chiefs were put in charge of maintaining peace and order within their respective jurisdictions. At the same time, the chiefs were left free to continue their traditional practices regarding allocation of lands for jhuming and collection of levies from their subjects. The composite Lushai Hills district was placed in the "Excluded Areas" category with its Inner Line Regulation.[62]

The first-half of the twentieth century was full of events which were formative in terms of the subsequent social and political developments. The English Baptist Mission and the Welsh Presbyterian Mission, followed by other denominations, opened schools, compiled Lushai language in Roman script, translated the Bible into Lushai, encouraged Mizo girls to

60. A victorious Lushai raid would bring back something like "20 heads and six captives". The heads of enemies were not just trophies of conquest for the Lushais, but essential for placing on the grave of a dead chief to ensure that the chief's soul was properly escorted, according to their traditional belief. In one British expedition 400 captives who were used for slave labour were freed.

61. Lengpunga succeeded in over-running the Aizawl post before he was arrested by the British and was sent to Hazaribagh jail where he committed suicide in 1891. Roupui Leni was captured and sent to Rangmati (presently in Bangladesh) where she died (Chatterjee, 1987).

62. Refer to note 9 of Chapter 1.

join schools along with boys, and thus gave a powerful momentum for the spread of education and Christianity. In 1901, less than1 per cent Mizos were converted to Christianity. By 1951 more than 80 per cent had adopted Christianity. Educated Mizos were welcomed by British administrators in government jobs. Some of them joined institutions outside Mizoram for higher education and thus benefited from wider interaction with ideas and people, and got acquainted with national developments. Some of them participated in the two world wars, which also broadened their outlook. The Government of India Act of 1935, which brought into focus questions of representation of hill tribal communities in the legislature of composite Assam created political awareness among the Mizos. It was no wonder, therefore, that Mizo Union, the first political party in Mizoram was born in 1946.

At another level, the question of who represented the Mizo people within Mizoram had acquired considerable significance in the context of growing distrust among Mizo commoners towards the feudal and autocratic structure of chieftainship. Against this background, the Mizo Union strongly opposed the British proposal that the Chiefs' Council, which included 20 chiefs, would represent all Mizo people.[63] The British District Superintendent then suggested that a larger District Conference would be constituted by including 20 representatives each of the chiefs and the commoners. This too was rejected by the Mizo Union. Meanwhile the Mizo chiefs formed a new party called United Mizo Freedom Organization, which had favoured merger of Lushai Hills district with the Union of Burma (present Myanmar). The Mizo Union was not swayed by this suggestion, nor did it favour A. Z. Phizo's bid to organize a united Naga-Mizo front in 1947. The Mizo Union's will to join the Indian Union finally prevailed.

POST-INDEPENDENCE PERIOD

Following the adoption of the Sixth Schedule of the Indian Constitution, the Lushai Hills District Council was formed in 1952. Furthermore, in 1953 the Pawi-Lakher Autonomous Region was constituted to meet the demands of minority ethnic communities. The District Council soon became the focal point for mobilizing public opinion for various social and political

---

63. During Second World War Mizo chiefs had tried to demonstrate their loyalty to the British by raising a Labour Corps and pledging their support to the British war effort. Needless to say, the chiefs would use the labour of their subjects, i.e. commoners. The British in turn, rewarded the chiefs by forming the Chief's Council, as a consultative body.

issues, as also the testing ground for political parties. The Mizo Union, which dominated the District Council after the 1952 general elections, lost no time in dismantling the system of chieftainship which had become an anathema in the new climate of democratic freedom. In 1952, the customary house-tax and levies in kind imposed by the Mizo chiefs on their subjects, as well as the system of forced labour were scrapped. In 1954, under the Lushai Hills District Acquisition of Chiefs' Rights Act, over 300 chiefs were paid monetary compensation in lieu of terminating the chieftainship. It is interesting to note that Mizo women, who had formed an organization called Mizo Hmeichhe Tangrual Pawl in 1946, played an active role in mobilizing public opinion for abolition of this institution. Once the autocratic and feudal system of chieftainship was abolished, the Mizos turned their attention to protection of Mizo identity and interests in composite Assam.

In 1954, the Lushai Hills district was renamed as Mizo Hills district. The Mizo Union had initially joined the Eastern Indian Tribal Union (EITU) and later the All Party Hill Leaders' Conference (APHLC) in their negotiations with the Central Government leaders to ensure a certain degree of autonomy for hill tribal communities and to preserve their ethnic identity and traditions. Two events, however, persuaded the Mizo Union to change its mind regarding the feasibility of a separate hill tribal State within Assam. When a terrible famine stalked the Mizo Hills during mid–1950s, the Mizos felt seriously let down by the Assamese leaders' perceived indifference towards the Mizos' hardships. Secondly, the enactment of a bill by Assam legislature adopting Assamese as the official State language in 1960 seemed to confirm the Mizos' misgivings about their fate in composite Assam. By this time the APHLC's initial proposal of a hill tribal State was losing its appeal. In this context, the Mizo Union left the APHLC and in 1962 voiced its demand for a separate State of Mizoram.

Not content with the seemingly slow movement toward Mizo aspirations for autonomy, a more radical party, Mizo National Front (MNF), was formed in 1962 by Laldenga, an ex-soldier and former accountant in the Mizo District Council. Laldenga, who belonged to Pawi tribe, had established Mizo Famine Front in 1958 and changed it to MNF and proclaimed the goal of a sovereign Mizo State outside the Indian Union, which would include other Kuki-Chin-inhabited areas, e.g. in Manipur. Mizo youth who were drawn by Laldenga's revolutionary appeal, were soon organized into a militant wing, Mizo National Army (MNA). In 1966 the MNA launched armed attacks on Aizawl and Lunglei and after holding Aizawl in siege, declared the establishment of an independent Mizo Government. Initially MNF activists received spontaneous local support in the form of food supplies and shelter. However, after a strong crack-down by the Indian security forces, Laldenga and his followers fled to East Pakistan (present Bangladesh) and continued armed insurgency from their bases in Pakistan with clandestine support from hostile powers across India's borders.

During the decade following turmoil, common people in Mizoram suffered a great deal. They had to bear the brunt of MNF violence, extortions, levies and murders of suspected informants on the one hand, and the strong-arm methods typical of army occupation on the other. In 1967 the Government of India launched the "re-grouping" operation whereby people living in 516 scattered and interior villages were evacuated and brought to 110 road-side clusters to protect them from the militants. The government also provided them rations, water, medical care, etc. This measure helped to cut off at least partly the food supplies and shelter to the militants. Nonetheless, the "re-grouping" scheme disrupted the life of nearly 23,000 families who were uprooted from their original habitats.[64]

After the Bangladesh war and emergence of friendly relations between Bangladesh and India in 1972, the MNF lost the support of arms and sanctuary for its guerilla operations. The Indian Government's policy of persuading the moderate sections of MNF to surrender, and of helping their rehabilitation, succeeded in weaning away many youths from MNA. Besides, splits within MNF leadership, failure to attract new recruits, and a growing popular desire for peace tilted the balance in favour of a negotiated settlement. With the enactment of the North-Eastern Areas (Reorganization) Act of 1971, Meghalaya, Tripura and Manipur attained full Statehood and Mizoram and Arunachal Pradesh were given Union Territory status, with elected legislatures and councils of ministers. In the subsequent conducive atmosphere, in 1976 the MNF and the Government of India concluded a peace accord, following which most of the MNF members surrendered, and an understanding was reached to resolve mutual differences through negotiations. Simultaneously with Mizoram

64. When there was relaxation in the "re-grouping" policy in 1971, several families returned to their previous villages, but many others migrated to other places and nearby towns in other States in search of employment, often as wage labourers (Nunthara, 1990).

getting Union Territory status, under the 1971 Act, Mizo District Council was dissolved. Under provisions of the Sixth Schedule of the Constitution, three Autonomous District Councils were created, viz. Mara, Lai and Chakma (the previous names Pawi and Lakher were changed to Mara and Lai, respectively) to give special protection to three disadvantaged groups.

In the meantime, the Mizo Union, which merged with the Indian Congress Party, lost its popular appeal and suffered defeat in the elections, which transferred political leadership to a new party, People's Conference, led by Brigadier Sailo. Within a relatively short period, however, it suffered reverses since it came to acquire an anti-MNF image and was unsuccessful in facilitating MNF-Government of India negotiations, which led Laldenga to resume insurgency in 1978. In the 1984 elections Mizoram Congress returned to power and successfully mediated in the resumed negotiations between MNF and Government of India. A historic agreement was reached in 1986 which cleared the way for full Statehood for Mizoram, and by a Constitutional Amendment on 20 February 1987, Mizoram attained full Statehood.[65]

Having thus achieved for Mizoram the cherished dream of Statehood, Laldenga emerged as a hero and became Chief Minister, though for a brief interlude. In 1988, however, Mizoram Congress defeated both the People's Conference and MNF, and retained power during the following decade. The much-needed peace and normalcy enabled the State to initiate several new policies and take rapid strides in development and well-being of its people.

Present Situation

SALIENT GEOGRAPHICAL AND DEMOGRAPHIC FEATURES

Mizoram covers an area of 21,081 sq km most of which is interspersed with north-south ranges of Mizo and western Patkoi hills, alternated with deep valleys. Blue Mountain, the highest peak, reaches an elevation of 2157 m. Mizoram shares an international border of 710 km with Myanmar's Chin Hills on the east and south, and with Bangladesh's

65. The 53rd Constitutional Amendment of 1986, which conferred Statehood on Mizoram provided that no acts of Parliament covering religion or social practices, customary laws, administration of civil and criminal justice, and ownership and transfer of land will apply to Mizoram unless so decided by the Mizoram legislature.

Chittagong Hills on the west. It has an adjoining border with Tripura on the north-west and with Assam and Manipur on the north. Nearly two-thirds of the State's total area is covered with forests. Among the several rivers which flow through the State, the major ones in the north are Dhaleshwari, Tuirial and Tuivawl, and in the south, Chimtuipui and Karnaphuli. Previously, the State was divided into three districts, viz. Aizawl, Lunglei and Chimtuipui. The present districts are: Kolasib, Aizawl, Champhai, Serchhip, Saiha, Lawngtlai, Lunglei, Mamit (Census of India 2001, Paper 1 of 2001).

Mizoram's population, according to 1991 Census was 689,756, the smallest among the N-E States. Over two-thirds of the State's total population is clustered in Aizawl district, while Chimtuipui and Lunglei are rather thinly populated. As mentioned in Chapter 1, Mizoram's urban population rose from 24.67 per cent in 1981 to 46.10 per cent by 1991, mainly due to expansion of the capital town Aizawl and of district headquarters. Mizoram's total population, which was 3.32 lakh in 1971 rose to 6.89 lakh in 1991, i.e. more than doubled. This was partly due to the influx of Chakmas and Muslims from Bangladesh, and Kuki-Chin tribal groups from Myanmar (Nandy, 1997). The percentage of STs in 1991 was 94.75 and that of SCs 0.10. The 2001 Census placed Mizoram's population at 8.91 lakh (Provisional Population Totals).

The Lushais constitute the most numerous group in Mizoram's population, and the process of assimilation of other tribes and sub-tribes, such as Paite, Kuki, Pawi, Lakher, Hmar, Ralte, etc. into a comprehensive Mizo identity has been progressing steadily. Hmars, a non-Lushai group belonging to the broader Kuki-Chin family, consider themselves as autochthones, but are gradually being assimilated in the larger Mizo ethnos. Same is true of the Raltes, who are believed to have different historical origins from the Lushais. On the whole, in comparison with other N-E States, the Mizos have achieved a high degree of social integration. The only exceptions are Chakmas and Reangs, who are concentrated on the southern side of the State near the western border with Bangladesh. A small number of Chakmas initially migrated to Mizoram in 1905 following a famine in Chittagong Hill Tracts (CHT), their previous habitat, and were allowed to settle down as subjects of Mizo chieftains. After partition in 1947, Chittagong Hill Tracts (CHT) were attached to East Pakistan. The adverse policies of East Pakistan Government, and later Bangladesh Government threatened their security and they continued to migrate to India in search of shelter.[66] By 1987 their number in Mizoram was 45,000. MNF and Laldenga are believed to have taken a hostile attitude towards Chakmas and killed many who were suspected to have positive links with Indian security forces. They are Buddhists and constitute an educationally and economically backward community in Mizoram, along with the Reangs, majority of whom follow a religion which is a mixture of Hinduism and some animistic elements from their original faith.

The religious distribution of Mizoram's population as per 1991 Census was: Christians 85.73 per cent, Buddhists 7.83 per cent, Hindus 5.05 per cent, Muslims 0.66 per cent, other religions and persuasions 0.27 per cent.

CURRENT ECONOMIC AND SOCIAL CONTEXT

Mizoram's economy is predominantly agricultural, jhuming being the major mode until recently. With rapidly shortening jhuming cycle, fast denudation of forests, quick run-off of water and heavy soil erosion, productivity of land is low. According to NEC data, the average yield of rice for 1993-94 was 1547 kg per ha as against the all-India average of 1879 kg. Out of the total sown area in 1990-91, only 12.30 per cent was irrigated, as against all-India average of 33.35 per cent (NEC 1995). In 1989-90 total food grain production was expected to reach 71,500 metric tonnes, against the requirement of 99,000 metric tonnes, thus necessitating imports from other States at high cost annually. The State Government has therefore launched a scheme to stop jhuming and replace it by settled cultivation, through providing a package of assistance including seeds, improved implements and technical assistance, etc. to groups of participating families for a period of five years (Menon, 1988). Such programmes are resulting in notable increases in food production, which rose from 81,500 metric tonnes in 1990-91 to 1,33,800 metric tonnes in 1996-97 (Chatterjee, 1999).

After abolition of chieftainship in 1954, a new class of powerful and enterprising landowners including some ex-chiefs who know how to capture maximum share of benefits from Government-sponsored agricultural development programmes, has emerged. They have acquired sizeable

66. See note 28 for history of Chakmas' immigration into India. In 1986, 5000 Chakma refugees were forcibly sent back to CHT. After establishment of friendly relations between Bangladesh and India, attempts are on to prevail upon Bangladesh government to arrange the return of Chakmas to their native place in Bangladesh.

additional lands and have undertaken commercial cultivation by employing poorer Mizos or Reangs as agricultural labourers. Guhathakurta (1999), on the basis of a field survey, has noted a trend toward marginal landholdings and even landlessness, which have been unknown in Mizoram until recently.

The steep rise in urban population in Mizoram, 46.10 per cent of the total State population in 1991, has not been due to growth of industries in urban areas, but mainly because of push factors: poverty and unemployment in rural areas. Besides, rural areas are devoid of most basic amenities. For that matter, even several urban areas lack elementary services such as piped water supply, sanitary latrines, covered drainage, and transportation, etc. (Bhattacharjee, 1995). Up to 1988, out of 722 inhabited villages in the State, 261, i.e. 36.15 per cent were electrified, and by 1992 this percentage rose to 71.71 (NEC, 1992 & 1995). The per capita consumption of electricity in the State was a modest 126.1 KWH, as compared to all-India average of 330.6 KWH (NEC, 1995).

Poor transportation continues to be a major handicap in Mizoram's economic development. After 1947 partition of the country and creation of East Pakistan (later Bangladesh) the State's direct communication link with the mainland was disrupted. In the absence of any rail link, the 180 km circuitous Silchar-Aizawl highway remains its sole link with the rest of the country. When this road gets blocked by floods or landslides, or other disturbances such as the 1994 week-long blockade by Assamese truck operators, Mizoram faces formidable difficulties. High transportation costs hike the prices of essential commodities imported from other States, and simultaneously reduce profit margins of goods produced in Mizoram and sent outside the State. The total road length in 1992 was 3708 km, the lowest among N-E States (NEC, 1995).

So far, almost all of Mizoram's meagre industrial development has been in the small-scale sector, and until 1994 there was only one medium-scale industrial unit in the State. By 1988, there were 918 small-scale industrial units which included handloom weaving, handicrafts, rice and flour mills, saw mills, aluminium casting and machine repair units, etc. Other units which provide employment, usually of a supplementary nature are poultries, piggeries, sericulture, cultivation of ginger, vegetables and fruits, restaurants and tea stalls, etc. The Net State Domestic Product (NSDP) for 1993-94 was Rs.562 crore, and per capita NSDP Rs.7517 according to *Indian Economic Survey, 1996-97*, and provisional estimate for 1995-96 was Rs.761 crore for the State and per capita Rs.9570. (State Directorate of Economics and Statistics and Central Statistical Organization). The Expert Group appointed by the Government of India estimated the number of persons living below the poverty line in 1987-88 in Mizoram to be 2.01 lakh or 32.52 per cent (1.68 lakh rural and 0.33 lakh urban). In 1993-94, this number came down to 1.94 lakh or 25.66 per cent (1.64 lakh rural and 0.30 lakh urban).[67]

The intense competition for limited employment opportunities combined with aspirations for Western styles of living, loss of old moorings and deep frustration, particularly among Mizo youths, are believed to be responsible for a high incidence of alcoholism and drug addiction. The proximity to Myanmar, with a highly lucrative drug trade across the border, increases their vulnerability to this evil. There is a growing concern among the older generation over erosion of their typical community ethos and egalitarian social traditions, described in the Mizo term "tlawmngaihua" which urges people to be unselfish and helpful to others. In recent years Mizoram, like other N-E States, has witnessed some "anti-foreigner" and "anti-outsider" agitations, directed against Chakmas, Bangladeshi Muslims and non-Mizo traders from Assam and other States (Ghosh, 1995). A large number of Reangs, although natives of Mizoram, have fled to Tripura due to threats from a militant outfit in Mizoram, and have been living in relief camps in Tripura since 1987.[68] Recently, the National Human Rights Commission has directed Mizoram Government to ensure conditions for the Reangs' return to their homeland (*Times of India*, 29 May 2000).

Barring these few disturbances, however, Mizoram has continued to enjoy considerable peace and political stability since attaining Statehood in 1987. The State Government has undertaken important steps to modernize agriculture by promoting terracing and water-shed management, as a viable alternative to jhuming. Modern technologies are being introduced in vegetable production, horticulture, and plantation crops, like rubber, coffee, cardamom, as also in fisheries, sericulture, etc.

---

67. Refer to note 11 for details of methodology.

68. The Reang's demand of an Autonomous District Council was believed to have provoked angry reactions among some Mizo sections. When faced with threats from the Bru National Liberation Front, a militant group, nearly 30,000 Reangs sought shelter in Tripura, where the Reangs constitute the second most numerous tribal community.

More significantly, Mizoram Food and Allied Industries Corporation (MIFCO) was set up in 1989 for processing and preservation of vegetables, fruits, milk, ginger, fish, etc. Its small and village industries will undoubtedly receive a boost with the establishment of two industrial estates and three more in various stages of planning. With the setting up of Mizoram Handloom and Handicrafts Development Corporation, the prospects of providing support in qualitative improvement and profitability of handloom and handicraft products are bright (Aggarwal, 1999). The recent border agreement between India and Myanmar opens up for Mizoram new opportunities for serving as a conduit for expanding trade between the two countries (Ahmed, 1994).

Mizoram has achieved a spectacular increase in its literacy rate, standing at 82.27 per cent in 1991, next only to Kerala which ranks as the highest in the country. In yet another area, Mizoram has set before the whole country a rare example of peaceful and trouble-free State Assembly elections in November 1998 and displayed impeccable political decorum.[69] In terms of human resources, Mizoram has valuable organizational assets out of which two are noteworthy. The YMA (Young Mizo Association), a non-sectarian, non-political State-wide network of branches, which organizes young men and women in a variety of community self-help activities is one example. The other is MHIP (Mizoram Hmeichhe Insuihkhawn Pawl) — Mizoram Women's Federation (MWF) — with over 500 branches extending to distant villages. These groups take-up various activities for women and children in need, and are often engaged in mobilizing public opinion for action against injustice to women.

NAGALAND

Historical Perspective

EARLIER HISTORY

The history of the Indo-Mongoloid tribes inhabiting the Naga hills and known as "Kirata" to distinguish them as non-Aryan, prior to thirteenth

---

69. The atmosphere in Mizoram during the 1998 poll campaign was devoid of bitter rivalry and violence among opposing political parties. In fact, rival parties often operated from election offices in close proximity. The Church and community organizations played an important role in creating awareness about responsible political behaviour (Banerjee, 1998).

NAGALAND

★KOHIMA

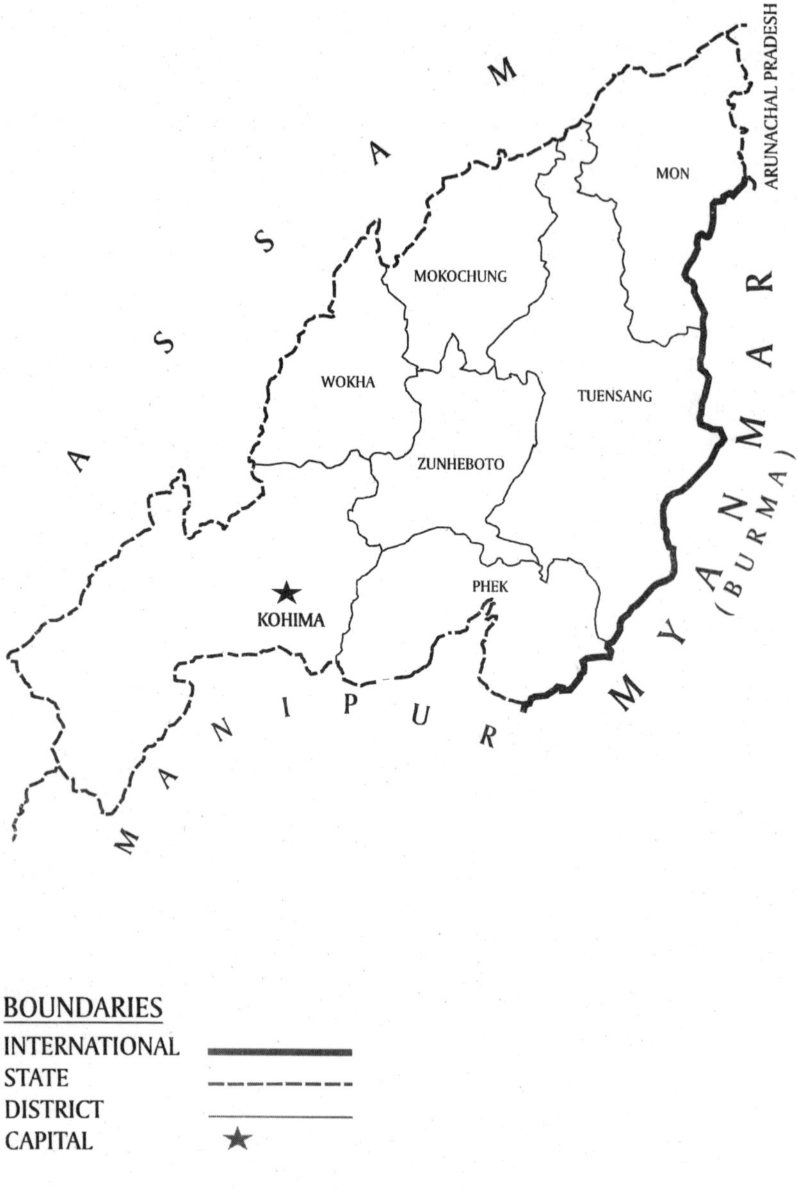

century CE, is shrouded in uncertainty.[70] Some Naga tribes are believed to have migrated from the south through Myanmar and Manipur on their way to Naga hills, and a sizeable number of Kabui, Tangkhul, Mao and Maram tribesmen settled down in Tamenglong, Ukhrul and Senapati districts of Manipur since the twelfth century. Some Nagas also settled down in Tirap area of Arunachal Pradesh and North Cachar and Karbi Anglong districts of Assam. Between thirteenth and nineteenth centuries, there were a number of conflicts among Nagas and other tribes in the Brahmaputra Valley. At the same time there were some positive respites marked by military and matrimonial alliances among Nagas, Ahoms and Manipuris. The dominant aspect, however, seems to be the Nagas' subjugation and confinement to Naga hills by the Ahoms, whenever the former raided the plains for plunder. Following the British occupation of Assam after 1826 treaty of Yandabo, the Naga hills came under increasing British control.

BRITISH PERIOD

The various Naga tribes traditionally lived in separate and in some cases, fortified village settlements and spoke their own dialects. Inter-tribal wars leading to capturing of territories and head-hunting were prevalent well into the last quarter of the nineteenth century. After the Ahoms' decline whenever the Nagas raided plains villages, the British had to assume responsibility of protecting the victims against looting, kidnapping and enslavement of persons by the Nagas. The British found that their intermittent punitive expeditions were not adequate to control Naga raids. The British, therefore, strengthened their administrative control over Naga hills area by constituting it as a separate district in 1866, and setting-up district headquarters at Kohima and sub-divisional headquarters at Wokha and Mokokchung by 1879. Naga Hills district was annexed to Assam in 1881, and placed under the control of a British Deputy Commissioner. While the British put a ban on tribal raids and head-hunting, they refrained from interferring in the tribes' customary ways of life within their respective boundaries. It is important to note that initially, the various tribes did not have any awareness of a common identity, and the name "Naga" was given to them by others.

70. According to one account, different Naga tribes came to Naga hills from Manchuria, Indonesia and Phillipines at different times and by different routes through Myanmar and Manipur (Sen, 1987, p. 21).

The American Baptist Church began its work in the Naga hills in the last quarter of the nineteenth century, no doubt with the blessings of British administration. Besides converting the Nagas to Christianity, the missionaries started schools, prepared scripts for Naga languages, opened hospitals, and generally helped to break the Nagas' isolation.

In 1918, under British patronage, the Naga Club was established to bring together government employees and others educated in Christian missionary institutions. This was about the first opportunity for persons belonging to different tribes to come together. When the Simon Commission visited Kohima in 1929, in the course of proposing Constitutional reforms for India, a delegation of Nagas submitted a memorandum to the Commission. It expressed its apprehension about alien laws interferring with their customs and traditions in case of integration of Naga hills with India. The Naga delegation also expressed its misgivings about the possible outcome of the proposed scheme of provincial autonomy, in view of their likely under-representation in Assam legislature because of the small size of Naga community and their educational backwardness. Furthermore, the Nagas were quite unsure whether they would be able to preserve their newly acquired Christian faith and preferred to be excluded from the scheme. They would rather be left alone, if the British were to leave.[71]

There is little doubt that the British had purposely stoked the Nagas' apprehensions in order to drive a wedge between them and leaders of the Indian national movement. As noted in Chapter 1, following the Government of India Acts of 1919 and 1935, as well as other legislative and administrative measures preceding these Acts, Naga Hills were placed in the category of "Excluded Areas," and governed by Inner Line regulation, which continued their isolation from other areas of the country. The 1946 British proposal to create a "Crown Colony" comprising all hill areas of N-E region and adjoining areas of Myanmar, under British protection, and independent from India, was thus consistent with their policy.

At the initiative of Charles Pawsey, the Deputy Commissioner of Naga Hills district, the Naga Club was replaced in 1945 by Naga Hills District Council, and further changed into Naga National Council (NNC) in 1946.

71. The Naga Club memorandum submitted to the Simon Commission included the following sentence, "You (British) are the only people who ever conquered us and when you go, we should be as we were" (Das, 1982, p. 42).

This development marked the creation of a joint political forum for various tribes and also an important beginning in evolving a composite Naga identity. The spread of Christianity particularly after the 1940s and modern education accelerated this process. During Second World War the Japanese occupation of Kohima, the district headquarters, caused great hardships for the Nagas. The epidemics which ravaged Naga Hills, and the perceived lack of concern by Assamese leaders lowered their morale. It is not surprising, therefore, that on the eve of Indian Independence, the danger of their small community and the emerging ethnic identity getting lost in the vast multitudes of India made the Nagas very anxious about their future.

The NNC was not established as a separatist organization. In fact, in 1946 it had opposed a Muslim League proposal to join Assam to East Bengal and had demanded the retention of Assam as a separate State within India. After British declaration in February 1947 to grant independence to India, a delegation of NNC had presented a memorandum to Lord Mountbatten, the Governor General of India and to Indian leaders to grant the Nagas greater autonomy within Assam for a trial period of ten years, at the end of which the arrangement was to be reviewed (Dube, 1982). By June 1947, negotiations between NNC representatives and Sir Akbar Hydari, the Governor of Assam, on a nine-point memorandum were nearing an agreement when differences cropped up between two sections of NNC regarding the implications of the trial period of ten years. Did the NNC have the freedom to decide extension of the agreement, or enter into a new agreement, or secede from the Indian Union? Angami Zapu Phizo, who led the more radical section of NNC, took a drastic decision and unilaterally declared Naga independence on 14 August 1947, a day prior to Indian Independence.

POST-INDEPENDENCE PERIOD

Phizo was arrested in 1947 and released in 1949. Phizo, who led the militant section of NNC, soon began to mobilize Naga youth and all types of disgruntled people who had lost their traditional privileges, ex-convicts, etc. and collected arms and ammunition including those left by the armies during Second World War. He held a so-called "referendum" on the issue of Nagaland's separation from the Indian Union, and claimed 99 per cent opinion in favour of Nagas' independence. In 1954, Phizo announced formation of People's Sovereign Republic of Free Nagaland. A violent phase began with Phizo and his followers going underground, terrorizing people and forcing collections from them. In the anarchy which followed, many people suspected to be pro-government, suffered extreme brutality at the hands of Phizo's lieutenants.[72] The Naga Peace Organizing Committee formed in 1956 at the initiative of Church leaders and others tried to bring about unity between the two factions of NNC in order to achieve a settlement with the Government of India. Phizo agreed to cease militancy for a while to buy time, and organized Naga Youth Movement and Naga Women's Organization.

The First Naga People's Convention held in 1957, demanded amalgamation of Tuensang area, referred at that time as "Naga Tribal Area" (previously clubbed with NEFA) with Nagaland, and this was accepted by the Government of India. One of the other demands, included in the nine-point 1947 NNC memorandum was to join to Nagaland forest areas in Sibsagar and Nagaon districts of Assam. This continues to remain as a contentious issue between Assam and Nagaland, among some other disputes regarding the dividing line.

Several rounds of negotiations between Government of India and Naga representatives were held until the latter reached an agreement with the then Prime Minister Jawaharlal Nehru in 1960. This was followed by the passing of a Constitutional Amendment (Thirteenth) Act of 1962, which provided a special status for Nagaland by stipulating safeguards for its religious and social practices and customary laws.[73] In 1963, Nagaland became the sixteenth State of the Indian Union. Meanwhile, despite brief lulls, militancy continued to plague Nagaland, and the Government had to deploy the army to protect people from the depredations of the insurgent groups. Phizo went into exile and the dissident group previously led by Phizo split into two factions : pro-Phizo Naga Federal Government and the Revolutionary Government of Nagaland. While the former wanted to fight for a sovereign Nagaland,

72. In 1955, Kaveho, a ruthless Phizo associate is reported to have punished residents of a supposedly non-co-operative Chakhesang village 14 miles away from Phek, by killing 48 innocent men and rounding up and distributing all women and children as slaves and concubines among his community (Singh, 1987).

73. The Thirteenth Constitutional Amendment provided that no act of Parliament in respect of the religious and social practices of the Nagas, their customary law and procedure would be applicable to the State of Nagaland unless the State assembly approves it by a resolution passed by a majority.

the latter was more interested in finding a peaceful solution through negotiations.

A peace mission under the leadership of the Late Jayprakash Narayan, and including Rev. Michael Scott from UK and B.P. Chaliha, the then Assam Chief Minister, tried to bring peace in 1964. It could not achieve reconciliation between the two opposing factions and was dissolved in 1967. The army, which had agreed to a ceasefire in 1964 had to be deployed again when normal life in Nagaland was completely disrupted due to extortions and murders by the militants. Meanwhile, the peace initiatives were revived again with the support of church leaders and others. Finally, the Shillong Accord was signed in 1975, with the Revolutionary Government faction agreeing to a group surrender. Phizo later repudiated the accord, however, and went into exile in UK. Some of his followers gave up underground hostilities due to disenchantment with the objectives of their struggle, and also because of weakening popular support.

Five years after the 1975 Shillong Accord, Issac, Muivah and Khaplang, former Phizo collaborators who were disillusioned with Phizo's policies, established National Socialist Council of Nagaland (NSCN) to resume the struggle for a sovereign Nagaland. In 1988, NSCN split into two factions, NSCN (I-M), led by Issac Swu and T.H. Muivah (belonging to Sema and Tangkhul tribes, respectively), and NSCN (K), led by Khaplang, a Burmese Konyak Naga. These groups have bases in Nepal, Bhutan, Bangladesh, Myanmar, etc. and receive arms and funds from some foreign powers. They continue to cherish their old dream of uniting all 34 Naga tribes settled in Nagaland, Manipur, Assam, Arunachal Pradesh and Myanmar into an integrated Sovereign Greater Nagaland. The rival NSCN factions continue their raids not only in Nagaland, but also in Manipur where they are trying to flush out the Kukis from areas crucial for control over the clandestine narcotics trade across the border with Myanmar.

The penchant for a consolidated Nagaland inevitably creates flutters among the States whose territories are involved. For instance, Manipur government has vehemently rejected the idea of separating its Naga-inhabited districts. An additional source of anxiety for Assam are the skirmishes over disputed borders between Assam and Nagaland. In 1979, Naga civilians backed by armed police raided Assamese villages and inflicted considerable violence. In 1985, the conflict at Merapani was more organized and police forces on either side fought a pitched battle. The separation of Naga Hills from Assam into an independent State, thus, has not ended the tensions between these two "Sisters."

Present Situation

MAJOR GEOGRAPHICAL AND DEMOGRAPHIC FEATURES

Nagaland's total area of 16,579 sq km spreads over a series of north-south ranges of Naga hills flanked to the east by Patkoi hills which form the watershed between India and Myanmar. There is considerable variation in the elevation of the ridges and the direction of slopes which result in changes in climate and rainfall. Towards the eastern side Saramati peak rises to 3826 m along with a few other peaks with around 3000 m and to the west in Kohima hills the highest peak has an elevation of 2995 m. Nagaland is bounded on the east by Myanmar, on the south by Manipur, on the west and north by Assam, and shares a small boundary on the north-east with Arunachal Pradesh. Even after Indian Independence, some areas beyond Dikhu and Tizu rivers adjoining thick forests towards Patkoi hills, which were referred as "unadministered" areas by the British, have remained fairly isolated from contacts with the rest of India. Head-hunting cases were reported from some interior Konyak villages even until 1979 (Sen, 1987). Nagaland is divided into following districts: Kohima, Dimapur, Mokokchung, Mon, Phek, Tuensang, Wokha and Zunheboto.

Nagaland population according to 1991 Census was 12.09 lakh, the percentage of STs being 87.70, and of urban population 17.21. Of the 34 Naga tribes scattered over the N-E region, principal tribes of Nagaland proper are Angami, Ao, Chakhesang, Konyak, Kabui, Khiamnungan, Lotha, Mao, Phom, Rengma, Sema, Tangkhul, Yimchunger, Zeliangrong. Some smaller tribes have merged together to form a larger composite group. For instance, Chakhuma, Khezama and Sangtam groups joined together in 1948 to form the Chakhesangs who inhabit Phek district. While most tribes are clustered in specific districts, some tribes have large concentrations in other States, e.g. Tangkhuls in Manipur. The Semas dominate Zunheboto district, while Mokokchung has a predominance of Aos. The Konyaks in Mon district maintain kinship ties with the Konyaks in the adjoining Myanmar. On the other hand, a large number of Kukis have lived in Nagaland for a long time and are listed as a major group in this State. There are wide variations in the social and technological development of various Naga tribes. The Angamis, the largest tribe, are most advanced and have adopted terraced cultivation, whereas the Konyaks still continue rather primitive *jhum* cultivation, after just leaving the food-gathering and hunting stage. The British are known to have introduced poppy cultivation in Mon valley to tame the Konyaks through addiction to opium. The social and cultural variations are reflected in customs related to marriage and the position of women in the family, as will be noted in Chapter 4.

The Naga tribes traditionally followed various kinds of indigenous faiths, some of which included propitiation of spirits and sacrifices for their appeasement. Christian missionaries started their activities here in the last quarter of nineteenth century, and only a small number, less than 4 per cent of Nagas were Christians by the end of nineteenth century. Conversions to Christianity gathered momentum during the 1940s, and besides American Baptists, other sects include Pentacostal Church, Assembly of God, Roman Catholic Church, etc. As of 1991 Census, the religious distribution of Nagaland population was: Christians 84.47 per cent, Hindus 10.12 per cent, Muslims 1.71 per cent and other religions and persuasions less than 1 per cent. The 2001 Census placed Nagaland's population at 1.98 million as per Provisional Population Totals.

ECONOMIC AND SOCIAL CONTEXT

One of the crucial steps to counter over five decades of insurgency and unrest in Nagaland is to promote speedy economic development, generate adequate employment opportunities and improve the quality of life of its people. Presently, about three-fourth of the State's workforce is engaged in agriculture, mostly of the jhuming type. The Angamis and Chakhesangs are exceptions, and have been practising terraced cultivation for a long time. In the N-E region Nagaland had the highest number of families, 1,16,046, practising *zhum* cultivation, according to Ministry of Agriculture Task Force report in 1983. In 1990-91 irrigation facilities were available for only 31.05 per cent of net sown area. The yield of rice per hectare in 1993-94 was 1343 kg as compared with the all-India average of 1879 kg (NEC, 1995). Annual food grain production in 1990-91 was 193.8 thousand tonnes, and remained at 211.9 thousand tonnes in 1996-97, indicating very modest growth (Chatterjee, 1999). As a result, Nagaland faces serious food deficits requiring imports from other States at high cost annually.

Nagaland is endowed with mineral resources in limestone, coal, oil, sulphate and magnelite. There is considerable potential for horticulture and plantation crops. But both of these resources remain undeveloped and only partially utilized. As per NEC (1995) sources, in 1994 the State had 16 large and medium-sized industrial units, which included a paper mill, sugar factory, a distillery and some units processing forest products. In 1992 there were 509 small-scale units in handloom weaving, sericulture, piggery, poultry, etc. which require technical, financial and marketing support to utilize their full employment potential.

Nagaland has made some progress in infrastructural services. By 1992, out of 1112 villages in the State 1099 were electrified (NEC, 1992), and presently it has the distinction of being the first State in the N-E region to achieve 100 per cent rural electrification. When Nagaland attained Statehood in 1963, it had only 56 km of surfaced road. By 1997, the length of surfaced road was 7800 km which compares very favourably with other N-E States (*Times of India*, 20 August 1997). In the area of literacy, Nagaland has made considerable progress as is evident in the percentages of literacy. From 1981 when it was 50.1, the percentage rose to 60.4 in 1991, and according to a 1997 report (*Times of India*, 20 August 1997) it had gone up to 65 per cent. Out of 649 villages which had no access to safe drinking water in 1980, 541 villages were provided with this facility by 1987 (NEC, 1990). The NSDP at current prices for 1993-94, according to *Indian Economic Survey* (*1996-97*) was Rs.880 crore, and per capita NSDP Rs.6638. The provisional estimate for 1996-97 for the State was Rs.1727 crore and per capita NSDP Rs.11,174 (State Directorate of Economics and Statistics and Central Statistical Organization).

In the context of traditions of community ownership of a high proportion of lands, emphasis on shared responsibility and an essentially subsistence type economy, there were no marked inequalities in incomes in the past. With the growth of markets and substantial infusion of funds by Central and State Governments and inflow of a variety of goods from other States, a class of rich traders, businessmen, contractors and politicians has emerged in Naga society, and not all of them are "outsiders." In 1993-94, according to estimates by an Expert Group appointed by the Government of India, 37.92 per cent of Nagaland population, or 5.05 lakh persons were living below the poverty line. The number of rural poor was 4.85 lakh and that of urban poor 0.20 lakh.[74] A type of absentee landlordship has been noted among some well-to-do farmers who raise cash crops and manage them through middlemen or contractors. For instance, some well-off Angami farmers have captured sizeable lands in villages at some distance and lease them to poor tribal peasants or to migrant landless labourers from other States, like Bengal and Bihar, who are given a paltry share of the produce in lieu of their labour. There are some other instances of extreme exploitation which survive to this day due to a combination of factors: geographical isolation, poverty and ignorance. In a Zunheboto village some fifty Sema tribesmen continue to live in slavery which they inherited from their parents and grandparents. They cultivate land which is owned and allocated by a chieftain and are unable to buy their freedom.[75]

The State Government has initiated some projects to promote settled cultivation in areas where jhuming is practised. Most of these efforts have failed in the absence of a sustained and comprehensive approach, including selection and rotation of crops to suit different locations, financial assistance for terracing and irrigation and competent technical support through agricultural extension services (Hussain, 1987). A welcome development which capitalizes on the community ethos in Nagaland is the establishment of Village Development Boards through Nagaland Village and Area Council Act of 1978 (Roy Burman, B.K. 1984). These Boards have introduced some significant elements in the highly male-dominated administration of Nagaland. The Village Development Boards must have at least one woman member, and 25 per cent of the allotment of funds must be set aside exclusively for the benefit of women. Naga women in some villages have displayed excellent initiative in promoting schemes, like community drinking water wells, granaries and forest paths which are vital for the convenience of families. The Boards have given rise to a new leadership and have created a mechanism for devolving government funds directly to Village Development Boards. This helps to avoid seepages and motivates local communities to create productive community assets according to their own priorities (Roy Burman, J.J. 1988).

---

74. See note 11 for details of methodology.

75. Each of these Sema Nagas is obligated to provide to the chieftain of Sukhalu village 12 days of labour annually by 12 family members, part of the agricultural produce, and choicest part of the meat of hunted animals (Chinai, *Times of India*, 12 September 1999).

There is an urgent need at a broader level, to develop ssuitably adapted development strategies, keeping in mind the particular systems of community ownership of land as well as areas where the traditional chiefs still wield considerable power. The experience of Village Development Boards has indicated some hopeful pointers. Another imperative need is to develop local technical and managerial competence to boost industrial development. These tasks, however, require peace and stability. In contrast, the whole of the 1990s decade has been full of violent raids by insurgent groups and intense in-fighting among rival militant groups which are identified with particular tribes to which their respective leaders belong. Furthermore, there are alignments among Naga militant groups for acquiring funds, arms and training, and insurgent groups from other States, e.g. ULFA (United Liberation Front of Assam), UNLF (United National Liberation Front of Manipur), and indeed hostile elements outside India's borders. This aspect has seriously complicated the task of controlling insurgency. So far it has never been possible for the Central or State Government to get even the two factions of NSCN — led by Issak-Muivah and Khaplang, to join together in negotiations, let alone other insurgent groups.

The NSCN (I-M) and NSCN (K) maintain underground armies organized like regular army units. The NSCN (I-M) is reported to collect taxes for their maintenance from households, shopkeepers, businessmen, government contractors and indeed all sections including government departments, besides tolls from vehicles plying on highways (Banerjee, *Times of India*, 19 July 1997). If there is resistance from any section to these extortions, the militants resort to murders and arson. The extortionists view such collections as perfectly legitimate "taxes" levied by the "Government of the Peoples' Republic of Nagaland." The civilian population is caught in the crossfire of militants and security forces deployed by the Government to protect them. The invocation of Armed Forces Special Powers Act gives wide powers to security personnel to kill even on suspicion of an imminent law and order problem, and arrest persons for interrogation. There have been cases where excesses cannot be ruled out. On the other hand, the police, paramilitary forces and army personnel too have been innocent victims of the wrath of militants as well as hostility of the civilians.

There is no doubt that people of Nagaland are completely exhausted as a result of the long turmoil, particularly since the intermittent spells of ceasefire have been short-lived, because it has not been possible so far to achieve unanimity among various insurgent groups. Moreover, as the leaders of underground groups like NSCN operate from bases in Myanmar, Thailand, Nepal, Bhutan, Pakistan, etc. they suffer considerable loss of credibility among Naga public. Meanwhile, rampant corruption at all levels of bureaucracy and politics has sapped the State's vitality. The serious underdevelopment of Nagaland is often blamed entirely on the Central Government's neglect. The lack of employment opportunities in the State has added to the frustration of the youth, and has made them more vulnerable to alcoholism and drug addiction, as well as to the enticements of underground outfits. There are some valiant attempts to revive the traditional community ethos by re-orienting the typical Naga institutions such as the "Khel" (sub-section of village, usually based on clan and lineage) and "Morung" (youth dormitory) in new incarnations (Banerjee, 1997).

Interestingly, the old dream of bringing together all the 34 Naga tribes scattered in Nagaland, parts of Manipur, Assam, Arunachal Pradesh and northern Myanmar into a sovereign "Greater Nagaland" is still alive at least among some Naga Sections.[76] The common people, however, are yearning for peace. Several organizations, e.g. the Naga "Ho-Ho"s (tribal parliament), Naga Students Federation, church leaders, Naga Mothers' Association, Naga Peoples' Movement for Human Rights, and Naga intellectuals have been making fervent appeals for peace (Manecksha, 1997). One of the prerequisites for this is honest introspection, unanimity and consensus among various insurgent outfits and other sections before an acceptable solution can be worked out through negotiations with the Central Government. For that to happen the Nagas will have to rise above their narrow loyalties to their tribes and evolve an overarching Naga identity.

While prospects of a lasting solution to the imbroglio are being explored, the people of Nagaland must make a sincere effort to achieve a modicum of unity among its splintered society. Above all, they must realize that economic and social development cannot be conferred on

76. "Greater Nagaland" concept upheld by the Nagas implies joining to present Nagaland the following areas: Naga-inhabited Khonsa and Changlang areas of Arunachal Pradesh, parts of North Cachar Hills and Karbi Anglong districts of Assam, the hill districts of Manipur, i.e. Senapati, Tamenglong, Ukhrul, Churachandpur and Chandel, some areas of Myanmar.

them by a benevolent Central Government. It has to be achieved by their own efforts, facilitated no doubt by a flexible and imaginative support from the Central Government. The key to such transformation lies with the Naga peoples' own initiative and determination.

TRIPURA

Historical Perspective

EARLIER HISTORY

Tripura, the smallest State in the N-E region, has a long and eventful history, though somewhat hazy as it goes back to the fifth century CE. Tripura once formed a part of larger kingdoms covering East Bengal, parts of Cachar and Karimganj, known variously as Samatata, Vanga, Harikela, etc. and Tripura was then referred to as the district of "Tippera" or the highlands of Bengal. Tripura is mentioned in ancient travelogues and inscriptions relating to several dynasties which ruled over these kingdoms.[77] When Bengal suffered the onslaught of successive Muslim invasions from the thirteenth century onwards, Tripura too faced many vicissitudes, although its tribal communities remained relatively unaffected, probably because of their isolated habitats in interior hills.

The next phase in Tripura's history began when Chengthung Fa, the Chief of Tripuri tribe defended his territory against Muslim rulers of Bengal and after conquering other tribes inhabiting Tippera Hills, established an independent Tripura kingdom around the thirteenth or fourteenth century.[78] He adopted the Hindu title of Maha Manikya, according to one account, and ruled over a kingdom which extended up to Chittagong in the south and Sylhet in the north. According to one version, his son Dharma Manikya (1431-62) was a devout Hindu who patronized brahmins, built

---

77. Huien Tsang, the Chinese traveller, who visited the Gupta king of Samatata in the seventh century CE referred to this kingdom which included central Bengal and the district of Tippera. Burmese chronicles and inscriptions of the eleventh century mention a prince of Pattikara in the district of Tippera, along with Sweinthi, a Burmese princess (Gan Chaudhuri, 1980).

78. There is some doubt among scholars regarding the dates of a few events mentioned in *Rajmala* and Tripura *Vamshavali* — the old texts that document royal chronicles prior to fifteenth century. One version traces introduction of Hindu culture into Tripura to king Ratna Manikya who encouraged 10,000 Bengali settlers to come into Tripura with the objective of introducing plough cultivation and organizing the administrative system of Tripura.

TRIPURA

★AGARTALA

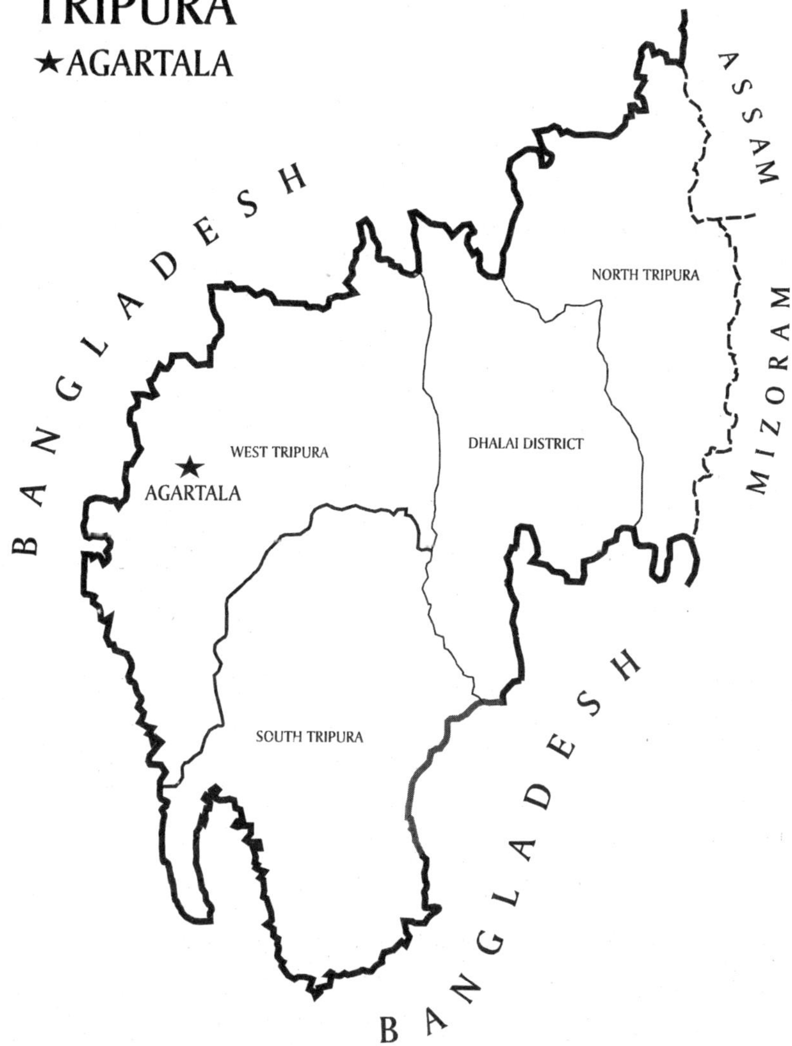

BOUNDARIES

INTERNATIONAL

STATE

DISTRICT

CAPITAL ★

temples, and initiated a firm Hindu tradition in Tripura.[79] During the successive regimes covering the rule of over 70 kings there were undoubtedly some reverses when the Muslims conquered parts of Tripura kingdom. On the other hand, some brave Tripura kings, viz. Dhanya Manikya (1490–1515) and Vijaya Manikya (1535-63) inflicted crushing defeats on the Muslim satraps of Bengal and even on their allies, the Mughs of Chittagong. Tripura kingdom at one time included Chittagong, Noakhali, Comilla and Sylhet (presently in Bangladesh), and extended up to Manipur in the east. Tripura rulers came into contact with other kingdoms in the Brahmaputra Valley and were defeated by the Koch king in the sixteenth century. They forged matrimonial and political alliances with the Ahoms and Manipuris, and had a specially close relationship with the Cachar kingdom due to their common Bodo lineage.

Tripura's close interaction with Bengal and other kingdoms in the Brahmaputra Valley resulted in the former imbibing various religious influences, e.g. Shaivism, Vaishnavism, Shaktism and Tantricism.[80] Since Tripura was regarded as one of the *pithas* (centres), it became an important place of Shiva-Parvati worship.[81] Tripura's religious customs also display a synthesis of its original tribal as well as Hindu traditions. For instance, the worship of "Chaturdash Devata" (fourteen deities) is regarded as an example of syncretic practice of tribal animism and Hindu doctrine of multiple incarnations of God.[82] Another important aspect of Tripura's

---

79. Dharma Manikya in the fifteenth century encouraged the adoption of Hinduism in Tripura, and also Bengali as the official language. He patronized the excavation of Dharmasagar tank at Comilla (presently in Bangladesh) and construction of artistic temples.

80. The "Tantric" sect upholds belief in a supreme reality that has male (Shiva) and female (Shakti) aspects. On a popular level, it revolves around the worship of Goddess Kali, or some other incarnations like Chandi, usually rather fierce and awesome. Tantric practices are associated with acquisition of occult powers, symbolic rituals, and animal and human sacrifices.

81. According to a Hindu legend, Parvati when humiliated by her father Daksha for marrying the strange and eccentric Shiva, jumped into the sacrificial fire. This sent Shiva into a cosmic rage that threatened annihilation of the universe, causing Vishnu, the God of Protection, to follow Shiva and cut to pieces the dead body of Parvati being carried by Shiva. Tripura, being one of the places where the pieces fell, acquired the status of a major centre of Shiva-Parvati worship.

82. The images of "Chaturdash Devata" (fourteen deities) in Tripura temples are believed to be transformations of the previous tribal spirits of mountains, rivers, crops, etc. into Hindu gods and goddesses, e.g. Shiva, Ganga, Lakshmi, etc. The Reangs, for instance, call themselves Hindus of the Shakta cult, worship goddess Kali while retaining some of their original animistic rituals.

history relates to its adoption of Hindu social structure in some respects. The Tripura kings appropriated for themselves the kshatriya caste, and conferred it on other tribal communities who were close to them through lineage or through services rendered, like the Jamatias and Noatias. The Reangs, who were Palki-bearers (palanquin-bearers) of the kings, and serfs of the Mizos, had an inferior social status *vis-à-vis* the Tripuris.

By the first quarter of the seventeenth century, Tripura kingdom began to decline due to its inadequate fighting power as well as internal rivalries and intrigues within the ruling family. By 1625, both the Mughals as well as the Mughs defeated Tripura forces and plundered the kingdom. The next Mughal invasion in 1658 virtually brought Tripura under Muslim rule. Although there were brief interludes when Tripura kings tried to resurrect their independence, they were defeated by the Mughals in 1727. The Nawab of Bengal, Shajauddin, gave Dharma Manikya II, Tripura king, "zamindari" rights over the district of Roshanabad on a yearly rent in the same year. (Gen. Choudhary, 1980). By 1743, most of the plains areas were annexed to the Mughal territory, and Vijay Manikya II had to surrender all revenues to the Mughal Nawab, while retaining limited control over the hill areas, in return for a small monthly allowance (Saigal, 1978).

Tripura was subjected to another upheaval when the East India Company defeated the Mughal Nawab Siraj-ud-Daula at the Battle of Plassey and concluded a treaty with the latter in 1759. The British lost no time in attacking Tripura and by 1765 the State came under British control. By this time Tripura was reduced to less than 10,000 sq km and a population of less than 50,000.

BRITISH PERIOD

Tripura continued as a princely State under British hegemony, ruled by a succession of kings who paid regular tributes to the British. During this period Tripura faced many hardships due to epidemics, famines, Kuki raids and internecine rivalries which led to the surrender of 850 miles of territory to the British and appointment of their Political Agent in 1871.

A chronic problem caused by seriously depleted State revenues drove Tripura kings to adopt a policy of encouraging cultivators from Noakhali and Comilla areas (previously within their domain) and Chittagong Tracts to reclaim forest lands in the hills and plains of Tripura. The immigrants who had superior skills in settled cultivation (with which native tribal jhumias were unfamiliar), were given liberal tenures and titles to reclaim lands in the hope of increasing yields and opening export markets for cotton and oilseeds. Similarly, tea planters from neighbouring States were invited to develop tea plantations as plenty of land was available. In 1939 Tripura Maharaja provided shelter to a large number of East Bengal refugees who left their homes in the wake of communal disturbances. This group proved to be the vanguard of much larger waves of Bengali refugees before and after Partition of India in 1947. The influx of immigrants into Tripura rapidly outnumbered tribal population, reducing the latter to a minority in their own State.

The social and economic consequences of the entry of such large numbers of immigrants into Tripura were extremely damaging for the native tribal groups, who could not easily make necessary adaptations to settled cultivation, nor did they possess adequate business acumen. As pressure on land increased, many tribal peasants who were very poor and indebted, either sold their lands for a pittance, receded into interior areas or became wage labourers. Within a short period, non-tribal Bengali cultivators occupied most vacant lands and continued to acquire tribal lands often through fraudulent deals. They also established control over trade, markets and credit, thus making tribal communities extremely vulnerable to exploitation. The point to be noted here is that tribal jhumias were exploited not just by non-tribal Bengali settlers, but also some better off tribal jhumias who owned more lands and could employ poorer jhumias on low wages as agricultural labourers, and who could also influence trading and markets (Das Gupta,1986). By 1930 some tribal peasants were ready to adopt settled cultivation, and at least one Tripura king, Bir Bikram Manikya (1923-47), had tried to encourage his tribal subjects to learn improved agriculture but land had already become scarce by that time. Moreover, the Tripura ruler's dependence on Bengali settlers was not just for augmenting agricultural yields and thereby State revenues, but also for administrative manpower. Within a short period, from among the immigrant settlers there emerged a class of landlords, traders and moneylenders who wielded considerable power, not to mention the Bengali dominance in the State administration. Numerically, the tribal population of Tripura even by 1931 was already on the verge of being outnumbered in their own State (forming 50.26 per cent of the total). It is not surprising, therefore, that tribal sections began to develop a strong hostility towards non-tribal "outsiders," and held Tripura rulers responsible for their plight.

By the latter half of the nineteenth century, the initially close relationship between the tribal communities and Tripura kings (who belonged to Tripuri tribe) showed signs of strain. In an effort to replenish State revenues, when Tripura rulers began to collect taxes from tribal groups, the Kukis and other disgruntled sections protested through a series of revolts in 1850 and again in 1860-61, when the Kukis plundered some villages in British-held territory. In 1863, Parikshit Jamatia led another tribal uprising to oppose the discriminatory system of taxation, but this was suppressed with the help of Kukis. In yet another effort to raise State funds, Tripura kings adopted the policy of establishing themselves as ultimate owners of all lands and forests through measures like the 1887 Reserved Forests Order. Such measures restricted tribal groups from using lands for jhuming and forests for their various sustenance needs, which meant a denial of their traditional community rights. Ironically, such measures did not prevent unscrupulous non-tribal contractors from plundering the forests.

In an obvious effort to appease tribal backlash, Tripura Maharaja issued orders in 1930 and 1943 declaring a huge area as a tribal reserve, intended for the exclusive use of five native tribal communities, viz. Tripuri, Jamatia, Noatia, Halam and Reang. Despite this official decree, non-tribal encroachments on tribal lands continued, thanks to inefficient implementation and collusion between unscrupulous individuals and corrupt State officials. In 1942-43, the Reangs rose in an armed rebellion under the leadership of Ratanmani, a Noatia, who declared himself as a king in a southern sub-division. Like other previous revolts, this provoked strong British disapproval and pressure on the Maharaja to put down the uprising. The mood among the tribal sections around 1940s was thus marked by strong resentment towards the affluent and exploitative sections among non-tribals, as also towards Tripura royalty who demanded free services from their subjects and seemed totally indifferent to the poverty and deprivation of their tribal subjects.

Around the 1930s, the emergence of the freedom movement under Gandhiji's leadership, growth of the Indian National Congress, as well as other struggles against capitalist and feudal forces in several parts of India created strong repercussions in Tripura. The State Congress organized a movement to demand responsible government in 1936 and tried to mobilize popular resentment against the feudal and autocratic style of Tripura's royalty. Tribal sections, which had felt completely disillusioned with their rulers and other oppressive sections, were trying to find an effective way of expressing their anger, and were drawn towards the Communist Party banner. The more radical elements among them formed Sengkrak, an extremist group of hill tribals in 1943, which soon joined hands with Mizo National Front. Developments in Manipur, particularly the valiant role of Manipuri women in the second "Nupilan" (women's movement) in rousing public opinion against British colonial regime as well as the seemingly self-seeking Manipuri royalty, inevitably found their reverberations in Tripura. The mounting popular pressure thus forced Tripura Maharaja to agree to the State's merger with the Indian Union after India's Independence.

POST-INDEPENDENCE PERIOD

Tripura's merger agreement with the Indian Union was signed in 1949 and in 1950 it became a part "C" State with a Commissioner appointed by the Central Government to be responsible for its administration. After its people rejected a States Reorganization Commission's recommendation to incorporate Tripura into Assam, it became a Centrally Administered Territory in 1954. Towards the end of 1960, the demand for full Statehood gathered momentum in the context of similar demands in Manipur and Meghalaya. In response, the Central Government, under provisions of the Union Territories Act of 1963, initiated the process of replacing the previous Territorial Council by an elected legislature and a popular ministry. This step undoubtedly strengthened the political clout of tribal sections in the State's population. After enactment of the North-Eastern Areas (Reorganization) Act in 1971, Tripura became a full-fledged State on 21 January 1972.

One of the major issues for Tripura's tribal population in the post-Independence period has been its desire to assert its separate identity in the context of increasing dominance of non-tribals in the State's economic, demographic and political spheres. The Tripura Government launched several programmes to improve the economic condition of its tribal sections. Unfortunately, most of these efforts failed to achieve the desired objectives due to serious flaws in their design or strategy of implementation. A couple of examples should suffice: An attempt was made in 1951-52 to stop jhuming among tribal peasants, in view of its destructive ecological consequences, and to encourage them to adopt settled cultivation in allocated plots of land. Within a short period, however, most of the tribal participants left the project area, because they found it too stifling to remain within an earmarked enclosure, after being accustomed to the freedom of a nomadic lifestyle. Furthermore, the sum of Rs.500 each of them received in lieu of signing a bond to give up their traditional jhuming rights was far too inadequate to meet their financial needs, not to mention the technical support services which they lacked.

In 1960 the State Government passed the Tripura Land Revenue and Land Reforms Act for the purpose of protecting the land rights of tribal communities.[83] The apathy and incompetence of the implementation machinery, however, permitted vested interests to deprive tribal groups of extensive areas of communally owned tribal lands and transfer them to Bengali refugees who poured into Tripura after the 1964 Indo-Pak conflict. Much more shocking, however, was the finding that some unscrupulous immigrant settlers managed to regularize their fraudulent acquisition of tribal lands by subverting the official registration procedure, sometimes with the connivance of corrupt government officials.

Many of the social, economic and political problems which confront Tripura today are related to the demographic changes since late 1940s. Partition of the country and creation of East Pakistan in 1947 brought enormous problems for Tripura: disruption of communication links with the rest of India, and successive waves of Bengali refugees, first around 1947, then again following Indo-Pak conflict in 1964. The 1971 Bangladesh war brought more Bengali refugees into Tripura, and the competition for limited employment opportunities became more and more intense for tribal youths. The decade of the 1960s saw large scale alienation of tribal lands as noted before. In 1971, the tribal population constituted 28.94 per cent of the total State population, i.e. less than one-third. In the atmosphere of seething discontent and insecurity, tribal leaders formed Tripura Upjati Juba Samiti (TUJS) in 1967 and renewed their earlier demand for formation of an Autonomous District to cover

83. The 1960 Act provided that all natural resources, not owned by individuals, were to be government property. As a result of tribal people's ignorance and inability to provide adequate documentary proof of ownership, 35592 ha of tribal-owned lands were turned into "Khas land." Furthermore, a 1974 amendment to this Act legalized land transfers from tribal to non-tribal persons effected before 1969, thus aiding and abetting the perfidy, and permitting review of only post–1969 cases.

tribal area. Another off-shoot of the mood of ethnic assertion was the formation of Tripura Students Federation (TSF) and the Kak-Borak Sahitya Sabha, which demanded official recognition for Kak-Borak, a language spoken by a majority of Tripura's tribal people.[84] Major political parties, viz. the Congress and CPI(M),[85] now began to vie with each other in wooing tribal voters.

When the CPI(M) came to power in 1978 the government made determined efforts to reach tribal people in order to help them benefit from various national and State employment and poverty alleviation schemes. Special efforts were also made to restore tribal lands, fraudulently acquired by non-tribals, to their rightful owners, but these achieved very limited success due to a number of administrative hurdles.[86]

The government, however succeeded in meeting a long standing demand for creation of an Autonomous Tribal District, after protracted efforts. A Bill introduced in 1979 to constitute Tripura Tribal Areas Autonomous District Council was held up due to a writ petition. It was ultimately passed after a Constitutional Amendment in 1984, which enabled application of the Sixth Schedule to Tripura. An area of 7131 sq km was demarcated for this purpose, and provision made for an elected council with 21 tribal and seven non-tribal members, having powers over allotment, occupation and use of land, regulation of money-lending and trade by non-tribals, education, health, etc.[87] In 1994, when CPI(M) came to power, the government passed an amendment to the 1974 Tripura Land Revenue and Land Reforms Act to strengthen provisions for restoring tribal lands acquired by non-tribal persons to their original owners.

The growing organizations among tribal people and the pro-tribal measures of the State Government generated hostility and insecurity among Bengali settlers, who founded a militant organization — Amra

84. Kakborak has no script of its own and initially Bengali script was used. However, in later years Kakborak in Roman script became a symbol of ethnic assertion for some tribal sections. Recently, members of some radical groups have brought disruption of education by burning books and forcibly closing schools that use Bengali script (Banerjee, 1997).

85. The Communist Party split in 1964 into two parties: CPI (Communist Party of India) and CPI (M), Communist Party of India (Marxists).

86. Out of 15,982 petitions received, only 1439 cases involving 1291 acres were resolved satisfactorily (Mukherjee and Singh, 1982).

87. The boundaries of the Autonomous District area and powers of the Council have continued to be contentious issues for a long time.

Bangali — in 1969. Meanwhile, the more extremist factions among the tribal people formed new militant outfits, like the Tripura Tribal National Front (TTNF) and Tripura Sena, led by Hrangkhawl, a Baptist missionary educated in Shillong. The antagonism between tribal and non-tribal populations led to several conflicts, the most tragic being the carnage at Mandai in 1980. This episode left nearly 1500 persons dead, several villages torched and over three lakh persons — tribal and non-tribal — homeless. Since this outrage, sporadic outbursts of violence between existing and new militant groups have been a regular feature of life in Tripura. Meanwhile, basic development tasks essential to ensure a minimum acceptable level of living for large sections of Tripura's tribal and non-tribal population continue to take a back seat.

Present Situation

MAJOR GEOGRAPHICAL AND DEMOGRAPHIC FEATURES

Tripura's total area of 10,486 sq km, nearly two-thirds of which is hilly, includes six main hill ranges running north-south, increasing in height towards Jampui range in the east, the highest peak being Beltingsib at 939 m on Tripura–Mizoram highway. Tripura is an enclave surrounded by 840 km border with Bangladesh on three sides, with a small corridor on the east connecting it with Mizoram and Assam. By land route, one has to cover a circuitous stretch of nearly 500 km to reach Guwahati and 1500 km to reach Kolkata. Several rivers originating from its hills provide some communication, although a bit hazardous, by country boats. Tripura is divided into four districts: North, South, West and Dhalai. The hills cover most of North Tripura district, while the South and West districts include the plain areas, bounded by Atharamura range running north-south, and two out of six ranges (Deotamura and Baramura) to the left of Atharamura range.

Tripura's population according to 1991 Census, was 2,757,205, with an average population density of 263 per sq km, the second highest (next to Assam) in the N-E region. During 1951 and 1981, the population increased from 6.45 lakh to 20.53 lakh, primarily due to refugees from East Pakistan (later Bangladesh) who sought shelter in Tripura. Consequently, the population of STs has become a minority and forms 30.95 per cent of the total. The percentage of SCs is 16.36 and that of urban population 15.30. Tripura's non-tribal population includes, besides Bengali Hindu settlers and refugees, persons from other States who went to Tripura to seek employment opportunities in government departments, various professions, trades and businesses. Muslims constitute a small minority and include descendents of soldiers who went to Tripura with Muslim invasions and stayed on. This group also includes settlers from East Bengal who migrated from the "zamindaris" (landlordships) previously belonging to Tripura kings, lured by cultivable land. Another segment consists of Santhals, Oraons, Mundas and such other groups from Madhya Pradesh, Bihar, Orissa and Bengal, who migrated into Tripura to work as tea garden labourers. The Provisional Population Totals of 2001 Census place Tripura's population at 3.19 million.

Tripura's tribal population, which presently forms about one-third of the total population of the State, consists of about 19 tribes and a few sub-tribes, the major ones being Tripuri, Jamatia, Reang, Noatia and Halam.[88] Kukis, Lushais, Uchais, Chakmas[89] and Mughs[90] are later entrants. After Partition of India, a sizeable number of tribal people came into Tripura from erstwhile East Pakistan, particularly from Chittagong Hill Tracts. In addition, there is a sprinkling of Khasis, Garos, Hajongs, some of whom follow their indigenous religions. Reangs, who originally belonged to the Kuki family, are believed to have come originally from Shan State of Myanmar, and later came under Hindu influence due to their close contact with Tripuri kings. They worship the Goddess Kali while retaining some of their native animistic rituals. A few Reangs who have long been in servitude of the Mizos, have accepted Christianity. A majority of Lushais belong to New Zealand Baptist Church, while a small break-away group which resented the dominance of foreign missionaries, are affiliated to Independent Church. Since the 1960s, some other tribal

88. For instance, the Halams include a number of sub-tribes such as Morshem, Kaipeng, Hrangkhawl, Koloi, Kursum, Rupini, etc. Halams originally were southern Kukis, who adopted Vaishnavism due to their close relations with Tripura kings.

89. About 4000 Chakmas are believed to have left their homes in Chittagong Hill Tracts and come to Tripura around 1884 in search of fertile lands after being pushed out by Lushai raids. Their influx into Tripura further snowballed with their persecution first at the hands of East Pakistan army and later the adverse policies of Bangladesh Government, which wanted to settle Muslim peasants in the area that was previously Chakmas' homeland. Refer to R. Menon, "Chakma: Shattered Lives," *India Today*, 15 March 1987, for details.

90. Mughs originally lived in the Arakan region but were driven out from there by Burmese invaders in 1783-84 and came to Chittagong area, from where they came to Tripura. In English and Burmese accounts they are referred to as Marma refugees.

people have been converted to Christianity. The Chakmas and Mughs are Buddhists. As per the 1991 Census, the percentages of religious distribution of Tripura's population was: Hindus 89.35, Muslims 6.16, Christians 1.21, Buddhists 2.66, other religions and persuasions less than 1 per cent.

CURRENT ECONOMIC AND SOCIAL CONTEXT

Tripura's economy is primarily agricultural, with low productivity, and poor industrial development, resulting in high unemployment. In the absence of modern technology, the yields in most crops are insufficient. According to NEC (1995) sources, the State's total food grain production in 1990-91 was 5,16,000 tonnes which is seriously inadequate to meet the needs of its population. Common food items like rice, wheat, sugar, salt, potatoes, onions, as well as other essential commodities such as kerosene and cement have to be imported from other States. By 1990-91, out of a total 2,70,000 ha of area sown, only 41,000 ha, i.e. 15.18 per cent (which was the lowest percentage in the N-E region) were irrigated. By 1994, Tripura had only one industrial unit in the large and medium category (NEC, 1995), while the small-scale industrial units in 1992 numbered 3523 and included paper and jute mills, units producing tea, cane and bamboo products, rubber, handloom cloth, etc. Tripura's hilly terrain is suitable for horticulture, tea and rubber plantations. A small beginning has been made to boost production of mangoes, lichis, oranges, pineapples, guavas, besides bananas and jack-fruits which were grown for some time. There has been a significant increase in production of rubber, which rose from 147 tonnes in 1984-85 to 5029 tonnes by 1993-94. There is a slight increase in area brought under tea plantation from 5411.33 ha in 1986 to 6152.87 ha by 1993 (Directorate of Statistics, Govt. of Tripura, 1994, 1995). Furthermore, a promising beginning has been made in modernizing this industry.

An important reason for Tripura's underdevelopment is the inadequate coverage of basic amenities and infrastructural services. The per capita consumption of electricity in 1992-93 was 83.9 KWH, the lowest in the N-E region, as compared to the all-India figure of 330.6 KWH. By 1988, out of Tripura's 4727 inhabited villages, 2329, constituting 49.30 per cent, had been electrified according to NEC (1990) sources. By 1992, 3028 villages, i.e. 64.06 per cent villages were electrified. By 1991, 33.72 per cent rural and 52.10 per cent urban population had access to potable water. The problem is specially acute in hilly areas where women face severe hardships since many previous water sources are drying up due to rapid denudation of forests, besides causing scarcity of fuelwood. In the context of Tripura's hilly terrain, limited rail and road network and circuitous communication links to the rest of India, as referred to in Chapter 1, pose a formidable challenge for economic development.

As if Tripura's existing problems are not enough, it continues to suffer from infiltration of foreigners in view of its porous border with Bangladesh. Tripura Upjati Juba Samiti (TUJS) and Tripura National Volunteers (TNV) have frequently raised their voice to demand State Government action to identify and expel these infiltrators. Luckily, the longstanding problem of nearly 70,000 Chakma refugees living in Tripura might be nearing a solution following the 1997 accord between India, Bangladesh and Chakma leaders. Furthermore, thousands of Reangs from Mizoram have been living in refugee camps in Tripura, as noted in the section on Mizoram (39,000 as per *Times of India* report of 9 July 1998). The wide cultural diversity among huge numbers of refugees who have sought shelter in Tripura since a long time — Bengali Hindus, Buddhist Chakmas from Chittagong, Mughs from Arakan region, and Reangs from Mizoram — says a great deal about its compassionate and remarkably tolerant social milieu.

Tripura government has launched a number of programmes for improving the conditions of its tribal population, most of which continues to live in acute deprivation. These include preparation of tribal sub-plans, schemes for resettlement for jhumias, social forestry projects, special assistance for artisans and farmers, promotion of rubber plantation in Tripura Tribal Area Autonomous District Council (TTAADC), etc. But the numbers of tribal households which were rehabilitated have been small. The fact that in spite of the appallingly low incomes from jhum cultivation, thousands of tribal families continue to pursue it, in addition to wage labour employment, other cottage industries and collection of forest produce, indicates their desperate situation.[91]

It is important to note that Tripura's underdevelopment is reflected in the large numbers of people — both tribal and non-tribal — who suffer

91. For details on the findings of three studies on jhumias between 1958 and 1982 by Ganguly, National Sample Survey and Agricultural Finance Corporation, see Malabika Das Gupta, 1986.

from high levels of malnutrition and poverty. In 1983-84, the Planning Commission had estimated that 23 per cent of Tripura's population lived below the poverty line, whereas the State Government's estimate placed it at 60.70 per cent. According to the Expert Group appointed by Government of India, in 1993-94, this percentage was 39.1 constituting a total of 11.79 lakh persons (11.41 lakh rural, and 0.38 lakh urban).[92] For a long time, Tripura has remained a revenue-deficit State with heavy dependence on Central grants. Between 1980-81 and 1985-86, the NSDP at current prices declined from Rs. 77.31 crore to 77.11 crore, according to the State Directorate of Statistics. Fortunately, this situation has changed, although it still continues to be far from satisfactory. The NSDP, at current prices, for 1993-94 was Rs. 1244 crore and per capita NSDP Rs. 4252, according to *Indian Economic Survey* (*1996-97*). The provisional estimate for 1996-97 for the State was Rs. 1703 crore and per capita NSDP Rs. 5432 (State Directorate of Economics and Statistics and Central Statistical Organization).

While the need to step up the pace of development of the State is extremely urgent, tribal discontent continues to flareup in sporadic outbursts of arson, murders, robberies and kidnappings by extremist organizations like National Liberation Front of Tripura (NLFT), All Tripura Tribal Force (ATTF) and the like. Recently, the encounters between NLFT and United Bengali Liberation Front (UBLF) have kept Kalyanpur and Teliamura areas in extreme turmoil (*Times of India*, 22 May 2000). Unfortunately, whenever an underground organization reaches an accord with the government to lay down arms and to surrender, another group springs up to keep insurgency alive. The victims of extremist violence are mostly non-tribal people, police, government officials, security personnel, and at times members of rival tribal organizations. As the government is heavily pre-occupied with law and order situation and with controlling insurgency, developmental programmes inevitably fail to receive the attention and resources needed, which in turn intensifies discontent with the government.

A supreme irony in recent times is the manner in which elections to TTAADC in May 2000 were completely subverted by Indigenous People's Front of Tripura (IPFT), a new alliance of tribal organizations. The major objective of empowering tribal people to plan and execute developmental programmes in a democratic framework was completely vitiated by the

---

92. For details of methodology used by the Expert Group, refer to note 11.

strong-arm methods reported to have been used by IPFT to win elections by suppressing public opinion (Chakravarti, 2000). It is important to ensure that the State Government does not permit such set-backs to deflect them from the original objective of enabling the Autonomous Council to manage its programmes independently. The tendency of State Government bureaucracy to control TTAADC's funds and plans will therefore have to be resolutely curbed (Subramanian, 2000).

The State Government currently faces formidable challenges in the context of continuous drain on its resources due to frequent outbursts of insurgency and violence, high level of poverty and unemployment and ethnic tensions. The Central allocation for Seventh Plan (1985-90) of Rs. 440 crore went up to Rs. 1130 crore for Eighth Plan (1992-97), and this trend will have to be continued in the light of Tripura's problems of resource mobilization. Meanwhile the State Government can initiate various measures for augmenting employment and incomes through various programmes, like modernizing handloom weaving, cane and bamboo crafts and such other small-scale ventures, improving and expanding agriculture, horticulture, pisciculture, rubber and tea plantations, poultry-keeping, animal husbandry, etc. Moreover, the unused gas and oil potential can be harnessed to promote industrial development and thus generate more employment for the State's burgeoning population. The style of implementing development programmes will have to pay much greater attention to training and skill development, and promotion of enterprising spirit. This is especially crucial in the management of tribal development programmes in order to develop self-reliance and confidence among tribal people. When their trust and self-respect are restored, the fascination for extremist outfits with their lure of power and weapons would disappear. This would herald an important step towards social amity and progress for Tripura.

OVERVIEW

The foregoing accounts of the seven N-E States reveal a number of differences in their socio-political evolution as well as similarities in their developmental backlogs. A few illustrations should suffice. The histories of these States, which help to understand their present situation in the Indian polity, show a great deal of variation. Assam, Manipur and Tripura have recorded histories which go back at least to the medieval period, if not farther back. These States have had considerable interaction with other parts of India, and particularly with Hindu religion and culture, resulting in intermingling of these with their indigenous tribal cultures. Meghalaya, Mizoram, Nagaland and Arunachal Pradesh, on the other hand, can trace their recorded history mainly from nineteenth century, more precisely from the British period. Reference to earlier period are mostly in the form of racial memory preserved through popular legends and anecdotes. Meghalaya, Mizoram and Nagaland were exposed to Christianity through foreign missionaries who received the patronage of British rulers. Introduction of education and health services by Christian missionaries facilitated the adoption of Christianity by native populations of these States, besides providing them access to knowledge, new ideas and contacts with the world outside. Arunachal Pradesh remained isolated to a great extent initially due to its geographical inaccessibility and later because of deliberate British policy to restrict outside contacts. After Indian Independence, the political and administrative integration of Arunachal Pradesh was initiated. While none of the N-E States have remained immune to outside social influences, a majority of Arunachal tribal societies today follow their respective indigenous faiths and cultural practices.

Despite wide differences in their historical and political backgrounds, the N-E States share some common features which set them apart from the rest of India. Their geographical isolation, hilly and difficult terrain, poor communications, difficulties of transportation and inadequacy of the most basic amenities like access to safe drinking water and electricity present major handicaps. Besides, primitive agriculture with low productivity, lack of industrialization, poor infrastructure for training, marketing and credit facilities pose formidable problems in development. What is holding the N-E States back from making a determined effort to overcome their problems? A handy but woefully incomplete answer is to blame the Centre for neglect and poor financial support for N-E States. A more relevant factor hindering development is the recurring insurgency and communal violence which keep some N-E States in turmoil. It could well be a series of ULFA sabotage of rail tracks in Assam, a fresh wave of Naga-Kuki conflicts in Manipur, a massacre of non-tribal villagers by Tripura National Volunteers (TNV) in Tripura, or a bloody encounter between rival factions of NSCN near the border between Nagaland and Myanmar. Fortunately, except for a few disturbances, Meghalaya and Arunachal Pradesh have remained fairly peaceful.

Surprisingly, after more than two decades of insurgency, after attaining full Statehood in 1987, Mizoram has enjoyed uninterrupted peace. Thanks to the exemplary sagacity of its political leadership, which kept their political differences aside in the interest of presenting a united front in negotiations with Central Government in order to attain full Statehood for Mizoram. It has been making steady progress in modernizing its agriculture and promoting industrialization. And what is more, it has been scrupulously avoiding political differences from disrupting social harmony, as exemplified in the congenial atmosphere during the last State Assembly elections. There is no doubt that the key to Mizoram's promising start lies in the type of its leadership which has shown evidence of keeping in check personal ambitions and narrow group loyalties in the interest of the State.

The N-E States today are a home to nearly 209 STs and several sub-tribes, speaking over 420 languages and dialects, in addition to immigrant groups from other Indian States, Bangladesh, Nepal and Myanmar. Many of these groups are clamouring for protection from exploitation, opportunities for advancement and ethnic identity. The situation demands leaders who can rise above constricted tribal identities and particular class interests and galvanize their societies in the pursuit of overarching goals of well-being of all and progress of the States. Indeed a daunting task, but something that cannot be postponed.

3

Economic Status of N-E Women

Introduction

INDIAN CONSTITUTION recognizes the fundamental right of all individuals "to practice any profession or to carry on any occupation, trade or business." Furthermore, the Constitutional Right to Equality prohibits discrimination among citizens in public employment on the basis of sex. In spite of such safeguards, Indian women suffer from many limitations in the enjoyment of these rights. The level of economic development in the country as a whole and within its various regions set the broad parameters of occupational options for both men and women. Within these, however, certain social and cultural factors, such as perceptions of gender roles and of division of work between men and women, access to preparation for occupations, prevailing customs, etc. determine women's entry into certain occupations and access to resources, and women of N-E region are no exception to this.

This chapter examines the economic status of women in N-E region from three perspectives given in three sections. Section I presents analysis of the activity status of N-E women as defined and reflected in Indian Census data for 1991. Section II depicts the types of activities in which N-E women are engaged. Section III considers their situation with respect to rights of property ownership and inheritance, and the nature of their participation in allocation of household resources and in financial decisions. Emerging trends with respect to new occupations have also been indicated wherever possible.

As has been noted earlier, N-E region includes a multiplicity of communities having their own customs and cultural traditions in diverse ecological settings. It is virtually impossible to arrive at generalizations that are almost universally applicable. While keeping in mind this limitation, we highlight the most dominant trends and patterns, and indicate examples of variations.

SECTION I
Economic Activity Status of N-E Women as per 1991 Census

This Section examines the economic activity status of women in N-E region as reflected in 1991 Census data. Specifically, we first look at women's distribution into "workers" and "non-workers", and then the former are subdivided into "main" and "marginal" workers. Further, we also look intos the various industrial categories of "main workers," and changes, if any, since the last decadal Census of 1981. We also highlight how women in N-E region compare with women in the rest of India, as also major inter-State variations within N-E region.

It is necessary to note the definitions and concepts used in classifying persons as "worker," "non-worker," "main worker," and "marginal worker" in the 1991 Census, which remained unchanged from the 1981 Census, thus facilitating comparisons. [1] Furthermore, the concept of "usual status" of a worker was considered more appropriate than "current status," the reference period being the year preceding the Census. "Work" was defined as "participation in any economically productive activity. Such participation may be physical or mental in nature. Work involves not only actual work but also effective supervision and direction of work. It also includes unpaid work on farm or in family enterprise." This elaboration, viz. "unpaid work on farm or in family enterprise" was specially added to net women and children who are often engaged in unpaid family labour, and otherwise likely to be excluded from "worker" category.

Work Participation Rate

The percentage of workers to the total population of females, i.e. female "Work Participation Rate" (WPR), has been regarded as an important indicator of women's economic status. Table 3.1 presents total, male and female WPRs for India and for N-E States in 1981 and 1991. The female WPR for India as a whole (excluding Assam and Jammu & Kashmir) for

1. "Worker" is a person "who had worked anytime at all during the year preceding the Census" and "Non-Worker" is a person "who had not worked at all during the year preceding the Census." "Main workers" are defined as "those who had worked in some economic activity for the major part of the year, i.e. for a period of six months (183 days) or more." "Marginal workers" are defined as "those who had worked for some time during the last year, but not for the major part," i.e. for less than 183 days. *Source: Census of India 1991, Final Population Tables*, Series-1 of 1992: pp. 27-31.

Table 3.1 Work Participation Rates by Sex in India & N.E. States, 1981–1991, as percentage of Total Population

India/States	*Total Persons*		*Males*		*Females*		*Difference in Male & Female WPRs in 1991 in percentage points*
	1981	*1991*	*1981*	*1991*	*1981*	*1991*	
* India (Excluding Assam and Jammu & Kashmir)	36.70	37.50	52.62	51.61	19.67	22.27	29.34
Arunachal Pradesh	52.63	46.24	58.63	53.76	45.67	37.49	16.27
Assam	NA	36.09	NA	49.45	NA	21.61	27.84
Manipur	43.20	42.18	46.80	45.27	39.48	38.96	6.31
Meghalaya	45.92	42.67	53.96	50.07	37.49	34.93	15.14
Mizoram	45.44	48.91	52.54	53.87	37.72	43.52	10.35
Nagaland	48.23	42.68	52.58	46.86	43.20	37.96	8.90
Tripura	32.27	31.14	50.71	47.55	12.78	13.76	33.79

Source: Census of India 1991, *Final Population Totals*, Series 1, Paper 2 of 1992.

*1981 Census was not conducted in Assam, and 1991 Census was not conducted in Jammu & Kashmir due to disturbed conditions.

N.A = Not Available

1991 was 22.27. For five out of seven N-E States, viz. Arunachal Pradesh (37.49), Manipur (38.96), Meghalaya (34.93), Mizoram (43.52) and Nagaland (37.96), they were significantly higher. Assam (21.61) and Tripura (13.76) on the other hand, had lower female WPRs than the national average. Both of these States have the lowest proportions of STs populations (12.83 per cent and 30.95 per cent, respectively) in the N-E region. All N-E States have lower female WPRs than male WPRs, which is consistent with the national pattern both for 1981 and 1991. However, the differences in the male and female WPRs are much smaller in five N-E States, viz. Arunachal Pradesh, Manipur, Meghalaya, Mizoram and Nagaland than for India as a whole, most probably because of tribal women's heavier involvement in agriculture, as compared to that of non-tribal women. Conversely, Tripura shows a wide disparity (33.79) in percentage points between male and female WPRs for 1991.

Women's WPR for India shows a decadal increase of 2.60 percentage points. Arunachal Pradesh, Manipur, Meghalaya and Nagaland have registered a decline in 1991 as compared to 1981. For Mizoram, there is a significant increase of 5.80 points over the ten-year period. In fact, Mizoram's 43.52 female WPR for 1991 is the highest among all States in the country and next only to the Union Territory of Dadra and Nagar Haveli with 48.79.[2] Tripura registered a very slight increase (0.98 points).

Main Workers and Marginal Workers

Table 3.2 presents the percentage distribution of population into main workers, marginal workers and non-workers by sex in India and N-E States for 1981 and 1991. In 1991 the percentage of female main workers in India (excluding Assam and Jammu & Kashmir) was 16.03. The corresponding percentages for Arunachal Pradesh (35.57), Manipur (32.65), Meghalaya (30.67), Mizoram (33.95) and Nagaland (37.32) are significantly higher than the national average, while Assam (12.57) and Tripura (10.14) are much lower. As against the 1991 percentage of female marginal workers for India of 6.24, Assam (9.04) and Mizoram (9.57) are higher, Manipur (6.31) nearly the same, while those for Arunachal Pradesh, Meghalaya, Nagaland and Tripura are much lower.

2. The female WPRs of Arunachal Pradesh, Manipur, Meghalaya, Mizoram and Nagaland for 1991 compare very favourably with those for Punjab (4.40), West Bengal (11.25), Uttar Pradesh (12.32), Kerala (15.85), Bihar (14.86) and Haryana (10.76).

As compared to 1981, the percentage of female main workers for India showed an increase of 1.96 points in 1991, whereas for Arunachal Pradesh, Manipur, Meghalaya and Nagaland, there was a decline despite the more inclusive definition of female work participation. The 1991 percentages of male main workers are consistently lower than those for 1981 in six N-E States (Assam data not available for 1981), which indicate a general deterioration in the employment situation in these States, as men have a prior claim on available work opportunities. This largely explains the decline in female main workers' percentages in the four N-E States. In Manipur, in the context of a decline in female WPR and percentage of female main workers in 1991 over 1981, the slight increase in percentage of female marginal workers does not give much cause for optimism. In Mizoram however, both the percentages of female main and marginal workers have registered an increase in 1991, which indicates a favourable trend in women's employment. Tripura too has registered an increase in female main workers' percentage for 1991.

Distribution of Female Main Workers in Production Sectors

All persons enumerated as main workers in the 1991 Census were classified into nine industrial categories. These were further grouped into three sectors: Primary, which includes industrial categories I, II, III, IV; Secondary, which includes categories V(a), V(b) & VI; and Tertiary, which includes categories VII, VIII & IX. In an industrially underdeveloped country or region, a predominant majority of main workers are necessarily employed in the primary sector, while with industrial development, employment opportunities in the secondary and tertiary sectors progressively expand.

For India as a whole, the distribution of female main workers in 1991 was: Primary sector 81.09 per cent, Secondary 8.07 per cent, and Tertiary 10.84 per cent (Table 3.3). Among the N-E States, the percentages of female main workers in the Primary Sector were: Arunachal Pradesh 89.92, Assam 86.50, Manipur 76.50, Meghalaya 83.75, Mizoram 78.36, and Nagaland 92.14, i.e. more than three-fourths of women main workers, while in Tripura it was 72.64. This is the sector where working hours tend to be long and remuneration fairly low because the tasks are generally unskilled, involving manual labour. The 1991 percentages of women main workers in the secondary sector in most N-E States are much lower than the national average of 8.07 per cent,

Table 3.2 :Main Workers, Marginal Workers and Non-workers as Percentages of Total Population by Sex in India and N-E States, 1981–1991

India/States		*Main Workers*		*Marginal Workers*		*Non-Workers*	
		1981	*1991*	*1981*	*1991*	*1981*	*1991*
*India (excluding Assam and Jammu & Kashmir)	Female	14.07	16.03	5.60	6.24	80.33	77.73
	Male	51.62	51.00	1.00	0.61	47.38	48.39
Arunachal Pradesh	Female	40.55	35.57	5.12	1.92	54.33	62.51
	Male	57.42	53.52	1.21	0.24	47.37	46.24
Assam	Female	NA	12.57	NA	9.04	NA	78.39
	Male	NA	48.38	NA	1.07	NA	50.55
Manipur	Female	34.59	32.65	4.89	6.31	60.52	61.04
	Male	45.94	44.21	0.86	1.06	53.20	54.73
Meghalaya	Female	33.29	30.67	4.20	4.26	62.51	65.07
	Male	53.11	49.54	0.85	0.53	46.04	49.93
Mizoram	Female	32.32	33.95	5.40	9.57	62.28	56.48
	Male	50.39	49.59	2.15	4.28	47.46	46.13
Nagaland	Female	42.45	37.32	0.75	0.64	56.80	62.04
	Male	51.91	46.69	0.67	0.17	47.42	53.14
Tripura	Female	8.95	10.14	3.83	3.62	87.22	86.24
	Male	49.23	46.99	1.48	0.56	49.29	52.45

Source: Census of India 1991, Final Population Totals, Series 1, Paper 2 of 1992.

*1981 Census was not conducted in Assam and 1991 Census was not conducted in Jammu & Kashmir due to disturbed conditions.

NA=Not Available.

the only exception being Manipur with 14.06 per cent. This is accounted for by the substantial number of women engaged in handloom weaving. Here again, there is a sharp decline from the 1981 figure of 21.47 per cent suggesting shrinking employment opportunities for Manipuri women in handloom weaving.[3] With the invasion of mill-made cloth from other States into Manipur, the demand for handloom materials is declining.

In the tertiary sector, 1991 figures show higher percentages of female main workers in all N-E States than those for 1981. The percentages for Meghalaya (14.71), Mizoram (19.89) and Tripura (22.43) are quite significant. With expansion of education among women and widening networks of schools, health institutions and government bureaucracies, more women in N-E States are employed in teaching, health services and secretarial and professional jobs. As is to be expected, the proportions of male main workers in the secondary and tertiary sectors are substantially higher than those for women in all N-E States, the only exception being Manipur where the percentages of women main workers in the secondary sector are higher than those for males both for 1981 and 1991.

As noted earlier this is due to the large number of women engaged in handloom weaving in the household segment.

Distribution of Cultivators and Agricultural Labourers

In India generally, a preponderant majority of women main workers are engaged either as cultivators or agricultural labourers. In the context of the Indian Census, the term "Cultivator" includes any person who works on land owned by his/her family or taken on lease. It however excludes persons who work in orchards or plantations who are covered under industrial category III.[4] An agricultural labourer is defined in the 1991

---

3. In Manipur, the total number of male main workers in the secondary sector in 1991 was 27,140 whereas the corresponding number for female main workers was 41,262 out of which 35,065 were engaged in household industry, according to 1991 Census, Series 1, Paper 2 of 1992: pp. 134-35. With the introduction of power looms and new technology, men are entering this field.
4. In Indian Census a person is a "Cultivator" if "he or she is engaged either as employer, single worker or family worker in cultivation of land owned or held from government or held from private persons or institutions for payment in money, kind or share. Cultivation includes supervision or direction of cultivation." The cultivation here refers to "cereals and millet crops such as wheat, paddy, jowar, bajra, ragi, etc. and other crops such as sugarcane, ground-nut, tapioca, etc. and pulses, raw jute and kindred fibre crop, cotton, etc. and does not →

Table 3.3 Percentage Distribution of Male and Female Main Workers in Primary, Secondary, & Tertiary Sectors (§) in India and N-E States, 1981-1991

India/States	Year	*Total Main Workers*		*Primary* [I+II+III+IV]		*Secondary* [V (a) + V (b)+VI]		*Tertiary* [VII+VIII+IX]	
		Male	Female	Male	Female	Male	Female	Male	Female
*India (Excluding 1991 Assam and Jammu & Kashmir)	1981	100.00	100.00	66.28	81.61	13.96	9.04	19.76	9.35
		100.00	100.00	63.37	81.09	13.30	8.07	23.32	10.84
Arunachal Pradesh	1981	100.00	100.00	63.21	95.11	13.13	2.00	23.66	2.89
	1991	100.00	100.00	54.60	89.92	12.34	2.21	33.06	7.87
Assam	1981	100.00	100.00	NA	NA	NA	NA	NA	NA
	1991	100.00	100.00	70.99	86.50	6.09	3.34	22.92	10.16
Manipur	1981	100.00	100.00	68.76	70.75	7.42	21.47	23.82	7.78
	1991	100.00	100.00	95.40	76.50	6.54	14.06	28.06	9.44
Meghalaya	1981	100.00	100.00	74.86	87.96	5.54	2.03	19.60	10.01
	1991	100.00	100.00	69.51	83.75	5.03	1.54	24.46	14.71
Mizoram	1981	100.00	100.00	65.18	88.72	6.67	1.98	28.15	9.30
	1991	100.00	100.00	58.18	78.36	7.17	1.75	34.65	19.89
Nagaland	1981	100.00	100.00	58.92	94.28	5.43	0.39	35.65	5.03
	1991	100.00	100.00	63.31	92.14	5.11	1.18	31.58	6.68
Tripura	1981	100.00	100.00	69.37	74.96	7.57	6.40	23.06	18.64
	1991	100.00	100.00	62.34	72.64	6.71	4.93	30.95	22.43

Source: Census of India 1991, Final Population Totals, Series 1, Paper 2 of 1992: pp. 176-89.

*1981 Census was not conducted in Assam, and 1991 Census was not conducted in Jammu & Kashmir due to disturbed conditions.

N.A. = Not Availalble.

Note: (δ) *Primary Sector:* I Cultivators; II Agricultural labourers; III Livestock, forestry, fishing, hunting and plantations, orchards and allied activities; IV Mining and quarrying; *Secondary*: V(a) Manufacturing, processing, servicing and repairs in household industry; V(b) Manufacturing, processing, servicing and repairs in other than household industry; VI Constructions; *Tertiary:* VII Trade and Commerce, VIII Transport, storage and communications; IX Other services.

Indian Census as "a person who works on another person's land for wages in money, kind or share."

The consistently lower proportions of cultivators and higher proportions of agricultural labourers among women main workers as compared to men main workers in India has been regarded as a strong indicator of women's lower economic status. In 1991, the percentage of cultivators among male main workers for India was 39.63 and that of agricultural labourers 21.05, whereas these percentages among women main workers were 34.22 and 44.93, respectively (Table 3.4). Agricultural labourers who work for wages on someone else's farm are usually poorer than persons from landowning households and therefore more vulnerable to exploitation than cultivators who work on land owned or taken on lease. As will be noted from Table 3.4, in all N-E States except Tripura, the percentages of cultivators among women main workers for 1991 are significantly higher than those among men main workers. This may be explained by the trend among men to shift to alternative and more lucrative employment, leaving major responsibility for cultivation with women. On the other hand, the percentages of agricultural labourers among female main workers are smaller than those among male main workers in Arunachal Pradesh, Assam, Mizoram and Nagaland, whereas in Meghalaya, Tripura and Manipur these percentages are higher. The significance of this mixed picture is not clear.

For 1991, the percentages of cultivators among women main workers are significantly higher than the country average of 34.22 in all N-E States except Tripura (where it is higher only by 3.32 per cent) and those of agricultural labourers lower than the national average of 44.93. This suggests that women in the N-E States engaged in agriculture are better off than women in the rest of India in terms of their economic status. The other side of the coin, viz. the heavier involvement of N-E women main workers in agriculture than that for India as a whole, indicates that N-E women have fewer employment alternatives and have to continue working in a sector where returns are generally low and work fairly more strenuous.

→ include fruit-growing, vegetable growing or keeping orchards or groves or working on plantations like tea, coffee, rubber, cinchona and other medicinal plantations." *Source: Census of India 1991*, *Final Population Totals*, Series 1, Paper 2 of 1992: p. 31.

Table 3.4 Percentages of Cultivators and Agricultural Labourers Among Total Main Workers by Sex in India and N-E States, 1981–1991

India/States	1981				1991			
	Cultivators		*Agricultural Labourers*		*Cultivators*		*Agricultural Labourers*	
	Male	*Female*	*Male*	*Female*	*Male*	*Female*	*Male*	*Female*
*India (Excluding Assam and Jammu & Kashmir)	43.71	33.09	19.57	46.34	39.63	34.22	21.05	44.93
Arunachal Pradesh	58.22	92.69	2.79	2.00	46.98	83.78	5.14	5.12
Assam	NA	NA	NA	NA	50.89	50.93	12.10	12.01
Manipur	63.96	63.10	3.31	7.29	58.64	66.18	4.65	9.61
Meghalaya	57.83	70.49	9.42	10.91	50.75	63.02	11.60	14.03
Mizoram	61.38	86.31	2.67	2.16	53.30	74.10	3.47	2.98
Nagaland	57.01	93.92	1.15	0.32	59.77	90.83	1.71	1.00
Tripura	44.15	38.27	22.62	32.07	38.20	37.54	21.93	30.539

Source: Census of India 1991, *Final Population Tables*, Series 1, Paper 2 of 1992 (Tables 4.2 & 4.3), pp. 155-88.

*1981 Census was not conducted in Assam, and 1991 Census was not conducted in Jammu & Kashmir due to disturbed conditions.

NA=Not Available.

When we compare the situations of women main workers in 1981 and 1991 for India, there was a slight increase in the percentage of cultivators and a small decline in the percentage of agricultural labourers in 1991. In the N-E States (barring Assam for which 1981 figures are not available), the percentages of cultivators among women main workers in 1991 have declined in five out of six States, viz. Arunachal Pradesh, Meghalaya, Mizoram, Nagaland and Tripura since 1981. Furthermore, the percentages of agricultural labourers among women main workers have increased since 1981 in Arunachal Pradesh, Manipur, Meghalaya, Mizoram and Nagaland, which suggests a negative trend. In the context of reports of land grabbing by unscrupulous and affluent landowners and increasing land alienation among poorer sections in N-E States this indicates that a declining proportion of women are working on family-owned lands. However, if one compares the percentages of agricultural labourers among women main workers for 1991 for some major Indian States, such as Andhra Pradesh (60.33), Bihar (59.29), Gujarat (45.08), Karnataka (49.69), Maharashtra (43.70), Tamil Nadu (53.79), the corresponding proportions are much smaller in all N-E States.

Regardless of the somewhat favourable situation of N-E women in agriculture, it is necessary to view their high participation from another perspective. Table 3.3 brings out the substantially higher percentages of male main workers in the tertiary sector in all N-E States as compared to women workers for 1981 and 1991, indicating new and more diverse employment avenues for men in these States. The high proportions of women main workers in agriculture, i.e. cultivators and agricultural labourers taken together, reflect lack of other occupational choices open to women, as compared to men. For 1991 out of a total of 60 districts covered by all N-E States, in 23 districts, or over one-third, the percentage of women main workers in agriculture was more than 90, and in the remaining 37 districts, it was more than 80 for rural areas (Refer to Appendix Table 3.A1) given at the end of this book.

Women Workers in Non-Agricultural Sectors

Let us now look at women's employment in non-agricultural industrial categories in 1981 and 1991 (Tables 3.5 and 3.6). For India, one significant change over the last decade was increased percentage of female main workers in the industrial category IX — "Other services." Similar situation was seen in six N-E States, viz. Arunachal Pradesh, Manipur, Meghalaya,

Table 3.5 : Distribution of Female Workers in Industrial Categories as Percentages of Main Workers in India and N-E States, 1981–1991

India/States	Industrial Category											
	Year	Total	I	II	III	IV	V(a)	V(b)	VI	VII	VIII	IX
*India (Excluding Assam and Jammu & Kashmir)	1981	100.00	33.09	46.34	1.83	0.35	4.57	3.60	0.87	2.04	0.37	6.94
	1991	100.00	34.22	44.93	1.60	0.34	3.53	3.88	0.66	2.26	0.32	8.26
Arunachal Pradesh	1981	100.00	92.69	2.00	0.42	0.00	0.13	0.58	1.29	0.28	0.01	2.60
	1991	100.00	83.78	5.12	1.02	0.00	0.15	0.65	1.41	0.63	0.05	7.19
Assam	1981	100.00	NA	NA	NA	NA	NA	NA	NA	NA	NA	NA
	1991	100.00	50.93	12.01	23.45	0.11	2.17	1.02	0.15	0.99	0.28	8.89
Manipur	1981	100.00	63.10	7.29	0.32	0.04	20.17	1.02	0.28	3.69	0.03	4.06
	1991	100.00	66.18	9.61	0.69	0.02	11.95	1.73	0.38	3.35	0.12	5.97
Meghalaya	1981	100.00	70.49	10.91	6.25	0.31	1.01	0.58	0.44	2.54	0.25	7.22
	1991	100.00	63.02	14.03	6.43	0.27	0.47	0.47	0.60	4.29	0.27	10.15
Mizoram	1981	100.00	86.31	2.16	0.22	0.03	1.05	0.73	0.20	3.21	0.08	6.01
	1991	100.00	74.10	2.98	1.26	0.02	0.86	0.68	0.21	7.83	0.04	12.02
Nagaland	1981	100.00	93.92	0.32	0.03	0.01	0.33	0.31	0.05	0.34	0.05	4.64
	1991	100.00	90.83	1.00	0.30	0.01	0.52	0.30	0.36	0.58	0.08	6.02
Tripura	1981	100.00	38.27	32.07	4.60	0.02	2.45	3.33	0.62	1.06	0.18	17.40
	1991	100.00	37.54	30.53	4.49	0.08	2.54	1.97	0.42	1.23	0.23	20.97

Source: Census of India 1991, Final Population Totals, Series 1, Paper-2 of 1992, Table 4.3, pp. 162-68.

*1981 Census was not conducted in Assam, and 1991 Census was not conducted in Jammu & Kashmir due to disturbed conditions.

NA-Not Available.

For definitions of Industrial Categories refer to Note (δ) below Table 3.3

Table 3.6 : Female Workers in each Industrial Category as Percentages of Female Workers by Rural-Urban Residence in India and N-E States, 1991

India/States		Industrial Category										
		I-IX	*I*	*II*	*III*	*IV*	*V(a)*	*V(b)*	*VI*	*VII*	*VIII*	*IX*
*India (Excluding Assam and Jammu & Kashmir)	Total	100.00	34.22	44.93	1.60	0.34	3.53	3.88	0.66	2.26	0.32	8.26
	Rural	100.00	38.58	49.32	1.61	0.29	2.93	2.34	0.27	1.10	0.08	3.48
	Urban	100.00	5.13	15.61	1.52	0.68	7.53	14.14	3.30	10.01	1.94	40.14
Arunachal Pradesh	Total	100.00	83.78	5.12	1.02	0.00	0.15	0.65	1.41	0.63	0.05	7.19
	Rural	100.00	86.47	5.17	0.97	0.00	0.14	0.48	1.25	0.53	0.03	4.96
	Urban	100.00	16.29	3.71	2.46	0.00	0.46	4.81	5.42	3.21	0.57	63.07
Assam	Total	100.00	50.93	12.01	23.45	0.11	2.17	1.02	0.15	0.99	0.28	8.89
	Rural	100.00	53.69	12.59	24.56	0.08	1.99	0.80	0.07	0.62	0.07	5.53
	Urban	100.00	4.66	2.28	4.80	0.51	5.17	4.80	1.49	7.31	3.68	65.30
Manipur	Total	100.00	66.18	9.61	0.69	0.02	11.95	1.73	0.38	3.35	0.12	5.97
	Rural	100.00	73.71	8.97	0.48	0.01	10.44	0.90	0.19	1.70	0.08	3.52
	Urban	100.00	31.23	12.56	1.69	0.06	18.96	5.61	1.26	11.00	0.32	17.31
Meghalaya	Total	100.00	63.02	14.03	6.43	0.27	0.47	0.47	0.60	4.29	0.27	10.15
	Rural	100.00	69.00	15.08	6.99	0.24	0.42	0.30	0.42	2.66	0.07	4.82
	Urban	100.00	6.11	4.06	1.03	0.61	0.98	2.13	2.31	19.82	2.10	60.85
Mizoram	Total	100.00	74.10	2.98	1.26	0.02	0.86	0.68	0.21	7.83	0.04	12.02
	Rural	100.00	92.46	1.43	0.34	0.00	0.21	0.04	0.07	1.41	0.02	4.02
	Urban	100.00	44.17	5.51	2.75	0.06	1.91	1.72	0.44	18.29	0.08	25.07

contd.

Indian/States		Industrial Category										
		I-IX	*I*	*II*	*III*	*IV*	*V(a)*	*V(b)*	*VI*	*VII*	*VIII*	*IX*
Nagaland	Total	100.00	90.83	1.00	0.30	0.01	0.52	0.30	0.36	0.58	0.08	6.02
	Rural	100.00	94.12	0.97	0.13	0.00	0.41	0.22	0.19	0.32	0.04	3.60
	Urban	100.00	29.00	1.53	3.40	0.18	2.47	1.81	3.55	5.47	100	51.59
Tripura	Total	100.00	37.54	30.53	4.49	0.08	2.54	1.97	0.42	1.23	0.23	20.97
	Rural	100.00	43.11	34.70	5.15	0.07	2.63	1.72	0.28	0.89	0.11	11.34
	Urban	100.00	0.89	3.13	0.16	0.14	1.97	3.59	1.32	3.43	1.05	84.32

Source: Census of India 1s991, *Final Population Totals*, Series 1, Paper 2 of 1992, Table 4.3, pp.162-68.

*1981 Census was not conducted in Assam, and 1991 Census was not conducted in Jammu & Kashmir due to disturbed conditions.

NA=Not Available.

For definitions of Industrial Categories, refer to Note (δ) below Table 3.3.

For numbers of female main workers in Industrial Categories in India and North-Eastern States, 1991 refer to Appendix 3 B-II, and for 2001 data to Appendix C (i).

Mizoram, Nagaland and Tripura (Assam data not available for 1981). If we examine the rural-urban distribution of women main workers (Table 3.6), much of this increase has gone to urban areas. This can be explained by the new employment opportunities for women in educational institutions, health and medical care facilities which tend to be clustered in urban areas, administrative centres at district headquarters and State capital towns. In spite of this trend, out of the total number of employed women, only a small number are employed in the organized sector.[5]

Another observation relates to a small increase in 1991 over 1981 in employment for women workers in the industrial category VII — "Trade and Commerce" — in Meghalaya and Mizoram (Table 3.5). On the other hand, there has been some decline in Manipur in the percentages of women workers in trade and commerce, as also in category V(a) — "Manufacturing, processing, servicing and repairs in household industry" for 1991 which is explained by a decrease in handloom weaving as noted earlier. Since Manipuri women are known to have occupied a strong position in the past in retail trade in vegetables, agricultural produce, groceries, handloom fabrics, etc. lower percentages in this category suggest a weakening of their position. This could probably be the result of emergence of new businessmen — both outsiders and Manipuri — who have access to larger outside markets and more capital, resulting in small women traders being edged out in the absence of adequate institutional and technical support.

Assam, Meghalaya and Tripura have significant proportions of female main workers in the industrial category III — "Livestock, forestry, fishing, hunting and plantations, orchards and allied activities." The large number of women working in tea plantations and orchards in Assam, Meghalaya and Tripura account for these.[6] It is not surprising that very few women in the N-E States are employed in manufacturing industries of non-household type [Industrial Category V(b)] in view of the low industrial development of

5. A quarterly employment review by Ministry of Labour, Govt. of India, reported that in September 1985, the number of N-E women employed in organized sector was 347.9 thousand (excluding Arunachal Pradesh for which data were not available). Out of these, 75.2 thousand were employed in public sector and 272.7 thousand in private sector. Refer to Dept. of Women and Child Development, Govt. of India, *Women in India: A Statistical Profile*, 1988: pp. 102-03.

6. The numbers of women workers in industrial category III that includes plantations in 1991 were: Assam 3,16,993, Meghalaya 17,094, and Tripura 6094. Refer to Appendix Table 3 A-II.

this region. Women employed in trade and commerce category VII in any significant numbers are located mainly in urban areas of Manipur, Meghalaya and Mizoram. (Table 3.6). The rural areas are characterized by a slow development of money economy and markets, and continue to rely partly on exchange of commodities and services through barter and reciprocity.

SECTION II
The Nature of Women's Work

In the preceding section we examined the work status of N-E women and their distribution in occupational categories as reflected in the 1991 Indian Census data. This section presents the various types of activities in which these women are engaged and some of the qualitative aspects of women's work. It refers not only to those functions which are included in the Census accounting but also to many others which are left out of even the enlarged definition of economic activity adopted in the 1991 Census, and which are crucial for sustenance of their households.

As noted in Chapter 1, *jhum* cultivation is the predominant mode in major part of the N-E region. It would therefore be useful to look at the broad division of work among men and women in this activity. In *jhum* cultivation that is prevalent in varying degrees in all N-E States wherever the terrain is hilly and forested, men undertake the clearing of jungles by felling and chopping trees and setting them on fire. Construction of houses, hunting — whether for food or recreation, keeping a night vigil to protect the fields from wild animals also fall in men's domain. Both men and women usually work together in clearing the burnt logs and bushes and spreading their ashes. In most N-E States women's tasks include sowing of seeds, weeding, harvesting, carrying bundles of harvested stocks home, threshing, winnowing and storing the produce in granaries. Although this is the broad division of work, in some tribes it is not rigid and both men and women join in these tasks. For instance, among the Adis of Arunachal Pradesh and Tripura tribes, both men and women join hands in sowing, harvesting and threshing paddy.

Where terrace cultivation is practised, like in Angami areas of Nagaland and Apatani areas of Arunachal Pradesh, generally men perform the more strenuous tasks such as terracing, preparing irrigation channels and dams, while women take care of sowing, transplanting, weeding, harvesting and all the later processing of grains. In the plains, ploughing is almost always done by men and very rarely by women, in case no male member is available. In fact, among many tribes women are forbidden from even touching the plough to avoid their so-called polluting effect. In all other tasks, however, women are heavily involved. Where new pest control technology has been adopted, men take charge of the operation. Women's chores, such as transplanting, weeding, harvesting, winnowing, etc. continue to be handled by manual labour and without the benefit of improved technology. While men's tasks are more strenuous and intensive at the beginning of agricultural season, women are engaged in tasks requiring continuous attention through sequential operations that permit few rest periods. In areas where men have taken up wet-rice cultivation or have developed orchards, women continue to assume greater burden of *jhum* cultivation. This is also true in cases where men have shifted to non-agricultural occupations.

The productivity of *jhum* cultivation is generally low as a result of shorter *jhum* cycles. In non *jhum* areas also, agricultural yields are low due to non-application of improved technology and of essential inputs such as irrigation, fertilizers and pest-control measures. Considerable time and energy, therefore, have to be spent by women to supplement family food resources by collecting edible roots, tubers and fruits from the forests and fodder for animals. In some areas, e.g. Garo Hills, households have a right to collect vegetables and fruits from the fallow areas that were under cultivation in previous years. Furthermore, it is women's responsibility to grow vegetables in *jhum* fields or in kitchen gardens, raise poultry, pigs and cattle for family consumption or for sale in order to earn cash for buying other household requirements.

Cooking for the family without access to basic amenities such as electricity, gas or running water is an arduous task for women. Collecting water from springs or rivers and firewood from forests are primarily women's jobs and only in a few groups men share these tasks with women. Various programmes to provide water through gravity feed schemes connected to mountain springs or rivers, storage of rain water and bore-wells have been in progress under Central and State Governments auspices for over 25 years. In Mizoram, for instance, nearly 72 per cent of villages were covered under various schemes by 1988-89. Even then many villages are still without access to safe water. Even in villages that are technically "covered" at some time, it has not been easy to keep the installed schemes in working order, due to inadequate maintenance, difficult terrain and high per capita costs in scattered habitations. When nearby mountain springs dry up in winter months, bringing water from considerable distances over hilly terrain becomes a strenuous operation for women. At present a small proportion of population in urban areas has the luxury of a piped water supply for limited hours of the day. Many families even in the capital town of Shillong in Meghalaya have to collect water from stand-posts at some distance, or purchase water by cans from water-carriers at a high cost.

Similarly, access to electricity is still a distant dream for many rural households in the N-E region. As of 1981, less than one-fifth of rural households in six N-E States (Assam was excluded from the survey) had access to electricity.[7] The situation has improved since in all States, as noted in Chapter 2 and progressively more villages are being electrified. And yet, the old *dhenki* (a wooden husking instrument operated with a foot lever) and manually operated oil presses are still not uncommon. In some areas power-driven huller mills and oil mills are bringing a lot of relief to women living in areas accessible to towns. But for women living in isolated villages accessible only by footpaths up and down hilly terrains, such as in Arunachal Pradesh, living conditions continue to be fairly primitive. Many of these women start their day at early dawn when the menfolk and children are still asleep, bring water from mountain springs, husk paddy, and prepare a meal for the family and leave for *jhum* fields after feeding the family, which includes cattle. At the end of a full day, they collect vegetable and fodder for cattle and firewood for cooking, on their way home. They must again go out to bring water, husk paddy before cooking and feeding the family at night.

After harvest and before major festivals such as "Bihu" and similar celebrations connected with agricultural cycle, women get very busy preparing rice or millet beer (variously called *apong* or *ju*), mostly consumed by men and offered to guests as a part of normal hospitality. When there is some let up in the busy agricultural season, most N-E women occupy themselves in weaving clothing for the family. Every N-E

---

7. The percentages of rural households having electricity in 1981 were: Arunachal Pradesh 10.99, Manipur 10.28, Meghalaya 7.44, Mizoram 4.96, Nagaland 19.97, Tripura 16.52. Assam data not available since 1981 Census was not conducted in the State due to disturbed conditions. *Source: Census of India, 1981,* Occasional Paper No.1 of 1989.

State, and indeed every major community or tribe in some States such as Nagaland has its own distinctive designs and styles of dress. Besides weaving cotton and woollen fabrics, women in several areas rear two special varieties of silk cocoons called *endi* or *eri* and *muga* in addition to those reared on mulberry. Efforts are currently being made to introduce scientific methods of raising and processing cocoons and thus enhance their income. Traditionally, weaving as a means of meeting the clothing requirements of the family has been regarded in most N-E communities as an essential skill in women. Much more recently, weaving is beginning to be perceived as a secondary or supplementary occupation for women. At present many Mishing and Manipuri girls pay for their education by handloom weaving, and may also earn some support for their families. During the days of hunting and tribal warfare, a *Kabacha* (an apparel worn by men) woven by the wife in a single night was considered as a protective cover for the man to ensure his safety and success. Even today, a Karbi wife is expected to weave a particular garment for her husband before her first child arrives.

The spinning and weaving instruments used by N-E women to a large extent continue to be fairly simple and primitive, and the loin loom (on which women weave narrow strips which are joined later), the pit loom and their variations still predominate. In Assam and Manipur, women have quickly adapted to fly-shuttle looms, and even power looms with sophisticated accessories that have recently made their entry into a few places. A lot of mill-yarn is currently imported in the N-E region to meet the requirement of handlooms. At the same time in areas somewhat remote from urban centres, women still undertake all the operations from carding cotton, preparing hanks, spinning the yarn, dyeing and then weaving. The same is true of weaving woollen fabrics.

The entry of mill-made cloth and synthetic fabrics and readymade fancy garments from outside the N-E region is beginning to affect the demand for handloom products. Secondly, with the introduction of modern weaving technology, men entrepreneurs are entering this occupation. There are some indications that women who have so far been home-based independent weavers may be under pressure to work in large weaving centres as wage earners. There is therefore an urgent need to provide technical and organizational support for women weavers to improve the quality and competitiveness of their products. Otherwise the trend visible in some communities to give up weaving since it is no longer economically viable may become entrenched and a unique source of ethnic identity and creativity may be irretrievably lost.

There are several miscellaneous activities in which women assume major or minor responsibility, depending on local traditions. These include raising poultry, pigs, milch animals, tending kitchen gardens, transporting agricultural produce to markets and trading it for purchase of other essential goods, fishing, rope-making, preparing cane and bamboo baskets, pottery, salt manufacture, etc.

SECTION III
Property: Ownership, Inheritance and Autonomy Regarding Management of Resources

In the preceding section, we looked at the various economic activities in which N-E women are engaged. This section examines another dimension of their economic status: ownership of property, including the kinds of property, women's right to inherit property from father/husband, the degree of autonomy in making decisions regarding management of household resources and access to occupations for earning income. Wherever possible, changes and emerging trends in their position have been noted.

In the light of this framework, the economic position of women in each N-E State will be reviewed. The focus will be on broad patterns, which will be presented with examples from some major and representative communities within each State to the extent possible. Variations or exceptions to the general practice will also be pointed out as illustrations. Women's economic status is viewed here in the context of customary laws, most of which have not been codified, as well as social and cultural aspects that influence the choices available to them.

ARUNACHAL PRADESH

Most tribes in Arunachal Pradesh follow patriliny. Immovable property such as land is owned by men and sons inherit it from their fathers. Adi is a major tribe of this State which includes a number of sub-groups, such as Gallong, Slimong, Padam, Minyong, Pasi, Galo and many others. The Adi women do not own land nor can they inherit it from their fathers. Widows have a right to use it but cannot sell it. If the widow has no male issue, the property goes to other male heirs of the clan. A father may occasionally gift a piece of land to a daughter, as a favour. Similarly, a son who inherits his father's land may allot a piece to his widowed mother, but she cannot claim it as a right. The widow and the daughters are usually given some maintenance. If the widow re-marries anyone outside the husband's clan, she loses the right to use any of her deceased husband's property. A Tagin widow acquires a right to use her husband's property, but cannot sell it to anyone except the relatives of the deceased husband. Among the Singphos who have adopted Buddhism, in the absence of sons, a daughter may inherit father's property and the son-in-law comes to stay at the girl's house. But in the following generation, the son would inherit property from his mother. In recent years, some Apatani farmers have acquired individual ownership over sizeable lands and have become fairly affluent, thanks to government schemes for promotion of settled and improved agriculture. Some of them have been transferring a part of their property to their daughters, particularly if the latter are not adequately provided for by their husbands. (Chowdhury, 1989).

At the same time, most tribes respect women's exclusive right over gifts received from parents in marriage, particularly jewellery. For instance, among the Wanchos of Tirap district, a girl has complete ownership over the clothes, ornaments, a basket, a scraper, an iron digging stick, a *dao* (a big chopper) and a grass rain cover gifted by her parents. The weaving instruments are also regarded as women's personal possessions. Apart from these, women generally have complete freedom to spend income earned by them through supplementary activities, such as, raising poultry, cattle, pigs, selling vegetable, rice-beer, etc. While they can do all minor purchases, for major purchases such as land, Tibetan beads or a *mithun* ("Bos Frontalis" — a tamed bison, akin to a buffalo), they must obtain either the husband's or the clan's permission. Idu Mishmi, a tribe that inhabits Dibang valley, provides one of the few exceptions, as they permit both sons and daughters to inherit their father's property.

Another and certainly more humiliating aspect of women's status is the attitude of viewing a wife as a part of man's property. It is customary among chiefs (where chieftainship prevails, e.g. Mishmi, Wancho, Nocte) and affluent persons to have several wives because it enhances their social prestige since it reflects their economic ability to pay the requisite bride-price. Another variation of the same pattern is to have several wives in order to possess more human labour for the fields and for the household to produce more food, more "apong" (rice-beer) and attain a higher standard of living in general. An Aka husband with ability to pay the requisite bride-price can thus entertain his guests generously if he has access to more labour through his wives. Among the Nishis and Mishmis, when a man dies, his widows are distributed among the deceased man's brothers, sons and other male relatives without even the formality of a marriage, since the widows are regarded as part of the deceased man's property. The Taraon Mishmi word for marriage is "Miyabraiya," which literally means "buying of a woman" (Misra, 1982). The stark economic implication of this practice is that a woman seeking dissolution of a marriage or a widow intending to marry a person other than the deceased husband's clan member must first arrange to repay the bride-price to the husband or his clan in order to obtain her release.

Despite their low formal economic status, women enjoy considerable autonomy in the day-to-day running of the household. Even within the polygynous framework, for instance, each Nishi wife has a separate cultivation plot, a separate granary and her own hearth. She rears her own poultry, pigs and goats that she can dispose of as she wishes. Women of most tribes have their own personal income and move about freely to make daily purchases for the household. Generally wherever the terrain is difficult and dependence on women's labour is high, women tend to enjoy a better economic status within the household. For instance, among Nishi, Tangsa and Sulung tribes, women are reported to be fully responsible for family budgets, although they have no right to own or inherit immovable property. It is a matter for conjecture how women's relative autonomy in the household would be affected as supply of hired farm labour is becoming increasingly available.

Within the generally disadvantaged status of Arunachal women with respect to ownership and inheritance of property, one of the positive aspects is that they do not suffer from any social restrictions on pursuing any household-based or outside occupations. They have complete freedom to spend money earned through growing vegetables, rearing poultry, pigs, handloom weaving (which is exclusively done by women). As new towns are coming up with the expansion of government administration and educational and commercial institutions, women have been finding new opportunities for trading in vegetables and other agricultural products. A few occupations are traditionally pursued by women. For instance carpet-weaving is exclusively women's occupation among the Buddhist Monpa and Sherdukpen tribes of Kameng. Among the Noctes of Tirap, women work along with men in salt making and portering (Dutta, 1989). A few affluent Miri fathers have allocated lands to their daughters. These young women have taken up pig-rearing besides cultivating their lands and have emerged as successful entrepreneurs in their own right, (Chowdhury, 1989). As opportunities for education and vocational training increase, women are entering new jobs as teachers, nurses, and employees in growing government bureaucracies. A small number are working as doctors, engineers, road and building contractors and business entrepreneurs. As girls display their initiative and achieve economic independence, there is already a beginning of some rethinking and change among the relatively enlightened parents regarding the unjust customary laws denying women a right to own and inherit property. Particularly when sons tend to be lazy and irresponsible with parents' money, some parents are inclined to give their daughters a part of their property.

ASSAM

In view of Assam being a composite State until early 1960s, even after the separation of Nagaland, Meghalaya, Mizoram and Arunachal Pradesh, its present population includes people belonging to diverse cultural origins. Some of these groups have retained their original traditions with respect to ownership and inheritance of property and economic status of women. Some other groups, however, have changed their practices in varying degrees as a result of interaction with new influences in their present environment. The second major source of heterogeneity is the large number of Muslim peasants and Hindu refugees who migrated to Assam from East Bengal, and later Bangladesh, and retained their strong patriarchal and patrilineal traditions after settling down in Assam. A third source that adds to the variety of the cultural mix is the adoption of Hinduism by a number of ruling tribes of Assam, and later the advent of Christianity introduced by the missionaries. These aspects also contribute to Assam's unique demographic composition with tribal population being 12.83 per cent of the total as of 1991. The economic status of women of Assam can be better understood by grouping Assam's population into three major categories: (a) Non-tribal, (b) Hill-tribal, and (c) Plains tribal societies.

NON-TRIBAL SOCIETIES

Assamese Hindus, who form the majority of non-tribal population of the State, are quite similar to the mainstream Hindu society of the country in their patriarchal and patrilineal traditions. In the non-tribal societies of Assam, Ahom aristocracy and the upper-classes owned land while the "paiks" or the toiling classes had the limited right to cultivate the land allocated to them, but did not possess the right to inherit or transfer land. Even after the British introduced a new system of land settlement, women remained a dispossessed category. Women generally had no right to own or inherit land or other immovable property. While the brahmins, kayasthas, and upper classes followed the Hindu traditions more rigorously, some local departures from the strictly patriarchal norms continued to survive among other groups, mainly because of their non-Aryan tribal past (Thakuria, 1988). After Indian Independence, the Hindu Succession Act recognized the right of a widow, mother and daughter to inherit property along with the sons, and their absolute right over property owned. Similarly, the Hindu Adoption and Maintenance Act of 1956 assures the wife a right to maintenance from her husband, and confers on a widowed daughter-in-law the right to maintenance from her father-in-law. Nevertheless, the lack of consciousness among women about these rights, loopholes in their enforcement and the force of social customs have deprived women of the full enjoyment of these rights.

Even among women who are employed and have an independent income, the effective control over such income does not rest with them and is mostly in the hands of men. The upper caste families tend to be more conservative and allow their women less freedom to work outside the home than families belonging to lower castes (Saikia et al., 1986). In the case of women whose family situation forces them to leave their families and seek employment in urban centres, the difficulties of safe living accommodation as also the lack of adequate child-care facilities pose formidable problems.

The expansion of education is opening up newer employment avenues as teachers, nurses, subordinate services in offices, etc. and urbanization is acting as a liberating force. Some women, even if a small minority, are beginning to enter new careers as doctors, engineers, officers in Indian Administrative Service, research officers, etc. Their enhanced status enables them to participate actively in making financial decisions for the household. What is equally significant, they now have more opportunities to become financially self-reliant in case their family situation turns out to be totally unhappy.

Assamese Muslims constitute over a quarter of Assam's total population. According to Islamic tenets, a Muslim woman inherits property as daughter, as wife and as mother. She has a right to maintenance by her father when unmarried and by her husband after marriage. Her right to property is absolute. Even then, Assamese Muslim women rarely assert their rights due to fear of social disapproval. They are worse off than their Hindu counterparts because they are less educated and less conscious of their property rights. Among the relatively upper strata, the influence of "Purdah" or seclusion is stronger and consequently women have less freedom of movement outside the home and more restrictions on the choice of occupations. For instance, they cannot go out for work to agricultural fields, nor can they undertake petty trading and marketing as freely, as Muslim women from lower economic classes. A small number of Muslim women who have attained college and university education are breaking out of the traditional barriers and are trying to arouse consciousness of their rights among other Muslim women (Sherfuddin, 1988).

Women tea garden labourers constitute a separate group because of their geographic isolation in upper Assam districts of Sibsagar, Dibrugarh and Lakhimpur. These women work full-time in tea plantations, in addition to doing all the household chores including child-rearing. Although women's superior dexterity in plucking tea leaves is considered as asset by tea garden managements, they are paid lower wages than men. They have no effective voice in labour unions, which are dominated by men. However, women's major contribution towards family income and their active role in keeping the family together give them an important status in the household and they are consulted by men in major financial decisions. One wonders if their tribal background might have been conducive to their relatively positive economic status in the domestic sphere.[8]

HILL-TRIBAL SOCIETIES

The Karbis and Dimasas who constitute the major component of Assam's hill-tribal population are concentrated in the two hill districts of Assam, viz. Karbi Anglong and North Cachar Hills, respectively, although some are scattered in Nagaon district and a few in Nagaland. They restricts the

8. The tea garden labourers belong to Santhal, Oraon, Munda and other tribes and migrated to Assam from Bihar, Chota Nagpur, Madhya Pradesh and Orissa between 1870s and 1930s. In Assam they are classified as Other Backward Classes (OBCs)

right of ownership and inheritance of immovable assets to men primarily but do not completely exclude women. Both Karbi and Dimasa fathers occasionally gift a piece of land to a daughter out of affection, but not as a right. The Dimasas have parallel systems of patri-clans (called Sengphong) and matri-clans (called Jaddi, Julu or Juluk), and while sons inherit their father's property, daughters inherit mother's property that consists of ornaments, clothes, weaving instruments, utensils, etc. This is evidently a vestige of matriliny that has survived the determined efforts to eliminate female clans system made by brahmin preceptors patronized by Dimasa rulers since late eighteenth century. If there are no sons, parents' property is inherited by daughters. Even otherwise, there is no rule that forbids daughters to inherit a part of their father's property. In fact, there is an emerging trend among Dimasas to give a rather handsome share of parental property to daughters at the time of marriage, which indicates a departure from the prevailing custom. This is attributed to a recognition of the significant contribution daughters make toward their parents' household before marriage (Nunisa, 1989).

Both Karbi and Dimasa women take a larger share of work than men in agriculture, in addition to their multifarious household chores such as bringing water and firewood, husking rice, preparing rice-beer, cooking, child-rearing, etc. Even then, the cash earned by selling surplus agricultural products belongs to men. The personal income earned by raising poultry, rearing *endi* (a kind of silk), weaving, etc. and the gifts given by parents in marriage belong exclusively to women and they can use them in any way they wish. Women generally spend their income to meet some household requirements and only rarely on things for themselves. Despite women's subordinate formal position *vis-à-vis* men with respect to property, they are consulted by men in matters related to purchase and sale of property, even if men have the final word. Karbi women are traditionally custodians of family heirlooms.

Despite the strenuous routine of Karbi and Dimasa women, family incomes remain low and there have been very few new and viable occupational choices. According to a sample survey by Sikidar (1990), until recently, 88 per cent of the population of Karbi Anglong and 93 per cent of North Cachar Hills depended on *jhum* cultivation where yields are low. In the broader context of a serious general under-development, women's access to income-generating opportunities is restricted due to several reasons: poor progress of alternative land-use schemes, e.g.

plantations and fruit orchards; unremunerative and primitive modes of production, e.g. in sericulture and weaving; depleting forest-based resources; geographic isolation and poor communications, etc.[9] Sikidar has suggested various measures some of which are directly relevant for improving the economic condition of Karbi and Dimasa women. These include: attaining self-sufficiency in food through substituting jhuming by improved agriculture and plantations; mobilizing women, through formation of groups to help them earn better incomes by supplying improved looms, yarns and dyes; training for scientific sericulture and adoption of *muga* and mulberry instead of *eri*, introduction of a number of agro-based industries, such as manufacture of paper boards and fuel briquettes from agricultural waste, extraction of edible oil from rice bran, etc.

On the whole, Karbi women have fared much better than the Dimasas who have remained rather isolated from external influences. The former have attained a higher level of education and participate more actively in various developmental schemes promoted by the government. For instance, they are increasingly adopting the fly-shuttle looms in place of the old loin looms. Access to water from bore wells and power-driven rice hullers are beginning to reduce some of their drudgery. Previously, the only avenue of employment for Karbi women who had attained middle or high-school level was teaching in primary schools. Now some of them are opting for higher education and becoming nurses and doctors, and a few have risen to executive positions in State Government hierarchy. There are also examples of Karbi women setting up successful enterprises in handloom weaving.

PLAINS TRIBAL SOCIETIIES

The principal tribes included in this group are Bodo Kachari, Rabha, Lalung, Deori, Barmans of Cachar, Sonowal Kacharis, Mishing, while other smaller groups include Tai Phake, Aitones, both originating from Myanmar. With the exception of Lalungs, most plains tribal societies are patrilineal and permit sons alone to own and inherit immovable property from father. For instance, the major groups, viz. Bodo, Mishing, Deori, Sonowal Kachari, do not allow women to own or inherit land as a rule. A Mishing woman may inherit land and other property from her father only

9. For details on causes of underdevelopment, shortfalls in achievement and suggestions for accelerating development of Karbi Anglong and North Cachar Hills districts, refer to Sikidar's survey of these two districts in *Economic Development of Tribal India*, New Delhi: Ashish Publishing House, 1990.

if no male heir is available, or if she bears the expenses of her father's funeral (Roy Burman, 1990:20). However, as elsewhere in the N-E region, women earn a personal income through poultry keeping, animal husbandry, raising vegetables, etc. which they use freely for household purchases and local trading. Husbands would not normally sell animals raised by women without the latter's consent, and women are consulted in major financial transactions. Although women do not own or inherit land, their ritual association with productivity of the soil is recognized by ensuring their presence in major agricultural events.

Tai Phake and Aiton, both Tai-speaking and Buddhist groups that migrated from Myanmar, although patrilineal, give an important place to women in decisions with respect to household resources. Women are responsible for all buying and selling of forest produce, vegetables, firewood, etc. If a Tai Phake woman divorces her husband, she gets half of his property and custody of children. Sons inherit deceased father's property and only a part is given to the widow. If there is no son, daughters divide father's property among themselves.

The Lalungs, who inhabit parts of Karbi Anglong and Nagaon districts, continue to follow matrilineal succession. The youngest daughter usually inherits land and ancestral house, and other daughters get a share in the parents' property. Land leases are always in the names of women. The husband manages the property on behalf of the wife and cannot dispose off any of the property without the wife's consent. On the other hand, a Lalung wife usually consults her husband or his brothers if she wishes to sell any part of her property. If a Lalung woman marries a non-Lalung and leaves her parental house, she forfeits her right of inheritance. The Lalungs who live in hilly areas still follow matriliny and courts do not recognize a land lease in the name of a male. In the plains, however, exposure to neighbouring patrilineal communities and to Christianity are reportedly creating a shift towards patriliny, and men are beginning to inherit parental property.

The Rabhas, another plains tribal group concentrated in South Goalpara and Kamrup districts, also followed matrilineal system in the past, but are moving towards patriliny. Their customary law permits women to inherit property of deceased father, but this may not be upheld by institutional law. At present, daughters inherit parental property if there are no sons. Generally, if a woman owns matrilineally inherited land, daughters may inherit it, but they cannot claim it by right as in purely matrilineal societies. The present picture is very mixed and a woman may give even her matrilineally inherited property to her sons, whereas a father may divide his self-acquired landed property among his sons and daughters.[10] Furthermore, a daughter and her husband may give matrilineally inherited property to their sons in the next generation. A widow cannot dispose of valuable property, such as land, without the consent of the deceased husband's nearest relatives. She loses even the limited right over her deceased husband's property if she remarries (Barooah, 1989). A social organization of the Pati Rabhas has recently taken the initiative to compile customary laws and practices. Surprisingly, these leaders have remained silent on the transition from matrilineal to patrilineal inheritance, and indeed on the whole subject of inheritance, probably because of the prevailing disagreement and inconsistency in the Rabha community regarding permitting women to inherit property (Goswami, 1979).

Sonowal Kacharis, who had traditionally accorded an equal status to men and women, began to subordinate the status of women when they adopted Vaishnavism, along with Hindu caste culture. A number of restrictions were imposed on women's participation in various spheres. For instance, although women are engaged in fishing, weaving, making bamboo articles, etc. they are not involved in selling any of their products. Property, such as land, is inherited only by sons. Exposure to modernization and western education has, however, initiated a process of reform in the community since the 1960s. There is a trend towards parents permitting their daughters, along with the sons, to inherit the formers' property (Mitra, 1989).

In general, women of plains tribal societies seem to be influenced by two major forces with respect to occupational choices. On the one hand, the steady alienation of land has reduced many plains tribal households, e.g. the Bodos, to accept wage labour employment on other people's farms, or migrate to other States in search of casual labour employment at mines, dams or road construction sites. The women of these families are especially vulnerable to exploitation by middlemen and contractors.

10. For case histories on how parents passed on property to sons and daughters and order or precedence in customary laws of inheritance, refer to Law Research Institute, Guwahati, *The Customary Laws and Practices of the Pati Rabha of Assam, 1979.*

On the other hand, the need to supplement meagre family incomes by undertaking various activities, e.g. animal husbandry, weaving, trading in vegetables and other agricultural products, has endowed these women with considerable initiative.

With increasing access to education, vocational training and resources provided by welfare and development programmes sponsored by the government, many women have found employment as teachers, nurses, child welfare workers, auxiliaries in rural and agricultural extension services etc. There are a small number of women working as doctors, officers in banks and government departments, engineers, lawyers, etc. among the Bodos, Mishing and Lalungs. It is truly remarkable that some women among the Barmans of Cachar, Sonowal Kacharis and a few other groups have established business ventures, such as pig farms, weaving, knitting and sewing centres, poultry farms, etc. While the number of these enterprising women is small, other women are bound to be inspired by them. Even at present, a number of Mishing girls are not only earning money to pay for their education, but provide support to their families. Mishing wives rear *endy* and other silk worms, poultry, pigs, spin yarn and weave and earn a substantial part of the family income and may even plough the field in the absence of men. As has been noted, women in most plains tribal societies do not own or inherit land and other immovable property. And yet, they are by no means meek and submissive and enjoy a respected place in the family. The factors contributing to this favourable position will be explored in Chapter 4. There is no doubt that if proper technical and infrastructural support is provided through government schemes, the innate spirit of enterprise and capacity for hard work should enable these women to make rapid strides in improving their economic autonomy.

MANIPUR

The situation of women in Meitei community, which constitutes a preponderating majority of the population of Manipur, and even more so in the central valley, presents some mixed elements in their economic roles and status. When Meitei rulers adopted Vaishnavite Hinduism in the early eighteenth century, and expected their subjects to follow suit, they also accepted the strongly patriarchal and patrilineal aspects of Hinduism. At the same time, they have retained some elements of the indigenous Meitei traditions. Thus, the right to own and inherit immovable property is primarily limited to men, but with some concessions to women. Generally a provision is made for the widow and daughters in a man's property. The syncretic practice of Hindu and Meitei cultures operates in yet another aspect. A daughter usually inherits mother's property, and may also get the mother's market stall, if the latter owned one (Chaki Sarkar, 1984). This practice may be explained by the simultaneous presence of both patriliny and matriliny in the pre-Hindu Meitei society (Tikoo, 1988). Although a wife cannot claim any share of husband's property while he is alive, a widow has a right to maintenance out of the property of her son. If a married woman acquires immovable property as an heir of her deceased father, she can use it in her lifetime. After her death, it goes to her son. She has absolute right only over property gifted by her parents or other relatives at the time of marriage or after the marriage and whatever she has purchased with money earned by her through her work (Raghumani, 1988).

Within the mainly patriarchal framework, Meitei women have managed to create a stronghold of power through their unique organizational skills. They form a number of "marups" or "Nupi-Palas" — women's associations, which give them a collective identity and enable them to overcome hurdles that are difficult to deal with individually. For example, their associations can bulk purchase raw materials such as yarn for weaving, send finished products to urban markets, obtain loans, and the like. Meitei women form co-operative teams with other women for performing various agricultural operations, rice husking, fishing, etc. Besides taking their full share of burden in family cultivation and housekeeping, Manipuri women have a strong tradition of active involvement in trading and commerce. There are sections in Manipur markets which are dominated by women who are members of several associations and handle retail as well as wholesale trade and commerce in local agricultural produce, groceries, woven materials, small carpentry items, etc. These women gave evidence of their solidarity and determination in the recent past when they refused to vacate their place in Thangal Bazar in Imphal (the State capital) to make room for a bank building until alternate market space was assured.

Several Meitei women provide a major source of income for their households and education of their children. Many young girls do weaving to pay for their education. Some educated girls take up jobs in towns and regularly send money to their parents who live in rural areas. Ironically, despite Meitei women's vigorous economic participation, men's writ prevails with respect to all major financial decisions in the household. Women from upper middle and affluent classes have less economic freedom than women from lower classes. Whether a girl will continue with her job after marriage depends on the wishes of the husband and in-laws. Meitei women from lower income groups have more freedom in pursuing an occupation and overcome to some extent the handicaps that stem from weak individual status in the family through their organizational strength. Meitei women are benefiting from a number of governmental schemes such as Development of Women and Children in Rural Areas (DWCRA) by starting new enterprises such as weaving centres, poultry units, cane and bamboo crafts, tailoring and embroidery, etc. They are receptive to adopting new technology, such as fly shuttle looms for weaving.

The tribal communities who inhabit the hill areas of Manipur follow their original strongly patriarchal and patrilineal Naga and Kuki traditions. Immovable property is owned by men and inherited by men in these groups. The Rongmei, a major kindred group of Zeliangrong Nagas, however, make a small concession to women in that if there are no sons, a father may give his land to his daughters as marriage gifts. Even when there are sons, in a few cases a Rongmei father may gift a piece of paddy land to a daughter, but not by way of a right. Among the Hmars, a Kuki group, women have no right to own property, and if there are no sons, the deceased man's land does not go to his widow, but to other male heirs in the clan.

Among the Tarao and Moyon communities, both of which are currently identified with the Naga groups, women take the major burden of *jhum* cultivation, but they have no right to own or inherit property, and have to be content with a symbolic gesture, probably to compensate for the lack of real status. A woman initiates the harvesting operation by cutting the first few stalks and stores the first basket in the granary for good omen. The reason why a Moyon woman cannot own or inherit property is strange, to say the least. When a Moyon woman marries, she is believed to be losing affiliation with her parent's clan, and she does not acquire her husband's clan affiliation after marriage. She is thus devoid of membership of any clan which makes her unfit to own or inherit property. It is surprising that the women of tribal communities of Manipur have not been influenced much by the enterprising spirit of the majority Meitei women. For instance, a Tarao woman may do weaving in her home, but cannot do any trading in finished products. The advent of Christianity and access to modern education have, however, been acting as progressive forces. There are signs of an emerging self-awareness among women of these communities and with education, new avenues of employment are opening out for women. Some Moyon women have become preachers and teachers. Some Rongmei women are now employed as doctors, nurses, and some have joined government service as judicial magistrates and a few have set up their own businesses. There are indications that women from a few tribal communities are becoming conscious of the inequities to which they have been subjected, and are beginning to raise their voices to demand a fairer deal.

MEGHALAYA

In the N-E region, Meghalaya continues to be one of the few surviving bastions of matriliny despite many kinds of stresses to which the system is exposed due to current economic and socio-cultural changes. Our presentation here will be focused on economic aspects of matriliny as it has functioned traditionally for women of the three major communities of Meghalaya — Khasi, Jaintia and Garo. In essence, a daughter inherits ancestral property from her mother, and children acquire their lineage and clan name from the mother. The Bhoi and Biate are the only exceptions to the rule, both groups being patrilineal, where sons inherit ancestral property, but daughters also get some shares. Among the Khasis and Jaintias, usually the youngest daughter, referred as the *Khadduh*, inherits major part of the ancestral property, e.g. the living house, lands and other family heirlooms from her mother. If she remains unmarried or has no female issue, her sister's daughter may succeed her. Among the Jaintias, in case the youngest daughter dies, and her sister or another substitute in the closest family branch is not available, the youngest son inherits the ancestral property. Among the Garos the male elders of the *Mahari,* i.e. closely related blood relatives within the mother's clan, select one of the daughters on the basis of her capability, to be the *Nokna* (meaning one who stays in the house to inherit the property). However, it is not unusual for sons to get some shares. It is customary for parents to gift pieces of land and other articles to daughters other than the heiress when they marry and help them set up their separate homes if they do not stay in the ancestral house. The daughter who inherits is perceived as a custodian of the property and not the sole owner, and has the obligation to provide care and sustenance not merely for her children but also aged parents, uncles and aunts, in fact any clan relative who is needy or destitute.

Although women in Meghalaya own and inherit property from their mothers, effective control over the property is exercised by men. Among the Khasis and Jaintias, the *Khadduh's* maternal uncle, brothers and parents, if living, constitute the family council that decides how the property is to be managed. The *Khadduh* cannot sell any of the lands or other property without the consent of the family council. Among the Garos, the *Mahari's* approval must be obtained before any action regarding the property is taken. The husband's role varies somewhat among the three communities. Among the Khasis, when the *Khadduh* marries, her husband comes to stay at her house and shares the decision-making powers regarding the wife's ancestral property with other males in the family council, his role generally being secondary to that of the council. The Jaintia husband visits his wife only at night and returns to his mother for the day. His role in the management of the wife's ancestral property is insignificant and responsibility towards maintenance of his children somewhat marginal. Among the Garos, the son-in-law comes to stay at his wife's house and manages her ancestral property on her behalf, of course with the consent of the *chras* (male maternal relations of the *Nokna*). In theory, the husband must consult the *nokna* before he can sell any part of the property including lands. In practice however since the wife's role is primarily centred in the household sphere and since average Garo women are not adequately educated and conscious of their rights, the husband often assumes a dominant position. Cases are reported where a husband squanders away the wife's property while the wife, who already takes the major burden of work in cultivation and the household, has to take up all kinds of extra jobs requiring physical labour to support her family. On the other hand, the *Nokna*, supported by the *Chras* may institute a legal proceeding against the husband objecting to his misuse of property, and the *Chras* normally represent her in the court.

Apart from the traditional family role perceptions, marriage customs also restrain women's ownership of property. If a Khasi or Jaintia woman marries a non-Khasi or non-Jaintia man and leaves the ancestral house, both she and her children forfeit the right to ancestral property. During the British rule, some British administrators had tried to confer on women the right to sell any of the ancestral property if they wished, but local leaders stoutly opposed such attempts. In recent years there have been court cases when the *Khadduh* has tried to sell any part of the ancestral property. In fact, Khasi women have faced opposition whenever they wanted to sell any lands even out of their personal property, i.e. lands or other possessions gifted to them by parents in marriage over which women are supposed to have an absolute right.

The matrilineal system of Meghalaya has recently come under attack from some quarters, particularly from men who believe that the practice of women holding ancestral property has been one of the major causes of economic stagnation and lack of entrepreneurial development in the State. The protagonists point out that in several cases where Khasi women have married non-Khasi men from patrilineal cultures, the husbands have usurped their wives' property and have abandoned them. The social pressures, which make it difficult for parents to gift or bequeath any of their property to their sons, are regarded as an impediment in helping the sons to set up a business or prepare themselves for a career, thus resulting in a general demoralization among men. A new legislation — the Meghalaya Succession to Self-Acquired Property (Khasi and Jaintia Special Provision) Act, 1984 — was therefore enacted by the State Government. It confers on Khasi and Jaintia men and women the right to distribute their self-acquired property according to their wishes by making a will. This is seen by some as a means of minimizing at least partially the inequity to which sons are subjected since Khasi and Jaintia customs do not permit inheritance of ancestral property by sons. A different view, presented among others by Nongbri (1988), is that the Succession Act weakens the position of women further, because it provides the husband a means of denying any part of his self-acquired property to his wife by passing all of it to his sons by a will. It is claimed that this makes her more vulnerable especially in view of all the onerous kinship and religious obligations customarily placed on her.

Although effective control over ancestral property remains with men, Khasi and Jaintia women do have complete freedom with respect to day-to-day household expenditures. Besides, in view of the *Khadduh's* role as custodian of the family property, she has some access to cash and other property for meeting expenditures for such matters as weddings, household rituals and funerals, etc. Although she cannot sell any part of the ancestral property without the consent of the family council, she and her sisters have control over possessions, including land, acquired by them as gifts or shares in the family's self-acquired (as distinct from ancestral) property. The matrilineal tradition and the responsible position assigned to women in the family and religion seem to have endowed women of Meghalaya with a high level of initiative. They feel free to undertake any work, jointly with their husbands or independently, to support the family. The matrilineal system requires the husband to remain loyal and responsible firstly to his mother's family including his sisters, and only secondly to his children and wife. This is also believed to be an important factor in making women unusually self-reliant and motivated for ensuring sustenance of the family and education of their children. On the other hand, this situation is believed to result in low self-esteem, irresponsible work attitude and a high prevalence of alcoholism among Meghalaya men.

Traditionally, Khasi-Jaintia women have enjoyed complete freedom in selecting any occupation of their choice. Besides *jhum* cultivation, women are engaged in sericulture, animal husbandry, spinning and weaving, trading in products of *jhum* cultivation, fruits, vegetables, betel-nuts, etc. With the advance of urbanization and better access to education and vocational training, women are increasingly finding entry into professions like teaching, medicine, civil service, secretarial positions as well as new businesses like construction, transport, tailoring, sale of books, stationery, video cassettes, etc. Growth of new towns, particularly Shillong after Indian Independence, first as capital of composite Assam and later of Meghalaya, has opened new and varied trades for Khasi women. Running tea stalls and restaurants, selling cane and bamboo articles, serving tea and snacks in offices, etc. provide lucrative occupations for many women. They have also been engaged in raising cash crops like potatoes, pineapples, oranges, betel-nuts, etc. It is reported that several of these trades are dominated by women (Sen, Saha and Mukherjee, 1982). The daily routine of many of these women, however, is a hard and long grind, starting at the crack of dawn and trudging 10-15 km up and down the hilly paths carrying baskets laden with vegetables or fruits to markets in Shillong and other towns. With the money they earn, daily necessities for the family, not to forget tobacco for the smoking pleasure of their husbands, must be purchased before their long trek back home at the end of the day, to begin cooking and feeding the family. In comparison with the Khasi-Jaintia women, Garo women are less educated, and have lacked exposure to new opportunities and motivation for improving their economic prospects. With the spread of education and adoption of Christianity, they too are entering new occupations. As they attain greater economic independence, their status with respect to economic as well as other decision-making in the family is beginning to improve (Marak, 1992).

The women of Meghalaya thus represent a unique situation where matriliny confers on them the right to own and inherit property, and yet systems of kinship and traditional definitions of gender roles have conspired to take away from them effective control, and placed it in the hands of men.

MIZORAM

Mizoram is one State in the N-E region that is characterized by a high degree of similarity in customs and social practices among its various tribes. As discussed in Chapter 2, this is explained by the Lushai political and cultural dominance over other tribes since the nineteenth century. Traditional Mizo culture is highly patriarchal and does not allow women to own land or other immovable assets, or inherit these from fathers or husbands. When a man dies, his youngest son usually inherits the former's property. In the absence of a son, the property passes on to the deceased person's brother or another nearest male relative. As a rule women are not involved in major financial decisions. In recent times, however, some change is noticed in this pattern. If the son happens to be unworthy for any reason, parents may pass on their property to daughters by making a will (Thomas, 1993). There are a few exceptional situations where women have access to the husband's property. If a husband abandons his wife and children, the wife retains the husband's property and assumes charge as the head of the household. In case he returns, the wife can decide whether to accept him. Furthermore, if a husband proves himself unworthy, or becomes incapacitated, the wife takes over his role and manages his property. If the husband turns her out of the house, she cannot claim alimony or maintenance from him.

A woman has right of ownership only on the possessions gifted to her by her parents at the time of her marriage, like clothes, baskets, weaving instruments, cash, etc. referred as *thuam* or dowry. In the past she had right also over the bride-price given by the husband, but this custom has eroded considerably in course of time. Although most of the Mizo marriages are solemnized in a church according to Christian ceremonies at present, traditional customs still govern divorces, separation, re-marriages, etc.

Mizo customary law lists 10-15 types of divorces (Nag, 1993) prescribing obligations of both parties to a marriage. However, the major trend is to absolve the husband of responsibility for giving the separated wife alimony or maintenance. If the husband divorces his wife, she retains right over the possessions gifted by her parents. However, if the divorce is due to her adultery, or is initiated by her, she loses her right even over her own possessions. If the wife is without any children at the time of divorce, and if the divorce is initiated by her, she has to return the bride-price paid by the husband. On the other hand if she has any children, these automatically belong to the husband, who can divorce her and pay only a pittance, if at all, as compensation. For more than 15 years, Mizo women have been protesting through organizations like MHIP (Mizo Hmeichhe Insuihkhawm Pawl) against the customary laws that deny them rights to own and inherit property and claim maintenance from a divorcing husband.

The disadvantaged economic position of Mizo women needs to be viewed in the context of a cultural role expectation that holds them fully responsible for day-to-day purchases for the household, care of children, in addition to their heavy involvement in *jhum* cultivation, the productivity of which is fairly low. Faced with this situation, Mizo women have always been engaged in a variety of economic activities, e.g. poultry and pig rearing, growing vegetables, collecting edible roots, fodder and firewood from forests, handloom weaving, etc. Whenever necessary and possible, they sell products of such activities in order to earn money with which they purchase other requirements of the household. The money so earned is treated as their own and they have full discretion to spend it according to their wishes.

With the growth of urban centres, trade and commerce and expansion of government bureaucracies, Mizo women have been quick to seize all possible avenues of earning money. They can be seen in the business of running tea stalls, restaurants, video cassette parlours, tailoring shops, transport contracts, in addition to new professions like teaching, health services, and secretarial services. A small number are working as officers in government departments, doctors, police officers, radio artists, research scientists, etc. The struggle to get a foothold in a field which has so far been exclusively male-dominated has, however, been tough. For instance, in 1986, out of a total of 24,029 government employees, only 4,303, i.e. 18.26 per cent were women, and most of them — 4287 — belonged to subordinate categories (*Statistical Handbook, Mizoram*, 1987).

The low level of industrialization of Mizoram limits employment opportunities in general, and specially for women. A hopeful beginning in promoting the growth of small and cottage industries was made during the decade following 1987 when Mizoram attained full Statehood, as discussed in Chapter 2. This is likely to open new prospects for women in fruit and vegetable processing, horticulture, plantations, and several handicrafts. An all-India Handloom Census in 1987-88 had revealed that out of a total of 1,03,794 handlooms in Mizoram, only 7.2 per cent were used for commercial purposes (Mazumdar, 1999). Mizo women have recently been setting up a few commercial handloom enterprises. With the newly established Mizoram Handloom and Handicrafts Development Corporation, there are better prospects of providing technical and financial support to handloom weavers. Fortunately, Mizo women enjoy full freedom in choosing their occupations. With their capacity for hard work and excellent enterprising spirit, they can be expected to seize any new economic opportunities that become available, provided they receive consistent and qualitative back-up support from the State Government.

NAGALAND

Naga tribes, as a rule, do not permit women right of ownership to immovable property like land, nor can women inherit the property of their fathers or husbands. The Zeliangrong (a composite group consisting of Zemei, Liangmei and Rongmei tribes), Tangkhul, Mao, Sema, Lotha, are illustrations of this rule. There are, however, some variations with respect to access to deceased husband's property for widows, ownership of land by women in exceptional cases, as well as women's right of ownership over dowry given by their parents at the time of marriage. According to customary law, sons inherit deceased father's property. However, a father may gift some land to his unmarried daughter, which reverts to her brother after her marriage. In exceptional cases a daughter may be allowed to keep the land after marriage during her lifetime. After her death, the land goes to her sons, and if she has no sons, the land reverts to her father or brother. Generally, women cannot own land unless they have bought it with their own personal income, and even then they cannot bequeath it as they please. After their death, the land automatically goes to their sons or other male heirs.

Most Naga tribes permit widows to use the deceased husband's property as long as they remain in the latter's household. Among the Semas, a widow is entitled to one-third of the deceased husband's movable property, if she does not re-marry and if she continues to stay in the deceased husband's household. She receives the benefit of free labour to which her husband was entitled, for three years, after which she may get free labour as a courtesy, but not by right. If the widow marries one of the husband's heirs, she can use all of her deceased husband's property during her lifetime (Zhimomi, 1988). Similarly, even though a Mao daughter has no right to her parent's immovable property, a Mao widow enjoys some rights over her deceased husband's property (Mao, 1988). Among the Lothas, a widow can use all of her deceased husband's property in her capacity as its custodian and as a person responsible for care of children. In traditional Lotha community gambling was a popular pastime for men and since their concept of property included wives, men would put a bet on their wives, and the winner had a right to keep the loser's wife for a certain agreed period (Tungoe Mhathing, 1988). The degraded status of Lotha women is reminiscent of Draupadi — the tragic heroine of *Mahabharat* — on whom the Pandavas lost a bet in a game of dice.[11] Happily, with the spread of education and modernization, this practice is reported to be on the way out. B.P. Misra (1982) has cited a late nineteenth century case of an Ao girl of 16 years who was deserted by her husband, and who was enslaved by a man because her father owed this man a debt of Rs. 2.50 for purchasing a pig.

In short, Naga women do not have the right to own or inherit property, nor do they participate in major economic decisions in the family. Probably to compensate for this, they have complete authority over the domestic sphere and are free to make daily household purchases. They may earn a small income through household activities such as poultry keeping, pig rearing, handloom weaving, etc. and can use such income according to their wishes. They have complete ownership over the gifts parents may give them in marriage, e.g. baskets, handlooms, clothes, ornaments, etc. Among some tribes, like the Konyaks, mothers' personal possessions go to their daughters. In general the Nagas tend to condone adultery among men. But if a wife is found to be guilty of adultery, she gets a heavier

11. This refers to the horrendous event in *Mahabharata*, the famous Indian epic, where the Kauravas, assisted by a scheming uncle who loaded the dice in a chess duel with the Pandavas, managed to win everything the latter possessed, their kingdom as well as their wife and queen Draupadi.

punishment and may forfeit even the limited right of ownership of property. For instance, if a Sema husband divorces his wife on grounds of infidelity or incompatibility within three years of marriage, the wife forfeits her ornaments received as gifts from parents, besides having to return the bride-price paid by the husband (Zhimomi, 1988).

While Naga women do not suffer from restrictions regarding choice of occupations they may select, the general underdevelopment of Nagaland seriously limits their employment opportunities. Although expansion of education and adoption of Christianity have acted as significant liberating forces for Naga women, their representation in higher education and vocational and professional training continues to be inadequate. Parents still give a higher priority to boy's education. At the same time, there is a trend to prefer educated and working daughters-in-law as this improves the standard of living of the family (Hunibou, 1988). Among tribal groups having a higher level of female education, e.g. Ao, Tangkhul, Mao, women are entering new fields, for example in teaching, nursing, medicine, Indian Administrative Service, etc. Some women have set up business ventures in handloom weaving. The number of women with professional or business careers is small, partly because of parents' poor economic condition, but also since their conservative attitudes tend to dampen women's initiative. To some extent, women's mobility is also restricted due to disturbed conditions caused by insurgency. However, with greater urbanization and social interaction with other societies, Naga women are beginning to venture into newer occupations and careers.

TRIPURA

Among the major tribes of Tripura, the general rule is to deny women a right to own or inherit land and other immovable property from their fathers or husbands. The Tripuris and Jamatias, however, make a small concession to widows and daughters. Tripuri fathers may give a small portion of land to their daughters if they wish or if the daughters demand it. But the sons always get the maximum share through inheritance from fathers. Widows may be given a nominal share in the deceased husband's property (Chakraborty, 1993). A Jamatia father may give one-eighth portion of land to a daughter if he wishes. When he dies, his unmarried daughters and the widow get a share of land for their maintenance, while the major part goes to his sons. In case a Jamatia man dies without having any children, his property remains in the possession of his widow, but if she re-marries, the property goes to close relatives of the deceased husband (Mandal, 1993).

Among other tribes, like Reang, Halam, Noatia, Mizo-Lushai, etc. the deceased father's property goes exclusively to the sons. Among Kukis and Mizos, the articles given by parents to their daughters at the time of marriage, like weaving implements, ornaments, clothes, baskets, and such other gifts are considered as the daughter's personal possessions and husbands have no right over these in general. Among the Mughs, who originally came from Myanmar, the eldest son inherits half of his father's property, while the eldest daughter inherits half of her mother's property, which consists of ornaments. The remaining half of the father's and mother's property is shared among the other sons and daughters (Choudhary, 1993).

Although Tripura's tribal women were generally denied right to own and inherit land and other immovable property, they had traditionally enjoyed some degree of economic security and autonomy within the family due to communal ownership of land and forests and their substantial role in *jhum* cultivation. Several recent developments have, however, deteriorated their economic status. The policies adopted initially by Tripura kings and later by State Government encouraged large scale occupation of lands by Bengali settlers, besides fraudulent transactions by unscrupulous traders and moneylenders resulting in eviction of tribal groups from their lands (Mukherjee and Singh, 1982). Furthermore, State Government schemes to stop jhuming and to promote settled cultivation have resulted in eliminating communal ownership of lands and forests from which tribal households obtained their subsistence (Ganguly, 1990). Some lands have been shifted from community to individual ownership which generally have been claimed by men. In many cases where questions of ownership and succession have remained unresolved since most customary laws have not been codified, local community leaders who are always men, have been left with the discretion to decide on contentious issues. Where women have tried to assert their rights over land traditionally cultivated by their households, intimidation and devious means are frequently adopted to suppress their rights (Dasgupta, 1993).

Wherever a shift from jhuming to settled cultivation has taken place, the role of tribal women has become secondary. Furthermore, with rapid denudation of forests and government policies of reserving large forest areas, tribal women's access to edible forest products and firewood has been severely limited, thereby eroding women's substantial contribution towards family's subsistence. Supplementary activities such as raising vegetables, rearing of poultry and pigs, handloom weaving, cane and bamboo crafts provide only modest earnings. Tripura's industrial growth being negligible, there has been little scope for employment in industrial sector. The low educational level of tribal women and lack of vocational skills provide few opportunities in salaried employment. A small number of Lushai women who have received education in Christian missionary institutions have been working as teachers, extension workers in government programmes and as health professionals. Presently, considerable potential in horticulture, plantation crops, pisciculture, animal husbandry and handicrafts remains unutilized due to want of technical and financial support. If this is developed, it could provide substantial employment both for tribal and non-tribal women, and thus give them some degree of economic autonomy.

While Tripura's tribal women's economic status is unsatisfactory, non-tribal women, who constitute a preponderant majority, are worse off because of the dominance of patriarchal Bengali Hindu culture. Their participation in economic activities is much less and a girl child is regarded as a liability by parents because of the practice of demanding dowry by the groom's party. Girls face discrimination in access to education and vocational preparation at the hands of parents and boys receive a preferential treatment. Non-tribal women have less freedom to participate in economic activities outside the family and much less voice in economic decision-making within the household. A small number of women who have received education and vocational or professional training are employed as teachers, health auxiliaries, research workers, secretaries in government offices, and a smaller number as doctors, professors, officers in civil service and the like. Unfortunately, Tripura is devoid of a strong tradition of entrepreneurship that explains the relative absence of independent business and industrial ventures among women.

OVERVIEW

Economic status of N-E women has been analysed from three perspectives presented in three sections. Section 1 examines their work participation on the basis of Indian Census classification. The Work Participation Rates WPRs as well as percentages of main workers (as distinguished from marginal workers) among women for 1991 in five N-E States, viz. Arunachal Pradesh, Manipur, Meghalaya, Mizoram and Nagaland, were significantly higher than the average for India as a whole, but in Assam and Tripura, both having a predominantly non-tribal population, these were lower (21.61 and 13.76 per cent, respectively). Within the N-E region, however, in four States the 1991 female WPRs and percentages of female main workers showed a decline from the 1981 situation. In Tripura and Mizoram, on the other hand, there was an increase in percentages of female main workers in 1991 (Assam 1981 data not available). In spite of this mixed picture, in comparison with some larger states in India (e.g. Punjab, W. Bengal, Uttar Pradesh, Kerala, Bihar, Haryana), the female WPRs in five N-E States were much higher than the Indian average, 22.27 per cent.

Chart I : Female Work Participation Rates in India and N-E States, 1991

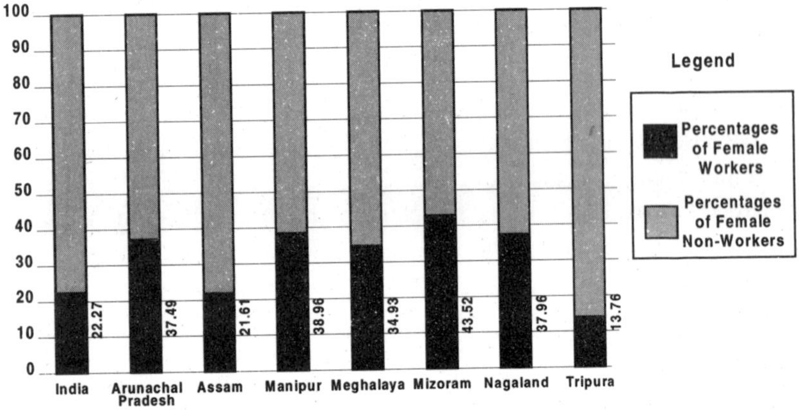

As regards the distribution of women main workers in production sectors in 1991, nearly two-thirds and above (over 72 per cent) in all seven N-E States were engaged in the primary sector, which is consistent with the national pattern. Women main workers engaged in the secondary sector constitute a much lower percentage than the national average, except in Manipur. A hopeful trend is the slow but definite increase in women's employment in the tertiary sector, particularly in Meghalaya, Mizoram and Tripura. This is explained by an increasing number of women in N-E States employed in educational, health and community development fields, secretarial jobs and occupied in various trades and small business enterprises, predominantly in urban areas. An overwhelming majority of women workers in the N-E region are engaged in the unorganized sector, like in India as a whole.

Chart II : Distribution of Female Main Workers in Production Sectors for India and N-E States in 1991

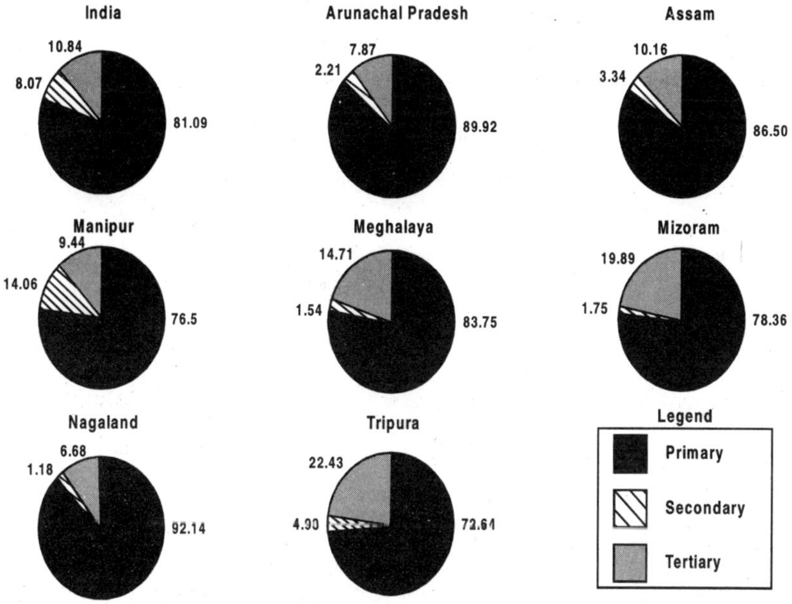

In terms of distribution of female main workers into cultivators and agricultural workers and other categories, the percentages of cultivators are higher than those of agricultural labourers in all N-E States, which indicates their better economic status, as compared to the situation in India as a whole. The percentages of agricultural labourers are significantly smaller in six N-E States. In several Indian States, e.g. Andhra Pradesh, Bihar, Kerala, Orissa, Tamil Nadu and W.Bengal, the situation is reverse, with larger percentages of agricultural labourers and smaller ones for cultivators. (see note 5). As compared to the situation in 1981, in five out of six N-E States, the percentages of cultivators among female main workers declined and those of agricultural labourers increased (Assam data for 1981 not available), which shows a negative trend in the economic status of N-E women.

Another observation with respect to the relative involvement of men and women in family cultivation highlights N-E women's heavier involvement than that of men. For India as a whole, the percentage of men cultivators among total main workers for 1991 was 39.63 and for women, 34.22. In six N-E States, the percentages of women cultivators

Chart III : Distribution of Female Main Workers into Cultivators, Agricultural Labourers
and Other Categories in India and N-E States, in 1991

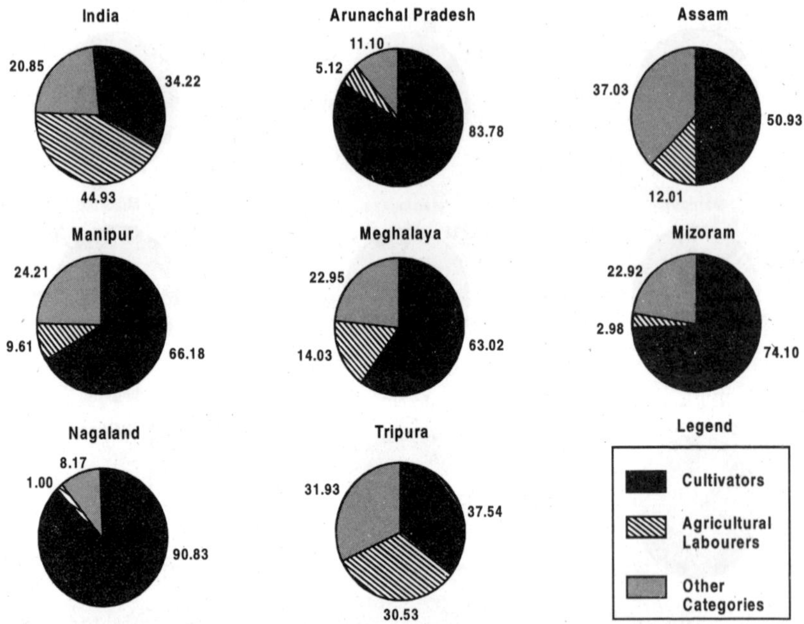

among female main workers are higher than those for men for 1991 and in Tripura, it is smaller by less than one per cent. This highlights N-E women's higher involvement in family cultivation, as compared to men. It is also explained by another factor. When men migrate to cities or to other States in search of more lucrative employment, women often end up taking on a heavier burden for family cultivation, besides their already major burden of household duties, so they have much lesser mobility as compared to men.

Section II looks at the multifarious tasks N-E women perform in addition to their main pre-occupation with agriculture, particularly *jhum* cultivation where they assume a major burden. Since the yields are generally insufficient to meet family requirements, women have to undertake many time-consuming and strenuous tasks to supplement their meager resources, which are not included in the Census definition of work, e.g. collecting edible roots and tubers, fodder for cattle and firewood for cooking besides bringing water over hilly terrain. Since they

Chart IV : Comparative of Cultivators Among Male & Female Main Workers in India and North-East States 1991

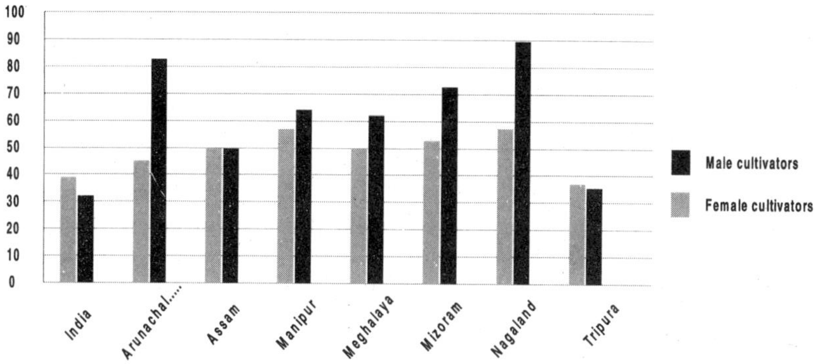

need cash to purchase some essential household requirements, they raise poultry, pigs and other animals, raise vegetables both for family consumption and for small trading. Many women are engaged in petty trading in fruits, vegetables, betel nuts, eggs, groceries, etc. in order to supplement household resources. Other means of income are: handloom weaving, sericulture, cane and bamboo crafts, most of which use rather primitive tools involving considerable time and effort and yet the profits are meager. A majority of N-E women undertake these type of activities in addition to their daily preoccupations like cooking, cleaning and feeding the family, child-care, feeding the cattle, which are undertaken for the most part without the benefit of running water, gas or electricity.

Section III analyses the extent to which N-E tribal women possess the right to own and inherit property, particularly immovable property such as land and living house. Except Meghalaya, women in N-E communities cannot own or inherit father's or husband's property after the latter's death and only sons and other male heirs have this right. In a few cases, a widow is allowed to use the deceased husband's property to maintain herself and her children, although she is not the owner, and after her death, the property goes to male members of the husband's clan. Even this limited right is withdrawn in case she re-marries a man belonging to another clan than her husband's. A small number of communities such as the Lalungs and Pati Rabhas who in the past had matrilineal traditions seem to be shifting towards patriliny as a result of surrounding social influences. On the other hand, some communities like the Meiteis of Manipur continue their matrilineal traditions whereby a daughter generally inherits her mother's possessions, like ornaments or a market stall. Women's property is limited to the few articles received from their parents in marriage, e.g. some agricultural tools, clothes, household articles, a handloom, ornaments, etc. Generally, women have exclusive right over money earned by them through supplementary activities such as handloom weaving, raising poultry, vegetables, etc.

The three matrilineal communities of Meghalaya — Khasis, Jaintias and Garos — provide an exception to the strongly patrilineal traditions among N-E communities. In these three groups, one of the daughters, usually the youngest, is chosen to inherit ancestral property including lands, the living house and other possessions from her mother. She continues to live in her parent's house after marriage and is joined by her husband. The girl who inherits — *Khadduh* among Khasi-Jaintias and *Nokna* among the Garos — however does not enjoy absolute right over disposal of the property and is expected to abide by the advice and decisions taken by the family council consisting of her maternal uncles, brothers and other maternal kins besides her husband. Other daughters are assisted through gifts of land and property to set up their own homes after their marriage if they do not wish to live in the ancestral house. Within this broad framework, the Khasi-Jaintia inheritress enjoys some autonomy to spend money on traditional ancestral and religious obligations and day-to-day expenditures. In comparison, the Garo inheritress (*Nokma*) is in a weaker situation, and all decisions are taken by the family council or by her husband who also enjoys the position of *Nokma,* i.e. the chief of the clan's territory.

Women from non-tribal sections, particularly Hindus and Muslims, who together constitute majorities in Assam and Tripura, are generally denied their legal rights to inheritance and maintenance. Moreover, the pressures of traditions, their own helplessness and ineffective legal procedures generally prevent them from asserting their rights.

Within the general patrilineal as well as patriarchal framework, N-E women enjoy considerable autonomy with respect to day-to-day management of the household. All important financial decisions, however, like the sale of land, buying of a *mithun* (tamed bison) or determining the bride-price for a daughter, generally rest with men. A number of N-E women have been expanding their economic autonomy through successfully pursuing various activities such as handloom weaving or pig and poultry rearing. Perhaps, most effective means of improving their economic, and thereby overall status, seems to be through pursuing an independent occupation out of a variety of businesses and trades, or salaried jobs as teachers, health workers, government employees. Professional careers — like doctors, engineers, civil servants, research officers, etc. have definitely enhanced their status.

4

Women's Status in Marriage, Family and Religion

Introduction

THIS CHAPTER examines women's status in the context of marriage, family and religion in each of the seven N-E States. The presentations include salient patterns among major population groups, referring to specific instances primarily to highlight the issues. In Chapter 3, we looked at women's economic status as reflected in: (1) activity status as defined and reflected in Census data, (2) types of tasks women perform for family's economic sustenance, and (3) ownership and inheritance of property and participation in family's economic decision-making. The present chapter does, at times, refer to a few practices discussed in Chapter 3, but the context is different. For instance, we view the practice of bride-price here with regard to its influence on parents' attitude towards daughters. Similarly, the extent of women's contribution to family's economic sustenance is reviewed here in terms of their position in family relationships.

It will be useful to explain the composite sense in which the term "religion" is used in the following analysis. "Religion" here refers to man's ways of coping with situations that seem to be beyond human control and, therefore, calls for intervention from some superhuman beings or powers. These may include, for instance, beliefs in a supreme all-powerful god who governs the whole universe, several gods and goddesses embodying special attributes like prosperity or wisdom, or spirits — both benevolent and evil — responsible for various phenomena, e.g. rain, lightening, famine, epidemics, etc. Activities like prayers and sacrifices for propitiating gods, rituals to appease evil spirits, offerings to invoke the souls of dead ancestors by persons claiming to possess occult powers, etc. are regarded here as part of religion.

A broad framework used for analysing women's status with respect to marriage, family and religion is presented here. The findings of each of the seven N-E States are presented under appropriate headings. As noted earlier, we see some unevenness since some N-E States, and within them a few societies, have received more attention of academicians and other writers, while others have attracted less interest. Each State presentation includes a recapitulation listing salient observations, which, it is hoped, should meet the needs of both types of readers — those who are knowledgeable as well as those who are not very familiar about the situations in N-E States.

A Framework for Analysis

MARRIAGE

Relative perceptions regarding birth of a girl and a boy in the family and reasons for preferences.

Process of girl's growing up through childhood and adolescence, family tasks assigned, nature of socialization, access to playmates, recreation and education.

Age at marriage, selection of marriage partner by girl, or by parents and whether girl's consent regarded necessary, customary restrictions on selection of mate, e.g. clan exogamy and tribal endogamy, consequences of violating rules, elopement of lovers, unmarried motherhood.

Transactions between bride's and groom's parties, e.g. bride-price and dowry or service by groom for prospective father-in-law's household, marriage ceremony, matri-local or patri-local residence.

Practices regarding monogamy/polygamy, grounds for husband's taking other wives, relationship among co-wives, ways of dealing with unpalatable marital situation for wife and husband.

Grounds for dissolution of marriage for wife and husband, redress against ill-treatment by husband, consequences for wife and husband, freedom to re-marry, custody of children.

Widowhood, freedom to re-marry and to select another man, access to maintenance and protection by family, restrictions on widows, if any.

FAMILY

Wife's major roles in the family (other than economic ones presented in

Chapter 3), e.g. house-keeping, child-care, day-to-day household management, such as shopping for daily requirements, storage of grains after harvesting, etc.

Responsibilities towards supplementing inadequate family food resources.

Participation in important family events, e.g. births, deaths, marriages, major festivals.

Wife's relationships with husband and other family members and role in family's decision-making (other than in major economic matters presented in Chapter 3).

Women's access to family's resources, e.g. land, harvested grains, poultry, pigs, dowry received from their parents in marriage.

Position in case of abandonment or ill-treatment by husband, redress from village councils, clan elders, etc.

RELIGION

Women's participation in worship at : (a) family, and (b) community levels and restrictions, if any, on participation and on acting as priests.

Effects on women's participation due to adoption of external religious influences, e.g. Hinduism, Buddhism, Christianity.

Roles performed by women in family and community events having religious significance, e.g. child birth, marriage, funeral, community festival to propitiate the goddess of fertility.

Position of women believed to possess magical or occult powers, e.g. to appease evil spirits causing epidemics, to communicate with souls of deceased persons.

ARUNACHAL PRADESH

Arunachal Pradesh, as noted in Chapter 1, covers the largest area among N-E states (83,578 sq km), inhabited by about 26 major tribes and 110 sub-tribes. We examine women's status in this sprawling State with respect to marriage, family and religion in some major clusters of tribes. Among them they represent a wide socio-economic and cultural diversity. For instance, several tribes that inhabit difficult terrains with high mountain slopes and deep gorges, such as the Nishis of East Kameng and Lower

Subansiri areas, pursue primitive *jhum* cultivation with low yields in order to eke out a precarious existence. The Apatanis of Subansiri, on the other hand have been practising terraced cultivation for quite some time, and a few of them own vegetable and fruit orchards and fish farms and can flaunt a fashionable lifestyle. The Monpas and Sherdukpens of Kameng have been Buddhists of Mahayana sect due to their close association with Tibetan theocracy. The Khamtis and Singphos of Lohit and Tirap on the eastern side, however, follow Hinayana Buddhism because of their Myanmar origins. The Adis, the most numerous group, have welcomed modernization and social reforms on the whole, and yet include among their fold a few subgroups living in interior areas, like Gallongs who still cling to oppressive social customs like child marriages. The difficult communications have resulted in social and physical isolation of some groups, leading to perpetuation of outmoded traditions.

Attitudes Towards Girls

In the context of tribal warfare, raids and hunting expeditions, in the past sons were always eagerly desired among most tribes. At the same time, birth of a girl has always been welcomed since women were seen as essential to produce sons and to replenish the population, especially so among tribes like the Akas and Wanchos who were frequently engaged in warfare and head-hunting. In the present context, at least one son is desired to ensure continuity of the family and clan. If this is assured, the birth of a girl is greeted with joy since from her early childhood she begins to help her mother with household chores and care of younger siblings, collecting water, fire-wood, edible roots and leaves, taking care of poultry, pigs, guarding crops from birds, etc. Older girls help mothers in cultivation tasks and do weaving. In fact, girls are such a valuable asset to the household that parents are often reluctant to send them to schools, and if the girls are enrolled, they are withdrawn before reaching the high school level. Boys' education receives a much higher priority, which explains why girls' enrolment beyond middle school and above remained much lower than that of boys until 1960s. This situation is beginning to change slowly. Young girls learn the art of spinning and weaving from their mothers. Among the Monpas and Sherdukpens, mothers teach their daughters their special traditional arts of carpet-weaving and embroidery (Dutta Choudhury, 1989).

Girls grow up in an atmosphere of freedom and can go out with their playmates — both boys and girls. Some Adi sub-tribes, e.g. Padams and Miniyangs follow the practice of sending young boys and girls to dormitories, called "Rasheng" and "Moshup" where girls entertain their boy-friends at night and select their life-partners. Among the Wanchos, boys around twelve years are sent to a dormitory called "Pa (payn)" which serves one unit of a village covering 50 to 60 houses, while the biggest dormitory is called "Panu (paynu)." The girls do not have a separate dormitory but sleep in a compartment of the chief's house and boys are allowed to visit them (Goswami, 1982). Even though youth dormitories are on a decline as schools have come up, most villages have youth clubs or associations which provide useful training for young girls and boys in undertaking community responsibilities, such as preparing pathways to water points, helping needy families with harvesting, etc. thus inculcating qualities of leadership, initiative, co-operation and discipline (Sarkar, 1982). It is customary for young girls and boys to sing and dance together at various community festivals, e.g. "Solung" or "Mopin" celebrations among Adis, where they meet their life partners. Unmarried motherhood does not pose a serious problem and children born out of wedlock are usually taken care of by the girl's family.

Selection of Marriage Partner

Arunachal Pradesh presents a mixed picture with respect to the process of selecting marriage partners. A number of Adi tribes, e.g. Padam and Minyong, and other tribes such as Wancho and Apatani give considerable freedom to girls to mix with boys and to select their partners. At the same time, some parents even among these same tribes may select grooms for their daughters and ascertain the latter's consent. As long as rules of clan exogamy and tribal endogamy are followed, parents on both sides generally go along with their children's choices and begin negotiations for marriage, which include bride-price to be given by the groom's parents to the bride's parents. In some cases the young lovers may elope if they apprehend parents' opposition. In general, since elopement is not a very uncommon event, parents regularize such unions in a brief marriage ceremony. In fact, as long as customary rules of exogamy and endogamy are not violated, some parents may actually welcome elopements. For instance, among the Akas, such a short-cut method spares the parents the expenses and cumbersome routine of visits and exchanges, and they may prefer this method (Sinha, 1962). The situation may not be so smooth in all cases of elopement, however. Among the Wanchos, if the parents have already fixed the engagement of a girl and a boy, and if the girl elopes with another man, parents try to locate the young lovers, and if they succeed, the boy with whom the girl has eloped is very heavily fined. On the other hand, if the young lovers escape the parents' search for three or four days, they are accepted as man and wife (Goswami, 1982). Among some tribes, however, parents fix their daughters' marriages when the latter are infants or very young and receive a bride-price, which may develop into a tragic situation, as we will see later.

Among the Nishis of East Kameng and lower Subansiri, although young girls move freely outside the home, parents keep a watchful eye to ensure that their daughters do not indulge in pre-marital sex, since chastity is valued in fixing the bride-price. At the same time, unmarried motherhood is not considered a calamity. Among the Singphos of Tirap, parents generally select a groom for their daughter whose consent is not regarded as essential. According to a Singpho custom, a father may find it difficult to reject a marriage proposal for his daughter from his sister's son, and the girl's personal preference may be overruled (Koing, 1989).

Bride-Price

The most common practice in Arunachal Pradesh is for the groom's side to give bride-price to the girl's parents. Bride-price is paid in various forms that include: cash, *mithuns* (tamed bisons) or other animals and articles given by the groom and his parents. In some cases instead of a lump-sum payment at one time, the groom's parents periodically supply meat, fish and *apong* (fermented liquor) to the girl's family over a period. Among the Pasi-Padam groups, the groom gives his services to the prospective father-in-law for a fixed period (Jogendra Nath, 1989). In some tribes, viz. the Akas and Nishis, if a groom is too poor to pay the bride-price in cash, he gives his service to his father-in-law for an agreed period. Some writers on Arunachal Pradesh have tried to emphasize that bride-price essentially represents a form of token compensation or consideration given by groom's side to bride's parents who lose a valuable asset when a girl leaves them after marriage. (Dutta, 1989). While this may be correct in principle, the custom of bride-price sometimes results in oppression of women, as noted from traditional practices in some communities.

Child-Marriage

In some tribes, e.g. Nishing[1] and Gallong, children's marriages are sometimes viewed as a means of forging alliances between families, clans or villages, rather than just a union of a boy and a girl. This practice is more prevalent in interior areas where people have little contact with more advanced societies. Child marriages occasionally take place even among tribes such as the Minyongs, who are relatively more progressive and generally permit daughters to select their marriage partners, and ascertain their consent when parents select grooms. This practice leads to tragic circumstances, e.g. a girl of fifteen years suddenly finding herself married to an old man who already has several wives, or to a person distasteful to her. Jogendra Nath's portrayal (1994) of a young Adi girl dragged forcibly to her father-in-law's house, since the latter had paid bride-price to her father when she was three years old, depicts the tyranny against women.[2] Mishra (1991) has noted that organizations of Nishing girls and boys have been exerting pressure in recent years on Nishing husbands and in-laws to persuade them to release girls forced into marriages in their childhood by parents. Moreover, in disputes arising out of girls' refusal to accept husbands to whom they were married or betrothed in childhood, Indian jurisprudence has tried to uphold the girl's individual rights whenever customary laws have denied justice.[3] Some of the more advanced tribes, e.g. Apatanis, have been trying to mobilize public opinion to ban the practice of child marriage in their communities. In the midst of these cross-currents of tradition and modernity, Arunachal Pradesh State Assembly passed a Bill titled "Protection of Customary Laws and Social Practices" in November 1994. Women's organizations

1. The term "Nishing" meaning hill people, has emerged recently as a symbol of a composite identity consciousness and covers several groups previously called Dafla, Bangni, Tagin, Nishi, Nishing, Sulung, etc.
2. *Kanyar Mulya*, the original book in Assamese by Lummar Dai, an Adi author, has been translated into English by Dr. Jogendra Nath (1994) as *Bride-price*. It depicts how an Adi village council deals with the dilemma of endorsing the father-in-law's customary right to demand a girl's return to his house on the strength of bride-price he had paid, or to release the girl from the bondage of an imposed marriage.
3. Abhijit Chowdhary (1989) reports on a case of a Gallong girl, betrothed at the age of five years, who refused to go to her husband's house since she found him repugnant. After the village council's failure to settle the case, it was taken to the District Magistrate of Along, who upheld the girl's right to freedom and dignity since her betrothal at the age of five, could not be presumed to have her consent.

in the state had raised protests against the bill, since they fear that it could be used for perpetuating unjust social practices under the name of protecting indigenous culture.

Practices related to Marriage

Most Arunachal tribes have the practice of ascertaining the girl's consent to a marriage arranged by parents, however, some groups seem to be clinging on to past associations with times when men regarded it as their privilege to abduct a girl they wanted to marry. An Aka marriage perpetuates this old tradition in a symbolic manner, by enacting a mock fight between the groom's and the bride's parties on the first day, ending with the bride's party pretending to yield. On the following day, however, women from the bride's party take a subtle revenge by playing some practical jokes on members of the groom's party (Sinha, 1962).

In some tribes, e.g. Miniyong (a sub-tribe of Adi group), a married girl may continue to stay with her parents for some years, during which time the husband visits her and some children are born. Her final departure for husband's place is planned to coincide with completion of a crop-cycle. She would carry with her seeds of various crops, besides pigs and other animals given as gifts by parents (Jamoh, 1989). Among most tribes when a married girl leaves for her husband's place, parents generally give her clothes, household articles, precious beads and ornaments, a *dao* (chopper), grass rain-cover, weaving instruments, etc. which are treated as her own personal property. Among Gallongs, daughters are given dowry in proportion to bride-price received from groom's side (Choudhury, 1989). Most tribes recognize women's exclusive right over dowry given by their parents in marriage.

Monogamy: Polygyny

While monogamy is the rule among several tribes of Arunachal Pradesh, polygyny is widely practised for numerous reasons, ranging from "understandable" to the frivolous. Besides the frequent need in the past for replenishment of population which was constantly at risk due to warfare and head-hunting, polygyny is more prevalent among tribes inhabiting steep mountain slopes and deep valleys where cultivation requires more human labour. Wherever chieftain system still exists (as among *Apatanis*, Wanchos and Mishmis), the chiefs and other affluent persons acquire as many wives as they can afford, with the bride-price often paid in *mithuns*.

A wife being childless, or producing "very few" children is often considered a good enough excuse for acquiring another wife! A wife who does not bear a son is automatically regarded as responsible for the failure, justifying the husband's taking another wife. One should not be surprised about this, however, since this erroneous notion prevails in many other parts of India, even among the educated.

As hired agricultural labour is becoming increasingly available, the need to have several wives to augment labour has diminished. Simultaneously, with the advance of education and contacts with more modern societies, polygyny being viewed as a means of gaining social prestige is becoming less relevant. Some tribes, e.g. Akas and Singphos, require a man to seek his first wife's consent before bringing another wife. A defaulting Singpho husband is fined by his wife and her brothers (Koing 1989). An Aka wife would sometimes ask her husband to bring another wife so she could entertain her husband's guests more lavishly with meat and *apong* (fermented beer). The more highly patriarchal tribes like Nishis, however, do not consider it necessary to consult the first wife.

Divorce

Many of the grounds for a husband divorcing his wife and for taking another wife are common, e.g. wife's childlessness or not bearing a son. A Wancho husband can divorce his wife if he finds her incompetent in cultivation tasks (Dutta, 1987). Most tribes permit divorce to either party to a marriage on grounds of incompatibility, impotence and adultery. Among the Adis, if a wife feels neglected or ill-treated by the husband, she can obtain a divorce. The necessary condition, however, is that the "Kebang" — the village council — must give its approval. While the "Kebang" is hailed as a democratic institution, women are not permitted to be its members, and there is no guarantee that their case would be adequately represented. However, if the "Kebang" concludes that a husband is guilty of ill-treating his wife, the latter gets a divorce and the husband has to forfeit the bride-price he paid (Nyori, 1989). Women may also get a divorce on grounds of husband's insolvency, neglect of wife, addiction to drugs and adultery. But when women initiate the process of divorce, in most tribes they have to return the bride-price to the husband. In general a man who initiates divorce has to pay only a token compensation, as compared to what a woman seeking divorce is required to pay.[4]

Male Dominance in Marital Relationship

The Nishis, who represent the second largest group next to Adis, relegate women to a distinctly subordinate position, almost to the point where a wife becomes part of the property of the husband since the latter has paid bride-price. If she dies within a short period after marriage without bearing a child, the husband can reclaim the bride-price from her parents. In case the husband is displeased with her for any reason such as adultery, he can inflict physical punishment on her. Even if he kills her, her family or community cannot question him as this is treated strictly as a personal matter (Phukan & Phukan, 1989). As noted before, cases of young girls betrothed or married in their childhood to older men with several wives are not unknown, and equally common are instances when the young wife would elope with a young lover. In such cases, the girl is forced to return to the husband, and cannot get a reprieve until her lover or parents repay the bride-price or compensation demanded by the husband. Despite differences among tribes regarding customs related to divorce, one thing is fairly common. A husband guilty of adultery can generally get away with a mild punishment, e.g. a small fine, whereas a woman with a similar guilt is treated much more harshly by the "Kebangs" (village councils) or the chief's councils, which are exclusively male preserves. Verrier Elwin (1953) has reported on the inhuman punishments imposed on women guilty of adultery,[5] which hopefully are a thing of the past.

When ordinary women in some tribes receive such unkind treatment, it is not surprising that women belonging to the class of slaves received even greater humiliation. Although slavery was officially abolished in 1955, some of its vestiges have lingered even to this day (Mishra, 1982). The Khamtis of Lohit, who are immigrants from Myanmar, had a traditional hierarchical structure, with the royal family and nobility at the top,

4. A Wancho man who divorces his wife is required to pay a fine of either an "endy" (a kind of silk) cloth, or a pig to the wife's parents. A Wancho woman seeking to divorce her husband has to pay a much heavier fine, which includes besides an "endy" cloth nine additional items, e.g. a pig, spear, war shield, silver belt, armlet, *dao* (a chopper), etc. (Singha, 1982).

5. Verrier Elwin in *Democracy in NEFA* (1953), has given a description of how Daflas (currently referred as Nishing) had the practice of stripping an adulterous woman and beating her, or mutilating her private parts. A later account by Shailendra Kumar narrates how a girl guilty of immoral behaviour was paraded around the villages after stripping her naked and cutting off her hair (Bormundi; 1989).

commoners in the middle and slaves at the bottom. According to the customary Khamti law, a master having illicit sex relations with a slave woman got away without any punishment. In case the woman's husband was a slave, although the woman was not a slave, the guilty master was let off with a minor expiatory ritual (Sarkar, 1993). The woman was thus subjected to a double insult: firstly due to belonging to the slave class, and secondly, because of being the wife of a slave.

Widowhood

There is no bar on widows re-marrying, although among some tribes the brother of the deceased husband has the prior claim to the widow and she needs the latter's permission to marry another man. The Nishis carry this rule to the point where the widows of the deceased man are distributed among his brothers, sons and other male relatives and the widows have no choice. If the widows are in the child-bearing age, they are assigned to various clan relatives, and a formal marriage is not considered necessary (Phukan and Phukan, 1989).

The bride-price thus reduces a widow into a commodity, a part of the deceased husband's property. The other and positive side of this picture is the protection the widow receives as long as she continues to live in her deceased husband's family. Some tribes also give a widow limited property rights. An Adi widow can use and even sell a part of the deceased husband's property in order to maintain her children (Rukbo, 1989). Similarly, a Tagin widow can use and sell some of the deceased husband's property to his relatives (Choudhury, 1989). If an Adi widow has no son, the husband's property goes to male relatives of the clan but she can claim maintenance for herself and her children (Jogendra Nath, 1989).

If a widow marries a person outside her husband's family or clan, she loses her right of using the deceased husband's property, the family's protection, as well as custody of children. Her new husband must return the bride-price paid by the deceased husband to the family of the woman. Until the bride-price is returned, the widow cannot even return to her parents. The children belong to the deceased husband's family and are looked after by them.

Women's Family Roles

The dominant pattern in Arunachal Pradesh is the nuclear family. Among exceptions are the Nishings who often have large families accommodating

100-150 members, including grandparents, parents, sons and their wives and children living under one roof, called the long-house. It has separate compartments with hearths for each couple and their unmarried children. When a married girl leaves her parents' house to join her husband, she leaves behind a relatively care-free and relaxed life and begins an unending routine full of varied chores, besides her heavy preoccupation with cultivation tasks, detailed in Chapter 3. Before leaving for the fields in the morning, she collects water from mountain streams, cooks and feeds the family, pigs and poultry. After a busy day at the fields, she must collect firewood, bring water, husk the grain, gather all the livestock, cook and feed the family and animals. She is fully responsible for child care, and for supplementing inadequate food grains by growing vegetables, collecting edible roots and tubers from the forests, and by raising poultry and pigs. She takes charge of drying and storing the grains, and if any person in the family goes hungry, it is treated as her lapse. Besides being industrious herself, she must also groom her daughters to strive hard to augment family resources (Nyori, 1989). She may get a helping hand from men in catching fish from mountain streams and in collecting edible forest produce, but the major responsibility of feeding the family belongs to her.

In areas characterized by steep mountain slopes where productivity from *jhum* cultivation is low, men resorted to raids on the plains of Assam or hunting expeditions to augment meagre resources of food and man-power almost until the fourth decade of the twentieth century. This forced women to assume major responsibility for household and cultivation tasks. This traditional division of labour among men and women has continued even though the dependence on hunting and warfare for survival has receded. In-between short spells of intensive activity when men clear areas for jhuming, or get busy with terracing and preparing water channels in areas under terraced cultivation, men have more leisure than women, whose tasks have remained essentially unchanged. When women return home from the fields in the evening, it is time for men to relax with their friends, and women must provide adequate quantities of *apong* (fermented liquor) and tobacco for men's smoking pleasure. Is it any wonder then, that a Nishing or an Aka woman would urge her husband to bring another wife to share her labour so that she can ensure for her husband and guests proper hospitality?

Despite the fact that major burden of cultivation is borne by women, they do not have a right to own or inherit land or other property, as noted in Chapter 3. The produce resulting from their hard toil belongs to their husbands. *Mithuns* are generally owned by men. The only discretion women may have is to sell some of the produce to purchase other household requirements. Sometimes, Nishing women are allowed to use part of the produce to organize co-operative labour from villagers for some agricultural operations, or for specific tasks such as construction of a house (Phukan & Phukan, 1989). Women generally receive ornaments from their parents as gifts, and these are treated as heirlooms and their personal possessions that they may give to their daughters in marriage.

Living with Co-wives

In the context of polygyny prevalent among many tribes, among the co-wives, the first wife has a special position. She generally keeps the keys to the granary and has custody of family heirlooms. Among the Adis, the senior-most wife has the discretion of making day-to-day household purchases, but must obtain the husband's or the clan's permission to make bigger purchases, e.g. Tibetan beads, lands, *mithuns*, etc. even out of her own personal income (Jogendra Nath, 1989). The income earned by women by selling vegetables grown in kitchen gardens, poultry or pigs raised by them, or through selling handloom articles woven by them is treated as their personal income. Among the Nishis, generally each wife has a separate cultivation plot, her own hearth, poultry, pigs, as well as her granary. The co-wives as well as the husband generally adopt a policy of mutual non-interference. Husbands normally live and dine with the senior-most wife and sleep with each wife in turn (Phukan & Phukan, 1989). There is sometimes rivalry among co-wives over getting the husband's help on their respective jhum plots. K. Mishra (1991) has cited a case of four sisters married to one man and the sisters reporting that the arrangement was quite satisfactory. She has also reported on a Nishing husband who had adopted his own method of keeping peace in the household by giving a mild beating to all his nine wives periodically. A completely non-discriminatory method of keeping the women in their place ! The Wancho society has a system of chieftainship and two major divisions — Wangham (Chiefs) and Wangpan (commoners). Every village chief marries a daughter of another chief (Wangsia), who is the principal wife or "Rani." He generally acquires other wives from the commoners' group. In the chief's house, each wife has a separate room but he takes his food, only with the chief wife (Singha, 1982).

Despite the highly authoritarian attitude of men towards wives and the controlling power men acquire by paying bride-price, Nishi women manage to express their rebellion effectively when they are displeased. For instance, they would wail loudly or use abusive language from the back balcony of the house in order to attract the attention of neighbours and thus embarrass the husband. Cases of adultery among young women married to old husbands are not unknown. If the lover is too poor to return the bride-price to the husband, he may agree to give his labour to the husband's household for an agreed period.

Family Solidarity at any Cost

While most Arunachal Pradesh tribes permit polygyny, among some Adi sub-tribes, a limited polyandry is reported to be prevalent. For instance, a Gallong woman marries only one husband, but shares intimacy with his brothers and cousins, if the husband permits. This continues even after the brother-in-law gets married, and he, in turn, is allowed to have close relations with his sisters-in-law. This practice is also prevalent among other Adi sub-tribes, e.g. Galos, Ramos, Pailbos, Bakars and Tangams, and is based on mutual understanding and not considered a right (Nyori, 1989). It is explained as a means of developing family solidarity, essential for survival in difficult and adverse living conditions due to dependence on hunting and primitive cultivation. This is interesting in the context of a highly patriarchal culture of the Adis. The point to be noted is that while women do not have a right to own or inherit property, nor any place in traditional village councils or the councils of elders, they command a certain degree of authority and respect in the household sphere. This is probably related to Adi religious philosophy, which will be discussed later.

How the Family views Women

The Akas present a rather unique illustration of a group that gives women a fairly respectable status in the household. She is not considered as a drudge, unlike for instance, the Nishis who often treat her as part of the husband's property. The reason for this favourable situation is not clear, although some authors have attributed it to Aka women's substantial contribution towards the household's economic sustenance (Sinha, 1962). Furthermore, Aka women who are descendents of the royal families who ruled over some Aka areas in the past are called "Nugum" or "Aka

Ranis."[6] They enjoy a special status as patrons of their villages, and can attend meetings of village councils, which ordinary Aka women cannot do. "Aka Ranis" are expected to help needy people in their respective villages (Sinha, 1962).

As regards the general picture of women's position in the family, although women cannot own or inherit family property, in most tribes they enjoy a certain degree of autonomy and respect in the household sphere. While men take major financial decisions, e.g. purchase or sale of land, ornaments or *mithuns* (tamed bison), women have the authority and discretion over the use of money they earn by raising vegetables, poultry or pigs or by weaving and petty trading. In polygynous families, the senior-most wife acts as the custodian of the granary as well as of family heirlooms.

Women's Position in Religion

In the sphere of religion, women's status shows a wide variation among different tribal communities of Arunachal Pradesh. The Nishing women, for instance, have little active role in religious rites, and merely assist men by preparing fermented liquor and other special foods required in rituals. The priests are always men and sacrifices can be performed only by men (Dutta, 1989). In case a Nishing woman is found guilty of sexual misconduct with a person who does not belong to her tribe, the matter becomes a concern for the whole community. Such a woman may be debarred from participating, howsoever perfunctorily, in all religious rituals, and may even be ex-communicated. The Akas, who are known to give a more respectable position to women in the family than many other tribes do not permit women to be priests, (Jha, 1989). Furthermore, they associate menstruation in women with evil influence. In case a man leaving for a hunting expedition eats food prepared by or touched by a woman in menses, this is believed to impair his hunting ability and even to cause death (Sinha, 1962).

In general Buddhist tribes are more liberal towards women's participation in religious activities although they too restrict women from some religious rites, and women cannot become "Lamas" or priests. The

6. Two Aka villages, Jamiri and Hushigaon continue the tradition of giving a special status to women descendents of former Aka ruling families, called "Aka Ranis" whose advice on social and political matters is sought in village meetings (Singh, 1962).

Monpas, Sherdukpens, Membas and Khambas, who are clustered in Kameng and northern Siang areas, permit women to participate in community prayers and veneration of the Buddha. These tribes belong to Mahayan sect and are influenced by Buddhist traditions of Tibet and Bhutan that are highly patriarchal and tend to view women as impediments in man's spiritual pursuits.

The Singphos and Khamtis of Lohit and Tirap districts on the eastern side of the State follow the Hinayan Buddhism due to their Myanmar origins, and tend to be more liberal towards women in religious matters. The Singphos allow women to participate more actively in religious events as compared to Buddhist tribes on the western side who follow the Mahayana Buddhist tradition. For instance, besides participating in community worship at temples, Singpho women customarily offer prayers at the family level before meals are served. They are permitted to take "Panchsheel" and "Ashtasheel" (ethical vows). Furthermore, in the absence of men, Singpho women are allowed to perform Buddhist religious rituals too, which was never permitted in their indigenous faith (Koing, 1989).

Adis, who represent the most numerous group in Arunachal, present a rather unique example of an indigenous religion that, after its recent revival, has become a symbol of uniting several smaller tribes under a new Adi identity. It is more liberal towards women than most tribal faiths, as well as the more established traditional religions like Buddhism and Hinduism. According to Adi mythology, man is the son of mother Pedong Nane and father Yidum Bote. Pedong Nane is the mother of the twins, Donyi-Polo, representing the synthesis of female and male principles, Sun and Moon, who illuminate the world and symbolize law and truth (Choudhury, 1971). At the instance of Pedong Nane, Kine Nane or Mopin gave man the means of subsistence, i.e. agriculture, and Mopin is therefore viewed as a respected goddess in the Adi pantheon (Jogendra Nath, 1989). Fecundity of the woman is believed to be synonymous with fertility of the earth. This explains why Adi magical and religious rites to ensure fertility of the fields are entrusted to women.

In the "Solung" and "Mopin" festivals, both of which are connected with agriculture, Adi women play a major role, and some dances are performed exclusively by women. There is a belief that women, because of their gentle hearts and sweet voices, can more effectively invoke gods and goddesses (Rukbo, 1989). Women participate with men in all religious events. Furthermore, Adi women can become priests and perform all religious rites as well as divinations. Besides preparing *apong* and special food for religious events, they participate in singing and dancing that accompany religious ceremonies. Among the Galos, an Adi sub-tribe, the ritual that marks initiation of harvesting is performed by young girls in the family (Nyori, 1989). The favourable position of Adi women in religion seems to be related to Adi mythology, which gives an exalted place to Pedong Nane, the mother of man and of Donyi-Polo, and to Mopin, the goddess of agriculture. With the progress of scientific knowledge and modern technology, whether the Adis would tend to attribute good harvests to quality seeds and fertilizers, rather than to Mopin, is a matter for conjecture. Would Adi women then continue to retain their high profile in rituals connected with agriculture? Another important area of inquiry is the position of women among some Adi sub-tribes, e.g. Padams of Dibang valley and Pasighat areas who have been converted to Christianity.[7]

Recapitulation

MARRIAGE

Most tribes in Arunachal Pradesh have a positive attitude toward the birth of a girl child, even though one son is desired to ensure continuity of the family in this patrilineal and patriarchal society. Girls are valued because they help their families substantially in household and agricultural chores and fetch a bride-price. They also give birth to progeny, particularly sons who, until the recent past, were coveted in the context of the tribes' major preoccupation with hunting and warfare. Girls grow up in an atmosphere of freedom in most tribes and can select their marriage partners. Elopements of young lovers are not uncommon and as long as the rules of clan exogamy and tribal endogamy are not violated, parents generally regularize such marriages. In a few tribes, e.g. Nishis and Gallongs who live in interior areas, parents arrange marriages of their children as a means of forging alliances between families and clans. Sometimes young girls or infants are married or betrothed for a bride-price which may result in young girls being married to old men with several wives or to persons distasteful to the girls. Although bride-price is interpreted as

---

7. Arunachal Pradesh, according to 1991 Census, included 10.29 per cent Christian population. Unfortunately, no information regarding Christian women's position was available from the papers presented at the 1989 seminar on Status of Women in Arunachal Pradesh.

compensation to the girl's parents who lose a precious asset, in practice it often deteriorates into the price paid for buying a wife.

While divorce in principle is available to both husband and wife, in practice it is much easier for husbands to get a divorce. Furthermore, most tribes permit men to have several wives if they can afford the required bride-price. Women's plea for divorce has to be accepted by the village council in which women have no representation, nor even an opportunity to plead their case. In most cases of divorce initiated by women, they or their parents must arrange to repay the bride-price to the husband. Furthermore the children, in most cases, remain in the custody of the husband's family. The position of widows in most tribes is somewhat humiliating. The brothers of the deceased husband have the first right to marry the widow and she needs the brother-in-law's permission to marry a man of her choice. If she succeeds, she or her new husband must return the bride-price to the brother-in-law's family. In some tribes, e.g. the Nishis, the widows are automatically distributed among the brothers, sons, or other relatives and treated like part of the property of the deceased. In a few groups, a widow is allowed to marry a man of her choice but in that case she loses the privilege of receiving the protection and maintenance of her husband's family, and has no claim on her deceased husband's property. On the positive side neither a divorcee nor a widow suffers from any social stigma and can remarry.

FAMILY

Women's position in the family varies widely among the Arunachal Pradesh tribes. Among Nishis, for instance, the position of a woman is not very different from that of a servant, according to some authors. A Nishi husband has the authority, according to customary laws, to inflict physical punishment or even to kill his wife if she were guilty of adultery. On the other hand, among the Adis, women and particularly mothers are given a respected place in the family. While women have no place in important decisions such as the purchase of land, ornaments, *mithuns,* etc., they enjoy autonomy in the day-to-day running of the household. They play an important role in the grooming of their daughters. While they do not own the produce from cultivation despite their major participation in cultivation tasks, they are free to use the money raised through ancillary activities such as growing vegetables, poultry-keeping and similar avenues. They have exclusive right to gifts, including ornaments, received from their parents at the time of marriage and generally pass them on to their daughters.

RELIGION

In the sphere of religion women's participation and status varies according to the systems of faith of the various tribes. Among tribes that follow their indigenous faiths, excepting the Adis, women are restricted from participating in most religious ceremonies. Apart from being expected to supply *apong* and special foods necessary in certain rituals, women remain mere spectators. They can never act as priests nor can they perform sacrifices. In the tribes which follow Mahayana Buddhism and Hinduism, e.g. Sherdukpens, Membas and Noctes, women can participate in many rituals and join men in the worship of the Buddha or Vishnu, but cannot act as priests. The Hinayana Buddhist tribes, e.g. Singphos, are less restrictive towards women and in the absence of men, permit women to perform all rituals. The priests, i.e. Lamas and Purohits, however, are always men. Adi tribes are by far the most progressive and not only consider women as more effective communicators with their deities, but require that some rituals, e.g. those connected with sowing and harvesting, must be performed by women. Adi women can officiate as priests, which indicates the respected place given to women.

ASSAM

In view of the high degree of heterogeneity of Assam's population, as described in Chapter 2, the status of women in marriage, family and religion is described in the context of three major constituents: (1) Non-tribal, (2) Hill-tribal, and (3) Plains tribal societies.

Non-Tribal Societies

COMPOSITION AND GENERAL SOCIAL CONTEXT

Assam's non-tribal population constitutes a preponderating majority of 87.17 per cent of the State's total population as per 1991 Census. Hindus and Muslims form two major segments of this group, while Christians, Sikhs, Buddhists, Jains and other religions together account for less than 5 per cent. It is useful to keep in mind some salient social aspects, referred in details in Chapter 2, which have a direct relevance to women's status. The impact of Hinduism and that of Shankardeva's Vaishnavism have influenced women's participation in religion as well as their family roles, and equally important, social perceptions of women. The Burmese invasions of Assam, particularly in early nineteenth century, prior to the beginning of British rule, were accompanied by plunder, social and political turmoil and violence against women, which led to a serious decline in women's status. The demographic changes in Assam which started in the nineteenth century and became accentuated by the massive influx of immigrants from Bengal, later East Pakistan, just prior to and after Partition of India in 1947 led to dividing Assam into two major cultural zones. The Barak Valley and parts of lower Assam are characterized by strong Bengali and traditional culture. The Brahmaputra Valley, on the other hand, retains to some extent its original tribal and non-Aryan traditions. The following presentation of Assam's non-tribal societies deals with two major segments: Hindus and Muslims. The tea garden labourers, although belonging to tribal groups prior to their migration into Assam, are officially listed under "Other Backward Classes" in Assam, which explains their inclusion in non-tribal category.

Assam's Hindus

ATTITUDES TOWARDS GIRLS

Both Assamese or indigenous and immigrant Hindus[8] have an unfavourable bias against girls, and birth of a girl child hardly evokes the enthusiasm which is evident when a son is born. The attitude of immigrant Hindus is relatively more negative because the custom of dowry to be provided by girl's parents makes a girl a burden on parents. Moreover, since she leaves her parents after marriage, any investment on her education tends to be viewed as futile, and she is not seen as a potential support for her parents. Among Kaibartas, for instance, a fishermen community from East Bengal settled in Chatla Howr, acute poverty, ignorance and increasing prevalence of dowry system combine to make parents look upon daughters as a liability. If girls are enrolled in schools, few complete even middle school level, since most of them are withdrawn by parents so the girls can help their mothers in housework and in taking care of younger siblings. Mothers, in their anxiety to get their daughters settled in marriage, observe "Vratas" (days of abstinence of food and prayers) in the hope that their daughters make a good adjustment to their in-laws

8. The terms "Indigenous" or "Assamese" and "Immigrant" in relation to Hindus and Muslims of Assam are admittedly relative. Their connotation in the present context has been explained in Chapter 2.

(Bhattacharjee, S. 1988). The tea garden labour community provides a happy exception in this respect since a girl from an early age begins to look after younger children and household work, which relieves the mother to work in tea gardens. Furthermore, when the girl reaches early adolescence, she starts working in the tea gardens, thus becoming an economic asset for the family (Phukan, 1988).

AGE AT MARRIAGE

Among Assamese Hindus generally, child marriage has never been prevalent, but among brahmans and kayasthas the practice of arranging marriages of girls between 10-13 years was common by early nineteenth century. Among immigrant Hindus, and especially among relatively disadvantaged groups, girls are married during early adolescence. This difference in the patterns regarding the age of marriage of girls among Assamese and immigrant Hindu communities was noted even by the Age of Consent Committee Report of 1928-29.[9] It is interesting to observe that Vaishnavite preceptors had advocated raising the minimum age of marriage for girls, and a minimum waiting period of three years after puberty before consummation. Chandraprova Saikiani, a prominent public figure, had urged the Age of Consent Committee to fix the minimum age of marriage for girls at 16 years. In 1926, she also led women to issue "cancellation notices" in cases of child marriages (Barooah, 1993). In present times, marriages of daughters, excepting a small minority, are arranged by parents, and the consent of girls may not always be regarded as essential, unlike in most tribal societies. With the spread of education, parents are becoming more favourable towards supporting their daughters' education, and the number of girls enrolled in higher education is slowly increasing, particularly in Assamese Hindus. Even among immigrant Hindus, some parents allow their daughters to continue education beyond high school, and where the daughters take up employment and begin to augment family income, the parents' previously negative attitude towards daughters begins to change. In general, with increasing levels of education, there is greater acceptance among parents of girls selecting their marriage partners, as also the need to obtain girls'

9. The Age of Consent Committee, a non-official body appointed by the government and headed by Moropant Joshi, in its report of 1928-29 noted that except for brahmins and Ganaks, pre-puberty marriages of girls were few in Brahmaputra Valley Hindus.

consent to marriages arranged by parents, although this situation by no means represents the majority.

PRACTICES RELATED TO DOWRY AND BRIDE-PRICE

While the Assamese Hindus do not have the custom of dowry or bride-price, it is customary for the groom's parents to give some clothes, ornaments and other gifts to the bride before marriage in a ceremony called "Jurun," meaning a blessing. Among relatively well-to-do urban sections, a practice of girl's parents giving jewellery, clothes and household articles as gifts is becoming common, and this trend seems to be spreading in rural areas. In fact, a slight shift towards dowry has been noted in rural areas among richer sections by Saikia, Gogoi et al. (1986). Among immigrant Hindus in the Barak Valley, however, the practice of girl's parents giving dowry is very common. At the same time, exorbitant dowry demands from the groom's side, or oppression of girls by in-laws to extract dowry are reported to be absent (Choudhury, 1988). Assamese writers take justifiable pride in asserting that Assam has remained free from some pernicious practices like female infanticide and oppression of women due to dowry demands. However, a small number of dowry deaths have unfortunately been reported from some remote villages in Kamrup district and some urban areas. According to a 1994 National Crime Records Bureau report (Govt. of India, Ministry of Home Affairs), there were 14 dowry deaths in Assam in 1991.

ATTITUDES TOWARDS DIVORCE, WIDOWHOOD AND REMARRIAGE

Hindu communities of Assam did not completely escape the influence of traditional degraded status of women in medieval India.[10] They adopted the Indian ideal of a married woman being an obedient, self-effacing and forbearing wife in spite of ill-treatment by her husband. Divorce is not common even in cases of a bigamous marriage or ill-treatment by husband. Despite the Hindu Marriage Act of 1955, which prohibits bigamy, very few women, excepting a small number of urban, educated and economically

10. Women's status, which had started deteriorating even during the Vedic period, declined rapidly through the medieval period and this was reflected particularly among caste-dominated societies of Assam, e.g. brahmins, kayasthas and other Sanskritized sections. Even Shankaradeva, hailed for his liberal attitude, preached through neo-Vaishnavism, equated woman to a "shudra" (a person of low origin), bird or animal, and viewed her as an evil distraction in spiritual pursuits (Gogoi, 1988).

independent women seek divorce. Unfortunately Assam's Hindu communities are strongly under the influence of yet another Indian tradition, viz. widowhood being viewed as a symbol of austerity and self-denial. Many Assamese widows take to wearing white dresses and give up meat and fish. Widow re-marriages became socially disapproved by nineteenth century. From about 1870 onwards, Gunabhiram Barua, Anandaram Dhekial Phukan, Laxmikant Bezbarua, Hemchandra Barua, among others, tried to create public awareness regarding the injustice and undesirable consequences of child marriages and of inhibitions regarding widow re-marriages. They tried to encourage widow re-marriages. In spite of these efforts, widow and divorcee re-marriages are few, and when these occur, they do not receive full social approval. A number of legislative provisions try to give protection to women from injustice and cruelty.[11] And yet few Hindu women seek legal remedies to obtain their right to maintenance from the deserting husband, or to get their share of parental property in cases where brothers usurp their sisters' share. Among Assam's Hindus, there has so far been a strong tradition of parents and brothers assuming responsibility for maintenance and protection of unmarried, widowed or dependent daughters. Most women, therefore, are inhibited from seeking legal remedies in cases of injustice due to cultural pressures, as also ignorance of laws and financial inability to engage in expensive litigation.

FAMILY ROLES AND PARTICIPATION IN FAMILY DECISIONS

Assam's Hindu women have a clearly subordinate position in the household. They take care of all house-keeping chores and child care, and in rural areas they are responsible for care of animals, raising vegetables, weaving, in addition to their heavy involvement in family cultivation. They also take up wage employment periodically, especially in rice-cultivating areas. In areas devoid of electricity and piped water supply or tube wells, women have to spend enormous time and energy in threshing and de-husking rice and in collecting water for the household. Women may also do weaving, tailoring, sericulture, petty trading in household goods and such other activities to augment family income. Most women spend long hours in work, but most of the time is spent in unpaid work, which does little to enhance their status in the family. Anuva Saikia (1988) has commented

11. The relevant laws include : Hindu Marriage Act, 1956; Hindu Succession Act 1956; Hindu Adoption and Maintenance Act, 1956; Dowry Prohibition Act, 1961; Hindu Women's Right to Property Act, 1937.

on the urgent need to develop opportunities for gainful employment in rural areas. In Barak Valley women's situation is worse since there is no tradition of self-employment. Perhaps, one of the few exceptions is that of Manipuri women who are economically quite active, and besides their involvement in harvesting and sowing, they are also engaged in petty trading and weaving (Choudhary, 1988). When women contribute to family income, their status in the family improves substantially. It is therefore important to initiate programmes of vocational training and entrepreneurship along with infrastructural services such as banking, credit and marketing facilities to substantially increase non-tribal women's ability to earn incomes.

Non-tribal Hindu women participate actively in events such as marriages, important celebrations like *Bihu, Durga Puja,* and may be consulted regarding major family expenditures and purchases, but men usually take final decisions. In urban areas, whether women, especially newly married daughters-in-laws, would take up salaried employment or other remunerative work depends on the wishes of the husband and in-laws. Here the steep increase in cost of living, rising aspirations, and a shift away from joint to nuclear families have contributed to making women's employment outside the home more acceptable. In families where women are qualified and employed in professional and higher administrative positions, they have a greater say in important family decisions, e.g. those related to children's education, and men tend to be more favourable towards sharing women's household and child care tasks (Saikia, Gagoi et al., 1986). Women in tea-garden labour communities present a different picture from other non-tribal Hindu families, and enjoy greater equality with men in taking household decisions and have more control over household expenditures. This is undoubtedly related to their very substantial contribution to family incomes, facilitated by their superior skills in plucking tea leaves. Even then, they have to carry a dual burden of whole-time labour and household chores with almost no help from husbands in house-keeping or child care (Phukan, 1988).

WOMEN'S POSITION IN RELIGION

Assam's non-tribal Hindu women have tried to appropriate whatever space religion could provide in an effort to make up for their otherwise lowly status in the family. As noted in Chapter 2, the adoption of Hinduism has been a major factor in the de-tribalization of the Mongoloid groups inhabiting Assam. Women's position in religion was strongly influenced by medieval and highly patriarchal Hindu concept of women being equated to "shudra" (person of low status), slave, even lower animals. Shankaradeva, the founder of neo-Vaishnavism too, imbibed much of the negative bias against women, and viewed them essentially as impediments in man's spiritual endeavours.[12] Even then, this new faith brought a liberal influence with its emphasis on community worship of one God — Vishnu — and elimination of elaborate rituals and the mediation of priests. Women found it appealing because it showed a way to achieve direct communion with God through devotion and participation in singing and listening to prayers in "Namghars" (community prayer halls). Women persuaded their men-folk to join this new faith so that they could find a legitimate place in community worship.

Shankaradeva was initially opposed to including a multiplicity of gods and goddesses but had to make a concession to women who had so far played an important part in worshipping goddesses like Lakshmi and Durga. It is a tribute to women's tenacity that "Ai-Nam" or goddess worship found a place in Vaishnavite *Namghars* on specified days. However, at the institutional level, Shankaradeva and his disciples restricted women's participation on the plea that women are incapable of rising above mundane concerns. The officials of Vaishnavite *Satras* (centres of religious training and administration) are always men, often celibate monks. Women cannot enter certain areas of *Satras* and are denied entry to some *Satras*, e.g. Barpeta. This restriction is related to the concept of menstruation and pregnancy being polluting, which is completely in contrast with tribal societies where onset of puberty in girls is celebrated as a happy occasion (Mahanta, 1988). Ironically, a recent attempt by members of a women's organization, "Lekhika Samaroha," to enter Barpeta *Satra* was thwarted by women of Barpeta. Indeed a strange instance of women turning against women to perpetuate male-dominance.

Assam's non-tribal Hindu women play an active role in festivals connected with sowing and harvesting, such as *Bihu,* daily worship of family gods and goddesses, as well as propitiation of deities and spirits to ward off or cure illness of family members or animals. Obviously, as medical

---

12. Despite the highly derogatory attitude of Shankaradeva and his disciples towards women, Shankaradeva's *Rukmini Harana* and *Parijat Harana* and Madhavadeva's *Jasoda* portrayed their main women characters as playing key roles in the household, highly respected and actively participating in important family decisions.

and veterinary sciences make treatment of diseases more dependable, women are likely to lose their position in rituals to protect family members and animals from sickness. It would be desirable to empower them with scientific training to become auxiliary health workers or veterinary workers so that they can be assets to their families and neighbours in preventing and curing simple ailments of family members and animals.

Women in Barak Valley provide an interesting instance where women have used a religious ritual to assert their position that was sought to be denied by a politically powerful group. Along with the Hinduization of Assam's tribal societies came the adoption of caste-dominated structure where brahmins and the warrior classes assumed a higher position than trading and agricultural groups, while women and those performing menial jobs were placed at the lowest stratum (Gogoi, 1988). When "Yaudheyas" or the warrior classes, who were not favourably disposed to women, tried to impose on peasant classes, "Kartik Puja," the glorification of a misogynist Kartik, peasant classes asserted their protest by performing a ritual called "Usha Bhasani" (immersion of Usha). Peasant women in Cachar bring river clay and grow paddy in a container in which an effigy of "Usha" — a symbol of fertility — is hidden. On the last day, they immerse it in the river as a part of Kartik Puja. Traditionally, women avoid visiting a Kartik temple due to a belief that he might curse them into maidenhood or widowhood (Choudhary, S. 1988).[13]

In short, Assam's non-tribal Hindu women have appropriated for themselves a space in religion by several means: using the eclectic temper of Hinduism which accommodated in its fold a multiplicity of gods and goddesses and forms of worship to satisfy the needs of a heterogeneous society which included a range of religious beliefs and practices; expanding the scope of their participation by stretching as far as possible the democratization and liberalization introduced by neo-Vaishnavism of Shankaradeva, and preserving from their tribal heritage elements which gave them a useful role in religion.

---

13. "Usha Bhasani," according to one version reinforces the belief that rituals to secure fertility of the earth fall in the domain of women. Another version presents the story of Karttika and Usha as follows: Karttika, the son of Shiva and Durga, while returning home after several victories, falls in love with Usha and proposes to her. He promises to return to marry her after obtaining the consent of his mother Durga, who expresses her disapproval. The dismayed Karttika, in his anguish, vows not to marry. Usha is heart-broken and in her grief decides never to show her face to a living being (Choudhary, S. 1988).

EMERGING PROBLEMS OF VIOLENCE AND DESTITUTION

Assam's non-Aryan and tribal heritage has spared Assamese women some of the worst indignities presently inflicted on Hindu women in the rest of India, such as female infanticide. There have been a few cases of dowry deaths, although the number is small. They have not, however, escaped altogether atrocities like rape and molestation.[14] With increasing social disorganization and weakening of family solidarity, unmarried mothers, women ill-treated or deserted by husbands, widows and single women devoid of protection and maintenance by families, etc. are posing a challenge for society. Many of these women migrate to urban areas in search of employment and seek shelter in rescue homes or residential care institutions. These institutions, however, cannot provide adequate rehabilitation services, vocational training and job placements. The difficult employment situation also poses serious problems for their inmates. It is no surprise that some of these women are lured or trapped into prostitution.

In recent years, the rising incidence of insurgency and political unrest have necessitated heavy deployment of army and security personnel in several areas of the State. This has unfortunately resulted in instances of violence against women. In communal conflicts that have rocked Assam in recent past some women have sadly been victims of revenge by hostile communities.

Assam's Muslims

Muslims account for 28.43 per cent of the total population of Assam, as of 1991 Census. The socio-cultural background of the different segments of Muslim population (presented in Chapter 2 under demographic aspects), influences position of women in certain respects. The descendents of soldiers who came to Assam during Muslim invasions between thirteenth and seventeenth centuries, will be referred as Assamese Muslims, to distinguish them from immigrant Muslims who came into Assam mostly from Bengal in the twentieth century. The Manipuri Muslims or "Pangans" who number over 40,000, are concentrated mainly in Cachar and Karimganj districts and have retained some cultural elements from their previous habitat in Manipur, although in most other respects, they are

14. According to National Crime Records Bureau, Ministry of Home Affairs, Govt. of India, for 1994, 508 cases of rape and 146 cases of molestation were registered in Assam.

very similar to immigrant Muslims.

ATTITUDES TOWARDS GIRLS

Girls are regarded as a liability by most Muslim families and parents usually arrange their marriages during early adolescence. Barring a small minority of enlightened and well-to-do parents, most of them give a low priority to girls' education. Among Manipuri Muslims, who form a fairly backward section of Muslims, most girls between 6-13 years go to nearby mosques in the morning, where they are expected to memorize and recite verses from the holy Quran. They rarely get an opportunity to learn to read and write, much less to understand the meaning of the scriptures (Huda, 1988). A large proportion of Muslims in Assam have low economic and educational levels and get their daughters married early, leading to early and repeated maternity and poor health of women.

MARRIAGE, DIVORCE, POLYGYNY IN ISLAM

On the positive side, the payment of dowry is rare among Muslims of Assam and cases of oppression of girls due to dowry are unusual (Huda, 1988). Polygyny is reported to be prevalent among Muslims from lower middle classes, but rare among educated and elite classes. Islam in principle puts severe restrictions on polygyny and divorce, places a high value on women's education and gives daughters and wives a right to inheritance in property and also a right to protection from their fathers and husbands, respectively. In practice, however, divorce by men is easy and often a unilateral affair, keeping women in a perpetually vulnerable situation. Barring a very small number, majority of Muslim women do not seek legal redress in cases of ill-treatment, desertion and failure to provide maintenance by husbands, or of denial of property rights by male members of their parental families. This is due to a combination of factors: fear of social disapproval, lack of education and awareness of their rights under Muslim personal law, lack of financial resources needed for legal procedures, etc. Above all, a cultural conditioning which glorifies the image of a woman being completely subservient to men in spite of extreme personal suffering, acts as a strong impediment for Muslim women raising their voice against injustices in the family and marriage.

MUSLIM WOMEN'S FAMILY ROLES

Muslims of Assam view man as the protector and provider of the family and assign a subordinate role to women. While women have some freedom in deciding on day-to-day domestic matters, all major decisions are taken by men. In rural areas, most Muslim women are heavily involved in household chores, upbringing of children, agriculture, weaving, etc. but trading and commercial activities are not favoured as a source of income for women (Sherfuddin, 1988). Among conservative and elite sections, women are not expected to go to the farms (Saikia et al., 1986). Manipuri Muslim women often work as vendors of eggs, poultry, puffed rice, woven materials, etc. A few Manipuri Muslim women along with many Bengali Muslim women observe *purdah* (seclusion) and do not go out unescorted. *Purdah* system limits Muslim women's access to education and vocational training, in addition to self-employment opportunities that are urgently needed to augment family income and equally to improve Muslim women's status in the family (Choudhury, Aparajita, 1988). A small number of Muslim women who are educated and hold professional and prestigious jobs enjoy considerable autonomy in their families and greater share in decision-making with their husbands. Some of them are beginning to raise questions about conventional interpretations of Quranic texts and Muslim personal laws (Roy, Shibani, 1988).

MUSLIM WOMEN'S POSITION IN RELIGION

As noted earlier, for many Muslim girls, daily attendance at nearby mosques where they recite Quranic verses without understanding their meaning sums up their exposure to religion. The original Quran being in Arabic, its various translations in other languages and their various interpretations, combined with generally low educational levels makes Muslim women vulnerable to injustice in a highly male-dominated society (Sherfuddin, 1988). Islamic texts, as interpreted by *maulavis* (authorities on religion) govern both religious and secular spheres for women, and their participation rarely goes beyond attendance in congregational prayers.

Hill-Tribal Societies

Karbi and Dimasa tribes are the major constituents of hill-tribal societies of Assam. They are concentrated in Karbi Anglong and North Cachar Hills Districts, although a few are scattered in other districts, e.g. Nagaon, Jorhat, Kamrup, Darrang, Sonitpur, etc. The two hill districts also have a sprinkling of Naga, Kuki, Garo, Khasi, Hojai, Lalung and some other tribes. The Karbis, one of the largest hill-tribes of Assam, racially belonging to Mongoloid and linguistically to Tibeto-Burman group, are believed to have migrated from Central Asia, and settled in several other habitats including Jaintia Hills, from where they were pushed out by the Kacharis before coming to Karbi Anglong (Borah, 1989). Dimasas, an Indo-Mongoloid group, belonging to the larger Bodo family (originally called "Dilaosa" meaning sons of the river "Dilao Tilao Lutt," i.e. Brahmaputra), previously ruled over Dimasa kingdom that was also known in the past as Cachar or "Heramb" kingdom (Bhattacharjee, J.B. 1987).[15]

GROOMING OF GIRLS

Both Karbi and Dimasa societies have a positive attitude towards girls, and birth of a girl child in the family is warmly welcomed. From an early age of five or six years onwards, young girls begin to assist their mothers in bringing water from mountain streams, carrying meals for their parents, working in *jhum* fields, collecting firewood from the forests, looking after younger siblings, care of poultry and other animals, gathering edible roots and vegetables from the forests, etc. Weaving is considered an essential part of the grooming of young girls in both of these communities. When there is a lull in agricultural operations, mothers use this opportunity to ensure that their daughters acquire proficiency in weaving. A Karbi mother's lullaby for her baby girl reflects her fervent wish that the girl may grow into an accomplished weaver and produce beautiful clothes for her family (Medhi, 1989). A married Karbi woman is expected to weave a special apparel for her husband before her first child arrives (Terangpi, 1989). Karbi and Dimasa girls are also engaged in various cultivation activities along with their parents.

The early socialization of Karbi and Dimasa girls is facilitated by two types of institutional arrangements: youth organizations and youth dormitories for girls and boys. Until recently, Karbi girls normally spent three years in a youth dormitory called "Jirkedam" where they were admitted as associate members. Each girl was designated as a kind of assistant to a boy who was responsible for specific tasks, e.g. bringing water, clearing the jungle, bringing harvested crops to the dormitory. The

---

15. According to legends, Dimasas initially established a kingdom in lower Kamrup sometime after CE1000 and in the subsequent political turmoil shifted to Sadiya, and then to Dimapur (now in Nagaland). When routed by the Ahoms in 1536 they settled down in Maibong for two centuries, were pushed out again by Ahoms in 1705 and after a period of political wilderness, moved southwards in Cachar plains in 1745. In Cachar, Dimasas who came under the influence of brahmins came to be known as Barmans (Bhattacharjee, 1987).

wife of the junior headman of a village generally selected the pairs in consultation with the girls, after ensuring that the boy and girl concerned belonged to different clans. With the emergence of formal school system, youth dormitories have suffered a decline. Even then, every village has youth organizations which train young boys and girls not only in various house-keeping and cultivation tasks, under the supervision of the village headman, but more importantly, in assuming responsibility for community needs such as looking after an ailing person, helping a needy family in harvesting, religious functions or death rituals, etc. Girls cook food, prepare rice-beer, welcome guests and participate with boys in singing and dancing in religious events, post-harvest festivals like *Bihu* or *Baisakhi,* or death ceremonies like *Chomangkan*. Besides the youth organizations ("Jirasong" of Karbis, and "Naudrung" of Dimasas), both of these communities assign a special role to older and experienced women. For instance, the "Hojaijiks," i.e. older Dimasa women take upon themselves the jobs of teaching young girls correct dance steps, new and intricate weaving designs, as well as social graces like the art of conversation (Nunisa, 1989). Karbi and Dimasa girls thus learn the essential tasks of a housewife as well as those of a responsible member of the community in a relaxed and free atmosphere.

SELECTION OF MARRIAGE PARTNER

Since girls are expected to be more responsible than boys for household tasks, their schooling gets a lower priority than that of boys in Karbi and Dimasa tribes. Their experience in youth organizations, particularly where girls are expected to take care of personal comforts of boys with whom they work as assistants, would seem to prepare them to accept the supremacy of men. At the same time, girls move about freely with friends and select their life partners. Even where marriages are arranged by parents, girls are consulted before engagements are fixed. Girls generally get married between 15-20 years.

Karbis do not have the practice of bride-price or dowry. Dimasas, however, follow the practice of the groom's side paying bride-price to the girl's parents, and the amount of cash and articles to be given are fixed during negotiations between the parents. When a boy wishes to marry a girl, his father or some other relatives approach the girl's parents with a proposal accompanied by a gourd full of beer. In both communities, women take active role in negotiations and acceptance of the gourd signifies confirmation of the proposal initiated by the groom's party. In both communities the traditional practice has been for the groom to live and work in the prospective father-in-law's place for one to three years, but this practice is declining rapidly, and may be observed in a token manner. At the end of the stipulated period, a Karbi girl can still refuse to marry the boy, and there is no liability of any kind for the girl's parents. Illegitimate child brings no stigma for the girl and she can get married without any difficulty. At the time of wedding, girls usually receive clothes, ornaments and spinning and weaving instruments from their parents. Dimasa girls may sometimes get a share from their fathers' property. In both Karbi and Dimasa groups, major share of wedding expenses including a feast for bride's party has to be borne by the groom's party. During the wedding ceremony the bride's parents receive a place of honour and the groom has to bow before them as a mark of respect.

CLAN EXOGAMY AND TRIBAL ENDOGAMY

The rule of clan exogamy and tribal endogamy must be obeyed and infringements are punished by the village council with fine or ex-communication. Dimasas have a bivalant system of patri-clans called "Sengphong" and matri-clans, called "Jadi" or "Julu." A Dimasa girl is prohibited from marrying a boy having an affiliation either to her mother's clan or father's clan. Furthermore, a Dimasa girl marrying a non-Dimasa boy faces strong disapproval and may even be excommunicated. A Dimasa boy marrying a non-Dimasa girl is frowned upon, but generally gets a lighter punishment (Nunisa, 1989). The village council generally decides on the action to be taken in cases of such violations. Ironically enough, a guilty woman, even after paying a fine or undergoing an expiatory ceremony of re-conversion, may still face rejection by relatively older Dimasa women who usually represent a strongly conservative section. A Karbi girl having an adulterous relationship with a man belonging to her own clan is considered a serious offence and she has to pay a heavy fine, at times face excommunication and may even be subjected to a symbolic death ceremony. However, after suffering the punishment, the girl can lead a normal life. But if she has adulterous relationship with a man belonging to a permissible clan, the punishment is nominal (Phangcho, 1989).

POLYGYNY, DIVORCE, REMARRIAGE

Both Karbis and Dimasas follow the rule of monogamy, although there is no absolute ban on polygyny, and when the first wife is childless or without a son, a man may acquire a second wife. Divorce is rare, and the village council, in which women have no representation, decides cases of divorce and adultery. If a Dimasa woman obtains a divorce because of the husband's fault, she does not have to return the bride-price to the divorced husband. Cases of ill-treatment and oppression of women are reported to be rare. Divorcees and widows can remarry, and although the general practice is for a widow to marry the deceased husband's younger brother, she is free to marry any other man.

FAMILY RESPONSIBILITIES AND RELATIONSHIPS

After marriage the relatively carefree and relaxed life of Karbi and Dimasa girls changes into a strenuous routine. The general level of development in Karbi Anglong and North Cachar Hills districts is low, living conditions continue to be harsh, the terrain is hilly and the predominant mode of cultivation is jhuming, with low productivity.[16] While men clear the forest and set the logs and brush on fire, women undertake all the remaining agricultural operations, besides the usual house-keeping chores of cooking, bringing water, collecting firewood and edible roots, brewing rice-beer, raising vegetables, poultry and other animals, rearing *endy* (a kind of silk), spinning, weaving, etc. Men on the other hand, are reported to have a relatively easy and relaxed routine, and more time for relaxation.

Men occupy a dominant position in the family. The choicest foods are saved for men. Karbi legends depict women as instruments of labour, and therefore substitutable (Terang, 1989). Loyalty and devotion to the husband is regarded as the greatest virtue among women. Women walk a few steps behind the husband as a mark of respect for him. Among the Karbis, a woman does not talk directly to the husband's brother and may cover her head in his presence. As discussed in Chapter 3, among both Karbis and Dimasas, ownership and inheritance of immovable property, e.g. house and land, and control over agricultural produce rest exclusively

---

16. According to a study by S. Sikidar, (1990), 88 per cent of population of Karbi Anglong district and 93 per cent of North Cachar Hills district depended on *jhum* cultivation. The study highlighted absence of technological improvements in agriculture, low family incomes, non-utilization of mineral resources, lack of agro-based industries, ineffective implementation of government development programmes, etc.

with men. A new trend among fathers towards giving a share of their lands to daughters has been noted recently, but this is by no means a general practice. Income earned by Karbi and Dimasa women by raising and selling vegetables, poultry, goats or *endy*-weaving and such other activities is regarded as exclusively their own along with presents received from parents at the time of their marriage. Husbands as a rule would not sell any of these products without consulting their wives. Despite their weak formal economic position, they are portrayed as having an important place in the family, and marital relationship is highly valued. Women usually are entrusted with safe-keeping of family valuables.

Karbi and Dimasa women play an active role in family events like marriages, child-births, deaths. At the time of celebration of community festivals like Bihu, women get busy preparing rice-beer and husking rice for the hospitality of guests. Both Karbi and Dimasa women act as negotiators of marriage proposals. In fact, Dimasa women play a crucial role in fixing bride-price, and men would make it a point to consult the bride's mother and other relatives before fixing a marriage. A Karbi woman from the groom's side usually goes to the girl's mother with a marriage proposal, and arranges details of the marriage ceremony. At child-birth, Karbi and Dimasa women fulfil important functions, like conducting deliveries, performing ceremonies like feeding the new-born for the first time at the breast and other purificatory routines. Older and experienced women, called "Hojaijiks" among Dimasas give useful tips to young mothers on child-rearing.

Karbi and Dimasa women cannot be village headmen, nor can they participate in meetings of village councils that decide matters concerning the community besides cases of infringement of customary laws, and disputes among individuals. Some exceptions are, however, made: like among the Karbis, the "Sarathi's" (headman) wife is consulted before taking important decisions. Dimasa village councils sometimes permit women to attend meetings if they are directly involved. As noted earlier, Karbi and Dimasa women have no right to own or inherit immovable property from their fathers, and may own a piece of land only if given as a gift by a father. Despite this weak formal position, they are not pictured as weak and subservient. There is an interesting story of Rongpharpi Rongbey, a Karbi woman who was cutting fire-wood when accosted by attendants of a Kachari king who wanted breast-milk of nursing mothers for his pet tiger-cubs. She was so incensed by this demand that she killed one of the king's men with her axe, after which she led her people to a safe habitat to escape the king's retaliation (Terangpi, 1989). The matri-clan system among Dimasas is believed to have given women a feeling of security and assurance. A son inherits father's property and takes his clan name, and a daughter inherits mother's property and takes her clan name. Besides, she has exclusive right over the dowry received from parents in marriage, which may include a piece of land gifted by her father.

WOMEN'S POSITION IN RELIGION

Karbi and Dimasa women have a rather marginal role in religion. The priests are always men. At the family level, women perform some rites at child-birth, marriage ceremony and deaths. In both Karbi and Dimasa communities, certain women are supposed to have special abilities of invoking appropriate deities and spirits to ward off and cure illnesses of family members. Some Karbi women (as well as men) are believed to get into a trance-like state called "Palodep" in which they profess to acquire powers to predict the future and to communicate with the souls of dead ancestors. When there is death in the family, an older woman credited with divining powers, called "Uchepi," takes care of the dead body, which includes cooking special food for two-and-a-half days before cremation. The "Uchepi" leads the funeral procession, carries gifts that are placed on the funeral pyre and lights the fire. Another woman, designated as "Char-he-Abang" sings the funeral dirges to ensure safe journey of the soul to its final resting place. Women vie with one another to be designated as "Uchepi" and "Char-he-Abang" since these women are highly respected. They provide their services free, but members of concerned families give them food and specially prepared rice-beer (Terangpi, 1989).

Among Dimasas, an older and experienced woman who is a professional mourner leads the funeral procession and sprinkles paddy and cotton along the way to the cremation ground, ostensibly to create a bridge between the living and the dead. The melodious voice of women who sing funeral songs is believed to facilitate the soul's final journey to its destination. This practice is similar to the one among the Rabhas, a plains tribe of Assam, who like the Dimasas, belong to the larger Bodo family. Women who perform purification rites at child-birth and death occupy an honoured place in Dimasa society and people who invite them offer clothes, money, betel nuts and specially prepared rice-beer (Chetia, 1989).

It is important to note that both Karbi and Dimasa communities have been exposed to various cultural influences as a result of interaction with other communities in the course of shifting their habitats. Even after these groups settled down in their present locations, they show considerable variations in their integration of outside religious and social influences. Thus, those groups who have lived in a more hilly terrain tend to be governed more by their native religions, whereas the groups living in plains have imbibed more influence of Hinduism as well as other cultures.

In general Karbi and Dimasa women's participation in indigenous tribal religions is very limited. Exposure to Hinduism has expanded their scope, particularly with respect to participation in community worship. It is important to note, however, that there are many differences in the extent to which Karbis and Dimasas have imbibed Hindu influences. For instance, Dimasas who have lived in isolated hill areas have remained more conservative in their religious attitudes as compared to the Dimasas living in the plains who have imbibed many Hindu elements through their contacts with Assamese Hindus. This explains why there are differences within sections of Karbis and Dimasas with respect to position of women in indigenous religious events. While Karbi and Dimasa women occupy a dominant position in family-level religious ceremonies like child-birth and death, they are restricted from participating in community worship in their indigenous faiths (Duara,1989). Despite the heavy involvement of Karbi women in agricultural activities, they cannot participate in the worship of "Hemphu" — the deity of agriculture, nor can they join the "Ronkar" festival, which is observed for ensuring the village community's well-being, or enter the place of communal worship. A Karbi woman may chant sacrificial *mantras* (verses), but cannot kill the sacrificial animal. Interestingly, the Karbis who live in the plains are losing their rigidity as a result of contacts with Hindu communities and permit women to participate in communal worship of Hindu goddesses — "Ai-Nam." In fact, knowledgeable Karbi women in the plains can perform many religious ceremonies, related to worship of Hindu goddesses and are highly respected, although the official priests are always men (Chetia, 1989). In comparison, Dimasa women participate more actively in communal worship due to greater exposure to Hinduism.[17]

17. Dimasas were exposed to Hinduism between fifteenth and eighteenth centuries. But a more direct interaction took place during the reign of Maharaja Krishna Chandra (1780–1813), who arranged a special ceremony to convert →

SOURCES OF CONSERVATISM AMONG DIMASA WOMEN

A comparison between the present status of Karbi and Dimasa women reveals considerable difference in their respective positions. Karbi women today are educationally more advanced, and are entering new professions like teaching, medicine, administrative services, etc. and have welcomed the benefits of amenities like electricity, tube wells and rice mills to improve the quality of life. Dimasa women in isolated hill areas, on the other hand, have resisted exposure to new influences and ironically represent forces of conservatism in their society, although both Karbi and Dimasa women live in similar ecological settings and until recently were nearly similar in their educational status.[18] The relative backwardness of Dimasa women is attributed to "Gusu-g-thar" (literally "pollution — purity" code), which was introduced by a non-Dimasa preceptor from Cachar to prevent epidemics believed to be caused by indiscriminate social mixing between Dimasas and other neighbouring groups, and ostensibly as a means of preserving ethnic purity.[19] Another reason of rigidity was the vehemence with which brahmin preceptors of Dimasa ruler, Maharaja Krishna Chandra (1780-1813) tried to push Hinduization of Dimasas and rejection of Dimasa customs and culture, including matri-clan system.[20] Infringements of "Gusu-g-thar" were punished by ex-communication. The Dimasas, however, resisted the brahmans' attempts and have retained the matri-clans to this day, probably as a defensive reaction to external pressures. Dimasas rigorously observe rules of clan exogamy as well as "Gusu-g-thar" — the pollution-purity code, which has resulted in their social isolation and

---

→ a large number of Dimasas to Hinduism. A point to be noted, however, is that the king's brahman preceptors advocated the Sakta cult, as distinguished from the more liberal Vaishnavism.

18. As per 1971 Census, the percentage of literacy among Karbi women was 4.95 (Sharma Thakur, 1989) and among Dimasa women 9.36 (Duara, 1989). At present Karbi women have out-stripped Dimasa women not only in education but also in occupational advancement.

19. When a massive epidemic spread in North Cachar hills during the British period, a non-Dimasa emissary blamed it on indiscriminate mixing among kshatriya Dimasas and other supposedly inferior neighbouring communities. To remedy this situation, "Gusu-g-thar" — a pollution-purity code — was adopted by Dimasas to preserve ethnic purity, resulting in severe restrictions on social contacts which led to isolation and conservatism (Nunisa, 1989).

20. An insistent demand of brahmin preceptors of Maharaja Krishna Chandra was elimination of matri-clan system of the Dimasas. They performed a purification ceremony for the Maharaja to eliminate the debility supposedly caused by female clan system (Bhattacharjee, 1989).

preoccupation with punishing those who violate the rules regarding contacts with other clans and sub-groups. It is a strange irony of fate that Dimasa women, who are themselves victims of patriarchal injustice, have assumed the role of dispensing punishments to the guilty.

While Dimasa female clans system is believed to give women a sense of identity, with increasing contacts with their Hinduised neighbours, there is an unmistakable shift towards patri-clan system. Most writers on Karbi and Dimasa women have presented a positive picture of women's position in the family. Instances of neglect and ill-treatment of women and divorces are reported to be rare. Undoubtedly, Karbi and Dimasa women's early socialization in the family as well as in youth organizations prepares them to accept a subordinate role with respect to men. The second factor seems to be women's indispensable position in family events like marriage, birth, death, etc. even if many of the roles are largely ceremonial. The present situation is beginning to change as these women have better access to education, vocational preparation, outside careers and contacts with other communities and new ideas. The question is : How long will they continue to remain content with their subordinate position?

Plains Tribal Societies

The tribes which inhabit Brahmaputra and Barak valleys, referred to as plains tribal societies mainly include: Bodo / Bodo Kachari, Deori, Sonowal Kachari, Barman Kachari, Lalung, Hojai, Hajong, Mech, Rabha, Miri/Mishing, Aiton and Tai-Phake. These groups reveal in their lifestyle varying degrees of inter-mixture of their original tribal culture and later influences brought about by their contacts with non-tribal communities of Assam. The resulting outcomes for women have thus been mixed. In some cases, there has been an erosion of their previous advantageous position, whereas in some others women have acquired new freedom and access to opportunities that were earlier denied to them. The plains tribal population formed nearly one-tenth of the total State population in 1971, but with a large influx of Bengali and other immigrants in the last three decades, this proportion has decreased. A majority of plains tribes belong to the larger Bodo ethnic group, although there are some exceptions, e.g. Mishings[21] Aitons[22] and

21. Mishings, also known as Miris, originally settled in Siang region, and were akin to Adis of Arunachal Pradesh. They migrated to Assam in search of fertile lands and took to settled cultivation. Their original religion, like the Adis, was based on the twin principle of Sun representing the female and the Moon →

Tai Phakes.[23]

ATTITUDE TOWARDS GIRLS

The plains tribal groups of Assam have a basically positive attitude towards a girl child, and mothers take a lot of care in her upbringing to ensure that she acquires necessary skills that are desired in a woman. Among the Bodos, traditionally, a woman's status depended on the number of her children, particularly girls. In plains tribal households, girls start helping their mothers even from four years onwards with care of siblings. They begin to help in other chores, such as bringing water and other house-keeping chores besides agricultural operations, and by early adolescence they become important assets to their families. Daughters have a special place in Rabha community, which previously was matrilineal. A Rabha gentleman on his way to an important mission considers it auspicious to come across a young Rabha girl. The eldest Rabha daughter is entrusted with the task of being a custodian of family income. Proficiency in spinning and weaving is regarded as an essential skill for girls in most plains tribes, and Bodo and Mishing mothers pay special attention to teaching these skills to their daughters.

Adolescence

Besides sharing responsibility for household work and family agriculture, Bodo girls are encouraged to raise their own poultry, pigs and other animals and may even have their own agricultural plots with which they earn an independent income. Indeed, some Mishing girls not only earn money for their education but may help support their younger brothers and sisters. Girls may rear *endy* to produce a kind of silk and do weaving

→ representing the male element. While they adopted Hinduism, and later Vaishnavism, they have retained some elements from their original religion and culture.

22. Aitons are a small community of about 5000 people, settled mainly in Golaghat and Karbi Anglong. Aitons are also known as "Man" in Karbi Anglong and are officially recognized as a plains tribal group. They came from Myanmar, speak Tai language and belong to Hinayan sect of Buddhism (Buragohain, 1989).

23. Tai Phake, a Tai-speaking Hinayan Buddhist group came from Hukawng valley in Myanmar around 1775 and are concentrated in Dibrugarh, while some inhabited areas in Tirap and Lohit (Arunachal Pradesh). When parts of Tirap were transferred to Assam in 1950, Tai Phakes were not officially recognized as a separate tribe in Assam, but were regarded as a sub-tribe of Khamtis or Miris.

not only to prepare their own *Dokhna* (wedding dress), but also to give financial help to the family. Besides acquiring resourcefulness and economic independence, young girls also get their training in sharing community responsibility. For instance, young Mishing girls are members of youth organizations in their community, and during the celebration of important festivals like *Bihu* and *Porag*, assume responsibility for a variety of jobs like preparing food and "apong" (rice-beer), welcoming guests, collecting materials for religious ceremonies, etc. Above all, with their colourful dresses, singing and dancing they bring a lot of cheer and spirit of festivity (Pegu, 1989).

SELECTION OF MATE AND MARRIAGE

Young girls enjoy freedom of movement among plains tribal groups. They often meet and select their marriage partners at community festivals related to soil fertility and prayers for bountiful harvests, such as *Porag* and *Bihu*. Even among groups like Tai Phake among whom marriages are arranged by parents, the girl must be above 15 years and her consent is ascertained. A girl is never forced to marry against her wishes (Gohain, A.K. 1989).

The Mishings in the past had a practice, although occasional, of abduction of a young girl by the groom's party. This is no longer prevalent, and even where parents may arrange their daughter's marriage, the girl's consent is obtained. Among Mishings elopement of young lovers is not only frequent, it may even be preferable since it spares parents on both sides cumbersome negotiations and expensive rituals. Generally, a love affair between a boy and a girl, and even elopement, is regularized by parents through a simple procedure of groom's parents offering a modest bride-price to the girl's parents. The bride-price, among the plains tribal groups, is viewed more as a symbol of dignity of the girl and of respect towards the girl's parents, and not as a price for buying a wife. Among the Bodos and Mishings, it is not uncommon for young girls to buy clothes and ornaments with their own earnings. The form of bride-price has recently been modified to a custom of a feast arranged by the groom's parents to honour the bride and her parents (Brahma, 1989). Among Dibongiyas too, a territorial sub-group of the Deoris,[24] there is an

24. Dibongiyas are one of the territorial groups of Deori Chutias, the other groups being Borgoniyas, Tengapaniyas and Patargoniyas. Deori Chutias performed priestly functions in the royal temples of Chutia kingdom. They originally came →

increasing preference for marriages by elopement, since this avoids expenses and elaborate rituals for parents of both parties (Saikia,1976). They regularize such unions by a ritual offering of rice-beer to the deities and to the souls of deceased ancestors. Simultaneously, groom's clan members formally make a future commitment for performing funeral rites for the girl, thereby ending her parents' obligation in this respect. For the girls parents, this ceremony confirms that their daughter is thereafter placed under the protection of her husband's clan.

None of the plains tribes have a practice of demanding a dowry from the girl's parents. However, bride's parents may give clothes, ornaments, household articles or cash as gifts to the girl in marriage, which remain as the girl's exclusive possessions. The rule of clan exogamy and tribal endogamy is followed among some tribes, e.g. Mishings and Rabhas, but the clan system is declining among the Rabhas along with their greater acculturation with neighbouring societies. Among Tai Phakes, a small Buddhist tribe that is struggling to get recognition and to overcome its backward status, young girls are marrying outsiders. Similarly Barman Kachari girls who are unable to find educated young men in their own community are marrying Bengali educated men, and are entering new careers to improve their status (Bhattacharjee, 1988). Marriage is a religious sacrament among most plains tribes. Among the Tai Phake however, a Buddhist group, it is a civil affair conducted before village elders.

RESIDENCE AFTER MARRIAGE

Most plains tribal groups follow the practice of patri-local residence, the only exception being Lalungs and Rabhas, who have a past tradition of matriliny. Among the Lalungs, the youngest daughter inherits land and the house from her mother, and her husband becomes the resident son-in-law who takes over as head of the family after his father-in-law's death. Other daughters get share of land from their mother, and their husbands construct homes on these lands. If a girl selects a non-Lalung man as her mate, she inherits maternal property only if her husband agrees to stay in

→ from areas adjoining Dibong river in Lohit, Arunachal Pradesh. While Deori Chutias or Deoris are listed officially as a plains tribe in Assam, other groups of Chutias are listed among OBCs. Dibongiyas have remained fairly isolated and retain many elements of their native religion. Their exposure to Hinduism and Vaishnavism led to a process of re-identification of their original with Hindu deities such as Kundi being equated with Shiva, and Mama with Parvati (Saikia, 1976).

her house (Gohain, B.K. 1989). The Rabhas have given up many of their matrilineal traditions due to influences of their patrilineal neighbours, and daughters generally go to their husbands' houses after marriage. However, if a Rabha father has no sons, he may give his lands to his daughters. A Rabha mother may also give her inherited lands to a daughter, whose husband becomes a *ghar-jamai* — a resident son-in-law (Goswami, 1979). However there is a new trend, as an evidence of increasing patrilineal influence: The former rather submissive *ghar-jamai* who was expected to render services to his father-in-law now comes as an honoured guest, entitled to special attention from his hosts. Furthermore, a beginning of change from bride-price to dowry has also been noted (Pal, 1993).

MONOGAMY : POLYGAMY

Although monogamy is the preferred norm among most plains tribes, the practice of polygyny exists to some extent. While barrenness in wife is a common and acceptable ground for a husband to take a second wife, this same reason, i.e. childlessness, is not used by a woman for taking a second husband. Among the Mishings, however, a wife can get a divorce if her husband is impotent (Taid, 1989). The Tai Phake husband is expected to obtain consent of the first wife before bringing a second wife. A Pati Rabha gentleman can marry a second wife if the first wife produced only girl children, thus perpetuating the traditional injustice to women. Until recently, it was customary for Rabha men to have several wives, since it gave them social prestige, besides additional farm labour. Rabha women were reported to be reconciled to this practice. With better availability of hired agricultural labour and expansion of education, monogamy is increasingly becoming the accepted norm (Barooah, 1989).

GROUNDS FOR DIVORCE

The grounds on which divorce can be obtained by either party include adultery, unsound mind, desertion, and as noted earlier, impotence. Among the Mishings, a wife can seek divorce if the husband fails to pay the agreed bride-price, or if he is unable to feed and clothe her, or is guilty of neglect or polygyny (Taid, 1989), and she can claim compensation if the husband divorces her, which indicates her relatively stronger position in the marital relationship. If a Rabha husband tortures his wife, destroys her weaving instruments or breaks her conch bangles, he is regarded as a serious offender (Rabha, 1989). The Rabhas also permit a divorce by mutual consent on grounds of incompatibility that is significant, particularly because unlike a husband, a Rabha wife cannot obtain separation from an adulterous husband unless the village council agrees. The wife is at a disadvantage since she may not be able to present her case adequately before the council, whose membership in restricted to men. Furthermore, the council may decide whether the husband may be fined or ordered to pay compensation to the wife for wedding expenses. Occasionally, the council may order a divorce even against the wife's wishes, simply because she could not present her case adequately (Barooah, 1989).

An interesting exception to the usually harsher attitude towards wives guilty of adultery as compared to husbands among most tribal groups, is provided by the Tai Phakes. Here, while the guilty woman gets a scolding from the village council the paramour of the adulterous wife is regarded as the more guilty person and the community imposes a fine on him. The woman's marital status is protected, but if she wants to divorce her husband, she is permitted to do so, the only condition being that she cannot claim any financial consideration from the husband. But if the husband divorces her, she gets half of his property and the custody of children (Gohain, A.K. 1989). Another noteworthy feature of the Tai Phakes is the provision that in such cases, the woman retains her exclusive right over money earned by her prior to marriage and the gifts received, including landed property, if any, received from her parents. Furthermore, when a man takes more wives, the legal status of previous wives is recognized.

REMARRIAGE OF DIVORCEES AND WIDOWS

There are no restrictions on divorcees and widows re-marrying and they do not suffer any social stigma. The practice of junior levirate — the younger brother of the deceased man marrying the widow — is prevalent among some groups, e.g. Mishing, Rabha. But the widows are not forced into such marriages, and can marry other men of their choice, the only condition being that they lose their rights over a share in the deceased husband's property. Some groups, however, have imbibed from their neighbouring non-tribal communities negative attitudes towards widows. Among Sonowal Kacharis, widows are expected to adopt an austere lifestyle, give up wearing the vermilion mark on the forehead and coloured dresses, and stop eating fish, meat and eggs, if not forever, at least for a year (Mitra, 1989). The Rabhas, because of their adoption of Hindu culture, do not favour widow remarriage, although there is no bar against it and some widows do remarry.

WOMEN'S ROLES IN THE FAMILY

Women occupy an important place in the family in plains tribal groups, which is undoubtedly related to the significant contribution they make towards the family's economy, besides their role in maintaining family solidarity. As noted in Chapter 3, except clearing the jungle and ploughing, which is men's task (in the absence of men Mishing women may even plough the fields), women are engaged in all agricultural operations such as sowing, transplanting, harvesting, threshing, storing of grains, husking, etc. They are responsible for all house-keeping jobs such as cooking, cleaning, bringing water, child-rearing, care of poultry, pigs and other animals, sericulture, vegetable cultivation, preparing rice-beer, etc. Many plain-tribal groups, e.g. Mishings, Bodos, Rabhas, etc. give great importance to women's skills in spinning and weaving and mothers are expected to ensure that their daughters acquire proficiency in these activities. Daily shopping and petty trading in domestic products is women's responsibility. Sonowal Kachari women also do fishing and weave baskets. Great prestige is attached to being competent and hospitable housewives and able mothers who teach their daughters all the house-keeping skills, as well as weaving.

Women in Plains tribal groups serve as an important focus to keep the kinship group together, whether living in separate houses or under the same roof. Among the Rabhas, for instance, the senior-most woman, i.e. the mother serves as a vital link among married sons who usually set up separate households. Among the Mishings some of whom still have the traditional household with 100-150 persons living together, women are expected to preserve solidarity and harmony among members. In a Bodo household, in the absence of the father, the mother enjoys a greater authority than the eldest son. Although a Bodo woman does not own or inherit property, she is custodian of the granary, and the husband would not sell any produce, poultry or pigs, without consulting her (Brahma, 1989). Among the Rabhas, it is customary for the mother to be the keeper of all valuables and family heirlooms, and none of the men have any knowledge about the secret hideout, which is transmitted to the daughter at the right time (Rabha, 1989). Aiton women, who take the major burden of financial sustenance of the family, are also responsible for buying and selling at nearby markets, and have an important voice in making household decisions (Buragohain, 1989).

Women have an important place in special events in the family, such as births, marriages and deaths, among Plains tribal communities. Experienced women usually conduct deliveries in areas where modern health workers are not available. In marriages, elderly women in the family often initiate negotiations between the bride's and groom's parties. Among the Rabhas, women called "Sirajik" act as professional mourners. Women generally do not have any role in deliberations of the village council, which is entrusted with the task of settling disputes among individuals, or issues concerning the whole village. Aitons are probably the only exception where in the absence of the husband, the wife represents her household at village meetings (Buragohain, 1989). While women are consulted in all important family matters, the final decisions generally rest with the men.

OBLIGATIONS OF THE FAMILY

When it comes to the family's obligations towards maintenance of women who for any reason become dependent, perhaps the Rabhas seem to be more careful and particular about ensuring that women do not become destitute in adverse circumstances. This seems to be related to their prior matrilineal culture. When a married daughter goes to live with her husband and in-laws, the girl's family assigns the task of safeguarding her interests to the "Boro-Mahari" — a group of men and women relatives of the girl. Similarly, a "Patir Bap" — a sacred bond father — is designated to ensure the girl's well-being at the in-law's place (Rabha, 1989). As the Rabhas are shifting towards patriliny, these traditions are declining in importance. A Rabha husband who divorces his wife is under obligation to provide for her maintenance. Similarly a widow is entitled to maintenance from the deceased husband's property as well as from her sons. But if the divorced or widowed daughter returns to her parents, her father must maintain the dependent woman and her children (Borooah, 1989). Among the Tai Phakes, when a husband dies, his sons inherit father's property, and a part is given to the widow (Gohain, 1989). In plains tribal groups generally, although there is usual expectation that divorcees, widows and unmarried daughters will be maintained by the family, it is only the Rabhas who specifically lay down responsibility for their maintenance. This is probably due to this community's efforts to codify their customary laws (Barooah, 1989). It is important that other tribal communities undertake similar exercises. This is likely to protect women's interests especially when women have no representation in meetings of village councils or of village elders, and they may be subject to injustice on the basis of misinterpreted customary laws and traditions.

WOMEN'S PLACE IN RELIGION

Women in plains tribal societies in general occupy an important place in religion. In most cases, this is due to their syncretic practice of elements from their indigenous tribal faiths and adoption of Hindu or Vaishnavite religion, and in a few cases conversion to Buddhism. This is true in spite of the fact that both Hinduism and Buddhism tend to perpetuate patriarchal attitudes and deny women access to some ceremonies, besides limiting priestly functions to men. A significant aspect of several tribal faiths is their belief that fecundity of a woman and fertility of the soil belong to the same genre, which explains the important place assigned to women in all ceremonies connected with sowing and harvesting which have a crucial place in predominantly agricultural communities. At the same time several tribal religions restrict women from community level worship. The combination of indigenous and external religions has been utilized by plains tribal women to expand their space in religion, as described in the following examples.

Mishing women occupy a significant place in the major "Porag" festival, which includes propitiating certain spirits to ensure plentiful harvests and for seeking the blessings of deceased ancestors. A young Mishing girl who is selected as a "Borpuwary" (the chief worshipper) initiates the sacrifice of a female pig and the brewing of "apong" (rice-beer). Furthermore, all married women, including those who have moved to their husband's villages, are invited to a sumptuous feast, as their good wishes are believed to ensure prosperity and good fortune for the community (Pegu, 1989). Among the Bodos, a respected older woman initiates the planting of paddy and also the harvesting that is marked by special rituals. During the period of growth of paddy, a young Bodo girl performs a ceremony to ensure a healthy crop by touching the tips of plants. The presence of two young girls as "Bairathis" is regarded as very auspicious. Besides the daily worship of family gods, selected Bodo women play the role of "Deodini" (the priestess). The role of Bodo women in religion has been strengthened due to their contact with Hinduism, with the creation of "Brahma" faith — a revivalist system of beliefs — initiated by Kalicharan Brahma, as well as by starting a new Hinduised sect by Guru Rupamani.[25] Bodo women who are well-versed in the Vedas can now act as priests. Similarly, those women who have adopted Christianity and have studied the Bible, can conduct Christian church service. Barman Kachari women, who have a much wider scope in Hindu festivals, participate with great enthusiasm in *Sankranti* and *Rajasik Puja* which are related to removing sins and evils and bringing prosperity to their villages (Bhattacharjee, Bimalendu 1988).

Women from a few plains tribal groups are restricted from participating in some religious ceremonies in their indigenous tribal faiths. For instance, Deori women cannot enter the "Midiku" — the abode of their community gods, nor can they take part in "Makan Chibba," a sacrificial ritual to invoke the goodwill of ancestors before using newly harvested grains, which is rather surprising in view of the women's heavy contribution to family cultivation (Saikia, P.C. 1976). Deori women cannot partake of the special feast arranged on this occasion. However, they have special place in singing "Ai Nam" — songs in praise of the goddesses. Surprisingly, Lalung women, who enjoy a central position in their household and have a matrilineal tradition, do not have an entry to some religious ceremonies, nor can they officiate as priests (Gohain, B.K. 1989). The Tai Phake women, who enjoy a strong position in the household *vis-à-vis* men, are prohibited from worshipping "Chao-suo," the tribe's village deity, because menstruation in women is regarded as impure. Women in most plains tribal groups have improved their position after adopting a new religion. For instance, Deori women take active part in the community worship of Hindu goddesses like Lakshmi (Saikia, P.C. 1989). The Tai Phake women can participate along with men in community worship of the Buddha, their adopted religion. According to Buddhist doctrines, men and women attain salvation entirely on the basis of their own deeds. Women can seek their spiritual fulfilment independently, and do not have to obtain it through unquestioning devotion to their husbands, as prescribed by Hinduism. Despite this highly equitable principle, Buddhism too has tended to regard women as an impediment in man's spiritual endeavours. Until

25. Kalicharan Brahma propounded the "Brahma" religion around mid-nineteenth century, in an effort to revive the authentic roots of the Bodos' religion and remove irrational and superstitious elements which had crept in. The promotion of Brahma faith gave a new impetus to education and social reform and recognized women's right to education. At a later point, a new Hinduized version of the "Bathou" system of Bodos was popularized by Guru Rupamani, who attracted mostly Bodo women disciples (Mukherjee and Mukherjee, 1982: 253-80).

almost the end of 1960s, women from Tai Phake and Aiton societies had no access to education since Buddhist monasteries remained until then about the only place to receive education and women had no entry to monasteries (Gohain, A.K. 1989).

The adoption of Hinduism, and particularly neo-Vaishnavism has helped women not only to expand their religions participation, but also to improve their overall position in social spheres as well. When the Sonowal Kacharis, who adopted Shankaradeva's Vaishnavism in 1603, women got an entry to Vaishnavite *namghars* (community prayer halls), although with some conditions (e.g. some centres restricted their attendance to alternate days). This experience helped considerably in their integration with neighbouring Hindu societies, and more importantly, improving their access to modernization. Barman Kachari women provide another example where exposure to brahmin preceptors, despite the latter's downgrading of the matri-clan system, endowed them with an enhanced status of kshatriyas (Bhattacharjee, Bimalendu 1988). Barman Kachari women have been benefiting a great deal from the new educational and developmental facilities and have greatly enhanced their position in the family and society. Dimasa families take pride in receiving Barman Kachari brides in their families.

Recapitulation

The status of Assam's women has been viewed in the context of three major components of the State's population: Non-Tribal, Hill Tribal and Plains Tribal Societies.

NON-TRIBAL SOCIETIES

This component, representing 87.17 per cent of Assam's total population, constitutes a heterogeneous mix which includes Hindus, Muslims and tea-garden labourers as important segments, besides sizeable groups of Nepalis and migrants from other Indian States who came to Assam in search of economic opportunities. Indigenous or Assamese Hindus reflect in their attitudes and practices twin influences which stem from their non-Aryan tribal origins and absorption of medieval Hinduism brought by brahmin preceptors from outside Assam. They tend to view girls as inferior to boys and give a lower priority to their education. Among immigrant Hindus, who hold even more conservative attitudes towards women, girls are viewed as a burden on parents, who have to give dowry to the groom's parents, and girls are usually married during adolescence and their consent may not be regarded as essential. Assamese Hindus are free from the custom of dowry, although a trend to give expensive presents from the bride's side is emerging among urban well-to-do sections. Among Muslims, parents are generally apathetic towards girls' education and get their daughters married during early adolescence, and their consent may not be regarded as necessary.

Both Hindu and Muslim women are expected to assume full responsibility for house-keeping and child care. In rural areas, women share with men considerable burden for agricultural chores, and may also take up wage labour employment particularly in rice-cultivating areas. Women also earn supplementary income through weaving, sericulture, raising poultry and other animals, petty trading in vegetables and agricultural produce, etc. Among brahmins, better economic classes and traditional Muslim families, particularly those in Barak Valley who are governed by *purdah* (seclusion) system, women generally do not go out for agricultural work, nor work as vendors and traders.

Hindu women participate actively in important family events such as births, marriages, major festivals, etc. and may be consulted by men in important family matters, but the final decision rests primarily with men. Among a small section of educated women holding professional jobs, there is a change in the direction of joint consultation and decision-making between husbands and wives. Women from tea-garden labour communities have an important role in controlling household matters, which is undoubtedly related to their crucial role in the family's economic sustenance. Despite various legislative provisions and safeguards, several Hindu women continue to suffer from injustice in the form of polygyny, ill-treatment and desertion by husbands. Very few of such women seek legal remedies. A small number of widows and divorcees re-marry, while many are thwarted by psychological and social inhibitions caused by traditional Hindu ideals of self-denial and austerity. Muslim women too are subject to injustice by husbands due to unilateral divorce and desertion (despite Islamic injunctions against injustice to women) because of their vulnerable social and economic situation. Few Muslim women assert their right to a share in their fathers' or husbands' property.

Assam's non-tribal Hindu women participate in family-level worship and rituals connected with family events such as births and marriages.

However, their participation in institutional level religious events is limited and the priests have always been men. The introduction of Shankaradeva's Vaishnavism eliminated the monopoly of brahmin priests along with several rituals and popularized communal worship of one God — Vishnu — without distinctions of caste. Women used this development to legitimize their participation in community prayers at *namghars*, and more significantly, in "Ai-Nam" (worship of the goddess), where they enjoy a privileged position. Assam's Hindu women are happily free from the worst manifestations of untouchability and oppressive caste system to which women in other parts of India are subject. This is due probably to Assam's original non-Aryan heritage and also the more egalitarian ethos of Shankaradeva's Vaishnavism. Assam's Muslim women, like their counterparts in the rest of India, are severely handicapped due to lack of awareness of the true meaning of Quran, and are conditioned to being governed in their religious and secular spheres by Islamic tenets, as interpreted by *maulavis* (religious preceptors). Their religious participation is largely limited to attendance in congregational prayers at mosques. In general, Assam's non-tribal Hindu and Muslim women are very similar to their counterparts in the rest of India in terms of their position in marriage, family and religion, except that the former have escaped some of the worst indignities like child-marriage, oppression due to dowry demands and dowry deaths and *sati* (immolation of the widow on the funeral pyre of her husband).

HILL TRIBAL SOCIETIES

This segment mainly includes Karbis and Dimasas who inhabit the two hill districts, viz. Karbi Anglong and North Cachar Hills. Among these communities, the birth of a girl child is greeted with joy and girls are carefully groomed by mothers to acquire proficiency in household chores, agricultural tasks and weaving. The former youth dormitories where girls spent their adolescence have suffered a decline with the emergence of schools. However, youth associations exist in most communities, and boys and girls learn to assume responsibility for community events such as special festivals, funeral ceremonies, relief for needy households. Girls select their marriage partners and parents on both sides finalize marriages. Rules of clan exogamy and tribal endogamy must be observed. Among Dimasas, who have parallel systems of matri-clans and patri-clans, violations are strongly disapproved and punished. Karbis do not exchange bride-price or dowry, but Dimasas have the practice of groom's parents giving bride-price to the girl's parents. The groom's side bears major part of marriage expenses. Both Karbis and Dimasas follow the rule of monogamy, although a man may take a second wife if the first one does not produce a child or a son. Divorces are rare and marital disputes are decided by village councils. Cases of ill-treatment and oppression of women are rare, and divorcees and widows can re-marry. No stigma is attached to unmarried mothers and they can get married without difficulty.

After marriage, Karbi and Dimasa women enter an extremely busy schedule with total responsibility for house-keeping tasks, child care, weaving, brewing rice-beer, care of poultry and other animals, besides taking major share of agricultural work. Men occupy a dominant position in the family and women take pride in being loyal and dutiful towards their husbands. Even though men take important financial decisions, women occupy an important place in the household and enjoy autonomy in day-to-day running of the household as well as in the use of their possessions and earnings. In indigenous religion Karbi and Dimasa women are responsible for family level worship and rituals connected with births, marriages and deaths. But they are restricted from participation in community worship, e.g. propitiation of "Hemphu" — the deity of agriculture, or "Ronkar" — a festival to ensure well-being of the community. Both Karbi and Dimasa women play important roles in leading funeral processions, singing funeral dirges and performing rituals believed to facilitate the soul's final journey. These communities also give a special position to women claiming to possess certain special and occult powers to do unusual things, such as, communicating with spirits to prevent future disasters. The marginal status that the Assam's hill tribal women occupy in religion is reflected in the keen competition to get the chief mourner's position in cremations of the dead.

PLAINS TRIBAL SOCIETIES

This group includes tribes which inhabit Brahmaputra and Barak valleys which mainly cover: Bodo/Bodo Kachari, Deori, Sonowal Kachari, Barman Kachari, Lalung, Hojai, Mech, Rabha, Miri/Mishing, Aiton, Tai-Phake and a few smaller groups. These groups have a very positive attitude towards girls, and mothers take great care to teach them house-keeping tasks and weaving. Girls are encouraged from an early age to undertake small enterprises such as raising vegetables, rearing poultry and other animals, weaving, etc. and earn independent incomes. They are members of youth associations and learn to assume joint responsibility along with boys for various tasks in celebration of major festivals like *Bihu* and *Porag*, besides bringing cheer through their singing and dancing. Young girls have freedom to select their marriage partners, however, elopement of young lovers is common and parents generally regularize such unions. Even among groups where parents arrange marriages, girl's consent is always ensured. Bride-price is the common practice, and is viewed more as a symbol of respect for the girl's parents than price for buying a bride. Girl's parents usually give her clothes, ornaments, household articles or cash as gifts and these remain as girl's exclusive possessions. The rules of clan exogamy and tribal endogamy are followed by most tribes but with varying rigour and instances of girls opting to marry educated boys from other communities are not rare. Tribes which had a tradition of matriliny and girl's matri-local residence after marriage, e.g. Lalungs and Rabhas, are moving towards patriliny and patri-local residence as a result of increasing interaction with patrilineal societies.

Monogamy is the preferred norm among most plains tribes, although polygyny exists to some extent, the usual reasons being, the first wife being childless or being without a son. Divorce can be obtained by either party on grounds such as adultery, unsound mind, desertion or impotence. In most of these societies, the husbands usually initiate divorces, and wives generally happen to be at the receiving end. Furthermore, village councils that decide on divorce cases have no representation of women. The Mishings and Rabhas present rather interesting exceptions where women's position is somewhat stronger. A Mishing wife can get a divorce if her husband neglects her, fails to feed and clothe her properly or takes another wife. A Rabha woman can seek divorce from her husband if he tortures her, or destroys her weaving instruments or breaks her conch bangles. The Tai Phake, a Buddhist tribe from Myanmar, represents another example where women guilty of adultery and divorce are treated with some sympathy. Here, the paramour of the woman involved in adultery is regarded as more responsible for the lapse than the woman. Furthermore, if her husband decides to divorce her, she gets half of his property and the custody of children. While most plains tribes recognize the right of widows and divorcees to remarry, some tribes, e.g. Sonowal Kacharis and Rabhas do not favour widow remarriages, and expect widows to adopt an austere lifestyle as a result of imbibing conservative Hindu cultural norms.

Women in plains tribal societies assume a heavy burden of housekeeping chores in addition to their major share in agricultural operations. Although women in most of these societies, with the exception of matrilineal groups like the Lalungs, do not own or inherit immovable property, they make a substantial contribution towards the economic sustenance of the household. They enjoy considerable autonomy in day-to-day management, while the major financial decisions rest with men. Women play an important role in maintaining family solidarity, and are usually the custodians of family heirlooms and treasury. Besides, they have important roles in family events such as birth, marriages and deaths. The family is expected to reciprocate this valuable contribution of women by giving them protection in case of need. It is the obligation of the family to provide maintenance and shelter to widows, deserted wives, unmarried daughters, etc.

Women in plains tribal societies occupy an important place in daily family level worship, as well as religious rites at major family events like births, marriages and deaths. Furthermore, the close association between women's procreative ability and fertility of the soil has given them considerable prominence in various religious ceremonies connected with sowing and harvesting. They are however, restricted from participating in some community-level ceremonies that are a part of their indigenous tribal faiths. To a considerable extent this is compensated by their adoption of community worship of Hindu goddesses such as Laxmi in Vaishnavite *namghars*. Although plains tribal women seem to enjoy a much better status in religion than non-tribal and hill-tribal women, they are not allowed to be priests and this privilege is restricted to men in most tribes. About the only exception to this is the "Brahma" faith of the Bodos where women are allowed to be priests. Plains tribal women thus seem to have benefited from the liberal elements in their indigenous faiths as well as the more inclusive and encompassing features of Vaishnavite Hinduism.

MANIPUR

Meitei Hindus constitute a predominant majority in the central valley that holds nearly two-thirds of the State's total population. The major focus here is on Meitei Hindu women's status with regard to family, marriage and religion. References to other communities in the valley, e.g. Manipuri Muslims, are mostly to illustrate Meitei influence on other ethnic groups. The hill areas surrounding the central valley, accounting for almost nine-tenths of the total State area, are inhabited by not less than 29 STs belonging mainly to Naga and Kuki-Chin ethnic groups. Only a few of these groups have received the attention of academics and researchers. The present analysis of women's status mentions a few of these communities, such as, the Tangkhul, Rongmei, Hmar, Moyon, Anal, but the references are mainly for comparative and illustrative purposes.

General Attitudes towards Women

The status of Meitei women with respect to marriage, family and religion reflects the influence of two important features of Manipur's history. The Meitei society in its early history was characterized by matriarchy and matriliny, which were replaced in later period by patriarchy and patriliny, resulting in a serious decline in women's position. And yet some vestiges of the former seem to have survived to this day (Bimala Devi, 1988). Secondly, the adoption of Vaishnavite Hinduism as the state religion by Manipuri royalty in the eighteenth century, and its super-imposition on the fairly sophisticated Meitei or Sanamahi faith and culture led to a syncretic social acceptance of both Hindu and Sanamahi elements. These simultaneous influences have resulted in somewhat unique and, at times, paradoxical perceptions about women.

One image of a woman is that of a loving, tender and protective mother figure capable of ensuring safety for a man from any possible evil and this is guaranteed when he carries a piece of her *phanek* (woman's garment). The other image portrays woman as an evil deceitful being, a source of unpredictable misfortune and whose *phanek* carries a polluting effect (Arunkumar, 1988). The derogatory attitude towards women is shared by some tribal groups in Manipur. For instance, among the Tarao tribe that is settled in Chandel district, men setting out for a hunting expedition consider a chance encounter with a woman as a bad omen (Bokul Singh, 1988). Similarly, the Moyons, a Naga sub-tribe inhabiting Chandel district and the foothills near Thoubal district, also share a generally negative attitude towards women. "Women and kids" are equated and some of their proverbs refer to them as being unreliable and not worthy of attention. Rongmei men consider women as inferior, e.g. persons "with long hair but limited knowledge." The great irony is that many Rongmei women are conditioned to regard men as inherently superior, and worthy to be served by women (Gailangam, 1988).

Attitudes towards Girls

A girl child is a great asset in a Meitei family, because from an early age she begins to help her mother in numerous household chores. She looks after younger siblings, thus relieving the mother to leave home for agricultural work or trading activities. Girls move about freely with boys of their age at schools or at various community festivals. Mothers take great care to ensure that their daughters learn weaving. In fact, many Manipuri girls start earning money by weaving and thus pay for their education. Until recently parents did not value education of girls and withdrew them from schools at an early age. Boy's education has always received a preferential treatment. A number of Meitei girls who have attained high school level or acquired degrees take up jobs and support the education of their younger brothers and sisters. It is not uncommon for educated Meitei girls to find jobs in government offices or schools in urban centres and to send regular remittances to their families in rural areas. Such developments have brought about a more favourable attitude towards girls' education, resulting in their improved enrolment in schools. In spite of this remarkable initiative and family responsibility among girls, Manipuri parents crave for a male child to continue the family line.

Selection of Mate

As against the past practice of arranged marriages, most boys and girls now prefer to choose their own life partners. Generally, girls are expected to be demure, and to let boys take the initiative. In cases of opposition from parents, the lovers may elope and this often leads to a formal marriage later, which is becoming socially quite acceptable. In fact, the girl's mother may well be an ally in the elopement as there is usually a close bond between the two, and the mother would help to ease the tensions in the family following her daughter's elopement. It is interesting to note that even among Manipuri Muslims, a rather conservative community, marriages by elopement are not uncommon (Khanam, 1988). The old practice of clan exogamy is no longer strictly followed among the Meiteis.

Most tribal communities of Manipur have a tradition of girls selecting their marriage partners with complete freedom. The Hmars, who are concentrated in Churachandpur district allow complete freedom to young girls to entertain their lovers for the night and pre-marital sex does not invite social disapproval. Some sections of Hmar society believe this permissiveness to be the cause of low priority for education among young people and the birth of illegitimate children (Lalremasang Hmar, 1988). Among the Tangkhul Nagas, one of the largest tribal groups in Manipur, young boys and girls assemble in youth dormitories after evening meals. Boys also meet their girl friends in their houses at night. Most marriages follow romantic love, although elderly ladies may initiate negotiations among parents on both sides to arrange marriages. Among the Tarao tribesmen, the traditional practice was for a girl to marry the son of her father's sister, and the son was expected to marry the daughter of his mother's brother. This practice has lost its rigour after Taraos accepted Christianity and young persons now have more freedom to choose their life partners (Bokul Singh, 1988). The Moyons allow young girls to select their marriage partners, but not to initiate marriage proposals (Sangkham, 1988).

Bride-Price and Dowry

The Meitei bridegroom's family may give bride-price in the form of cash and ornaments, besides assuming major responsibility for expenses of marriage feasts. Though the groom's side does not demand a dowry, the girl's parents generally give their daughter gifts, e.g. clothes, ornaments and household articles. It is reported that there is a growing trend towards giving a handsome dowry as a matter of prestige, and this may well create problems for parents with modest means (Tikoo, 1988). Although Meitei women do not have the right to own or inherit immovable property, as mentioned in Chapter 3, they retain absolute right over gifts given by their parents, other relatives or husband at the time of marriage, besides whatever income they have earned by their own efforts. A daughter generally gets a share in her mother's property, and inherits the market stall owned by mother after the latter's death. This is clearly a carry-over of the previous matrilineal tradition among the Meiteis. Furthermore, in case a daughter needs protection and maintenance after her father's or husband's death or following divorce, a brother is expected to provide her shelter and support. It is interesting to note that during the reign of the Manipuri king Chandrakirti (1834-86), a new annual festival called "Ningon Chakoba" — meaning Daughters' Day — was started. On this day, married daughters visit their parents' house and receive a warm welcome. This new practice was a fitting complement to the already prevalent "Bhratru-Dwitiya" — Brothers' Day.

The Anals and Moyons, both currently identified with the Nagas (although historically and culturally believed to be akin to Kuki-Chin-Mizo group), follow the practice of the bridegroom working in the prospective father-in-law's place for about three years. This custom is losing its rigour and the period is getting shorter (Gangmumei, 1985). The Moyons, however, still follow the practice of a special farewell feast for the bride's relatives and clan members, which marks the end of the girls' affiliation with her maiden clan and departure for her husband's house (Sangkham, 1988). The girl's separation from her parental clan is used as a justification for denying her right to inherit property, as well as for barring her from participating in several religious ceremonies, as we will see later. Although the Tangkhul Nagas limit the right to own and inherit immovable property to men, some parents give a piece of land to a daughter as a marriage gift. The groom's parents usually build a new house for the couple. She also gets presents such as rice, chillies, baskets, shawls and other household articles from her parents.

Polygamy

With the decline of matriarchy and matriliny and consolidation of patriarchy and patriliny, Meitei women's position in marriage and family suffered a serious setback. The already prevalent polygyny was reinforced by the Manipuri kings. Pamheiba, who assumed the title "Garib Nawaz" (1709-48) after his initiation into Hinduism by brahmin preceptors, married ten wives. His grandson Bhagyachandra who assumed the throne in 1763 had 94 wives. While the Brahma-Sabha (Council of brahmin preceptors) did not restrict men especially from the royal family and upper classes to have several wives, it tried to restrict widows from re-marrying and introduced the practice of *sati* (immolation of the widow on the deceased husband's funeral pyre) in the royal family and among brahmins. Thanks to the counteracting Sanamahi influence in Manipur the custom of *sati* was never adopted by the commoners, and was discarded rather quickly by the royal family and other elite classes before end of the eighteenth century.

Polygyny at present is believed to be more common in urban areas than in rural, and more prevalent in affluent sections. It is not uncommon for a man to have a second wife or just to keep a mistress. One hears of urban men having affairs with maids from rural areas, and if the latter became pregnant, the men offer money either to arrange for an abortion or for delivery (Salam, 1988). There are cases of Meitei men having four wives, and in some cases, all of them may live in the same house. The more usual practice is for the first wife to keep a separate house. If she feels insulted, she may leave the husband, but unless she obtains a divorce she cannot take another husband. Polygyny is also prevalent among affluent Manipuri Muslims or Pangans. Meitei personal law prescribes that a man must not have more than five wives. It does not however tolerate a woman having more than one husband (Raghumani, 1988). A Tarao man was customarily permitted to indulge in polygyny. Since the adoption of Christianity by the group, there is a strong public opinion against it. When it comes to a second marriage, a widower can marry any woman, but a Tarao widow is allowed to marry only a widower (Bokul Singh, 1988). Among the Hmars, one of the largest Kuki-Chin tribes of Manipur, a married man can flirt with another woman without incurring any serious social disapproval, but the woman involved in the same adultery is punished severely and treated as the main culprit. Similarly, a widower's re-marriage is celebrated with great jubilation and the society takes active interest in finding a suitable match. But if a widow re-marries, she is condemned by the society, including other women, who do not hide their disapproval (Lalremasang Hmar, 1988).

Divorce

Divorce is not difficult to get for either party of a Meitei couple, provided parents on both sides consider and confirm the decision, although the Meitei personal law is more liberal towards men in permitting divorce. A Meitei husband can divorce a wife who is childless, disobedient, handicapped, immoral or if she creates any discord over a co-wife. If for any reason a wife ceases to please her husband or if he begins to dislike her, she can be divorced (Raghumani, 1988). With the grounds for divorce being so hopelessly non-specific and at times vague, the odds are heavily loaded against the woman. If the husband initiates divorce he gives bride-price to the divorced wife, and when the wife initiates it, she returns the bride-price paid by the husband. If she takes another man without obtaining a divorce from the first husband, the second husband must pay compensation to the first husband. In cases of separation of spouses, the father has a stronger claim over children, the exception being children under four years, whose custody is granted to the mother.

In Islam, marriage is a contract that can be dissolved if both or either party fails to satisfy the terms agreed upon. Among Manipuri Muslims divorce is available to both husband and wife, which is important in view of the fact that while Muslim men practice polygyny rather freely, women are more restricted (Khaanam, 1988). Manipuri Muslim women seem to enjoy greater freedom in seeking divorce than Muslim women in Assam who are immigrants from Bengal. Among the Tangkhuls, a Naga tribe settled mostly in Ukhrul district, a husband is free to marry another woman if his wife is childless, guilty of adultery or if she leaves her husband on grounds considered as flimsy and fails to return soon. If she divorces her husband and takes another husband and if the village council decides against her, she or the second husband has to pay the prescribed fine. In some disputes, besides members of the village council, all members of the village may participate in taking a joint decision (Pearson, 1993). It is interesting to note that so far the village councils did not permit women to be members. It is only recently, probably due to spread of education and influence of Panchayati Raj, that a few women have been given membership of some village councils. A Tangkhul couple can obtain a divorce by mutual consent. Among the Tarao group (a Naga sub-tribe), although both marriage partners have a right to get a divorce, women rarely initiate the process, but men generally do. If a wife seeks divorce, she repays marriage expenses to the husband.

Meitei brahmins, under the influence of brahmin preceptors, have tended to discourage re-marriage of widows. In other Meitei sections, however, remarriage of widows and divorcees does not pose any problem. Most tribal communities continue to have a relaxed attitude towards remarriage of widows and divorcees. Until recently, Tangkhul Nagas had a custom that gave a deceased husband's brother a right to marry the widow. With the spread of education and modernization, a Tangkhul widow is now free to marry a person of her choice (Thomas, 1988). Notwithstanding the highly patrilineal system of present Meitei society, probably as a vestige of its past matrilineal tradition, the parental family, i.e. parents and brothers of Meitei women provide shelter and maintenance for widows, divorcees and unmarried daughters (Chaki Sircar, 1984).

Family

After marriage, when a young Meitei woman leaves her parental home and joins the husband's family, her life turns into a long and arduous routine full of diverse responsibilities. As referred in Chapter 3, women are heavily involved in family farming, besides trading and exchange of local agricultural produce. They are fully responsible for all house-keeping chores such as cooking, cleaning, bringing water, child-rearing, without any help from husband. Even when women hold full-time outside jobs in urban areas, they are still responsible for all house-keeping jobs generally without hired help. Weaving is exclusively women's activity, undertaken usually for supplementing family resources. In rural areas, women often work in groups in various agricultural operations and fishing. As children become older, women spend lesser time in cooking and house-keeping tasks, and engage themselves in trading, small enterprises in weaving, running tea-stalls and the like.

Despite the heavy burden of household and cultivation tasks carried by Meitei women, they have little decision-making authority in major concerns such as purchase of property involving substantial family expenditure, marriages, family or kinship level matters, etc. Although women may be consulted in a few cases, husbands and in-laws take final decisions. In lower and middle income groups women have considerable autonomy regarding day-to-day purchases for the household. In relatively affluent sections, women may not have even this freedom. For instance, whether a woman will continue her education or her employment after marriage are matters which are decided by husbands and in-laws. It is reported that many married women having special academic interests or artistic talents fail to get any scope to pursue their careers if the husbands and in-laws are not supportive (Salam, 1988). Women are expected to spend their earnings for maintaining the family, which includes care and education of their children. The husbands' earnings are spent to meet the requirements of their parental family, e.g. education of his brothers and sisters. The significant point to note is the assumption that mothers rather than fathers are regarded among the Meiteis as primarily responsible for the upbringing of children (Bimala Devi, 1988).

An interesting feature of Meitei family is the differential family and social roles for and expectations from women at different stages of life. As women approach their forties, they are no longer confined to their house-keeping roles, but extend their sphere to outside trading activities and become members of various "Marups" and "Nupipalas," i.e. women's associations, clubs, chit-fund type of co-operatives. Apart from the economic support functions these groups fulfil, as mentioned in Chapter 3, they serve a crucial purpose of establishing solidarity among women in the context of male dominance in Meitei families. Women who spend major part of the day away from home at markets selling vegetables, fruits, groceries, etc. need small comforts like tea and snacks which are arranged by these associations. They can get loans for special occasions such as weddings or for purchase of household utensils and the like. Even more importantly, these groups provide valuable emotional and social support during periods of stress. For instance, when the husband keeps a mistress or brings another wife, other women in the neighbourhood or association members express their solidarity for the first wife and disapproval towards the husband and the second wife. When women get older, they are relieved of domestic responsibility and spend more time in social and economic activities. Apart from joining credit associations, they join groups which are engaged in recreational and cultural activities, e.g. "Shumang Leela" — theatre presentations, which earn some money through roving performances (Chaki Sircar, 1984). Older and mature women also use their experience in undertaking joint projects for the benefit of their community, such as construction of community centres and weaving sheds. As women get older, they exercise greater authority also over family budgets.

General Image of Women in the Family

Despite the overt male dominance in the Meitei family, women have managed to ensure a respectable place for themselves, by dint of their industriousness and substantial earning capacity. Besides assuming responsibility for house-keeping and child care, they contribute significantly to family income, and also find time to involve themselves in groups and associations promoting co-operative self-help and social solidarity. They exude an air of self-confidence and even though men like to exclude them from important family decisions, the women exert considerable influence without seeming to be overtly influential.

In comparison, the Anal and Moyon women (both Naga sub-tribes), both of whom assume major responsibility in cultivation tasks, have to be content with a symbolic recognition in the sense of women initiating the storing of grains after a new harvest. The Rongmei women perceive men as superior beings and consider serving them as their main function. Of course, Rongmei men reinforce this self-deprecatory attitude of women and perceive women as inferior.

The Tangkhuls, a major Naga tribal group concentrated in Ukhrul district, present a happy exception in the sense that men concede women's contribution in some respects as useful. Tangkhul wives are consulted in all important family matters (Horam, 1977). Among Tangkhuls, the festival called "Chumphu" which marks the beginning of using newly harvested grains, is an exclusively women's preserve and men must scrupulously avoid to be around, and even accidental presence is regarded as unlucky. On the other hand, if the grains fall short of the family's requirements, a Tangkhul woman is held mainly responsible for the lapse. Family disputes are decided by village council or courts which until recently have excluded women from membership. The adoption of Christianity and spread of education are believed to have created greater awareness among the Tarao community regarding women's inferior traditional status. As a result some outmoded practices unfair to women have been discontinued, and women have a wider choice of economic activities than before. It is reported that there is an improvement in Tarao women's status in the family and they have more voice in family affairs (Bokul Singh, 1988).

Religion

Any assessment of Meitei women's status in religion has to bear in mind Meitei matrilineal and matriarchal past, which was replaced later with patriliny and patriarchy, and secondly, co-existence of the original Sanamahi faith over which Vaishnavite Hinduism was superimposed since eighteenth century. Quite significantly, at a time when brahmin preceptors were trying to suppress and eliminate old Meitei religion from Manipuri society with support from Manipuri kings, women steadfastly continued worshipping Sanamahi deities at the family level, while adopting Vaishnavite Radha-Govinda worship socially at temples. The Sanamahi movement, which was aimed at revival of Sanamahi rituals and a repudiation of Brahma-Sabha's insistence on adoption of Vaishnavite Hindu practices and culture, as discussed in Chapter 2, acquired the form of Meitei nationalism during the 1930s and 1940s, and provided a boost to Meitei women's position. At the same time, a continuing strand runs through Manipur's social history, both in Sanamahi and Hindu contexts, to exclude women from some rituals by picturing them as inferior to men. It is a tribute to the tenacity of Meitei women that they have continued to resist their exclusion and have often won their battles.

Despite the predominant Hindu influence in Meitei society following adoption of Hinduism as State religion during the reign of Garib Nawaz in eighteenth century, Meitei personal law is based on Sanamahi religion. Pakhamba and Sanamahi, two sons of the Supreme Creator — Atiya Sidaba, and the Eternal Mother — Ima Laimaren, continue to occupy an important position in Meitei household worship, which is performed essentially by women. Simultaneously, Meitei women play an important role in the worship of Radha-Govinda, particularly. "Ras-Leela" and "Sankeertan," the devotional dancing and music, which is an integral part of religious festivals. King Bhagyachandra created a new "Loishang" (department) in 1776 to enhance artistic excellence of "Ras-Leela" by infusion of talents from north India, and expertise in Meitei traditional music, thereby enriching existing repertoire by addition of newly choreographed items (Chaki Sarkar, 1984). Another factor which endowed a high prestige to "Ras-Leela" was the royal patronage of king Bhagyachandra's daughter Bimbavati, who played the central role of Radha. Later Dhanamanjaridevi, the queen of Churachand (1891–1941) who was an accomplished artist — led women in dance and music with great aplomb. Under these circumstances, Meitei women found a highly respected avenue for participation in important religious events, besides providing a legitimate expression for artistic excellence. In addition to this highly professional artistic expression, religion also provides common Meitei women another satisfying avenue. At *Holi* festival which is associated with the new harvest, several groups of women — some having nearly 150 members — come from distant villages singing devotional songs and accompanied by male drummers to converge at Govindaji temple in the capital city Imphal. As Chaki Sircar (1983) has commented, the unique blend of Meitei traditional lore with Vaishnavite devotional themes combining aesthetic refinement has endowed the singing and dancing a high respectability.

It is interesting to note that for some time around early nineteenth-century men, specially brahmin priests, had succeeded in prohibiting women from using cymbals and drums and from singing and dancing before Radha and Govinda images. Meitei women continued a relentless battle for over a century to resist this ban. Their determination and self-confidence have compelled the religious authorities to withdraw this unjust exclusion of women. They now sing and dance and can use drums and cymbals before appreciative audiences in temples. But there still remain restrictions on Meitei women's participation in some rituals. For instance Meitei men alone can perform Apokpa-Khurumba, an offering to the original ancestor of a lineage. Women cannot perform this, and more so they are not permitted to partake of the fruits offered in worship, since they are believed to be without a lineage and therefore inferior. Only the married lady of the house may eat the fruit. An unmarried daughter is regarded not only as unworthy but also dangerous because there is a belief that her eating the fruit might destroy the lineage (Arunkumar, 1988). The negative attitudes towards women are manifested in yet another aspect. The priests who perform religious rituals in temples must always be men. And yet, Sanamahi religion has institutionalized a female functionary called "Maibi" who plays an important role in Meitei society, as seen in the celebration of Lai Harouba, which has currently acquired the image of Meitei identity.

The Meitei religion equates women's procreative power with fertility of the Mother Earth. The annual "Lai Harouba" (meaning "In pleasure of the Deities") festival, while asserting male supremacy, simultaneously acknowledges female sexuality and fertility and interdependence of the sexes. It includes several ritual dances, which symbolize formation and birth of a baby from the mother's womb. Two groups of male and female dancers are led by the "Maiba" (male priest) and "Maibi" (female priestess). Ironically, the Maiba's role is not as prominent as that of the Maibi, although both receive training in various rituals. From among 240 Maibis, one is assigned to preside over the ceremonies in various places in the state, according to Chaki Sircar (1984). The Maibi is typically pictured as a stubborn woman, who breaks away from usual family tradition, and after receiving a divine call, undergoes rigorous training in dance and rituals from experienced teachers. She is believed to possess unusual divining powers and ability to communicate with the deities.

A reference has been made earlier to the exclusion of Meitei women from some ceremonies on the plea that they have no permanent lineage. A similar notion regarding women not possessing a fixed clan affiliation, and therefore considered inferior, prevails among the Moyons, a Naga sub-tribe settled in Chandel district. Moyon women are not permitted to perform some customary rituals at community festivals, and the general belief is that they are good enough only for the routine household chores and the diverse cultivation tasks and nothing else. In fact, a Moyon proverb asserts that since women have no permanent clan, they have no principles! (Sangkham, G., 1988). The irony of the situation is that Moyon women take great pride in helping their husbands perform "Ikam" — a feast of merit which enhances their social status, and the wives must be content to bask in the reflected glory! The introduction of Christianity among the Moyons since 1910, and along with it the spread of education, are reported to have made a dent in the stronghold of old beliefs and some Moyon women have become preachers and teachers in rural areas.

The Tarao tribe also assigns women an inferior ritual status on the plea that they do not belong to a permanent clan. Tarao women must not touch a spear which is set aside for killing an animal in a ritual sacrifice. There is a taboo on women eating certain types of meat of a sacrificed animal. Men must not eat the meat of an animal killed by a woman. Among the Anal community, a sinner, widow or widower are not allowed to perform sacrifices before their traditional deities (Kabui, 1985). The Rongmei women, who otherwise enjoy a better family status as compared to Moyon and Tarao women, have to be content with fairly minor rituals like seeking divine blessings when drawing supplies from the granary and offering token sacrifices of food when a family member is ill or when the family performs a religious event. Among the Tangkhuls, one of the largest Naga tribes in Manipur, while women enjoy a better status in the family than among most Naga groups, in many religious ceremonies connected with agriculture, women's major function is to ensure adequate supplies of rice-beer and supply of sticky rice. The village priest, always a male, performs religious rites and sacrifices at community events, presided over by the "Avunga," the hereditary chief of the village (Pearson, 1993). As among other Naga tribes Tangkhul women are assigned the ceremonial role associated with drawing on stocks from the new harvest. At the family level, unlike the Meities, the head of the household acts as the family priest, worships the family altar and makes offerings to the family deity (Horam, 1977). Although a predominant majority of tribal groups in Manipur have now been converted to Christianity some of the rituals which were part of their indigenous faiths have survived. It would be interesting to study whether adoption of Christianity has changed in any way the man-woman equations in indigenous religious ceremonies. Equally significant, whether women continue to face the same problems of male dominance in the observance of Christian ceremonies or whether they have used this opportunity to make a break with past traditions.

Recapitulation

The major focus in Manipur presentation has been on Meitei women although some observations on women from tribal groups have also been included. Meiteis have a positive attitude towards girls, who start helping mothers with household chores from an early age, and many start working to earn financial support for their families. Boy's education receives a higher priority over girls' education, none the less. The past practice of parents selecting marriage partners has virtually been replaced by young girls selecting their mates, and elopement of young lovers is not only common but socially acceptable. Among Kuki-Chin as well as Naga tribes, girls choose their own partners and in most tribes, bride-price is the practice. Among the Meiteis, the usual practice is for the groom's parents to give bride-price and pay for wedding expenses. But lately, the traditional practice of the bride's parents giving some presents to their daughter is deteriorating into pressure on girl's parents to give a rather lavish dowry. The practice of Meitei husbands having three or four wives, or keeping a mistress is more prevalent in urban rather than rural areas. While divorce is not difficult for either party, men are more likely to seek divorce, and the usual grounds are: wife's childlessness, disobedience, conflict with a co-wife or disability of some sort. Furthermore, Meitei personal law allows a man to divorce his wife on fairly vague or indeterminate grounds, e.g. if he loses interest in her or if she ceases to please him. After either party seeks a divorce, parents on both sides must consider and confirm the divorce. If a Meitei woman takes another husband without obtaining confirmation of the divorce, she or her second husband may have to pay a heavy compensation. Despite the brahmin preceptors' strong condemnation of re-marriage, Meitei widows and divorcees can re-marry without any difficulty.

Meitei women, like all N-E women carry full responsibility for household chores and child-care, besides their heavy involvement in agricultural operations, weaving, fishing, etc. When the children are a bit older and mothers reach their forties, they take up trading in agricultural products, fruits, vegetables, woven articles and a variety of other household goods, and earn a substantial part of household income. A small number of women are also engaged in wholesale trade and commerce. Traditionally, while husbands are more concerned with the education of their brothers and sisters, Meitei mothers generally assume responsibility for their children's education. Despite this heavy family burden women carry, husbands have the authority to take decisions with respect to marriages, purchase or sale of property, kinship obligations, and even whether a working wife would continue her job after marriage. The overt male dominance and the weak formal position of women are mitigated to a great extent by the financial autonomy of women and the social and emotional support they receive from the various self-help and co-operative groups to which they belong.

Meitei women have a strong presence in religion, despite their exclusion from some rituals by male priests. When Vaishnavite Hinduism was adopted as a state religion by Manipuri king Garib Nawaz in the eighteenth century, Manipuri women accepted Hindu rituals and the worship of Radha-Govinda. Simultaneously, they continued Sanamahi worship at the family level. When Sanamahi revival movement gained momentum in the twentieth century, women's participation in Sanamahi practices received a boost. The strong royal patronage for enhancing the artistic excellence of singing and dancing, which became an integral part of both Hindu and Sanamahi religious festivals, provided Meitei women a highly respected and emotionally fulfilling avenue for religious participation. They appropriated this space in religion fully to enhance their status and have struggled persistently and steadily to eliminate certain restrictions on women using cymbals and drums, and singing and dancing before the images of Radha-Govinda. In Lai Harouba festival, a Maibi — a priestess — gives a lead in the ritual dances, along with the Maiba — a priest, thus asserting the interdependence of the sexes. On a more popular level, large groups of Meitei women from distant villages come singing to the Govindaji temple in the State capital to participate in *Holi* festival. In comparison, the position of tribal women of Manipur in indigenous religions is insignificant and they are restricted from taking part in several important rituals. Since a large majority of tribal groups have recently adopted Christianity, perhaps these women might be able to break away from their traditional shackles. But this is not likely to be an easy step. They will have to make an organized demand for equality with men in religious practices, like their Meitei counterparts.

MEGHALAYA

Introduction

Meghalaya is unique in the N-E region because of the matrilineal system which prevails in the three major communities of the state, viz. Khasis, Jaintias and Garos. Descent is traced from the mother's side, with children taking their mother's clan name and maternal kin have an important place in the family. One of the daughters inherits ancestral property from her mother, and when she marries, her husband comes to stay with the wife's household. In Chapter 3, it was noted that the daughter who inherits the ancestral property is viewed more as a custodian rather than an absolute owner of the property and men from her maternal kinship and her husband wield effective control over use of the ancestral property. We will now examine the position of Meghalaya women with respect to marriage, family and religion among the three principal communities of the state: Khasis, Jaintias and Garos.

Attitudes towards Girls

Since the Khasis and Jaintias have a similar culture, we will review the position of women in these two communities jointly, while indicating the few aspects in which they differ. A girl child is welcomed among these communities in view of her potential for proliferation of the tribes, and particularly so among the Jaintias, who are specially sensitive about their small numbers. There is no discrimination in the manner in which girls and boys are brought up. If at all, girls are reported to have an edge over boys since they are seen as continuators of the lineage and the clan, and get a preferential treatment in terms of better clothes, ornaments and schooling. Young girls are carefully groomed to acquire house-keeping skills. The only exception to the preference for girls are the patrilineal Biates and Bhois who prefer boys over girls. In the traditional Khasi-Jaintia culture, men are perceived as warriors, whereas women are viewed essentially as home-makers. This explains why at the time of naming ceremony of a girl child, a sling basket for carrying things at the back and a rope are used, whereas in the case of a boy, a bow and arrow are used as auspicious symbols (War, 1992).

Among the Garos, the generally inferior status assigned to women is evident even from the manner in which a Garo family treats the birth of a girl child. This event is completely devoid of that special rejoicing which marks the arrival of a son. Until recently, most Garo parents have had a rather limited goal for their daughters, viz. settling down as a housewife after marriage. Naturally, from early childhood girls are kept engaged in house-keeping chores, and they do not get adequate opportunities for play and education. While education for boys is regarded as essential preparation for future careers, girls' education receives a lower priority. In rural areas, parents may enrol their daughters in primary or middle schools, but withdraw them early if high schools and colleges are located at a distance. During their childhood Garo girls are often dominated by their brothers, as a result of the preferential treatment boys receive in the family.

Selection of Marriage Partner

Khasi and Jaintia girls have always been allowed to mix freely with young boys through childhood and adolescence, and girls have complete freedom to select their marriage partners. In the past the rule of tribal endogamy was more strictly followed. For instance, a Jaintia woman marrying a non-Jaintia man was frowned upon and the offspring of such a marriage may still be restricted from participation in some traditional religious practices. Similarly, pre-marital sex was considered a serious offence in the past. (Sen, 1992). In present times these restrictions have lost their rigidity. It is not unusual for a boy and girl to live together for some time before getting married formally. No stigma is attached to children born out of wedlock. Relationships between boys and girls have generally been open and relaxed, and cases of rape are rare.

Among the Garos, however, the situation is very different. Marriage signifies a permanent bond between two clans. Individual choice of a girl regarding her marriage partner is less important than the joint decision of the *Mahari* (closely related maternal kin residing in the same village). Neither the girl concerned nor other women in the family may be consulted. While the *Mahari*, and especially the *Chras* (elderly male members of the *Mahari*) have a dominant position in decisions regarding marriage as well as divorce, they also play a protective and proprietary role in such affairs. A girl can depend on the *Chras* in difficult situations. Until recently if a girl had set her heart on a marriage partner, the *Chras* would take it upon themselves to procure him, even by capture, if necessary (Goswami and Majumdar, 1972). Among the Garos, pre-marital sex is not regarded as a serious deviation and illegitimate children do not suffer from social disapproval.

In view of the peculiar Garo concept of marriage as an unbreakable union between two clans which even death cannot break, they follow what is known as the law of *akim*, i.e. in case of one of the partner's death, a relative of the deceased person is to be given as replacement. In case a suitable adult relative is not available in the clan, sometimes young girls, e.g. even 12 years old, are forced into marriage with old widowers, often under physical threat (Marak, 1992).[26] This custom sometimes may result in a young man being given to an older widow as a replacement husband on the condition that the widow's daughter, regardless of the girl's wishes, is promised to be given as his second wife. This custom, called *dokchapa*, is reported to be prevailing even today, more commonly among non-Christian Garos, both in rural and urban areas. Since the 1980s, the spread of education is believed to have weakened the practice of *akim* and *dokchapa,* and enlightened sections are trying to create social awareness in order to eliminate the injustice.

Marriage and Girl's Matri-Local Residence

Among the Khasis and Jaintias when a boy and a girl decide to marry, the groom's parents initiate marriage negotiations. As long as rules of clan exogamy are obeyed, parents on both sides solemnize the marriage in a simple ceremony. No dowry or bride-price is involved. The parents of the girl may, however, give her some clothes, ornaments and part of their property as a gift. A Jaintia marriage includes a ritual where oblations of wine from the girl's and the groom's side are offered to deities and ancestors with prayers for prosperity of the clans and for birth of many children. Unlike typical patrilineal societies, in a Jaintia wedding, the groom assumes a subservient role towards members of the girl's clan in various ceremonies symbolizing his acceptance of responsibility for her clan and obligation towards sharing its adversities when necessary.

An important aspect of the matrilineal system of Meghalaya is the practice of a girl continuing her stay with her parents after marriage and the son-in-law coming to live in his wife's household. In the case of the Garos, if a girl is selected by her *Mahari* as a replacement wife for a widower according to the law of *akim*, she has to join the widower's household. Barring this exception, the practice is for daughters to continue

26. A girl of 12 years was subjected to five hours of harrassment, including a threat of beating in Tura in 1957 to extract her agreement to marry her brother-in-law, as a replacement of a deceased sister (Marak, 1992).

their stay with their parents after marriage. As discussed in Chapter 3, one of the daughters — *Khadduh* among the Khasis and Jaintias, and the *Nokna* among the Garos — inherits ancestral property from their mothers. Other daughters may continue to stay with their parents. Alternately, in case they have to set up separate households, parents usually give them some lands and other property in their marriage and help them to set up their households. When the *Nokna*'s husband gets old, he brings his sister's son as the resident son-in-law to replace him since it is necessary to ensure that the male head of the household and the son-in-law belong to the same lineage.

A Khasi-Jaintia woman who marries a non-Khasi or non-Jaintia man loses not only ritual status, but also right of inheritance, as has been mentioned in Chapter 3, besides losing her Khasi status, as recognized by the customary law. A Khasi-Jaintia man marrying a non-Khasi or non-Jaintia woman, however, does not suffer from these disabilities, as confirmed by the Land Reforms Commission For Khasi Hills, 1975 (Mathew, 1980). Among the Garos, a young girl may be married to an elderly person as a replacement for a deceased relative by the former's *Mahari*, and she has no avenue of redress (Goswami & Majumdar, 1972).

Attitude Towards Adultery, Polygamy, Divorce, Remarriage

Although monogamy is the norm, childlessness in a woman permits a man to take a second wife. While adultery is considered a serious offence in both men and women, adultery in women causes more serious consequences among all communities of Meghalaya. Among both Khasis and Jaintias, an adulterous woman and her children lose ritual status and when she dies, her bones are not placed in the common family ossuary. An adulterous Jaintia woman is automatically separated from her husband and is excluded from all social and religious affairs of the husband's clan. However, if she leaves her paramour and children born out of such relationship, she is accepted back in the community and her usual rights are restored (Gassah, 1992). According to an old Khasi tradition, a husband whose wife was adulterous, theoretically had the right to inflict death on her, unless he chose to forgive her (Syiem, 1992). The Khasi and Jaintia society's attitude towards men guilty of adultery, or having several wives, is fairly tolerant. A second wife, however, does not have the same status as the first wife, which penalizes the woman rather than the man guilty of bigamy. It is not uncommon for Khasi-Jaintia men to have two or even three wives. A man having children from different wives or from extra-marital relationships is described rather indulgently as a "man with many flags"! (Nongbri, 1988).

Divorce is common and easily obtained. Khasi and Jaintia women can divorce their husbands on grounds of adultery and impotence. Divorcees and widows do not suffer from social prejudice and can re-marry. The matrilineal system endows women with a stronger right over children than men.

Among the Garos, however, a widow has low status, next only to a destitute (Goswami & Majumdar, 1972). Adultery and polygyny are not uncommon among Garo men. In case a husband wishes to bring a second or a third wife, he is supposed to obtain the permission of his first wife. In practice, however, this formality has little meaning in view of the deep-rooted subservience of average Garo women towards their menfolk. The husband obtains the consent of his wife as well as her *chras* without much difficulty since the only other option is separation. Although the Garos permit divorce and re-marriage very few women seek separation from a bigamous or adulterous husband, unlike Khasi-Jaintia women. Garo women have to obtain the permission of their *Mahari* for divorce (Goswami & Majumdar, 1972). There are more cases of Garo women being deserted by their husbands than those seeking divorce, because of their weak social and economic position and no alimony is paid to them (Marak, 1992). There is one positive aspect of the joint responsibility of the *Mahari* which protects a Garo woman in case of serious mismanagement of the ancestral property by her husband. The male elders of the *Mahari* stand behind her and represent her in court if necessary. If her husband commits adultery with an unmarried girl, the latter may have to pay compensation to the aggrieved wife, whose *Mahari* would ensure that it is received. On the other hand, if the woman is fined by the court for any reason, the *Mahari* jointly pays the fine.

Women's Position in the Family : Traditional Perceptions

In the Khasi-Jaintia matrilineal culture mother has a highly exalted position, since God is believed to have created woman to procreate and multiply the clan. In the unique Khasi-Jaintia perception of the process of procreation, the primary function of nurturing a child during nine months of incubation, which provides the substance, is performed by the mother with her own blood. In comparison, the father's role is viewed as rather secondary, viz. giving merely the form and stature to a child (Nongbri, 1988). In the traditional Khasi-Jaintia society, with their preoccupation with inter-tribal warfare, men were perceived as warriors, protectors, hunters, administrators, priests. Women, on the other hand, were viewed essentially as mothers, house-keepers, helpers in the fields, custodians of family property, preservers of ancestor worship and religion. The mother is referred as "Ka Blei Ing," meaning goddess of the house, an embodiment of virtue and purity, a central figure in the clan and the family (War, 1988). As we will see later, this glorified image places enormous burden of responsibilities on women despite some redeeming features.

Garo creation myths bestow an important place for goddesses, although Tatara Rabuga, the supreme god, is credited with creation of the earth. It was however the goddess Nostu Nopantu who retrieved the earth which was submerged under deep water, and created mountains and plant life. Another goddess created animals and the sun and other spirits. Rokkime, a goddess, is invoked annually to endow every rice-field with good harvest and prosperity (Marak, 1992). Garo legends depict women as pure, beautiful and noble. During the Garo tribe's sojourn from Tibet to their present habitat, and through several wars with enemy tribes, Garo women are believed to have ably supported their menfolk, including taking part in warfare. Like Khasi-Jaintias, Garo mythology gives an honoured place to women as progenitresses of Garo clans. In view of the respected position enjoyed by women both in Khasi-Jaintia and Garo cultures, it is not clear what intervening influences might account for the difference in their current status in the sphere of family and religion, particularly the injustice and male dominance to which Garo women are presently subjected.

Women's Family Chores

A reference has been made in Chapter 3 to the substantial burden Khasi-Jaintia and Garo women carry in family cultivation, whether *jhum* or wet-land type. In addition, they also work in plantations of fruits, betel-nuts, pineapple, carry agricultural produce to markets for sale over long distances and bring back household requirements at the end of the day over hilly tracks. They bring water, collect firewood, tubers, edible roots, cattle fodder, take care of cooking and feeding the family besides cattle, and cleaning. In areas where there are no husking mills, they also have to husk paddy until late at night. In areas which have become urbanized like, for instance, Shillong, many Khasi women are engaged in petty trading, and have started small businesses like tailoring, groceries, restaurants and tea-stalls and earn major part of family's subsistence. Similarly, Garo women often seek employment as labourers in house construction or may take small contracts, e.g. cutting and transporting wood, etc. The traditional glorification of mother as a symbol of continuation of the clan has contributed to holding women primarily responsible for children. In cases of father's failure to earn a steady income or to assume responsibility for children, mothers have to work harder to raise and educate their children.

Position of Inheritness in Matrilineal Framework

Since matrilineal system in Meghalaya provides the framework within which family relationships operate, it will be useful to refer briefly to its major economic aspects, which have been presented in detail in Chapter 3. Among the Khasi-Jaintias, the *Khadduh*, and among the Garos, the *Nokna* inherits ancestral property from her mother and continues to stay in her parental house, where her husband joins her after marriage. The *Khadduh* is viewed mainly as a custodian rather than absolute owner of the ancestral property, and requires approval of the family council — which includes her maternal uncles, brothers, parents if living, and husband — for any major expenditures or disposal. Among the Garos, the *Mahari* selects the *Nokna*, who too is regarded as a custodian of the inherited property, and her husband exercises authority over its use. Although in principle he requires her consent in all matters regarding its use or disposal, in practice the *Nokna* is without power. The *Mahari* would intervene only in cases of serious abuse of the property by her husband. In other family matters, even non-financial, the *Mahari*, and particularly the *Chras*, have the final authority for decisions, even those which personally concern the *Nokna*.

Family Relationships

There is considerable difference in the manner in which the *Khadduh* and the *Nokna* are viewed, as well as their obligations and family relationships, their participation in family decisions and the degree of autonomy they enjoy. In the Khasi-Jaintia society, the maternal kin of the

Khadduh, particularly maternal uncles and brothers and parents, if living, form a solid front standing behind the *Khadduh*, and the resident son-in-law has to strive to establish his equation with the family council in order to create a space for himself in family decisions. If he is weak and unsure, maternal relatives of the *Khadduh* take a dominant role not only in financial matters but also in other family issues like raising of children. If this happens, the *Khadduh's* husband may begin to absolve himself from responsibility for children. Among the Jaintias, since the husband visits his wife only at night and returns to his mother's house in the morning, he feels even less responsible for his children and may often limit his role to making a token financial contribution. The husband's minor role in raising children places a heavier responsibility on Khasi-Jaintia women for children's care and education.

In comparison, the position of the *Nokna* among the Garos is much weaker. To begin with, her *Mahari* and parents decide which daughter is selected to be the *Nokna*, and also the person who becomes her husband. As noted earlier the *Nokna*'s husband, i.e. the *Nokma*, manages the ancestral property on her behalf. When he gets old, he usually brings his sister's son as the new resident son-in-law, thus maintaining the continuity of his clan's relationship. When the *Nokma* happens to occupy the position of *A'khing Nokma,*[27] i.e. village headman, he can exert even greater control over his wife's property, and has a definite edge over the *Mahari* in terms of position in the family. When he dies, the *Chras* take over management of the property. The widowed *Nokna* does not have the right to transfer her landed property to anyone she wishes, including her son, but she is allowed to use it during her lifetime. As noted earlier, the *Mahari* takes sides with the *Nokna* only in extreme cases, e.g. when the *Nokma* squanders or mismanages the property. In day-to-day matters the *Nokna* may have to put up with humiliation by the *Nokma* and at times has to work harder to make up for his financially irresponsible behaviour. Besides, the *Mahari* usually is highly dominated by men, and women in the family, including the *Nokna* have very little say in important family decisions, including marriages of *Nokna*'s children.

---

27. The term *A'khing Nokma* means a person who is husband of the *Nokna* as well as headman of the *A'khing*. As noted in Chapter 2, the British administrator of Garo Hills demarcated the boundaries of each *A'khing* land, i.e. land belonging to a clan or tribe in 1872, to prevent inter-tribal conflicts and issued documents of possession to the headmen, who were assigned some administrative functions.

While neither the *Khadduh* nor the *Nokna* is absolute owner of the inherited ancestral property, and both are viewed as its custodians, the *Nokna* is far more vulnerable to its misuse, has virtually no access to its use and has less support from her *Mahari*. Although the *Khadduh* requires consent of the family council in major financial decisions, she has considerable autonomy in using the property to fulfil traditional obligations such as expenditures for ceremonies connected with child-births, marriages, deaths, community festivals, etc. Besides, she is also expected to and can help any person belonging to the clan who is needy or destitute. Over and above this, the *Khadduh* has full authority to use her personal property, which may include lands and other articles gifted by her parents and her personal income any way she wishes. The Garo *Nokna* in comparison does not have any economic autonomy to use the ancestral property, nor does she enjoy freedom to take even non-economic decisions due to the dominant role of the *Nokma* and male members of the Mahari. The position of ordinary women, i.e. those who are not inheritresses of ancestral property, in Khasi-Jaintia and Garo societies also reveals major differences. While women in both communities take major responsibility for economic support and family sustenance, Khasi-Jaintia women have greater freedom in deciding family matters than Garo women. Besides, Garo women are far more inhibited by a low self-image, lack of occupational options and rigid traditions, in resisting abuse and injustice from husbands and maternal kin groups. Khasi-Jaintia women have full freedom with respect to decisions regarding household management and day-to-day expenditures, whereas Garo women have to work within limits set by the *Mahari*, and most of the time do not even have access to *Mahari*'s meetings.

Position in Religion

The Khasi-Jaintias believe in one Supreme God who gave them their religion, which emphasizes righteousness, love of one's fellowmen and close bonds among maternal and paternal relatives. God is believed to have created woman in order to procreate and multiply the clan, which elevates marriage to a sacred bond (Kynpham Singh, 1980). Mothers are perceived as important links between the past and present clan members and preservers of the clan's continuity and ancestor worship. It is, therefore, women's responsibility to ensure performance of sacred ceremonies at the time of events such as birth of children, where the paternal grandmother is supposed to bless the new-born. On specific occasions, women must see to it that oblations of food are offered to the souls of clan's ancestors. At the *Behdienkhlam* festival of the Jaintias, special rituals are performed to seek the blessings of ancestors in order to drive away evil spirits and to ensure soil fertility. It is women's task to prepare special food and liquor, provide sacrificial animals, etc. The actual performance of rituals is, however, reserved for men, usually brothers. While Khasi-Jaintia women perform family worship, community rituals are always performed by men. The priests are always men. The annual *Nongkrem* festival of Khasis is celebrated to invoke the blessings of the ancestress of the Syiem's clan and other founding ancestors, and women take active part in preparations for various rituals, and in the accompanying dances.

Khasi religion in its pristine form did not have priesthood as a formal institution, according to Rymbai (1980). The emergence of male priests as separate functionaries may have been a later development. During the days of Khasi Syiemships (principalities with Chiefs), the Syiem's mother, sister or niece was assigned the role of "Syiem Sad" — the state priestess — who was responsible for preparations for various rituals and sacrifices, besides being the custodian of the Syiem's property, (War, 1992). Among the Jaintias, a woman priestess is supposed to help the "Langdoh" (religious leader) in preparing for communal sacrifices (Gassah, 1992). The significant point to note is that while women are responsible for various preparations men alone perform all major rituals.

At Khasi-Jaintia cremations, women prepare special food and other offerings, while the eldest male member of the deceased person's clan lights the funeral pyre. Women collect bones and ashes after the cremation and put them in the family ossuary. If a woman's husband dies, she has the religious obligation to return his bones to his mother or sister for interment at his maternal family's ossuary.

While Khasi-Jaintia women's position in traditional religion may be described as inferior to that of men, Garo women's participation in most religious ceremonies is even more minimal. The priests are always men. At the most, Garo women may sing traditional songs, mostly dirges. Ironically, women are involved in the final burial of the bones after cremations. About the only ceremony in which Garo women participate is the "Gana" — a magico-religious ritual Garo men perform to enhance their social status. Garo wives perform the ceremonial "Gana" dance with their husbands (Goswami & Majumdar, 1972). In community religious festivals, Garo women are mostly busy with fetching water, cooking and preparing rice-beer, and cannot participate in religious ceremonies.

Impact of Christianity

Adoption of Christianity by a preponderant majority of Meghalaya population (64.58 per cent as per 1991 Census) definitely changed the nature of women's participation in religion, thus influencing their religious status. More importantly, Christianity was instrumental in causing important modifications in their general life as well, which in turn changed their overall status. As noted in Chapter 2, Christian missionaries were instrumental in promoting education, particularly girls' education since the latter half of nineteenth century. It has been a long and persistent struggle against parents' opposition and apathy towards girls' education. Today most parents want to educate their daughters, even if boy's education still continues to have a higher priority among the Garos. Even then a few Meghalaya women have obtained higher education and a few can hold their own in academic, administrative and professional positions. For many women, expansion of education and vocational training has opened many occupational avenues. Access to education has undoubtedly empowered women to resist injustice and oppression, whether in the form of a husband's ill-treatment, or the *Mahari* pressurizing them into marrying an old widower under the law of *Akim*. Christian churches too have opposed unjust social customs like *Akim* and *Dokchapa* and polygyny. The expansion of education has brought Meghalaya into closer interaction with other societies, both more advanced as well as highly patriarchal. The consequences have been a mixed bag: access to new and progressive ideas, at the same time re-enforcement of its own prejudices about women.

A decline in the indigenous religion after conversion to Christianity has significantly altered the traditional roles of Khasi-Jaintia women in several customary rituals, e.g. offerings made to the souls of ancestors, collection and interment of bones after funerals in family ossuary and other ceremonies related to the roles as procreators and multipliers of the lineage. Many of such ceremonies have either been discarded or have lost their significance. This is believed to have reduced the importance of maternal kin, leading to changes in family members' attitudes towards them. Such changes have diminished the glorified image of women as central figures in the clan. Some writers believe that women's status now depends more on their own social position and that of their husband's, rather than on their traditional position as an important link between past and present clan members (Syiem, 1992).

Acceptance of Christianity has given Meghalaya women equal access with men to church services. However, they feel disappointed that not a single Khasi-Jaintia or Garo woman has been ordained by Christian churches to become a pastor or deacon, and men continue to lead services. The Baptist church has, however, been debating the ordination of women for quite some time. Women are very active in social services sponsored by churches. Since the 1980s, thanks to the efforts of two enlightened men among others, a few Garo women have been allowed to speak at regular services and annual church conventions (Marak, 1992).

Emerging Trends

A number of socio-economic, cultural and demographic changes are today responsible for unsettling old family traditions in Meghalaya. Advancing urbanization, new occupational choices and employment options for men and women are leading to residential mobility, loosening of the joint family bonds and a trend toward nuclear family. With the adoption of Christianity there has been a decline in the importance of traditional religious roles of women and a dilution of matrilineal practices. As families become increasingly nuclear, the *Khadduh* has less support from her maternal kin, which places a heavier burden on her to take care of aged parents and needy and destitute clan members. At the same time, this enhances the role of the husband which may result in his sharing more responsibility for the family with his wife. Among the Jaintias, the practice of husbands visiting their wives only for the night is beginning to be replaced by the former staying permanently with their wives and taking a greater share in raising children and providing economic sustenance of the family. Since social changes and related roles of family members do not always follow in a rational manner, in some cases these may result in unreasonable stresses on some family members. For instance, when the *Khadduh* or the *Nokna* is saddled with a highly irresponsible and at times an alcoholic husband, the woman has to work harder to support the family and raise her children without help from her maternal relatives. Significantly, some *Maharis* have made a beginning to allow women to express their views in meetings regarding matters concerning them — indeed a hopeful sign.

As mentioned in Chapter 3, the matrilineal system of Meghalaya is criticized by some sections as the root cause of economic under-development of the State, which is attributed to lack of initiative and enterprising ability among men. It is argued that since women inherit ancestral property they tend to be rude and overbearing, whereas men have no access to capital and are therefore handicapped and tend to become demoralized and irresponsible. Those who advocate this view suggest a restructuring of Meghalaya society on patrilineal basis. The Meghalaya Succession to Self-Acquired Property Act of 1984 empowers parents to give their self-acquired property to sons by making a will. This reduces the economic power matriliny confers on Meghalaya's women.

Recapitulation

A quick recapitulation of Meghalaya women's position with respect to marriage, family and religion brings out some major differences between Khasi-Jaintia and Garo women. The matrilineal system has been functioning differently in the two groups despite a few similarities. In neither group, the *Khadduh* and *Nokna* are absolute owners of the ancestral property inherited from their mothers, and are viewed in both primarily as custodians. Both have to seek the consent of their maternal kin and husbands before taking any major decisions regarding use of the inherited property. In the case of the Khasi-Jaintia women, however, the *Khadduh* in her role as the "Goddess of the Household," and an important link between the past and present clan members, has important roles in ensuring performance of certain ceremonies and religious rituals on behalf of the extended household. Simultaneously, she also enjoys some autonomy in using family resources for raising children, performance of religious obligations, care of needy and old clan members, besides day-to-day management. She receives the support of the maternal kin and her husband in these tasks. A Garo woman, on the other hand, has none of this exalted position in the household, nor any operational freedom to use family resources. Her husband, the *Nokma*, has much greater authority in using the ancestral property on behalf of his wife, the *Nokna*, and while he needs the latter's approval, it has no real meaning in view of the subservient role of a Garo wife. She has very little voice in influencing the *Mahari*'s decisions.

Khasi-Jaintia girls have full freedom to select their marriage partners. Among the Garos, the *Mahari* generally takes the lead in selecting marriage partners, and marriage is viewed primarily as a union of two clans. Even if a girl selects a partner, the *Mahari*'s approval is essential. Similarly, if the *Mahari* decides to give a daughter as replacement according to the law of *Akim*, the girl has no choice. Polygyny prevails among Khasi-Jaintias and Garos to some extent, although Christian churches disapprove this practice. While Khasi-Jaintia women have more freedom to decide on divorce and re-marriage, Garo women need *Mahari*'s approval for both. Even otherwise, Garo women rarely seek divorce in view of their weak economic and social situation, and the fear of social disapproval discourages re-marriage. Khasi-Jaintia widows can re-marry if they wish, whereas Garo widows are relegated to a low status in society. In traditional religion, both Khasi-Jaintia and Garo women occupy a subordinate position and religious rituals are performed by men. The priests are always men. Khasi-Jaintia women, however take active part in preparations for rituals and perform family worship. Moreover, the *Khadduh*, who is traditionally assigned the role of a link between the past and present clan members, performs rituals connected with oblations for the souls of past ancestors, as well as those connected with child-births. With the adoption of Christianity, some of these rituals have lost their importance. While both Khasi-Jaintia and Garo women participate in church services and social services promoted by churches, so far not a single woman has been ordained as a pastor or deacon. While the adoption of Christianity, in view of its disapproval of bigamy and oppressive social customs like *Akim* and *Dokchapa*, has been a boon for women in resisting injustice, it tends to perpetuate the conservative and male-dominated religious practices in Meghalaya.

As noted in the foregoing analysis, despite many drawbacks, Khasi-Jaintia women's position is much better in comparison with that of Garo women with respect to marriage, family and religion. A small number of Garo women who have shown the determination to acquire higher education, vocational or professional training have, however, demonstrated in a small way what the majority can achieve if they organize themselves. They need to develop a resolve to overcome obstacles, whether in the form of oppression or lack of co-operation by husbands, *Chras* or *Mahari*, and utilize to the maximum the new opportunities opening up before them. For this to become a reality, they must develop a strong motivation for change and self-confidence.

MIZORAM

The present Mizo society is more homogeneous, in comparison with the communities of other N-E States, and is characterized by a reasonable similarity in practices and customs related to marriage, family and religion. After the Lushai tribe established its supremacy over other tribes during the latter half of nineteenth century, a more or less composite Lushai culture emerged. The development of a written Mizo script by Christian missionaries in 1897 and the later conversion of majority of Mizos to Christianity undoubtedly hastened the process of social integration. Probably the only exceptions were Reangs and Buddhist Chakmas who have remained educationally and economically backward and socially isolated in Mizo society.[28]

Childhood and Marriage

In traditional Mizo society, birth of a girl child has never been regarded as unwelcome. At the same time there is no denying the fact that a boy's arrival is greeted with greater enthusiasm. The difference in attitudes was evident since old times when the "Upas" or community elders blessed the new-born boy and girl. For a boy, the "Upa's" wish would be that the former would grow into a valiant son, capable of killing elephants and defending the tribe. A girl child, on the other hand, was greeted with a hope that she would grow up into a beautiful and accomplished girl who would fetch a *mithun* (tamed bison) in bride-price ! In present times, although a girl is viewed as an asset to the family by parents, a boy enjoys preferential treatment in terms of access to education and opportunities for play and leisure.

From an early age Mizo girls accompany their mothers and learn various household chores like collecting firewood, taking care of younger siblings, cooking, cleaning, care of poultry, pigs, etc. Today, while travelling in Mizoram it is a common sight to come across groups of girls ranging from six years to adolescents with conical baskets strapped to their back, carrying bamboo cylinders filled with water from mountain springs or vegetables, fodder for animals, etc. The boys were traditionally sent to

28. Unfortunately, observations on Reang and Chakma women were not included specifically in the Mizoram seminar on status of women. Even in general literature on Mizoram, information on Reang and Chakma women is virtually negligible. For information on these two communities, refer to Section on Religion in Tripura in this Chapter and notes 28 and 89 at the end of Chapter 2.

the *Zawlbuk* — youth dormitory, although with the spread of modern education, schools have replaced the *Zawlbuk*. In some communities, the *Zawlbuk* is now being used as a community centre and a focal point for recreation and social services.

When Christian missions began to open schools in Mizoram in the last decade of the nineteenth century, it was hard enough for the missionaries to persuade parents to send their boys to schools. It was infinitely more difficult to get them to send their girls to school because girls were needed at home for various chores. In 1899, out of 56 pupils in the solitary school at Aizawl, only six were girls and these too could attend only part-time since girls were busy in *jhum* fields and in household work (Hluna, 1988). There has been a sea-change in this situation and presently enrolment of girls in schools is only slightly lower than that of boys, and parents are keen to get their daughters educated.

Mizo girls mix freely with young boys and select their marriage partners. At the end of a long day when a Mizo girl returns home from the *jhum* field and the evening meal is over, she is free to entertain young men who visit her and sometimes stay for the night. Another traditional practice in Mizo society is for an adolescent girl to select a working partner — "Lawnpa," who assists her in arduous agricultural tasks. The girl is expected to wash his clothes, carry his implements, take care of not only his meals but also other creature comforts, e.g. tobacco and cigarettes. In other words, she acts as his unfailing and loyal assistant. Girls learn from their early socialization that their role is to serve and please men. It would be considered disgraceful if the young man, i.e. the "Lawnpa" left the girl.

When a girl and a boy decide to marry, the parents negotiate the bride-price. In the past, a simple ceremony which included offering of a sacrificed chicken solemnized the marriage. The bride-price usually consisted of a *mithun*. Customarily, the girl's parents give her clothes, ornaments, household articles such as baskets, a weaving loom, etc. which is called *thuam,* or dowry. Neither party is pressurized regarding the amounts of bride-price or dowry and these are left to be decided by the respective parents according to their capacity. In recent times, there have been occasional cases of dowry becoming rather extravagant and taking the form of expensive presents to the groom's relatives as a status symbol, obviously a result of influences from neighbouring non-tribal societies (Thomas, 1993). Presently, most Mizo marriages are solemnized in Christian churches. Although church leaders continue to express disapproval of the custom of bride-price, upward trend in the amounts has been noted recently.

The traditional freedom enjoyed by young Mizo girls to select their marriage partners also enjoined on them observance of a certain decorum. In case a girl became pregnant, the young man concerned was under pressure to marry her. If he refused to do so, the usual custom is to force him to pay compensation in the form of cash to the girl. Children born out of wedlock were taken care of by the family or the community, and did not suffer from destitution or social stigma. In the present circumstances when social cohesion is somewhat fragile, cases are reported where putative fathers have failed to pay the prescribed compensation to the concerned women (Thomas, 1993). Similarly, the customary fines imposed for breaking an engagement are not always insisted upon.

During the two decades of insurgency after the mid-1960s and the consequent deployment of the army and security personnel in Mizoram, a number of illegitimate children were reported to have made their appearance. There is some concern among older Mizos that exposure to western influence and contacts with other communities have caused a decline in previous moral codes and have led to laxity in sexual relationships of young Mizo women and men. Rape and violence against women, which were unknown in traditional Mizo society have recently been reported. When cases of rape do occur, the tendency among aggrieved women and their parents is not to approach the police. The culprit may get away unpunished by a token act of asking the girl's father to forgive him.[29] Thanks to the efforts of Mizo women's organizations, in 1987 out of 37 reported cases of rape, 30 were brought to trial in courts (Liandingi, 1988).

Polygamy, Divorce and Remarriage

Somewhat in contrast to the freedom enjoyed by an unmarried Mizo girl in deciding whom and when to marry, after marriage she does not get a

29. The author recalls an incident in the mid-1980s when a Mizoram Government officer had raped a young girl employed for a secretarial job in the same office. The father of the rape victim had not reported the case to the police because, according to him, the guilty officer had asked the former's forgiveness. Members of the women's organization (MHIP) had been trying to persuade the father and the rape victim not to let off the guilty officer without punishment.

fully fair deal. Polygamy was usual among the chiefs, and has prevailed to some extent among the commoners as well. At present, monogamy is the most common pattern, although polygyny exists to some extent despite the disapproval of Christian churches. Similarly, even though divorce is regarded as undesirable by Christian churches, both divorce and separation have traditionally been frequent and are known to have become even more so at present. Women who are divorcees or widows can remarry without any difficulty. Since adoption of Christianity, most marriages are solemnized in churches and notwithstanding the Christian churches' efforts to emphasize the sanctity and permanence of the marriage tie, it continues to be a somewhat fragile arrangement, mostly influenced by customary practices.

Mizo customary law refers to eleven types of divorce (Nag, 1993). Broadly, the consequences depend on whether the husband or the wife initiates the process, and the grounds for seeking the divorce. If a wife initiates divorce, she must return the bride-price paid by the husband. In case the divorce is sought because of adultery on her part, the wife must return the bride-price and forfeit all her personal property including the gifts given by her parents at the time of her marriage. If the husband seeks a divorce, and if the wife did not have any children, he can reclaim the bride-price paid by him. If she had children, the bride-price must be fully paid by him in case it was being paid in instalments. If the husband seeks a divorce from his wife due to his involvement with another woman, he must pay the full agreed bride-price in addition to giving the wife compensation, which traditionally took the form of some paddy, earthen pots and tubers. The important point to note is that the husband is not obliged to pay regular maintenance to the divorced wife. If the divorce takes place by mutual consent, the husband and wife may agree to share the bride-price equally or maintain a *status-quo*, i.e. neither return of the bride-price nor any new payment. Divorce can be sought on grounds of insanity of either partner or impotence of the husband.

Protection against Desertion

The customary law gives Mizo woman some protection in case the husband deserts her and has been absent from home for a long period. In such cases, she is allowed to use the family property to maintain her children. She also has a right to decide whether to accept him in case he returns to her. In actual practice, the husband can unilaterally turn the wife out of the house without any obligation on him to give her a regular maintenance. She has no right over children. Since Mizo woman generally does not own or inherit family property, this places her in considerable hardship. Mizo women's organizations have been trying to create public awareness regarding the need to change this situation.

Family

The gender-based division of work had its roots in the lifestyle which characterized Mizo society until the end of nineteenth century. Up to the time when the British prohibited encroachments into rival tribes' territories, Mizo men were preoccupied with inter-tribal and inter-village conflicts and hunting. Women therefore had to manage the home front. The traditional division of work between men and women in jhuming operations has remained more or less unaltered to this day. Men are responsible for cutting down trees and clearing the forest. Women take care of planting, weeding, harvesting, storing of grains, in addition to all household chores, child care, animal husbandry, etc. When there is a lull in agricultural operations in autumn, women are busy with storing fire wood for the next rainy season. They also weave clothes for the family before winter sets in. Men, on the other hand, either rest or go hunting, often as recreation, when free from the tasks of clearing *jhum* lands or community tasks such as preparing paths to water sources. Women remain busy from dawn to late at night and depend heavily on their daughters for sharing their workload. With the recent government efforts to replace jhuming with settled cultivation, introduction of new agricultural technology and new crops, the respective roles of men and women are likely to change in the near future.

Family Relations

In traditional Mizo families, men generally dominate decision-making not only in economic matters (as noted in Chapter 3, ownership of property and inheritance are denied to women) but also in other family matters such as marriages, religious events, etc. While women are responsible for daily marketing, decisions regarding purchase or sale of land fall entirely in men's domain. Typically men are not supposed to help women in household chores, and are teased by their friends if they do. A number of Mizo proverbs reflect men's contemptuous attitude towards women's intelligence. For instance: "A wife and an old fence need to be replaced without much concern." "A woman's wisdom does not go beyond the village water-source."

It is surprising that Mizo men have traditionally treated women with such low regard. During times when men were away due to wars or hunting expeditions, women took over complete responsibility of managing the household as well as *jhum* cultivation. In present times, if a husband is unable to assume his role due to disability or incompetence, a Mizo wife takes over the former's burden fully and confidently. Relatives and neighbours may give a helping hand to women deprived of male support in agricultural operations, house construction, etc. But Mizo women are known to be extremely hard-working and rise to the occasion when called upon to shoulder full family responsibility without men's support.

In spite of general male dominance, Mizo women are far from being meek and subservient in their family relationships. Unlike in traditional Hindu societies, Mizo women do not suffer from inhibitions due to false prestige considerations. For instance, an educated middle-class housewife would consider it perfectly sensible to accumulate a decent kitty by raising and selling pigs in order to buy a new refrigerator she has set her heart on. Similarly, members of a women's group would prepare and sell snacks at a stall in a local festival to raise money for a hamper full of gifts for a child whose mother died in an illness. Of course, women in urban areas and those with a better education have wider options of income generating activities than their rural counterparts. None the less, there is no denying the fact that Mizo women in general are industrious and full of initiative, and can therefore create their own space within a male-dominated family.

Religion

A Mizo proverb — "Women and crabs have no religion" — just about sums up the position of women in the traditional Mizo religion. At the centre was belief in one supreme god and several good and evil spirits which governed natural phenomena, death, disease, destiny of the clan, prospects of hunting expeditions, etc. A male priest presided over propitiation rites and animal sacrifices which were performed exclusively by men. Women were completely excluded from these ceremonies. When Christian missions came to Mizoram in late nineteenth century, Mizo men strongly resisted women's participation in the missions' activities, including attendance at churches. It was felt that if at all, men could adopt Christianity, but for women it was totally unnecessary.

Against this background, it is easy to understand why some of the earliest women converts to Christianity were victims of oppressive social customs and traditional practices. In 1902, Rev. Rowlands provided refuge to two slave girls of about 14 years who had escaped from their master, a Zote chief, and came to the mission centre sponsored by the Welsh Presbyterian Church.[30] Prior to that in 1894, Rev. Lorrain, representing the Arthington mission of the Baptist Church of England, succeeded in persuading a woman who was a village witch and her daughter, to give up witchcraft and accept Christianity in the face of stiff opposition by the villagers (Laltlani, 1988).[31] When the Christian missionaries baptized a few women, initially they were prohibited by Mizo men from reading the Bible and attending the church and even if they did, women had to sit with their faces towards the walls.

Access to Education Through Christianity

Mizo women welcomed Christianity and along with it an opportunity to attend schools, since learning to read and write was necessary to read the Bible. The Christian missionaries adopted a very imaginative approach in tackling the initial reluctance of parents to spare their daughters from housework for attending schools. Along with learning the alphabets, the girls were taught useful skills like stitching, knitting, care of animals, etc. This idea was extended with the appointment of Bible Women since 1913 to teach local women methods of safe delivery and child care. The women were given their first lessons in collection of funds for social causes through introduction of "Buhfai Tham" — a system of collecting tin-fuls of rice.

Today Mizo women are in the forefront of collecting funds for a variety of church-sponsored activities, such as establishment of a mental asylum, maternity services, shelters for the destitute, etc. Mizo women have taken active part in strengthening the facilities of a theological college and since 1972 when the college started admitting women, several women have acquired their Bachelor's degree in Divinity.

---

30. Rev. Rowlands paid the price of a *mithun* — Rs. 40 to the Zote chief to redeem Hnunziki from her slavery. In the second case, viz. Pawngi, the girl's freedom was obtained since the British administration rejected the chief's claim on her (Hluna, 1988).

31. Thangchhumi's mother had traditionally performed witchcraft to avert the wrath of evil spirits. The villagers, therefore, did not want her to give up her profession and accept Christianity. To dissuade her they withheld customary gifts of rice, vegetables, fowls, etc. and refused help in the field and in constructing her house (Laltlani, 1988).

Mizo women have been participating enthusiastically in revivalist meetings of the church and have contributed substantially to the phenomenal spread of Christianity in Mizoram, from less than 1 per cent in 1901 to over 80 per cent of the total population by 1951. Out of about 580 missionaries and other regular workers attached to the Mizo Presbyterian Church, about 150 were women in 1988 (Lalbiaktluanga, 1988). They have displayed a high degree of dedication in evangelical work among the Chakmas and Reangs, who constitute disadvantaged sections of Mizoram population.

Despite this high profile participation of Mizo women in religious activities, neither the Presbyterian nor the Baptist Church has so far ordained a single Mizo woman as a pastor or a minister. The Baptist church has ordained a few women as elders. While a few women are allowed to preach in churches, they are not included in important committees, nor are they generally chosen as delegates for the Synod conferences. This is a matter of considerable disappointment for Mizo women, particularly because the parent churches elsewhere in India and abroad have ordained women as pastors and have included some women in decision-making bodies.

Recapitulation

An overall summing up of Mizo women's status with respect of marriage, family and religion reveals some contrasts as well as new possibilities. Mizo parents have always shown a favourable attitude towards girls, even if birth of a boy evokes greater jubilation. Girls become assets for the family because of their substantial participation in household chores from an early age. Furthermore, they fetch a bride-price. Nevertheless girls' education receives a lower priority as compared to that of boys, but this situation is changing and girls' enrolment has steadily risen. Mizo girls have complete freedom in selecting their marriage partners, and they are allowed to mix freely with boys. Pre-marital sex is on the increase and there is growing laxity regarding boys' responsibility in case a girl becomes pregnant. This is a cause for concern in Mizo society.

With the transition of a Mizo girl into a married housewife, life becomes very demanding and harsh because of the multiple and strenuous household tasks a woman is expected to fulfil, besides her heavy preoccupations with cultivation. Men occupy a dominant role in financial as well as other decisions. Although women have access to divorce and re-marriage, the customary laws allow men greater freedom to take a second wife or keep a concubine, and to divorce their wives. The penalty for divorcing husbands is much greater for women. Similarly, adultery in men is condoned more easily in Mizo society, but in women it results in much harsher punishment. Quite ironically, while marriages are solemnized in Christian churches, customary laws continue to govern separation, divorce, re-marriage and polygamy.

Mizo traditional religion assigned a very low status to women. They could not participate in most rituals nor could they become priests. With the adoption of Christianity, Mizo women can participate actively in church services as well as other social activities sponsored by churches. In fact, Mizo women can now play leadership roles in organizing collection of funds for various humanitarian causes sponsored by churches and have also been active as missionaries. Their one persistent handicap is that they are not ordained as priests or pastors and are mostly excluded from important policy-making meetings and conferences organized by important church organizations, viz. the Baptist and Presbyterian churches.

Adoption of Christianity is likely to prove a positive factor in terms of Mizo women's status in the family because Christianity has consistently expressed disapproval of Mizo customs of polygyny and divorce. Another significant gain for women has been access to education which Christianity strongly supported. The spread of education has brought about dramatic changes in Mizo women's lives. It has opened the doors to many types of vocational and professional training as well as self-employment in trades and businesses. With the diverse occupational choices now opening up for Mizo women, as well as greater interaction with new ideas and experiences, Mizo women are achieving greater economic autonomy. Simultaneously, they are gaining greater self-confidence and a legitimate place for themselves in the family. A very significant change in the attitude of parents towards their daughters is noticeable in recent years. Parents have found their daughters much more dependable and caring than sons who tend to take a more casual approach towards educational opportunities provided by parents, and in some cases, dissipate their lives in drinking and drugs. Daughters on the other hand, tend to use facilities for education and vocational preparation far more responsibly and often prove a valuable support for old parents.

NAGALAND

Nagaland, with 88 per cent Sheduled Tribes population, is similar in this respect to Mizoram where the corresponding figure is 95 per cent. Until the end of nineteenth century the Nagas, like the Mizos, were engaged in warfare — inter-tribal, inter-village, as well as raids on villages in Assam plains. Nagaland, however, differs from Mizoram in one important respect. In Mizoram, following the Lushais' conquest and assimilation of other tribes, a fairly homogeneous Mizo culture emerged. In the absence of such a unifying force, Naga tribes retain to this day many of their individual traditions, customs and dialects. The range is wide: while some tribes have a fairly sophisticated and highly Westernized lifestyle, others have only recently graduated from food-gathering and hunting stage to primitive *jhum* cultivation. In the following analysis, we try to present common features with respect to the situation of women in marriage, family and religion among major Naga tribes, and to indicate wherever significant, the range of variations among them.

Attitudes towards Girls and Boys

The Naga attitudes towards men and women were strongly influenced by the reality of warfare and hunting as essential aspects of the community's survival. These required a constantly replenished army of men who were brave warriors and intrepid hunters. Physical strength and courage were essential to wrest a living in the inhospitable and hilly terrain. It is, therefore, easy to understand why the Nagas welcomed the birth of boys rather than of girls. This preference for male children continues to this day. Furthermore, in the context of patrilineal descent, a male child is perceived as a continuator of the lineage and, therefore, preferred over a female child. When a male child is born after a succession of girls, the Mao Nagas celebrate the event with great pomp, which includes killing a bull in order to treat villagers to a sumptuous feast (Mao, X. 1988). The Lothas assign a strength of six to a man, and five to a woman. Consequently, a male child is christened on the sixth day after birth, and a girl child on the fifth (Tungoe, 1988). A Zeliangrong husband regards it justifiable to divorce his wife if she fails to give birth to a son.

While the Nagas prefer sons rather than daughters, the birth of a girl child is certainly not regarded as a misfortune. In most Naga tribes, girls fetch a bride-price from the groom's side and can never be a liability to their parents. Besides, girls learn household chores from a young age and are assets to their parents. Furthermore, girls as potential mothers who give birth to valiant sons have always commanded a certain respect in Naga society. Despite the basically preferential attitude towards boys, girls grow up in an atmosphere of love and freedom and move about without inhibitions with their friends — both boys and girls. Mothers teach their daughters various house-keeping tasks, weaving, making cane and bamboo articles, etc. Among some tribes, e.g. the Semas, young girls are sometimes sent to the chief's house to earn their keep by working for the chief's household (Zhimomi, 1988). Until almost the end of 1960s, most Naga parents were quite apathetic towards their daughters' education, and often withdrew them from schools after completing the primary stage. Even at present boys' education receives a higher priority and poorer parents tend to view investments on girls' education as wasteful, since girls leave their parents' house after marriage. During the last two decades, however, parents have been showing greater interest in educating their daughters. The number of girls enrolled at middle and higher levels of education is steadily rising.

In the past most Naga tribes sent young girls and boys to separate dormitories called "morungs," which provided them training for social responsibility and leadership, besides opportunities to select their marriage partners. Girls also received training in household tasks, weaving and other arts from older and more experienced women during their stay in the dormitories. With the expansion of formal school system, youth dormitories suffered a decline. Christian missionaries have also been opposed to the system in view of its free mixing of boys and girls. A small number of youth dormitories have survived, particularly in non-Christian Naga villages, albeit with many changes. In some villages, "morungs" serve the purpose of community centres where boys as well as men may assemble in the evenings. Naga boys and girls participate in singing and dancing together at community festivals, and enjoy a relaxed relationship. Courtship among boys and girls is acceptable in Naga community. Despite the freedom Naga boys and girls enjoy at community dancing, they are reported to display a high degree of decorum (Horam, 1977).

Selection of Mate

Most Naga tribes allow their daughters to select their marriage partners. At the same time, the practice of parents arranging their marriages, sometimes through elderly women acting as intermediaries between the girl's and the boy's families, is equally prevalent. Even when parents arrange marriages, girls are consulted and not forced into marrying persons against their wishes. There are very few exceptions where the girls may not be consulted, e.g. the Zeliangrongs and Konyaks, among whom men take all important decisions without consulting women (Hunibou, 1988, Sen, 1987). Rules of exogamy apply to a clan as well as a *Khel* (a sub-division of a village co-ordinated with the clan and lineage systems) and as long as these are complied with, parents generally give their consent to love marriages arranged by their sons and daughters. Persons violating these rules may be exiled from the village or fined. Child marriages are absent in Naga tribes. Among the Khiamnungans, girls are married between 20-25 years, and early marriage is believed to result in weak progeny (Sardeshpande, 1987).

Although chastity is valued, pre-marital sex is not uncommon among girls. If a girl becomes pregnant and the boy belongs to a permissible clan, they are under pressure from relatives to get married. If, however, they belong to non-permissible clans, the girl always receives a harsher punishment than the boy. The Maos turn her out of the village, and she is allowed to return later, but without the child (Mao, X. 1988). Among the Konyaks, unmarried mothers sometimes kill their children with the help of a *Sheepa* (a person believed to possess occult powers to communicate with evil spirits) (Sardeshpande, 1987). Although pre-marital motherhood brings some degree of disgrace, it is not a serious obstacle for the girl to marry.

It is incumbent on a chief's son to marry only a chief's daughter. The Yimchungers, who are settled in Tuensang district, until recently were known to follow the practice of marriage by capture. For instance, if a boy happens to like a girl, he abducts and marries her (Sen, 1987). In the past the Khiamnungans too were known to have had the custom of marriage by capture. Even today their marriage ceremony includes a routine of a mock abduction of the girl by the groom's relatives and her running away a couple of times. A simple ceremony follows thereafter in which the girl and the boy take oaths of mutual loyalty (Sardeshpande, 1987). The marriage ceremony in most Naga tribes is simple and brief.

Bride-Price

The most common practice among Naga tribes is for the groom's parents to negotiate bride-price with the girl's parents. Sometimes a groom works for the prospective father-in-law for a specified period, during which the girl may be invited to visit the groom's family to give her future in-laws an opportunity to observe her. A groom may also visit the girl's family during the engagement period (Sardeshpande, 1987). There is a system of hierarchy regarding the amount of bride-price. A girl from a respectable clan, and having competence in house-keeping chores and skills in weaving fetches a decent bride-price. The chief's daughter attracts the highest bride-price, but if she is found guilty of some misbehaviour, the fine imposed on her is also high. A girl known to have had several affairs, or is notorious as a flirt fetches the lowest bride-price. The Lothas assign a lower status to a spinster than to a widow (Tungoe, 1988). A woman who is divorced due to some misconduct fetches only a nominal bride-price. The Semas pay a rather high amount as bride-price (Randip Singh, 1987). The bride-price may be in the form of cash, precious stones, domestic animals or landed property. Among the Zeliangrongs, the bride-price received from the groom's side is distributed among relatives and friends on the bride's side, and the latter, in turn, are expected to support her and protect her interests in case of any marital problem (Hunibou, 1988).

Among the Tangkhuls, Angamis and Maos, the custom of bride-price does not exist, but presents are exchanged between the groom's and the bride's sides. Tangkhul parents on both sides give household articles to the newly married couple. The groom's parents, assisted by clan members, build a new house for the couple. Alternatively, the groom's parents give their house to the young couple, and move, with unmarried children, into a new house built with the clan's help. The custom of bride-price is disapproved by Christian churches, and may suffer a decline in days to come.

Naga tribes have never had the practice of demanding a dowry from bride's parents. But it is customary among parents in most tribes to give her ornaments, clothes, a loom, baskets, shawls, etc. Women have exclusive right over these possessions, and they may pass these on to their daughters. In a Konyak wedding, a woman from the bride's side leads a party to the groom's house with presents for the groom's clan members. The next day, the groom's party returns the favours, usually in the form of money (Sardeshpande, 1987).

Polygyny

Although polyandry is unknown among Nagas, polygyny prevails to varying extent among many tribes. It has been customary for the chiefs of tribes, e.g. Konyak, Tangkhul, and other affluent persons to have several wives. A Konyak chief, called the "Ang," lives like a king in a large house, with several villages under his control from whom he gets tributes and free labour and generally has several wives (Randip Singh, 1987). Since having several wives presupposes ability to pay the requisite bride-price, it is a matter of prestige. Besides, this provides more labour for cultivation. Usually the eldest wife is designated as the principal wife, whose son generally enjoys certain hereditary rights to chieftainship and property. Co-wives may live in separate houses or share a joint household (Zhimomi, 1988). Some tribes, e.g. Mao and Khiamnungon, favour monogamy, whereas polygyny prevails among the Semas and Lothas, especially among traditional sections. A Lotha husband may take a second wife without divorcing his first wife if she is childless (Tungoe, 1988).

Christian churches have been trying to promote monogamy among the Nagas, and are making it a requirement to obtain prior permission of the church before a second marriage. The younger Nagas are reported to have welcomed this change since it is expected to curb the traditional chiefs from using their feudal authority to take away any young woman they fancied even if it entailed separating young lovers.

Divorce and Remarriage

Divorce is generally easily available among the Nagas in case of marital problems and divorcees can re-marry without any difficulty. The common grounds for divorce are : mutual incompatibility, affliction by an incurable disease, adultery, ill-treatment, barrenness of the wife or failure to give birth to a son. Divorce is disapproved among some tribes, e.g. Khiamnungan and Lotha, which is a strange irony since in both of these groups men wield absolute authority to summarily dismiss their wives on even minor and at times unfair grounds. A Khiamnungan husband can simply order his wife to leave if she incurs his displeasure due to the slightest pretext (Sardeshpande, 1987). As mentioned before, a Lotha husband can take another wife, or divorce his first wife, if she is childless on the tacit assumption that she and not the husband is responsible for childlessness. This practice of holding the wife automatically responsible for childlessness prevails among other Naga tribes too. Sometimes, a husband may divorce three wives in succession, and it is only when a divorced wife remarries and gets a child that the first husband's deficiency gets exposed. And yet, he can get away without paying any penalty for causing unjustifiable anguish to his previous wife. A Sema husband can unilaterally ask his wife to leave his house on grounds of incompatibility or some minor fault, and can reclaim bride-price from her family within three years of marriage (Zhimomi, 1988). In several Naga tribes, men can divorce their wives on fairly vague and indeterminate grounds, e.g. being overbearing or disrespectful, and this arbitrariness increases where the stakes are high, i.e. when the bride-price is high as among the Semas.

It is not so easy for Naga women to get a divorce without paying a penalty. If an aggrieved Tangkhul wife leaves her husband for what might be considered by husband or others as flimsy grounds, and does not return soon, the husband is free to marry another wife. If the first wife takes another husband, and the village council decides that she is guilty, the second husband is fined heavily (Horam, 1977). Besides, she is fined double the amount of bride-price paid by her first husband and is forbidden to take with her any possession from his house (Pearson, 1993). A Lotha wife who is considered by her husband or his relatives as overbearing, probably because she is educated or comes from a well-to-do family background, is warned by the latter and may even be divorced summarily by paying ten rupees (Tungoe, 1988). In the case of a woman, however, if she wants a divorce because of ill-treatment by husband, she may get it only if permitted by the village council.

If the husband divorces a Lotha wife on grounds of adultery or immorality, it is difficult for her to find another husband. Adultery in women, as noted earlier, attracts a much heavier penalty as compared to adultery in men. A Sema husband who divorces a wife on grounds of adultery can claim return of bride-price, in addition to her dowry (which is generally treated as her personal property) besides one head of cattle from her father (Zhimomi, 1988). The wife can reclaim her ornaments only if the village council finds the husband guilty of serious ill-treatment, and in such cases, the council may impose a fine on the husband.

Divorce cases initiated by women can be brought to the village council or to the chief (where the chieftain system prevails) who is generally assisted by village elders or council members. Membership of these councils is restricted to men. However, clan members, and sometimes the whole village may participate in deciding the cases. As noted in Chapter 1, certain legal and Constitutional safeguards protect the jurisdiction of traditional village authorities. However, some changes have been made in the existing arrangements whereby district magistrates and sub-divisional commissioners were given authority to decide appeals against the village authorities' decisions. Among the Zeliangrong Nagas, a wife seeking a divorce is required to produce witnesses before the village council and village elders. Only when the latter jointly come to the conclusion that the husband is guilty of adultery or ill-treatment is she free from the obligation to return the bride-price to the husband (Hunibou, 1988). In general, the bride-price which is regarded as a symbol of women's dignity, is thus used as a stick to punish the wives even for relatively minor lapses, while the husband in most cases can usually get away without having to compensate even for serious misdemeanour.

Women's Family Chores

When Naga girls get married and join the husband's family, they leave behind a care-free and enjoyable life filled with happy times and dancing with friends, and enter a strenuous and hectic routine. Cooking, cleaning, collecting and bringing home water and firewood, growing vegetables, rearing poultry, pigs and other animals, preparing rice-beer, spinning from cotton and nettle fibres and weaving clothes, making cane and bamboo articles, etc. keep them very busy. As mentioned in Chapter 3, excepting clearing of jungles and guarding crops from wild animals, which are performed by men, women undertake major cultivation tasks, such as sowing, transplanting, weeding, harvesting, drying and storing of grains. In areas where husking mills are not available, women spend considerable time and energy in de-husking rice daily.

During the days of tribal warfare whenever men were away, women are reported to have taken complete responsibility for *jhum* fields, holding posts for providing essential supplies to the fighting men and construction of houses which is usually men's job. It is interesting to note that Sema men, despite their usual attitude of superiority towards women, inwardly regarded women as strong and warrior-type, and women in fact accompanied men in tribal feuds in case of need (Zhimomi, 1988).

Women's Participation in Decisions

Naga women enjoy considerable autonomy with respect to day-to-day household management. They do daily shopping for the family and petty trading in poultry or vegetables or other *jhum* products in order to purchase other family necessities. A Lotha man who seems to take interest in household details is teased by his friends, who would regard hunting or gambling as more appropriate pastimes for men (Mhathing, 1988). It is women's job to ensure that there is no shortage of grains and the family is fed properly. A Zeliangrong husband may not consult his wife regarding the groom he has selected for their daughter, but concedes the wife's right to decisions regarding day-to-day running of the household. He would refrain from disposing of animals reared by his wife without seeking her approval, and respect her right to use her own money (Hunibou, 1988).

When it comes to important family concerns, there are wide differences among various Naga tribes with respect to women's participation. The Tangkhul women are actively involved in important family matters. The Khiamnungan men, who are known to be rather aggressive outside the home, are reported to be somewhat submissive within the household and consult their wives in family matters such as cultivation, livestock and marriages (Sardeshpande, 1987). This picture changes considerably with respect to Zeliangrong men who consider it perfectly normal to take all important family decisions such as inheritance, social events, even marriages with which the women may be directly involved (Hunibou, 1988).

Family Relationships and Role Expectations

Relationships in the family are generally characterized by male dominance, but vary considerably within a wide range. For instance, the Lothas expect their women to be docile and obedient. If a Lotha wife who is educated expresses a negative reaction about some family decision, she may be criticized for interfering in what are regarded as the husband's affairs, and is likely to be warned by the husband or his relatives. If her behaviour still seems assertive, she is likely to be divorced summarily after paying her a token compensation. A reference has been made in Chapter 3 to the old practice of Lotha men placing a bet on their wives in gambling, and the loser having to turn his wife over to the winner for a fixed period (Tungoe, 1988). In a Tangkhul household, on the other hand, a wife has considerable influence on important family matters, and the mother has a key role in ensuring proper care of all family members. In important community festivals men and women dance together, and it is reported that the participants display perfect propriety and decorum.

When it comes to deciding on important matters such as maintenance of community water sources, or implementing decisions affecting the whole tribe, or deciding on punishment for a person violating clan exogamy rules, women are not included in village councils or meetings of the chief assisted by village elders (Horam, 1977). The Khiamnungans, who live in the relatively isolated terrain in the vicinity of the Patkoi ranges, have classified two types of leaders: first, the brave, warrior-type, regal in their bearing, and second, persons having wisdom, sagacity and knowledge. Since women are believed to be devoid of either type of qualities, they are excluded from all joint decision-making (Sardeshpande, 1987). Both Naga men and women are so conditioned that both accept the superior and inferior position of men and women respectively. For instance, Sema men typically consider women incompetent in dealing with social, economic, political and religious matters, and men are regarded as the backbone of society. In the folklore, women are portrayed as inspirers who dedicate songs to men and thus motivate them to victory and achievement (Zhimomi, 1988). The ideal Naga wife is depicted as conscientious in performing her responsibilities towards the household and careful in looking after her husband's comforts. Her conscientiousness does not, however, find reciprocation. Women are, for instance, forbidden to eat the meat of a monkey or bear, due to a belief that they might acquire the qualities of those animals.

Position of Widows

When a woman becomes a widow, her situation becomes unenviable in Naga society. As mentioned in Chapter 3, a widow has no right to own or inherit her deceased husband's property. Some customary practices, however, mitigate to some extent this harsh reality. In some tribes, e.g. the Semas, a widow is entitled to a part of the husband's movable property. She also gets the benefit of labour and other services due to her deceased husband for a limited period as a courtesy. Zeliangrong men provide labour in certain strenuous cultivation tasks to widows as a social obligation. They cannot, however, demand any of these benefits as a right. If a widow re-marries the deceased husband's brother, or remains unmarried in the deceased husband's house, she can continue to use his property without having ownership. The previous custom requiring a widow to marry the deceased husband's brother, which prevailed in several tribes, e.g. the Lothas and Tangkhuls, has lost its rigour. Similarly, the practice among the Sema sons to divide their step-mothers after the father's death has virtually disappeared (Randip Singh, 1987). A widow can now marry a man of her choice, however, if the latter belongs to a clan other than that of her deceased husband's, she loses the protection of her deceased husband's clan. She also loses right over her children. Among the Konyaks, if a widow is not liked by the deceased husband's family, and happens to have only daughters but no son, she may be asked to return to her parents' house after she is given some grains and a pig as compensation (Sardeshpande, 1987).

A positive aspect of Naga societies, however, is that widows do not suffer from any social stigma, nor is remarriage disapproved. Equally important is the general family ethos of giving protection to widows, which safeguards them against destitution. In case a widow, a divorcee or an unmarried girl for any reason becomes dependent, her parental family and clan give her protection.

Naga Attitudes Towards Women : A Perplexing Mix

The Naga attitudes towards women seem to be a complex mixture: strong elements of distrust and disdain side by side with a certain degree of grudging respect and protectiveness. Nowhere is this demonstrated more obviously than in the customs and beliefs related to head-hunting, tribal warfare and hunting expeditions. In the past, it was considered inauspicious for men setting out on wars to have any contact, even accidental, with women before leaving. The practice was for men to sleep in the boys' dormitory to avoid temptation. Lotha men are supposed to avoid sleeping with their wives before going on a hunting or fishing expedition to avoid mishaps (Tungoe, 1988). Contact with women or accepting anything from women before leaving on a tiger-hunt is believed to be unlucky. It was customary for Zeliangrong men to give a warning yell before attacking an enemy village, and killing women and children was considered cowardly (Hunibou, 1988).

At the same time, women's heads were regarded as more coveted trophies than men's heads and were believed to draw the *Aren* (Spirit of Fortune) from enemy villages (Horam, 1977). The Tangkhul warriors who brought back enemy heads were given a ceremonial welcome which women were not permitted to attend. At the most, they could watch the ceremonies from a distance. Women traditionally did not participate in dances related to head-hunting, warfare and deaths, all of which suggest a concern for avoiding emotionally disturbing occasions for women. Women's movements were restricted when their village was at war. Among the Konyaks, a newly married couple enjoyed immunity from enemy attack during inter-village wars (Sardeshpande, 1987).

During the days of head-hunting and tribal warfare, Naga women often assumed roles of peace-makers and of a neutral force in order to end further violence. As referred earlier, Sema women were known to accompany their men in tribal feuds when needed (Zhimomi, 1988). During the head-hunting raids, if women came in between warring parties waving leaves or cloths, the fighting had to stop immediately among the Maos. Even in the course of ordinary fights between two men, women act as peace-makers. They were also known to negotiate a treaty between the warring parties (Mao, X. 1988). When two Tangkhul parties engaged in head-hunting, reached a point when one of them was about to suffer a crushing defeat, a neutral force — "Pukhareila" — in the form of one or more ladies came in between to stop the fighting and thus save men's lives (Thomas, 1988). They were respected for their neutrality and were never harmed. It would indeed be very fortunate if Naga women could invoke these past associations with their role as peace-makers and negotiators to bring about amity and reconciliation among the different militant groups which have kept Nagaland in a state of turmoil for over half a century.

With the rapid expansion of education, and a beginning of vocational and professional training, Naga women are entering employment as doctors, nurses, teachers, and a small number have entered Indian Administrative Services and similar prestigious positions. Contrary to the previous apathy towards girls' education, more people now welcome educated and working daughter-in-laws, since they augment family incomes. More importantly, if women hold respectable jobs, this significantly improves their status in the family and social life. Simultaneously another significant change is evident in Naga parents' traditional preference for boys. Naga boys are no longer content with pursuing family cultivation and prefer to migrate to urban areas in search of employment and a more modern lifestyle. In the process, they are leaving behind their old parents, unmarried sisters, and other needy relatives such as widowed or deserted women. This type of situation compels people to re-think and revise traditional expectations regarding women and parents are more willing to give their daughters a fairer deal.

Women's Place in Religion

Most Naga tribes, according to their indigenous religions, believe in the existence of one supreme, all powerful God and good and evil spirits which are propitiated with prayers, offerings and sacrifices. There are no idols, nor places of worship like shrines or temples (Horam, 1980). In the Mao mythology, for instance, the blue sky represents the father and the earth the mother, who lays on her back, and all living creatures are believed to be born out of their union. Another Mao belief attributes the birth of God, man and tiger to the ancient ancestress, who came into contact with a cloud. The Maos observe a ceremony at the time of harvesting called "Belu Kotow" — intended to seek a blessing for prosperity — which is performed by women. (Mao, X. 1988). When the Tangkhuls begin to draw on the new harvest they celebrate "Chumphu" — a harvesting festival — in which women perform a certain ceremony, which Tangkhul men must scrupulously avoid witnessing (Horam, 1977).

In the past, important events such as head-hunting and hunting of tigers and other animals were associated with religious ceremonies. For instance, among the Konyaks, there are rituals associated with washing the hands of head-hunters. Another category of religious events was connected with agricultural events, e.g. sowing and harvesting. The sacrifices and other rituals connected with both kinds are performed by religious leaders who are always men. Women generally have no place in performing these, the only exceptions being a few symbolic events during harvesting (Sardeshpande, 1987). The marginal role assigned to women in the sphere of religion is illustrated by a practice followed by the Khiamnungans to seek protection from evil spirits who are believed to cause illness or death. Some women who are supposed to possess special powers to communicate with evil spirits through their dreams, called "Eins" are approached to avert an apprehended disaster. The "Ein" is also invited to persuade the evil spirit not to harm a couple desiring a child (Sardeshpande, 1987). The Konyaks assign a similar role — that of a "Sheepa" — to persons who are believed to possess special powers to intercede with malicious spirits and prevent a misfortune, and "Sheepas" can be women.

The Chakhesangs, a group inhabiting Phek district, select two elderly and wise persons, a man and a woman, to fix "gennas" — special days when certain rules, such as fasting, prayers, abstention from work, etc.

— are to be observed. The male leader is responsible for fixing the days to mark important community festivals and special events. The elderly woman leader fixes "gennas" related to agricultural operations (Sen, 1987). Among the Tangkhuls, the male head of the family acts as the family priest, worships at the family alter and performs all rituals intended to propitiate the deities. The Tangkhuls, like most other Naga tribes, assign to women the incidental role of preparing rice-beer and sticky rice needed at religious events. The Khiamnungan folklore refers to a devastating flood which threatened their existence, and how the tribe appeased the deities by offering the sacrifice of a beautiful maiden. They therefore hold Yakko peak in the Patkoi range as their saviour deity (Sardeshpande, 1987). Formerly, it was customary for Khiamnungan men to hunt for heads and hang them outside the *morung* (boys dormitory) to ensure a good crop and to avert illnesses, and women's role was limited to appeasing the evil spirit "Paiyakova," with whom a few selected women were believed to be able to communicate. Some Naga tribes, e.g. Tangkhuls and Aos, believe in life after death in the form of souls. The supreme god of the Aos, "Kovatso," it is believed, decides whether the souls of men and women would live in his house or face rejection, depending on whether they have led a virtuous or a vicious life. A delightful Ao legend about a couple relates how a husband, while dying, whispers to his wife to wait and not to re-marry, assuring her of a reunion and a happy and peaceful life in the form of souls (Ao, 1980).

Impact of Christianity

By the beginning of the twentieth century, a predominant majority (96 per cent) of Nagas belonged to their indigenous tribal faiths (Sen, 1987). Their conversion to Christianity which made a small beginning in the last quarter of the nineteenth century gained momentum by 1950s, and by 1991 less than 1 per cent of the State's population belonged to traditional religions. For Naga women whose position in traditional religion had been marginal, adoption of Christianity has meant a fortunate break with the past. Naga women can participate on an equal footing with men in regular church services. But no woman has so far been ordained as a priest or deacon. Significantly, women have been actively involved in social activities sponsored by Christian churches, e.g. campaigns against social problems such as alcoholism, polygyny and in providing services for persons in special need. The association with the church helps Naga women to overcome traditional social barriers and some of them now address public meetings. A concomitant and probably more basic change brought about by the early Christian missionaries was promotion of girls' education at a time when many Naga parents were indifferent in this respect. The expansion of educational facilities has opened many new employment opportunities and vocations for women, and equally significantly, raised their status in the family. It has given them an opportunity to interact with more progressive cultures and new ideas.

On the negative side, it is argued that Christianity has altered the content of several Naga religious ceremonies having a strong community orientation (Ao, 1972). The question raised by some Naga thinkers is whether Christianity, with its emphasis on personal salvation, hastened the erosion of the Nagas' traditional community ethos, which had provided Naga women protection against destitution and desertion. It is worth noting that Naga persons seeking divorce and re-marriage are expected to obtain churches' permission since Christianity places emphasis on the sanctity of marriage.

Recapitulation

The Nagas' preference for a male child over a female is a carry-over of their past dependence on brave warriors and hunters for survival. However, birth of a girl was never regarded as a misfortune, since she would be a great asset for parents in household chores since early years, besides fetching a bride-price when she marries. Although parents usually give girls' education a lower priority in comparison with boys, girls grow up in an atmosphere of love and freedom to mix with boys and girls. Mothers teach them various house-keeping tasks and arts like weaving. The past practice of sending adolescent girls and boys to live in youth dormitories which played a vital role in their socialization, has suffered a major decline with the expansion of school system, and also because of disapproval by Christian missions. In most Naga tribes, girls select their own marriage partners and as long as clan exogamy rules are obeyed, parents agree to the marriage. Even where parents take initiative in arranging marriages, girls are consulted, and exceptions to this practice are very few. In most Naga tribes, the groom's side pays bride-price to the girl's parents, and among a few tribes, e.g. Tangkhuls and Angamis, parents on both side exchange presents. The marriage ceremony is usually very simple, with both the girl and the boy pledging mutual loyalty.

Polygyny exists among most tribes, and particularly among chiefs and affluent persons. Divorce is easily available among most Naga tribes and divorcees can re-marry without any difficulty. On the whole, men are more likely to initiate a divorce and can obtain it even on rather vague or non-specific grounds, such as the wife being quarrelsome or overbearing, as also wife's childlessness on the assumption that she is responsible. It is more difficult for a woman to obtain a divorce, and when she initiates it she generally has to repay the bride-price, and can get it if the village council is satisfied about her claim. Women have no representation in these councils. Christian churches disapprove of divorce and polygyny, and some churches require their prior permission before obtaining a divorce and also for remarriage. Children's custody generally goes to the father, and women do not get any of the family property.

After marriage, Naga women get tied to a hectic routine which includes many household chores like cooking, cleaning, bringing water and collecting fuel, weaving, care of children, besides their major responsibility for family cultivation. In most Naga tribes, women enjoy more or less complete autonomy in day-to-day household management and disposition of resources raised by them. In some tribes, e.g. Zelinangrong and Konyak, men consider it unnecessary or useless to consult women regarding important family matters such as inheritance, marriages and other family events. Since women are regarded incapable of comprehending matters which concern the whole community, they do not represent their family in village councils. Ironically, most Naga women are reconciled to their subordinate position and are keen to fulfil their responsibilities towards the family and dutiful towards their husbands. Women participate with men in community dancing at special festivals, although they do not participate in dances related to deaths.

In indigenous Naga religions women have a very marginal position as exemplified by some of them acting as interlocutors with evil spirits. The priests at community and family worship have always been men. Women were excluded from religious ceremonies related to welcoming victorious warriors who brought enemy heads. About the only religious rituals which women perform are those related to harvesting, and that too only in some tribes. Since the adoption of Christianity, Naga women's position not only in religion but also in other social spheres has improved considerably. Christian churches so far have not ordained any woman as priests. But women participate fully in church worship as well as social activities promoted by churches, and they can now address public meetings. Naga women have benefited immensely from educational facilities which were initially promoted by Christian missions. Expansion of education opened before them important avenues of personal and social development. Access to education and occupational training has equipped women for new and varied opportunities of employment, which in turn is enhancing their status in the family and society.

TRIPURA

Tripura's indigenous tribal population, as stated in Chapter 2, was outstripped by Bengali immigrants even prior to mid-twentieth century, and by 1991 declined to 31 per cent of the total State population. The State's non-tribal population consists of two major constituents : (i) Bengali cultivators who kept coming to Tripura particularly since the last quarter of the nineteenth century in search of cultivable land and (ii) huge waves of Hindu refugees from erstwhile East Pakistan, and later Bangladesh, who sought shelter in Tripura due to communal strife prior to and after Partition of India. The status of women among Tripura's non-tribal population is mostly similar to that of Bengali Hindu society. The following analysis of the situation of women with respect to marriage, family and religion deals primarily with the State's tribal population which has some distinctive and unique features, and references to non-tribal society are mainly for illustrations and comparisons.

Attitude towards Girls

Girls grow up in a relaxed atmosphere among Tripura's tribal communities. Child marriage is unknown, girls move about quite freely and are allowed to mix with boys. They participate actively in community festivals which include a lot of singing and dancing. In the bamboo-dance called "Cherolam" for which the Lushais and their sub-tribes are well known, girls charm audiences with their colourful dresses and graceful movements. Simultaneously, however, while boys are free to play football and other games, girls have to spend more time in doing various household chores and weaving. The Tripuris, for instance, who generally give a lot of freedom for girls and boys to move together, expect girls to be more responsible for various family tasks and to learn stitching and making cane and bamboo articles. Tripuri boys get better food and clothes, and their education receives a higher priority than that of girls (Saigal, 1978). The generally dismal female literacy rates among Tripura's tribal women, the low enrolment of tribal girls in schools and high wastage rates until the late 1980s are indicative of tribal parents' lack of concern regarding girls' education (Choudhary, 1993). This situation is slowly beginning to change in recent times. The Mughs do not discriminate against girls and are reported to be treating boys and girls as equals, and both grow up in a free and relaxed atmosphere (Saigal, 1978). This can be understood in the context of their Myanmar origins and the relatively favourable attitudes towards women in South-East Asian culture.

Selection of Marriage Partner

Most marriages are negotiated by parents, sometimes with the help of middle-men, among the older tribes who originally inhabited Tripura, e.g. Tripuris, Reang, Jamatia Noatia. At the same time love-marriages are quite common among all tribes, old and new. Cases of young lovers' elopement seems to be a familiar occurrence, judging from the fact that most tribal groups have well established rules to deal with elopement. Among the Tripuris, for instance, parents may show their disapproval by asserting their right to have their daughter brought back home. If the girl is abducted against her wishes, the village council takes a serious view and the delinquent boy may be heavily fined. Besides, young lads of the girl's village have their own way of teaching the abductor a lesson by giving him a sound thrashing. Some tribes, e.g. Rupini and Chakma regard it essential to obtain parents'consent even after the young boy and girl have chosen each other, or have eloped. Most parents, however, give their consent to the marriage if the young people elope once again. In such cases, parents presume that they are man and wife, and even if the girl becomes pregnant, the child does not pose any problem of illegitimacy. The whole village community and village council exert pressure on the boy to marry the girl. If, however, the boy refuses to marry the girl after he has eloped with her, he is fined heavily by village councils, who usually deal with civil and criminal cases. Among the Halams, if the girl is regarded as more responsible than the boy in the act of elopement, she is fined more heavily (Saigal, 1978). On the other hand, if a boy proposes to an already engaged girl, he is fined and the amount is handed over to the aggrieved young man (and not to the girl). The Halams, and indeed most tribal groups belonging to Lushai family, allow complete freedom to young girls to entertain their boy-friends in their homes in the evenings, and pre-marital sex is not uncommon. The extent of initiative taken by parents on the one hand and young boys and girls on the other, in arranging marriages, varies among different tribes of Tripura. Among Reangs and Halams, a majority of marriages are arranged by parents. While Tripuri girls are known to display considerable poise and spontaneity in social relationships, they are reported never to cross the limits of propriety (Choudhury, Pratap 1993).[32]

Most tribes in Tripura follow rules of clan exogamy and tribal endogamy, and some tribes tend to be more rigorous than others. Among the Rupinis, marriageable girl and boy must be unrelated for five previous generations. The Mughs prohibit cross-cousin marriages. On the other hand, among the Garos, cross-cousin marriages are preferred, the only condition being that the boy and girl must not belong to the same maternal clan and lineage (Choudhury, Pratap 1993). Jamatia girls are not permitted to marry boys from the Reang, Morsum or Kaipeng groups because the Jamatias regard themselves as of superior class (Mandal, 1993). Generally, the rules regarding permissible clans and tribes have lost their rigidity among persons who have adopted Christianity, e.g. the Lushais. Among Noatias, girls are married when they are of 14 years and boys at the age of 18, while in most other tribes they tend to marry at a much older age.

Bride-Price, Jamai-Khata and Dowry

Traditionally, "Jamai-Khata," i.e. the practice of the groom giving his service in the prospective father-in-law's house for about three years, (the period to be determined by the girl's parents) was common among the Tripuri, Jamatia, Reang, Uchai, Koloi. In recent times the duration is considerably reduced or replaced by cash to be paid by the groom to the girl's father. Among the Lushais, and kindred sub-tribes, e.g. Halams, Rupini, Koloi, Kaipeng, etc. bride-price is the common practice, the amount generally varying between Rs. 80 and Rs. 1,000. At times it can be still higher. The important point to note is that the consent of the girl is the

32. Most current writers on Tripura's tribal societies have drawn on two valuable but old British sources of detailed information: (1) Captain T. H. Lewin, Deputy Commissioner of Chittagong Tracts, *The Hill Tracts of Chittagong* (1869) and *Wild Races of South Eastern India*, 1870, reprint edition, Calcutta: Firma K.L.M. Private Limited, 1978, and (2) W. W. Hunter, *A Statistical Account of Bengal*, vol. VI, 1887, reprint edition, Delhi: D. K. Publishing House, 1973. The frequent references to these old sources by present-day writers suggest their relevance even after a long time-gap.

main consideration in fixing the match.

The practice of Jamai-Khata or bride-price, and simultaneously the absence of dowry system among Tripura's tribal groups are a confirmation of the concept of a daughter being viewed as an asset to her parental family. In complete contrast, most non-tribal groups of Tripura have to pay a hefty sum as dowry to the groom's side, which makes parents view girls as liabilities. Unfortunately, among some tribal groups of Tripura, there is an emerging trend for the groom's side to demand expensive gifts or dowry from girls' parents. It has been noted that among Jamatias, this trend has emerged, probably in their eagerness to imitate non-tribal customs to gain status (Das Gupta, Manas 1993). Girls from non-tribal society of Tripura do not have much freedom to mix with boys and to select their marriage partners. Inter-caste and inter-community marriages face considerable opposition. Furthermore, some cases of dowry deaths or suicides due to harrassment by husbands or in-laws are reported, although hardly any cases are filed in courts under the Dowry Prohibition Act of 1961.

Marriage Ceremony

Traditional marriage rites among Tripura's tribal groups are very simple and consist mainly of sharing of liquor between the bride and groom. These are very similar among the Tripuri, Jamatia, Reang and Noatia tribes and vary only in minor details. Among the Lushai and Kuki tribes, marriage is a civil contract which can be dissolved by mutual consent. In all cases, marriages are celebrated with a lot of feasting, drinking and dancing among the respective communities.

Monogamy : Polygamy

Monogamy is the general rule among Tripura's tribes, although among a few tribes, e.g. Noatia and Kaipeng, polygamy is not unknown. The Jamatias permit one re-marriage, but if a person marries more frequently, the village council imposes a fine. There are no restrictions on re-marriage of widows and divorcees. It is interesting to note that although polygyny was prevalent among some Tripura rulers — Udai Manikya (1585–96) had 240 wives — their tribal subjects remained largely monogamous.[33] Among non-tribal groups, however, there are instances of men deserting

33. The Tripura king Udai Manikya (1585-96), punished some of his 240 wives by having them trampled by elephants on charges of infidelity (Saigal, 1978).

their first wife and taking another one. It is reported that the aggrieved women do not often seek legal remedies either due to ignorance of law or the inability to bear expenses of litigation. A number of cases where deserted or oppressed women have sought alimony or maintenance from husbands are usually pending before Tripura courts for a long period.

Adultery and Divorce

Most Tripura tribes strongly disapprove of adultery and it is uncommon among their societies. In the past it was punished by death, as reported by Lewin, Deputy Commissioner of Chittagong Hill Tracts, in 1869. Among Lushais or Kukis, adultery was punished with life-long slavery of the chief of the tribe. Among the Chakmas, if a man runs away with another man's wife, the former repays to the aggrieved husband all expenses of the marriage in addition to a fine. Among Jamatias, adultery is regarded as highly reprehensible and the chief generally decides the amount of fine to be paid to the partner seeking divorce. On the whole, a husband's adulterous behaviour is treated with some lenience, whereas illicit sex relations of a wife are strongly disapproved and considered sinful and criminal (Chakraborty, Manik 1993).

Divorce is permitted in all tribal groups of Tripura. Generally, if it is sought by only one of the marriage partners, it can be obtained by paying a penalty usually prescribed by the village council. Among the Lushais and kindred groups, since marriage is a civil contract, if both parties wish to divorce, the girl repays the amount of bride-price to the boy and the marriage is dissolved. The divorced woman is free to marry again among all tribes. Among the Chakmas, if a man divorces his wife without any fault on her side, the man has to return the ornaments and clothes which she brought with her at the time of her marriage, as gifts by her parents. Very young children in the breast-feeding stage are given to the wife. Older children are given the option to decide whether they wish to stay with the mother or father. As long as the divorced wife remains single, she is entitled to compensation, and her children inherit father's property. If the divorced wife re-marries, she forfeits all rights on her first husband's property (Saigal, 1978). This humane treatment of the aggrieved woman among the Chakmas, though not wholly consistent with the generally patriarchal bias among Tripura's other tribes, could perhaps be traced to the relatively more liberal attitude towards women in the Burmese Buddhist origins of the Chakmas. For a more representative account of Tripura's indigenous tribes, we may turn to an eyewitness account by a British Official, Captain Lewin (Choudhury, Pratap, 1993) of a village council meeting of another Tripura tribe, where a woman subjected to habitual cruelty by her husband sought divorce. After verifying the facts and granting the divorce the jury members did not wish to send a wrong signal to women who might malign their husbands on minor grounds. They therefore held her guilty of wanting to abandon her lawful husband and ordered her to return all her ornaments to her husband, besides paying a fine and providing a pig and plenty of liquor. Tripura's tribes already had a patriarchal bias and it has been reinforced due to interaction with the Bengali Hindu culture of the majority non-tribal population.

The Family

The family is a strong and well-knit institution among Tripura's tribes. The eldest male member is the head of the family where joint family is the general rule, as among Reangs and Kaipengs. In nuclear families, main authority is the husband and major family decisions regarding sale or purchase of land and other property are taken by the male head. Within this framework, women may be consulted by husbands in varying degrees. For instance, in a Lushai household, women enjoy considerable respect. A Lushai widow occupies an important place in her son's family because of which Lushai widows seldom re-marry (Choudhury, P., 1993). Among the Halams, a kindred tribe, relations between men and women in the family are reported to be relaxed and women have complete authority in internal household matters and have a clearly defined position. In the Reang tribe — the second most numerous among Tripura's tribal groups — the eldest male wields ultimate authority in the family. He has to ensure that the family fulfils its functions of multiplying the progeny, educating and inculcating the tribe's culture among children and ensuring adequate resources for the family. Within this framework, husband-wife relationship is based on mutual respect, love and trust (Choudhury, P., 1993).

Women's Tasks

As stated in Chapter 3, the division of functions between men and women among Tripura's tribal communities where *jhum* cultivation is practised is pretty similar to that of other N-E States. While men cut trees, set the logs on fire and clear the area, women take care of all other operations such as sowing seeds, harvesting, carrying, husking and storing the grains.

Where jhuming has been replaced partly or wholly by settled cultivation, women's workloads have increased. Where men have shifted to other occupations, women's workload in *jhum* has generally increased. Even where the household has adopted settled cultivation wholly, women join men in sowing, harvesting, threshing, transporting products to homes or markets, etc. Some tasks have remained as women's exclusive responsibility, e.g. husking paddy, extracting oil from oil-seeds, collecting firewood, spinning and weaving, fetching water, brewing rice-beer, cooking and cleaning the house, etc. Child care is almost exclusively women's responsibility. Care of poultry and pigs is also women's job (Ganguly, 1993). The Kaipengs provide a rather unique exception in the sense that a husband may occasionally share the responsibility of cooking or taking care of children, if the wife is away in the fields (Choudhury, P., 1993).

Some of women's tasks are becoming more strenuous due to changing environmental factors and lack of basic amenities such as water and electricity. The rapid denudation of forests and restricted access have made the task of collecting firewood more arduous. Similarly, the drying up of natural water sources in some areas causes enormous hardships for women in collecting and carrying water over hilly terrains. Whenever food grains are in short supply, women have to work harder to collect edible tubers, stems, roots and leaves from forests.

Protection of Women against Crimes

As noted in Chapter 3, women from tribal societies of Tripura do not have a right to own or inherit land or other immovable property, and the exception among Tripuris and Jamatias to permit daughters and widows to possess nominal shares in father's and deceased husband's property does not substantially change the picture. Women cannot buy, sell or mortgage lands. Against this background the manner in which women are depicted in Tripura's folk tales and mythical stories present images of helplessness and misery. Here are some illustrations: A young girl drowning herself in desperation when her father kills the husband chosen by her against his wishes; a woman whose husband happened to be a king discards her after cutting her nose and ears just because she could not keep her promise to beget seven sons; a forlorn wife whose drunken husband ill-treats her and marries another woman (Choudhury, P., 1993). These vignettes of Tripura's tribal women present a picture of women's utter helplessness in the face of absolute and unbridled male dominance. Even then, their position in the family and marriage is better than that of non-tribal women, who have virtually no access to divorce or to remarriage in practice, even if these exist in law. It is interesting to note that Maharaja Bir Chandra Manikya (1862-96), who is credited with the first codification of criminal laws, enacted laws prescribing death penalty for some types of crimes against women. Mizos, Kukis and some other tribes in north Tripura district have customary laws which punish men guilty of having sex with a minor or an unwilling girl, or of seducing a married woman to commit adultery. Furthermore, if a Kuki-Mizo wife seeks shelter with another man to escape being thrashed by her husband, their tribal customary law gives immunity to the protector for forcibly restraining the husband (Choudhury, P., 1993).

Religion

It is useful to review the religious affiliation of Tripura's tribal groups in order to examine women's religious status. As noted in Chapter 2, most indigenous tribal groups adopted Hindu beliefs and practices under the influence of Tripura rulers who had accepted Hinduism since fifteenth century, while retaining some elements of their tribal faiths. Another factor which accelerated the incorporation of Hindu practices was the influx of Bengali Hindu immigrants into Tripura. Since the various tribal groups' relationship with the ruling family and exposure to Bengali Hindu settlers varied, their religious beliefs and customs reflect some variations. Some are followers of Shiva, while some are Vaishnavites and some worship goddess Kali, and many retain vestiges of their indigenous animistic beliefs. For instance, the Reangs (who originally belonged to Kuki family and are believed to have come from Shan region of Myanmar) follow a religion which is a mixture of Hindu and tribal forms of worship. Their religion includes worship of Rama, Sita, Shiva along with propitiation of spirits representing natural elements (Saigal, 1978). They call themselves Hindus of the "Shakta" cult and are worshippers of the Goddess Kali. The Jamatias, who are believed to be a branch of the Tripuri tribe, and were closely identified with Tripura rulers, had occasionally adopted the practice of *sati* (immolation of the widow on the funeral pyre of her deceased husband). The British Political Agent's persistent inquiries regarding the few cases of *sati* around 1884-88 finally compelled Maharaja Bir Chandra Manikya to issue a royal proclamation prohibiting *sati* in 1889.[34]

34. "Rajamala" — the royal chronicles of Tripura kings — refers to instances of *sati* in the royal family. Around 1888 British administrators had conveyed →

While Tripura's tribal women participate in both tribal and Hindu religious ceremonies, i.e. *Ker Puja, Kharchi Puja, Garia Puja,* as well as typical Hindu festivals like *Durga Puja* and *Kali Puja,* their role is rather limited. They can never officiate as priests. In some groups, e.g. the Kaipengs, even family-level rituals must be performed by the male head of the family (Choudhury, P., 1993). The Chakmas call themselves Buddhists, although their beliefs reflect some mixture of Hinduism and animism. Generally, their attitude to religious participation of women tends to be slightly more liberal than that of other tribal and traditional Hindu groups.

Among the Lushais and Mizos, a predominant majority are Christians and belong to New Zealand Baptist Church. While Lushai women participate in church services and related social activities, they cannot act as priests or pastors. However they have benefited significantly from educational facilities supported by Christian missions. In comparison with other tribal women, Lushai women have a better access to professional and vocational training which in turn has expanded their occupational options.

Tripura's tribal women in general have very limited participation in traditional religion and while adoption of Hinduism has widened their scope, it does not seem to have given them an important place in religion, as is the case of some other N-E women, e.g. Meiteis and Plains Tribal Assamese women. In comparison, non-tribal women play a more active role in family level worship as well as traditional festivals like *Durga Puja.*

Recapitulation

The position of young girls among tribal societies of Tripura is fairly positive as is evident from the manner in which they are brought up by parents. They have freedom of movement and mix with their playmates; they can select their marriage partners within the rules of clan exogamy and prohibited degrees of relationship within the girl's and boy's family, and are not viewed as liabilities by parents since they fetch bride-price or benefit of "Jamai-Khata" (bridegroom giving free service to the prospective

---

→ their concern over three cases of *sati* in Sonamura Division amongst the Jamatias. While the Tripura king Bir Chandra Manikya (1862-96) banned *sati* officially in 1889, he had conveyed to the British that the instances in question were voluntary actions of the widows, and there were no indications whatsoever of external pressure on the women concerned (Choudhary, D.K. 1989).

father-in-law). Even where parents negotiate and settle the match, a girl is never married without her consent. On the negative side, girls get less freedom to play as compared to boys because of their preoccupation with household chores as well as parents' lower priority for girls' education. Non-tribal parents generally regard girl children as a burden because parents have to give dowry to the groom's side, and this negative attitude towards daughters is usually reflected in the denial of opportunities of play, education and selection of marriage partners. Compared to non-tribal groups, Tripura's tribal communities are far more liberal in permitting divorce and re-marriage for women. While most tribal groups observe monogamy, polygyny is not completely absent. Among non-tribal groups, although divorce is permissible and monogamy is prescribed by laws, few deserted and neglected women seek justice through courts, and even fewer obtain legal justice due to cumbersome and expensive legal procedures.

As regards position in the family, Tripura's tribal women have a stronger position in the sense that they enjoy some autonomy in the household sphere even if they have no voice in financial and other important decision-making. The situation of non-tribal women in the family is weaker than their tribal counterparts. While patriarchal attitudes manage to keep women in both tribal and non-tribal societies of Tripura in subordinate roles, tribal women's position is better because of their higher economic autonomy. In groups which follow *jhum* cultivation, women's contribution is substantial. But even where *jhum* cultivation is replaced by settled cultivation, tribal women make substantial contribution by taking wage employment, rearing pigs and other animals, collecting forest produce, making rice-beer, selling their products in local markets, etc. Non-tribal women do not have access to most of these activities and avenues of outside employment are limited (Ganguly, 1993). It might not be out of place to mention a special category here: Women in tea-garden labour. Since heavy drinking is common among men tea-garden labourers, women have to assume major responsibility for sustaining their families with their meagre earnings. This is not all. They also become victims of ill-treatment by drunken husbands.

In the sphere of religion, while Tripura's tribal women are marginalized in traditional religious faiths and are excluded from performing most rituals, adoption of Hindu worship has improved their position. Women belonging to tribes like Lushais, and some Hindu tribesmen who were converted to Christianity around 1985 by Tripura Baptist Christian Union are better off in the sense that they can participate in church services freely along with men. Non-tribal women who are governed mainly by East Bengal Hindu culture may be slightly better off than tribal women in the sense that the former play a more active role in family level worship as well as some important festivals like *Kali Puja* and *Durga Puja*. Women both in tribal as well as non-tribal Tripura groups cannot however become priests. For that matter, even Baptist and other Christian churches do not allow women to be priests or pastors.

5

Health and Education

THIS chapter examines N-E women's position with respect to health and education, presented in Sections I and II, respectively. The method of presentation regarding health and education in this chapter is somewhat different from that in the preceding chapters. The analysis of health and educational situation uses some important statistical data as indicators of women's status — some positive and some negative, some direct and some indirect.

SECTION I – HEALTH

In order to examine N-E women's health status we present some statistics on aspects related to health in many different ways. For instance, data on extent of access to safe drinking water reflects women's and their families' vulnerability to water-borne diseases. Proportions of women married before 18 years of age indicate the likely effect of social customs regarding age at marriage on the growth of women and their progeny. Some statistics show mothers' access to preventive measures to avoid major hazards to maternal and child health. We also examine data on educational levels of women that is an indirect but very crucial measure of their knowledgeability regarding health matters, and even more importantly, their accessibility to various media for health messages. Our major source of information is the National Family Health Survey-1(NFHS-1), from which we have chosen selected data. This has been supplemented to some extent by another series of surveys — Health Conditions of Mothers and Children, some findings from which have been used primarily for comparison. We have also drawn on reports published by the Registrar General of Census of India and Sample Registration System, as well as reports prepared by Ministry of Health and Family welfare, Government of India, as a supplementary source. Some basic information on our major sources of information follows:

The National Family Health Survey-1 (1992-93)

The NFHS-1[1] was a countrywide representative survey, which included 88,562 households and 89,777 ever-marmried women of age 13-49. The main objective of the survey was "to collect reliable and up to date national level and State-level data on fertility, nuptiality, fertility preferences, knowledge and practice of family planning, the potential demand for contraception, the level of unwanted fertility, utilization of antenatal services, breast-feeding and food-supplementation practices, child nutrition and health, vaccinations, and infant and child mortality," (NFHS, *India-Summary Report, 1992-93*). The survey was initiated by the Ministry of Health and Family Welfare, Government of India, funded by the United States Agency for International Development, co-ordinated and technically guided by the International Institute of Population Sciences and conducted by a few specialized and field level agencies. The data collection in N-E States was organized during December 1992–March 1993 in Assam and during February 1993–June 1993 in Arunachal Pradesh, Manipur, Meghalaya, Mizoram, Nagaland and Tripura, covering representative samples of households and women of age 13–49 years. For various reasons, we have limited our scope to NFHS-1, and have not included NFHS-2.

Health Conditions of Mothers and Children (HCMC) Surveys: 1980-82

We draw upon another source of information, viz. Surveys of Health Conditions of Mothers and Children, referred hereafter as HCMC, undertaken during 1980–1982,[2] primarily to note the situation prevailing a decade earlier and major changes, if any, by NFHS-1. HCMC Surveys

---

1. From NFHS-1 data series, we have relied on the following reports : NFHS-1, 1992-93, *India: Summary Report*, August 1995; *Assam*, June 1995, *North-eastern States*, (*Arunachal Pradesh, Manipur, Meghalaya, Mizoram, Nagaland and Tripura*), December 1995, International Institute of Populations Sciences, Bombay.
2. The Series — *Health Conditions of Mothers and Children* (HCMC) surveys undertaken during 1980-82 included the following reports on N-E States : *Assam* 1987, *Manipur* 1984; *Meghalaya* 1985; *Mizoram* 1985; *Nagaland* 1984; *Tripura* 1985, UNICEF East India Office, Calcutta.

were undertaken as a collaborative venture of UNICEF East India Office (Calcutta), All India Institute of Hygiene and Public Health (Calcutta), and respective State/UT Governments. Unfortunately, Arunachal Pradesh government did not join the project. The surveys were large-scale and covered rural areas of Assam, Manipur, Meghalaya, Mizoram, Nagaland and Tripura (besides Sikkim and Andaman and Nicobar Islands). A common set of schedules used for data collection covered the following: State/UT profiles; structure and extent of services provided by respective State/UT Health departments; a general background of sample households, maternal care, health and nutrition status of mothers between 15-49 years in ante-natal, natal and post-natal period having children below five years, and children below 14 years. Undoubtedly, there were some differences in the scope and methods of data collection between NFHS-1 and HCMC, but there were several common aspects on which comparative observations have been made.

Access to Basic Environmental Amenities

We look at the extent to which households in N-E States included in NFHS-1 lacked two very basic amenities of living: safe drinking water and toilet facilities. Households which do not possess piped water supply must use water from a variety of sources, such as streams, wells, ponds, etc. which may contain pollutants. Similarly, houses without some kind of a toilet, be it a pit latrine or dug-well type, leave no option for its occupants except defecation in the open without proper excreta disposal, which makes them vulnerable to many kinds of infections.

As noted in Table 5.1 (Column II), in five out of seven N-E States, less than half, or between 40-48 per cent households had access to drinking water from pumps and piped sources. Arunachal Pradesh and Nagaland occupy the top positions, with 76 and 72 per cent households, respectively, having this facility, which is noteworthy in view of the Indian average of 68 per cent. Assam and Tripura, the two most populous States in the group, stand in the middle with 43 and 44 per cent, respectively, along with Manipur (47) and Meghalaya (48), while Mizoram stands at the bottom with 40 per cent.

As regards households with no toilet facility (Column III, Table 5.1), Assam has the highest percentage (50.4), which means more than half of its population has no access to any type of latrine. Mizoram stands at the opposite end with less than 2 per cent of households without a toilet

Table 5.1 : Basic Environmental Amenities, Education, Nuptiality and Fertility Indicators, India and N-E States : NFHS-1 (1992-93)

	Drinking Water and Sanitation		Education Level Females		Female Nuptiality	Fertility Indicators	
India/N-E States	*Per centage of households with drinking water from pump/pipe*	*Percentage of households with no toilet facility*	*Percentage of illiterate females age 6 +*	*Percentage of attending school (females 6-14)*	*Percentage of women between 20-24 married before age 18*	*Crude birth rate (*)*	*Total fertility rate (*)*
I	II	III	IV	V	VI	VII	VIII
India	68.2	69.7	56.7	58.9	54.2	28.7	3.39
Arunachal Pradesh	75.8	26.6	57.9	65.3	43.9	34.6	4.25
Assam	43.2	50.4	49.3	56.0	44.4	30.4	3.53
Manipur	47.0	16.9	37.0	36.8	14.3	24.4	2.76
Meghalaya	47.6	45.7	39.8	75.7	28.1	31.9	3.73
Mizoram	40.1	1.7	11.1	88.5	13.3	20.8	2.30
Nagaland	72.1	20.7	28.2	89.0	16.4	31.3	3.26
Tripura	44.1	20.6	35.6	76.7	41.1	23.1	2.67

Source: NFHS -1, *India: Summary Report, 1992-93*, International Institute of Population Sciences, Bombay.

(*) Based on births to women aged 15-49 during the three years preceding the survey.

For comparable data from NHFS-III (2005-06), refer to Appendix C (ii).

Table 5.2

Basic Environmental Amenities and Literacy Levels Among Mothers: HCMC 1980-82

N-E States	Percentage of households with drinking water from pump/pipe	Percentage of households with no toilet facility	Percentage of Illiterate mothers
I	II	III	IV
Assam	29.98	71.13	67.0
Manipur	38-49 in 3 districts 2-12 in 3 districts	29.4	75.36
Meghalaya	16.0	82	55.1
Mizoram	1.4	33.9	19.0
Nagaland	47.0	71.8	48.9
Tripura	43: West; 5.4: North; 40.6: South District	47.0	62.9

Source: Health Conditions of Mothers and Children (HCMC): 1980-82. Reports on Assam, Manipur, Meghalaya, Mizoram, Nagaland and Tripura, UNICEF, East India Office, Calcutta.

facility. Meghalaya ranks next to Assam with 46 per cent households with no toilets. Arunachal Pradesh, Nagaland, Tripura and Manipur ranged between 26 and 17 per cent. It is useful to remember that only a small number of households have flush toilets, and a majority have to settle for some kind of a pit or trench latrine where disposal of excreta may not always be safe. But people without even this elementary facility have no other option but to defecate in open fields. The lack of privacy creates enormous hardships especially for women, besides the health hazards involved. While the situation in N-E States is far from satisfactory, when one notes that over two-thirds of households in India are without toilet facility, the N-E States do not seem so badly off.

A comparison of NFHS-1 findings with those of HCMC (which was conducted during 1980-82 and limited to rural areas) indicates considerable improvement in the availability of drinking water from hand-pumps and piped sources by 1992-93 in most N-E States (see Table 5.2 for HCMC figures). In Meghalaya, the percentage of households with drinking water from piped sources rose from 16 to 48, in Mizoram from less than 2 to 40, in Nagaland from 47 to 72. In two out of a total of three districts of Tripura (West and South), in 1980-82, the percentages were 43 and 41, and in the remaining north district, it was at an appallingly low level of five. By NFHS-1 the State percentage rose to 44. In Manipur, in three out of six districts (Central, Tengnoupal and West) between 2 and 12 per cent households had a perennial piped water supply, while in the remaining three districts (east, north and south), between 38 and 49 per cent households had access to piped supply of drinking water in 1980-82. And by the time NFHS-1 was undertaken, the State percentage had reached 47, which hardly seems impressive. In Assam, the percentage rose from 30 to 43 by NFHS-1, which again leaves little room for complacency, particularly when we remember that women have to bear the brunt when the common water sources, such as springs, mountain streams and ponds dry up during some months annually. In Manipur, for instance in 1980-82, more than one-third of the households had to put up with inadequate water supply, and women in these households had to bear the brunt of trudging more than half a km to reach a water source (Deodhar and Srivastava, *Manipur : HCMC*, 1984, p. 43). In Meghalaya, more than half of the households had to traverse between one-fourth to more than 1 km of hilly terrain daily to bring water (Khandekar et al., *Meghalaya: HCMC*, 1985, p. 41). After a decade, the situation had improved a little, but more than half of the total population of these two States still continued to be without a piped source of water at the time of NFHS-1.

We now look at changes with respect to availability of toilet facilities since the HCMC surveys, conducted between 1980-82. These inquiries had revealed that between 71 and 82 per cent of households in Assam, Nagaland and Meghalaya had no toilet facilities and people had to use open fields for defecation. In the three remaining States, viz. Manipur, Mizoram and Tripura, households without toilets ranged between 29 to 47 per cent. During the decade preceding NFHS-1, the situation in five N-E States showed some improvement and this percentage stood between 2 and 26, although in Assam and Meghalaya nearly half the households were still without toilet facilities in 1992-93. When we remember that a preponderating majority of present toilets are of the pit or dug-well type, the goal of ensuring safe excreta disposal is still a long way off.

Illiteracy and School Attendance

A close relationship has been observed between women's educational level and ability to protect themselves and their families, and especially young children from various common health hazards and to adopt health-conducive practices. NFHS-1 inquired into levels of illiteracy among females of 6+ age in sample households. In six N-E States, as presented in Table 5.1, column IV, the percentage of illiterates among 6+ females, (barring Arunachal Pradesh where it is 58), ranges between 11 in Mizoram to 49 in Assam, as against the Indian average of 57. Mizoram has the lowest percentage of illiterate females, viz. 11 and it outranks even Kerala with its 18 per cent as per NFHS-1 (1992-93). A closely related indicator is the percentage of girls of 6-14 age attending schools (Table 5.1, column V). While the national average is 59 per cent, all seven N-E States exceeded this and ranged between 65 for Arunachal Pradesh and 89 for Nagaland, while for Mizoram it is 88.5 per cent.

When we compare the illiteracy levels among age 6+ females in NFHS-1 with those among mothers in the HCMC series (1981-82), the situation prevailing a decade earlier seems quite depressing, even after making a concession to the difference in the base population. While NFHS-1 figures deal with percentages of illiterate females of 6+ age among sample households, in total State populations (Table 5.1, Col. IV), HCMC illiteracy percentages refer to 15-49 year old rural mothers in antenatal, natal and post-natal stages having children below 5 years [Table 5.2, Col.(IV)]. We should therefore make some allowance for the likelihood that illiteracy percentages based on 6+ female population in HCMC sample households could have been lower than those among mothers alone. Even then there is no doubt about considerable reduction in illiteracy among female population in all N-E States in the 1981-91 decade. The HCMC (1981-82) had revealed that excepting Mizoram where the percentage of illiterate mothers was 19, in the remaining five States, it varied between 49 for Nagaland and 75 for Manipur, with Meghalaya, Tripura and Assam standing between 55 to 67 per cent.

The situation regarding school attendance among girls of 6-14 years (Table 5.1, Column V) as per NFHS-1 certainly seems quite optimistic with all N-E States showing 65 and above percentages. In the following Section on Education in this Chapter, we will see a more updated picture.

The data regarding illiteracy levels and school attendance are relevant here particularly in view of their relationship with practices related to age at marriage and fertility that follow.

Nuptiality

Women's age at marriage and child-bearing have a close relationship with their own health, as well as that of their children. Child Marriage Restraint Act of 1978 prescribes 18 years as the minimum legal age at marriage for women and 21 years for men. NFHS-1 investigation revealed that except for Mizoram where some awareness of this legislation was noted, there was widespread ignorance regarding its existence and significance, and particularly so in the N-E region as a whole. Table 5.1 column VI presents NFHS-1 percentages of women age 20-24 who were married before 18 years. While these are much lower for N-E States than the Indian average of 54.2, these are 44.4 for Assam, 43.9 for Arunachal Pradesh and 41.1 for Tripura.

For Mizoram, Manipur, Nagaland and Meghalaya, the percentages range between 13 and 28. In the N-E States generally girls are not married at an early age, especially among tribal communities. In Tripura that has a high majority of non-tribal population, NFHS-1 shows that 21 per cent of women of age 20-49 years were married before they were 15 (NFHS-1, *North-Eastern States*, Table 4.3, p. 63). In Assam, where non-tribal population forms even a higher percentage of the total, this number was 25 (NFHS-1, *Assam*, Table 4.3, p. 50). This finding seems consistent with that of HCMC, *Assam* (1981–82), at which time more than 46 per cent were less than 18 years at their marriage. Furthermore, the percentages of women married before 15 years were 14, 15 and 16 in Kamrup, Goalpara and Nagaon districts of Assam, respectively (HCMC, *Assam*, Table 8.04, p. 84). While the NFHS-1 percentages of women married before they were 18 years seem high for Arunachal Pradesh, Assam and Tripura, these do not appear so bad when we compare them with the percentages of some other States, e.g. Madhya Pradesh (73.3), Rajasthan (69.5), Bihar (69.1) and Andhra Pradesh (68.6).

We now compare NFHS-1 data on nuptiality with findings of another study based on 1991 Census data, by Prakasam, Murthy and Chowdhury on behalf of International Institute of Population Sciences (IIPS), Mumbai (FRHS, *Health Monitor,* 1998). Although this analysis uses slightly different age-groups, viz. 10-14 years and 15-19 years, its findings on six N-E

States are worth examining. The percentages of married females in age-groups 10-14 and 15-19, respectively, were as follows. Arunachal Pradesh 2.2 and 25.5, Manipur 1.3 and 9.0, Meghalaya 1.4 and 16.8, Mizoram 7 and 9.7, Nagaland 1.3 and 7.7, Tripura 1.2 and 24.4. Although NFHS-1 presents statistics on women married before 18 years, which is a smaller age-range than the one used in this analysis, viz. 19 years, the percentages here are smaller in all six N-E States. We present data on percentages of women married before 19 years based on 1981 Census from an SRS report (Registrar General, Occasional Paper No. 2 of 1989) which gives the following figures : Arunachal Pradesh 29.5, Manipur 11.8, Meghalaya 21.5, Mizoram 10.8, Nagaland 9.7 and Tripura 26.4. As will be noted, while the percentages of women married before 19 years presented here for 1981 and 1991 are derived from different methods from that of NFHS-1, the figures are consistently smaller than those of NFHS-1. It might not be out of place here to look at more recent data on Assam, with respect to percentages of women less than 18 years of age at effective marriage (age at effective marriage meaning age at couple's cohabitation which is reported to be very close to age at marriage, for Assam). The SRS figures are: 1994 – 25.6, 1995 – 15.7, 1996 – 13.7. It is evident that in Assam, the number of women married before 18 years is declining. In all N-E States, there is a definite decline in the percentages of early marriages of girls, as noted from comparisons among 20-24 and 45-49 age cohorts in Table 4.3 in NFHS-1 reports on Assam (p. 50) and N-E States (pp. 62-63). This trend is confirmed by percentages of currently married women whose age at marriage was below 18 years during two time periods: 1981-86 and 1986-91 at 1991 Census. The percentages of women married before 18 years were consistently lower for 1986-91 than for 1981-86 for all N-E States (1991 Census, *Selected Indicators on Female Nuptiality, State Profile 1991: India*).

It was observed from NFHS-1 findings that generally age at marriage was higher among the educated as against the illiterate, and among the urban as compared to rural women. Differences were also noted among groups belonging to different religions. Thus, girls among Muslim communities tended to get married at an earlier age than among Hindus, and among Christians the age at marriage was higher than among Hindus (NFHS-1, Assam, Table 4.4, p. 51). In Meghalaya, for instance, it has been noted that among some tribes, e.g. Garos, girls are married at a younger age than among Khasis.

Fertility

CRUDE BIRTH RATES (CBRS)

We now examine NFHS-1 data on two summary measures of fertility, viz. Crude Birth Rate (CBR) and Total Fertility Rate (TFR),[3] computed from the birth history information in the Woman's Questionnaire, and presented in Columns VII and VIII, respectively, of Table 5.1. The CBR of Arunachal Pradesh is 34.6, the highest among seven N-E States, followed by Meghalaya (31.9), Nagaland (31.3) and Assam (30.4). Manipur, Tripura and Mizoram CBRs range between 24.4 and 20.8, all of which are lower than India's average CBR of 28.7. Arunachal Pradesh, Assam and Meghalaya also have higher percentages of illiteracy among 6+ females. Arunachal Pradesh and Assam are also States with high percentages of women between 20-24 years married before 18 years. Manipur, on the other hand, has 37 per cent illiterate females of 6+ age, but is probably compensated by a low rate (14.3) of women age 20-24 married before 18 years of age. Tripura has a medium rate of illiterate females of 6+ age (35.6) but a high percentage of women age 20-24 married before 18 years (41.1 per cent) and still has a modest CBR of 23.1. Mizoram has the lowest rate of illiteracy among females 6+ age, lowest percentage of women of 20-24 years cohort who were married before age 18, and the lowest CBR, 20.8, among all N-E States.

It is obvious that besides education and age of marriage, fertility is influenced by some other factors.

---

3. CBR is calculated in the NFHS-1 "as a sum of products, who's each product is an age-specific birth rate multiplied by the ratio of females in the specific age group to the total *de facto* population." TFR is calculated "as five times the sum (over five-year age groups) of the age-specific fertility rates. The TFR is interpreted as the number of children a woman would bear during her reproductive years if she were to experience the age-specific fertility rates prevailing during the three-year period preceding the survey." (NFHS 1993, *Northeastern States*, pp. 70-71). The procedures of calculating CBR and TFR are as follows :

$$\text{Crude Birth Rate (CBR)} : \frac{\text{Number of Live births during the year}}{\text{Mid-year Population}}$$

$$\text{Total Fertility Rate (TFR)} : \frac{5 \times \sum_{15-19}^{45-49} \text{ASFR}}{1000}$$

(ASFR refers to Age-Specific Fertility Rate).

Table 5.3 Comparative Estimates of CBRs and TFRs for India and N-E States: 1992–2002

	NFHS-1 1992-93		*SRS 1996-98**		*Guilmoto-Rajan 2002*	
India/N-E States	*CBR*	*TFR*	*CBR*	*TFR*	*CBR*	*TFR*
India	28.7	3.39	27.1	3.3	25.9	3.16
Arunachal Pradesh	34.6	4.25	21.9	2.8	29.9	3.92
Assam	30.4	3.53	27.9	3.2	27.0	3.19
Manipur	24.4	2.76	19.4	2.4	21.0	2.59
Meghalaya	31.9	3.73	29.9	4.0	33.6	4.45
Mizoram	20.8	2.30	15.3	N.A.	27.3	3.36
Nagaland	31.3	3.26	N.A.	1.5	24.1	3.16
Tripura	23.1	2.67	18.1	2.1	21.2	2.48

Source : Table adapted and compiled from NFHS-1 and Guilmoto and Rajan, *Economic and Political Weekly*, Feb. 16, 2002, p. 667. N.A.: SRS data not available. *SRS data compiled by Guilmoto-Rajan from reports of Sample Registration System.

TOTAL FERTILITY RATES (TFRs)

NFHS-1 indicates that TFR is highest at 4.25 for Arunachal Pradesh, and Mizoram's is lowest at 2.30 among N-E States (Table 5.1, Column VIII). Here again, Arunachal Pradesh, Meghalaya and Assam have higher TFRs than for India as a whole (3.39), while Nagaland, Manipur, Tripura and Mizoram have lower TFRs than the Indian average, and range between 3.26 and 2.30.

Comparison with Other Fertility Estimates

Two other estimates of CBRs and TFRs are presented in Table 5.3 that are derived through different sources, for comparison with NFHS-1 data. The first is by Guilmoto and Rajan *(Economic and Political Weekly,* 16 February 2002), which uses the "reverse survival technique" on 1991 Census data on population below seven years, and the just released 2002 Census population data. The second is the Sample Registration System (SRS) estimate for 1996-98.

As compared to NFHS-1 estimate of Arunachal Pradesh CBR of 34.6, both Guilmoto-Rajan as well as SRS estimates, 29.9 and 21.9, respectively are considerably lower for the following 4 to 10 years period. Except for

Meghalaya and Mizoram, where Guilmoto-Rajan estimates of CBR are higher than those of NFHS-1, they are lower for all remaining N-E States. The SRS estimates too are lower than those of NFHS-1 for six N-E States (Nagaland CBR is not available among SRS data).

When we look at TFRs, Meghalaya has the highest figures (4.45 and 4) among all N-E States both according to Guilmoto-Rajan and SRS. Arunachal Pradesh, which had the highest TFR (4.25), according to NFHS-1, shows lower ones in both Guilmoto-Rajan and SRS estimates (3.92 and 2.8, respectively). Guilmoto-Rajan estimates of TFR are lower than those of NFHS-1 for Assam, Manipur, Nagaland and Tripura, and higher for Mizoram than NFHS-1 estimate. With the exception of Meghalaya, SRS estimates of Total Fertility Rate are lower than those of NFHS-1 for the remaining five States (SRS estimate not available for Mizoram).

We now look at N-E States' CBRs and TFRs in comparison with other States in the country. According to NFHS-1 (1992–93) Arunachal Pradesh CBR 34.5 and TFR 4.25 were second highest in the country, and next only to Uttar Pradesh with CBR 35.9 and TFR 4.82, with Bihar trailing behind Arunachal Pradesh with CBR 32.1 and TFR 4.0. Within less than a decade, according to SRS figures (1996–98), Meghalaya emerged as fourth highest among all States, with TFR of 4, following Uttar Pradesh (4.8), Bihar (4.4) and Rajasthan (4.2). With respect to CBRs, according to the same source, the top four States were : Uttar Pradesh (33.3), Madhya Pradesh and Bihar both 31.6 and Meghalaya 29.9. The Guilmoto–Rajan findings (1994–2001) present Meghalaya as having the highest CBR of 33.6, followed by Bihar (33.4) and Rajasthan (32.1), and rank Meghalaya as the second highest with TFR of 4.45, led by Bihar (4.54), with Uttar Pradesh (4.36) closely following Meghalaya.

In short, Arunachal Pradesh seems to have discarded its notorious position of having very high CBR and TFR, and Meghalaya currently seems to be ranking high among States having top positions with respect to CBR and TFR according to SRS and Guilmoto-Rajan estimates. The possible causes for these changes need to be investigated, and obviously seem to go beyond female literacy and school attendance, as well as age at marriage of women.

USE OF CONTRACEPTION

Women's use of contraception is important from the point of control over too frequent and unwanted pregnancies. NFHS-1 inquired into women's use of any traditional or modern contraceptive methods. Table 5.4 column II presents percentages of women in N-E States and India using any contraceptive method. Surprisingly, Tripura, at 56 per cent occupied the top position among N-E States, followed by Mizoram at 54. Arunachal Pradesh, Meghalaya and Nagaland occupied the bottom group with 24, 21 and 13 per cent, respectively, i.e. less than one-fourth of women, while Manipur at 35 and Assam at 43 occupied the middle group. The rates were found to be higher in urban areas than in rural, and lower among illiterate women than among the educated in all States. This finding highlights the importance of improving access to contraceptive services and the need for more vigorous efforts to educate women regarding various contraceptive methods.

While the NFHS-1 findings on the whole seem somewhat discouraging, a comparison with the situation prevailing during HCMC surveys (1980-82) reveals the considerable changes occurring during the decade of 1980s. In Mizoram, for instance, as many as 88 per cent of interviewed women, as per HCMC had reported that they did not use any family planning method. Out of less than 8 per cent who had adopted contraception, nearly three-fourths had used sterilization, and only about one-fourth had used condoms or oral contraceptives, indicating that a very small minority of women were aware of temporary and modern methods of contraception. In Tripura, the percentage of women using contraception, according to HCMC, did not go beyond three, which rose to 56 by NFHS-1 and in Mizoram, it increased to 54. In Nagaland, although the HCMC interview schedule for mothers included a question listing various modern and traditional contraceptive methods, no findings were reported, very likely because of poor responses. However, a separate question on contraceptive use solicited from heads of households revealed that 8 per cent of households had some member who had undergone sterilization. For Manipur, during HCMC inquiry (1980-82), only 3 per cent of women had reported on using contraception, and more than half of even this small number using it irregularly. As has been noted earlier, by NFHS-1, 35 per cent of women were using contraception. For Assam, from less than 6 per cent, according to HCMC, the percentage rose to 43 by 1992-93. On the whole, the responses to questions in HCMC surveys on contraceptive methods revealed that a large number of women did not seem fully aware of the various temporary and modern methods of contraception.

Besides increase in the use of contraception over the following decade, the NFHS-1 findings indicated that there was a better awareness of the various methods, which is a prerequisite for their adoption. NFHS-1 findings on knowledge about any modern contraceptive method, among currently married women were as follows: In Assam nearly all (99 per cent in urban and 97 per cent in rural areas) women knew at least one modern contraceptive method, e.g. pill, IUD, condom, injection, vasectomy, etc. In Manipur, Mizoram and Tripura, the percentages were over 90, for Arunachal Pradesh and Meghalaya 77 and 78, respectively. In Nagaland, however, it was the lowest at 44 per cent.

CARE DURING ANTE-NATAL PERIOD

We now look at the extent to which women in N-E States receive adequate advice and care during pregnancy to protect them from malnutrition, anaemia and tetanus which are common hazards and which are amenable to prevention by a few simple measures. Government health services are expected to provide for registration of expectant mothers for periodic check-up and treatment if necessary, provision of iron and folic acid supplements to prevent anaemia and two tetanus toxoid injections, provided either at the time of visits by expectant mothers to government health centres or through home visits by government health workers. NFHS-1 explored the extent to which mothers received these services, and we present the findings with respect to two indicators, viz. percentage of mothers who received ante-natal care and two doses of tetanus toxoid vaccine. The percentages refer to live births in the 4 years preceding the NFHS-1 (1992-93), and include, besides care received at government health centres, private care availed of by mothers.

A mixed picture becomes visible from NFHS-1 findings presented in Table 5.4 Columns III and IV, with Mizoram being at the top with 89 per cent of mothers receiving antenatal care, and Tripura (64.9 per cent) and Manipur (63.4 per cent) following next, with nearly two-thirds of mothers receiving care. Meghalaya (52 per cent) is in the middle, and at the lower end are Assam and Arunachal Pradesh (49.3 and 48.9) and Nagaland (39.3), implying that more than half of pregnant women were not receiving ante-natal care. The situation with respect to receiving two tetanus toxoid injections is not very encouraging. Here, Tripura leads N-E States with 59 per cent coverage, and other States range between 32 and 48 per cent, thus leaving more than half of pregnant women unprotected.

Table 5.4 :Women's Use of Contraception, Ante-natal Care, Place and Assistance in Delivery, Child Care during Diarrhoea and Immunizations, India & N-E States, NFHS-1 (1992–93)

India/N-E States	Percentage of women using any contraceptive method[1]	Percentage of mothers receiving ante-natal care[2]	*For Births in the last four years* Percentage of mothers receiving two doses of tetanus toxoid vaccine	Percentage of births delivered in a health facility	Percentage of deliveries assisted by health professional[3]	*Per cent of children* Children who received either ORS or RHS for diarrhoea[4]	Fully Immunized (age 12-23 months[5]
I	II	III	IV	V	VI	VII	VIII
India	40.6	62.3	53.8	25.5	34.2	30.6	35.4
Arunachal Pradesh	23.6	48.9	31.9	19.9	21.3	33.3	22.5
Assam	42.8	49.3	34.9	11.0	17.9	35.2	19.4
Manipur	34.9	63.4	48.0	23.0	40.4	63.1	29.1
Meghalaya	20.7	51.8	30.0	29.6	36.9	40.7	9.7
Mizoram	53.8	88.9	42.5	48.9	61.5	24.5	56.4
Nagaland	13.0	39.3	33.0	6.0	22.2	24.6	3.8
Tripura	56.1	64.9	58.7	30.7	33.5	*	19.0

Source : NFHS–1, *India: Summary Report*, 1992–93. *Percentage not shown since based on fewer than 25 children.

1. Per cent of currently married women age 13-49;
2. Ante-natal care refers to pregnancy-related health care provided by a doctor or a health worker in a medical facility or at home;
3. Allopathic doctor or nurse/midwife;

Note: For complete data from NFHS - III (2005-06), refer to Appendix C (iii).

4. For children who had diarrhoea in the past two weeks, per cent receiving a solution made from an Oral Rehydration Salt (ORS) packet, or a Recommended Home Solution (RHS) made from sugar, salt and water;
5. Per cent who have received BCG, measles and three doses DPT and polio vaccines.

PLACE AND ASSISTANCE DURING DELIVERY

It is important to ensure that deliveries take place in hygienic conditions and are assisted by trained health personnel to safeguard the mother and the new-born from possible infections and hazards due to delayed or obstructed delivery or excessive bleeding. NFHS-1 collected information on per cent distribution of live births during the four years preceding the survey by place of delivery and assistance during delivery. In the N-E States, where many areas are hilly and devoid of adequate transport facilities and not sufficiently covered by properly equipped health services, it is not surprising that a majority of deliveries are conducted in homes and without the support of trained medical practitioners. According to NFHS-1 findings (Table 5.4, Columns V and VI) Mizoram leads N-E States with 49 per cent deliveries being conducted in a health facility. Tripura (30.7), Meghalaya (29.6) and Manipur (23) follow next, while Arunachal Pradesh (19.9), Assam (11.1) and Nagaland (6) are way behind.

The situation is slightly better with respect to deliveries both institutional and home, assisted by health professionals. Here again, Mizoram leads with 62 per cent, followed by Manipur (40.4), Meghalaya (36.9) and Tripura (33.5). Nagaland, Arunachal Pradesh and Assam stand at the lower end with 22, 21 and 18 per cent, respectively. A picture that has emerged from NFHS-1 findings indicates that as of 1992-93, in six out of seven N-E States, nearly half to two-thirds of pregnant women received ante-natal care, and in six States less than half of the mothers received two doses of tetanus toxoid. Furthermore in six N-E States less than one-third of deliveries were conducted in a health facility and in six States, about a third or less of the deliveries received the assistance of trained health professionals. These observations for N-E States seem consistent with all-India situation as reflected in SRS report: In 1992, 24.4 per cent of births took place in health institutions, and out of the remaining ones taking place in homes, 22.9 per cent were attended by trained professionals and the rest 52.7 per cent by untrained persons (SRS, *Fertility and Mortality Indicators,* 1992).

HCMC Findings : A Comparison

If, however, we compare NFHS-1 findings with those of HCMC studies conducted during 1980-82, considerable improvement in ante-natal care is noticeable over the decade, although care during delivery still continues to be fairly unsatisfactory. In the HCMC, the samples included rural women in ante-natal, natal and post-natal period having any child below 5 years.

In Meghalaya, Mizoram, Nagaland and Tripura, all women in sample households were asked questions regarding ante-natal care, whereas for questions on delivery care, the scope included the last delivery of all mothers and expected delivery of pregnant women. The percentages of mothers who received regular ante-natal care administered by both trained health personnel and untrained *dais* were as follows: Meghalaya 26.5, Mizoram 47.6, Nagaland 22 and Tripura 9. The respective percentages of women who received two doses of tetanus toxoid during pregnancy in these same States were : 9.3, 29, 16.4 and 10.3. The respective percentages of deliveries conducted in health facilities were: 6.2, 15.9, 4.2 and 14.4, whereas the respective percentages of total deliveries (institutional and home) assisted by trained health personnel (which included doctors, auxiliary nurses midwives and *dais* if specified as trained) were: 13.1, 40.3, 15.1 and 9.4. Nagaland survey report mentioned the crucial role of *dais* in deliveries conducted at home, but since it did not clarify whether the *dais* had received training, they were not included among trained health personnel. We will have occasion to take up this point later.

In Assam and Manipur, information on percentages of mothers receiving ante-natal care and two tetanus toxoid injections was solicited only from expectant women. In Assam 82 per cent of the expectant women registered themselves at various health institutions for ante-natal care, and only 23 per cent made more than two visits, which was quite unsatisfactory, in view of the standard of a minimum of four ante-natal visits (NFHS-1, *North-eastern States*, p.161). Only eight per cent of pregnant women in the Assam sample received two tetanus toxoid injections. In Manipur, out of 270 pregnant women in the sample, 9 per cent reported on receiving regular ante-natal care, while 86 per cent received it irregularly and 11 per cent received two tetanus toxoid doses. As far as care during delivery was concerned, in Assam only 7 per cent of the last deliveries of all mothers were conducted in health institutions, and 14 per cent of the total were handled by trained health personnel. In Manipur, out of the total number of last deliveries and expected deliveries of currently pregnant women, 3 per cent would be in health institutions and 10.5 per cent of total deliveries (both institutional and home) were assisted by trained health personnel. Once again, *dais* were believed to be making a valuable contribution in conducting deliveries, especially in rural areas of Manipur. In this particular instance, however, whether *dais* were trained was not mentioned.

In comparison with the situation prevailing in early 1980s, NFHS-1 findings certainly appear encouraging, although access to health facilities for deliveries still continues to be somewhat difficult. But there are psychological barriers also, which need to be removed. For instance, the Manipur HCMC inquiry brought to light that more than half of the mothers were not aware of the need for ante-natal care. (HCMC — *Manipur*, p. 83). The Nagaland study showed that nearly two-thirds of mothers who did not avail of ante-natal care reported that ante-natal care was either contrary to their tradition or they did not know the need of such care. (HCMC — *Nagaland*, p. 65). In addition to these problems that were noted in most N-E States, some mothers mentioned unavailability of time as the reason for their not availing of ante-natal care. Education will certainly help to overcome these barriers, as is evident from the noteworthy progress made by Mizoram women with respect to ante-natal care as well as deliveries supervised by trained health personnel revealed by HCMC and confirmed by NFHS-1.

Mother's Awareness of Health Protection of Children

We now look at two types of health hazards for children for which simple treatment and preventive measures are available. When children suffer from diarrhoea, the depletion of water and electrolytes caused by frequent motions can be countered by giving them a solution of Oral Re-hydration Salts (ORS) mixed with water, or by giving them a Recommended Home Solution (RHS), which contains sugar, salt and water in prescribed proportions. The percentage of children who received either ORS or RHS during diarrhoea episodes in the two weeks preceding the inquiry was noted by NFHS-1 to gauge the awareness of mothers (Table 5.4, Column VII). Among N-E States, Manipur had the highest percentage of children, 63, who received either ORS or RHS during diarrhoea episodes. Other States ranged between 25 and 41. Surprisingly, there was hardly any difference between Nagaland (25.6) and Mizoram (24.5), contrary to the expectation that Mizoram, with its high female literacy rate, would out-do not just Nagaland, but other N-E States as well.

We will look at one more index of mothers' awareness of the importance of immunizations of children less than 2 years: BCG, measles, three doses of DPT and polio (Table 5.4, Column VIII). Mizoram comes to the top of N-E States, with 56 per cent of children between 12-23 months. Meghalaya and Nagaland, with 10 and 4 per cent represent the lowest performers, while Manipur (29.1), Arunachal Pradesh (22.5), Assam (19.4) and Tripura (19.0) occupy the middle position.

It might be interesting to see where N-E States stand with respect to complete immunizations of children between 12-23 months in relation to other States in India. The States were divided into four classes on the basis of percentages of complete immunization coverage as of 1996-97, in terms of BCG, OPV, DPT and measles. The top group includes 90 and above percentage, to which Mizoram belongs along with Kerala and Tamil Nadu. Tripura falls in the second group with coverage between 60-79, while Meghalaya, Manipur and Assam find a place in the third group with 40-59 percentage points. In the lowest group, with less than 20 per cent coverage are Nagaland and Arunachal Pradesh in the company of Bihar. (Ministry of Health and Family Welfare, *Evaluation of Routine Immunization, 1997-98*). While these two States seem to be lagging far behind, the remaining five States appear to have taken great strides in providing immunizations to children by 1996–97.

Prevalence of Addictions among Mothers

HCMC surveys inquired if mothers included in the six N-E States samples were addicted to alcohol, opium and smoking. Addiction was defined as regular consumption without reference to the quantity or dependence on the substance concerned. Besides the three, a question aimed at eliciting information on "other addictions" was included, in response to which consumption of betel-nut, *pan* (a green leaf usually wrapped around some condiments) and tobacco was mentioned by some mothers. In the absence of specific responses, we cannot present information regarding "other addictions." Table 5.5 presents data on percentages of mothers responding positively to questions regarding addiction to alcohol, opium and smoking.

As noted from Table 5.5, addiction to alcohol among mothers was highest in Tripura, 20 per cent, followed by Assam and Meghalaya with 13 per cent each. It was nil in Mizoram, while Manipur and Nagaland were in the middle range, both at 7 per cent. HCMC survey provided additional district-wise information on some States. Inter-district variations within most States were sizeable. For instance, with respect to alcohol, in Jaintia Hills district of Meghalaya, over 49 per cent of women reported

Table 5.5: Mothers with Addiction to Alcohol, Opium and Smoking in N-E States, HCMC, 1980-82

Percentages of Mothers Reporting Addiction			
States	Alcohol	Opium	Smoking
Assam	12.96	0.09	7.93
Manipur	6.58	0.56	25.60
Meghalaya	12.80	1.50	30.30
Mizoram	—	1.40	41.00
Nagaland	6.60	2.10	5.00
Tripura	19.70	1.00	33.10

Source: HCMC reports on Assam, Manipur, Meghalaya, Mizoram, Nagaland and Tripura (1980-82), UNICEF, East India Office, Calcutta.

on addiction, while the percentage was less than four in West Garo Hills district. In the Mizoram sample, while about 3 per cent kept quiet when asked if they took any alcoholic drink regularly, all others replied in the negative. In Tengnoupal district of Manipur, 34 per cent of mothers and in south Tripura district 24 per cent reported on addiction to alcohol.

It is necessary to remember that social and cultural attitudes towards alcohol consumption are different in N-E States from those prevailing in the rest of India. For instance, in the HCMC survey in Meghalaya, 26-30 per cent of mothers in West Garo Hills district recommended alcoholic drinks for expectant, post-natal and nursing mothers in response to a question on preferred foods. As noted in Chapter 4, fermented liquor is an essential ingredient in several religious ceremonies such as sacrificial offerings and solemnization of weddings and it is not uncommon to offer it to guests — both men and women. We have also noted in Chapter 4 how among several tribal communities in Arunachal Pradesh, women consider it essential to have an adequate stock of *apong* (fermented beer) when their husbands and their guests want to relax in the evenings. Cases are reported where women may urge their husbands to bring a co-wife as an extra hand, so that there would be plenty of *apong* available to keep their husbands in good humour.

Addiction to opium was highest (2.1 per cent) in Nagaland and lowest (0.09 per cent) in Assam. Other States ranged between 1.5 per cent

(Meghalaya) and 0.56 per cent (Manipur). Here again, districts reflected considerable variations. For instance, while four out of six districts in Manipur reported nil, West district came out with a little over 2 per cent of mothers being addicted to opium. In Phek district of Nagaland, 23 per cent of mothers reported on being addicted, while five out of the six remaining districts reported zero per cent. While the State percentage for Meghalaya was fairly low at 1.5, Jaintia Hills district reported 2.5 per cent. Tripura reflected a similar pattern with State percentage being one, while South Tripura district came out with 2.4 per cent mothers reporting on being regular opium consumers.

HCMC did not include a specific query regarding addiction to narcotic drugs among women. However, the proximity to Myanmar, and States like Manipur, Mizoram and Nagaland being used as conduits for large-scale narcotic traffic make them particularly vulnerable to addiction to narcotic substances. It is widely believed that some young women in these States, particularly those used to free mixing with young men, become addicted to narcotic drugs. In fact, some relatively better-off parents prefer to send their daughters to Calcutta, Delhi and such other places for higher education with a view to protect them from the drug menace.

We now look at addiction to smoking, where Mizoram tops the list with 41 per cent of mothers reporting to be regular smokers. The percentages for Tripura, Meghalaya and Manipur are fairly high with 33, 30 and 26, respectively. Surprisingly, the lowest positions are occupied by Assam with 8 and Nagaland with 5 per cent. Here again, some districts have very high percentages of smokers: for instance, Jaintia Hills and West Garo Hills district of Meghalaya 90 and 35 per cent, respectively, South Tripura 65 and south district of Manipur 61 per cent.

Let us look at HCMC findings (1980-82) in the context of an all-India survey conducted by National Sample Survey Organization (NSSO) on smoking and/or consumption of tobacco in any form, in its 43rd round, 1987-88. According to the NSSO survey, the number of rural women who were regular smokers was highest in the country in Mizoram (300 per 1000 women), followed by Manipur (125 per 1000 women). Among urban women again, Mizoram occupied the top position among all States in India with 206 regular smokers per 1000 women, with Manipur following next with 101 regular smokers per 1000 urban women. Among women in rural areas who were regular consumers of tobacco in any form, once again Mizoram occupied the top position in the country with 353 per 1,000 women, while Orissa and Maharashtra followed with 322 and 242, respectively per 1000 women. For urban areas, Mizoram assumed once again the top position with 378 per 1000 women, while Lakshadweep and Orissa followed with 198 and 196 per 1000 women, respectively. Among other N-E States, Meghalaya came out with 104 regular smokers per 1000 women and 213 regular consumers of tobacco per 1000 women in rural areas. In urban areas, once again, Manipur and Meghalaya stood among the top group with 141 and 129 regular consumers of tobacco per 1000 women, respectively. Arunachal Pradesh reported on 173 regular consumers of tobacco in rural areas per 1000 women, while the corresponding number in urban areas for Tripura was fairly high at 124 (India, NSSO, 43rd round, 1987-88, September 1990).

It is necessary to remember that smoking among women in N-E States, particularly among tribal communities, is viewed differently from other Indian States. Here, it is not confined to younger and highly sophisticated women, but is common among women of all ages and socio-economic strata. For instance, one can see a number of Meghalaya rural women of all ages who bring agricultural products for sale in Shillong bazars or Manipuri women at their market stalls in Aizawl smoking as they relax after a strenuous trip from their villages. One notices relatively better off Mizo women too smoking as they discuss an important club activity. The author recalls her meetings with Mizo women in remote villages which frequently included two or three wizened old women watching the proceedings with a detached amusement as they smoked a *hookah*.[4]

There is no doubt that all addictions among N-E women are injurious to health. Efforts to persuade women addicted to alcohol, opium and smoking must include information regarding their deleterious effects on health. Simultaneously, the social and cultural aspects that make these addictions so widespread must be taken into account in devising strategies for their eradication.

Health Service Facilities

So far, we have reviewed health conditions of N-E women from various

---

4. *Hookah* is a tobacco pipe with a small water chamber through which tobacco smoke is filtered before being inhaled and carried through a long tube to the smoker.

preventive and curative aspects. We now look at the important point of availability of and access to services, since these determine to a large extent what health measures can be adopted by women.

HOSPITALS AND DISPENSARIES

Table 5.6 gives the distribution of hospitals and dispensaries in each N-E State and bed capacity available as of 1994. Assam had 268 hospitals and 325 dispensaries (80 hospitals and 8 dispensaries out of the total being under private sponsorship) with a bed capacity of 12,703. More than half (151) of the hospitals and nine-tenths of dispensaries in Assam are located in rural areas. Other N-E States have a small number of hospitals, ranging between 9 and 31, all except four each in Manipur, Meghalaya and Mizoram being under government auspices. Excepting Tripura that has 474 dispensaries, all under government auspices, other N-E States have between 16 and 42 dispensaries, all government administered. Two-third or more of hospitals in Arunachal Pradesh, Manipur and Nagaland are located in rural areas, while in Meghalaya, Mizoram and Tripura, urban areas receive a favourable share, and considering that they constitute a much smaller area than rural, the latter receive a much smaller share of total hospital services.

BASIC RURAL HEALTH INFRASTRUCTURE

A three-tier organization, prescribed by the Ministry of Health, Government of India, along with staffing and population norms, exists in all N-E States to provide basic health care for rural populations, of course with some variations. At the base is the sub-centre, serving a cluster of villages and population between 3000-5000, staffed usually with one or two paramedical workers, supported by periodic visits by a doctor. The next in the hierarchy is the Primary Health Centre (PHC), intended for a population between 20000-30000, usually staffed with one or two doctors and a public health nurse, pharmacist and health assistants. Community Health Centre (CHC) is the next higher referral point, intended to serve a population of about one lakh, and better staffed and equipped than the PHC. Hospitals located at the State and district headquarters not only serve as higher referral facilities, but also provide specialized medical services for diseases like Malaria, Leprosy, Tuberculosis, besides surgical care and specialized facilities such as ophthalmic care, X-ray, etc.

Table 5.6

Number of Hospitals, Dispensaries and Bed-strength, and Rural-Urban Distribution, N-E States, January 1993.*

	Hospitals				*Dispensaries*				
North-East Region and States	*Hospitals Total*	*Rural*	*Urban*	*Hospital Beds Total*	*Dispensaries Total*	*Rural*	*Urban*	*Dispensary Beds Total*	*Total Number of Beds in Hospitals and Dispensaries*
Arunachal Pradesh	18	12	6	1,091	36	30	6	62	1,153
Assam	268	151	117	12,661	325	297	28	42	12,703
Manipur	29	25	4	1,561	42	39	3	0	1,561
Meghalaya	9	0	9	1,867	21	19	2	0	1,867
Mizoram	17	6	11	1,304	18	18	0	180	1,484
Nagaland	31	21	10	1,050	16	16	0	64	1,114
Tripura	25	12	13	1,730	474	468	6	0	1,730
Total No. in N-E region	397	227	170	21,264	932	887	45	348	21,612

Source: Central Bureau of Health Intelligence, Directorate General of Health Services, *Health Information of India, 1994.*

* As on 1 January 1992.

Table 5.7 : Basic Rural Primary Health Infrastructure and Average Population and Area Covered N-E States and India, 1997*

India & N-E States	*Number Functioning*			*Average population (in thousands)*			*Average area coverd (sq km)*			*Average radial distance (km)Covered*		
	Sub Centre	*PHC*	*CHC*	*Sub-*	*PHC*	*CHC Centre*	*Sub-*	*PHC*	*CHC Centre*	*Sub*	*PHC Centre*	*CHC*
All India	138615	22962	2708	4.6	27.4	232	22.9	136.4	1156.5	2.7	6.6	19.2
Arunachal Pradesh	245	47	9	3.1	16.0	84	N.A.	N.A.	N.A.	N.A.	N.A.	N.A.
Assam	5280	619	105	3.8	32.2	190	14.7	125.4	739.1	2.2	6.3	15.3
Manipur	420	72	16	3.2	18.5	83	52.8	308.1	1386.4	4.1	9.9	21.0
Meghalaya	377	82	13	3.8	17.6	111	59.1	271.7	1713.5	4.3	9.3	23.4
Mizoram	324	38	6	1.1	9.8	62	63.5	541.8	3431.3	4.5	13.1	33.0
Nagaland	244	33	5	4.1	30.3	200	67.3	497.9	3286.4	4.6	12.6	32.3
Tripura	537	56	11	4.3	41.7	212	19.3	184.6	939.9	2.5	7.7	17.3

Sources : *Rural Health Statistics in India*, December 1997, Rural Health Division, Director General of Health Services, Ministry of Health and Family Welfare, Govt. of India. Foundation for Research in Health Systems, *Health Monitor*, 1999.

*Data Provisional.

N.A. : Not Available; PHC : Primary Health Centre; CHC : Community Health Centre.

Table 5.8
Para Medical Female Health Workers in Position in N-E States up to 31 December 1997

States	*MPW(F)/ANM*	*HA(F)/LHV*	*Trained Dais*
Arunachal Pradesh	296	14	513
Assam	4037	310	14229
Manipur	490	77	2162
Meghalaya	568	50	2328
Mizoram	315	81	1036
Nagaland	162	31	N.A.
Tripura	517	31	1507

Sources : *Rural Health Statistics in India*, December 1997, Rural Health Division, Directorate General of Health Services, Ministry of Health and Family Welfare, Govt. of India. N.A.: Not available. Foundation for Research in Health Sciences, *Health Monitor*, 1999.

MPW(F)/ANM : Multi-purpose Worker (Female)/Auxiliary Nurse Midwife
HA(F)/LHV : Health Assistant (Female) / Lady Health Visitor
Trained Dai : Woman trained in delivery

Table 5.7 provides a picture of the situation prevailing as of 1997. Looking at the average populations served in N-E States against the national norms, Assam, Meghalaya, Nagaland and Tripura need more community health centres, while the situation with respect to PHCs, except in Tripura, seems fairly satisfactory. In the N-E States, accessibility becomes a vital consideration in view of the difficult and hilly terrain. On the point of average area covered and radial distance, the available facilities, particularly the PHCs and CHCs, seem quite inadequate. In addition, there are problems of having sufficient number of qualified doctors to provide the needed referral services.

Table 5.8 presents numbers of some categories of paramedical staff in position in N-E States, particularly needed to meet maternal care requirements. As will be noted, their numbers are far too small to be able to provide the needed basic ante-natal and delivery care of mothers. In view of the formidable difficulties in transporting patients to referral facilities, it is necessary to considerably augment the number of paramedical female staff and properly equip them with kits and training to improve the quality of care of patients in their homes.

A number of experiments in training local village women in safe delivery, and equipping them with an inexpensive kit containing a small bottle of disinfectant, sterilized razor-blade for cutting the umbilical chord after delivery and clean dressing material have been successfully tried out. In Manipur, an enterprising PHC doctor had trained small batches of local women in remote villages in conducting normal deliveries in a hygienic manner, and equally important, in advising families of pregnant women to seek the PHC doctor's help in case certain symptoms indicated possible complications.

In the context of generally inadequate medical care facilities and formidable difficulties of transporting patients from remote villages to district or State hospitals in major part of the N-E region, it is essential to adopt a pragmatic approach of giving a higher priority to preventive and primary health care. Equally important, it is necessary to emphasize upgrading the training of paramedical health staff and equip them with suitable portable kits to deliver basic health care to rural families in their own homes. They must emphasize motivating families, and particularly women, regarding protective health measures. Simultaneously, doctors at PHC and CHC level must play a highly supportive role in providing referral services and in training local paramedical staff regarding proper preventive and follow-up care.

SUMMARY AND HIGHLIGHTS

We start summarizing N-E women's health situation by looking at access to two most basic pre-requisites — safe drinking water and toilet facilities attached to households. According to NFHS-1 (1992-93) findings, nearly three-fourths of the households had access to water supplied through pipes or pumps in two States, viz. Arunachal Pradesh and Nagaland, while in the remaining five States, this facility was denied to more than half the households. Mizoram was the only State where almost all households had some type of toilet facilities, howsoever elementary, in four States close to four-fifths had this facility, and in two States (Meghalaya and Assam) nearly half had no option but to defecate in open fields. Absence of literacy can be a major obstacle in receiving health messages. In this respect, Arunachal Pradesh was in the most disadvantageous position, with nearly 3 out of 5 females of 6+ age being illiterate, and Mizoram in the most desirable situation with 9 out of 10 being literate. In the remaining five States, illiteracy among 6+ age females prevailed between roughly one-fourth to one-half.

Women aged 20-24 who married before completing 18 years, formed on the whole a minority in N-E States, although in Tripura, Arunachal Pradesh and Assam, a little over two out of five women were married before 18 years. This trend is, however, definitely declining. With respect to Crude Birth Rate (CBR), Arunachal Pradesh had the highest among N-E States (34.6), with Meghalaya, Nagaland and Assam trailing behind, all being higher than the Indian average of 28.7 while Manipur, Tripura and Mizoram had lower CBRs. Total Fertility Rate (TFR) too for Arunachal Pradesh was highest among N-E States (4.25) and Mizoram's was the lowest. Meghalaya and Assam followed Arunachal Pradesh with higher TFR than the Indian average of 3.39 while Nagaland, Manipur, Tripura and Mizoram were lower.

Use of contraceptives by women was highest in Tripura (56 per cent), followed by Mizoram (54 per cent), while in four other States, about one out of every 3 women used contraceptive, with Nagaland being dismally low at 13 per cent. Assam represented the middle position (43 per cent) and yet, surprisingly almost all women here knew about at least one modern contraceptive method. Except Nagaland where about three out of every five women showed ignorance, in other States more than three-fourth of women knew about contraceptive methods.

As regards access to ante-natal care from public as well as private sources, Mizoram, Tripura and Manipur occupied the most favourable position with 63-89 per cent of mothers receiving such care, while in Assam, Arunachal Pradesh and Nagaland less than half of the mothers received it. Meghalaya occupied the middle position. When we look at the situation with respect to receipt of two tetanus toxoid injections, however, the picture was fairly gloomy. Barring Tripura where the coverage of mothers was 59 per cent, in the remaining six States more than half of the mothers did not receive this protection. The safety of deliveries being conducted in health institutions was available to less than a third of the deliveries in six States, including Nagaland where only 6 per cent received this care. Mizoram was the only State where 49 per cent of deliveries received this benefit. Once again, Mizoram was in the most favourable position with nearly two out of every three deliveries being assisted by health professionals. In Nagaland, Arunachal Pradesh and Assam just about one out of five, and in Manipur, Meghalaya and Tripura nearly two out of five deliveries received this benefit. NFHS-1 findings on mother's use of two preventive and treatment measures for children revealed a rather disappointing situation. The administration of ORS or RHS during children's diarrhoeal episodes was highest in Manipur (63 per cent of children), while in the remaining States the percentages ranged between 25 and 41. As regards complete immunization of children between 12-23 months. Mizoram topped N-E States with 56 per cent, followed by Manipur 29 per cent while the remaining States ranged between 4 and 23 per cent, with Nagaland taking the lowest rank.

PREVALENCE OF ADDICTIONS

HCMC surveys (1980-82) revealed the following data on addictions among N-E women. Addiction to alcohol was high among mothers in Meghalaya, Assam and Tripura, while addiction to smoking was highest in Mizoram, followed by Tripura, Meghalaya and Manipur. Addiction to opium was highest in Nagaland, followed by Meghalaya.

HEALTH SERVICE FACILITIES

Out of a total of 397 hospitals in N-E States, as of 1994, a little more than half (227) were located in rural areas, whereas a predominant majority of dispensaries, 887 out of 932, were located in rural areas. Barring a small number, most of these facilities are administered under government auspices. The establishment of basic rural primary health infrastructure has had a late start in N-E States. Even then, it meets the population norms, with a few exceptions, with respect to sub-centres, PHCs and CHCs. It is, however, seriously deficient with respect to access to services due to difficult terrain, poor transportation, weaknesses in referral services, shortage of doctors and trained paramedical workers, particularly female health assistants, ANMs and trained nurses.

SECTION II – EDUCATION

This section reviews N-E women's educational status. While it is conceded that formal education by itself does not ensure rational behaviour, there is no doubt that it enhances a person's access to information and general understanding of the situation around, which improves chances of adopting behaviour which is conducive to one's well-being. We will look at some indicators, such as, percentages of literacy among N-E women, male-female and rural-urban differentials in literacy, enrolment of girls at various stages, dropout rates, number of schools in each N-E State, type of teachers available, etc.

Literacy Among N-E Women

Literacy rates for total populations of N-E States and India, for male and female populations separately for 1981 and 1991, and the male-female differentials are presented in Table 5.9. It is necessary to note a methodological departure in the 1991 Census by calculating literacy rates on the basis of population aged 7 years and above, unlike the 1981 Census which used population aged 5 years and above as the basis of calculation. Table 5.9 presents 1981 figures adjusted to 7+ population to ensure comparability. Female literacy rates for 1991 were 45 or above in Manipur, Meghalaya, Mizoram, Nagaland and Tripura. Assam female literacy rate (43.03), although lower, was better than the Indian average of 39.19 per cent. Arunachal Pradesh with 30 per cent female literacy stood in the low-literacy group with Rajasthan, Bihar, Uttar Pradesh and Madhya Pradesh ranging between 20 to 30 per cent. Mizoram (78.60 per cent) occupied second highest position in the whole country, and second only to Kerala with 86 per cent.

When we compare the 1991 female literacy rates with the situation in 1981, in five out of six N-E States (Assam data not available since Census was not conducted), there was an increase of 10 to 15 percentage points and in Meghalaya it was 8. In 1981, Arunachal Pradesh had 14.2 per cent female literacy, and was the second lowest in the country, while Rajasthan, with 14 per cent occupied the lowest rank.

The male-female differential in literacy rates in 1991 (Col. V & IX in Table 5.9) was smaller than the national average of 25 percentage points in all N-E States. In comparison with 1981, excepting Arunachal Pradesh, where it increased slightly (from 21.10 to 21.76) in the remaining five N-E States, it declined by about one to five points in 1991. In 1981, among six N-E States, the percentage difference between male and female literacy ranged between 9 and 29 points, whereas in 1991, the lowest was for Mizoram with 7 points and the highest was for Manipur with 24 points. Mizoram attained top rank among all States and Union Territories with respect to the lowest percentage difference between male and female literacy in 1991. We may look at the difference in male and female literacy rates from another angle: female literates per 1000 male and female literates (columns X, XI, of table 5.9). The sex-ratio among literates in 1991 registered an increase over 1981 in six N-E States (Assam data for 1981 not available). In six N-E States, it is over 600 for

Table 5.9 Literacy Rates for India and N-E States by Sex for Population aged 7 and above, 1981–91

	1981				*1991*				*Sex ratio (female literates per 1000 male literates)*	
	Literacy rate (7+)			*Male-Female difference in literates*	*Literacy rate (7+)*			*Male-Female difference in literates*		
India/States	*Persons*	*Male*	*Female*		*Persons*	*Male*	*Female*		*1981*	*1991*
I	*II*	*III*	*IV*	*V*	*VI*	*VII*	*VIII*	*IX*	*X*	*XI*
India (Excluding Assam & J&K)	43.67	56.37	29.85	26.65	52.19	64.20	39.19	25.01	491	564
Arunachal Pradesh	25.55	35.12	14.02	21.10	41.59	51.45	29.69	21.76	331	478
*Assam	N.A.	N.A.	N.A.	N.A.	52.89	61.87	43.03	18.84	N.A.	632
Manipur	49.66	64.15	34.67	29.48	59.89	71.63	47.60	24.03	523	634
Meghalaya	42.05	46.65	37.17	9.48	49.10	53.12	44.85	8.27	752	799
Mizoram	74.26	79.36	68.61	10.75	82.27	85.61	78.60	7.01	781	836
Nagaland	50.28	58.58	40.39	18.19	61.65	67.62	54.75	12.87	578	701
Tripura	50.11	61.49	38.01	23.48	60.44	70.58	49.65	20.93	582	661

Source: Census of India 1991, Series 11, Paper 2 of 1992, *Final Population Totals: Brief Analysis of Primary Census Abstract*, Registrar General & Census Commissioner, India.

*1981 Census not conducted in Assam.

Table 5.10 : Female Literacy Rates (7+ age) in N-E States and India by Rural-Urban Residence, 1991

I	II	III	IV	V
India/N-E States	*Urban Population as Percentage of Total Population*	*Literacy Rates Rural*	*Literarcy Rates Urban*	*Rural–Urban Differential in Percentage Points*
* India	26.13	30.35	63.94	33.59
Arunachal Pradesh	12.80	25.31	62.23	36.92
Assam	11.10	39.19	73.32	34.13
Manipur	27.52	43.26	58.67	15.41
Meghalaya	18.60	37.12	77.32	40.20
Mizoram	46.10	67.03	91.61	24.58
Nagaland	17.21	50.36	79.10	28.74
Tripura	15.30	44.33	76.93	32.60

Source: Census of India 1991, Series 1 : India *Final Population Totals,* Paper 2 of 1992, Series 1.

*Excludes Assam and Jammu & Kashmir

1991, which indicates that for every five literate males, there were at least three literate females. Mizoram figures indicate that there were four literate females for every five literate males. Arunachal Pradesh is the only N-E State where the sex ratio among literates is 478, i.e. less than 500 (although, it showed considerable improvement over the 1981 ratio of 331), which means that it does not have even one female literate against two male literates. Rajasthan and Uttar Pradesh in 1991 had lower than 400 sex-ratio among literates, which means there were less than two literate females for every five literate males, which indicates that the N-E States were in a much better situation with respect to male-female literacy differentials.

Rural-Urban differentials in literacy are an important dimension of female literacy, especially since in N-E States accessibility to schools in rural areas is closely related to girls' school attendance. Table 5.10 indicates the large differentials in terms of percentage points — 33 to 40

— for Tripura, Assam, Arunachal Pradesh and Meghalaya. For the remaining three States, viz. Manipur, Mizoram and Nagaland, urban female literacy rates are higher than rural rates by 15-29. Outside the N-E region, the high rural-urban differential States were: Madhya Pradesh (39.19), Rajasthan (38.65) and Bihar (37.99), while at the other end, Kerala had the lowest differential of 3.94.

The above findings regarding rural-urban literacy differentials must be viewed in the context of N-E States' special demographic features: In five States, urban populations were relatively small, between 11 and 19 per cent as of 1991 Census, as compared to India's 25.7 per cent. Secondly, with the recent growth of administrative centres at district and capital towns, educational institutions also tend to cluster around these new urban areas.

Pockets of High Female Illiteracy and Literacy

Despite considerable improvement in female literacy levels in N-E States, as reflected in 1991 Census data, some pockets of high female illiteracy continue to nag this region. If we compare the 1991 situation with that of 1981, however, the improvement seems significant. For instance, in 1981, 10 out of 11 districts of Arunachal Pradesh and West Garo Hills district of Meghalaya had less than 20 per cent female literacy. By 1991, this number came down to three districts of Arunachal Pradesh, viz. East Kameng (14.02 per cent), Tawang (16.83 per cent) and Tirap (18.52 per cent). Besides this, districts with less than 30 per cent female literacy included: Upper Subansiri and Changlang of Arunachal Pradesh, Dhubri of Assam and Mon of Nagaland. On the positive side, Aizawl (85.51 per cent) and Lunglei (72.58 per cent) in Mizoram and Mokokchung district (74.88 per cent) in Nagaland had higher than 70 per cent female literacy. One of the significant observations of 1991 Census was: districts with high female literacy had lesser percentages of population between 0-6 years, indicating lower fertility rates.

Male–Female Literacy Differential Among SC and ST Populations

As noted from Table 5.11, SC populations in five N-E States are very small — less than 1 per cent in four states and 2 per cent in Manipur. The question of male-female literacy differential is not very significant for these States. At all-India level female literacy rate for SC population is lower

Table 5.11: Literacy rates of SCs and STs, 1991 N-E States and India

India/N-E States	*Schedule Castes*			*Schedule Tribes*			*Percentage of total SC population*	*Percentage of total ST population*
	Total	*Male*	*Female*	*Total*	*Male*	*Female*		
India	37.41	49.91	23.76	29.6	40.65	18.1	16.73	7.95
Arunachal Pradesh	57.27	66.25	41.42	36.45	44.0	24.94	0.47	63.66
Assam	53.94	63.88	42.99	49.16	58.93	38.98	7.40	12.83
Manipur	56.44	65.28	47.41	53.63	62.39	44.48	2.02	34.47
Meghalaya	44.27	54.56	31.19	46.71	49.78	43.63	0.51	85.53
Mizoram	77.92	77.54	81.25	82.71	86.66	78.7	0.10	94.75
*Nagaland	0.00	0.00	0.00	60.59	66.27	54.51	0.00	87.70
Tripura	56.66	67.25	45.45	40.37	52.88	27.34	16.36	30.95

Source: Department of Secondary Education and Higher Education, Ministry of Human Resource Development, Govt. of India, *Selected Educational Statistics,* 1998-99, Studies in Educational Statistics No. 1-2000, Table 14.

*Nagaland does not have SC Population.

than male literacy rate by 26 percentage points. Tripura has a sizeable proportion of SC population (16.36 per cent, which is very close to India's 16.73 per cent) followed by Assam's 7 per cent, and the female literacy rates are lower than male literacy rates by 22 and 21 percentage points, respectively. Interestingly, in Mizoram female literacy is higher than male literacy by 3.71 percentage points among SC population.

When we come to differentials in male-female literacy among ST populations, it is 23 per cent for India, which is exceeded only by Tripura's 26 per cent. In Mizoram, Nagaland and Meghalaya, which have over 85 per cent tribal population, the male-female literacy differential is lowest, ranging between 6 and 12 points. For Assam and Manipur, it is 20 and 18 respectively. Arunachal Pradesh, which has 64 per cent ST population, does not fit into the pattern of Mizoram, Nagaland and Meghalaya, and shows a higher male-female literacy differential of 19 points.

For comparison, we may look at the situations in some other States. Bihar, as per 1991 Census figures, had an SC population of 14.55 per cent and ST population of 7.66 per cent. The male-female literacy differential for SC segment was 23.57 (Male literacy 30.64 per cent, female literacy 7.07 per cent) and for ST segment, it was 23.65 (Male literacy 38.4 per cent, female literacy 14.75 per cent).

We may look at Uttar Pradesh and Rajasthan, which had 21 and 17 per cent SC populations and the male-female literacy differentials were 30 and 34 points, respectively. Looking at these figures, along with those from N-E States, perhaps a common feature can be discerned. In States where the status of SCs and STs is lower than the majority non-SC-ST community, there is a larger difference between male and female literacy rates in the former. On the other hand, in Meghalaya, Mizoram and Nagaland where tribal communities have a dominant social position, male and female literacy rates are comparatively closer, suggesting lesser discrimination against women in education. It must be conceded, however, that other factors do influence the participation of women in education. For instance, in States like Arunachal Pradesh that have had a late start in developing formal education systems, girls continue to get a lower preference in education, as compared to boys.

Changes in Female Literacy by 2001

We now turn to the 2001 Census (Table 5.12). Although the findings are provisional, they certainly indicate broad changes and trends. For India, there is an increase of 13 percentage points by 2001 in total literacy rate, while female literacy has increased by 15 points over the 1991 figures (39.28 per cent). When we look at N-E States, except Arunachal Pradesh, all are better off than India as a whole. During previous decade, Manipur, Assam, Arunachal Pradesh, and Meghalaya registered increases of 12, 13, 15 and 16 percentage points, respectively. In 1991, Tripura, Nagaland and Mizoram had joined the higher female literacy group ranging between 50 to 79 per cent. In 2001, these States continued to retain their favourable position at 65, 62 and 86 per cent, respectively. Arunachal Pradesh in 1981 had female literacy rate of 14.02 and in 1991, 29.69 per cent. The 2001 rate of 44.24 per cent thus represents a highly creditable increase of over 30 points within two decades.

Geographical Distribution of Populations of N-E States

Before looking at enrolment of girls in N-E States, which reflects a more current aspect of education, we would quickly review the geographical distribution of populations in N-E States (Table 5.13), since this influences people's access to schools. It will be noted that a number of States, e.g. Arunachal Pradesh, Manipur, Meghalaya, Mizoram and Tripura, have set up new districts, which expands infrastructure for educational administration. The increase in the number of towns tends to improve access to schools, which is reflected in higher enrolment of children in schools located in urban areas.

Factors Influencing Enrolment of Girls

A reference has been made in chapter 4 to the pervasive tendency among parents in N-E States (as in the rest of India) to give a lower priority to girls' education as compared to boys'. Furthermore, since girls customarily help their mothers in various household and agricultural chores, parents are often reluctant to enrol them in schools, or withdraw them from schools at an early stage. Besides these attitudinal problems, the N-E terrains pose some special problems related to accessibility of schools. In Arunachal Pradesh, for instance, which has a population density of 13 per sq km, populations are scattered in small villages and often in locations interspersed with hills, valleys and rivers, requiring children to cover long distances and difficultt terrain to reach schools. Mizoram, Meghalaya, Nagaland and hill districts of Manipur, where population densities are relatively lower and

Table 5.12 : Total Population and Literacy Rates for N-E States and India by Sex 1991 and 2001 (Provisional)

India/N-E States	*Total population in thousands*	*Total population in thousand*	*Literacy rate (Population 7 and above)*			*Literacy rate (Population 7 and above)*		
			Persons	*Male*	*Female*	*Persons*	*Male*	*Female*
	1991	2001	1991			2001		
1	**2**	**3**	**4**	**5**	**6**	**7 8**		**9**
*India	846388	1027015	52.20	64.13	39.28	65.38	75.96	54.28
Arunachal Pradesh	865	1091	41.59	51.45	29.69	54.74	64.07	44.24
Assam	22414	26638	52.89	61.87	43.03	64.28	71.93	56.03
Manipur	1837	2389	59.89	71.63	47.60	68.87	77.87	59.70
Meghalaya	1775	2306	49.10	53.12	44.85	63.31	66.14	60.41
Mizoram	690	891	82.27	85.61	78.60	88.49	90.69	86.13
Nagaland	1210	1989	61.65	67.62	54.75	67.11	71.77	61.92
Tripura	2757	3191	60.44	70.58	49.65	73.66	81.47	65.41

Source: Census of India 2001, *Provisional Population Totals,* Series 1, Paper 1 of 2001. *In order to make 1991 and 2001 data comparable, figures for Jammu & Kashmir, entire district of Kachchh, Morvi, Maliya Miyana and Wakaner Talukas of Rajkot district, Jodiya Taluka of Jamnagar district of Gujrat and entire Kinnaur district of Himachal Pradesh were excluded, since census operations could not be conducted either in 1991 or 2001 due to difficult conditions.

Table 5.13: Area, Nuber of Districts, Towns and Inhabited Villages India and N-E States

I	II	III	IV	V	VI	VII
India/States	*Area in sq km*	*No. of districts*	*No. of towns (Statutory & Census)*	*No. of inhabited villages*	*Density per sq km 2001*	*Sex ratio (females per 1000 males) 2001*
India	3287263	572	4689	587226	324	933
Arunachal Pradesh	83743	13	10	3649	13	901
Assam	78438	23	93	24685	340	932
Manipur	22327	9	31	2182	107	978
Meghalaya	22429	7	12	5484	103	975
Mizoram	21081	8	22	698	42	938
Nagaland	16579	8	9	1216	120	909
Tripura	10486	4	18	855	304	950

Sources: (1) *Census of India 2001*, *Provisional Population Totals,* Series I, Paper1 of 2001,
(2) *Census of India 1991, State Profile, 1991 : India.*

terrains are hilly, share this same problem in varying degrees. In looking at enrolment of girls, we also need to keep in mind the low sex ratios of some States, e.g. Arunachal Pradesh (901) and Nagaland (909), as noted in Table 5.13.

Government Policies Regarding Girls' Enrolment

After adoption of Indian Constitution in 1950, Article 45 directed the State to provide, within a period of ten years, free and compulsory education for all children below the age of 14 years. While the goal of providing compulsory education for all children is still far off, education departments of N-E States have been providing free education to children initially up to VI or VII standards and are extending this policy to progressively higher standards. For instance, Nagaland and Assam governments provide free education to boys and girls up to class X, and Arunachal Pradesh and Tripura up to class XII. In addition, some States offer special concessions for girls, e.g. Manipur, where education for girls is free up to X standard, and Arunachal Pradesh, where school uniforms for girls are free. Against this background, we will now look at enrolment of girls in India as a whole, followed by N-E States.

Enrolment of Girls

Students joining educational institutions "for undergoing systematic instructions in a course of study" are classified as enrolment in official statistics. At all-India level, the negative bias against girls' enrolment has been evident in enrolment data on boys and girls at different stages of school education. However, the gap in boys' and girls' enrolment has narrowed over the past 50 years, as is evident from Table 5.14.

Table 5.14, besides highlighting the narrowing gap between boys' and girls' enrolment, brings out the substantial increase in girls' enrolment over nearly five decades since 1950-51 at primary, middle and high/ higher secondary stages. The respective figures for 1998-99 are: nine times, 32 times and 52 times those for 1950-51. We will now review the current girls' enrolment in N-E States.

Enrolment of Girls in N-E States (1998-99)

As will be noted from Table 5.15, enrolment of girls at all three levels, i.e. primary, middle and secondary, is lower than that of boys in all N-E

Table 5.14
Sexwise Enrolment by Stages : 1951–1999 (In Million) India

Year	*Primary*		*Middle/Upper Primary*		*High/Hr.Sec./Inter/ Pre-Degree*	
	Boys	Girls	Boys	Girls	Boys	Girls
1950-51	13.8	5.4	2.6	0.5	1.3	0.2
1980-81	45.3	28.5	13.9	6.8	7.6	3.4
1993-94	55.1	41.9	20.6	13.5	13.2	7.5
*1998-99	62.7	48.2	24.0	16.3	17.26	10.50

Source: Dept. of Secondary Education and Higher Education, Ministry of Human Resource Development, Govt. of India, *Selected Educational Statistics: 1998-99,* compiled from data in sub-table XXXIV.
* Provisional

States. The differences are comparatively higher in Tripura and Assam and very small in Mizoram, Meghalaya and Nagaland. Meghalaya provides the only exception where at middle level, enrolment of girls is higher than that of boys. Arunachal Pradesh, which has had a later start in opening schools (since it remained quite isolated up to Indian Independence), seems to be making a reasonable progress in enrolment of girls at all three levels. The situation will be clearer when we examine enrolment ratios a little later.

A comparison of enrolment of girls in 1998-99 with that in 1992-93 (Ministry of Human Resource Development, *Education in India: 1992-93*) shows considerable improvement in the situation. For instance, during the intervening six years, enrolment of girls at primary stage rose from 52,217 to 69,103 in Arunachal Pradesh, while in Assam it rose from 14,19,936 to 17,19,815. At middle stage too, enrolment of girls increased within this period as follows: in Meghalaya from 32,897 to 45,905 and in Tripura from 52,407 to 64,305. While these statistics on enrolment are encouraging, it is necessary to remember that like for India as a whole, these are inflated by students who fail in the examinations and repeat the same class, or drop out in the middle of an academic year. For instance, the girls' enrolment figure for Assam in 1992-93, which was 4,28,845, included 46,470 repeaters as per official records.

Enrolment at high/higher secondary level quite expectedly is much smaller than at primary and middle levels. But the differences in boys' and girls' enrolment are relatively smaller in Manipur, Meghalaya, Mizoram and Nagaland, as compared to those in Arunachal Pradesh, Assam and Tripura.

Enrolment of Women in Higher Education: 1998-99

We will now look at enrolment of women in courses at degree level and above, presented in Table 5.16. They include women enrolled for bachelor's, master's and doctorate level in various disciplines, e.g. arts, science, commerce, engineering, architecture, medicine, etc. and represent potential leaders for women's development.

The figures in Table 5.16 reveal the negative bias against girls' enrolment in higher education generally in all N-E States, and especially in Arunachal Pradesh, Assam and Tripura, where it is 347, 509 and 601, respectively per 1,000 boys enrolled and lower than the Indian average of 635 (Column V). Meghalaya, Mizoram and Nagaland, all of which have nearly 85 per cent and above tribal population, reflect a more favourable situation regarding girls' enrolment, which is lower, but not so markedly lower than boys' enrolment, viz. 899, 783, and 708, respectively per 1000 boys enrolled. A comparison between absolute figures for girls' enrolment in Manipur (12,955) and Meghalaya (6,783) as shown in Column III of Table 5.16 brings out an anomalous situation, however. These two States had nearly equal population in 1991 (18.37 lakh, and 17.75 lakh, respectively), and in 2001 (23.89 lakh and 23.06 lakh, respectively (refer to Table 5.13). Tribal population formed 34 per cent and 86 per cent of Manipur's and Meghalaya's total population in 1991. And yet, the number of girls enrolled in higher education is nearly double, 12,955 for Manipur, as compared with that for Meghalaya, 6,783.

This discrepancy is surprising for one more reason. In Meghalaya, Christian missionaries started their activities, including opening schools and colleges, since the first half of the nineteenth century, albeit with the blessings of British administrators. In fact, girls from other N-E States, e.g. Mizoram, came to Meghalaya to pursue high school education until 1920. Meghalaya girls went to Calcutta and abroad to pursue higher education and held important positions in educational and other institutions on their return. Meghalaya seems to have lost the momentum in women's

Table 5.15 : School Enrolment by Stages 1998-99; N-E States and India

India/ N-E States	*Primary/Jr. Basic (Classes I-V)*			*Middle/Upper Primary (classes VI-VIII)*			*Secondary/higher sec./pre degree (classes IX-XII)*		
	Boys	Girls	Total	Boys	Girls	Total	Boys	Girls	Total
India	62710059	48275818	110985877	24008332	16345026	40353358	17265562	10501887	27767449
Arunachal Pradesh	82918	69103	152021	26597	22027	48664	16625	10711	27336
Assam	2107200	1719815	3827015	701034	504809	1205843	496586	357014	853600
Manipur	137230	119440	256670	60300	52720	113020	38750	32780	71530
Meghalaya	157302	156676	313978	43302	45905	89207	26384	23664	50048
Mizoram	70869	63901	134770	23529	22585	46114	14847	14263	29110
Nagaland	106150	99136	205286	34137	32866	67003	22239	18498	40737
Tripura	245780	206641	452421	78673	64305	142978	51545	35727	87272

Source: Dept. of Elementary Education & Literacy, Dept. of Secondary Education and Higher Education, Ministry of Human Resource Development, Govt. of India, *Annual Report: 1999-2000.*

Table 5.16: Enrolment of Boys and Girls: Degree Level and Above N-E States and India;1998-99

I	II	III	IV	V
India/ N-E States	*Boys*	*Girls*	*Total*	*Girls per 1000 Boys*
India	43,42,584	27,57,858	71,00,442	635
Arunachal Pradesh	2,913	1,011	3,924	347
Assam	1,26,329	64,427	1,90,756	509
Manipur	14,737	12,955	27,692	872
Meghalaya	7,541	6,783	14,324	899
Mizoram	4,771	3,739	8,510	783
Nagaland	3,969	2,811	6,780	708
Tripura	11,490	6,915	18,405	601

Source: Dept. of Elementary Education and Literacy, Dept of Secondary Education and Higher Education, Ministry of Human Resource Development, Govt. of India, *Annual Report: 1999–2000.*

education somewhere along the way, and the reasons need to be identified. In comparison, Manipur had a much later start. Prior to 1898 there were very few schools for girls and a small number that were started later only provided primary and middle level education. Maharaja Churachand opened the first high school for girls in Imphal in 1935. Christian missionaries started the first high school that developed into Pettigrow College in Ukhrul in 1898 and found it sufficiently challenging to attract boys, let alone girls, for quite some time.

Perhaps, the high sense of responsibility among Manipuri girls towards providing economic support for their parents and the need to support education of their brothers and sisters, referred in Chapter 4, account for the high motivation for education, both general and professional, among Manipuri women.

Enrolment Ratios of Girls

Enrolment ratio for primary and/or middle level is defined as "percentage of the enrolment in classes I-V and VI-VIII and/or I-VIII to the estimated child population in the age-group 6-11 years and 11-14 and/or 6-14 years respectively." Since enrolment may include under-age or over-age children, besides inaccurate estimates of child population, the percentages may be more than 100 in some cases. At all-India level, girls' enrolment ratios in 1950-51 were as follows : primary — 24.8 and upper primary 4.6. By 1998-99, these rose to primary 82.85 and upper primary 49.08 (Ministry of Human Resource Development, *Selected Educational Statistics — 1998-99*). We will now look at enrolment ratios of boys and girls in N-E States at primary and upper primary/middle stages in 1998-99 presented in Table 5.17.

We will focus attention mainly on differences in enrolment ratios of boys and girls after noting that at primary level girls' enrolment is high in all N-E States and exceeds 84 per cent. At upper primary level, girls' enrolment registers a sharp decline and ranges between 52 (Assam) and 78 (Mizoram) per cent. This pattern applies, however, to boys as well.

As will be noted from Table 5.17, at primary stage for 1998-99, girls' enrolment was 18 per cent lower than that for boys for India as a whole. For two N-E States, viz. Assam and Tripura, the differentials are larger, i.e. 19 and 21 percentage points. For the remaining five States, the differentials vary between 3 (Nagaland) and 14 (Arunachal Pradesh) percentage points. Coming to middle level, for India as a whole, boys' enrolment was higher than that of girls by 16 percentage points, which is exceeded slightly by Assam's 17. For the remaining N-E States, the differences range between 0.55 (Mizoram) and 11 (Tripura) points. The noteworthy aspect is, that for Nagaland and Meghalaya, girls' enrolment ratios are higher than those for boys by four and five points, respectively. Once again, the differentials for Assam and Tripura are highest among N-E States.

Tables 5.18 and 5.19 give enrolment ratios for boys and girls for primary and middle levels for ST and SC population segments for N-E States, and for India as a whole. The enrolment ratio for girls belonging to ST population for primary level is 73 and 40 at middle level for India as a whole. For six N-E States (Assam data not available) girls' enrolment ratios at primary level are higher than the Indian average and at middle level higher than the Indian average for five N-E States, Tripura being the one exception where enrolment ratio is lower (37.42 per cent). Boys' enrolment ratio at primary level is higher than that of girls by 24 percentage points for India as a whole. The differentials for the three predominantly tribal population States, viz. Meghalaya, Mizoram and

Nagaland, are lower, varying between 4 and 11 points, while for the remaining three States they range between 14 and 28 points. Since Assam data for 1998-99 was not available, we may look at corresponding figures for 1999–2000 (provisional), which are as follows : boys' enrolment ratio 151.09, girls' ratio 119.22, indicating a huge difference of 31.87 points.

At upper primary/middle level, the difference between boys' and girls' enrolment among ST population is 23 percentage points for India as a whole. Once again, the differentials are small for Meghalaya, Mizoram and Nagaland, ranging between 2.93 and 8.50 points, and significantly for Meghalaya, girls' enrolment ratio is higher than that of boys by 3.46 points. Arunachal Pradesh has a much lower girls' enrolment ratio than that of boys, although it has 64 per cent ST population and does not fit into the pattern of Meghalaya, Mizoram and Nagaland. The differentials for Manipur, Arunachal Pradesh and Tripura are larger and range between 11 to 20 points. For Assam, since 1998-99 figures are not available, we may look at 1999–2000 provisional figures, which place boys' enrolment at 122.99 per cent, and girls' at 96.57 per cent, thus indicating a difference of 26.42 points.

The enrolment ratios for boys and girls in the three predominantly tribal population States, viz. Meghalaya, Mizoram and Nagaland show smaller differentials both at primary and middle level, as noted earlier. Furthermore in the case of Meghalaya, the enrolment ratio of girls is higher than that for boys at middle level. Does this suggest that in these three States there is greater equality for girls between 6 and 14 years in opportunities of education? This observation does not seem to hold for Arunachal Pradesh while ST population constitutes almost two-thirds of the total State population, which raises questions regarding possible reasons.

Table 5.19 gives enrolment ratios of SC boys and girls at primary and middle level. As will be noted from Column II of this table, in four N-E States, viz. Arunachal Pradesh, Meghalaya, Mizoram and Nagaland. SC populations do not constitute even 1 per cent of the total population of these States, and Manipur's SC population is 2 per cent. Tripura is the only State with a sizeable SC population (16.36 per cent), Assam comes next (7.40 per cent). At All-India level, girls' enrolment ratio is 78 at primary and 51 at middle levels, and their enrolment is lower than that of boys by 19 and 21 percentage points, respectively. For Tripura, the corresponding differences are 30 and 5 and for Manipur 6 and 10 points,

Table 5.17: School Enrolment Ratio in Classes I-V and VI-VIII N-E States and India (all students) 1998-99

India/N-E States	*Classes I-IV (6-11Years)*			*Classes VI-VIII (11-14 years)*			*Differential between boys' and girls' enrolment ratios (percentage points) Primary level*	*Differential between boys' and girls enrolment ratio (percentage points) Middle level*
	Boys	*Girls*	*Total*	*Boys*	*Girls*	*Total*		
Arunachal Pradesh	121.94	107.97	115.17	68.20	64.90	66.66	13.97	3.30
Assam	118.78	100.16	109.63	69.41	52.42	61.12	18.62	16.99
Manipur	100.17	84.11	92.00	77.31	68.47	72.92	16.06	8.84
Meghalaya	119.17	113.53	116.29	56.98	62.03	59.47	5.64	+5.05
Mizoram	133.72	120.57	127.14	78.43	77.88	78.16	13.15	0.55
Nagaland	111.74	108.94	110.37	63.22	67.07	65.05	2.80	+3.85
Tripura	118.73	97.47	107.98	66.67	55.92	61.36	21.26	10.75
India	100.86	82.85	92.14	65.27	49.08	57.58	18.01	16.19

Source: Dept. of Elementary Education and Literacy, Department of Secondary Education and Higher Education, Ministry of Human Resource Development, Govt. of India, *Annual Repot: 1999-2000.*

Table 5.18 :Enrolment Ratio of Students belonging to Scheduled Tribes in General School Schools Classes I-V and VI-VIII, N-E States and India 1998-99

I	II	III	IV	V	VI	VII	VIII
India/N-E States	*Percentage of ST Population 1991*	*Enrolment Ratios — Classes I-V 6-11 Years*			*Enrolment Ratios — Classes VI-VIII 11-14 Years*		
		Boys	*Girls*	*Total*	*Boys*	*Girls*	*Total*
Arunachal Pradesh	63.66	120.05	94.02	106.30	87.67	69.66	78.29
Assam	12.83	N.A.	N.A.	N.A.	N.A.	N.A.	N.A.
Manipur	34.41	96.13	80.77	88.48	62.82	51.49	57.16
Meghalaya	85.53	89.28	85.57	87.38	54.16	57.62	55.94
Mizoram	94.75	123.37	112.68	117.80	78.00	69.50	73.58
Nagaland	87.70	111.81	102.59	107.17	76.48	73.55	75.01
Tripura	30.95	108.45	80.61	94.50	56.97	37.42	47.25
India	7.95	96.89	73.22	85.09	63.37	40.48	52.20

Source: Dept. of Elementary Education and Literacy, Department of Secondary Education and Higher Education, Ministry of Human Resource Development, Govt. of India, *Annual Report: 1999-2000.* N.A. – Not Available.

Table 5.19: Enrolment Ratio of Students belonging to Scheduled Castes in General Schools: Classes I-V and VI-VII, N-E States and India 1998-99

India/N-E States	*Percentage of SC Populaton 1991*	*Enrolment Ratios — Classes I-V 6-11 Years*			*Enrolment Ratios — Classes VI-VIII 11-14 Years*		
		Boys	*Girls*	*Total*	*Boys*	*Girls*	*Total*
I	II	III	IV	V	VI	VII	VIII
Arunachal Pradesh	0.47	32.78	29.57	31.45	29.45	34.38	31.45
Assam	7.40	N.A.	N.A.	N.A.	N.A.	N.A.	N.A.
Manipur	2.02	91.95	85.57	88.75	67.76	57.86	62.77
Meghalaya	0.51	110.56	107.72	109.24	103.08	109.53	106.08
Mizoram	0.10	49.41	86.17	54.88	55.60	53.44	55.28
Nagaland	0.00	0.00	0.00	0.00	0.00	0.00	0.00
Tripura	16.36	107.42	87.11	97.54	61.72	57.20	59.50
India	16.73	96.55	77.95	87.57	72.12	50.96	62.09

Source: Dept. of Elementary Education and Literacy, Department of Secondary Education and Higher Education, Ministry of Human Resource Development, Govt. of India, *Annual Report*: *1999-2000*. N.A. – Not Available.

respectively. Assam data are not available.

It is interesting to note, despite very small SC populations, that in Mizoram at primary level and in Arunachal Pradesh and Meghalaya at middle level, girls' enrolment ratios are higher than those of boys.

Dropout Rates

While steadily increasing school enrolment of girls in N-E States is a positive development, the high dropout rates are a serious cause for concern, and measures to ensure their reduction need to be undertaken. Table 5.20 gives dropout rates of boys and girls at primary, elementary and high school levels. Dropout is defined as percentage of children to total enrolment dropping out of the school educational system.

Let us examine dropout rates at primary level (Classes I-V, Columns II and III of Table 5.20). In Mizoram, Assam, Manipur and Tripura, girls' dropout rates are higher than those of boys, but the range is small, varying between 0.51 for Mizoram and 4.25 points for Tripura. In the remaining three States girls' dropout rates are lower than those for boys by the following percentage points : Meghalaya (1.10), Nagaland (3.72) and Arunachal Pradesh (5.05). At the middle level (Classes I-VIII, Columns V & VI), dropout rates of girls are higher than those of boys for Meghalaya, Tripura, Manipur and Assam by a small margin varying between 0.40 (Meghalaya) to 4.05 (Assam) percentage points. Once again, for Arunachal Pradesh and Nagaland, girls' dropout rates are smaller than those of boys, and Mizoram joins this group with smaller girls' dropout rate. For I-X classes (Columns VIII and IX) again, three States, viz. Assam, Mizoram and Nagaland have lower dropout rates for girls, the differences ranging between 1.23 and 2.86 percentage points. The remaining four States have higher girls' dropout rates than those for boys ranging between 0.39 (Manipur) and 4 (Tripura) points. Dropout rates for India as a whole, interestingly, are higher for girls than those for boys at all three levels, viz. I-V, I-VIII, and I-X.

The dropout rates for girls in N-E States are higher in some States and lower in some others than those for boys. Furthermore, no consistent pattern of higher girls' dropout rates at higher school levels seems evident. These figures do not therefore support the commonly held view that parents generally withdraw their daughters from schools as they approach adolescence, while boys are more likely to continue schooling. This matter requires further scrutiny.

Table 5.20: Dropout Rates in Classes I-V, I-VIII and I-X for the year 1998-99 (Provisional) N-E States and India

N-E States and India	*Classes I-V*			*Classes I-VIII*			*Classes I-X*		
	Boys	*Girls*	*Total*	*Boys*	*Girls*	*Total*	*Boys*	*Girls*	*Total*
I	II	III	IV	V	VI	VII	VIII	IX	X
Arunachal Pradesh	51.74	46.69	49.59	67.47	65.86	66.78	76.09	78.67	77.20
*Assam	40.87	42.43	41.56	68.26	72.31	70.08	76.55	75.32	76.00
Manipur	43.71	46.38	44.97	45.36	47.02	46.15	76.35	76.74	76.54
Meghalaya	58.43	57.53	57.98	77.71	78.11	77.91	62.12	63.74	62.89
Mizoram	51.56	52.07	51.80	68.50	65.75	67.20	73.85	71.10	72.56
Nagaland	32.11	29.83	31.03	46.46	38.95	42.98	63.84	60.98	62.59
Tripura	49.44	53.69	51.42	69.58	71.06	70.26	79.94	83.95	81.78
India	38.62	41.22	39.74	54.40	60.09	56.82	64.44	70.22	67.44

Source: Dept. of Elementary Education and Literacy, Dept. of Secondary Education and Higher Education, Ministry of Human Resource Development, Govt. of India, *Annual Report: 1990-2000.*

* *Rates for Assam are for 1997-98.*

If we compare girls' dropout rates among N-E States with those of other States of India, a mixed picture emerges. For instance, at primary level (Classes I-V), six out of seven N-E States show girls' dropout rates between 42 and 58 per cent (Column III). These rates are much higher than those for Karnataka (27.77) and Kerala (5.20). At middle level (Classes I-VIII) five out of seven N-E States reveal girls' dropout rates between 66-78 per cent (Column VI), which are above the Indian average of 60 per cent. The corresponding rates for some other States are: Kerala (3.46), Maharashtra (44.09), Rajasthan (61.59), Bihar (80.12). Dropout rates for Classes I-X for girls in five N-E States (Column IX) range between 71-84 per cent. Girls' dropout rates for Kerala (19.16), Maharashtra (64.22), Bihar (87.26) and Indian average (70.22), indicate that the situation in N-E States is far from satisfactory. The dropout rates for girls in N-E States are closer to educationally backward states like Bihar and Rajasthan.

High dropout rates are generally attributed to the poor quality of education imparted by schools and its lack of relevance to life. An important input for increasing enrolment of children in schools ensuring their retention relates to the quality of teachers available in schools. We now look at the situation of teachers in N-E States.

Teachers and their Training

Table 5.21 provides information on male-female distribution of teachers at primary, middle and high school level in N-E States and India as of 1992-93. It is generally believed that availability of women teachers is conducive to girls' enrolment in schools. Furthermore, whether teachers have received training for their profession is also a relevant consideration.

At all levels, i.e. primary, middle and high school, women teachers constitute a minority among the total number of teachers in all N-E States, which is consistent with the picture for India as a whole. In Meghalaya at all three levels, and in Mizoram at primary level, the percentages of women teachers in the total number are somewhat better (Columns IV, VIII and XII). With respect to women teachers who had received training, in Mizoram at primary and middle levels, they constituted nearly three-fourths and at high school level almost half of the total number of women teachers. In Assam at primary level, more than half of women teachers were trained, while in other States, trained women teachers form a minority

Table 5.21 Numbers, Percentages and Sex of Teachers at Primary, Middle and High School Levels, N-E States & India 1992-93

	Primary				*Middle*				*High School*			
N-E States and India	*Men teachers (% trained)*	*Women teachers (% trained)*	*% women teachers to total no. of teachers*	*% trained women teachers to total no. of trained teachers*	*Men teachers (% trained)*	*Women teachers (% trained)*	*% women teachers to total no. of teachers*	*% trained women teachers to total no. of trained teachers*	*Men teachers (% trained)*	*Women teachers (% trained)*	*% women teachers trained) no. of teachers*	*% trained women to total teachers to total no. of traind teachers*
I	II	III	IV	V	VI	VII	VIII	IX	X	XI	XII	XIII
Arunachal Pradesh	1935 (40.05)	567 (37.57)	22.66	8.51	1409 (44.78)	379 (26.91)	21.20	5.70	811 (47.10)	266 (40.23)	24.70	9.94
Assam	50187 (68.08)	17609 (58.14)	25.97	15.10	30036 (27.87)	7629 (29.57)	20.25	5.99	30138 (29.00)	7932 (22.71)	20.84	4.73
Manipur	7611 (53.66)	3373 (31.43)	30.71	9.65	4828 (32.52)	2261 (19.64)	31.89	6.26	5508 (33.51)	2982 (24.31)	35.12	8.54
Meghalaya	4948 (39.41)	3899 (32.55)	44.07	14.34	2195 (20.41)	1390 (23.74)	38.77	9.21	2193 (25.08)	1811 (39.26)	45.23	17.76
Mizoram	2039 (82.74)	1802 (85.85)	46.91	40.28	2621 (81.23)	641 (73.79)	19.65	14.50	1618 (47.47)	344 (49.13)	17.53	8.61
Nagaland	4673 (49.13)	1770 45.03)	27.47	12.37	2861 (29.61)	790 (26.96)	21.64	5.83	2582 (30.91)	1227 (27.87)	32.21	8.98
Tripura	7459 (27.51)	2113 (36.73)	22.07	8.11	3977 (24.82)	1195 (27.87)	23.11	6.44	4489 (32.03)	1839 (34.37)	29.06	9.99
India	1137147 (83.12)	514269 (84.46)	31.14	26.30	709423 (86.93)	375878 (88.05)	34.63	30.50	568357 (86.70)	281101 (87.19)	33.09	28.35

Source: Department of Education Ministry of Human Resource Development, Govt. of India, *Education in India :1992-93*, compiled from data in tables XII, XIII, XIV.

at all three levels (Columns III, VII and XI). When we consider the percentages of trained women teachers to the total number of trained teachers at all three levels, the former represent a tiny minority, except for Mizoram at primary level (Columns V, IX and XIII). At All-India level, trained women teachers form roughly between 26 and 30 per cent of the total number of trained teachers, indicating that the situation in N-E States is worse off.

Teacher-Student Ratio

Teacher-pupil ratio is considered a relevant dimension of the quality of education. Table 5.22 presents average number of students per teacher in N-E States and India as of 1992-93. A smaller average number of students per teacher permits greater individual attention to students and is therefore regarded as desirable. At primary level, against the all-India average of 43 students per teacher, five N-E States have much lower average (18-31) and Meghalaya and Assam averages are 40 and 41 respectively. At middle level, while all-India average is 38 students per teacher, all N-E States fall within 13-24 range. At high school level, while the all-India average is 30, N-E States are happily within 16-27 range.

Development of Educational Institutions

We will now review the distribution of various types of educational, vocational and professional training institutions in N-E States. The figures in Table 5.23 present a rather dismal picture as regards pre-primary/ pre-basic schools, except in Tripura, where their number is 3406. In Manipur, Meghalaya and Mizoram, virtually no institutions are listed. It must be recognized, however, that kindergartens or balwadis (pre-school institutions) may exist under voluntary auspices, without seeking government recognition. The importance of properly designed pre-school experience for children in developing appropriate learning attitudes and skills and social abilities hardly needs justification. The rather sharp decline in the number of institutions from primary to middle and high school level (Columns III, IV and V) in all N-E States (Tripura, where number of high schools exceeds that of middle, being the only exception) suggests that for many children education ends at primary level, which is confirmed by high dropout rates by middle and high school level noted earlier.

As far as colleges for general education are concerned (Column VI),

Table 5.22: Number of Teachers in General Education Institutions and Average Number of Students Per Teacher (1992-93) in N-E States and India

N-E States/India	*Primary/Jr. Basic Schools*		*Middle/Sr. Basic Schools*		*High/ Post Basic Schools*	
	Total no. of Teachers	*Average no. of Students*	*Total no. of Teachers*	*Average No. of Students*	*Total no. of Teachers*	*Averge no. of Students*
Arunachal Pradesh	2502	31	1788	23	1077	23
Assam	67796	41	37665	24	38070	23
Manipur	10984	18	7089	16	8490	19
Meghalaya	8847	40	3585	18	4004	19
Mizoram	3841	26	3262	13	1962	16
Nagaland	6443	19	3651	21	3809	27
Tripura	9572	24	5172	23	6328	21
India	1651416	43	1085301	38	849458	30

Source: Dept. of Education, Ministry of Human Resource Development, Govt. of India, *Education in India : 1992-93*, compiled from data in Table X (pp.93-95).

Table 5.23: Total Number of Recognized Educational Institutions (1998-99) India and N-E States

India/ N-E States	*Pre-Primary /Pre-Basic Schools*	*Primary/ Junior Basic Schools*	*Middle/ Senior Basic Schools*	*High/Higher Secondary Schools Pre-Degree /Jr. Colleges (10+2;New Pattern)*	*Arts Science & Commerce Colleges*	*Engineering/ Technology/ Architecture/ Medical Colleges*	*Teacher Training Schools*	*Teacher Training Colleges*	*Polytechnic Institutes/ Technical/ Industrial/ Arts & Craft Schools*	*Universities/ Deemed Universities/ Institutions of National Importance*
I	II	III	IV	V	VI	VII	VIII	IX	X	XI
Arunachal Pradesh	46	1277	326	171	7	1	0	0	3	1
Assam	199	33236	8019	4590	265	8	1	24	40	6
Manipur	1	2570	630	582	50	1	1	2	7	2
Meghalaya	0	4679	946	493	33	0	10	1	4	1
Mizoram	0	1244	741	378	27	0	2	2	3	0
Nagaland	28	1469	470	295	29	0	2	1	5	1
Tripura	3406	2065	414	589	16	2	2	2	5	1
India	51569	626737	190166	112438	7494	1295	1319	818	5237	237

Source: Department of Secondary Education and Higher Education, Ministry of Human Resource Development, Govt. of India, *Selected Educational Statistics*: 1998-99 (compliled from data in Table 15).

Arunachal Pradesh has only seven, which is understandable in view of its late start in education. For Tripura their number, which is 16 is small in view of its population, in comparison to Manipur, Meghalaya, Mizoram and Nagaland. There is a very high deficit of teacher training schools and colleges (Columns VIII and IX), which is confirmed by the dismal percentages of trained teachers in all N-E States except to some extent in Mizoram and Meghalaya, as noted earlier in Table 5.21. Arunachal Pradesh does not have a single teacher training institution, while there are hardly three or four such institutions in four other N-E States. According to a Ministry of Human Resource Development source (*Education in India: 1992-93*), Tripura had the lowest percentage of trained teachers at primary level, Meghalaya at middle level and Assam at high school level in India, as of 1992-93. One crucial deficit is the disappointingly small number of institutions providing technical and professional training (Columns VII and X). Barring Assam where their combined number is 48, all other N-E States reflect a serious deficiency in this respect. It is not surprising that the total number of universities or higher learning institutions for N-E region does not go beyond 12.

Summary

FEMALE LITERACY RATES

According to 1991 Census, female (7+) literacy in six N-E States out of seven was above 43 per cent, against the Indian average of 39.19, Arunachal Pradesh being the only exception with 30 per cent. Mizoram, with 79 per cent, ranked second highest in the country, next only to Kerala. Male-Female differentials ranged between seven and 13 percentage points in Meghalaya, Mizoram and Nagaland, the three States with more than 85 per cent ST populations. In the remaining four States, these stood between 19-24 points. The rural-urban differentials were high, between 33-40 points for Tripura, Assam, Arunachal Pradesh and Meghalaya. For the remaining three States, these ranged between 15-25 points. These figures must be viewed in the context of relatively small urban populations in N-E States. The N-E region, like India as a whole, includes some pockets with extremely low female literacy rates, e.g. East Kameng, Tawang and Tirap districts in Arunachal Pradesh having less than 20 per cent. On the other hand, some shining examples of high female literacy districts were: Aizawl and Lunglei (Mizoram), and

Mokokchung (Nagaland), having above 70 per cent female literacy. As per provisional 2001 Census findings, Aizawl district of Mizoram has 96.64 per cent female literacy, and Serchchip, Champhai, Kolasib and Mamit districts have achieved over 80 per cent (District-wise Indicators, National Commission on Population, Govt. of India, 11 July 2001, p. 58).

Male-female literacy differentials for Scheduled Caste (SC) populations for Tripura and Assam (having 16 and 7 per cent SC populations) were 22 and 21 points, respectively. For the remaining five States with 2 per cent or less SC populations, this is not a very significant consideration. Coming to male-female literacy differentials in Scheduled Tribes (ST) populations, for Meghalaya, Mizoram and Nagaland, these are lowest, ranging between 6 and 12 points. For the remaining four States these stood between 18 and 23 points. Arunachal Pradesh, even with its 64 per cent ST population, does not fit into the pattern of predominantly ST population States.

A hypothesis emerging from the lower male-female literacy differentials for Meghalaya, Mizoram and Nagaland, worth further scrutiny is the following: In states where ST segments enjoy a respectable social status, women enjoy greater freedom from discrimination in educational opportunities.

The 2001 Census data (provisional) indicate that all N-E States, except Arunachal Pradesh, have achieved female literacy rates ranging between 56-86, i.e. above the Indian average of 54 per cent. Nagaland, Tripura and Mizoram continue to maintain their previous leading positions.

ENROLMENT OF GIRLS IN SCHOOLS

In N-E States, as in the rest of India, parents give a lower priority to girls' enrolment. Furthermore, girls from an early age are given heavy responsibilities for household and agricultural tasks. Girls' enrolment is lower than that of boys at primary, middle and high school level in all States as per official 1998-99 figures with one exception in Meghalaya at secondary level where boys' enrolment is lower. The differences between boys' and girls' enrolment, within the general pattern and declining numbers from primary to middle to high school, are relatively small for Meghalaya, Mizoram and Nagaland, as compared to other N-E States.

Enrolment ratios for girls, as per 1998-99 official figures, ranged between 84 and 121 at primary level, and between 52 and 78 at middle level, as against Indian averages of 83 and 49, respectively. Differences between boys' and girls' enrolment ratios at primary level were greater for Assam, Tripura, Manipur and Arunachal Pradesh (14-21) than those for Meghalaya, Mizoram and Nagaland (3-13). At middle level, enrolment ratios for girls were lower than those for boys by 9-17 percentage points for Manipur, Tripura and Assam. The differentials ranged between 0.55 to 5.05 for Mizoram, Nagaland, Arunachal Pradesh and Meghalaya, with an interesting difference: for Meghalaya and Nagaland, girls' enrolment ratios at middle level were higher than those for boys. Coming to enrolment ratios among ST populations, for six N-E States (Assam data not available), girls' enrolment ratios at primary level are fairly high, ranging from 81 to 113. At middle level, while there is a sharp drop in both girls' and boys' enrolment ratios, girls' ratios stand between 51 and 74 for five States (higher than the Indian average of 40), Tripura being the only exception where it is 37. Once again, the differentials between boys' and girls' enrolment ratios are smaller for Meghalaya, Mizoram and Nagaland both at primary and middle level, than for the remaining States. An interesting observation: girls' enrolment ratio at middle level is higher than that for boys in Meghalaya.

Enrolment ratios for girls in SC population for Tripura, which has 16 per cent SC population were 87 for primary and 57 for middle level and girls' ratios were smaller than those for boys by 30 points at primary and 21 points at middle level, respectively. In the remaining five N-E States (Assam data not available) this issue is not very significant since SC populations constitute less than 1 per cent in four states and 2 per cent in one.

Dropout rates for girls at various levels in N-E States do not reflect a consistent pattern, and some States have higher and some lower dropout rates for girls than those for boys. On the whole, dropout rates are high both for girls and boys in all N-E States, and measures to improve their retention in schools are needed.

TEACHERS AND EDUCATIONAL AND TRAINING INSTITUTIONS

N-E States have a shortage of women teachers, who form about one-third of the total number of teachers at primary, middle and high school levels. Furthermore, trained teachers as a whole, and trained women teachers particularly, constitute a minority. There is a sharp decline in the numbers of schools from primary to middle, and to high school level. N-E States also suffer from a shortage of teacher training institutions. Furthermore, institutions providing vocational, technical and professional training are very few in six N-E States, and are predominantly located in Assam.

6

Social and Political Status

Introduction

THIS chapter examines N-E women's social and political status. Chapter 3, it may be recalled, presented their economic status, while Chapter 4 reviewed their status with reference to three important institutions: marriage, family and religion. Chapter 5 examined their situation on the basis of some important indicators with respect to health and education.

Concept of Social and Political Status

The terms "social" and "political" status have broad connotations, and it is therefore essential to state the sense in which the terms are used in the present context. Women's social status here refers to their position or relative ranking in their respective communities or societies. Their political status refers to their standing in groups or councils constituted to determine the rules and procedures for ensuring the internal integrity and external security of the community or society concerned. Having said this, one would be hard put to refer to women's social and political status that is not influenced by their status in other spheres. For instance, a woman's social status goes up if she belongs to an affluent family. Or again, if she has attained high educational qualifications, her status as a candidate for Panchayat election would certainly be higher. The interrelations between different aspects of a woman's status are varied and complex. Furthermore, social and political spheres sometimes intersect and merge together, so that activities perceived initially as social may in course of time acquire political significance and vice versa.

It is necessary to recognize that social status, to some extent, is a relative concept operating within a particular society. For instance, in some N-E societies living in remote and isolated areas, women's role is viewed mainly as multipliers of the clan through their procreative capacity and as sustainers of the family. These societies may find it a bit difficult to let their women form a "Mahila-Mandal" (Women's Association) to meet the latter's own needs of companionship and relaxation away from the household grind. In such a context, when women form a group and assert their needs, it is indicative of their status.

The seven N-E States within them represent a wide range in terms of social status assigned to women. The same is true of women's political status. Admittedly, the framework for analysing social and political status presented here is illustrative and not exhaustive. Nor is it completely applicable to all N-E States, both due to variations in women's situations as well as in the availability of information.

Framework for Analysing Social and Political Status

PARTICIPATION IN SOCIAL EVENTS

The nature of women's participation in social events, e.g. festivals to mark the onset of spring, or celebrations associated with certain agricultural operations, such as sowing or harvesting reflects their status. Some of these events may include a religious component (e.g. a ritual offering to a deity believed to be responsible for a bountiful harvest), but for the major part, they are social occasions that include feasting, singing and dancing. Women's social status is reflected in the nature of their participation, the type of tasks assigned to them *vis-à-vis* men, and equally importantly, women's exclusion from certain occasions.

WOMEN'S MEMBERSHIP OF VOLUNTARY ASSOCIATIONS

When women form or join groups formed to promote common social interests, this is indicative of their social status. For instance, when women, whose entire time is spent in *jhum* cultivation and house work such as cooking and feeding the family, form a women's group to meet their recreational and fellowship needs, this in itself is indicative of their self-assertion and confidence. Furthermore, when such groups widen their interests and for instance, undertake construction of a community centre, this gives them a higher status in their community.

DEMONSTRATIONS OF PROTEST

Women have been using this method for a variety of reasons: e.g. to show condemnation of an atrocity on a woman, such as rape, by a person in authority. Sometimes demonstrations are organized to express strong opposition to an action or policy adopted by a public authority. Occasionally, demonstrations sparked by stray events may assume political significance when opposition parties get involved to turn the initial event into a policy issue.

WOMEN'S PARTICIPATION IN TRADITIONAL VILLAGE/COMMUNITY COUNCILS

Most tribal communities in N-E States have village or community councils which decide on social and political matters of concern to the clan/tribe/community inhabiting a defined geographical area. Where Chieftainship or village headmanship systems prevail, such councils may include the Chief's or headman's assistants and village elders. Other councils generally include representatives of each household/clan/tribe. These councils decide action to be taken in cases of social offences (e.g. a young boy marrying a girl belonging to the same clan in communities where the rule of clan exogamy prevails), as well as political matters, such as infringement of territory by another community.

SUPPORT FOR POLITICAL CAMPAIGNS AND ISSUES

As far as modern political institutions are concerned, women's political status is reflected in their participation in political activities or movements launched by political parties, e.g. campaigning for candidates, voting in elections, writing in support of policies or persons. For instance, Mizo women took an active part in the movement for abolition of chieftainship system in early 1950s. While Tangkhul women in Manipur may not contest election to district councils, they actively canvas support for men candidates of their choice.

PARTICIPATION IN ELECTIVE BODIES

A fairly concrete indication of women's political status is the number of women who contest and get elected to representative political bodies at national, State and local levels. We will therefore review how many women contest and win elections for (i) Lok Sabha and Rajya Sabha, (ii) State Legislative Assemblies, (iii) Zila Parishads, Panchayat Samitis, Gram Panchayats for rural areas and Municipal Corporations, Municipal Councils and Nagar Panchayats for urban areas. Indian Constitution has provided a different administrative structure for local governance of areas that are inhabited primarily by tribesmen. Furthermore two Constitutional provisions, viz. 73rd and 74th Amendments have made special provisions with respect to reservation of seats for women, SCs and STs in rural and urban local bodies. A brief summary of major Constitutional provisions which are applicable to various N-E States is provided here.

Major Constitutional Provisions

We list below major Constitutional provisions, some of which apply to vulnerable sections such as SCs (Scheduled Caste) and STs (Scheduled Tribes) in the whole of India, while some are specific to N-E States. In view of the majority ST populations in four and sizeable ST populations in two N-E States, the following Constitutional safeguards are relevant considerations for social and political status of women.

1. Certain Articles of the Indian Constitution, viz. 46, 15(4), 16(4) and 19(5) direct the State to promote educational, social and economic interests of SCs and STs through measures such as reserving seats for them in educational institutions, protect them from social injustice, exploitation and discrimination in government employment.

2. Fifth Schedule, under Article 244(D), provides for special administration and control of Scheduled Areas, empowers the Governor, with the approval of the President, to suitably adopt or modify State Acts, or enact special legislation to protect STs against exploitation by moneylenders, and to safeguard their interests in land. It also provides for creation of Tribes Advisory Councils which may advise the Governor regarding administration of Scheduled Areas.

3. Sixth Schedule [under Articles 214(2) and 275(1)] provides for special administration of tribal areas of Assam, Meghalaya, Mizoram and Tripura through Autonomous District Councils for major and Regional Councils for smaller areas. It is aimed at conferring greater autonomy on tribal populations in specified areas and providing for self-governance through elected representatives, and for safeguarding their customs and traditions. District councils have legislative, administrative and financial powers with respect to several matters such as, use of land, unreserved forests, water courses, appointments of chiefs and headmen, inheritance of property, marriage, divorce and social customs, etc. These councils have a term of five years, and may constitute village councils, town committees, manage primary schools, dispensaries, assess and collect revenues and taxes (Dutta Ray, 1999)

4. The Fifty-first Amendment of 1984 provides for reservation of seats for tribesmen in Arunachal Pradesh, Meghalaya, Mizoram and Nagaland in Lok Sabha and in State Assemblies of Nagaland and Mizoram.

5. The 73rd Constitutional Amendment Act, passed in December 1992 and brought into force on 24 April 1993, provided for Gram Sabhas and a three-tier system, consisting of Gram Panchayat, Panchayat Samiti and Zila Parishad for all States/UTs except those having a population of less than 20 lakh. The Act specifies areas excluded from its application, e.g. hill districts of Assam, Meghalaya, Autonomous District Council area of Tripura, Nagaland, Mizoram, hill areas of Manipur where District Councils have been established. The major provisions include the following: direct elections for all posts, except those of Chairmen of Panchayat Samiti and Zila Parishad; tenure of Panchayats to be five years; reservation of seats for SCs / STs in Panchayats (Chairmen and members) in proportion to their population, and most importantly, reservation of one-third seats (Chairmen and members) for women as a mandatory requirement. State Governments may decide what financial powers may be given to Panchayats and also the extent of devolution of functional areas. State Governments were required to alter their existing laws, if any, and bring them in conformity with 73rd Amendment by 1994.

6. The 74th Amendment of 1993 added a new Part IX A relating to Municipalities, i.e. Nagar Panchayats for areas in transition from rural to urban, Municipal Councils for smaller urban areas, and Municipal Corporations for large urban areas (Twelfth Schedule). There are similar provisions for reservation of seats for SCs and STs (Chairmen and members) in proportion to their populations and for reservation of one-third seats (Chairmen and members) for women, as in 73rd Amendment. Similar provisions regarding elections, tenures, delegation of financial powers and subjects to municipalities by State Government, as in 73rd Amendment referred previously, have been made here.

When 73rd and 74th Constitutional Amendments were passed in 1993, it was felt that for the tribal areas which were excluded from their coverage a suitable system which was consistent with tribal traditions be prepared. The Central Government, therefore, appointed a committee under the chairmanship of Dileep Bhuria to devise a suitable system. While this committee submitted its recommendations, the decision was held up due to differences between the Law and Rural Development

Ministries. Meanwhile some N-E States have been exploring whether and with what modifications, the general legal provisions could be used, while some other States have adopted special legal measures governing local administration.

Some Limitations in Data Available

Admittedly, the numbers of women in representative political bodies do not tell the story of their qualitative contribution towards decision-making, about which data are not available. Even with respect to numbers of women who participate in representative bodies at below-district level, there are some gaps which need to be stated. Data on number of women who contested and were elected to the Lok Sabha, Rajya Sabha and State Legislative Assemblies were obtained from the Secretariat of the Election Commission of India and periodic reports published by this office. The objective has been to find out the general patterns in terms of number of women who contested and won various elections, and no attempt has been made to include data on all elections and bye-elections. There are several gaps in information with respect to women's representation at district level and below, and particularly for tribal areas which are exempted from the purview of 73rd and 74th Constitutional Amendments, i.e. both rural and urban local bodies. Most books and reports on Panchayati Raj and urban local government deal with larger Indian States, and information regarding N-E States tends to be either absent or incomplete, and not fully up to date. Some useful information was available from reports prepared by the Institute of Social Sciences, New Delhi, viz. *Status of Panchayati Raj in the States of India*, 1995, 1997 and 2000 versions. Several efforts were made to contact State Government officials and other knowledgeable persons to obtain information on women elected or nominated to urban local bodies, autonomous district and regional councils and other district and village councils not covered by Sixth Schedule (e.g. Manipur). Despite repeated efforts, complete information was not available.

ARUNACHAL PRADESH

Women's Position in Traditional Community Councils

In most tribes of Arunachal Pradesh, women traditionally have no share in decision-making at community level. In some tribes, women could not even set foot in places where community meetings were held, e.g. the

Adis' "Kebang," Noctes' and Wanchos' "Nongthun," or the Apatanis' "Buliong" (Jha, 1989). The grounds on which this ban on women was put were many. For instance, the Adis, the most numerous community in Arunachal Pradesh, clubbed "slaves and women" as unworthy of participation in the "Kebang." One reason why women have no place in community councils is that they are believed to be without a permanent clan affiliation, since in an exogamous marriage system, a woman's clan status is merely temporary and she is therefore regarded as undependable in terms of keeping the clan's secrets. Besides, in the past, since community council meetings were held to plan matters related to warfare and defence or hunting campaigns, women's presence would be considered completely unnecessary. Furthermore, women during menses and childbirth have been regarded as unclean and liable to have a polluting effect. It is important to note that these beliefs have been prevalent among Adis, which is by far a relatively progressive community and one which gave women an important place in religious and cultural spheres (Nyori, 1989). The attitude towards women has been even more disparaging in some other tribal groups.

Some Traditional Perceptions about Women

As noted in Chapter 3, most Arunachal tribes do not permit women to own or inherit immovable property. Much worse, however, has been the general attitude towards women. Among the Nishings, the second largest community in the State, as noted in Chapter 4, when a man pays bride-price and marries a woman, he earns a claim over her body for sexual gratification, her life-long service and her procreative powers. Furthermore, when a Nishing husband dies, his widows are distributed among his brothers and sons without the formality of a marriage and the widows have no choice. Among the Wanchos of Tirap district, a wife's status depends on the number of children she produces. A husband is free to divorce a childless wife and re-marry (Dutta, 1987). Among the Daflas, it was customary to purchase slaves or procure wives by exchanging *Mithun* (tamed bison) in order to ensure more labour to produce sufficient food grains in a hilly terrain (Misra, 1982). Having more wives has been a sign of man's affluence and respectability.

Winds of Change

Against this traditional picture describing the situation of a majority of Arunachal Pradesh women, a number of important changes are already beginning to influence women's social and political status. With Indian Independence in 1947, a number of political and administrative measures, noted in Chapter 2, have been taken which are conducive to greater integration of Arunachal Pradesh in the Indian polity. The introduction of NEFA Panchayati Raj Regulation in 1967 and the awareness that women could vote for candidates of their choice, the first Lok Sabha election in 1977 and Legislative Assembly election in 1978 when women could not only vote but also become candidates for election — these were important landmarks in women's social and political awareness. The expansion of women's education has been another factor in helping women to break the shackles of age-old traditions. During the last two decades, i.e. between 1981 and 2001, female literacy in Arunachal Pradesh rose from 14.2 per cent to over 44 per cent. A few illustrations indicate the type of changes in women's social and political status.

An important development spear-headed by education is women's entry in employment in various fields such as education, health, community development, administrative services as well as business ventures and small trades, as noted in Chapter 3. With women's entry in employment outside the family, and the introduction of new representative political institutions such as the Panchayati Raj, Lok Sabha, Rajya Sabha and State Legislative Assembly, women are reported to be interested in elections. They relish the experience of being wooed by contestants and a small number has been elected in panchayats. Quite remarkably, one woman was elected to the Rajya Sabha and another woman has been a minister in State Government. Women's participation in business activities, politics, employment in government and private services and professions, even in small numbers, indicates their determination to overcome the obstacles which have traditionally denied them opportunities to enhance their social and political status.

Individual Revolts Against Oppressive Practices

There are significant indications that Arunachal women are beginning to question some traditional practices and customary ways which are grossly unjust for them. For instance, a number of girls who were married off in their infancy or early childhood by parents for a bride-price from the in-laws have been resisting their parents' and in-laws' pressures, without inviting any significant protests for repudiating marriages performed without their consent. Increasingly, such girls have refused to accept the verdict of traditional "Kebangs" pressurizing them to return to their husbands and in-laws. Significantly, whenever such cases are referred to District Magistrates, the civil law has supported the girl's individual right not to be forced into a marriage performed when she was too young to consent (Chowdhury, 1989). Similarly, marriages between persons belonging to different tribes, or between persons belonging to the same clan, which were considered invalid by customary laws, seem to have been accepted by the society particularly when the women involved enjoyed respectable social status and economic independence. Besides instances of individual repudiation of oppressive customs, some groups are also raising their voices.

Group Protests and Organized Resistance

The emergence of local groups and organizations which have been drawing their communities' attention to injustice perpetuated by some traditional practices is a very positive development. For instance, Yazali Girls Association in Subansiri region, joined by a local youth club have managed to secure the release of some girls forced into marriages by parents against their wishes due to betrothals performed when the girls were very young or because of financial obligations due to receiving bride-price from the groom's parents. The young people have at times used some novel methods like camping in the groom's village and refusing to budge until the groom and his parents released the girls (Misra, 1991). The Apatanis, a fairly advanced and educated community, have adopted a rule in the council of elders strictly prohibiting child marriages as well as marriages of girls against their wishes (Haimendorf, 1982). The Adis in Siang district have formed District Social Welfare and Cultural Society which has been trying to eliminate pernicious customs which harm women from their society.

Changing Parental Attitudes

Perhaps one of the significant factors in changing parental attitude to their daughters' education has been their daughters' sense of responsibility and loyalty towards parents. Young boys, on the other hand, have often tended to leave their ageing parents in penury and migrate to towns or to other States in search of a better life or a more lucrative job. Some parents are beginning to give a higher priority to girls' education, which is an important factor in improving women's status. Needless to say, expansion in girls' education is an important avenue not only in opening before them a variety of occupational options but also promoting responsible social attitudes. Some parents are beginning to give pieces of land to their daughters, instead of sharing their property only among sons. Among the Hill Miris of Subansiri, where some parents have allotted lands to their daughters, the latter have acquired sizeable property due to their industriousness and initiative and are unlikely to leave the question of selecting their partners to their parents (Chowdhury, 1989).

Women Protest Perpetuating Unjust Customs

It is evident that several traditional notions and practices and customary laws in Arunachal Pradesh have degraded women's position. In Chapter 4, many instances of seriously unfair customary laws relating to marriage, divorce and traditions with respect to the position of widows, and women in general have been cited. Against this background, when Arunachal Pradesh Assembly passed in 1994 Arunachal Pradesh (Protection of Customary Laws and Social Practices) Bill, women's groups in Arunachal along with some national women's organizations, raised their voice in protest, and expressed their misgivings. There is understandable fear that such a legal measure would tend to endorse and perpetuate undesirable customs like child marriage, polygyny and domestic slavery. It would be extremely important for women's organizations to undertake and present systematic documentation with respect to cases of ill-treatment and oppression of women in family and society (Rajalaxmi, *Frontline*, 1995).

Participation in Representative Political Institutions

We now look at one important measure of social and political status of women: their representation in national and State Legislatures and Panchayati Raj Institutions.

LOK SABHA AND RAJYA SABHA

Arunachal Pradesh has allocation of two seats in Lok Sabha and one seat in Rajya Sabha. Ever since the first Lok Sabha elections in Arunachal Pradesh in 1977, there has been no representation of women until the last election held in 1999. In the Rajya Sabha, however, one woman, Omem Deori, got elected in 1984. Between 1990 and 2002, there has been no woman contestant in the Rajya Sabha elections.

STATE LEGISLATIVE ASSEMBLY

Following separation from Assam and creation of the Union Territory of Arunachal Pradesh in 1972, and provision of a Legislative Assembly in 1975, general elections were held for the first time in 1978. Quite remarkably, two women contested during 1978-79, and one was elected. The Janata government decided to give representation to a woman from a minority group, the Singphos, who had passed seventh standard. In 1982-83, there were no women contestants. In the 1984-85 elections however, five women contested and two were elected (Nyari Welli and Komoli Mossang). In 1995 elections, four women contested but only one was elected.

WOMEN IN PANCHAYATI RAJ INSTITUTIONS

In 1967, Arunachal Pradesh government adopted Panchayati Raj Regulation with the object of bringing some uniformity in the divergent systems prevailing in different areas of the territory. Basically, this was a three-tier structure consisting of Gram Panchayats at village level, Anchal Samitis at block level and Zila Parishads at district level, with direct elections at Gram Panchayat and indirect ones at the remaining two levels. After the 73rd Constitutional Amendment was passed in 1992, Arunachal Pradesh Legislative Assembly adopted Panchayati Raj Ordinance in 1994, which was sent by the Governor of the State for President's assent, following which the State Legislative Assembly was to adopt Panchayati Raj Bill to replace the Ordinance.

It is at this stage that a stalemate had stopped further development. Arunachal Pradesh Ordinance did not include reservation of seats for SCs in proportion to their population. It may be noted that their population in the State is less than 1 per cent. A Constitutional Amendment Bill in 1999 has sought exemption from SC reservation, and when passed it will resolve the deadlock. Meanwhile, the panchayat institutions formed according to the old Panchayati Raj Ordinance of 1967 were given maximum extension by the Governor, but in September 1997 the State Government had to order their dissolution. The State Assembly adopted Arunachal Pradesh Panchayat Raj Bill on March 6, 1994 and ratified 73rd Amendment Act. Pending resolution of the stalemate caused by absence of reservation of seats for SCs, it is worthwhile to note the position of women elected to Panchayati Raj bodies at village, block and district level as of 1992, particularly when reservation for women was not

Panchayati Raj Institutions: Results of 1992 Elections

	Total no. of Bodies	*Total No. of Elected Members*	*SCs*	*STs*	*Women*
Gram Panchayats	2012	5733	0	5733	86 (15%)
Anchal Samitis	79	1205	0	1205	39 (3.20%)
Zilla Parishads	12	77	0	77	—

mandatory at that point. The percentage of women elected at Gram Panchayat level was 15, at Anchal Samiti level three and at Zila Parishad level zero (Talukdar, 2000).

As noted from the above table, the number of women elected at Gram Panchayats is small (15%). At the same time, it is significant, considering the odds against Arunachal women in view of the traditional ban against participation of women in village community councils in most tribes. Although small, the number of women elected at Anchal Samiti level is significant. It would be extremely interesting to note women's performance in elections after incorporation of the provision of reservation of one-third seats for women, particularly since they were reported to be enthusiastic about Panchayati Raj when the 1967 Regulation was adopted.

Arunachal Pradesh does not have municipal legislation or urban local bodies.

ASSAM

Women's Position During Ahom Period

While we are concerned primarily with Assamese women's present position, it may be useful to keep in mind the major ups and downs in their social and political status during Assam's better-known history since the Ahom period. We will refer briefly to some events and personalities which convey a great deal about women's position in Assam's chequered history. Mula Gabharu, the wife of Ahom army commander is known to have rushed to the battlefield with her five companions when her husband died while defending the Ahom kingdom against Muslim invasion in 1532. As she fought on horseback until death, she is believed to have impressed the enemy with her fighting skills. Examples of brave and intelligent women were noted among other communities too, e.g. Morans, Koches, Kacharis, etc. Sadhani, the wife of Chutia King Nitipal, who was known to be devoid of political acumen, guided her husband in state affairs and diplomacy, and when the Chutias were defeated in 1523, jumped with her family heirlooms from Chandangiri hill, preferring death to humiliation of defeat (Borah, 1992). Phuleswari, the wife of Ahom king Siva Singh (1714-44), for whom the astrologers had predicted a disastrous spell, accepted the reins of the kingdom from her husband, and left her mark as a talented and competent queen of a prosperous and benevolent kingdom. This glorious epoch, however, was followed by a dark period due to in-fighting and political intrigues to which Burmese invasions dealt the last blow in the first quarter of the nineteenth century. During this period, marked by death and destruction, Assamese women experienced a spate of rampant violence, insecurity and many restrictions on their freedom.

Impact of Social Reform Movement

Towards the end of the nineteenth century and early twentieth century, social reformers like Gunabhiram Barua, Anandram Dhekial Phukan, Hem Chandra Barua and others, as noted in Chapter 4, began to arouse social conscience against injustice to women, and tried to promote reforms like re-marriage of widows and abolition of child marriages. While some schools imparted elementary education to girls since the latter half of nineteenth century, the first quarter of the twentieth century saw a number of men and women, as well as Christian missionaries opening high schools and colleges for girls, as noted in Section II of Chapter 5 (Barooah, 1993).

Assamese Women Get Drawn into Independence Movement

When Mahatma Gandhi visited Assam in 1921, the ground was thus ready for a vigorous resurgence among women. When he noticed the extensive practice of handloom weaving among women, his spontaneous comment was "Every woman in Assam is a born weaver and she weaves fairy tales in cloth." Gandhiji's confidence in their ability, and the organization of 1926 Indian National Congress Session at Pandu had a magical effect in drawing Assamese women of diverse backgrounds and age groups towards various social causes. They cast aside their traditional inhibitions and initiated a number of political activities as well as "constructive" programmes — a classification popularized by Gandhiji to distinguish activities such as education, cottage industries, etc. from agitations, boycotts of foreign goods and the like. Assamese women began to form organizations to promote their various objectives. The Tezpur Mahila Samiti was formed in 1921 and adopted a formal constitution in

1928. Asom Mahila Samiti emerged under the presidentship of Chandraprova Saikiani in 1926 and began to issue cancellation notices in cases of child marriages. When Saikiani pulled down the bamboo curtain which separated women from men in Assam Sahitya Sabha (Assam Literary Association) in 1925, it was a symbolic act to remove restrictions on social participation of women (Barooah, 1993). In the Barak Valley, women's awakening resulted in the creation of Karimganj Mahila Sangh and Sylhet (which was a part of Assam before Partition) Mahila Sangh in 1930. Another significant development was the creation of women's department within the Indian National Congress for Assam in 1940, with Pushpalata Das and Amalprova Das as Joint Secretaries of the State unit. Many smaller women's organizations merged their activities with this women's unit of the Congress.

As noted before, women participated in a variety of programmes. Some educated and urban women gave a lead in organizational activities and succeeded in mobilizing a large number of rural and uneducated women in activities promoted by Gandhiji and Indian National Congress. Many women took part in processions and picketing of shops selling alcohol, opium and foreign goods. Some little known women in remote areas fought these battles singly, without the support of organizations. For instance, Mungri, a tea garden labourer near Tezpur became a martyr in the cause of boycotting liquor (a chronic evil among tea garden labourers) in 1921. Dariki Dasi from Golaghat was imprisoned while in an advanced stage of pregnancy, in an anti-opium demonstration and died in a jail hospital in 1932 (Sharma, Dipti, 1988). Birgashri, a Bodo woman who was revenue collector for the British administration, refused to collect revenues during Non-cooperation Movement and died while fighting British soldiers (Brahma, Kameshwar, 1989). A large number of women, both rural and urban, participated in promotion of literacy, spinning and weaving, creating awareness about freedom movement, training of women for rural health, mother and child care, etc. Several women joined the Satyagraha (non-violent non-cooperation) phase, as well as the Quit India movement in 1942 and faced police beating, firing, imprisonment and death. They belonged to different age groups, e.g. Kanaklata Baruah — a 16-year-old girl from Barangabari village in Sonitpur district — to Bhogeshwari Phukanani — a 60-year old woman, both of whom sacrificed their lives. There is a general feeling of disappointment among Assamese women that the great martyrdom of many women who died in police firing, or languished in prisons or were maimed due to police atrocities has not received due national recognition.

Post-Independence Period

A major political event involving a large number of women in post-Independence era was the Assam Movement during 1979-85, as noted in Chapter 2, which was directed at driving away immigrants from other States, and particularly Muslim immigrants from East Bengal, and later East Pakistan. A large number of Assamese women, particularly from middle-class participated in the movement. They would finish their household work in the morning and join processions and demonstrations to express their support. The agitation was fuelled by an apprehension that the continued inflow of immigrants from other countries and States would reduce the native Assamese to a minority. Since the basic human and economic issues got mixed with emotional ones, the movement is reported to have failed to achieve substantial results.

The disillusionment with the Assam Movement prompted some sections to adopt the radical path of ULFA, as noted in Chapter 2. During the second half of 1980s ULFA started building an organizational cadre, which included young women trained as nurses to function as couriers of secret messages and weapons among their branch units. Between 1991 and 1996, many of these women activists left the organization, probably quite disillusioned. However, a small number, which includes wives of ULFA office-bearers continue to operate from their hideouts in Bangladesh and Bhutan, as they cherish their dream of re-creating an autonomous Assam of the glorious Ahom period.

Women's Involvement in Social Causes

The establishment of women's organizations after Gandhiji's visit in 1921 and numerous subsequent programmes generated by the Independence movement, as noted earlier, gave a new social and political status to women. As new social needs emerged, some of these organizations modified their earlier programmes. Around the time of Partition of India, communal unrest and violence assumed serious proportions near the eastern border. Karimganj Mahila Sangh, under its able leader Matangini Das, organized "Suraksha Samitis" (defence committees) and trained women members to defend themselves mentally and physically during communal disturbances (Bhattacharjee, Manjulika, 1988). The post-Independence period gave rise to a new awareness of services needed for optimum development of women and children. Despite a huge expansion in Government-administered basic services, there are a number of gaps which create difficulties for women. Women's organizations have been trying to provide services to fulfil these unmet needs. For instance, Assam Pradeshik Mahila Samiti, a statewide organization having several branches, provides maternal and child health, pre-school and nutrition services for populations which are not covered by government services, besides vocational training, social education, family planning, etc. An organization started by Bodo women — Mahila Lakhi Bhandar — has set up a community grain bank which provides grains to families to tide over occasional shortages on a loan basis.

An important function of women's organizations has been to arouse social conscience whenever there are instances of violence or injustice against women. For instance, in late 1980s, tribal women in a little-known community were reported to be tortured by the police. Organizations of non-tribal women in Assam as well as other parts of India joined forces to raise their voice against this outrage in an emphatic manner. In Dhaman Salmari, women's organized resistance in a peasant struggle forced the police to withdraw (Borkataky, 1988). During the Assam Movement, there were reports of violence by State law enforcement agencies, e.g. rape of women in North Kamrup by Central Reserve Police (CRP) men, and police firing on peaceful student demonstrators. Women expressed their strong protest against these outrages through demonstrations, speeches, use of written media, etc. The fact that such instances continue to recur is a sad travesty of our democracy. At the same time, women's organizations need to devise more effective ways of preventing such episodes.

Women's Situation in Plains Tribal Groups

After noting some aspects of women's social status (a predominating majority of them belong to non-tribal groups), we will take examples of some tribal communities to highlight how women's status in other spheres influences their social as well as political status, and the factors which determine the outcome. The Bodos, a plains tribal community, have always given a respected position to women in the household in matters of family's economic sustenance, important events like birth, marriage, death, daily worship of household gods and goddesses, major agricultural events like initiation of sowing and harvesting etc. After the adoption of Brahma cult, women well-versed in sacred hymns are permitted to officiate as priests. Consequent to a new social awareness of their original culture among the Bodo community, Bodo women have established Mahila Samitis (women's groups) in many villages, which are actively involved in eliminating alcoholism among men (a deep-rooted social evil) while some women's groups have established cooperative arrangements to enhance profits from handloom weaving. Bodo women take active interest in Panchayat and State Assembly elections, and there is an instance of a Bodo woman becoming a State cabinet minister (Brahma, K., 1989). Bodo women have set up organizations like All Bodo Women's Welfare Federation and Bodo Women's Justice Forum.

Women from Mishing community — another plains tribal group — illustrate how their social status is linked to their position in other spheres. As noted in Chapters 3 and 4, Mishing women make a very substantial contribution towards household economy. They occupy an important place in the family as well as religion and major community festivals like "Porag" and "Bihu," both connected with earth's fertility and thanks-giving for annual harvest. But Mishing women have no place in the "Kebang" or "Mel" — community councils — which settle cases of disputes. Their meetings are attended by "Gaonbura" — the village chief, community elders (none of these positions can be occupied by women) and other men. Women have, however, found a way of conveying their views through larger community organizations to which they belong, e.g. Mishing Bane Kebang (All Mishing Conference) or Mishing literary organizations (Pegu, 1989). There is an important change in Mishing women's social and political status due to another recent development. Their heavy pre-occupation with household chores and economic activities had so far tended to deny them access to education. The percentage of literacy among Mishing women was less than eight by 1971. This is changing rapidly and girls' enrolment in schools and colleges has been rising steadily. As a result, more women are getting employment as teachers, as ministerial and administrative staff in government bureaucracies and a few occupy positions as doctors, engineers and officers in Assam Civil Service (Taid, 1989). Mishing women now participate in tribal development programmes, and Panchayat affairs. Women from Sonowal Kachari tribe, like Mishing women, are making rapid advances through entering new occupational avenues. They are emerging as entrepreneurs in running pig farms, poultry units, knitting and sewing centres, weaving units, etc. besides taking up professional careers as doctors, bank officers, teachers, etc. A Sonowal Kachari woman has won the election to State Legislative Assembly (Mitra, 1989). A significant development related to their improved educational and social status reflects a new outlook — Sonowal Kachari girls are beginning to inherit a share in their father's property. This community, prior to adopting Vaishnavism, had accorded equal status to women in terms of inheriting property. With the new reforms introduced after expansion of education and new awareness, there is a new and powerful trend to eliminate discrimination and injustice for women.

Women's Situation in Hill Tribal Groups

In comparison, the change in women's status in Hill Tribal communities is slower due to their physical and social isolation. A Karbi woman, for instance, carries the whole burden of running the household and a major share of family cultivation, which in the context of meagre food resources, turns out to be a very arduous task. As noted in Chapters 3 and 4, she has no right of inheritance in father's property. She has no place in the worship of "Hemphu" — the deity of agriculture, nor in "Ronkar" — the ceremony to ensure well-being of their community. A woman whose husband is a tribal chief or village headman has a higher social status than a common woman who might be a government officer. She has no place in the District Council, nor can she hold any office such as a village priest or a headman.

Although the Karbis continue their old social and family traditions, some change, even if slow, is taking place as a result of contacts with other communities, spread of education and creation of new government programmes and political institutions. Karbi women in the plains who are exposed to contacts with other communities, have adopted the worship of Hindu gods and goddesses and perform religious rituals if they are knowledgeable, something which their original tribal faith did not allow. By the end of 1980s, three Karbi women were executive magistrates and one was appointed as a Block Development Officer. In comparison with Karbi women, Dimasa women from the adjacent North Cachar district continue to suffer from a lower social status, at least some of which can be attributed to Dimasa women's own conservatism. They have so far been defenders, probably unwittingly, of a pollution-purity code (Gusu-g-thar) imposed on their society by non-Dimasa preceptors, and have been acting as law-enforcing agents. They have thus failed to benefit fully from interactions with neighbouring communities, which could bring about progressive changes in their social status (Thaosen, 1989).

Representation in Lok Sabha, Rajya Sabha and State Legislative Assembly

LOK SABHA

Six women from Assam contested the first Lok Sabha election in 1952 and Bonily Khongmen was the only woman elected. In the next five elections, i.e. during 1957-77 out of 12 women who contested, eight were elected, some of them more than once. Many of them were educated, e.g. Jyotsna Chanda, Bonily Khongmen and Renuka Devi Borkataki, and most were connected with women's organizations or other community groups or political parties. Bonily Khongmen, one of the early women graduates, born in Jowai and married to Khongmen (a Khasi) served as Vice-President of Khasi-Jaintia National Conference and was member of the Advisory Council of Khasi-Jaintia Hills and Mikir Hills (former name of Karbi Anglong). Rani Manjula Devi, wife of Raja of Sidh, was president of Assam Pradeshik Mahila Samiti. Renuka Devi Borkataki was General Secretary of Guahati District Moina Parijat, while Jyotsna Chanda, who was elected three times to the Lok Sabha, was Chairman of Silchar School Board and a member of Advisory Board on Women's Education. Mofida Ahmed from Jorhat was convenor of Women's wing of the Congress at Golaghat and Assistant Secretary, Tezpur District Mahila Samiti. A few of these women (e.g. Jyotsna Chanda, Renuka Devi Borkataki) were elected to the State Legislative Assembly prior to their Lok Sabha election (Satyanarayan Rao, 1996).

The major part of 1980s was disrupted due to Assam agitation, because of which elections covering the whole state could not be held, and in the 1985 elections, only one woman contested but was not successful. In the 1991 and 1996 elections, eight women contested each time but none was elected. Three women contested in 1998 elections and Ranee Narah was the only woman elected. In the last, i.e. 1999 elections, out of nine women who contested, Ranee Nara was re-elected and Bijoya Chakravarty, a student activist and lecturer, was also elected.

RAJYA SABHA

Assam has been allotted seven seats in Rajya Sabha. On the whole, representation of women has been very low so far. The 1986 Rajya Sabha which included 28 women members from the whole country, included one woman from Assam, Bijoya Chakravarty, who was later elected to the Lok Sabha, as noted earlier. During the 1990s only two women (Basanti Sharma and Jayasree Goswami Mahanta) were elected to the Rajya Sabha from Assam.

ASSAM STATE LEGISLATIVE ASSEMBLY

In the first Legislative Assembly election in 1952 out of six women contestants, two were elected (Jyotsna Chanda and U. Borthakur). In the next four elections in 1957, 1962, 1967 and 1972, out of 10, 4, 9 and 12 contestants, 5, 4, 5 and 8 women, respectively were elected. In 1957 election, the two women winners from 1952 election were re-elected besides three new candidates. In the 1978 elections, out of 20 women candidates, only one, Syeda Anwara Taimur, was elected as Congress (Indira) nominee, despite the Janata party wave at the Centre. Quite significantly, during 1978–82, four chief ministers ruled the State, and A. Taimur also occupied the chief minister's seat for six months. Following a period of violent disturbances and political unrest during which proper elections could not be held, the 1985 elections were conducted when normalcy had returned. Twenty-nine women contestants were in the fray in this election and five were elected. The number of women contestants which had remained between four and 20 during 1952 and 1978 elections, seems to be rising since 1985. In comparison the number of men contestants which varied between 202 and 918 during the same period, women candidates still continue to be a small minority. In 1996 Legislative Assembly elections, out of 45 contestants six were elected. In the 2001 elections, nine women were elected, which is perhaps the highest so far.

Panchayati Raj Institutions

It would be useful to review briefly the important points in the evolution of the present Panchayati Raj system in Assam. The first legislation, Assam Rural Panchayat Act of 1948, which introduced a two-tier structure — village and revenue *mouza* (a cluster of villages constituting a revenue collection unit) — was followed by 1959 version based on three tiers: Gaon Panchayat, Anchalik Panchayat and Mahkuma Parishad. This was replaced by another Act in 1972 reverting to two-tier system, and substituted by 1986 Assam Panchayati Raj Act, which replaced the three tiers. Elections were held in 1992 under provisions of the 1986 Act, which provided 30 per cent reservation of seats for women at each of the three levels. The 1992 Panchayat elections were held after 13 years' gap, and the results were as follows:

Panchayat Elections, 1992

	Total No.	*Elected Members Total*	*SCs*	*STs*	*Women Members (Percentage to Total No.)*
Gaon Panchayats	2489	24860	-	-	7458 (30%)
Anchalik Panchayats	196	2486	-	-	745 (29.97%)
Mahkuma Parishads	21	-	-	-	

Source : Mathew, George (ed.), Institute of Social Sciences, *Status of Panchayati Raj in the States of India*, New Delhi, Concept Publishing, 2000.

After adoption of 73rd Constitutional Amendment, 1986 Act was amended and 1994 Assam Panchayat Act incorporated the needed changes, e.g. replacement of Mahkuma Parishads by Zila Parishads and reservation of one-third seats for women in addition to one-third Chair person's positions, besides reservation of seats for SCs and STs proportionate to their share in the total population. The task of demarcating the boundaries of constituencies necessitated by adoption of Zila Parishads to replace Mahkuma Parishads has been considerably delayed, as a result of which elections were postponed for a long time. Meanwhile the existing panchayat institutions were dissolved in 1997. Here are some results of 2001 elections: Out of 378 members of Zila Parishads, 131 were women, i.e. 34.6 per cent; Anchalik Parishad members: total number 1959, women members 570, i.e. 34.3 per cent; Gram Panchayat Presidents, total number 1930, women 567, i.e. 34 per cent. The available information is incomplete and does not include total number of institutions at each of the three levels, the number of presidents of Zila Parishads and Anchalik Samitis and women in each category, and the total number of elected members of Gram Panchayats. However, there is no doubt that the statutory requirement of one-third seats for women is met.

Despite several gaps in available information on Assam's Panchayat elections of 2001, the indications that one-third of total seats are reserved for women at Zila and Anchalik Panchayats is a notable development. Considering the formidable odds against women in getting a foot-hold in panchayat bodies, it would be important to study women's participation in some detail. A sample study in Nalbari district conducted by Omeo Kumar Das Institute of Social Change and Development, Guwahati (Goswami and Sharma, 1995) has come up with interesting findings. The absence of decentralization of authority and funds at Gram Panchayat level and concentration of power at the Block office, as well as ignorance and lack of training of elected women members have been found to be major obstacles in the effective functioning of elected women members.

Urban Local Bodies

After adoption of 74th Constitutional Amendment, an amended act, Assam Municipal Act was passed in 1994. Elections to 24 municipal boards and 38 town committees were held in June 1997, after a gap of 16 years. A circular dated 15 May 1997, addressed to concerned officials by Municipal Administration Department indicated the wards in 62 towns included in the June elections, to be reserved for women candidates of general category, SCs, STs and women of SCs and STs. Out of 545 members which were to be elected, 212 constituting more than one-third, were earmarked to be women. While the statutory requirement was thus fully met, there has been criticism about the quality of women candidates elected. Evidently, their performance was found to be not satisfactory, which suggested that vigorous efforts will be required to provide adequate training for elected women, besides administrative support from Municipal Administration Department. The Assam Act empowers State Government to nominate persons with expertise as members of municipal bodies. Furthermore, a 1997 amendment enables State Government to nominate women and SCs, if they are not adequately represented. Data on women elected to Guwahati Municipal Corporation are not available, although it is noteworthy that this body has so far elected women mayors twice.

Autonomous District Councils

As per provisions of the Sixth Schedule of the Constitution tribal areas of Assam are exempted from the coverage of 73rd and 74th Amendments, as noted earlier. It is reported that four seats are reserved for women in both autonomous district councils, viz. Karbi Anglong and North Cachar Hills. Unfortunately neither individual women contestants nor political parties seem to be interested in utilizing the seats. There is one instance when Autonomous State Demand Committee (ASDC) supported the election of one lady in Karbi Anglong District Council, but even the provision for nominating women has not found any takers, according to an official of the council. Complete information was not however available, despite requests.

Besides North Cachar Hills and Karbi Anglong districts, several tribal communities in other districts of Assam have formed regional or village councils. For instance, hill tribes living in 515 villages in Cachar, Karimganj and Hailakandi districts formed Barak Valley (Hill Tribes) Development Council with the objective of promoting economic, social, educational and cultural progress of hill tribal people residing in these districts. Assam government has constituted 44 Lalung village councils covering 425 villages in Marigaon, Nagaon and Kamrup districts in 1996. Mishing Autonomous Council covers 1200 villages organized under 177 village councils with a population of 40 lakh. The Rabhas too, spread over 885 villages are covered under 44 village councils including 3 lakh population. It is significant that Lalung Autonomous Council has demanded end of Panchayati Raj administration on the basis of an agreement Lalungs concluded with Assam Government. In 2003, the Bodo Liberation Tigers, Assam State Government and Central Government concluded an agreement regarding Bodo Autonomous Council which will include 40 members. In view of the exemption of tribal areas from the purview of 73rd Amendment, the question is whether women will find representation in these tribal councils.

MANIPUR

The following analysis of the social and political status of Manipuri women deals mainly with Meiteis who constitute nearly two-thirds of the total State population. References to women from some Naga and Kuki-Chin and other communities like the Pangans are also included for illustrative purposes.

Self-Help Associations Meet Various Needs

Meitei women are members of several friendly associations or "Marups" or clubs which meet their needs of companionship as well as social solidarity. Some of these groups are of the "Chit-fund" type where women pay a monthly membership fee and draw lots in turn to receive a lumpsum which may come handy for meeting some family need, e.g. buying utencils or daughter's wedding purchases and the like. A reference has been made in Chapter 3 to groups of women following the same occupation, like handloom weaving or trading in local markets, where bulk purchases and credit needs of members can be met. Some of these groups also meet their other needs, such as tea and snacks during working hours. Membership of various types of groups helps to give Meitei women some economic security and enhances their social status. As noted earlier, Manipuri market women's group solidarity has helped them in the past in exerting effective pressure on local administration not to force them to vacate their market space until adequate alternative accommodation was assured.

Women Assert Right of Artistic Expression

Manipur, among N-E States, enjoys a rather unique place due to the excellence achieved by women in dancing and music, thanks to the strong patronage and artistic contributions received during Maharaja Bhagyachandra's reign in the latter half of eighteenth century. A reference has been made in Chapter 4 in the context of religious participation, indicating how Manipuri women persistently struggled to regain their freedom to present dance, music and theatrical performances, including use of cymbals, before mixed audiences in Radha-Govinda temples. At present groups of women meet for rehearsals and sometimes travel to other towns for dramatic performances, and may even earn some money. They meet the expenses of refreshments and travel out of their own earnings, and apart from the creative satisfaction, get a chance to forget their domestic troubles for a while (Chaki Sarkar, 1984).

How Women Mobilize Community Contributions

While Meitei women do not own or inherit immovable property, nor have the right to make important family decisions, their substantial contribution to family sustenance gives them some autonomy to participate in health, nutrition and child welfare programmes implemented by State Government, sometimes with support from outside organizations such as UNICEF. The author had the privilege of collaborating with groups of rural women who were provided modest UNICEF grants for constructing community centres, on the condition of matching local contributions. Thanks to the initiative and organizational leadership provided by a Manipuri woman official, Pramodini Devi, local women's groups mobilized substantial donations in the form of free land, building materials, skilled and unskilled labour for construction. In a majority of cases, local women managed to involve whole-hearted participation of local men with the result that the community centres provided accommodation and facilities far beyond venues for women's activities. Some of them provided additional accommodation for a *balwadi* (kindergarten) for children, a room for local young men's band and space for a weaving centre or adult education classes. Besides, the centre could be used for larger community functions on very modest rent. These community centres thus provided women an opportunity for learning to involve the whole community in resolving conflicts over location and eliciting their cooperation, besides enhancing their social status.

Protests Against Injustice

An interesting feature of Manipuri women's social status is their ability to organize themselves to voice their protest about events, government policies or social problems. The first *Nupi-lan* (women's movement) goes back to 1904, almost 100 years back, when a British Political Officer had demanded compulsory labour from Manipuri men to rebuild the house of an assistant which was damaged by some unruly elements. This action sparked a powerful outburst among Manipuri women, which forced the officer to withdraw his order. The second *Nupi-lan* in 1939, was precipitated by the British administration's policy to export rice from Manipur at a time when local population faced acute shortages. Manipuri women, led by a small number of urban educated women, sent a representation to the Maharaja expressing their resentment. When they lay down before trucks carrying rice for Marwari traders who showed utter insensitivity to local shortages, the Maharaja was forced to stop the export of rice (Bimala Devi, 1988). Perhaps this uncommon ability among Manipuri women to raise their voice against perceived injustice might have its roots in the old tradition of women's courts which were presided over by the ruling king's mother during the period when monarchy was strong. Cases of wife beating, adultery, divorce, etc. were brought before such courts, and where men in authority were believed to have failed in doing justice to the women concerned, it was customary for older women to lodge a joint protest with the king against the men concerned (Chaki Sircar, 1984).

Fighting Social Evils

Manipuri women have formed groups like "Mairapaigi" — meaning torch-bearers — which organize protests against socially harmful practices and outrages such as rape by security forces personnel. A remarkable aspect of Manipuri women's expression of concern over undesirable events or social trends is the uncommon and forceful manner in which they express their determination to deal with the same. During the 1970s, they expressed their resolve to curb the disturbing menace of alcoholism and drug addiction, especially among the youth. So they formed groups at many places in the state and kept night vigil on streets to catch men found in an inebriated condition or under the influence of narcotics. In some villages, women destroyed club houses which in fact had become gambling dens enticing young men with alcoholic drinks and narcotic substances. These women were so determined that they even held some adolescents captive in camps for 8-10 days and put them through a rigorous daily routine of physical exercises and moral instruction. One may question the efficacy of their treatment methods, but their sincerity and determination to salvage these youngsters were beyond doubt.

Participation in Struggle for Responsible Government

As far as participation in matters with direct political significance, urban educated Manipuri women seem to have taken the lead, particularly since 1940s onwards. They formed an organization called Mahila Sammelini under the guidance of H. Irawat Singh. During the period when the struggle for Indian Independence was entering a crucial phase, many women joined Manipur Congress. In the post-Independence period during which Manipur became a Part C State and later a Union Territory with a Territorial Council, Manipuri women took active part in the movement for responsible government. The Territorial Council was elevated in 1963 to Territorial Assembly to be constituted by elected representatives. Meanwhile, from 1960 onwards Manipuri women, especially urban educated women, took active part in the movement for demanding a responsible movement, as noted in Chapter 2, and participated in the popular agitation, which later culminated in Manipur attaining full statehood in 1972.

Women from Some Tribal Communities

After this review of the situation of Meitei women, we will now focus our attention on some of the tribal communities who occupy the hill areas surrounding the central valley. The advent of Christianity, and along with it introduction of education seem to have helped women from some of these communities to make a break with several discriminatory old traditions. The changes, however, are not uniform and besides Christianity, some other variables seem to have played their part, as will be noted from the following observations.

The Moyons, who inhabit the foothills near the State's south-eastern border have, until early 1900s, denied women the right to participate in several religious and social events because women were believed to have no permanent clan affiliation. They could not perform the customary ceremonies at village festivals, nor could they participate in village councils. The traditional division of roles prescribed that it was women's duty to do all the back-breaking cultivation chores besides every household task, while men had to be spared from discomfort and were expected to be revered. After the entry of American Baptist Mission in 1910 and Roman Catholic religion in 1956, Moyons adopted Christianity and along with it education. Moyon women avidly used these opportunities to make a break with the past traditions in the face of stiff resistence and even punishments. They became preachers and teachers in schools, and soon started their own organizations to promote social and economic development of Moyon society. They also joined the crusade against alcoholism, drug addiction, and other social problems. While women still suffer from sex discrimination in many respects such as right to inherit property, they have initiated a process of change in their status (Sangkham, 1988).

The Taraos, a tribe settled in Chandel district, has so far treated their women as vastly inferior to men. For instance, women's mere touch was believed to have a polluting effect in religious rituals. Although women worked equally hard in cultivation along with men, and took care of all household tasks, besides weaving, embroidery, etc. they were not allowed to engage themselves in any trade or business. They were strictly excluded from matters related to village administration. Conversion to Christianity has enabled Tarao women to break away from many traditions, such as compulsion to marry their father's sister's sons. The access to education has eliminated some of the occupational barriers for women. They can now take up trading in various articles, including woven materials, or set up small units for knitting, embroidery, basketry, tailoring, etc. Women's enhanced economic status, due to diversification in occupations has positively influenced their social status, as evident from their presence in village meetings, even though as spectators. While women are still far from getting an equal status, they have managed to obtain some space for themselves (Bokul Singh, 1988).

The Rongmei, a Naga community which produced the legendary Rani Gaidinlieu who led the Zeliangrong movement to challenge the mighty British in 1930s (as noted in Chapter 2) had initially resented the proselytizing activities of Christian missionaries. Ironically, however, the introduction of Christianity and modern education has initiated important improvements in the status of Rongmei women. While older Rongmei women continue to view men as inherently superior and regard more freedom for women as dangerous, younger and educated women strongly resent their subordinate social status. With better educational opportunities, some Rongmei women are entering professional careers as teachers, doctors, government officers, etc. and some are making their mark in business enterprises. While Rongmei women still cannot attend meetings of village councils, they manage to convey their views through their own associations. They can express their resentment against polygyny and can exercise greater influence in limiting the size of their families. The days of unquestioning obedience towards men are fast being replaced by women beginning to expect men to treat them as social partners (Gailangam, 1988).

For the Hmars, who occupy a part of Churachandpur district, the struggle for existence is tough and educational facilities inadequate. Although they adopted Christianity quite a while ago, women continue to suffer from rank discrimination. Parents give a low priority to girls' education and are unwilling to spare their time, normally used for household chores and cultivation, to attend schools. Even girls have such low self-esteem that they want their parents to give preference to their brothers' schooling. A married Hmar woman has no right over family property, nor even over her own children. If her husband dies, she cannot claim maintenance from his family. Hmar women's low family status and economic insecurity affect their social status as well. For instance, while a widower's re-marriage is celebrated with great pomp, a widow who wishes to re-marry faces social disapproval, even from women. In cases of adultery, the woman involved is punished severely, while the adulterous man gets away lightly (Lalremasang Hmar, 1988).

Manipuri Muslim Women

We now look at the situation in a non-tribal community, viz. the Pangans, or Manipuri Muslims. While Pangan women's status is low, they seem to have benefited to some extent from their Meitei origins. As noted in Chapter 2, Pangans emerged as a community due to unions of Muslim soldiers with Meitei women. Manipuri Muslim women are free from the customs of *purdah* (seclusion) and *burkha* (veiling of the face), the only exception being the wives of *maulawis* (religious teachers). They are active in agricultural work, rice-husking, weaving, rearing poultry, petty vending and trading. Their one basic handicap is their low level of education, as compared to Meitei and tribal women. Only a small minority of Manipuri Muslim women have acquired high school or college education, and hold professional jobs. These educated women are currently providing leadership for promoting Muslim women's education and social participation. Quite notably, some Pangan women joined movements like *nisha-bandh* (ban on alcoholism), and some are taking interest in Panchayat elections (Khanam, 1988).

Manipuri Womens Participation in Representative Bodies

LOK SABHA AND RAJYA SABHA

Excepting 1984 when one woman contested for Lok Sabha, until 1991 there have been no women contestants. In 1996 out of three women candidates no one was elected. In 1998, however, one woman contested from Outer Manipur constituency (which is reserved for STs) and won the election (Kim Gangte). Two women contested in the 1999 election but none was elected. Representation of Manipuri Women in Rajya Sabha has been nil so far.

STATE LEGISLATIVE ASSEMBLY

Prior to Manipur attaining full statehood in 1972, during 1957-67, when Manipur was a Union Territory, initially with a Territorial Council and later a Territorial Assembly, some women were nominated by the government as members. These included R. K. Mukhara, Akim Angnal, Lhingjaneng Gangte, Shiningla and A. Bimola Devi. The practice of nomination was discontinued when Manipur achieved statehood (Bimola Devi, 1988). Between 1970-83, 13 women contested for the Assembly seats but no one was successful. Up to the end of 1980s the only woman who was elected was Maharaj Kumari Binodini Devi. In 1990, out of five women who contested only one, Hangmila Shaiza, a Tangkhul lady won the election. A record number of 11 women contested the 1995 election but none was successful.

DISTRICT AND LOCAL BODIES: WOMEN'S REPRESENTATION

Two different systems of local administration at District level and below operate in the four valley districts, i.e. Imphal East, Imphal West, Bishnupur and Thoubal, and five hill districts, viz. Chandel, Churachandpur, Senapati, Tamenglong and Ukhrul.

VALLEY DISTRICTS: PANCHAYATI RAJ IN RURAL AREAS

Manipur Panchayati Raj Act, 1975 was adopted after Manipur attained statehood, although Panchayati Raj system was operational even prior to that in the valley districts. The five hill districts, however, were governed by the 1956 Manipur (Village Authorities in Hill Areas) Act. The 1975 Panchayat Act provided for a three-tier system: (i) Gram Sabhas for every 3000 population, with elected Gram Panchayats; (ii) Panchayat Samitis at block level consisting of *Pradhans* of Gram Panchayats; (iii) Zilla Parishads at district level constituted by presidents of all Panchayat Samitis. Significantly, each Panchayat Samiti and Zilla Parishad was to include two women, and one representative each of SCs and STs, to be nominated by State Government if not already elected. Nomination of women on panchayat bodies marked a significant development for women.

After adoption of 73rd Amendment, a new Manipur Panchayat Raj Act was passed by State Legislature on 23 April 1994 and an amendment in 1996 which incorporated a two-tier structure: Gram Panchayats and Zilla Parishads, which included provision for one-third seats to be reserved for women and increased the authority of popularly elected presidents of Zilla Parishads in planning and implementation of development schemes. The situation with respect to women elected in 1997 was as follows:

Total no. of Bodies	*Total No. elected persons*	*SCs elected*	*STs elected*	*Women elected*
3 Zilla Parishads	61	1	2	22 (36.02%)
166 Gram Panchayats	1.556	35	44	576 (37.02%)

Furthermore 55 seats of Pradhans of Gram Panchayats were held by women members (Mathew, 2000)

URBAN LOCAL BODIES

Within the provisions of the Fifth Schedule of the Constitution, Manipur Municipalities Act of 1994 provided for Municipal Councils and Nagar Panchayats to be constituted by the directly elected councillors, in addition to those appointed by the State Government on the basis of special competence in municipal administration. This act provides for reservation of seats for SCs and STs in proportion to their population and one-third seats for women (Singh, U.B. 1999).

HILL DISTRICTS: DISTRICT AND VILLAGE COUNCILS

The five hill districts of Manipur (Chandel, Churachandpur, Senapati, Tamenglong and Ukhrul) were excluded from the purview of 73rd Constitutional Amendment. The 1956 Manipur (Village Authorities in Hill Areas) Act provided for Village Authorities, similar to village Panchayats in valley districts. A later development was the Manipur (Hill Areas) District Council Act of 1971 (Act No.76) which provided for District and Village Councils with functions analogous to those under the Sixth Schedule (which covers hill areas of Assam, Meghalaya and Mizoram) except for a few differences. These councils do not have the authority to decide on matters related to the appointment and succession of chiefs, practices pertaining to marriage, divorce, inheritance and social customs.

As noted in Chapter 4, women in Manipur's tribal communities traditionally have never been permitted to be members of community or village councils or councils of elders, which are presided over by the chief or headman. Even where these councils are involved in deciding on matters in which women are directly involved, the women are represented by men of the family or clan elders. With the introduction of Christianity, which in 1991 covered between 83 and 97 per cent of the population of the five hill districts of Manipur, there has been some liberalization of the tribal traditions. The spread of education, accompanied by women's entry into new occupations and professional jobs have also helped to enhance women's social status. Besides, women from many tribal communities have formed their own associations through which they may try to voice their opinions or try to influence the village elders (Gailangam, 1988). For instance, although Tangkhul women cannot participate in *Tangkhul*

Long meetings, they have formed counterpart conclaves like *Tangkhul Shanao Long* through which they express their views on social and political matters.

While tribal women do not find a place in District Councils, women from some communities such as the Tangkhul are beginning to participate in election campaigns of men members of their choice and organize meetings and collect funds for supporting their election (Tikoo, 2000). Although the State Government has prescribed two reserved seats for women in village councils, the nominated women are more like observers in meetings presided over by the "Awunga" or the Tangkhul Chief (Philangam Ngakang, 1991). Women from Rongmei and Tangkhul groups, who are relatively more progressive, still suffer from traditional restrictions on participation in social and political affairs. The situation in some other tribal communities like the Tarao in Chandel district is understandably much worse. An accidental encounter with a Tarao woman by a men's hunting party is regarded as bad luck. Tarao men are not supposed to touch meat of animals killed by women (Bokul Singh, 1988). Is it any wonder then that Tarao women have no place in village affairs?

MEGHALAYA

Traditional Position

Women of Meghalaya have traditionally been denied entry to village or State Councils or "Durbars," which were open only to "Men with moustaches," meaning mature men. Women were clubbed with children and drunkards as unfit to participate, because such gatherings dealt with matters of warfare with other tribes, violation of rules of the community, disciplinary action against offenders, etc. Evidently, women were not trusted to maintain the requisite decorum and restraint. Women even at present cannot be *Syiems*, *Dolois* or *Nokmas* (Chiefs), *Sirdars* or village headmen, nor can they participate in the election of these officials. The typically contemptuous social attitude towards women who venture to dabble with social or political affairs is reflected in the local proverb : "If the hen crows, the world, including the family, has changed for the worse" (Syiem, 1992).

Historical accounts and folklore of Meghalaya mention the names like Ka Piang Sariang and Queen Latimpong, who were rulers of Jaintia states. Another woman, Ka Lar, was reported to be the Syiem of

Nobosohphah state (Syiem, 1992). Regardless of these exceptions, there has been a general belief that whenever women tried to meddle with political affairs, bad times were in store for the community (Gassah, 1992).

Women's position in traditional religion conveys their social position. For instance, in Khasi-Jaintia religion, woman's main function towards god was to procreate and multiply the clan, and she was viewed as a symbol of virtue and purity (Kynpham Singh, 1980). In actual practice, as noted in Chapter 4, women were responsible for procuring all necessary materials, like special foods, rice-beer, sacrificial animals, etc. Men alone could perform sacrifices and all rituals. Even the "Syiem Sad" (state priestess), who was generally the Syiem's sister or niece, or the woman priestess among the Jaintias, was to assist the Syiem or the Langdoh (religious leader), who alone could perform the rituals. Among the Garos, women's position in religion is even more marginalized. The priests are always men, while women undertake all the preparatory and strenuous chores like fetching water, providing rice-beer at religious ceremonies and the like. They sing dirges and collect bones at cremations (Marak, 1992).

Already Heavy Family Chores

On the one hand, the matrilineal system which enables women to inherit family property including the house from their mothers, and the sons-in-law who join their wives' household after marriage and references to women like "Ka Blei Ing" (goddess of the house) convey an image of Meghalaya women as strong and powerful. It is therefore somewhat puzzling that these same women accepted their complete exclusion from administration and political spheres. This paradox can be explained when one looks at the diverse and demanding responsibilities women must carry for the household. As noted before in Chapter 3 and 4, women are heavily burdened with daily household chores and work in family fields, besides the various income-generating activities like trading in agricultural products, bamboo crafts, vending liquor, selling dry fish, and many others with which they earn a substantial part of family's economic sustenance. In addition to their involvement in family events like child births and community festivals, they are mainly responsible for care and education of children. Even in families where women hold full-time outside jobs, they continue to take the full burden of child care, and if husbands try to help with menial tasks like sweeping the floors or looking after children, many women feel quite embarrassed, not to mention disparaging remarks of neighbours.

Contribution of Christianity and Education to Social Status

Two major factors which are responsible for many changes in the traditional scenario are the adoption of Christianity and introduction of women's education since the middle of nineteenth century. While the traditional Khasi-Jaintia and Garo religions gave women a special place within the clan, as we have noted earlier, it was mostly related to woman's procreative powers which were essential for continuation and multiplication of the clans and tribes, and women were assigned roles which were mostly secondary in relation to men's position. Although women lost the somewhat glorified past image, Christianity gave them an opportunity to participate in church services on an equal footing with men. Even more importantly, Christian missionaries actively promoted girls' education, and a few of these girls went outside the state to acquire higher education. Some of these women, on their return became head-mistresses of schools and colleges for girls, and a few others occupied high positions in different professions and social life. Expanding opportunities for higher education and new employment avenues have provided socially prestigious jobs for women as teachers, doctors, architects, magistrates, etc. and some women have joined State and Central civil service. Although the number of Garo women employed in professions is smaller than that among the Khasi-Jaintias, they are successfully running small and medium-sized businesses, e.g. construction, cutting and collecting timber, handloom weaving, etc. (Marak, 1992). The emergence of Shillong as the capital of composite Assam State initially, and later of Meghalaya, facilitated its growth as an important trading centre where women dominate a variety of small, medium and large businesses and trades. (Sen, Saha and Mukherjee, 1982). The point to note is the substantial contribution of women towards family income, which enhances their social status.

A notable result of adoption of Christianity has been the opportunities it provided to women for promoting a wide variety of educational and social organizations under the sponsorship of Christian missions. Meghalaya women today are actively participating in educational institutions, and a large number of social service organizations for the needy, handicapped and destitute individuals. Garo Mothers' Union, which completed 60 years of existence, has been operating three educational institutions for girls, besides its activities in creating public awareness regarding pernicious social customs. For instance, they have been raising their voice against traditional practices like *Akim* (replacement of a deceased marriage partner by his/her relative regardless of the latter's age and wishes — see Chapter 4 for details) and *Dokchapa* (daughter of a widow, being promised to a man married to the widow as per the rule of *Akim* — see Chapter 4 for details). Women are also active in drawing public attention to the large number of cases where husbands indulge in polygyny without getting divorce from previous wife and refuse to pay alimony.

Implications of Current Trends for Women's Status

A large number of factors are responsible for changes and disruptions in traditional family and social practices in Meghalaya. For instance, joint families are being replaced by nuclear families when husbands or wives have to shift to urban areas or to other States due to employment. Maternal kins' support is no longer available to women to the same extent as before, and they have to assume greater responsibility for their own families. Contacts with other communities, most of which may be patrilineal and more patriarchal, tend to raise doubts and questions regarding traditional definitions of roles in Meghalaya families. Such issues acquire new complexion when Meghalaya women marry men from other States, because questions of ownership of property and preservation of indigenous culture tend to arouse public passions thereby giving the incidents wider social and political significance. A reference has been made in Chapter 3 to the emergence of a group of individuals who hold matrilineal system of Meghalaya mainly responsible for economic backwardness of the State and for lack of initiative and enterprising spirit among men. They propose adoption of patriliny as a remedy. If Meghalaya women wish to enhance their social and political status, they need to develop attitudes and strategies which will promote well-being of the whole society and minimize conflict between the sexes.

Women's Entry into Politics

Indian Independence and the preceding freedom movement provided Meghalaya women an opportunity to make a break with the traditional ban on women's participation in political sphere. It is interesting to note that some Meghalaya women who were educated participated in representative national and State political bodies. Mavis Dunn Lingdoh was a member of the Sadulla government of composite Assam and served as Minister of Health Services from 1939-46. As noted in the context of Assam, Bonily Khongmen, born at Jowai in 1912, was elected as a member of the first Lok Sabha in 1952, prior to which she too was a member of Assam Legislative Assembly and Deputy Speaker. During 1946-52 she was Vice-President of Khasi-Jaintia National Conference, and a member of Advisory Council of Khasi and Jaintia Hills and Mikir Hills, i.e. present Karbi Anglong (Satyanarayan Rao, 1996). It is reported that some Meghalaya women participated in the movement demanding a separate hill State and for secession from the composite Assam.

Women's Participation in Representative Political Bodies

We will now look at women's participation in Lok Sabha, Rajya Sabha and State Legislative Assembly since 1972 when Meghalaya attained statehood. Under the provisions of Sixth Schedule, Meghalaya has constituted three Autonomous District Councils: Khasi Hills, Jaintia Hills and Garo Hills. Urban areas of Meghalaya are governed by two types of administration. Shillong and Tura have municipal administration provided under 1956 Assam Municipal Act which was adopted by Meghalaya. Other urban areas, e.g. town committees of Nongstoin and Jowai, are governed by respective Autonomous District Councils.

LOK SABHA AND RAJYA SABHA

Since 1972 when Meghalaya became a separate State, no woman from Meghalaya has been elected to the Lok Sabha or the Rajya Sabha. In 1996 and 1998 Lok Sabha elections, there were one and two women contestants respectively, but none was elected. In 1999 election, there was no woman contestant.

STATE LEGISLATIVE ASSEMBLY

Out of nine women contestants in the 1972 election, one woman was elected to the Legislative Assembly. Out of seven women contestants in the 1978 election, Miriam D. Shira was the only woman who was successful. Eight women contested during 1980-83, but no one was elected. In 1988, however, out of three contestants, two women, viz. Maysalin War and Miriam D. Shira were elected. Coming to more recent times, out of 15 contestants in 1998 three women were elected. In the last election to the Legislative Assembly in 2003, two women were elected.

Autonomous District Councils and Urban Local Bodies

Women's representation in the three Autonomous District Councils has been negligible, which shows the force of tradition which did not permit women in the Khasi and Jaintia Durbars presided over by the Syiems or chiefs. At present, there are seven District Councils responsible for seven districts. By 1982, only two women were reported to be members of Khasi District Council (Natarajan, 1982). A Jaintia woman was nominated to the Jaintia Council around 1990 (Passah, 1992). Currently no woman is reported to be member of Autonomous District Councils, according to a North-Eastern Hill University (NEHU) source. During 1977-78, one woman was selected to be an executive member of Khasi Hills Autonomous District Council.

As noted earlier, some urban areas in Meghalaya are governed by Autonomous District Councils and some, e.g. Shillong and Tura follow the pattern provided by 1956 Assam Municipal Act. Unfortunately, it has not been possible to obtain information regarding women elected to urban local bodies despite several requests to concerned government authorities. It is reported that during early 1950s a woman was nominated to Shillong Municipal Council, and in 1966 first woman was elected to this council. Interestingly, in 1971 Shillong Municipality had a lady chairperson for the first time for a five-month term.

MIZORAM

Mizo Women's Entry Into Politics

Traditionally, Mizo women had no entry to the Chief's councils or the councils of elders which dealt with political affairs. Their entry into politics dates back to 1946 when they joined their men in demanding abolition of the chieftain system. The Lushai Commoners' Union, later named Mizo Union, the first political party, took the lead in 1946 in urging the British administration to dismiss the chiefs and install a democratic administration in their place. Mizo women participated actively in demonstrations to voice their protest against the system. Mizo chiefs had the practice of marrying several wives, besides keeping some women as slaves. It was not surprising therefore, that Mizo women were eager to see the dismantling of the chieftain system, which was finally eliminated during 1952-54 after Indian Independence, as noted in Chapter 2.

When elected district and village councils were established to replace the chieftain system, Mizo women were reported to be taking active interest in their effective functioning. At present every political party in Mizoram has a women's wing at State, district and village level. Mizo politicians consider women a decided asset in door-to-door campaigns. And yet, Mizo women's direct participation as candidates for national legislative bodies, i.e. Lok Sabha and Rajya Sabha is almost nil and with respect to State Legislative Assembly fairly modest, as we will see later. Interestingly enough, a number of Mizo women are known to have participated in the insurgency operations led by Laldenga and Mizo National Front (MNF) and some even sacrificed their lives in police firing.

Christianity Opens New Social Avenues

Mizo women had no place in the traditional worship of gods and goddesses and various spirits, nor could they perform sacrificial rituals. Naturally, they responded very positively to foreign missionaries' efforts to introduce Christianity in Mizoram. As noted in Chapter 4, Mizo women have been very active in promoting activities of Christian missions belonging to Presbyterian, Baptist and other denominations. They are engaged in collecting public contributions towards augmenting the facilities of churches, adding new services in mission hospitals, setting up rescue homes for destitutes, all of which have enhanced their social status. Women can now address meetings organized on behalf of churches, something which they could not do before. Now Mizo women participate actively in social projects, and do not require the sponsorship of churches. Another, and perhaps even more fundamental change in women's status was brought about as a result of Christian missionaries' efforts to promote girls' education, as noted in previous chapter. Access to education has opened before them many occupational avenues and employment opportunities. Today, the main bazaars of Aizawl are dominated by women, who are running restaurants, modern hotels, book shops and some have been successfully working as contractors in transport and construction businesses. Some are placed in professions of teaching, medicine, nursing, Indian Administrative Service, etc. Apart from earning substantial part of family's economic support, some Mizo women have attained a high social status due to their respectable occupational standing.

Mizo women's close association with Christian Churches has opened before them a completely new and prestigious field — singing in church choirs. Today women's choirs are very popular, besides women singers' tremendous drawing power which is used by political parties at election meetings.

Participation in Social Organizations

Mizo women today are active in running a variety of services for different types of disadvantaged social sections. Their oldest organization — Mizo Hmeichhe Tangrual Pawl — set up in 1946 has been running a working women's hostel since 1980 and a home for destitute infants since 1970. Young Mizo Association (YMA), a statewide organization of young men and women, non-sectarian and non-political, has been active in various service projects for needy families, besides making valuable contributions towards maintaining communal amity in periods of social tension. Mizo Hmeichhe Insuihkhawn Pawl (MHIP) — Mizoram Women's Federation — another non-political statewide organization with over 500 branches spread over distant villages, has been active in promoting varied services for women and children in need. Other voluntary agencies include Roshni Association, Mahila Imdad Committee, Aizawl Juvenile Aid Society. These organizations have been receiving financial and consultancy support from Mizoram State Social Welfare Advisory Board for operating various social projects, e.g. craft centres, balwadis, creches, income-generating projects for needy women, family counseling centres, etc. (Liandingi, 1988).

Mizo women's organizations have received substantial support from the State Social Welfare Advisory Board in programmes aimed at redressal of offences against women, and creating awareness regarding elimination of unjust customary laws. For instance, organizations like MHIP have been persuading women victims of rape and their families to report such cases to the police and to take them to courts for trial of the guilty, besides providing legal aid in such cases. Similarly, campaigns are launched to educate Mizo society regarding the customary Mizo laws which have so far denied women right to own and inherit property, as also the need for women to obtain the right to claim alimony and maintenance from husbands who desert or divorce their wives arbitrarily. Some women's organizations have been active in creating public awareness about the evils of alcohol and drugs, besides providing counseling services for women victims of these addictions.

Women's Participation in Representative Bodies

LOK SABHA, RAJYA SABHA AND STATE LEGISLATIVE ASSEMBLY

Since Mizoram became a Union Territory in 1972, it has been allotted one seat each in Lok Sabha and Rajya Sabha. So far no Mizo woman has been elected to the Lok Sabha or Rajya Sabha, although one woman unsuccessfully contested Lok Sabha elections in 1977. In 1972, the District Council was replaced by Legislative Assembly, which presently provides 40 seats. In 1972, although four women contested the election, none was successful, while no woman was a contestant in 1977 election. In 1978, the only contestant, Thanmavii from Serchhip, was elected. Three contestants were in the fray during 1979-80, and one woman was elected. No one contested between 1980-83, In 1987, however, there were four women contestants out of whom Lalhimpuii was the only one who was victorious. She had the distinction of holding the post of Minister of State in charge of Social Welfare for some time. In 1989, out of four contestants, no one was elected. Same was the case in 1993 when three women contested but none was elected. Seven women contested the 2003 Assembly elections but no one was successful.

Women's Representation in Village Councils

Each village council has a three-year term, and five to seven members with two-thirds elected through adult franchise and the remaining to be nominated by executive committee. It is responsible for allotment of *jhum* land, adjudication of disputes and developmental functions.

There is no representative body between the State Legislative Assembly and Village Councils at district or block level, and there are no municipal bodies in urban areas. The situation in 1999 according to the District Council Affairs Department of Mizoram was as follows: Aizawl and Lunglei districts had 393 and 127 Village Councils respectively, thus making a total of 520. As of August 1999, the total number of elected Village Council members was 1987 and nominated members 561, adding up to a total of 2248, out of whom 14 women were elected and one nominated. A predominant majority of 11 women out of this number belonged to urban areas. The number of women holding position as Chairpersons were seven, all in urban areas and none in rural areas. The three autonomous District Councils of Mara, Lai and Chakma areas included one woman member each, the first two nominated and the

Chakma member elected. It seems evident that while Mizo women are reported to be taking interest in village affairs, they are only marginally involved in electoral politics.

As noted earlier, Mizoram was excluded from the provisions of the 73rd Constitutional Amendment, besides a special provision (Article 371G), which exempts the State with respect to application of laws made by the national Parliament. The existing situation with respect to the functions and powers of Village Councils is not satisfactory. The State Government is studying a draft bill prepared by the Administrative Reforms Committee which has proposed some changes with respect to village councils, keeping in mind the 73rd Amendment (Nunthara, 2000). If Mizoram succeeds in evolving a suitable system for village councils which incorporates the positive features of Panchayati Raj, including reservation for women, this might well prove to be a positive development for Mizo women, in addition to providing new directions for some other N-E States.

NAGALAND

Traditional Attitudes on Women's Place in Public Life

Women are assigned a very low social and political status in Naga traditional culture. In tribal or village councils which are responsible for social, political and judicial matters of the community, women have no entry. Tribes differ somewhat in terms of their organization. Among the Tangkhuls, the "Awunga" or the hereditary chief is like a king, while some tribes have village headman, elected or hereditary. In either case, the chieftain combines several functions, e.g. village defence, administration of civic amenities for his subjects, besides settlement of disputes. Where the chief or headman's post is hereditary, the eldest son of the seniormost wife, in case of several wives, inherits the position. A daughter never occupies the position, and where it is through election, a woman is not eligible. Usually, a village or community council and elders' council assists the chief executive in discharge of his responsibility. Generally, each *khel* (a territorial exogamous group) or clan sends its representative to these councils. Once again, a woman is not permitted to be a member of these councils. This exclusion of Naga women from social and political affairs is clearly related to how men perceive women's disposition and their roles in the family in a highly patriarchal culture. Some examples will illustrate this point.

Among the Khiamnungans, a community settled in the vicinity of Patkoi hills, each village selects two types of leaders: (i) warrior type, brave, having a regal disposition, capable of wielding executive power, and (ii) persons who can provide dependable advice with their knowledge, patience and wisdom. Women are strictly excluded from these positions due to a belief that they are apt to indulge in loose talk and cannot be trusted with confidential matters (Sardeshpande, 1987). The general attitude to women is reflected in the perception of women's purpose in life. For instance, among the Sema Nagas, a woman's role is viewed primarily as child bearing and rearing, taking care of husband's comforts and managing the household. While men are regarded as the backbone in social, political, economic and religious matters, women are considered very insignificant (Zimomi, 1988). This basically discriminatory attitude towards women seems to prevail among most Naga tribes, although with some variations, with respect to divorce. As noted earlier, village councils or elders' councils are also responsible for adjudication of disputes, e.g. encroachment on lands, violations of clan exogamy rules, or cases of marital discord. For instance, a Lotha husband can summarily ask his wife to leave the house if he finds her interfering. A Sema husband can divorce his wife unilaterally on such vague grounds as her being incompatible or not adequately respectful, and can reclaim the bride-price paid by him. As noted in Chapter 4, a Naga husband can divorce his wife on the plea of childlessness without having to prove that she was responsible for this situation. A Naga wife seeking a divorce on grounds of ill-treatment and neglect has to produce witnesses to substantiate her case before a council where she may not be allowed to participate. Among most Naga tribes, while adultery in women is severely punished, men guilty of adultery are treated with considerable lenience.

In the light of this strongly deprecatory attitude towards women in public life, it seems quite puzzling, as noted in Chapter 4, that Sema women sometimes joined their men in wars. Furthermore, Mao and Tangkhul women were known to play the role of peace-makers and ambassadors by appearing as a neutral force in between two warring sides, and the fighting had to stop, as described earlier. It is obviously difficult to reconcile these unusual practices with the more persistent image of Naga women as incapable of contributing towards social and political affairs of the community.

Changes in Naga Women's Situation

Various events and developments are changing this traditional situation, the two important ones being introduction of Christianity in the last quarter of nineteenth century, and promotion of girls' education initiated by Christian missionaries, as noted in Chapters 4 and 5. By 1991 over 99 per cent of Nagas had adopted Christianity, which enabled Naga women to make a break with traditional religions which excluded women from religious ceremonies. They can now participate in Christian church services on an equal footing with men and take active part in different activities promoted by churches. They can address public meetings and join campaigns initiated by churches, e.g. eradication of alcoholism and drug abuse, etc. which undoubtedly enhance their social status. As noted before, they continue to suffer from one handicap : they cannot be pastors or deacons. By 2001 Census, Nagaland's female literacy rate reached almost 62 per cent, from 40.39 per cent in 1981. Apart from the inherently liberating influence of education, Naga girls are beginning to enrol for higher education and a few are seeking technical and professional training. Education has helped immensely in ending their isolation and opening contacts with other and more advanced societies. An increasing number of women are engaged in setting up their own businesses, as well as seeking new careers in teaching, medicine, Indian Administrative Service, etc. They have thus found new avenues of enhancing their social status.

Naga Women's Organizations

Naga women have formed several organizations which have given them a corporate identity and helped them articulate their concerns and views on various matters. It is especially significant that while it has been extremely difficult for Naga women to voice their opinions on important social and political issues individually due to traditional constraints, they have been able to express their viewpoints through their organizations. For instance, Naga Women's Organization and All Naga Women's Federation are statewide organizations which have participated in important peace negotiations between the Government of India, State Government, representatives of militant groups, along with important organizations such as Naga Ho Ho and various peace missions. There are several women's organizations which belong to particular tribes. For instance, Sema women's organizations are active in fighting drug and sex abuse, and are trying to promote advancement of Sema community.

Lotha women are members of groups some of which are open to men and women, but women are still not allowed to be heads of these organizations (Tungoe Mhathing, 1988). Naga women are associated with a number of welfare services for physically or socially handicapped individuals. Some of these agencies are sponsored by Christian churches. They are also active in medical services sponsored by Christian missions. A small number of voluntary organizations, e.g. Gandhi Ashram in Mokokchung, are affiliated to national bodies which are active in promoting women's and children's well-being through health and welfare services.

Currently, educated Naga women are concerned about some attitudes and customary practices which are grossly unfair towards women. For instance, most Naga parents still give a greater priority to boys' education as compared to girls' education, despite the common observation that educated girls tend to be far more caring and responsible towards old parents, as compared to boys. Other concerns before women are polygyny, despite Christian churches' disapproval, and customary divorce laws which penalize women heavily and let off men who divorce their wives unilaterally, and often on vague and petty grounds.

Participation in Representative Political Institutions

LOK SABHA AND RAJYA SABHA

During the fifty years since the first Lok Sabha elections in 1952, so far Rano Shaiza has been the only woman who won the election in 1977. Born in 1928, Rano Shaiza, who belonged to Tangkhul community, went underground in 1953 before her detention for 19 months during disturbed conditions in Nagaland. During 1973-75 she was president of All Naga Women's Federation and Naga Women's Organization (Satyanarayan Rao, 1996). In 1980 one woman contested the Lok Sabha election but did not win. From 1980 onwards up to 2002, there has been no woman contestant for the Lok Sabha. The Rajya Sabha has not had any Naga woman member so far.

NAGALAND STATE LEGISLATIVE ASSEMBLY

In 1964, the State Legislative Assembly had been allotted a total of 40 seats, which were increased to 52 in 1969 and raised further to 60 in 1974. During 1970-80 there has been no woman contestant for Nagaland Assembly. During 1980-82, there was one woman contestant but she was not elected. Three contestants fought the 1987 elections and the only woman elected was Chubalemla. There was no woman contestant for the 1989 and 1998 elections. It is evident that Naga women's participation in national and State level electoral politics has been minimal so far.

VILLAGE DEVELOPMENT BOARDS

As noted earlier, Naga women have so far had no entry to traditional village or tribal councils or elders' councils. During the period between Indian Independence in 1947 and formation of the State of Nagaland in 1963, the insurgency leaders introduced their own system of village councils. In 1963, the first Nagaland State Legislative Assembly passed a law in order to introduce a hierarchical system of village, area and regional councils. The arrangement underwent a change in 1978 when Nagaland passed a new legislation, Nagaland Village and Area Council Act, which established a new system of Village Development Boards (VDBs). This new Act eliminated regional councils and an amendment of this act in 1990 removed area councils.

VDBs were intended to serve as a major mechanism to promote rural development. Some salient features of this new arrangement were as follows : Village Councils were to select members of VDB, who need not be members of Village Councils. At least one woman must be selected to be a member of VDB, which has a tenure of three years. The Deputy Commissioner is ex-officio chairman of all VDBs in his district. Since 1980 VDBs have become the chief agency for implementing various development programmes sponsored by Central and State Government. They can receive government grants and raise matching amounts through their own initiative. Another significant feature is a stipulation that at least one-fourth of government grants received are reserved for schemes selected by women (Gokhale, 2000). This new scheme has to some extent overcome the problems of exclusion of women from participating in development programmes. A review of this scheme after 1990 has highlighted the necessity of exposure of VDB members to new ideas and methods in order to promote maximum development. This observation is specially relevant for women in view of their heavy preoccupation with household and farm work and limited access to innovative projects and experiences of more advanced communities. At the same time, the VDB experience has highlighted the capacity of women to use this opportunity to promote programmes which are highly relevant for the well-being of their families. It is reported that traditionally Naga women have never been permitted to go beyond the outskirts of community meeting places — *morungs* — where they would bring rice-beer for their men. Women's membership of the new VDB, by selection or nomination cannot therefore be expected to please many Naga men (Sardeshpande, 1987). Quite interestingly, however, once the women join as members, they are reported to be participating actively in VDBs' functioning.

TRIPURA

The General Context

The following analysis focuses primarily on Tripura's tribal women, and references to non-tribal women have been made either for comparisons or to highlight some aspects of social and political status of Tripura's women in general. The tribal population of the State which formed a majority (56.37 per cent) in 1921 was reduced to a minority (28.44 per cent) by 1981 due to massive influx of Bengali refugees around Partition of the country in 1947 and again, the 1971 Bangladesh war. Emergence of ambitious entrepreneurs, landlords and unscrupulous moneylenders, at times aided by State Government policies, resulted in rapid alienation of tribal lands, often pushing tribal families to interior forests and hills, or to wage-labour employment or to migration in search of outside employment. Tribal women's access to forest resources, which previously contributed substantially to family's subsistence, has been severely restricted. According to 1991 Census, among N-E States, Tripura had the highest percentage of non-workers among women (86.24 per cent), and among women workers in the Primary Sector, the lowest percentage of Cultivators (34.54 per cent) and the highest percentage of Agricultural Labourers (30.53 per cent). Although these statistics pertain to total number of women, both tribal and non-tribal, they convey the general trend about women's social status.

Tripuri Women in the Past

Tripura's tribal women are known to have displayed unusual abilities in the eventful history of Tripura kingdom at least in its better-documented period since the fourteenth century. For instance, Tripurasundari, the wife of Tripuri Chief Chhengthung Fa, courageously led the army and repulsed a retaliatory attack by a Turkish Sultan of Bengal, Hirawat Khan, when her husband was inclined to surrender (Saigal, 1978). Some Tripuri queens are known to have displayed good statesmanship during periods of political unrest or crises. Kamla Devi, wife of king Dhanya Manikya who ruled in early sixteenth century, ably assisted her husband in removing pernicious caste restrictions which had vitiated the morale in their army. In the late eighteenth century, when Krishna Manikya died, his queen took over administration of the kingdom during 1784-85 when rival claimants to the throne created unrest and uncertainty.

Position in Traditional Village/Community Councils

In a stark contrast to women in the royal family, Tripura's tribal women in general have always been excluded from social and political bodies such as village councils, which deal with administrative matters, such as allotment of *jhum* plots, and settle disputes between individuals, including cases of marital discord. This practice still prevails in most tribal communities. Women are never allowed to participate in these councils as members or presidents. For instance, among the Jamatias, an all-male village authority called "Akra" decides action on matters such as elopement of a boy and girl, or a girl's abduction. Among the Tripuris, a traditional community council includes men representatives from each village, and while this body is reputed to be extremely democratic in its functioning, women have no place whatsoever in it (Gan Choudhari, 1980). Among the Chakmas, a village council decides a woman's right to compensation from a husband who has unilaterally divorced her, and also matters regarding custody of children (Saigal, 1978). Perhaps, the only exception Reangs make when they welcome a village guest, women decked with all their ornaments join men in the welcome. The Chief's wife presents the guest several bottles of wine, which are then shared by the assembled group (Saigal, 1978). With the emergence of representative political bodies since Independence, tribal women's scope for political participation has increased, as we will see later.

Some Changes in Women's Status

The increasing interaction between tribal and non-tribal communities has resulted in some changes in women's status — some positive and some negative. As noted in Chapter 4, tribal women had very limited participation in traditional religions. The adoption of Hinduism by a large section of Tripura's tribal population, and Buddhism or Christianity by some tribal groups has enhanced their status in religion. On the negative side, the beginning of dowry system in place of bride-price or "Jamai-Khata" (son-in-law giving service in his father-in-law's household) indicates a lowering of tribal women's status (Mandal, 1993). Tribal women are better off, however, than their non-tribal counterparts in matters of divorce. In tribal communities, divorce is more easily obtained. Furthermore, divorcees and widows can remarry more easily, and do not face the opprobrium non-tribal women have to bear in similar situations. Tribal women do not have the right to own and inherit property, except women from Tripuri tribe who have a limited right. Although non-tribal Hindu women have been granted this right by the Hindu Succession Act of 1956, in most cases they do not get it and in the few cases where the women try to assert their right, the lengthy and expensive litigation in which they get involved make a mockery of their right.

With the rapidly decreasing access to land for jhuming and State Government's policies to stop *jhum* cultivation and adopt settled cultivation, lands traditionally allotted by village councils and owned by communities are transferred to individual, i.e. men's ownership. The control over plant protection and ploughing has shifted to men. In some cases, tribal women have been facing difficulties due to the influence of a customary taboo against women touching the plough prevailing in non-tribal societies. (Chakravarti, 1993). Where men owners of the land are absent due to death or migration for seeking urban employment, tribal women who are left with the major burden of cultivation face many difficulties due to harassment by hostile elements in the community. Occasional cases of witch-hunting have also been reported (Das Gupta, 1989). Where women migrate with their husbands in search of alternate employment, they lose the sense of security enjoyed in their original habitat, and may have no option but to accept some low-paid wage employment, which definitely lowers their social status.

As noted in Chapter 3 a majority of non-tribal women who belong predominantly to immigrant Bengali families, are worse off as compared to tribal women, since a majority of them belong to low and lower middle classes and have less freedom to pursue economic activities outside the family. Most parents give a lower priority to girls' education, as compared to boys, which limits their career options. Despite these limitations, some changes are evident and an increasing number of women are employed in various government departments as teachers, health workers and extension workers in community development programmes. Many women are employed in secretarial cadres in State Government, and a small number as officers, doctors, professors in colleges, etc. There is no doubt that these women have a better social status.

A small number of educated women came under the influence of the national movement for Independence initiated by Gandhiji and the Indian National Congress. A few non-tribal women were actively involved in the tribal peasant movements led by the Communist Party. In fact, the small number of women who have been elected to Lok Sabha and Rajya Sabha and the State Legislative Assembly mostly came from this section.

Women's Struggles Against Injustice

In an essentially patriarchal culture, women are subjected to various types of subservience and exploitation. We will now look at how Tripura's tribal women have dealt with such challenges. One of the earliest women's organization, Tripura Nari Samiti, was established in 1949, with tribal women heading it as president and secretary. Tribal women joined their men to protest against a cess in the form of grains from *jhum* cultivators collected by agents of the royalty in 1949 and three women lost their lives in the firing on an unarmed group. In the following two decades, Ganamukti Parishad, an organization set up by a small number of tribal youth, who included Dasrath Deb, who later became chief minister of the State, provided leadership for a number of movements against exploitation by powerful landlords, rapacious moneylenders, and at times government functionaries. As noted earlier, when tribal peasants were unable to pay land-rents or repay debts owed to moneylenders, the latter often used drastic methods such as confiscating tribal lands, forcibly collecting their grains, demanding compulsory labour, besides adopting dishonest methods of registering tribal lands in their own names. Ganmukti Parishad in 1952 organized a strong peasant movement in which many tribal women joined, in order to resist collection of grains, to oppose exorbitant rates of interest by moneylenders and to oppose fraudulent registration of land ownership.

Ironically, at times tribal women have had to resist injustice and arrogance of government agents as well, since sometimes the latter have not only been indifferent towards the former's exploitation by the rich and powerful sections, but have at times been guilty of sexual harassment of women as a tool of breaking their resistance. In 1964 tribal women launched a determined fight against forest guards employed by the government who would forcibly confiscate the forest produce collected by women declaring the areas as "reserved forests." Furthermore, some forest guards were reported to have been guilty of sexual harassment and rape of tribal women. At Belonia, when women organized a peaceful protest, a member of the Nari Samiti was shot dead in police firing, but this incident strengthened the resolve of protesting women (AIDWA, 2000). When the food situation became critical for poor families around 1966, both tribal and non-tribal women joined hands in several demonstrations to put pressure on the State Government to open ration shops and introduce an effective public food distribution system. Another issue on which women, particularly tribal women organized a movement was the demand for creation of an autonomous tribal district under the provisions of the Sixth Schedule. The creation of Tripura Tribal Area Autonomous District Council (TTAADC) in 1984 represents fulfilment of a long struggle by tribal women and men.

As noted in Chapter 2, the emergence of a number of extremist organizations in Tripura, such as Tripura National Volunteers (TNV), National Liberation Front of Tripura (NLFT), All Tripura Tiger Force (ATTF), United Bengali Liberation Front (UBLF) have kept the State in complete turmoil for over two decades. Quite expectedly, women's movements to eliminate injustice and promote unity among tribal and non-tribal groups have received a set-back as a result of terrorist violence.

Women's Organizations

One of the earliest organizations which tried to promote education of tribal children was established in 1945 by some educated tribal youth. Their efforts to start schools in tribal areas received active support of tribal women. One of the largest women's organization, Tripura Ganatantric Nari Samiti, is affiliated to All India Democratic Women's Association (AIDWA). The Tripura association has 14 divisional and 153 local units, and 1925 primary committees, many of which are located in tribal areas. This organization promotes education of women, development activities in villages, besides bringing to the notice of State Government and people problems faced by women, such as, food shortages, intimidation by extremist groups, etc. Its affiliation with the national association AIDWA helped immensely in bringing to light many outrages on women by terrorists, and even by security forces. When tribal women were gang-raped by security forces at Ujan Bazar in 1988, AIDWA filed public interest litigation in Supreme Court which led to setting up inquiry commissions. This organization has been promoting the cause of unity among tribal and non-tribal women in Tripura. There are a large number of voluntary organizations in the State which have been implementing programmes for promoting the welfare of women, sponsored by the Central Social Welfare Board, e.g. maintaining protective homes for destitute and deserted women, condensed courses, vocational training and the like. Tripura Government has appointed a Women's Commission, which is involved in providing justice to women who are victims of ill-treatment, exploitation, dowry demands, etc.

Women's Participation in Representative Political Bodies

LOK SABHA AND RAJYA SABHA

Very few women have contested from Tripura for Lok Sabha seats. For instance, up to 1980 there was no woman contestant. In 1980, one woman did contest, but was not elected. In 1991 Maharani Bibhu Kumari Devi contested on Indian National Congress ticket and won a seat. Wife of Maharaja Kirit Bikram Kishor Manikya and a graduate, she had been a member of the State Legislative Assembly during 1983-91, and a minister during 1988-91, when the Congress was the ruling party. During the 1996 and 1998 elections, there were two and one contestants, respectively for Lok Sabha, but none was elected. The 1980 Rajya Sabha included one woman from Tripura, Ila Bhattacharjee, a teacher who was also chairperson of the State Social Welfare Advisory Board and active member of Tripura Teachers Association. She represented the CPI-M Communist Party of India-Marxist (CPI-M). There has been no other woman member from Tripura in the Rajya Sabha so far.

STATE LEGISLATIVE ASSEMBLY

Tripura Legislative Assembly with a council of ministers was established in 1962, initially with 30 seats which were raised later to 60. Between 1970-72, out of seven women contestants two were elected. In 1977, six women contested and one was elected (Gouri Bhattacharjee). During 1980-83, a much larger number of 11 contested and four (including Maharani Bibhu Kumari Devi) were successful. Out of seven women who contested in the 1988 election, two, viz. Maharani Bibhu Kumari Devi and Biva Rani Nath were elected. A surprisingly large number, 21 women entered the fray in 1998 elections and two were elected.

WOMEN IN PANCHAYATI RAJ AND AUTONOMOUS DISTRICT COUNCIL

The beginning of local self-government goes back to 1947, when Tripura adopted Uttar Pradesh Panchayati Raj Act with some minor changes. Under this Act 476 Gaon Sabhas and 138 Nyaya Panchayats functioned with some drawbacks, until 1983 when Tripura Panchayat Act replaced the existing arrangements. Gaon Sabhas were replaced by Gaon Panchayats and given a wide range of functions, e.g. rural employment programme, anti-poverty programmes, deployment of government lands for horticulture and pisciculture, etc. At block level, Block Development Committees, consisting of *pradhans* (presidents) of Gaon Panchayats, members of Legislative Assembly and Autonomous District Council, were formed. In 1988, the State Government superseded all Gaon Panchayats and placed the whole system under the supervision of the Directorate of Panchayats.

After the 73rd Amendment, Tripura Panchayat Act, 1993 was passed and a three-tier structure was established, which covered 525 Gram Panchayats, 16 Panchayat Samities and three Zilla Parishads. These figures have undergone some changes after creation of a new district — Dhalai. After 1993 when a CPI(M)-led State Government came into power, several steps were taken to improve the functioning of Panchayati Raj Institutions. These include provision of salaries and honoraria and travelling allowances to officebearers and support for construction of offices for panchayats and for meeting halls (Sharma, Sudhir, 2000).

The situation at 1999 elections under the new act was as follows:

	Nos	*Total no. of members*	*SCs*	*STs*	*Women*
Gram Panchayats	538	5685	1480 (26.03%)	286 (5.03%)	1895 (33.33%)
Panchayat Samitis	23	299	78 (26.08%)	15 (5.01%)	105 (35.11%)
Zilla Parishads	4	82	22 (26.82%)	4 (4.87%)	28 (34.14%)

It is reported that 185 women were elected as *pradhans* (presidents) of Gram Panchayats, 11 as chairpersons of Panchayat Samitis and two women as presidents of North and Dhalai Zilla Parishads (AIDWA, 2001).

There is no provision for reservation for women at District level in the Autonomous District Council which covers nearly three-fourths of the total state area. As per TTAADC Secretariat, West Tripura sources, two women were elected in 1995 on CPI(M) tickets, representing Dhalai and West Tripura districts. Another woman was nominated by the State's Governor in 1994, and she came from North Tripura district. At the Gram Sabha level, of which there are 408, one-third seats of members and chairpersons are reserved for women. The last election of the Autonomous District Council in 2000 was marred by considerable violence reported to have been used by Indigenous People's Front of Tripura (IPFT) to capture 18 out of 28 seats. It is also reported that National Liberation Front of Tripura (NLFT) and other extremist groups have unleashed terror causing disruption of normal life and many women are known to have been harassed, and beaten and some even raped and killed (AIDWA, 2001).

After passing of the 74th Amendment, one-third seats in Municipal bodies are reserved for women. In the last elections, out of a total of 143 seats in Municipal Council and Nagar Panchayats, 55 seats were won by women (AIDWA, 2001).

In short, the legal requirement of reserving one-third seats for women in Panchayats and Municipal bodies is quite adequately utilized by women. It is specially noteworthy that at the district level in the Autonomous District Council area where there is no provision for reserving seats for women, two women got elected and one was nominated by the Governor.

SUMMARY

A significant finding of this Chapter is that women's status in social and political fields is closely interrelated and this in turn is intimately connected with other aspects such as education, occupation and ability to earn an independent income. Women in N-E societies traditionally have been assigned a very low social and political status, as reflected in their exclusion from all types of community councils which have been responsible for matters of village or territory administration, defence from external aggression and disputes between individuals which included cases of marital discord. There are considerable variations in women's social and political status among different N-E States, and within different communities in the same State. At the same time, similar developments and forces in the N-E region have been changing the traditional situation and beginning to raise women's social and political status, although at varying paces within the region. These include the following:

Interaction between N-E women and outside communities which were more advanced. For instance, women of Assam got quite involved in the Non-cooperation Movement launched by Gandhiji and the Indian National Congress. Manipuri women were undoubtedly influenced by developments in the mainland in their anti-colonial and anti-feudal struggles.

Conversion to Christianity in Meghalaya, Mizoram and Nagaland opened for women the doors to religion and along with it to several social programmes launched by churches. Adoption of Hinduism and Buddhism by some tribal communities created new space for women in religious worship and enhanced their social status.

By far the most important factor in changing women's situation has been introduction of education. Apart from opening new mental horizons, education has been instrumental in creating many types of vocational and professional careers, entry into new businesses and trades and thus gain economic autonomy which has raised their social status.

An indication of women's rising social and political status is their expression of revolt against unjust practices. Some illustrations include: Arunachal women's struggles to seek release of girls from in-laws' oppression when they were married in childhood in exchange for bride-price by parents; Meitei women's Nupi-lans; Tripura's tribal women's refusal to allow landlords and moneylenders to collect forced levies.

An effective tool of N-E women for resisting social and political injustice has been the formation of groups and organizations. These vary a great deal in terms of size and area of influence, and include a wide range : from Manipuri women's "Marups" or neighbourhood self-help groups to statewide organizations such as the MHIP of Mizo women. Some of these groups may be organized around specific issues, e.g. Tripura women's protests against the high-handedness of forest guards. Furthermore, Tripura experience highlights the importance of national women's organizations such as AIDWA providing much-needed support to new and small women's groups until they get stabilized.

WOMEN'S REPRESENTATION IN POLITICAL BODIES

Women's representation in political bodies at various levels is both an indication as well as an instrument of enhancing their social and political status. It is necessary to remember that excepting Assam, all N-E States attained full statehood much later, and Mizoram and Arunachal Pradesh not until 1987. The process of electoral politics, therefore, is at various stages in these States.

LOK SABHA AND RAJYA SABHA

Three N-E States, viz. Arunachal Pradesh, Mizoram and Meghalaya have not had any woman elected to Lok Sabha, while Manipur, Nagaland and Tripura have returned one woman each so far. In Assam, between 1952 and 1977, nine women and between 1985 and 1999, three women were elected to the Lok Sabha. Manipur, Mizoram, Meghalaya and Nagaland have not had any woman elected to the Rajya Sabha so far, while Arunachal Pradesh and Tripura have sent one woman each. Three women from Assam have received this distinction so far.

STATE LEGISLATIVE ASSEMBLIES

Since the first Legislative Assembly elections were held in Arunachal Pradesh in 1978, about 15 women have been contestants and not more than five have been elected. In Manipur, between 1970 and 1995 only two women were elected to the Legislative Assembly, however, the number of contestants seems to be rising, as evident from 1995 elections when eleven women contested although none was elected. Since 1972 when Meghalaya became separated from composite Assam, nine women were elected and nearly 45 women have contested the elections so far. In Mizoram out of about 19 contestants until 1993, three were elected. Although seven women were in the fray in 2003, none was elected. In Nagaland, out of about five contestants during 1970-98, only one woman was elected up to 1987, and no one was elected in the 1998 elections. In Tripura, during 1970-88, out of 31 women contestants, nine were elected. In 1998, out of a fairly large number of 21 contestants, two women were elected. Assam, which started having Legislative Assembly elections since 1952 has had about 200 women contestants, and nearly 50 women have been elected so far. The number of contestants has been rising, as evident from the 1996 election which had 45 women contestants out of whom six were elected, and in the 2001 election, nine women were elected. Briefly, in four N-E States, viz. Arunachal Pradesh, Manipur, Mizoram and Nagaland the number of women elected to legislative assemblies ranges between one and five, Meghalaya and Tripura, about nine to 11, and Assam nearly 50.

WOMEN'S REPRESENTATION IN POLITICAL BODIES AT DISTRICT AND BELOW-DISTRICT LEVELS

The 73rd and 74th Constitutional Amendments are applicable to Arunachal Pradesh, Assam, Manipur, Tripura with the exception of areas specified as being excluded. Despite some Constitutional or administrative bottlenecks one-third of total seats at village, block and district level Panchayat bodies (members and presidents) are being reserved for women. Similar arrangements are in existence wherever urban representative bodies, e.g. municipal bodies or town committees are constituted.

In areas which are excluded from the above provisions, e.g. areas covered under the Sixth Schedule, e.g. Karbi Anglong and North Cachar Hills districts of Assam, Meghalaya, Mizoram and TTAADC (Tripura Tribal Area Autonomous District Council), women's representation in district and village councils is minimal. For instance, even if one or two women are nominated to Karbi Anglong or North Cachar Hills District Councils,they hardly participate in the councils' functioning. In Mizoram, out of a total number of 1687 elected Village Council members in 1999, only 14 were women, and out of 561 nominated members, only one was a women. Nagaland has chosen a different pattern — VDBs (Village Development Boards) — where the inclusion of one woman member is compulsory. It is evident that the traditional exclusion of women from indigenous community councils still exerts a strong influence even on newly constiituted representative bodies.

7

Recapitulation and Concluding Observations

Recapitulation

THE salient ecological, demographic, historical, political, social and economic features of the N-E region as a whole and its seven component States provided in the first two chapters present the context in which N-E women lead their lives. Nearly 70 per cent of the area in N-E region is full of high mountains, deep valleys and hill ranges, with several mighty rivers like Brahmaputra, Kopili, Barak, Subansiri and a large number of smaller rivers originating in the mountains and often causing devastating floods. Poor development of roads, railways and river transport create difficulties in travel and transportation of goods within the region, besides disruptions in communication links with the rest of India, resulting in physical as well as social and emotional isolation.

The original inhabitants of N-E States belong to Indo-Mongoloid races with various origins such as China, Tibet, Mongolia, Myanmar and South-East Asian region, represent some 209 STs and several sub-tribes, and speak more than 420 languages and dialects. The N-E region's total population, as of 2001 Census was 38.5 million, with Assam alone accounting for 26.7 million, and the remaining six States together having less than 12 million. Assam, Tripura and Manipur have been exposed to interaction, particularly with northern and eastern parts of India and Hinduism at least since the medieval period. Meghalaya, Mizoram and Nagaland have received Christian missionary influences since nineteenth century and are predominantly Christian. Arunachal Pradesh remained isolated from contacts with the mainland until about the middle of twentieth century, and a majority of its tribal groups follow their indigenous religions, while some communities follow Buddhism due to their Tibetan and Myanmar origins. The demographic profiles of these seven States show great variations. Meghalaya, Mizoram, Nagaland and Arunachal Pradesh populations belong predominantly to Scheduled Tribes. The heavy inflows of migrants from other Indian States, as well as from Bangladesh (former East Pakistan), Nepal and Myanmar have swamped Assam and Tripura, turning their original tribal communities into minorities. The central valley of Manipur is inhabited by Meiteis, who adopted Hinduism under the influence of their rulers, while the surrounding hill districts have populations belonging to Naga and Kuki groups constituting nearly one-third of the total State population.

Integration of N-E States into the Indian polity was preceded by greatly divergent and in some cases stormy political processes. Nagaland was incorporated as a State in the Indian Union in 1963 after a violent movement led by Phizo to assert its sovereignty went into a temporary lull, but the insurgency among some rebel sections continues even now. Manipur and Tripura, both princely kingdoms under British supremacy until 1947, achieved statehood in 1972. Meghalaya too became a separate State in 1972 after a Constitutional struggle to wrest its freedom from the hegemony of Assam. Arunachal Pradesh, which for a long time had remained an "unadministered territory" and later known as North-East Frontier Agency, attained full statehood in 1987 after a stint as a Union Territory. Mizoram, originally known as the Lushai Hills district of Assam, went through a difficult period of insurgency under the leadership of Laldenga, before attaining a Union Territory status in 1972 and becoming an independent State in 1987.

Against this backdrop of N-E region and its seven component States, we review major findings presented in Chapters 3, 4, 5 and 6 and suggest some approaches to improving N-E women's status.

Economic Status

N-E women's economic situation can be viewed from three perspectives outlined in three sections. Section 1 analysed their status from the point of view of their work participation, as reflected in 1991 Census and major changes as compared with 1981 Census. Women from five N-E States, viz. Arunachal Pradesh, Manipur, Meghalaya, Mizoram and Nagaland, have much higher work participation rates (between 35 and 44 per cent) than the average for India as a whole (22 per cent), as well as higher percentages of female main workers (as against marginal). For

Assam and Tripura, which have a predominant majority of migrants and non-tribal populations, both of these percentages are lower than the national average. Very high percentages (ranging between 72 and 89) of women main workers are engaged in Primary Sector and mostly in agriculture, like in India in general, which implies long strenuous labour and low returns. Within the primary sector, Assam, Meghalaya and Tripura have sizeable numbers of women engaged in plantations and orchards. Very small percentages of women find employment in the secondary sector, Manipur being the exception because of the sizeable number of women engaged in handloom weaving, with Assam and Tripura trailing behind, although the decline in percentages from 1981 is a cause for concern. A positive trend is noted in the increasing percentages of women, as compared to 1981, who are engaged in the Tertiary sector, particularly in a variety of trades and businesses in most States, but especially in Mizoram, Meghalaya and Manipur. "Other services" (category IX) in the tertiary sector shows sizeable percentages of women in all N-E States, and particularly in Tripura, Mizoram, Meghalaya and Assam, with urban areas accounting for a majority. As N-E women acquire educational and vocational qualifications, they are finding employment in government departments, e.g. education, health, community development, women's and children's programmes, and in government secretariats. A small but hopeful beginning can be noted in N-E women finding new careers as teachers in colleges and universities, doctors, engineers and as civil servants.

A notable feature of N-E women's work participation is the high percentage among women engaged in agriculture are cultivators, i.e. engaged in family farms, and a small minority are agricultural labourers. This is significant in comparison with the situation in several larger States, e.g. Andhra Pradesh, Bihar, Karnataka, Gujarat and Maharashtra, where women agricultural labourers constitute a high majority. When one compares the 1991 situation with 1981, however, the percentages of women agricultural labourers show an increase. This negative trend is explained by advancing land alienation among local and particularly tribal populations due to indebtedness, ignorance regarding government procedures, acquisition of tribal lands by enterprising individuals sometimes by fraudulent means, and through government acquisition for public sector projects, road development, etc.

Section II reviewed the various time-consuming and strenuous tasks

N-E women have to undertake, besides cultivation, mostly primitive and *jhum,* in which a high majority are involved, but which are not included in the official Census definition of work. Women are primarily responsible for collecting fuel, fodder for animals and edible roots and vegetables from forests to supplement insufficient food supplies from *jhum* cultivation, besides cooking and feeding the family, child care, etc. Barring a small minority who live in capital towns or other urban areas, a majority of N-E women do not have access to basic amenities like piped water supply, electricity or gas. Traditionally, ensuring adequate food for the family as well as procuring other essential household supplies are considered women's responsibility. This necessitates their undertaking several activities such as raising vegetables, poultry and pigs, handloom weaving, cane and bamboo crafts, sericulture, etc. in order to supplement family's food resources as well as to earn cash for purchasing some essential household necessities. The outputs of these activities are hardly commensurate with the time and effort women put in. This is an area that deserves careful thinking and planning to improve quality of products as well as profitability.

Section III reviews N-E women's situation with respect to right to own and inherit property, the extent of freedom women enjoy in managing the household resources, and access to means of earning independent income and economic autonomy. Excepting Meghalaya which follows matrilineal succession (which will follow later) all other N-E States restrict the right to own and inherit immovable property to men. Women cannot own or inherit lands or the living house from their fathers or husbands as a rule, although there are some exceptions.

The Idu Mishmis of Dibang Valley of Arunachal Pradesh have followed the practice of permitting both sons and daughters to inherit shares of land owned by deceased father. In some communities having matrilineal traditions, such as the Meiteis of Manipur, or Dimasas of Assam who have parallel matri-clans and patri-clans system, generally sons inherit father's property while daughters inherit mother's property. Among the Tai Phakes of Assam and the Singphos of Arunachal Pradesh (both originating from Myanmar), if there are no sons, daughters inherit deceased father's lands, but in the next generation the property goes to sons. Some Apatanis of Arunachal Pradesh have become quite affluent as a result of benefiting from government programmes for promoting settled cultivation, and have been gifting some lands to their daughters. Interestingly enough, some Naga and Mizo parents are reported to have been favourably impressed by the caring and responsible attitude of daughters towards their parents, in contrast with sons who seem to be fairly indifferent towards their parents and squander their parents' money. This has prompted many parents to revise their traditional attitude towards daughters and to gift some lands to their daughters.

Lest these observations convey a wholly optimistic prospect for N-E women, we may note the equally negative trends. Among the Lalungs and Rabhas of Assam, the original matrilineal traditions are rapidly being replaced by patrilineal ones as a result of their exposure to highly patriarchal culture of non-tribal Assamese societies. A few N-E communities, e.g. the Adis of Arunachal Pradesh and the Lothas of Nagaland permit a widow to use the deceased husband's property to maintain herself and her children, but she cannot sell it and if she remarries a person outside her husband's clan, she loses the right to use the property.

Most N-E communities acknowledge a woman's right over articles she brings with her when she leaves her parental home and joins her husband after marriage. The typical possessions include a digging stick and *dao* (a chopper), a grass rain-cover, a handloom, clothes, household articles gifted by parents and her own savings, if any. In some cases she receives ornaments as gifts from parents in marriage. In addition, if she earns any money by pursuing ancillary activities like pig or poultry-rearing or raising vegetables, whatever she earns is treated as her own personal possession over which she is supposed to have complete control. It is obvious, thus, that despite the long hours and strenuous daily routine of most N-E women, what they can count as their exclusive possessions are really minimal. One redeeming feature, however, is the freedom and autonomy they enjoy in running their households. Non-tribal women in Assam and Tripura, especially among the higher castes among Hindus, and Muslims generally do not enjoy this freedom to go out or take up some kinds of work, e.g. agricultural work or vending, and for that matter, even to spend the money earned by them freely and without the consent of men.

In some highly male-dominant communities such as the Nishis of Arunachal Pradesh, or the Semas and Lothas of Nagaland, men may even deprive women of their minimal personal possessions if the latter happen to fall in their disfavour. A Sema husband can divorce his wife on grounds like incompatibility or adultery, and if this happens within three years of marriage, he may keep the ornaments she received from her parents, besides making her return the bride-price paid by him. The custom permitting a Nishi husband to acquire several wives by paying the requisite bride-price (usually a *mithun*), and the practice of distributing the widows, after his death, among his male relatives, even without the formality of a marriage ceremony — these indicate how a woman is virtually turned into part of man's property.

While it is conceded that women from all N-E communities do not suffer from this kind of degraded status, the point remains that despite their long and strenuous daily schedules, their personal economic situation continues to be extremely weak. Measures for enhancing their ability to earn independent income need to be strengthened.

As far as Meghalaya's matrilineal system is concerned, it is a far cry from the Women's Kingdom where women enjoy unlimited economic power. The daughter who is selected to inherit ancestral property from her mother does not have absolute control over the property, and all major financial decisions are controlled by a family council consisting of her maternal uncles, brothers, parents if living and her husband. Among the Garos, her husband, who may also be occupying the position of head of the clan's territory (*Nokma*) is in a stronger role than among Khasi-Jaintias, and in a few cases, he may even squander the property while the *Nokna* (the inheritress) watches helplessly until the family council steps in to restrain him. Among the Khasi-Jaintias the somewhat secondary role of the husband places enormous burden on the *Khadduh* (the inheritress) of living up to the highly glorified traditional role of the protector of all old, ailing and needy members of the clan and fulfilling the various religious obligations in her capacity as continuator of the clan. Besides, she must also bear the major responsibility of educating and raising her children, without much support from husband, whose major involvement continues with his mother's and sister's household. Despite this rather demanding role women must fulfil, Meghalaya culture assigns equal status to women and men, and girls grow up in an atmosphere that is free from discrimination. (In fact, some Meghalaya men assert that boys are treated as inferior to girls!) Other sisters who do not inherit ancestral property are assisted by parents through giving some lands and are helped to set up their own homes in case they do not stay with mother's household. Probably due to a favourable cultural conditioning, Meghalaya women display remarkable self-confidence, ability for hard work and great initiative in pursuing a variety of trades, businesses, occupations and professions successfully.

In summing up, there is no doubt that N-E women face formidable difficulties in improving their economic status in the context of overall poor economic development of N-E region. Their situation is exacerbated due to discriminatory customary laws with respect to ownership and inheritance — a circumstance, which is not amenable to quick change. Notwithstanding this obstacle, a section of N-E women in each State has demonstrated their initiative and perseverance in benefiting from new educational and vocational training facilities, and they are entering into a variety of jobs, trades and businesses, and a few are making their mark in new professional careers.

Women's Status in Marriage, Family and Religion

The birth of a girl child in a family is a happy event in N-E tribal communities although some communities prefer the arrival of a boy. The Akas and Wanchos of Arunachal Pradesh, Nagas and Mizos, for instance, have generally shown a preference for boys because of their long past preoccupation with warfare and the consequent need for replenishment of warriors. Even then, they valued girls as a source of producing defenders of the tribe. The Khasis and Jaintias have always viewed girls as proliferators of the tribe and continuators of the lineage. Unlike the non-tribal Hindu communities of Tripura and Barak Valley who are worried over having to give dowry in daughters' marriages, for most tribal communities, girls are not seen as a liability, and in fact there is assurance that they would fetch at least a *mithun* as bride-price for parents.

Girls grow up in a relaxed atmosphere and move freely with friends, both boys and girls. From an early age, they start helping their mothers in household chores, look after younger siblings and begin to share with their mothers cultivation tasks. In fact, they prove to be such valuable assets to their families that parents often withdraw them from schools at an early age. Tribal communities permit their young daughters to mix with boys and participate in special events like festivals connected with harvesting of crops where they work and dance together and generally select their life partners. Mothers take great care to teach their daughters handloom weaving, since in many communities, e.g. the Meiteis of Manipur, Adis of Arunachal Pradesh, Karbis of Assam, etc. weaving is regarded as an essential skill for girls. In comparison with tribal-majority States, in a

State like Tripura, tribal parents tend to give boys a preferential treatment, e.g. better food, clothes, educational facilities, as compared to girls obviously due to the influence of the non-tribal majority population of the State, which has a generally negative attitude towards women.

The youth dormitories where young girls and boys used to be sent, e.g. the Mizo "zawlbuks," Naga "morungs," Padam-Miniyongs' "Rashengs" and "Moshups," etc. deserve a special mention (even if almost extinct now), because of their sound pedagogical approach combined with social concern. Here, young girls learnt to share house-keeping and cultivation tasks with other members, correct dance steps, new weaving patterns, and sound etiquettes under the supervision of experienced women, and selected their marriage partners in a free and relaxed atmosphere. Although modern educational systems have mostly replaced youth dormitories, several communities have established youth organizations or associations for young boys and girls. These groups take up useful community projects, help families in distress, assume responsibility for organizing important social events like "Bihu" or "Porag" among the Mishings, and may even bring social pressure on in-laws to release girls forced into unhappy marriages due to pernicious social practices.

Selection of Marriage Partners

Most N-E communities let young girls select their life partners and later arrange their marriage ceremonies. Among groups where parents arrange their daughters' marriages, girls' consent is ascertained and exceptions (e.g., Zeliangrong and Konyak Nagas) are very few. It is not uncommon for young girls and boys to elope, if they apprehend parents' disapproval. On the whole, there is greater acceptance of pre-marital sex as well as unmarried motherhood. As long as rules of clan exogamy and tribal endogamy are followed, parents go along with their children's choices. The rules of clan exogamy and tribal endogamy are quite strict among some communities, e.g. the Nagas, Adis, Karbis and Dimasas. In case of infringements, girls are punished more severely, while boys are let off with mild punishment. For instance, a Dimasa girl marrying a non-Dimasa boy faces strong rejection and may even be ex-communicated. A Karbi girl having an adulterous relationship with a boy who belongs to her own clan may have to pay a hefty fine, face ex-communication and even a symbolic death ceremony. A Dimasa boy marrying a non-Dimasa girl faces disapproval but gets a much lighter punishment. A Khasi woman marrying a non-Khasi loses her ritual status, right of inheritance and also Khasi status, whereas a Khasi man marrying a non-Khasi woman does not suffer from any of these disabilities. Among most plains tribal communities of Assam, as well as among the Meiteis of Manipur, rules of clan exogamy are not so strict.

Interestingly, in some communities, parents may welcome elopement by children, because it saves them from cumbersome negotiations and expensive marriage ceremony. Among the Meiteis, the practice of sons and daughters selecting their partners is gradually replacing the earlier custom of parents arranging their children's marriages, and what is more interesting, elopements by young lovers are becoming common not only among the Meiteis, but even among Manipuri Muslims, a rather conservative community.

Marriage ceremonies in most N-E communities are generally simple, and may include : invocation of blessings of certain deities and ancestors and oblations of wine, prayers for prosperity of the clans and for birth of many children, sacrifices of chickens, commitments of loyalty among marriage partners, etc. A few weddings (e.g. Anal, a tribal community residing in Manipur hills) include ceremonies that formally end the girl's affiliation with her parental clan. Ironically, several communities, such as Anal, Tarao, Meitei, etc. consider women as devoid of a permanent clan affiliation, and therefore untrustworthy and inferior and unfit to participate in some religious rituals. Marriage ceremonies in some communities, e.g. the Akas of Arunachal Pradesh, Mishings of Assam, and Khiamnungans of Nagaland, include a routine of mock abduction or capture of the girl by the boy's party, which reflects a fond desire to hark back to the times — even if temporarily — when a man's fancying a certain woman was good enough reason to capture her, without any regard for the girl's wishes! Perhaps, the saving grace in the Aka wedding ceremony is the opportunity for the girl's party to play some practical jokes with the boy's party, before the final surrender.

Bride-Price and Dowry

A majority of N-E tribal communities follow the practice of bride-price, which recognizes daughters as assets to their families. There are variations regarding the forms in which bride-price is paid — e.g., cash, ornaments, a *mithun*, a feast for members of the girl's clan, or service for a fixed period by the prospective groom in his father-in-law's household. Some groups, e.g. the Karbis, Tangkhuls, Angamis, Khasis and Jaintias, do not have the custom of bride-price, but presents may be exchanged between the groom's and the bride's families. The girl's parents give some gifts, e.g. agricultural tools, handloom, household articles, clothes, ornaments, etc. over which girls have complete ownership. While the Meiteis, and most Assamese Hindus do not have the practice of dowry, migrant Hindu communities in Barak Valley and Tripura follow the custom of dowry, which has negative implications in terms of parents' attitude towards daughters. Unfortunately, the banal influence of dowry system seems to be affecting communities which were so far free from it, e.g. Assamese Hindus, Mizos, Tripura tribal groups like Jamatias, etc. resulting in groom's side expecting expensive presents from girl's parents.

While the belief that daughters are a valuable asset for their parents implicit in the practice of bride-price elevates the status of women, in some communities, e.g. the Nishings, Semas, Lothas, especially among affluent persons and chieftains of tribes, such as Konyaks and Tangkhuls, bride-price is perceived literally as a price with which a bride can be purchased. A woman thus deteriorates into a possession to be acquired by giving a *mithun*, or an agreed amount of money, and discarded if it ceases to be useful, e.g. a Sema Naga ordering his wife to leave his house because she did not produce a son. A Nishing man may have married three women and acquired five widows when his brother died, his affluence being reflected in terms of the number of wives and *mithuns* he owned. In most cases, women alone are regarded as responsible for not producing children, or not producing sons, and it is only when the divorced wife re-marries another man and gives birth to children that the first husband's injustice is exposed.

While polygyny is not uncommon among several N-E communities, the reasons may vary. In mountainous and difficult terrains, the need for more labour in the fields can be a reason for bringing a second or a third wife, sometimes at the instance of the first wife, as among the Akas of Arunachal Pradesh. With increasing availability of hired agricultural labour, this practice is declining and a few relatively progressive groups, e.g. the Apatanis, are slowly adopting monogamy as the new norm. Some groups, e.g. the Karbis and Dimasas of Assam and the Maos and Khiamnungans of Nagaland have traditionally favoured monogamy and value fidelity and trust in marital relationships. On the whole, flaunting several wives as a form of showing one's affluence and therefore gaining prestige is on the decline, even though in several N-E communities, men having more than one wife or some mistresses is not uncommon and such men are viewed more indulgently than women having extra-marital relationships. The custom of bride-price sometimes proves to be a means of getting out of an unwanted marriage for women. If a women married to an older man having more wives finds a young lover with whom she elopes, she or her paramour can return the bride-price to the first husband in order to obtain her release from the previous marital obligation. Such instances are not however very common.

Divorce and Remarriage

On the whole, divorces are relatively easy and frequent among most N-E tribal communities, and divorcees, as well as widows can re-marry. This is quite different from non-tribal Hindu communities of Assam and Tripura, where even when the husband abandons or ill-treats a wife, she cannot easily get a divorce, and even if she does succeed, she faces strong social disapproval. In most tribal communities, the usual grounds for divorce for both partners are mutual incompatibility, infidelity, childlessness or affliction from an incurable disease. Among a few highly male-dominant tribes, however, men are known to just order their wives to leave, without any formality of divorce. For instance, a Nishi husband from Arunachal Pradesh may simply order his wife to quit on fairly vague grounds, such as incompetence in house-keeping or cultivation tasks. Among the Lothas of Nagaland, wives are expected to be docile and obedient, and if a man or his relatives feel that a wife is disobedient or overbearing, they may just order her out, after giving a token compensation like Rs. 10/-. A Sema Naga may unilaterally ask his wife to leave on such indeterminate ground as incompatibility, and reclaim bride-price from her parents (particularly since bride-price tends to be on the high side among the Semas) within three years of marriage.

Divorce cases in most tribal communities are settled by village councils or councils of village elders, where women have no representation. In general, women seeking a divorce must produce witnesses, and generally women end up paying heavy fines, besides having to return bride-price to the husband, because men in village councils are keen to avoid an impression that a woman can easily divorce her husband on a frivolous pretext. While men guilty of adultery get away with a light punishment, adultery in women invites a much heavier punishment. Even when a husband has initiated a divorce case, the divorced woman does not get maintenance in most cases. The Mishings and Rabhas of Assam stand out as somewhat special cases where wives subjected to neglect and lack of maintenance can get a divorce and compensation from guilty husband. The Tai Phakes (a Buddhist group of Myanmar origin) provide a unique example where in cases of adultery, the paramour is treated as the main culprit and punished more heavily than the woman involved in adultery.

In most N-E tribal communities, there are no restrictions on widows wishing to remarry, unlike in the non-tribal communities of Assam and Tripura, where widow re-marriages are disapproved among brahmins and other higher castes. The Nishings of Arunachal Pradesh and Lothas and Semas of Nagaland represent a few exceptions among tribal communities that treat widows more like pieces of property where brothers and sons of the deceased husband distribute the widows among themselves, even without the formality of a wedding. Fortunately, this practice is reported to be declining to some extent and widows are given the freedom to marry men of their choice. However, if a widow marries a man not belonging to her husband's clan, she loses the right of maintenance from the first husband's clan, and custody of children. In some tribes, the woman is required to return the bride-price to the first husband's clan members.

Women's Family Roles

Women in N-E tribal communities assume major responsibility for cultivation and for the various supplementary activities needed for family subsistence, as noted earlier, and this is taken for granted, so they do not get any special recognition for this. But even a minor lapse, such as a household member going hungry on some day, is regarded as disgraceful. Men occupy a dominant role in the family in some groups, such as Karbis and Dimasas of Assam and Rongmei Nagas, and women reinforce this by their loyalty and devotion to husbands. The choicest foods are given to men. Life in these families runs smoothly since both men and women fully accept mutual roles. In some other communities, however, women have a more dominant role in the household and men who seem rather aggressive outside the home (e.g. Khiamnungans) would not take decisions regarding purchasing livestock or marriages of children without consulting their wives. The intra-family equations between women and men thus include many variations. Bodo women are custodians of granaries, and husbands would not sell grains without their wives' concurrence.

Women occupy an important place in events like births, marriages, celebration of festivals, thus promoting solidarity in the family and clan members. In a number of groups, women act as negotiators of marriages between the girl's and the groom's families and may often have to ease tensions caused by events like daughter's elopement. As noted before, the *Khadduh* (Khasi inheritress) plays an important role in providing care and protection to aged and needy relatives and preserving solidarity of her clan. Among Khasi-Jaintias, major responsibility for children's education has to be assumed by women, unlike in non-tribal societies where this is regarded primarily as fathers' concern. This is also true of Meitei women, since husbands are more involved in supporting their mothers' and sisters' families. Meitei women to a large extent receive support not only in their economic, but also in family problems through organization of "Nupi-Palas" or "Marups" or self-help groups. Besides providing moral support in difficult family situations, such groups have expanded opportunities of participation in singing and theatrical presentations, which bring them much-needed relief from the daily grind as well as providing artistic expression.

In recent years, a change in parents' previously rather discriminatory attitude towards girls as compared to boys has been noted among several tribal communities e.g. Mizo, Naga, Apatani, Miri, etc. Parents seem to have realized that girls generally utilize educational opportunities more conscientiously, and show greater concern and responsibility towards ageing parents as well as younger siblings. This has lessened the parents' tendency to withdraw girls from schools at an early age. Because of their industriousness and perseverance, more and more girls are earning incomes out of which they are providing financial support for their parents as well as for the education of younger brothers and sisters. This is reported to be prompting an increasing number of parents to gift some lands to their daughters. As noted earlier a few women have been running successful economic enterprises in every N-E State, which may lead to equitable treatment of daughters by parents.

Women's Place in Religion

A majority of indigenous N-E religions have relegated women to low and insignificant positions, and exclude them from performing most religious rituals. The priests are always men and women's job is limited to getting together the materials needed in various rituals, e.g. *apong* (rice-beer), other food, sacrificial animals, etc. While a few communities, e.g. Meiteis, allow women to perform family level worship (the Tangkhul Nagas do not permit women to perform even household level rituals), community level rituals are always performed by men. Even the much-glorified Khasi "Syiem-Sad" (State priestess) is expected to assist the Syiem in performing religious ceremonies. The reasons given for women's exclusion are many and varied: e.g. women do not have a permanent clan, menstruation makes them unclean, etc. In any case, they are no more flimsy than the grounds on which orthodox Hinduism prohibited women from officiating as priests in major Hindu rituals. There are a few exceptions, however, among N-E religions with respect to women's exclusion. The Adi religion in Arunachal Pradesh — which popularized "Donyi-Polo" faith, permits women to be priests, and even regards women as especially capable of invocation of deities. The "Brahma" faith among the Bodos of Assam, propounded by Kalicharan Brahma, is another example where women are accepted as priests. Most of the Buddhist tribes, e.g. Sherdukpens, Membas, Khamtis and Singphos of Arunachal Pradesh permit women to participate on an equal footing in congregational prayers, although the priests are always men.

Many tribal women in N-E communities used exposure to Hinduism to expand their limited space in indigenous religions. This was often facilitated when several tribal chiefs or kings adopted Hinduism and urged their subjects to join. In a similar way, many non-tribal women of Assam, along with tribal women, welcomed Shankaradev's Vaishnavism, because by eliminating rituals and the mediation by priests, Vaishnavism offered them a simple faith to achieve direct communion with God — Vishnu — through devotion and participation in singing and prayers in *Namghars* (community prayer halls). Meitei women, faced with pressure from brahmin preceptors to give up Sanamahi religion and adopt Vaishnavism used a different tactic of retaining Sanamahi worship at family level and adopting Hindu worship at community level thus expanding their space in religion. In later years, when revival of Sanamahi religion by some Meitei leaders became a symbol of Meitei nationalism, for Meitei women, Lai Harouba, and the prominent role of "Maibi" symbolized an assertion of women's important and complementary role along with men. The interest and strong patronage given by some Meitei kings, like Bhagyachandra and Churachand since late nineteenth century onwards to women's participation in Ras-Leela and artistic excellence in dance and music provided Meitei women an important avenue to enhance their status — both religious and social — and women used this opportunity to resist discrimination in their use of cymbals and drums. And they won the battle!

The arrival of Christian missionaries during early years of the British rule in Meghalaya, Mizoram and Nagaland, and introduction of Christianity, have enhanced the religious status of women in these States, and they can participate on an equal footing in church worship. Perhaps even more significant is the introduction of girls' education by the missionaries that has made rapid advances in improving women's status in many respects — occupational, economic and social. Women's participation in Christian churches brought another development — they could actively participate in several church-sponsored social activities, e.g. orphanages for destitute children, shelters for needy women, hospitals and health services sponsored by Christian denominations, fund-raising campaigns on behalf of various Christian churches, etc. Women's participation in such activities has now opened for them avenues to promote other social causes — even without churches' support. There is, however an important limitation which stands in their way. Neither the Presbyterian nor the Baptist or any other churches have so far allowed women to hold positions of deacons, priests and pastors, although a few participate in some church committees but not the most prestigious ones. Some Mizo women have acquired Bachelor's degree in Divinity and a few are acting as missionaries among disadvantaged population groups. This is indeed a big leap from the times when women's religious role was confined to being communicators with good and evil spirits and warding off social calamities like epidemics or individual mishaps like illness and disease. Women in some remote communities continue to play such roles even today. For instance, the "Eins" and "Sheepas" continue to be invited to avert individual or social disasters among the Khiamnungans and Konyaks of Nagaland.

Quite significantly, women's procreative powers and along with it menstruation has caused some strange and often contradictory signals, particularly among a few tribal communities. Among the Akas of Arunachal Pradesh, menstruation in women has been associated with evil influence, and there is a belief that if a man leaving on a hunting expedition accidentally touches a menstruating woman or eats food prepared by her, he runs the risk of meeting with a disaster or even of death. Even in Hinduism, women's exclusion from some religious rituals is justified on the grounds of menstruation. On the other hand, some communities have given women a special place since with their powers of procreation, they are of the same genre as the fertile earth. The Adis of Arunachal Pradesh who give great importance to Mopin, the deity of agriculture, also consider women as specially suited to propitiate divine powers. The Mishings and Bodos, and indeed many plains tribal communities of Assam give significant roles to women in festivals connected with fertility of the soil and harvesting. On the other hand, among Karbis and Dimasas (hill-tribal communities of Assam), the ability to sing funeral dirges and thus ensure the soul's journey to its final resting place, qualifies women to lead funeral rites, and they are reported to be eager to get the position of "Uchepi" or the chief mourner!

Health Status

A few selected findings from the NFHS-1 (1992-93) on N-E women are used as indicators of their health status and the extent of access to health services. The access to water supplied through pipes or hand-pumps was available to nearly three-fourths of households in Arunachal Pradesh and Nagaland, while in the remaining five States more than half of the households did not have this facility. Mizoram was the only State where most households had some kind of a toilet facility — howsoever primitive, while in Meghalaya and Assam nearly half of the households did not have any. Although child marriages are not common in N-E societies, the survey revealed that in Arunachal Pradesh, Assam and Tripura, two out of five marriages took place when girls were less than 18 years of age. The Crude Birth Rates (CBR) in Arunachal Pradesh, Meghalaya, Nagaland and Assam were higher than the Indian average (28.7) and Total Fertility Rates (TFRs) were higher than the Indian average of 3.39 in Arunachal Pradesh, Meghalaya and Assam. Arunachal Pradesh had the highest CBR (34.6) and TFR (4.25), while for Mizoram, both rates were lowest, viz. 20.8 and 2.30 respectively.

Use of contraceptives by mothers was highest in Tripura (56 per cent), with Mizoram following close behind (54 per cent), while lowest (13 per cent) in Nagaland. Access to safe delivery in health institutions was available to less than a third of the mothers in six out of seven States, while in Mizoram, 49 per cent of mothers had such access. Nearly two-thirds of mothers could avail of services of health professionals during delivery, while this facility was accessible to 20-40 per cent of mothers in the remaining six States. As regards complete immunization of children below two years of age (BCG, measles, three dozes of DPT and polio), once again Mizoram came to the top position with 63 per cent coverage, while the remaining six States ranged between 25 to 41 per cent.

According to Ministry of Health (Govt. of India) sources, as of 1994, the N-E States had a total of 397 hospitals and 937 dispensaries. The basic rural primary health infrastructure available in 1997, including sub-centres, primary health centres and community health centres, generally met the government norms based on population, with a few exceptions. However, problems in access to services due to difficult terrain, poor transportation facilities, weaknesses in referral services, shortage of doctors and trained female health assistants, auxiliary nurse midwives (ANMs) and nurses remain fairly acute.

Educational Status

As per 1991 Census, female (7+) literacy in six N-E States ranged between 43 per cent and 79 per cent, i.e. above the Indian average (39 per cent), while Arunachal Pradesh lagged behind at 30 per cent. Mizoram, at 79 per cent occupied the second highest rank in the country. As per 2001 Census (Provisional figures), Arunachal Pradesh, despite considerable progress, remained at 44 per cent against female literacy rate for India as a whole — 58 per cent, while the remaining six States ranged between 56 and 86 per cent, and Mizoram retained its second highest position in the country at 86 per cent, next to Kerala with 88 per cent. Male-female literacy differentials for N-E States in 1991 ranged between seven percentage points for Mizoram and 24 points for Manipur, i.e. lower than the national average of 25 points. Male-female literacy differentials in ST populations for 1991 vary between 6 percentage points for Mizoram and 26 for Tripura. It is significant to note that the male-female literacy differentials are the lowest — between 6 and 12 points for Mizoram, Meghalaya and Nagaland — that have more than 85 per cent ST populations.

The 1998-99 official figures indicate that the enrolment of girls at primary, middle and secondary school levels is lower than that of boys in all N-E States, the differences being comparatively higher in Assam and Tripura (the two States with non-tribal majority populations), and fairly small in Meghalaya, Mizoram and Nagaland — States with predominantly tribal populations. Meghalaya provides a happy exception where girls' enrolment at middle level is higher than that of boys. Surprisingly, dropout rates for all three levels, as compared with those for boys do not reflect any consistent pattern, but high dropout rates for both boys and girls in N-E States, in comparison with some other States, are a cause for concern. The quality of teaching and access to schools are certainly important factors in retention of students and need careful consideration. N-E States have a shortage of trained teachers, and particularly trained women teachers, as well as inadequate teacher-training facilities. Furthermore, there is a need to augment training facilities for technical, vocational and professional streams, and ensure their proliferation in other States besides Assam, where they are concentrated at present.

Social and Political Status

N-E women have generally been excluded from participation in traditional village councils, or councils of elders which are responsible for administrative, social and political matters concerning the community, including cases of disputes between individuals, violation of customary rules, or marital disputes. The reasons given for women's exclusion are varied, e.g. that they do not have a permanent clan, or that they cannot maintain confidentiality and are apt to indulge in loose talk, or that they are devoid of wisdom and sound judgement, etc. A number of later events and developments have been making profound changes in the situation and have influenced N-E women's social and political status. Here are some examples:

Women's status in social and political fields is closely interrelated, and this in turn is strongly influenced by their status in other areas such as education and occupation. Mavis Dunn Lingdoh, Bonily Khongmen and Jyotsna Chanda — all of whom were among the early graduates and connected with the field of education — were elected to State Legislative Assembly or to the Indian Parliament. Furthermore, if women earn an independent income, their status in society also goes up, besides their family status. N-E women's substantial contribution in family cultivation and their numerous tasks undertaken to supplement insufficient food for the family are taken more or less for granted and do not give them any special recognition. But if they earn some money by taking up a salaried job, e.g. as a teacher or health visitor or start a business and earn profit, or occupy a professional position, not only their status in the family but also in society goes up significantly.

Women's Participation in Welfare Activities

Indian freedom struggle and Gandhiji's Non-cooperation Movement drew many Assamese women — and some from remote areas — into activities like boycott of foreign goods or resistance movements, and many courted arrests and some even braved police bullets. Equally important, many women initiated a variety of welfare activities under the "Constructive" programme. When foreign missionaries introduced Christianity in Meghalaya, Mizoram and Nagaland, they provided women an access to congregational services in churches, which in itself was a new experience for them, since in their native religions, women had a very marginal and subordinate status. Equally important, the missionaries introduced girls' education, which opened a new world for women. Besides, women also got an opportunity to participate in a variety of welfare activities sponsored by churches. At present, women in these States are active in organizing a number of programmes, e.g. homes for destitute children, relief for the aged and the sick, fund-raising campaigns on behalf of churches, etc. Although women in all N-E States participate in some welfare activities, in some States like Arunachal Pradesh, these are in early stages of development. In some States, women are active in educating their communities with respect to pernicious customs. For instance, Garo women's organizations have been trying to eliminate customs like "Akim" — replacement of a deceased marriage partner by another member of the clan, which at times results in a young girl of 12 years being married to an old widower.

Women Acquire a New Voice through Organizations

Formation of groups, associations and organizations has been an important means for N-E women to enhance their weak social and political status. The Meitei women's "Nupi-palas" or "Marups" provide one of the best examples of achieving a stronger self-image through identification with the group in a highly male-dominated society. Besides meeting members' requirements of small loans during family crises, and daily needs like tea and refreshments during long hours of work away from home, these groups can exert social pressure against a member's husband for bringing a second wife! Mizo women's federation — MHIP — is a statewide organization with over 500 branches at district and village level. When it takes up issues like Mizo customary laws that make no provision for maintenance to be given by a husband unilaterally divorcing a wife, this receives public attention. A number of Naga tribes such as the Sema, Lotha and Tangkhul have separate women's associations that can raise their voice against injustice. It is worth noting that Naga Women's Organization and All Naga Women's Federation, which are more broad-based bodies including members from several tribal communities, are invited to participate in negotiations among the State and Central Governments, Naga Ho Ho and various insurgent groups. Assam has a few organizations, e.g. Assam Pradeshik Mahila Samiti, with branches in various districts and towns. While Arunachal Pradesh has a small number of organizations representing women from local communities, the difficult terrain and problems of communications pose serious challenges for setting up large statewide or even district-wide organizations. Even then, women can improve their visibility and self-image by forming small groups of members, which may include like-minded men as well, residing in the same village.

Expression of Protests and Revolts

There are quite a few instances of N-E women offering resistance to actions or practices of the government or other powerful sections, considered unjust or oppressive. In some cases, the protests are immediate and spontaneous while in some others these have continued for relatively long periods. Some illustrations :

— Mizo women joined the movement for abolition of chieftain system, starting in late 1940s and continuing until early 1950s.

— A Rongmei Naga girl Guidinlieu continued to lead the Zeliangrong movement initiated by her cousin Jadonang and challenged the British rulers in 1931.

— Meitei women's two "Nupi-lans" — the first in 1904, to resist British officers' demanding compulsory labour from Manipuri men, and second in 1939, to stop export of rice by British administration at a time when local population faced food deficits.

— Tripura tribal women joined their men between 1949-64 in resisting forced levies by exploitative landlords, government agents and moneylenders. Another protest action was directed against the highhandedness of forest guards in confiscating forest produce collected by women and their use of force.

— Assamese women participated in large numbers in peaceful resistance during the Assam movement in early 1980s.

— There have been several instances of protests against rapes of women and arbitrary use of force by security personnel and police in Tripura, Assam and Manipur. In a few cases, women's organizations of a national stature, e.g. All India Democratic Women's Association and National Council for Women have provided support to arouse public concern and to institute legal proceedings against the guilty.

— Mizo women organized protest marches and public meetings during 1980s to express their outrage over rapes of women employees at the hands of employers, and the shocking absence of action against the culprits.

Women's Presence in Representative Political Institutions

After Indian Independence in 1947 and adoption of a new Constitution, for Indian women, and particularly N-E women, a new democratic era opened where they were assured equal opportunities with men to seek election to representative bodies at national, state, district and other local levels. As noted before, most N-E tribal communities had traditionally been denied entry to women in village or tribal councils and councils of elders which were responsible for social and political matters. We will summarize briefly how N-E women have fared in the new representative bodies.

Since the first Lok Sabha election in 1952 up to 1977 nine women, and between 1985 and 1999 three women were elected to the Lok Sabha from composite Assam. During this period Manipur, Nagaland and Tripura have returned one woman each, while the remaining three States, viz. Arunachal Pradesh, Mizoram and Meghalaya did not elect any woman. For the Rajya Sabha, between 1952-99 three women were elected from Assam, and one each from Arunachal Pradesh and Tripura, while not a single woman was elected from Manipur, Mizoram, Meghalaya and Nagaland.

Assam had its first legislative assembly election in 1952 and up to 2003, nearly 50 women have been elected so far. For Arunachal Pradesh, Manipur, Mizoram and Nagaland, the number of women elected to State assemblies ranges between one and five, while for Meghalaya and Tripura, it varies between nine and twelve.

When we review the situation of women's representation in local urban and rural bodies at district level and below, as per the 73rd and 74th Constitutional Amendments, one-third of the total number of seats (members and presidents) are being reserved for women in Arunachal Pradesh, Assam (with the exception of two hill districts), Manipur central valley and Tripura (excluding the Autonomous District Area). In areas covered under the Sixth Schedule, or by other similar legislative provisions, women's representation varies between none to one or two, and even where one of two women are nominated, they act as observers and not as full-fledged members. In Nagaland, there is a statutory provision of at least one seat in Village Development Boards being reserved for women, which ensures some representation, and women members are reported to be actively participating in village development programmes. In the five hill districts of Manipur, women's participation varies between nil to two, who more often than not act as observers, rather than active participants in village councils. Another illustration is Mizoram, where in 1999 women elected to village councils or nominated formed a very small minority, viz. 15 out of total 2248 seats, and one woman each in the three autonomous district councils. Quite interestingly, a small number of tribal women have been fighting elections to the Tripura Tribal Area Autonomous District Council, and in 1995, for instance, two women were elected. The support received from All India Democratic Women's Association has been extremely helpful in encouraging tribal women's participation in elections to the Autonomous Council.

Concluding Observations

MEASURES FOR ENHANCING ECONOMIC OPPORTUNITIES FOR WOMEN

The review of economic status of N-E women brings into focus the large number involved in jhum and other types of primitive cultivation, their heavy workloads, insufficient yields and the pressing need for several supplementary activities for meeting their families' basic requirements. The first two chapters have indicated the enormous potential for hydro-electric power, and rich mineral resources of N-E States that can be harnessed by the Central Government to promote the economic development of these States. Here, we will focus primarily on those areas where State Governments and local communities can jointly mobilize available resources in order to create conditions for maximizing the initiative of women and thus promote the economic wellbeing of their families.

While recognizing the need for changing over from jhuming to settled cultivation, some simple methods, e.g. using high-yielding varieties of seeds, constructing small bunds and diversion channels to better utilize water from mountain streams and rivers (as adopted by farmers in Nagaland) can improve yields even from *jhum* cultivation. However, Mizoram, Arunachal Pradesh and Tripura have adopted more productive strategies for land-use, e.g. tea, coffee and rubber plantations, and cultivation of fruits such as oranges, bananas, pineapple, jackfruit, guava, mango, leechi, etc. Preparation of extracts and oleoresins from ginger, basil, citronella, lemon grass, cinnamon leaves and a fungus which grows on agarwood trees, etc. has been found very lucrative in view of the industrial and medicinal uses of these extracts. And women can be usefully engaged in collecting raw materials and preliminary processing of the same. In most N-E States, transportation of vegetables, fruits and other perishable articles has so far been difficult and expensive. Mizoram has made a promising start by setting up Mizoram Food and Allied Industries Corporation which started production of fruit juice concentrates, and processing of vegetables, mushrooms, fish, pork, chicken, etc. Arunachal Pradesh has also set up a fruit-processing plant. If these facilities are expanded on a larger scale, women will have an assured market for their products, and therefore can take up production on a larger scale, besides finding new employment in food processing units. There is one aspect that has not received adequate attention from State Governments. For instance, whenever schemes are launched to promote orchards or plantations on hill slopes in place of jhuming, tribal families that adopt such changes require technical and financial support during the relatively long period of four to six years before the new types of cultivation starts giving returns. It is necessary to provide them sustained support during the gestation period. In the past many schemes of this type have failed in the absence of sustained support and tribal peasants have sold their lands for a pittance and have become agricultural labourers or have migrated to cities in search of wage labour employment.

As has been noted before, a majority of N-E women have to

supplement food resources from *jhum* cultivation by undertaking a variety of ancillary activities, such as raising vegetables, poultry, pigs, fishing, sericulture, handloom weaving, etc. There is enormous scope for improving the quality of products through infusion of modern technology, besides increasing returns in these activities. In the few places where women have adopted modern techniques of poultry and pig-rearing, their profit margins have increased due to more effective protection of the animals from diseases, and better growth. In sericulture, the adoption of better silk varieties like pat and mooga in place of eri, improved post-cocoon technology for reeling, dying and weaving can increase profits. In some N-E areas like Arunachal Pradesh, women still continue to use loin or pit looms, instead of fly-shuttle and even newer models like jacquard looms. All these supplementary activities need to be upgraded with improved tools, training, supply of raw materials, market outlets, credit facilities, etc. Some States have initiated pilot projects in most of these activities. What is needed is their expansion on a scale that can make a significant impact on their viability.

In the context of the heavy dependence of N-E tribal women on forests for supplementing their inadequate resources for household subsistence, it is useful to initiate measures for ensuring continued availability of fuel, fodder for animals and edible tubers and vegetables to supplement insufficient food supplies. There are a few good examples of joint forest management combining commercial and private interests that need to be multiplied. For instance, Tripura government has initiated schemes in partnership with tribal communities for cultivation of fruits, fodder for animals and medicinal crops (Das Gupta, 1999). Arunachal Pradesh government has initiated tree plantation in degraded *jhum* lands in collaboration with Anchal Parishads (counterparts of Block Samitis). The significance of this measure in a State that contributes nearly half of the total timber supply from N-E region is self-evident (Mitra, 1999). There is plenty of experience in several States, and an outstanding example is provided by a voluntary agency (Sadguru Water and Development Foundation, Dahod) in Gujarat that has launched successful joint forest management projects in areas that had remained totally barren due to scanty rainfall for a long time. Here, tribal women are emerging as successful fruit producers, nursery raisers, and most importantly, competent extension workers.

A discussion of improving N-E women's capacity for generating more income is incomplete without simultaneously giving thought to saving their time and energy in daily house-keeping chores and other activities undertaken to supplement inadequate resources. They have to spend considerable time and energy in collecting water from mountain springs and rivers which dry up in some seasons, and in collecting firewood for cooking, and in de-husking and grinding grains manually in the absence of gas and electricity. While the Central and State Government programmes to provide piped water and electricity to increasing number of villages make slow progress, some steps are necessary to reduce the physical strain and time women have to spend daily in these routine tasks. There are some examples in Himachal Pradesh where the flowing power of rivers and mountain streams is converted through simple devices to run flour mills. Similarly, considerable experimentation has gone into devising systems of storing water from streams into storage devices at different levels in order to meet shortage of water in dry months. However, the natural gas available in several N-E States is mostly flared away and only a small part is currently being used. It is necessary to find ways of deploying it to meet the fuel requirements of households, as well as for running small and medium-size industries in the N-E region. A number of innovative ventures in some other parts of India have developed devices like bio-gas plants, improved wood-stoves for cooking, use of solar as well as wind energy, more efficient handlooms, agricultural tools for transplanting and weeding, etc. For some reason, most of the appropriate technology centres have not paid much attention to evolving suitable devices to bring some relief into the life of many N-E women who continue to perform their daily chores with very primitive tools. Perhaps, the North-Eastern Council and institutions of technical training and research could give some thought to ways of reducing the enormous drudgery of many N-E women and release their energy for more viable and creative activities.

In this connection, an imaginative and heart-warming development — National Innovation Foundation (NIF) — represents the flowering of an idea cherished by Professor Anil Gupta of Indian Institute of Management, Ahmedabad, for providing technical and financial support to grassroot innovators in the country. Branches of Grassroot Innovations Augmentation Network (GIAN) are expected to facilitate scientific and entrepreneurial support to motivated innovators for fulfilling their cherished projects. Under this programme, a village carpenter from Darrang district in Assam has developed a wood-cutter that can reduce energy and time spent in cutting large wooden logs. A radio mechanic from Kamrup village in Assam has built an inexpensive water turbine that can generate up to two kilowatts of electrical energy.

EXPANDING EMPLOYMENT AVENUES FOR WOMEN

It has been noted repeatedly, that a large number of household activities undertaken daily by N-E women in order to supplement insufficient food supplied from *jhum* or other primitive cultivation are taken for granted as usual household chores and do not give women any additional status. But if they earn cash income by some work outside the home, their status in the family and society goes up. Our foregoing reviews of women's situation in education and health have highlighted several opportunities for women's employment. The high dropout rates among girls in most N-E States are a cause for serious concern, and the causes include shortage of trained women teachers and absence of boarding and hostel facilities for girls, both of which could generate employment opportunities for women in school. The review of health has indicated many gaps in preventive and protective measures. For instance, nearly half of mothers in four N-E States do not receive iron and folic acid supplements during pregnancy; less than half of total deliveries in six N-E States are conducted by trained health professionals; children below two years in six N-E States who received ORS or HRS during diarrhoeal episodes did not constitute more than two out of every five afflicted children. There are many instances of this type that indicate an urgent need for adequately trained women health auxiliaries who can visit mothers in their homes and provide such essential services. Similarly, State Government departments of community development and women's welfare can train and assign women extension workers to equip housewives with better tools and techniques, e.g. more efficient wood-stoves (*chulhas*), inexpensive sand water filters, recipes for preparing more nutritious food and conserving vitamins, etc. Women can also be taught improved techniques of raising poultry birds and pigs, and kitchen gardens. Such programmes can be supervised by adequately trained women extension officers. Assam and Manipur have demonstrated the utility of mobile units of two or three women extension workers equipped with sets of demonstration materials, audio-visual equipment and a jeep, who were assigned to different parts of the States. The economic activities suggested require the will, organization of training facilities and administrative actions by appropriate State Governments in collaboration with local communities.

INCREASING RETURNS FROM WOMEN'S ECONOMIC ACTIVITIES

A reference has been made earlier to the initiation of food-processing units in Mizoram and Arunachal Pradesh by the respective State Governments. A majority of food products, e.g. vegetables, fruits, poultry birds, etc. are raised by women to supplement inadequate food supplies from *jhum* cultivation, or to earn cash for purchasing other family requirements. It is in this area that a lot of scope is available for making profits through better marketing of the produce. Most women sell their products in local markets since access to larger markets in state or district capitals is not available due to problems of transportation.

It is useful to learn from the experience of some successful rural development projects in other parts of India. Once again, we refer to Sadguru Water and Development Foundation,(SWDF), Dahod, Gujarat that has transformed the life of local tribal communities through introducing better conservation and management of available water. SWDF has trained local men and women to take up cultivation of vegetables, fruits and flowers instead of conventional crops as off-season activity, and thus enabled them to earn substantial income through their sale in nearby town markets. The cultivators have formed small groups and assigned to a member the task of transporting members' products to an urban market where they get an assured profit, even after paying a certain percentage as sales commission. Women in N-E States can adopt this method not just for vegetables and fruits, but also for poultry and piggery units and facilitate transportation of products to urban markets through suitable co-operative arrangements.

UPGRADING QUALITY AND VIABILITY OF HANDICRAFTS

N-E women possess several skills in handicrafts, e.g. handloom weaving in cotton, silk and wool, cane and bamboo products, pottery, embroidery, etc. There is tremendous scope for improving the quality of their products, tools and equipment used, and above all the economic viability of their crafts. Some N-E State Governments have initiated programmes for introduction of new technology, training of artisans, sales emporia for craft products, etc. but these have been quite inadequate to meet the needs. It might be worthwhile for groups of women engaged in various crafts to initiate some steps by establishing contacts with organizations having expertise in different areas and identify their needs and then bring pressure on State Governments to take appropriate actions.

For instance, Khadi and Village Industries Commission can assist women weavers in N-E States to adopt new weaving techniques and improved looms and better dyeing of yarns. The National Institute of Design can demonstrate the adoption of improved designs. The N-E cane and bamboo crafts-persons can benefit from consultations with expert organizations like Dastkar to identify market requirements and appropriate changes in products. A large number of groups engaged in handicrafts have found new outlets to exhibit and sell their products by establishing contacts with Dastakari Hat Samiti. Self-Employed Women's Association (SEWA) in Ahmedabad has helped women engaged in Chikan embroidery work in Lucknow to improve profitability of their endeavours. N-E women need the help of banks to provide working capital and credit facilities to protect themselves from exploitation by middlemen. In short, if women engaged in various crafts take the initiative in seeking the support of appropriate organizations in the country, respective State Governments will be under pressure to undertake suitable supporting actions.

NEW POLITICAL CHALLENGES BEFORE N-E WOMEN

Indian society in general has relegated women to a low social and political status due to a pervasive and long-standing belief among men that women are neither interested nor capable of participating in social and political matters. Quite ironically, Indian women have to a great extent reinforced this assumption due to various reasons. Among N-E tribal communities the exclusion of women from village or community councils responsible for administrative, social and political affairs of the community is very explicit. Against this backdrop, when Indian Constitution opened the doors of all representative institutions to men and women without any distinction, it is interesting to note how N-E women have responded at various levels.

At least five women were elected so far to the Lok Sabha and Rajya Sabha from six N-E States and 15 women from Assam. Coming to the State Legislative Assemblies, nearly 30-32 women have been elected from six N-E States, and about 50 from Assam. Considering the negative bias against women, the numbers of women elected to national and State legislatures do not seem insignificant, and the increasing numbers of women contestants indicate an optimistic trend. Coming down to the district level and below, Arunachal Pradesh, Assam, Manipur and Tripura have been complying with the requirements of 73rd and 74th Constitutional Amendments with respect to reservation of one-third seats for women in rural and urban local government bodies. This provision of reservation for women does not however apply to areas included under the Sixth Schedule and the Manipur District Council Act, viz. Mizoram, Meghalaya, two hill districts of Assam, Tripura's tribal areas, and the hill districts of Manipur. In the Autonomous District Councils and village councils, women's representation is nil or minimal. Even where women are nominated, they act mostly like observers rather than full participants. In the District Councils of Meghalaya, a very small number of women get elected or nominated. In Mizoram too, a very small number of women are elected to village councils. It is necessary to examine whether Nagaland's VDBs which provide for one compulsory seat for women indicate any pointers. Would it help to fix a minimum quota of reservation of seats for women, as in Panchayati Raj Institutions?

After more than 50 years of the functioning of Autonomous District Councils in the N-E States, it is necessary to evaluate whether these have fulfilled their original objectives of ensuring optimum conditions for preserving the distinctive cultures and traditions of self-governance of tribal communities concerned or, they have perpetuated the tradition of exclusion of women from social and political affairs. Since Arunachal Pradesh adopted the Panchayati Raj pattern, what are the positive and negative aspects of its functioning? Can respective State Governments initiate objective assessment of the functioning of Autonomous District Councils and measures needed to strengthen the same? On the other hand, a question needs to be raised as to whether these councils should be replaced with Panchayati Raj Institutions, and thus facilitate the integration of tribal communities concerned within the mainstream Indian polity.

This also raises the point regarding proper orientation of Autonomous Council Members to educate them with respect to their responsibilities. In fact, such orientation programmes are organized for members of Parliament and Panchayati Raj Institutions in some States. Apart from helping members of Autonomous District Councils to become aware of the relevant aspects of their jurisdiction, they can be sensitized with respect to their attitudes towards women members as well as the situation of women in general in their communities.

NEED TO REMOVE OPPRESSIVE PRACTICES

In several respects, N-E women are better off than women from non-tribal societies in the rest of India. For instance, the freedom girls enjoy to select their marriage partner; the relatively easy divorce if for any reason the marriage does not work out; the social acceptance of remarriages of divorcees and widows, the absence of oppressive dowry system — many of these aspects need to be incorporated by non-tribal societies in the rest of India. At the same time, the vague and arbitrary grounds on which men in some N-E communities, e.g. Lotha, Sema, Nishing, can dismiss their wives is quite shocking. Furthermore, the Village Councils, which are exclusively male conclaves, tend to be grossly unfair to women, who cannot represent their cases. The strong bias against women seeking divorce generally leads to Village Councils imposing a heavy penalty on women, while men seeking divorce get away with a minor fine. Barring a few exceptions, most N-E tribal communities do not permit women to own or inherit immovable property. It is extremely important to create public awareness about such issues in order to generate reforms. There is a need to provide a fairer and impartial forum for adjudication of women's marital and other legal problems through the general legal procedures, such as courts presided over by District Magistrates. This highlights the question of encouraging N-E communities to undertake comprehensive reviews of their customary laws and traditions.

Some communities, e.g. the Adis of Arunachal Pradesh have initiated a cultural revival movement that has resulted in elevating the position of women especially in Adi religion. The Bodos and Sonowal Kacharis of Assam have removed several unjust customs from their society, leading to vast improvement in the status of their women. The Pati Rabhas of Assam have initiated a codification of their customs, which has resulted in improving the situation of women. For instance, a Pati Rabha woman who is divorced by her husband is now entitled to receive maintenance from her husband. It is necessary to create opportunities for both women and men to benefit from the experience of communities that have adopted more humane practices and eliminated injustice towards women. In fact, a number of organizations in the country have initiated documentation of cases where women are subjected to cruel and unfair treatment, which has highlighted the need for reforms. N-E women can benefit from contacts with groups and individuals — both women and men — in the N-E region and outside and learn from their experience in social and judicial activism. The Law Research Institute, Guwahati, has taken the initiative in codification of customary laws in a number of N-E communities. Such consultation need not be confined merely to legal expertise, and needs close involvement of individuals and groups interested in reforms of customs and structures that are unjust and unfair.

INTEGRATION — AN ESSENTIAL ASPECT

N-E women at present face many problems. The alarming incidence of alcoholism and drug addiction in the region, the large-scale drug trafficking across international borders, the rising unemployment and frustration among the youth and their exploitation by insurgent groups leading to violence — these factors present additional hardships for N-E women. The continued presence of the police and security forces and their combing operations create a new set of problems that add to women's hardships. There is no doubt that their isolation makes the situation even more difficult.

It is obviously outside our scope to go into the details of the respective responsibilities of the Central and State Governments. At the same time, it is extremely important to emphasize the need for both the parties not to get bogged down completely by the law and order situation, and keep their visions focused on the long term development of N-E States, to ensure a fuller and satisfying life for their inhabitants. An important aspect of this goal is to promote meaningful contacts and exchanges among persons engaged in various developmental programmes in different parts of India so that they can learn and benefit from each other. Coming down to the situation of N-E women officials in State Governments, there is no doubt that they would benefit greatly from contacts with their counterparts from other States in the region and the country.

An important prerequisite for establishing relationships is obviously adequate communications and transport facilities. As per government sources, as of 1991, more than three-fourth of the nearly 3400 villages in Arunachal Pradesh could be reached only by one to seven days or longer foot-march! It is obvious that Government of India and N-E State Governments need to give a higher priority to building roads, rail network and water-ways which simultaneously can also generate some employment which in itself can reduce discontent among the youth. It is important that the usual grouse of inadequate financial allocations from the Central Government is not used as an excuse for half-hearted implementation of development plans. A combination of vigorous State Government initiatives and peoples' participation can generate rapid development, as has been noted already from some successful experiences in the N-E region. What is needed is to continue such efforts on a sustained and coordinated basis.

While recognizing the many practical problems, the importance of breaking the isolation of N-E women and giving them an opportunity to get acquainted with the activities of women's organizations in other States can hardly be over-emphasized. A few examples may help to clarify this point. SEWA, Gujarat, has acted as an important link between poor and illiterate women in a drought-prone area of Gujarat and two specialized organizations — Gujarat Agricultural University and the Indian Petrochemicals Corporation — to teach the women how to store available rain water and select appropriate crop-cycles. The women could then produce crops which found a ready market (Banerjee, 1998). N-E women at present undertake most agricultural operations manually and without the benefit of efficient tools. If they have contacts with organizations that specialize in designing efficient tools, much of their labour and time, currently spent in digging, weeding, harvesting, threshing, etc. can be saved. Above all, they will experience a feeling of camaraderie and fellowship with other women, learn something from the latter and in turn give them something from their experience. In fact a number of individuals and groups are already active in promoting better mutual understanding and support. It is important that these efforts are multiplied and sustained in order to generate a powerful movement which ushers an era of mutual respect and cooperation between women from N-E region and the rest of India.

MEASURING HUMAN DEVELOPMENT

The foregoing analysis of N-E women's status has brought out the fact that while an increase in women's economic status helps to improve their status in other spheres, such as the family and society, it may not necessarily ensure an improvement in other aspects, e.g. health. In the field of human development, a similar kind of awareness has grown that while production of wealth is important, human capabilities are an equally integral part of development. In 1990, the U.N. developed a composite Human Development Index (HDI), which combined indices of life expectancy, educational level and income. A further adaptation of HDI, Gender-related Development Index (GDI) was developed by United Nations Development Programme (UNDP) by adjusting the three component indices for disparities in male-female levels of achievement. These two indices are used by UNDP to rank countries of the world in terms of human development. The Population Foundation of India prepared slightly modified versions of the two indices, HDI and Gender-related Health Index (GHI), the latter based on life expectancy at birth and educational attainment, and leaving out income disparities between males and females in view of the difficulty in getting gender-wise distribution of State Domestic Product. A third index, viz. Reproductive Health Index (RHI) is based on seven parameters:Total Fertility Rate (TFR), Age Specific Fertility Rate in 15-19 age group (ASFR), the proportion of order 4 and above births (B4+), Percentage couples effectively protected by contraceptives (sterilization), Perinatal Mortality Rate (PNMR), Proportion of births receiving skilled attention (SKAB) at the time of delivery, and Educational attainment of women (EAW).

The Population Foundation of India has presented indices for 16 major states of India in a report "State of India's Population" based on 1995 data. Assam is the only N-E State covered in this report, while the remaining six N-E States were left out in the absence of adequate data. Assam occupies 10th position on HDI, 11th on GHI, and 12th on RHI, while Kerala tops the lists in all three.

Another promising effort to measure development has been initiated by the National Commission of Population (*District-wise Indicators*, 2001) by ranking 569 districts out of a total of 593 districts on the basis of 12 indices on which fairly reliable data were available. The criteria include the following indicators: (1) Percentage decadal population growth rate, (2) Total Fertility Rate, (3) Percentage of current users of family planning methods, (4) Percentage of girls marrying below 18 years of age, (5) Sex ratio, (6) Percentage of women receiving skilled attention during deliveries, (7) Percentage of children getting complete immunization, (8) Literacy rate male-female, (9) Percentage of villages not connected with pucca road, (10) Percentage coverage of safe drinking water and sanitation, (11) (a) Percentage of births registered, (b) Percentage of deaths registered. Some additional items such as child mortality up to age of 2, maternal mortality rate, nutritional status of children below 6 years, etc. were dropped since district level data on these were not available at the time.

The States and districts of India have been ranked on the basis of a composite index. Despite the many limitations and adjustments on the quality of data available, this is a useful and worthwhile attempt. On a composite scale-value of 0-100, the 34 States of India and 569 districts have been ranked. The situation of seven N-E States among a total of 34 was as follows:

State	*Scale-value*	*Rank*
Mizoram	69.24	11
Tripura	64.17	17
Assam	56.35	22
Manipur	54.01	25
Meghalaya	50.51	27
Nagaland	48.31	29
Arunachal Pradesh	43.58	31

Goa with 83.71 scale-value occupied 1st rank, while Jharkhand, with 38.27 scale-value was assigned the last position 34th.

Among the 569 districts in India which were ranked on the composite index, the four N-E districts occupying the highest rank and four districts assigned the lowest rank were as follows:

Districts with Highest Ranking				*Districts with Lowerst Ranking*			
District	*State*	*Scale Value*	*Rank*	*District*	*States*	*Scale Value*	*Rank*
Jorhat	Assam	79.71	33	Chandel	Manipur	38.10	502
Nalbari	Assam	76.30	58	Upper Siang	Arunachal Pradesh	37.44	510
Serchhip	Mizoram	76.00	63	Upper Subansiri	Arunachal Pradesh	36.18	525
Mamit	Mizoram	75.82	67	Tuensang	Nagaland	32.57	552

The highest rank among 569 districts was occupied by Ernakulam district in Kerala, with the scale-value of 88.48, whereas Balrampur district of Uttar Pradesh, with the scale-value of 25.05 was assigned the lowest rank.

The development of indices to measure human progress in various aspects of life is a heartening initiative. At the same time, using a composite index that gives equal weight to different components such as life expectancy and income makes certain assumptions which are open to questions. Coming down to the task of assessing N-E women's status, the various indicators listed by National Commission of Population can prove an effective tool in identifying developmental backlogs in certain geographical areas and population groups, especially in aspects such as health and education. This will also help in drawing State Government's attention to aspects which are overlooked or where official records are inadequate. Our analysis of economic status of N-E women has highlighted and need to accurately assess women's substantial contribution towards their families' subsistence through their crucial roles in family cultivation, and equally important, the various supplementary activities, e.g. collecting fuelwood, fodder and fruits from forests, raising vegetables, rearing pigs and poultry, weaving, petty trading, etc. Despite attempts like National System of Accounts (NSA) it has not so far been possible to compute their economic contribution accurately.

There is one aspect of women's status, however, which does not lend itself to mathematical computation. For instance, women's status in the family is reflected in values, attitudes and relationships of other members and women's own subjective responses. And these cannot be measured in mathematical scores. Furthermore, to some extent these are culture-specific. Being the senior-most wife in an Adi household from Arunachal Pradesh might well give a woman an enhanced status. Among the Aos of Nagaland who favour monogamy, if a husband brings a second wife, it would be a humiliating experience for the first wife. One possible approach that may help to some extent in making judgements about women's status is to prepare sample inventories of positive and negative indicators of status. These can list, e.g. other people's responses towards women, as well as women's subjective responses towards others, somewhat on the lines of personality tests prepared by psychologists. Regardless of the difficulties N-E women face due to unfair customs and traditions, one thing is certain. There is enormous unutilized scope for improving their economic status, which will in turn enhance their status in the family as well as social and political spheres. Equally important, strengthening their health and educational status, which is entirely within the respective State Governments' power, will enable women to face adverse circumstances and simultaneously benefit fully from opportunities for their fullest potential, leading to socially enriched and personally fulfilling lives.

Appendix A

List of Seminars on Status of Women in North-Eastern States, 1988-89, Sponsored by ICSSR Regional Centre, Shillong

1. Seminar: *Status of Women — Arunachal Pradesh,* organized by Arunachal University in Collaboration with Jawaharlal Nehru College, Pasighat, 3-4 February 1989.
2. Seminar: *Status of Women —Assam: Non-Tribal Societies,* organized by Department of History, Dibrugarh University, Dibrugarh, 4-5 October, 1988. # S.L. Baruah (ed.), *Status of Women in Assam with Special Reference to Non-Tribal Societies,* New Delhi: Omson Publication, 1992.
3. Seminar: *Status of Women — Assam: Barak Valley,* organized by North-East Institute of Anthropological Research (Silchar), Karimganj, 26 and 27 November 1988.
4. Seminar: *Status of Women — Assam: Hill Tribal Societies: Karbi and Dimsasa,* organized by Dept. of Political Science, Diphu Government College, Diphu, 5 February 1989.
5. Seminar : *Status of Women — Assam: Plains Tribal Societies,* organized by Dept. of Folklore Research, Guwahati University, Guwahati, 19-20 January, 1989.
6. Seminar: *Status of Women — Manipur,* organized by Department of History, Manipur Universiity, Imphal and Churachandpur, 23-24 September 1988.
7. Seminar: *Status of Women — Meghalaya,* organized by Centre for Literary and Cultural Studies, North-Eastern Hill University, Shillong, July 1988. # Soumen Sen (ed.), *Women in Meghalaya,* Delhi: Daya Publishing House, 1992.

Seminar Reports are available in published form.

8. Seminar: *Status of Women —Mizoram: Tribal Societies,* Pachhunga University College, NEHU, Aizawl, 29 July 1988.

9. Seminar: *Status of Women —Nagaland: Naga Societies*, organized by Naga Students' Union, Nagaland House — Shillong, 23 November 1988.

10. Seminar: *Status of Women —Tripura: Tribal Societies,* Organized by Dept. of Analytical and Applied Economics, Tripura University, Agartala, 14 January 1989.

Appendix B

Table B-I: Proportions of Agricultural Workers* Among Female Main Workers in Districts in India and N-E States, Rural Areas, 1991

India/ N-E States	*A (Total no. of Districts)*	*B 70.00% or less*	*C 70.01% to 80%*	*D 80.01% to 95%*	*E 90.01% to 95%*	*F 95.01% & above*
India	446	84	38	108	134	82
Arunachal Pradesh	11	-	1	4	4	2
Assam	23	13	3	5	2	-
Manipur	8	2	-	2	4	-
Meghalaya	5	-	1	1	1	2
Mizoram	3	-	-	-	1	2
Nagaland	7	-	-	2	1	4
Tripura	3	1	1	1	-	-
N-E Region	60	16	6	15	13	10

Source : *Census of India 1991*, Paper 3 of 1991, *Provisional Population Totals*, Workers and their distribution : 44

* Agricultural Workers include Cultivators and Agricultural Labourers.

Table B-II: Numbers of Female Main Workers by Industrial Categories in India and North-Eastern States, 1991

India/N-E States	Total Female Main Workers	Cultivators	Agricultural Labourers	Livestock forestry, fishing hunting & Plantations Orchards & allied activities	Mining and quarrying	manufacturing Processing servicing and repairs: House-hold Industry	manufacturing Processing servicing and repairs: other than House-hold Industry	Construction	Trade & Commerce	Transport Storage & communications	Others Services
	I-IX	I	II	III	IV	V(a)	V(b)	VI	VII	VIII	IX
*India (Excluding Jammu & Kashmir)	64273909	22221404	28432997	1324709	214356	2249005	2453041	420737	1433612	207620	5316428
Arunachal Pradesh	142100	119056	7274	1453	2	211	924	2001	896	72	10211
Assam	1351869	688534	162391	316993	1395	29321	13821	2000	13426	3771	120217
Manipur	293471	194232	28199	2036	53	35065	5075	1124	9831	345	17511
Meghalaya	265962	167608	37315	17094	725	1251	1256	1590	11421	709	26993
Mizoram	112306	83223	3346	1413	27	961	762	235	8793	47	13499
Nagaland	212060	192623	2124	631	26	1095	634	756	1225	180	12766
Tripura	135776	50973	41456	6094	112	3451	2672	573	1660	314	28471

Source: Census of India 1991, Final Population Totals, Series 1, Paper 2 of 1992, Table 4: 126-147

* 1991 Census was not conducted in Jammu & Kashmir due to disturbed conditions.

Appendix C

Table C (i) : Numbers of Female Main Workers Classified by Industrial Categeory: India and N-E States, Census of India 2001

		A+B	*C*	*D*		*E*	*F*	*G*	*H*	*I*	*J & K*[1]	*L M N O P Q*[2]
				Manufacturing and Repairs								
Area Name	*Total Female Main Workers Rural & Urban*	*A – Agriculture Hunting and Forestry B – Fishing*	*Mining and Quarrying*	*House-hold Indus-tries HHI*	*Non-Household Industries Non-HHI*	*Electri-city Gas and Water Supply*	*Con-struction*	*Wholesale and Retail Trade*	*Hotels and Restau-rents*	*Transport Storage and Communi-cations*		
India	24999662	3617948	262928	4645780	4381139	67451	1064350	1857666	215187	368279	755870	7763064
Arunachal Pradesh	30557	3543	24	1520	522	1338	5072	1566	367	168	2972	13465
Assam	741170	318300	3070	72780	73540	1600	4950	22650	2970	7110	8240	225960
Manipur	97580	4350	220	27070	6120	510	1060	14270	1860	510	1900	39710
Meghalaya	78550	5900	560	4770	2170	510	1660	13740	2470	670	1740	44360
Mizoram	43031	2369	125	1614	2044	539	845	12760	1569	364	3186	17670
Nagaland	48412	1161	25	5614	1347	1152	1565	3661	439	361	7784	25103
Tripura	79240	12270	480	7830	4330	300	1390	3840	340	780	750	46930

1. J & K: J-Financial Intermediation; K-Real Estate, Renting and Business Activities.
2. L–Q: L-Public Administration and Defence, Compulsory Social Security; M-Education; N-Health and Social Work; O-Other Community Social and personal Service activities; P-Private Households with employed persons; Q-Extra — Territorial Organizations and bodies.

Source : Advance Table 1.1, Census of India 2001

Appendix C

Table C (ii): Housing Characteristics, Educational Attainment, Female Nuptiality and Fertility Indicators India & N-E States: NFHS -III, 2005 - 2006

India / N-E State Having	*Percentage of Households age 15-49 who have*			*Percentage of Women Nuptiality*		*Female*	*Fertility Indicators*	
	Electri-city	*Piped water*	*Toilet*	*No Education*	*Completed 10 years of education*	*Women age 20-24 married by age 18*	*Total Fertility rate (children per woman)*	*Median age at first birth for women age 25-49*
India	67.9	42.0	44.5	41.0	22.0	44.5	2.68	19.8
Arunachal Pradesh	76.9	70.4	66.4	42.0	15.0	40.6	3.03	19.9
Assam	38.1	11.6	76.4	30.0	19.0	38.0	2.42	20.7
Manipur	87.0	32.7	95.5	21.8	33.8	12.7	2.83	23.7
Meghalaya	70.4	42.2	71.3	30.0	23.0	24.5	3.80	21.7
Mizoram	92.3	60.8	98.0	5.6	27.5	20.6	2.86	22.3
Nagaland	82.9	40.1	85.4	21.7	21.5	21.1	3.74	21.7
Tripura	68.8	33.5	96.6	22.4	15.2	41.0	2.22	20.3

Source : Key Population and Health Indicators of NFHS-3, 2005-2006, Kamla Gupta , Sulabha Parasuraman, P. Arokiasamy, K.S. Singh and H. Lhungdim, *Demography India,* vol. 35, no. 2 (2006), pp. 193-217.

Appendix C

Table C (iii) : Key Indicators of Maternal and Child Health, India & N-E States: NFHS Þ III, 2005-2006

India/N-E State	*Contraceptive Prevalence Rate*[1]	*Any Atenatal Care*	*Mothers who had at least 3 antenatal care visits for their last birth*	*Institutional births*	*Births assisted by a doctor/nurse/ LHV/ANM/other health personnel*	*Mothers who received post-natal care from a doctor/nurse LHV/ANM/other health personnel within 2 days of delivery for their last birth*	*Children 12-23 months fully immunized, (BCG, measles, and 3 doses each of Polio/DPT*	*Children age 12-35 months who received Vitamin A dose in last 6 months*
India	56.3	76.9	50.7	40.7	48.2	36.4	43.5	21.0
Arunachal Pradesh	43.2	59.0	36.4	30.8	33.4	23.3	28.4	17.4
Assam	56.5	70.8	36.3	22.7	31.2	13.8	31.6	16.6
Manipur	48.7	87.7	70.1	49.3	61.7	49.1	46.8	15.4
Meghalaya	24.3	67.9	53.4	29.7	31.7	28.8	32.8	19.9
Mizoram	59.9	75.0	57.8	64.6	69.4	51.5	46.4	42.2
Nagaland	29.7	56.9	31.6	12.2	25.9	11.3	21.0	8.7
Tripura	65.8	79.1	58.7	48.9	50.0	26.7	49.7	38.8

1. Contraceptive Prevalence Rate refers to proportion of currently married women 15-49 years or husbands using any family planning method.

Bibliography and List of Sources Consulted*

Books

Abbi, B.L. (ed.), 1984, *North-East Region — Problems and Prospects of Development*, Chandigarh: Centre for Research in Rural and Industrial Development.

Acharya, S.K.,1988, "Ethnic Processes in North-Eastern India", *Economic and Political Weekly*, vol. xxiii, no. 21, May 21, pp.1068-76.

Agarwal, A.K., 1999, "Industry of Mizoram", in Amalesh Banerjee & Biman Kar (eds.), *Economic Planning and Development of North-Eastern States*, New Delhi: Kanishka Publishers, pp. 232-40.

——— 1999, "Energy for Economic Development : A Case Study of North East India", in Amalesh Banerjee & Biman Kar (eds.), *Economic Planning and Development of North-Eastern States,* New Delhi : Kanishka Publishers, pp. 181-92

Agarwal, Bina, 1981, "Agricultural Modernisation and Third World Women, Pointers from the Literature and an Empirical Analysis", Preliminary discussion paper produced for the Rural Employment Policies Branch, Employment and Develpment Department, ILO, Geneva, January, 1981.

———,1988, "Who Sows? Who Reaps? Women and Land Rights in India", *The Journal of Peasant Studies*, U.K., July 1988.

Agnihotri, S.K., 1992, "Formation of Sadulla Ministry in 1937", *Journal of North-East India Council for Social Science Research*, vol.16:1, April, pp. 27-37.

---

*For papers presented at the seminars on status of women in N-E States sponsored by ICSSR during 1988-89, which were available in a cyclostyled form, the following format has been used: Name of the author, title of paper, the state and the communities covered where applicable (e.g. Assam : Plains Tribal Societies). A list of the seminars giving details is attached as Appendix A.

Ahmed, Syed Zubair, 1994, "Winds of change blowing over Khasi Society", *Times of India*, January 28, 1994.

———,1994, Trade with Myanmar will benefit North-East", *Times of India,* May 11, 1994.

——— ,1994, "Naga Ultras Open Office in N.Y.", *Times of India*, May 28, 1994.

———,1994, "North-East's Potential Remains Untapped", *Times of India*, June 20, 1994.

All India Democratic Women's Association (AIDWA) 2000, *Women Against Terrorism: The Tripura Experience,* New Delhi: AIDWA, 31 December.

———2001, *"Tripura"* State Reports, 6th National Conference, November 24-27, Vishakhapatnam.

Ao, Alemchiba, 1972, "Problems of Re-adjustment to a New Situation (with special reference to Naga tribes)", in K.S. Singh (ed.), *Proceedings of a Seminar*, Simla: Indian Institute of Advanced Study, 1972.

Ao, P.J., 1980, "The Here-After: Traditional Ao Nagas", in Sujata Miri (ed.), *Religion and Society of North-East India*, New Delhi: Vikas Publishing House, pp. 63-68.

Arunkumar, M.C., 1988, "Sex Alienation in Meitei Society", *Status of Women Seminar,* Manipur.

Bandyopadhyay, Sabari and Debesh Chakraborty, 1999, "Migration in the North-Eastern Region of India during 1901-1991, Size, Trend, Reasons and Impact", *Demography India*, vol. 28, no. 1, pp. 75-97.

Banerjee, Amalesh 1999, " Regional Planning for Economic Development of North-Eastern India", Amalesh Banerjee and Biman Kar (eds.), *Economic Planning and Development of North-Eastern States,* New Delhi: Kanishka Publishers, pp. 13-41.

Banerjee, Amalesh and Biman Kar (eds.), 1999, *Economic Planning and Development of North-Eastern States*, New Delhi: Kanishka Publishers.

Banerjee, Nirmala and Swati Mitter, 1998, "Women Making a Meaningful Choice: Technology and New Economic Order", *Economic and Political Weekly*, December 1998.

Banerjee, Nirmalya, 1997, "Killing within Bodos Cause Concern", *Times of India*, 14 January 1997.

———,1997, "Row over script for Kokborok language takes a violent turn," *Times of India*, 21 February 1997.

———,1997, "NSCN Runs a Parallel Govt: Army", *Times of India*, 19 July 1997.

———, 1997, "Nagas are now bitten by the revivalism bug", *Times of India*, 26 July 1997.

———, 1998, "Riang refugees in Tripura may face difficulty in voting", *Times of India*, 17 November 1998.

———,1998, "Thou Shalt not buy votes, rig or spend wastefully . . .", *Times of India*, 29 November 1998.

———, 2000, "Tripura violence claims 45 lives, curfew clamped", *Times of India*, 22 May 2000.

Banerjee, Ruben, 1994, "Stoking Ethnic Terror", *India Today*, 31 August 1994.

Bareh, Hamlet, *The History and Culture of the Khasi People*, Shillong: Khasi Press, 1967.

———, "Khasi–Jaintia State Formation", in Surajit Sinha (ed.), *Tribal Polities and State Systems in Pre-Colonial, Eastern and North-Eastern India*, Calcutta: Centre for Studies in Social Sciences, 1987, pp. 261-305.

Barooah, Debo Prasad, 2000, "Assam", in George Mathew (ed.), *Status of Panchayati Raj in the States and Union Territories of India, 2000*, Institute of Social Sciences, New Delhi: Concept Publishing, pp. 66-74.

Barooah, Jeuti, 1989, "Women in Pati Rabha Society: An Appraisal in the Context of Customary Laws and Practices", *Status of Women Seminar — Assam, Plains Tribal Societies.*

———,1993, *Single Women in Assamese Hindu Society*, New Delhi: Gyan Publishing House.

Barthakur, Sheila and Sabita Goswami, 1990, "The Assam Movement", in Ilina Sen (ed.), *A Space Within the Struggle: Women's Participation in People's Movements*, New Delhi: Kali for Women.

Bhattacharjee, Bimalendu, 1988, "The Role of Barman Women in Barman Society", *Status of Women Seminar — Assam: Barak Valley.*

Bhattacharjee, J.B., 1987 "Dimasa State Formation in Cachar", in Sinha, Surajit (ed.), *The Tribal Polities and State systems in Pre-Colonial Eastern and North-Eastern India,* Calcutta: Centre for Studies in Social Sciences.

Bhattacharjee, Manjulika, 1988 "Participation of Women in Freedom Movement in Karimganj District", *Status of Women Seminar — Assam: Barak Valley.*

Bhattacharjee, P.R, Deb Ray, Amitabha Sinha and Anil Kumar Das, 1989, *An Analysis of the Situation of Children in Tripura*, A report prepared for UNICEF, East India Office (cyclostyled).

Bhattacharjee, Rakhee, 1995, "Regional Economic Imbalance of North-East India", *The Window : Journal of the Study Circle*, Special Issue on North East India, Shillong, no. 4, 1 March 1995, pp. 32-37.

Bhattacharjee, S., 1988, "Womenfolk of the Fishermen Community in Chatla Howr — An Overview", *Status of Women Seminar — Assam; Barak Valley.*

Bhattacharjee, Tanmay 1989, "The Dimasa Female Clans and Some Problems", *Status of Women Seminar Assam: Hill Tribal Societies: Karbi and Dimasa.*

Bhattacharjee, Tarun, 1989, "The Status of Women in Arunachal Pradesh", *Status of Women Seminar: Arunachal Pradesh.*

Bhattacharya, Rabindra Nath, 1999, "Economies of India's North East, Natural Resource Base and Globalization", Amalesh Banerjee and Biman Kar (eds.), *Economic Planning and Development of North-Eastern States*, New Delhi: Kanishka Publishers, pp. 103-14.

Bhaumik, Alok K., 1999, "Development Constraints and Possibilities in North-Eastern India : A Field Review", Amalesh Banerjee and Biman Kar (eds.), *Economic Planning and Development of North Eastern States,* New Delhi: Kanishka Publishers, pp. 68-77.

Bimala Devi, 1988, "The Study of the Urban Educated Elite Women in Manipur", *Status of Women Seminar — Manipur.*

Bokul Singh, M., 1988, "The Tarao Women: Whether Changing to Better Position?", *Status of Women Seminar — Manipur.*

Borah, Ashwini Kumar, 1989, "The Status of Women in Karbi Society: An Observation", *Status of Women Seminar — Assam : Hill Tribal Societies, Karbi and Dimasa.*

Borah, Bibha, 1992, "Women in Administration and Politics in Medieval Assam," in S.L. Baruah (ed.), *Compendium of the Proceedings of the Seminar on Status of Women in Non-Tribal Societies of Assam*, 4-5 October 1988, New Delhi: Omsons Publications.

Borah, Bimal, 1989, "Gaps and Variance in Tribal Society of Arunachal", *Status of Women Seminar — Arunachal Pradesh.*

Bordolai, B.N., (date unknown) "Management of Land and Forest in the Hill Areas of Assam: Retrospective and perspective and Traditional Land-Man Relations in the Zeme Naga Society of North Cachar Hills (Cyclostyled paper)", Tribal Research Institute, Guwahati, Assam.

Bordoloi, B.N., 1989, "Status of Plains Tribal Women in Assam from the Viewpoint of Education", *Status of Women Seminar, Assam : Plains Tribal Societies.*

Borkataky, Anju, 1988, "Women and Violence in Non-tribal societies of Assam", *Status of Women Seminar, Assam : Non-Tribal Soceties.*

Bormundi, Anjali, 1989, "Status of Women in Arunachal Pradesh", *Status of Women Seminar — Arunachal pradesh.*

Bose, Ashish, Tiplut Nongbri and Nikhilesh Kumar (Eds.), 1990, *Tribal Demography and Development in North-East India*, New Delhi: B.R. Publishing Corporation.

Bose, Saradendu, S. Ghatak and R.K. Bera, 1982, "Shifting Cultivation in India", K.S. Singh (eds.), *Economies of the Tribes and their Transformation*, New Delhi: Concept Publishing Company, pp. 216-25.

Brahma, Binoy Kumar, 1989, "The Status of Women in Tribal Society with Reference to the Bodo Society", *Status of Women Seminar, Assam : Plains Tribal Societies.*

Brahma, Kameshwar, 1989 "The Status of Bodo Women in the Society with particular reference to Kokrajhar District", *Status of Women Seminar, Assam : Plains Tribal Societies.*

Buragohain, Joya, 1989, "The status of women in Aiton Society : Past and Present", *Status of Women Seminar, Assam : Plains Tribal Societies.*

Chaki Sircar, Manjusri, 1984, "*Feminism in a Traditional Society : Women of the Manipur Valley*", New Delhi: Shakti Books, Women in Society Series.

Chakraborty, Manik, 1993, "Customary Laws and the Status of Tribal Women in Tripura", in Malabika Das Gupta (ed.), *Status of Tribal Women in Tripura*, New Delhi: Vikas Publishing House, pp. 1-4.

Chakravarti, Mahadev, 2000, "Tripura ADC Election, 2000 : Terror Tactics Win", *Economic and Political Weekly*, vol. xxxv, no. 30, July 22, 2000.

Chakravarti, Tapati, 1993, "Economic Role and Status of Tribal Women in Tripura", in Malabika Das Gupta (ed.), *Status of Tribal Women in Tripura*, New Delhi: Vikas Publishing House, pp. 12-22.

Chandrasekhar, C.P. and Abhijit Sen, 1996, "Statistical Truths: Economic Reform and Poverty", *Frontline*, 23 February 1996, pp. 100-102.

Chatterjee, Neera, 1965, "Tripura and Its Tribal Population", *Educational Miscellany*, vol. 1, no. 2 March 1965, pp. 71-78.

Chatterjee, Suhas, 1985, "*Mizoram under the British Rule*," Delhi: Mittal Publications.

Chatterji, A.K., 1999, "Development of Social Sector in the North Eastern States of India", Amalesh Banerjee and Biman Kar (eds.), *Economic Planning and Development of North-Eastern States*, New Delhi: Kanishka Publications, pp. 368-95.

Chetia, Jiban, 1989, "Status of Women Tribal Societies (Karbi and Dimasa)", *Status of Women Seminar, Assam: Hill Tribal Societies, Karbi and Dimasa.*

Childyal, V.C., 1982, "Tribe and Forest", K.S. Singh (ed.), *Economies of the Tribes and their Transformation*, New Delhi: Concept Publishing Company, pp. 133-43.

Chinai, Rupa, 1995, "ISI hand alleged in N-E Insurgency", *Times of India*, 24 January 1995.

———, 1995, "Bus Passengers Die in Naga-Kuki War", *Times of India*, 28 January 1995.

———, 1995, "Manipur may turn into India's Bosnia", *Times of India,* 30 January 1995.

———, 1999, "The Dream of Freedom", *Times of India*, 12 September 1999.

———,1999, "Talking Terms in Nagaland", *Times of India*, 24 September 1999.

Choudhury, Abhijit, 1989, "Women's Rights in Arunachal Pradesh: Customary Law in Relation to Civil Law (A Case Study)", *Status of Women Seminar — Arunachal Pradesh.*

Choudhury, Aparajita, 1988, "Changing Role of Women in Barak Valley", *Status of Women Seminar — Assam, Barak Valley.*

Choudhury, J.N., 1971, *A Comparative Study of Adi Religion*, Shillong, North East Frontier Agency.

———, 1989, "Status of Women in Preliterate Arunachal Society (In the Light of Social Sciences)", *Status of Women Seminar — Arunachal Pradesh.*

Choudhury, Pratap, 1993, "Status of Women in the Tribal Societies of Tripura", in Malabika Das Gupta (ed.), *Status of Tribal Women in Tripura*, New Delhi: Vikas Publishing, pp. 23-33.

Choudhury, Sujit, 1988, "A Female Rite of Barak Valley & its Social Significance", *Status of Women Seminar — Assam: Barak Valley.*

———, 1995, "The Bodos, The Tribe For Whom History Failed", *The Windows, Journal of the Study Circle*, Shillong, Special issue on North-East India, 1 March 1995, pp. 8-13.

Chowdhary, Dipak Kumar, 1993, "Sati in the Tribal Societies of Tripura", In Malabika Das Gupta (ed.), *Status of Tribal Women in Tripura*, New Delhi: Vikas Publisihing House, pp. 5-11.

Das, B.M., 1978, "*Variation in Physical Characteristics in the Khasi Population of North-East India*", New Delhi: D.K. Publishers.

Das, Gurudas, 1990, "The Pace of Development and Emerging Structural Constraints of the Agrarian Economy of Arunachal Pradesh", Paper presented at a Seminar on Constraints of Agricultural Develpment in North-East India, North-East India Council for Social Science Research, Shillong 2-3 July 1990 (cyclostyled).

Das, J.N., (date unknown) "Communal Tenure System in the North-Eastern Region with Speical Reference to Land Records and Rights of Women", paper presented at a seminar organized by National Institute of Rural Development, North-East Regional Centre Guwahati, (cyclostyled paper).

Das, N.K., 1982, "Agrarian Structure and Change in Nagaland", in K.S. Singh (ed.), *Economies of the Tribes and their Transformation*, New Delhi: Concept Publishing, pp. 314-22.

———,1982, "The Naga Movement", in K.S. Singh (ed.), *Tribal Movements in India*, New Delhi: Manohar Publishers.

———,1993, "Customary Law and Settlement of Disputes Among the Angami Naga of Nagaland", in K.S. Singh (ed.), *Tribal Ethnography, Customary Law and Change*, New Delhi: Concept Publishing, pp. 43-48

Das, N.K. and P. Gupta, 1982, "The Ahom Movement", K.S. Singh, (ed.), *Tribal Movements in India*, vol. 1, New Delhi: Manohar Publishers.

Das Gupta, Barun, 1997, "A Partial Truce", *Frontline*, 12 December 1997.

Das Gupta, Malabika, 1986, "Jhumias of Tripura", *Economic and Political Weekly*, vol. XXI, nos. 44-45, 1-8 November 1986.

———, 1989, "Bride-price and the Status of Riang Women in Tripura", *Status of Women Seminar — Tripura*.

———, 1999, "Planning for the Hill Economy of Tripura", in Amalesh Banerjee and Biman Kar (eds.), *Economic Planning and Development of North-Eastern States*, New Delhi: Kanishka Publishers, pp. 78-91.

———, (ed.), 1993, *Status of Tribal Women in Tripura,* New Delhi: Vikas Publishing House.

Das Gupta, Manas, 1984, "Tribal Unrest: Tripura", *Economic and Political Weekly,* vol. XIX, no. 11, 17 March 1984.

Deb, Dasrath, 1986, *Gana Mukti Parishad in Building the Peasant Movement in Tripura*, All India Kisan Sabha, 1936-86, Golden Jubilee Series, no.7.

Deb, Keya, 1979, *Impact of Plantations on the Agrarian Structure of the Brahmaputra Valley*, Occasional Paper, no. 24, Calcutta: Centre for Studies in Social Sciences.

Deb Roy, H.L., 1981, "*A Tribe in Transition: The Jaintias of Meghalaya*", New Delhi: Cosmo Publications.

Debnath, Chhanda and Sircar Bithi, 1993, "Riang Mothers at Risk : A Nutritional Case Study on Riang Women of North Tripura", In Malabika Das Gupta (ed.), *Status of Tribal Women in Tripura,* New Delhi: Vikas Publishing House, pp. 47-58.

Deka, R.,"The Other Backward Classes Movement in Assam", K.S. Singh (ed.), *Tribal Movements in India*, New Delhi: Manohar Publishers, pp. 295-305

Deodhar, N.S. and S.S. Srivastava, 1984, *Manipur: Health Conditions of Mothers and Children*, UNICEF, Calcutta: East India Office.

———, *1984, Nagaland : Health Conditions of Mothers and Children*, UNICEF, Calcutta: East India Office.

Deodhar, N.S., S.S. Srivastava and S.C. Seal, 1985, *Tripura: Health Conditions of Mothers and Children*, UNICEF, Calcutta: East India Office.

Desai, Neera and Vibhuti Patel, 1985, *Indian Women, Change and Challenge in the International Decade, 1975-85*, Bombay: Popular Prakashan.

Duarah, Dharmeswar, 1989, "The Traditional Status of Women in Dimasa Society", *Status of Women Seminar — Assam: Hill Tribal Societies*, Karbi and Dimasa.

Dube, S.M., 1982, "Inter-Ethnic Alliance, Tribal Movement and Integration in Norh-East India", K.S. Singh (ed.), *Tribal Movements in India*, vol. 1, Delhi: Manohar Publishers, pp. 1-25.

Dutta, Choudhury K., 1989, "Change in Women in Arunachal Pradesh as observed in 3 Decades", *Status of Women Seminar — Arunachal Pradesh*.

Dutta, P.C., 1987, "Social Organization of the Wanchos of Tirap District of Arunachal Pradesh", Manis Kumar Raha (ed.), *The Himalayan Heritage*, Delhi: Gyan Publishing House, pp. 3-26.

Dutta, Parul, 1989, "Status of Women in Arunachal Pradesh", *Status of Women Seminar — Arunachal Pradesh*.

Dutta, Ray B., 1999, "Autonomous District Councils and the Strategy of Development in North-East India", in Amalesh Banerjee and Biman Kar (eds.), *Economic Planning and Development of North-Eastern States*, New Delhi: Kanishka Publishers, Distributors, pp. 252-67.

Fernandes, Walter, and Geeta Menon, 1987, *Tribal Women and Forest Economy: Deforestation, Exploitation and Status Change*, New Delhi: Indian Social Institute, Tribes of India Series.

Foundation for Research in Health Systems, 1998, 1999, *Health Monitor*, 182, Ahmedabad: Azad Society.

Gailangam, K., 1988, "Status and Role of Rongmei Women", *Status of Women Seminar — Manipur*.

Gan, Chowdhary, 1980, *Tripura: The Land and its People*, Delhi: Leeladevi Publications.

Gandhi, Nandita and N. Shah, 1992, *The Issues at Stake: Theory and Practice of Contemporary Women's Movement in India*, New Delhi: Kali for Women.

Gangmumei, Kabui, 1982, "The Zeliangrong Movement", K.S. Singh (ed.), *Tribal Movements in India*, vol.1, New Delhi: Manohar Publishers, pp. 53-66

———, 1985, *Anal: A Transborder Tribe of Manipur*, Delhi: Mittal Publications.

Gangopadhyay, D.K., 1991, "Land Reforms in Assam", *Gramin Vikas Newletter*, July 1991, pp. 14-16.

Ganguly, J.B., 1990, "Pattern and Occupational Structure of Tribal Population of Tripura", in Ashish Bose, Tiplut Nongbri and Nikhilesh Kumar (eds.), *Tribal Demography and Development in North-East India*, Delhi: B.R. Publishing Corporation, pp. 103-19.

———, 1993, "Case study of Herma Village in West Tripura District", in Malabika Das Gupta (ed.), *Status of Tribal Women in Tripura*, New Delhi: Vikas Publishing House, pp. 69-79.

Gassah, L.S., 1992, "Status of Women in Jaintia Culture", in Soumen Sen (ed.), *Women in Meghalaya*, Delhi: Daya Publishing House, 36-45.

———, 1992, "Founding Clans: Their Role in Jaintia Traditional Polity Formation", *Journal of North-East India Council for Social Science Research,* April, vol. 16, no. 1, pp. 8-14.

———, 2000, "Meghalaya", in Mathew George (ed.), *Status of Panchayati Raj in the States and Union Territories of India* 2000, Institute of Social Sciences, New Delhi: Concept Publishing, pp. 206-13.

Ghosh, S.K., 1987, *Law Enforcement inTribal Areas*, New Delhi: Ashish Publishing House.

Ghosh, Santanu, 1995, "Fear of the Foreigner", *Sunday*, 25 JuneÝ1 July, 1995.

Gogoi, Janhabi Nath, 1988, "Social Attitude Towards Women in Medieval Assam", *Status of Women Seminar — Assam, Non-tribal Societies*.

Gohain, Hiren, 1987, "North-East, Roots of Separatism I," *Mainstream*, vol. XXVI, no. 11, 26 December 1987.

———,1988 "North-East: Roots of Separatism II", *Mainstream,* vol. XXVI, no. 13, 9 January 1988, pp. 8-10.

———,1997 "Ethnic unrest in the North-East", *Economic and Political Weekly*, vol. XXXII, no. 8, 22 Feburary 1997.

Gohain, Amiya Khang, 1989, "The Status of Tai Phake Women in Assam; Condition and Change", *Status of Women Seminar — Assam, Plains Tribal Societies*.

Gohain, B.K., 1989, "The Status of women in the Society of Matrilineal Lalungs of Assam", *Status of Women Seminar, Assam: Plains Tribal Societies*.

Gokhale, A.M., 2000, "Nagaland", George Mathew (ed.), *Status of Panchayati Raj in the States and Union Territories of India*, 2000, Institute of Social Sciences, New Delhi: Concept Publishing.

Goswami, A. and Archanna Sharma, 1995, *Working of Panchayats in Assam with Special Reference to the Role of Women Representatives*, Omeo Kumar Das Institute of Social Change and Development, Guwahati.

Goswami, Atul and Jayant Kumar Gogoi, 1984, "Migration and Demographic Transformation of Assam, 1901–1971", B.L. Abbi, (ed.), *Northeast Region: Problems and Prospects of Development*, Chandigarh: Centre for Research in Rural and Industrial Development, pp. 60-80.

Goswami, B.B., 1987, "The Mizos in the context of State Formation", Surajit Sinha (ed.), *Tribal Politics and States Systems in Eastern and N-E India*, Calcutta: Centre for Studies in Social Sciences.

Goswami, B.B. and D.P. Mukherjee, 1982, "The Mizo Political Movement", K.S. Singh (ed.), *Tribal Movements in India*, New Delhi: Manohar, pp. 129-50.

Goswami, M.C. (ed.), 1982, *The Customary Laws and Practices of Pati Rabhas of Assam*, Law Research Institute, Eastern Region, Guahati High Court, Guahati.

Goswami, M.C. and D.N. Majumdar, 1972, *Social Institutions of the Garo of Meghalaya,* Calcutta: Navabharat Publishers.

Goswami, P.C., 1984 "Foreign Immigration Into Assam," B.L. Abbi (ed.), *Northeast Region: Problems and Prospects of Development*, Chandigarh: Centre for Research in Rural and Industrial Development, pp. 35-59.

Guha, Amalendu, 1987, "The Ahom Political System: An Inquiry into State Formation in Medieval Assam, 1228-1800", Surajit Sinha (ed.), *Tribal Polities and State Systems in Pre-Colonical Eastern and North Eastern India*, Calcutta: Centre for Studies in Social Sciences, Calcutta, pp. 143-76.

Guha, Seema, 1997, "Bitter Battle for Bodo Leadership", *Times of India*, 7 January 1997.

Guhathakurta, S.N., 1999, "High Rates of Papulation Growth, Urbanization and Literacy in Mizoram", in Amalesh Banerjee and Biman Kar (eds.), *Economic Planning and Development of North-Eastern States*, New Delhi: Kanishka Publishing, pp. 343-67.

Guilmoto, Christophe Z. and S. Irudaya Rajan, 2002, "District Level Estimates of Fertility from India's 2001 Census", *Economic and Political Weekly*, vol. XXXVII-7, 16 February 2002, pp. 665-72.

Haimendorf, Christoph von Furer, 1982, "Change and Development among Tribes of Arunachal Pradesh", *Tribes of India*, Delhi: Oxford University Press, pp. 286-312.

[illegible]zari[illegible] K.N., 1997, "Development Finance in the North-East", *The Windows, Journal of the Study Circle*, Shillong, no. 5, March 1997, pp. 12-16.

Hazarika, Karabi Deka, 1988, "Status of Assamese Women in the Family and Society as Reflected in Assamese Literature", *Status of Women Seminar — Assam, Non-tribal Societies*.

Hazarika, Sanjoy, 1996, "Mizoram, The Accord That Worked", *Times of India*, 21 February 1996.

———, "Land Question Behind Bodo — Santhal Conflict", *Times of India,* 3 July 1996.

Hluna, J.V., 1988, "Education and Change: impact on Mizo Women", *Status of Women Seminar — Mizoram*.

Horam, M., 1977, *Social and Cultural Life of the Nagas*, Delhi: B.R. Publishing Corporation.

———, "Naga Religion: A case Study", in Sujata Miri (ed.), *Religion and Society of North-East India*, New Delhi: Vikas Publishing House, pp. 59-62.

Huda, Chabi, 1988, "Status of Manipuri Muslim Women in Barak Valley", *Status of Women Seminar — Assam: Barak Valley.*

Hunibou, Newmai, 1988, "The Status of women in Zeliangrong Naga Society", *Status of Women Seminar — Naga Societies.*

Husain, Majid, 1987, "Diffusion of Innovations in Shifting Cultivation in Nagaland: Prospects and Problems", *ICSSR, Research Abstracts Quarterly.* vol. XVI, nos. 3 and 4, July-December 1987

Hussain, Imdad,1992, "Mutiny years in Assam: A View from the Ranks", *Journal of the North-East India Council for Social Science Research,* vol. 16, no.1, April 1992.

Hussain, Wasbir, 1987, "Shillong in Turmoil", *The Telegraph,* 19 July 1987.

Ibochouba, K., 1988, "Anglo-Manipuri Relations (1762-1947)", N. Sanajaoba (ed.), *Manipur: Past and Present.* vol. 1, Delhi: Mittal Publications.

Jamoh, Yanung, 1989, "Status of Women in Adi Society with Particular Reference to Miniyong Subtribe of Arunachal Pradesh", *Status of Women Seminar — Arunachal Pradesh.*

Jaswal, I.L.S., 1982, "The Seng Khasi", in K.S. Singh (ed.), *Tribal Movements in India*, vol. 1, Delhi: Manohar Publishers, pp.173-80.

Jha, S.D.,1989, "Status of Women in Arunachal Pradesh", *Status of Women Seminar — Arunachal Pradesh.*

Nath, Jogendra, 1989, "Status of Women in Traditional Adi Society", *Status of Women Seminar — Arunachal Pradesh.*

———, 1994, *Bride-Price*, Patna and New Delhi: Himalayan Publishers.

Kagyung, Bhriguram, 1989, "Status of Women in the Mishing Community of Assam", *Status of Women Seminar — Assam, Plains Tribal Societies.*

Kanwar Randip Singh, 1987, *The Nagas of Nagaland,* New Delhi: Deep & Deep Publications.

Karat, Brinda, 1992,"Deb Commission Report on Tripura", *Economic and Political Weekly,* vol. XXVII, no. 3, 18 January 1992, pp. 80-84.

Karna, M.N., 1990, "Aspects of Tribal Development in North-Eastern India", Ashish Bose, Tiplut Nongbri and Nikhilesh Kumar (eds.), *Tribal Demography and Development in North-East India,* New Delhi: B.R. Publishing Corporation.

Kaushik, Susheela, 1995, *Panchayati Raj in Action: Challenges to Women's Role,* New Delhi: Fredrich Ebert Stiftung (India Office). D-9, South Extension, Part II, New Delhi 110 049.

Khanam, Mahmoodah, 1988 ,"The Status of Muslim Women in Manipur", *Status of Women Seminar — Manipur.*

Khandekar, Mandakini, N.S. Deodhar and Sindhu Phadke, 1985, *Meghalaya: Health Conditions of Mothers and Children,* Calcutta: UNICEF East India Office.

———,1985, *Mizoram: Health Conditions of Mothers and Children,* Calcutta: UNICEF East India Office.

Koing, Suman, 1989, "Status of Women in Singpho Society", *Status of Women Seminar: Arunachal Pradesh.*

Krishna Raj, Maitreyi (ed.), 1986, *Women's Studies in India: Some Perpectives*, Bombay: Popular Prakashan.

Kynpham, Singh, 1980, "Khasi Religion and Khasi Society", in Sujata Miri (ed.), *Religion and Society of North-East India*, New Delhi: Vikas Publishing House, pp.43-55.

Lahkar, A., 1990, "Social Status of the Koch in an Assam Village in the Local Social Hierarchy: A Case Study", *Social Sciences Ý An Inter-disciplinary Journal,* Silchar, vol.3, no.1 & 2, June- December, 1990, pp 165-70.

Lalbiaktluanga, C., 1988 "Mizo Women Through History", *Status of Women Seminar — Mizoram.*

Lalliankhuma, 1990, "Tribal Education in Mizoram", Ashish Bose, Tiplut Nongbri and Nikhilesh Kumar, *Tribal Demography and Development in North-East India*, New Delhi: B.R. Publishing Corporation, pp.169-75.

Lalremasang, Hmar, 1988 , "Modern Education and the Status of Hmar Women", *Status of Women Seminar — Manipur.*

Laltlani, P.C, 1988, "Mizo Women and the Church", *Status of Women Seminar — Mizoram*,

Liandingi, P., 1988, "Mizo Women and Social Control", *Status of Women Seminar — Mizoram.*

Luthra, Pran Nath, 1994, "All Aliens Must Go Back", *Times of India*, 30, October 1994.

Mahanta, Aparna D., 1988, "Women, Religion and Science in the Non-tribal Society of Assam", *Status of Women Seminar — Assam Non-Tribal Societies.*

Majumdar, D.M., 1982, "The Garo National Council", in K.S. Singh (ed.) *Tribal Movements in India*, vol.1, Delhi: Manohar Publications, pp. 199-214.

Majumdar, D.N., 1989, "Some Basic Points for Considering Regarding Status of Women Particulary Among the Plains Tribal Societies of Assam", *Status of Women Seminar — Assam, Plains Tribal Societies.*

Mali. D.D., 1988, "Development of Entrepreneurship in North-Eastern Region: NISIET's Experience", *Journal of the North Eastern Council*, vol. ix, no. 1 & 2, JanuaryÝJune, 1998, pp, 5-8.

Mandal, D.B., 1993, "Mechanism of Social Control and Some Aspects of Customary Laws of Jamatia", in K.S. Singh (ed.), *Tribal Ethnography, Customary Law and Change*, New Delhi: Concept Publishing, pp. 139-46.

Maneck sha, Freny, 1997, "Naga Tribals' Meet Favours Peace and Dialogue", *Times of India, 25 March 1997.*

Manikchand, Konsam, 1988, "The Evolution of Meitei State", Sanajaoba, Narorem (ed.), *Manipur: Past and Present*, vol.1, Delhi: Mittal Publications, pp. 145-59.

Mao, John, 1988, "Status of Women in Naga Society", *Status of Women Seminar — Naga Societies*,

Mao, Xavier, 1988, "The Status of Women in Mao-Naga Society", *Status of Women Seminar — Naga Societies.*

Marak, Caroline R. "Status of Garo Women in Souvenir: Mothers Union Golden Jubilee, 1914-1991, Tura, Meghalaya.

Marak, Caroline R., 1992, "Status of Women in Garo culture", in Soumen Sen, (ed.), *Women in Meghalaya*, Delhi: Daya Publishing House, 56-72.

Mathew, T., 1980, "Xth Report of the Land Reforms Commission of Khasi Hills: A Summary: 1980", T. Mathew (ed.), *Tribal Economy of North-Eastern Region,* Gauhati: Spectrum Publications, pp. 100-32.

Mathew, T. (ed.), 1980, *Tribal Economy of North Eastern Region.* (Proceeding of a Seminar at NEHU) Gauhati: Spectrum Publications.

Mathur, P.R.G., 1982, "The Khasi Solidarity Movement", in K.S. Singh (ed.) *Tribal Movements in India*, vol.1, Delhi: Manohar Publications.

Mazumdar, Debashis, 1999, "Handloom Industry, New Vistas of Growth Potential", Amalesh Banerjee and Biman Kar (eds.), *Economic Planning and Development of North Eastern States*, New Delhi: Kanishka Publishers, pp. 193-217.

Medhi, G.C., 1989, "Women — Their Training and Status in Karbi Society", *Status of Women Seminar — Assam, Hill Tribal Societies, Karbi and Dimasa.*

Menon, Ramesh, 1987, "Chakmas, Shattered Lives", *India Today,* 15 March 1987, pp.76-80.

———, 1988, "A Brave Attempt (Mizoram)", *India Today*, 15 January 1988.

Miri, Sujata (ed.), 1980, *Religion and Society of North-East India*, New Delhi : Vikas Publishing House.

Mishra, Kiran, 1991, *Women in a Tribal Community: A Study of Arunachal Pradesh*, Delhi: Vikas Publishing House.

Mishra, Udayan, 1987, "North-East Regional Parties, High Hopes and Hard Realities", *Economic and Political Weekly*, vol. XXII, no 24, 13 June 1987.

———, 1999, "Immigration and Identity Transformation in Assam," *Economic and Political Weekly*, vol. XXXIV, no. 21, 22 May 1999, pp. 1264-71.

Misra, Bani Prasanna, 1980, "The Spread of Christainity in North-East India", Sujata Miri (ed.), *Religion and Society of North-East India*, New Delhi: Vikas Publishing House.

———, 1982, "Kirata Karyokinesis: An Introduction to the Political, Econmy of Tribal Societies in North-East India", in K.S. Singh (ed.) *Economies of the Tribes and their Transformation*, New Delhi: Concept Publishing, pp 45-62.

Mitra, Amitava, 1999, "Planning for Forestry and Environment Development in Arunachal Pradesh", Amalesh Banerjee and Biman Kar (eds.), *Economic Planning and Development of North-Eastern States*, New Delhi: Kanishka Publishers, pp 115-24.

Mitra, Kalyan "Status of Women Among the Sonowal Kachari Tribe of Assam", *Status of Women Seminar — Assam, Plains Tribal Societies*.

Mukherjee, Bhabanand and K.S. Singh, 1982, "Tribal Movements in Tripura", in K.S. Singh (ed.), *Tribal Movements in India*, vol. 1 New Delhi: Manohar Publications, pp. 317-37.

Mukherjee, D.P. and S.K. Mukherjee, 1982, "Contemporary Cultural and Political Movements Among the Bodos of Assam", in K.S. Singh (ed.) *Tribal Movements in India*, New Delhi: Manohar Publications, pp. 253-80.

Mukherjee, D.P., P. Gupta and N.K. Das 1982, "The Zeliangrong or Haomei Movement", in K.S. Singh (ed.) *Tribal Movements in India*, vol. 1, New Delhi: Manohar Publications, pp. 67-95.

Munshi, Debashish, 1993, "Peace at Last", *Times of India*, 28 February 1993.

Nag, Chitta Ranjan, 1993, *The Mizo Society in Transition*, New Delhi: Vikas Publishing House.

Nag, Sajal, 1995, "North East India, Consturction and Deconstruction of Images", *The Window, Journal of the Study Circle*, Shillong, Special Issue on North-East India, 1 March 1995, pp. 3-6.

Nag, Tejimala Gurung, 1995, "Rejected Peoples, The Nepalese in North-East India", *The Window, Journal of the Study Circle,* Shillong, Special Issue on North East India, 1 March 1995, pp. 28-31.

Nair, Sukumaran, M K., 1999, "Constraints on the Development of a Land Market in Meghalaya", in Amalesh Banerjee and Biman Kar (eds.), *Economic Planning and Development of North Easten States*, New Delhi: Kanishka Publications, pp. 139-67.

Nandy, Sibdas, 1997, "Infiltration in North-East India, Fact and Fiction", *Window; Journal of the Study Circle,* Shillong, March 1997, pp. 21-34.

Natarajan, Nalini, 1982, "Cultural Revivalism Among the Christian Khasis of Meghalalya", in K. S. Singh (ed.), *Tribal Movements in India,* vol. 1, Delhi: Manohar, pp. 151-71.

Nayar, Kuldip, 1995, "The Scene in Nagaland", *Indian Express*, 25. November 1995.

Neog Maheswar, 1984, "Assam Agitates Against Foreign Nationals", B.L. Abbi (ed.), *North-East Region: Problems and Prospects of Development,* Chandigarh: Centre for Research in Rural and Industrial Development 1984, pp. 275-86.

Nigam, M.P., 1991, "Sericulture Extension and Mangement; Some Suggestions", *Journal of the North Eastern Council*, AprilÝJune 1991.

Nongbri, Tiplut, 1984 "Problems of Matriliny: A Short Review of the Khasi Kinship Structure", *Journal of the North East India Council of Social Science Research*, vol. 8, no. 1, April 1984.

———,1988, "Gender and the Khasi Family Structure: Some Implications of the Meghalaya Succession to Self-Acquired Property Act, 1984", *Sociological Bulletin,* 37(1&2), March-September, pp. 71-82.

North Eastern Council (NEC), *Journal of the North Eastern Council,* Shillong, North Eastern Council Secretariat. 1986, 1988, 1991, January-April 1986, July-August 1986, January-June 1988, April-June 1991, July-September 1991.

———, *Basic Statistics of North Eastern Region*, 1990, 1992, 1995, Shillong, North Eastern Council Secretariat.

Nunisa, Motilal, 1989, "Status of Women in Tribal Societies (Dimasa)", *Status of Women Seminar—Assam; Hill Tribal Societies*, Karbi and Dimasa.

Nunthara, C., 1990, "Social Aspects of Tribal Development", in Ashish Bose T. Nongbri and Nikhilesh Kumar (eds.), *Tribal Demography and Development in North East India*, New Delhi, B.R. Publishing Corporation.

———, 2000, "Mizoram", George Mathew (ed.), *Status of Panchayati Raj in India 2000*, Institute of Social Sciences, New Delhi: Concept Publishing, pp. 215-19.

Nyori, T., 1989, "The Position of Women in Adi Traditional Society", *Status of Women Seminar — Arunachal Pradesh*.

Pakem, B., 1992, "Megalithic Problem of Meghalaya: A Case Study of Megaliths of Jaintia Hills", *Journal of North-East India Council for Social Science Research,* vol. 16, no. 1, April 1992.

Pal, S.K., 1993, "The Rabha Customary Law in Transition from Matriliny to Patriliny", in K.S. Singh (ed.), *Tribal Ethnography, Customary Law and Change*, New Delhi: Concept Publishing, pp. 49-55.

Passah, P.M., 1992, "Status of Women in Jaintia Society and Culture", in Soumen Sen (ed.), *Women in Meghalaya*, Delhi: Daya Publishing House, 46-55.

Patel, Tulsi, 1987, "Women's work and their Status, Dialectics of Subordination and Assertion", *Social Action*, vol. 37(2), April-June, 1987, pp. 126-49.

Patel, Vibha J.,1994, "Naga and Kuki, Who is to Blame?", *Economic and Political Weekly,* vol. XXIX, no. 22, 28 May 1994.

Patowary, A.C. and N.S. Deodhar, 1987, *Assam: Health Conditions of Mothers and Children*, Calcutta: UNICEF East India Office.

Paul, M.C., 1989, *Dimensions of Tribal Movements in India,* New Delhi: Inter-India Publications.

Pearson, Hungyo, 1982, "Economic Life of the Tangkhul Naga with Speical Reference to Shifting Cultivation", in K.S. Singh (ed.), *Economies of the Tribes and Their Transformation*, New Delhi: Concept Publishing, pp. 240-48.

———,1993, "Chieftainship and Customary Laws Among Tangkhul Naga of Manipur", in K.S. Singh (ed.), *Tribal Ethnography: Customary Law and Change,* New Delhi: Concept Publishing, pp. 39-42.

Pegu, Indreswar, 1989, "Status of Women in the Mishing Society", *Status of Women Seminar — Assam: Plains Tribal Societies*.

Phadnis, Urmila and Indira Malani 1978 (eds.), *Women of the World: Illusion and Reality, New Delhi:* Vikas Publishing House.

Phangcho, P.C., 1989, "Status of Women in Karbi Society", *Status of Women Seminar — Assam Hill Tribal Societies; Karbi and Dimasa*.

Philangam, Ngakang 1991, "Education of Girls Among Tribals of Manipur", a project report submitted to Tata Institute of Social Sciences as part fulfilment of a training course (unpublished).

Phukan, J. and B.N. Phukan, 1989, "Status of Women in Nishi Society", *Status of Women Seminar — Arunachal Pradesh*.

Phukan, Minoti, 1988, "Status of Labour Women in the Tea Gardens of Assam", *Status of Women Seminar — Assam: Non-Tribal Societies*.

Population Foundation of India, 1998, *State of India's Population*, New Delhi.

Rabha, Heramb, 1989, "Status of Rabha Women in a Plains Tribal Society of Assam", *Status of Women Seminar — Assam: Plains Tribal Societies*.

Raghumani, Sanabam, 1988, "Meitei Personal Law", in Naorem Sanajaoba (ed.). *Manipur: Past and Present,* Delhi: Mittal Publications, pp. 329-48.

Raha, Manish Kumar and P.C. Coomar, 1989, *Tribal India: Problem, Development, Prospect,* New Delhi: Gian Publishing House.

Rajkalaxmi,T.K., 1995, "Arunachal Concerns: Harming Women in the Name of Tribal Customs?", *Frontline,* September 8 1995, pp.36-38.

Randip Singh Kanwar, 1987, *The Nags of Nagaland*, Nwe Delhi: Deep & Deep Publications.

Roy Burman, B.K., 1970, *Demographic and Socio-economic Profiles of the Hill Areas of North East India,* Census of India 1961: Monograph Series, New Delhi: Government of India Press.

———, 1984, *Towards Poverty Alleviation Programmes in Nagaland and Manipur,* Delhi: Mittal Publications.

———, 1990, "Social Ecology of Women's Roles in the Hills of Northeast India", Discussion paper series, Mountain Population and Employment, MPE Series no. 5, International Centre for Integrated Mountain Development.

———,1990, "Tribal Population and Development", in Ashish Bose, Tiplut Nongbri and Nikhilesh Kumar (eds.), *Tribal Demography and Development in North-East India,* Delhi: B.R. Publishing Corporation, pp. 67-82.

Roy Burman, J.J., 1988, "Tribal Tradition and Modern Development in North-East India", *Indian Journal of Social Work,* vol. XLIX, October 1988, pp. 409-13.

Roy, N.C. and P.K. Kuri, 1999, "Inequalities in Land Ownership and the Problems of Land Reforms in Arunachal Pradesh", in A. Banerjee and Biman Kar (eds.), *Economic Planning and Development of North East States,* New Delhi: Kanishka Publishers, Distributors, pp. 125-38.

Roy, Shibani, 1988, "Contemporary Indian Women with Special Reference to Muslim Women", *Status of Women Seminar — Assam: Barak Valley*.

Rukbo, Talom "The Traditional and Customary Status of Women Among the Tribes of Arunachal Pradesh in General and the Adis in Particular", *Status of Women Seminar — Arunachal Pradesh.*

Rymbai, R.T., 1980, "Some Aspects of the Religion of the Khasis-Pnars", in Sujata Miri (ed.), *Religion and Society of North-East India*, New Delhi: Vikas Publishing House, pp. 37-42.

Saha, R.K., 1982, "An Ethnic Movement in Manipur Valley", K.S. Singh (ed.), *Tribal Movements in India,* vol.1, New Delhi: Manohar Publishers, pp. 97-113.

———, 1987, "State Formation Among the Meiteis of Manipur", in Surajit Sinha (ed.), *Tribal Polities and State Systems in Pre-Colonial Eastern and North-Eastern India*, Calcutta: Centre for Studies in Social Sciences.

Saigal, Omesh, 1978, *Tripura: Its History and Culture,* Delhi: Concept Publishing Company.

Saikia, Anup, 1994, "Tension Over Chakma Issue — Arunachal Pradesh", *Economic and Political Weekly*, vol. XXIX, no. 53, 31 December 1994.

Saikia, Anuva, 1988, "Economic Status of Women in Rural Areas of Assam", *Status of Women Seminar — Assam; Non-Tribal Societies.*

Saikia, P.C., 1976, *Dibongiyas,* Delhi: B.R. Publishing Corporation

———, 1989, "Acculturation in the Mishing Society in Silapathar Town, Lakhimpur", *Status of Women Seminar — Assam; Plains Tribal Societies.*

———, 1989, "Status of Women in Deori Soceity", *Status of Women Seminar — Assam: Plains Tribal Societies.*

Saikia, P.D., 1982, "A Note on Shifting Cultivation in North-East India", K.S. Singh (ed.), *Economies of the Tribes and Their Transformation,* New Delhi: Concept Publishing, pp. 228-39.

Saikia, P.D. and U. Phukan, 1978, "Some Aspects of Agricultural Land- Use in North-East India", T. Mathew (ed.), *Rural Development in India,* Report of a NEHU Seminar, New Delhi: Agricole Publishing Academy, pp. 141-51.

Saikia, P.D., K. Gogoi and Anjali Lekharu, 1986, *Indian Rural Women: A Study on Role and Status of Rural Women in Assam,* Delhi: Mittal Publications.

Saikia, Sabina Sehgal, 1996, "Tension Between TribalsÝNon-tribals in North-East", *Times of India,* 4 March 1996.

Salam, Irene "Women of Imphal Valley", *Status of Women Seminar — Manipur.*

Sanajaoba, Naorem, 1988, *Manipur: Past and Present,* vol.1, Delhi: Mittal Publications.

Sangkham, Gina, 1988, "The Status of Women in Moyon Society", *Status of Women Seminar — Manipur.*

Sardeshpande, S.C., 1987, *The Patkoi Nagas,* Delhi: Daya Publishing House.

Sarin, V.I.K., 1984, "Socio-Economic Tensions: Insurgency in Tripura II", *Times of India,* 2 August 1984.

Sarkar, Jayant, 1982, "Economic System and Social Change in Arunachal Pradesh", K.S. Singh (ed.), *Economies of Tribes and Their Transformation,* New Delhi: Concept Publishing Company, pp. 287-302.

———, 1982, "Development of Identity Consciousness in Arunachal Pradesh", K.S. Singh (ed.), *Tribal Movements in India,* vol. 1. New Delhi: Manohar Publications, pp. 231-39.

———, 1993, "Customary Law of the Khamti of Arunachal Pradesh", in K.S. Singh (ed.), Tribal *Ethnography, Customary Law and Change,* New Delhi: Concept Publishing, pp. 29-35.

Sarma, Surendra Nath (date not given), "Status of Women in the Assamese Society", Research Scholar Guwahati University, Cyclostyled paper.

Satyanarayan Rao, Akula 1996, *Lok Sabha Elections and MPs. 1952–1996, First to Tenth Lok Sabha*, Hyderabad: Rakesh Publications.

Sen, Jyoti, N. Saha and S.K. Mukherjee, 1982, "Role of Women in Tribal Economy", K.S. Singh (ed.), *Economies of the Tribes and Their Transformation,* New Delhi: Concept Publishing Company: 95-103.

Sen, Sipra 1987, *Tribes of Nagaland,* Delhi: Mittal Publications.

Sen, Soumen, 1989, "Development in a Tribal Setting: A Case of Meghalaya", in M.K. Raha and P. C. Kumar (eds.), *Tribal India, Problems, Development, Prospect,* New Delhi: Gyan Publishing House, pp. 93-109.

Sen, Soumen, 1992, (ed.), *Women in Meghalaya: Papers presented in a Seminar on the Status of Women in Tribal Cultures of Meghalaya,* Delhi: Daya Publishing House.

Sengupta, Nirmal 1988, I "Reapparaising Tribal Movement: A Myth in the Making", *Economic and Political Weekly,* vol. 23, no. 19, 7, May 1988, pp. 943-45.

———, 1988, II "Legitimization and Spread", *Economic and Political Weekly,* 14 May 1998, pp. 1003-05.

Sharma, Chandan Kumar, 1995, "Poverty and Inequality: Case of Assam", *Economic and Political Weekly,* vol. xxx, nos. 6 & 7, February 18-25.

Sharma, Dipti, 1988, "The Women of the Brahmaputra Valley in the Freedom Struggle (1921-47)", *Status of Women Seminar — Assam, Non-tribal Societies.*

Sharma, O.P and R.D. Rotherfield, 1987, *Recent Literacy Trends in India,* Occasional paper no.1 of 1987, Office of the Registrar General and Census Commissioner, Ministry of Home Affairs, Govt. of India.

Sharma, Sudhir, 2000, "Tripura", George Mathew (ed.), *Status of Panchayati Raj in the States and Union Territories of India, 2000,* pp. 283-88.

Sharma, Thakur G.C., 1989, "Social Status of the Karbi Women as Reflected in the Socio-cultural Life and Legends of the Karbis", *Status of Women Seminar — Assam: Hill Tribal Societies: Karbi and Dimasa.*

Sherfuddin, Farida, 1988, "Status of Women in the Assamese Muslim Society", *Status of Women Seminar — Assam: Non-tribal Societies.*

Sikidar, Sujit, 1990, *Economic Development of Tribal India,*New Delhi: Ashish Publishing House.

Singh, Balmiki Prasad, 1988, "North-East India: Problems and Prospects", *Mainstream,* vol. xxvi, no.19, 20 February 1988.

Singh, K.B., 1978, "Social Stratification and Mobility in Manipur", in S.M. Dube (ed.), *North-East India: A Sociological Study* Delhi: Concept Publishing Company, pp. 61-66.

Singh, K.S. (ed.), 1993, *Tribal Ethnography, Customary Law and Change,* New Delhi: Concept Publishing.

Singh U.B., 1999, *Urban Governance in North-Eastern Region,* New Delhi: Gyan Publishing House.

Singha, N.K. (ed.), 1981, *The Customary Laws and Practices of the Wancho of Arunachal Pradesh,* Gauhati: The Law Research Institute, Eastern Region, Gauhati High Court.

Sinha, M., 1991, "A Systematic Plan for Fisheries Development of North Eastern States", *Journal of the North Eastern Council,* vol. xii, no. 2, AprilÝJune, pp. 6-17.

Sinha, Raghuvir, 1962, *The Akas,* Shillong: Research Department, Advisor's Secretariat.

Subramanian, K.S., 2000, "Tribal Insurgency and Rural Development in Tripura", *Economic and Political Weekly,* vol. xxxv; nos. 8 & 9, 19-26 February 2000.

Syiem, I. M., 1992, "Women in Khasi Society", in Soumen Sen (ed.), *Women in Meghalaya,* Delhi: Daya Publishing House, pp. 22-35.

Syiemlieh, D.R., 1990, "Education, Elite and Politicization in the Khasi-Jaintia Hills", in Ashish Bose, Tiplut Nongbri and Nikhilesh Kumar (eds.), *Demography and Development in North-East India,* Delhi: B.R. Publishing Corporation, pp. 177-85.

Synnah, Jacquiline, 1989, *Institution of Marriage in Pnar Society — A Study in Raliang,* unpublished project report, Bombay: Tata Institute of Social Sciences,

Taid, Tabu, 1989, "The Mishing Women: Rights and Responsibilities", *Status of Women Seminar — Assam: Plains Tribal Societies.*

Talukdar, A.C., 2000, "Arunachal Pradesh", in George Mathew (ed.), *Status of Panchayati Raj in the States and Union Territories of India,* 2000, Institute of Social Sciences, New Delhi: Concept Publishing.

Terang, Rong Bong, 1989, "The Place of Women in Karbi Society According to the Folk Tradition", *Status of Women Seminar — Assam: Hill Tribal Societies: Karbi and Dimasa.*

Terangpi, Tado, 1989, "The Role of Karbi Women in Society: Past and Present", *Status of Women Seminar — Assam: Hill Tribal Societies: Karbi and Dimasa.*

Tezpur District Mahila Samiti, 1995, *North-East India: Future Perspectives,* Tezpur, Assam (cyclostyled document)

Thakuria Reeta, 1988, "Legal Status of Women in Non-Tribal Societies of Assam" *Status of Women Seminar — Non-tribal Societies.*

Thaosen, J.L., 1989, "Status of Women in Dimasa Society", *Status of Women Seminar—Assam: Hill Tribal Societies: Karbi and Dimasa.*

Thomas, E.J., 1993, *Mizo Bamboo Hills Murmur Change,* New Delhi: Intellectual Publishing House.

Thomas, Lucy, 1988, "The Tangkhul Women Today", *Status of Women Seminar — Naga Societies.*

Tikoo, R., 1988, "The Socio-Economic and Political Profile of Meitei Women", *Status of Women Seminar — Manipur.*

Tikoo, Ratna, 2000, "Participation of Tribal Women in Politics: Prospects in the New Millenium", Paper in *Seminar on Tribals in the New Millennium*, Students Home, Manipur Univeristy, Canchipur, 28-29 April 1996.

Times of India, 1993, "Rabha Tribals Want Self-rule", 21 December 1993.

———, 1994, "Record haul of Agarwood", 3 September 1994.

———, 1996, "Bodo Leaders Fail to Agree on Agenda", 2 July 1996.

——— , 1996, "Bodos Concerned Over Increase in Violence", 18 October 1996.

———, 1998 "Army Busts Insurgents' Camps in the North-East", 31 March 1998.

———,1999, "Change of Govt. May Hit Talks with North-East Rebels", 21 April 1999.

———, 1999, "Ulfa Unleashes Vilence on Poll Eve", 3 October 1999.

———, 2000, "NHRC direct Mizoram Govt. to Take Back Reangs", 29 May 2000.

Tungoe, Mhathing, 1988 "Status of Women in Lotha Society," *Status of Women Seminar — Naga Societies.*

Upadhyaya, K.K., 1986 *Development Problems and Propects of Mizoram,* Tribal Studies of India Series T-117, New Delhi: Inter-India Publications.

War, Juanita, 1992, "Status of Women in Traditional Khasi Culture", Soumen Sen (ed.), *Women in Meghalaya,* Delhi: Daya Publishing House; 11-25.

———,1988, Report on the Consultation on "The Effects of the Matrilineal System on Present Day Khasi Society", 27-28 May 1988, Don Bosco Youth Centre, Laitumkhrah, Shillong (Cyclostyled paper).

Warjri, K.M., 1988, "Educational and Social Problems Faced by Women", *Status of Women Seminar — Naga Societies.*

Yashwant, Raj, 1998, "People Waging War Can Also Make Peace", *Times of India,* 1 November 1998.

Zimomi, Salomi, 1988, "The Status of Women in Sema Society", *Status of Women Seminar — Naga Societies.*

Reports

Child Mortality, Age of Marriage and Fertility in India, 1989, Occasional Paper No. 2 of 1989, Demography Division, Registrar General and Census Commissioner, India, Ministry of Home Affairs, New Delhi.

District-wise Soical Economic Demographic Indicators, 11 July 2001, National Commission on Population, Government India, 2001.

Education in India; 1992-93, Department of Education, Ministry of Human Resource Development, Govt. of India.

The Excluded and Partially Excluded Areas of Assam, Govt. of Assam, 1947, Shillong: Assam Government Press, No. 1 Hom (c) 525.

Final Population Total: Brief Analysis of Primary Census Abstract, 1991, India, Series 1: Paper 2 of 1992, Registrar General and Census Commissioner, India.

Health Conditions of Mothers and Children, *Assam* (1987) *Manipur* (1984), *Meghalaya (*1985*) Mizoram* (1985), *Nagaland* (1984), *Tripura* (1985), Calcutta, *UNICEF*, East India Office, 1984–87.

Health Information of India, 1994, 1997, 1998, Directorate General of Health Services, Central Bureau of Health Intelligence, Ministry of Health and Family Welfare, Govt. of India.

National Family Health Survey, 1992-93, India: Summary Report — Assam (June 1995) North-Eastern States (December 1995), International Institute of Population Sciences.

National Family Health Survey, 1992-93, *India: Summary Report,* Mumbai. International Institute of Population Sciences, 1995.

Provisional Population Totals, 2001, Series 1 of 2001, Registrar General and Census Commissioner, India.

Religion, 1995, Paper 1 of 1995, Registrar General and Census Commissioner, India.

Report of the Expert Group on Estimation of Proportion and Number of Poor, Perspective Planning Division, Government of India, 1993.

Rural Health Statistics of India: 1997, Directorate General of Health Services, Rural Health Division, Ministry of Health, Govt. of India.

Selected Educational Statistics,1998-99, Department of Secondary Education and Higher Education, Ministry of Human Resource Development, Govt. of India.

Some Basic Statistics of Tripura: 1994-95, Directorate of Statistics, Govt. of Tripura, Agartala, 1995.

State Profile, 1991, India, Registrar General and Census Commissioner, India.

Statistical Abstract of Arunachal Pradesh, 1998, Directorate of Economics and Statistics, Govt. of Arunachal Pradesh, Itanagar, 1998.

Statistical Handbook — Mizoram, Govt. of Mizoram, 1987.

Towards Equality: Report of the Committeee on Status of Women, Department of Social Welfare, Government of India, 1974.

Women in India: A Statistical Profile, Ministry of Women and Child Development, Govt. of India, 1988.